Fundamentals of Selling

The Irwin Series in Marketing

Consulting Editor
Gilbert A. Churchill
University of Wisconsin, Madison

Charles Futrell
Texas A&M University

Fundamentals
of Selling

1984

Richard D. Irwin, Inc.
Homewood, Illinois   60430

ISBN 0-256-03101-0

Library of Congress Catalog Card No. 83–82132

Printed in the United States of America

1 2 3 4 5 6 7 8 9 0 V 1 0 9 8 7 6 5 4

To my children Amy and Gregory, two of the best salespeople I know.

Preface

Fundamentals of Selling is written by a salesperson turned professor. For eight years I worked in sales with Colgate, Upjohn, and Ayerst. As a professor, I have taught selling to thousands of college students, business people, and industry sales personnel, developing and using the strategies, practices, and techniques presented in this text. Further, each year I spend time in fieldwork with sales personnel. In my classes and programs, I stress "learning by doing" examples and exercises, and video-tape role playing of selling situations. This text is the result of these experiences.

Fundamentals of Selling was conceived as a method of providing ample materials for readers to construct their own sales presentations after studying the text. This allows the instructor the flexibility of focusing on the "how-to-sell" approach within the classroom. Covering the basic foundations for understanding the concepts and practices of selling in a practical, straightforward, and readable manner, it provides students with a textbook for use in preparing sales presentations and role-playing exercises.

Many features have been included to stimulate interest. Each chapter contains numerous buyer-seller dialogues, actual industry examples, comments from successful salespeople and sales managers, as well as interesting profiles of sales personnel from Fortune 500 companies. Each company represented by a salesperson profiled in the book selected one of their outstanding salespeople to contribute to the learning of selling practices which can make a successful salesperson. Additionally, selling materials and photographs were provided by numerous companies whose contributions have greatly increased the educational quality of this text.

Further, each chapter provides chapter objectives, key terms, a chapter summary, and review and discussion questions to facilitate understanding. Projects and case problems presented at the end of each chapter have been carefully selected. The text, exercises, projects, and cases have all been classroom tested.

The 17 chapters contained in the text are divided into five parts:

1. *Selling as a Profession* emphasizes the career, rewards, and duties of the professional salesperson and illustrates the importance of the sales function to the organization's success.
2. *Preparation for Successful Selling* presents the background information salespeople use to develop their sales presentations.
3. *The Dynamics of Selling* covers the entire selling process from prospecting to follow-up and is the heart of the text. State-of-the-art selling strategies, practices, and techniques are presented in a "how to" fashion.
4. *Special Selling Topics* discusses the selling challenge and excellent career opportunities in retailing and industrial selling. The importance of the proper use of managing one's time and sales territory, as well as the social, ethical, and legal issues are also given thorough coverage.
5. *Functions of the Sales Manager* shows the challenging job of managing salespeople.

For the instructor, a large, comprehensive manual accompanies the text to aid in class preparation. A *video cassette* is available from the publisher upon adoption of the text, providing numerous sales presentation examples which can be shown in class to help students in preparing their sales presentation.

I have had the good fortune to receive excellent assistance in preparing this text from the following outstanding sales instructors: Professors Timothy W. Wright, Lakeland Community College; John R. Beem, College of DuPage; Lynn J. Loudenback, Iowa State University; Leslie E. Martin, Jr., University of Wisconsin—Whitewater; and Donald Sandlin, East Los Angeles College.

Additionally, many of the profiled salespeople made content suggestions which were incorporated throughout the text. They also answered many of the end-of-the-chapter exercises and cases.

For the use of their selling exercises and sales management cases, I am especially grateful to Professors Gerald Crawford, University of North Alabama; Dick Nordstrom, Western Illinois University; Rollie Tilman and James E. Littlefield, University of North Carolina at Chapel Hill; George Wynn, University of Arkansas at Fayetteville; and James L. Taylor, University of Alabama.

Special thanks go to Professor Jeffrey Sager for his content comments and editorial work. Cliff Defee will always be remembered for reading and rereading the manuscript, plus running my selling labs. Elaine Valagure did an outstanding typing job.

Finally I wish to thank the sales trainers, salespeople, and sales managers who helped teach me the art of selling when I carried the sales bag full time. I hope I have done justice to their great profession of selling.

I hope you learn from and enjoy the text. I enjoyed preparing it for you. Readers are urged to forward their comments on this text to me. I wish you great success in your selling efforts. Remember, it's the salesperson who gets the customer's orders that keeps the wheels of industry turning. America cannot do without you.

Charles Futrell

■ **Profiles**

Successful salespeople and sales managers profiled throughout this text greatly added to the educational value of the text and its lively, real-life examples. To these people—thanks!

Kim Allen—McNeil Consumer Products Company
Gary Brown—Richard D. Irwin, Inc.
Steve Gibson—United States Steel Corporation
Gary Grant—NCR Corporation
Martha Hill—Hanes Corporation
Mike Impink—Aluminum Company of America ALCOA
Bob James—American Hospital Supply Corporation
Cindy Kerns—Xerox Corporation
Patrick Kamlowsky—Hughes Tool Division
Jim Mobley—General Mills, Inc.
George Morris—The Prudential Insurance Company of America
Vikki Morrison—Century 21 Real Estate Corporation
Kathleen Paynter—Campbell Soup Company
Bruce Scagel—Scott Paper Company
Linda Slaby-Baker—The Quaker Oats Company
Sandra Snow—The Upjohn Company
Matt Suffoletto—International Business Machines IBM

Contents

Unsure. A *FAB*ulous Approach to Buyer Need Satisfaction: *The Product's Features: So What? The Product's Advantages: Prove It! The Product's Benefits Sell It. Order Can Be Important.* How to Determine Important Buying Needs—A Key of Success. Your Buyer's Perception. Buyer Perceptions, Attitudes, and Beliefs Are Learned: *Example of a Buyer's Misperceptions.* The Buyer's Personality Should Be Considered: *Self-Concept. Selling Based upon Personality.* You Can Classify Buying Situations: *Some Decisions Are Routine. Some Decisions Are Limited. Some Decisions Are Extensive.* View Buyers as Decision Makers: *Need Arousal. Collection of Information. Information Evaluation. Purchase Decision. Postpurchase.* To Buy or Not to Buy—A Choice Decision.

Cases

Profile: Kim Allen   *McNeil*

Communication: It Takes Two: *Salesperson-Buyer Communication Process Requires Feedback.* Nonverbal Communication: Watch for It: *Concept of Space. Communications through Appearance and the Handshake.* Body Language Gives You Clues. Barriers to Communication. Master Persuasive Communication and the Force Is with You. *Feedback Guides Your Presentation. Empathy Puts You in Your Customer's Shoes. Keep It Simple, You Silver-Tongued Devil. Creating Mutual Trust Develops Friendship. Listening Clues You In. Your Attitude Makes the Difference. Proof Statements Make You Believable.*

Cases

Profile: Patrick E. Kamlowsky   *Hughes Tool*

Where'd You Learn That: Sources of Sales Knowledge. Why Salespeople Require Knowledge: *Knowledge Increases Confidence in Salespeople. . . . And in Buyers. Know Your Firm. General Company Information.* Know Your Product. A Little Knowledge of Distribution Can Go a Long Way: *Conflict and Cooperation in Distribution Channels.* Advertising Aids Salespeople: *Types of Advertising Differ. Why Spend Money on Advertising?* Sales Promotion Generates Sales for You: *Point of Purchase Displays: Get'em Out There. Shelf Positioning Is Important to Your Success. Premiums.* What's It Worth? Pricing Your Product: *Types of Prices. Discounts Lower the Price.* Markup Represents Gross Profit: *Be Creative in Your Pricing Techniques. Customer Credit: Get'em to Pay on Time.* Know Your Competition, Industry, and Economy.

Cases

9. Objections Are Your Friends   268

Profile: Bruce Scagel *Scott Paper*

Welcome Objections! When Do Prospects Object? Who Is the Toughest Prospect. What Are Objections? Four Major Categories of Objections: *The Hidden Objection. The Stalling Objection. The No-Need Objection. The Money Objection.* Handle Objections as They Arise. Techniques for Meeting Objections. Rephrase an Objection as a Question: *Forestalling Objections Is Sometimes Necessary. Send It Back with the Boomerang Method. Ask Questions to Smoke Out Objections. Direct Denial Should Be Used Tactfully. Anticipating Objections Comes with Experience. Compensation or Counterbalance Method. Let a Third Party Answer.* Basic Points to Consider in Meeting Objections: *Anticipate Objections. Consider Objections as Opportunities. Be Positive. Understand Objections.* After Meeting the Objection—What to Do? *First, Use a Trial Close. Move Back into Your Presentation. Move to Close Your Sale. If You Cannot Overcome the Objection.*

10. Close, Close, Close   304

Profile: George W. Morris *Prudential Life Insurance*

When Should I Pop the Question. Reading Buying Signals. What Makes a Good Closer? *Ask for the Order and Shut Up! Get the Order and Get Out!* How Many Times Should You Close? Closing under Fire. Difficulties with Closing. Essentials of Closing Sales. Twelve Steps to a Successful Closing. Prepare Several Closing Techniques: *The Alternative Choice Close Is an Old Favorite. The Assumptive Close. The Compliment Close Inflates the Ego. The Summary of Benefits Close Is Most Popular. The Continuous-Yes Close Generates Positive Responses. The Minor-Points Close Is Not Threatening. The T-Account or Balance Sheet Close Was Ben Franklin's Favorite. The Standing-Room-Only Close Gets Action.* Prepare a Multiple Close Sequence. Close Based on the Situation. Research Reinforces Book's Sales Strategies. *Keys to Improved Selling.*

11. Winning in the Long Run: Building a Relationship through Service   334

Profile: Gary Brown *Richard D. Irwin, Inc.*

Super Salespeople Discuss Service. Account Penetration Is a Secret to Success.

Service Can Keep Your Customers. You Lose a Customer—Keep on Trucking! Increasing Your Customer's Sales. When You Do Not Make the Sale. Return Goods Make You a Hero. Handle Complaints Fairly. Build a Professional Reputation. Dos and Don'ts for Industrial Salespeople.

IV   **Special Selling Topics**

12.   Retail Selling Is Challenging and Rewarding   356

Profile: Kathleen E. Paynter   *Campbell Sales Company*

What Is Retailing: *Financial Rewards Are Excellent. Nonfinancial Rewards Are Many.* Retailers Sell like Industrial Salespeople. The Retail Salesperson's Role: *Accurately Completing Transactions Is a Must. Handling Complaints Satisfies Customers. Working Stock Is Necessary. Personal Selling Is Where It's At.* Basic Retail Selling Process: *The Approach Is Critical. The Retail Sales Talk Requires Creativity. Use the Sell Sequence.* Handling Objections. Closing the Sale: *Types of Closes.* Follow-Up with Service after the Sale. Challenging Situations in Retail Selling: *Selling to Several Customers at the Same Time. The Group Shopper. Substitutions Are Sometimes Necessary. Turning the Customer over to Another Salesperson. The Customer Who Does Not Buy. Trading up Increases Sales. Return Goods Selling Is a Must. Selecting Which Price Line to Show. Suggestion Selling Is Persuasive.* Dos and Don'ts of Retail Selling.

13.   Selling in the Industrial Setting   386

Profile: Stephen Gibson   *U.S. Steel*

What's Different about the Industrial Market: *Demand for Industrial Products. Major Types of Industrial Purchases. Product Characteristics.* Who Makes the Decisions around Here? Who Should I Talk To? Purchasing Agents Are Rational Buyers. Why Do Producers Buy: *Value Analysis: A Powerful Selling Tool.*

**14.   Time and Territory Management Is a Key
to Success   408**

Profile: Cindy Kerns   *Xerox*

What Is a Sales Territory? *Why Establish Sales Territories?* Elements of Time and Territory Management: *Salesperson's Sales Quota. Account Analysis. Develop Account Objectives and Sales Quotas. Territory-Time Allocation. Customer Sales Planning. Scheduling and Routing. Territory and Customer Evaluation.*

15. Social, Ethical, and Legal Issues in Selling   436

Profile: Sandra Snow   *Upjohn*

The Social Responsibility of Business: *Why Assume Social Responsibilities? How Managers View Ethics.* Ethics in Dealing with Salespeople. Are These Socially Responsible Actions? Salespeoples' Ethics in Dealing with Their Employers. Ethics in Dealing with Customers. What to Do?

V   Functions of the Sales Manager

16. Planning, Organizing, Staffing of Successful Salespeople   456

Profile: Martha Hill   *Hanes Knitwear*

Transition from Salesperson to Sales Manager. What Is the Salary for Management? Overview of the Job: *Managerial Skills.* Sales Management Functions. Sales Force Planning: *Sales Forecasting. The Sales Manager's Budget.* Organizing the Sales Force: *The Organizational Chart.* Methods of Organization: *The Line Organization. Specialized Design. Combination of Design Elements.* Staffing the Sales Force: *Personnel Planning. Employment Planning. A Sales Manager's View of the Recruit.* Training the Sales Force: *Purposes of Training. Training Methods. Where Does Training Take Place? When Does Training Occur? Who Is Involved in Training?*

17. Motivation, Compensation, and Evaluation of Salespeople   498

Profile: Bob James   *American Scientific Products*

Motivation of the Sales Force. The Motivation Mix: Choose Your Ingredients Carefully. Methods of Compensating Salespeople: *Straight Salary. Straight Commission Plans. Combination Plans. Bonus: Individual or Group.* The Total Compensation Package. Nonfinancial Rewards Are Many. Leadership Is Important to Success: *Trait Approach. Behavioral Approach. Situational Approach. Choosing a Leadership Style.* Performance Evaluations Let People Know Where They Stand: *Reasons for Performance Evaluation. Who Should Evaluate Salespeople? When Should Salespeople Be Evaluated? Performance Criteria. Evaluation Guidelines.*

Cases

Fundamentals of Selling

Selling Your Best Product . . . Yourself

Customer satisfaction means more than just satisfaction with your product or service.

The first time, perhaps, you sell the product by satisfying a need. But after that, you're selling *yourself*—your knowledge and effort. Because along with the product the customer buys you! Your success in selling yourself—in making the buyer identify *you* with the product and company, look forward to seeing *you*, ask for *you* when he calls, be grateful to *you* when a delivery is speeded up or a snarl untangled— determines when the buyer stops being a customer and becomes an account!

Selling as a Profession

1

The Life and Times of the Professional Salesperson

Profile

Matt Suffoletto
IBM

My name is Matt Suffoletto. I joined IBM as a marketing representative in 1969, after earning a bachelor's degree in management science from Rensselaer Polytechnic Institute in Troy, N.Y. Since then I have held a number of marketing line and staff positions. I am currently a marketing consultant on IBM's corporate marketing staff.

While in college, I decided that I wanted to pursue a sales career. My technical background led me to seek employment in a company with a high technology product line. In addition, I was looking for a growing company in a growth industry.

IBM was one of the companies that fit my criteria. They have a strong emphasis on marketing and customer service and offer a clear opportunity for advancement. I still believe that the first successful sales call of my professional career was selling myself to IBM.

Career opportunities for salespeople are unlimited. That statement is evidenced by the vast number of former salespeople who are in key executive positions with *Fortune* 500 companies. What young salesperson doesn't dream of becoming a corporate vice president of sales?

Within IBM, the first step in launching oneself into a sales management career is to establish a consistent sales performance and maintain it for several years. However, you must keep in mind that you will be competing with other outstanding salespeople for job promotion, so sales performance just gets you into the running. Qualities such as leadership, creativity, adaptability, intelligence, and dedication are the real "difference makers."

When I started in sales I had a very narrow view of my possible career opportunities. Through exposure to positions other than direct sales, I learned of a multitude of attractive alternatives. Though career alternatives are numerous, several areas that are closely related to sales are product development, marketing research, advertising, administration, personnel, business planning, and marketing support.

The rewards of a successful sales career are unparalleled by those of any other business career that comes to mind. First and foremost is the personal satisfaction derived from the culmination of a sale. Personal recognition is high on the salesperson's list of motivational needs, and sales management responds to those needs with a wealth of recognition programs. Second, the financial rewards for a successful salesperson are outstanding. It is not uncommon for the best salespeople to earn incomes equivalent to those of top corporate managers. Finally, there is a wealth of personal gain to be realized through a commitment to excellence, for no career has a better yardstick of excellence than sales. Sales, more than any other vocation, offers a close relationship between effort and reward.

He came on muleback, dodging Indians as he went, with a pack full of better living and a tongue full of charms. For he was the great American salesman, and no man ever had a better thing to sell.

He came by rickety wagon, one jump behind the pioneers, carrying axes for the farmer, fancy dress goods for his wife, and encyclopedias for the farmer's ambitious boy. For he was the great practical democrat, spreader of good things among more and more people.

He came by upper berth and dusty black coupe, selling tractors and radios, iceboxes and movies, health and leisure, ambition and fulfillment. For he was America's emissary of abundance, Mr. High-Standard-Of-Living in person.

He rang a billion doorbells and enriched a billion lives. Without him there'd be no American ships at sea, no busy factories, no 60 million jobs. For the great American salesman is the great American civilizer, and everywhere he goes he leaves people better off.[1]

The salesperson makes valuable contributions to our way of life by selling goods and services that benefit individuals and industry. Red Motley, who was a sales training consultant, once said, "Nothing happens until somebody sells something." Selling brings in the money and causes cash registers across the country to ring. For centuries the salespeople of the world have been causing goods and services to change hands.

More than ever, today's salespeople are a dynamic power in the business world. They are responsible for generating more revenue in our economy than workers in any other single profession. The efforts of salespeople have a direct impact on such diverse areas as:

- The success of new products.
- Keeping existing products on the retailer's shelf.
- Constructing manufacturing facilities.
- Opening businesses and keeping them open.
- Generating sales orders that result in the loading of trucks, trains, and ships, airplanes, and pipelines that carry goods to customers all over the world.

The salesperson is engaged in a highly honorable, challenging, rewarding, and professional career. In this chapter you are introduced to the career, rewards, and duties of the salesperson. The chapter begins by examining why people choose sales careers.

Why Choose a Sales Career?

Five major reasons for choosing a sales career are (1) the wide variety of sales jobs available; (2) the freedom of being on your own; (3) the challenge of selling; (4) the opportunity for advancement in your company; and (5) the rewards offered by a career in sales.

A Variety of Sales Jobs Are Available

As members of a firm's sales force, salespeople are a vital element in the firm's effort to market their goods and services profitably. Due to the importance of salespeople to firms of all types, a wide variety of sales jobs are available to qualified applicants. Some 6 million people are now employed in selling jobs, and industry will need an estimated half million to a million new salespeople annually for the remainder of this decade.[2] These individuals will be performing diverse job activities associated with their particular type of sales job.

Types of Sales Jobs—Which Is for You? While there are numerous specific types of sales jobs, most salespeople work in one of three categories: either as a retail salesperson, a wholesaler's salesperson, or a manufacturer's sales representative. These categories are classified according to the type of products sold and the salesperson's type of employer.

Retail salespeople are often considered to be strictly order takers, operating inside a place of business. Selling clothing, shoes, jewelry, and sporting goods are all examples of retail sales jobs. These salespeople generally stay in the store and let the business "come to them." While this situation is common, it is not always the rule. At times a retail salesperson is required to contact customers at their home or place of business. Furthermore, many retail salespeople are highly skilled professionals, commanding exceptionally high incomes for their ability to sell.

The **wholesaler's sales representative** works for a firm that carries the products of several different manufacturers. The wholesaler's salesperson sells these products to retail or industrial customers. There may be thousands of items available for customers to purchase.

This salesperson may obtain orders in three ways. One way is to ask customers what products they need. Second, a salesperson may check customers' inventories and suggest that they reorder products found to be in low supply. Finally, they sell new products.

The wholesale salesperson's main responsibility is to provide service to his customers. Customers should be contacted routinely, with a low-pressure sales approach. A friendly and service-oriented approach is better than an aggressive one. Sales typically come from orders, rather than special selling techniques for persuading a customer to buy.

The types of **manufacturer's sales representative** positions range from the order taker who delivers milk and bread, to the specialized salesperson selling highly technical industrial products. Working for the firm that manufactures a salesperson's products is considered to be the most prestigous type of sales job available. The salesperson working for a manufacturer may sell to other manufacturers, wholesalers, retailers, or directly to consumers. There are five main types of manufacturer sales positions:

Account representatives call on a large number of already established customers in—for example—the food, textile, and apparel industries.

Detail salespeople concentrate on performing promotional activities and introducing new products rather than directly soliciting orders. The medical detail salesperson, for example, seeks to persuade doctors, the indirect customers, to specify a pharmaceutical company's trade name product for prescriptions. The actual sale is ultimately made through a wholesaler or is made direct to pharmacists and hospitals who fill prescriptions.

Sales engineers sell products for which technical know-how and an ability to discuss technical aspects of the product are extremely important. Expertise in identifying, analyzing, and solving customer problems is another critical factor. This type of selling is common in the oil, chemical, machinery, and heavy equipment industries because of the technical nature of their products.

Industrial products salespeople, nontechnical sell a tangible product to industrial buyers. No high degree of technical knowledge is required. Packaging materials manufacturers and office equipment sales representatives are nontechnical salespeople.

Service salespeople, unlike the four preceding types of manufacturing salespeople, must be able to sell the benefits of intangible or nonphysical products such as insurance, advertising, or computer repair services.

Only a few years ago, many manufacturers required their salespeople to routinely contact their customers and take their orders. It was felt that the company's reputation, quality products, and advertising actually sold their products. Today, manufacturers want their salespeople to be **order-getters,** not simply **order-takers.** Manufacturers' salespeople are trained on the most current techniques for selling **tangible products** (manufacturing equipment, computers, or copy machines) or **intangible services** (insurance and advertising services). Jobs are always available for qualified manufacturer's sales representatives.

Freedom of Action: You're on Your Own

A second reason why people choose a sales career is the freedom it offers. A sales job provides possibly the greatest relative freedom of any career. Experienced employees in outside sales usually receive very little direct supervision and may go for days, even weeks, without seeing their bosses.*

Job duties and sales goals are explained by a boss. Then salespeople are expected to carry out these job duties and achieve their goals with minimum guidance. They usually leave home to contact customers. These customers may be around the corner or around the world.

Job Challenge Is Always There

Working alone with the responsibility of a territory capable of generating thousands (sometimes millions) of dollars in revenue for your company is a great personal challenge. This environment adds great variety to a sales job. Salespeople often deal with hundreds of different people and business firms over a period of time. It is much like operating your own business, without the burdens of true ownership.

Because of the unique challenges and duties of a sales career, the type of person who succeeds in sales might conceivably be the subject of the following quote from Tex Schramm, president of the Dallas Cowboys professional football team:

> you attract a unique kind of person; competitive by nature, he has to feed his ego with success and public recognition. He is judged by the public. His incentive comes on Sunday before the crowd . . . and at the end of the season when the playoff money is won.[3]

Sales personnel are much like Schramm's football players. They are competitive, need success, thrive on recognition, and want high financial rewards when they are successful.

Opportunities for Advancement Are Great

Successful salespeople have many opportunities to move into top management positions. In many instances this advancement comes very quickly. Companies like Procter & Gamble, Quaker Oats, and Xerox may promote successful salespeople to managerial positions such as district sales managers after they have been with the company for only two years.

A sales personnel **career path,** as Figure 1–1 depicts, is the upward sequence of job movements during a sales career. Occasionally people

---

* Outside sales usually are made off the employer's premises and involve person-to-person contact. Inside sales occur on the premises, as in retail and telephone contact sales.

Figure 1–1 A Sales Personnel Career Path

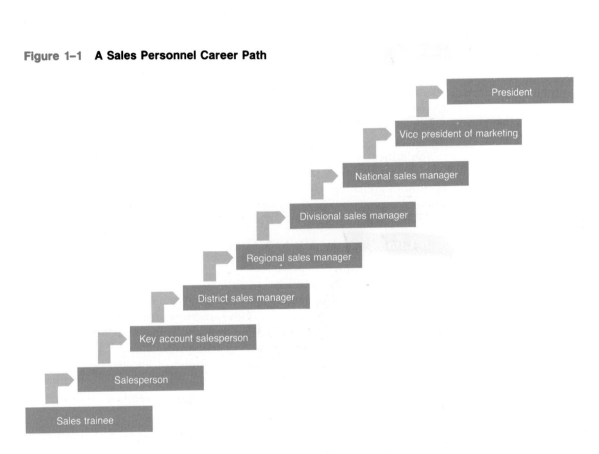

without previous sales experience are promoted into sales management positions. However, 99 percent of the time a career in sales management begins with an entry-level sales position. Firms believe that an experienced sales professional has the credibility, knowledge, and background to assume a higher position in the company.

Most companies have two or three successive levels of sales positions, beginning at the junior or trainee level. Beginning as a salesperson allows a person to:

Learn about the attitudes and activities of the company's salespeople.

Become familiar with customer attitudes toward the company, its products, and its salespeople.

Gain first-hand knowledge of products and their application, which is most important in technical sales.

Become "seasoned" in the world of business.

After training, a salesperson is given responsibility for a sales territory; he now moves into a regular sales position. In a relatively short time, the salesperson can earn the status and financial rewards of a senior sales position, contacting the larger, more important customers. Some companies refer to this function as a **key account** sales position. A person may choose to stop here, or may opt to move into sales management. Keep in mind that while most recruiters today want to hire a person who can sell, they also look for management potential in their salespeople.

The first managerial level is usually the district sales manager's position. From district sales manager a person may move into higher levels of sales management. However, it is also possible to move from any of the sales management levels into the sales training, product management, advertising, promotion, or marketing research areas customarily located at the company's home office.

Rewards: The Sky's the Limit

As a salesperson you can look forward to two types of rewards—nonfinancial and financial.

Nonfinancial Rewards.   Sometimes called psychological income or intrinsic rewards, **nonfinancial rewards** are generated by the individual, not given by the company. You know the job has been done well—for instance, when you have skillfully delivered a sales presentation.

When you successfully meet the challenges of your job, it produces a feeling of self-worth, and you realize that your job is important. Everyone wants to feel good about a job, and a selling career allows you to experience these good feelings, these intrinsic rewards, daily. Salespeople often report that the nonfinancial rewards of their jobs are just as important to them as financial rewards.

Financial Rewards.   Many are attracted to selling because in a sales career **financial rewards** are usually based solely on performance. Many professional salespeople have opportunities to earn large salaries. These salaries average even higher than salaries for other types of workers at the same organizational level. People with no experience can find sales jobs paying $12,000 to $35,000. With several years' experience, their earnings can rise to $45,000 or even more. In addition, their employers furnish them with cars and allowances for travel, customer entertainment, and meals.

A recent study conducted by the American Management Association showed that salaries for field sales personnel have been moving rapidly upward, with new sales trainees earning an average of $22,350 their first year (see Figure 1–2). This same upward trend was also found for sales managers' salaries.

Table 1–1 presents the percentage increases in salaries of field sales personnel for consumer and industrial products. Industrial salespeople were found to have higher salaries than their consumer salespeople counterparts, even though both groups of salespeople had sizeable increase in pay. This indicates that employers recognize the importance

Figure 1–2 How Salespeople's Total Compensation Is Growing

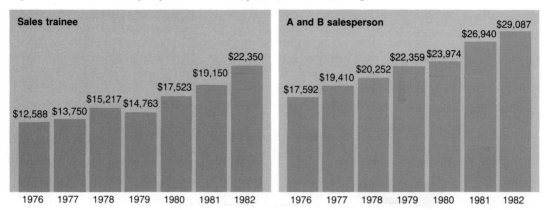

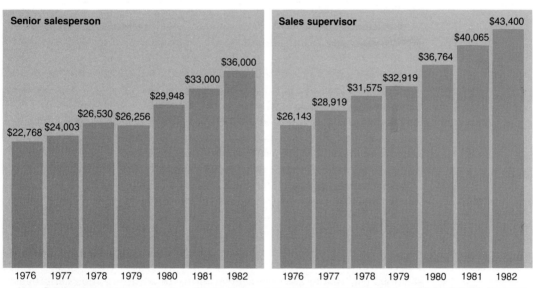

Note: Salaries plus commission incentives. Figures apply to consumer goods, industrial goods, and "other," that is, insurance, services, transportation, and utilities.

Source: Reprinted by permission of the publisher, from Executive Compensation Service, "Sales Personnel Report," 25th edition, 1982. © 1982 by American Management Associations. All rights reserved.

Definitions of field sales personnel

Sales trainee: Anyone who is learning about the company's products, services, and policies, as well as proven sales techniques, in preparation for a sales assignment.

Salesperson Grade A: A "regular" salesperson who has little or no selling experience except that which has been acquired in the company's sales training program. He contacts established and prospective customers to develop interest in the company's products and to sell them.

Salesperson Grade B: A salesperson who has broad knowledge of the company's products and services and sells in a specifically assigned territory. He maintains contact with established customers and develops new prospects.

Senior salesperson: A salesperson at the highest level of selling responsibility. He is completely familiar with the company's products, services, and policies; he usually has years of experience and is assigned to major accounts and territories.

Sales supervisor: A veteran salesperson who, because of abilities and experience, leads others. This salesperson's primary function is to direct the activities of and train salespeople and sales trainees, but he or she may also sell to selected key accounts.

Table 1–1 Salespeople's Annual Compensation

	Consumer Products			Industrial Products		
Salesperson Level	1982	1981	Percent Change	1982	1981	Percent Change
Sales trainee						
Straight salary	$17,400	$15,200	+14.5%	$17,646	$16,650	+6.0%
Salary plus incentive						
Salary	18,250	14,650	+24.6	18,063	17,375	+4.0
Incentive	2,200	1,250	+76.0	3,000	2,825	+6.2
Total	20,500	16,250	+26.2	23,113	20,600	+12.2
A&B salespeople						
Straight salary	21,500	18,100	+18.8	25,623	24,392	+5.0
Salary plus incentive						
Salary	20,980	19,060	+10.1	22,619	21,171	+6.8
Incentive	5,700	4,160	+37.0	6,013	5,753	−4.5
Total	27,640	24,320	+13.7	29,531	27,771	+6.3
Senior salespeople						
Straight salary	29,892	28,200*	+ 6.0*	33,942	30,357	+11.8
Salary plus incentive						
Salary	25,460	23,820	+ 6.9	28,600	25,765	+11.0
Incentive	5,600	4,560	+22.8	7,044	7,835	−10.1
Total	33,300	30,140	+10.5	36,919	33,724	−9.5
Sales supervisor						
Straight salary	32,500	32,500	N.C.	39,564	35,825	+10.4
Salary plus incentive						
Salary	30,760	30,080	+ 2.3	34,014	31,687	+7.3
Incentive	5,020	5,420	− 7.4	8,607	9,120	−5.6
Total	36,780	35,420	+ 3.8	44,050	41,147	−7.1

Note: Some differences between years reflect changes in the organizations that reported data. It should also be noted that in the "salary plus incentive" category, the "total" compensation will not equal the sum of the "salary" and "incentive" components because not all respondents provided information for each of the components.

N.C. = No change.

* Estimated.

Source: Reprinted, by permission of the publisher, from Executive Compensation Service, "Sales Personnel Report," 25th edition,1982–83. © 1982 by American Management Association. All rights reserved.

of their salespeople and are willing to pay them an above-average salary year after year. This leads to an important question. What are the main job activities salespeople perform to receive such high salaries?

The Salesperson's Activities as a Territorial Manager

The salesperson's roles or activities can vary from company to company, depending on whether sales involve goods or services, the firm's market characteristics, and the location of customers. For example, a salesperson selling *Encyclopedia Britannica* or Avon products performs similar, but somewhat different, job activities than the industrial salesperson making sales calls on General Electric or RCA.

Most people believe that a salesperson only makes sales presentations, but there is much more to the job than person-to-person selling. The salesperson functions as a **territory manager**—planning, organizing, and executing activities that increase sales and profits in a given territory. A sales territory is comprised of a group of customers assigned within a geographical area. Figure 1–3 indicates just a few of the typical activities

Figure 1–3   Examples of a Salesperson's Activities

Starting with an early-morning sales meeting, these photographs depict the activities of a Scott Paper Company Consumer Sales Representative (1) meeting with his supervisor, (2) checking a report, (3) preparing for a customer call, (4) planning an in-store promotion with the store manager, (5) getting product from the store's backroom, and (6) with the permission of the store manager, stocking the shelves with specially marked packages of ScotTowels.

Source: Scott Paper Company; used with permission.

of a salesperson working for the Scott Paper Company. As manager of a territory, the salesperson performs the following seven functions:

1. Provides Solutions to Customer's Problems. Customers have needs that can be met and problems that can be solved by purchasing goods or services. Salespeople seek to uncover potential or existing needs or problems and show how the use of their products or services can satisfy those needs or solve those problems.

2. Provides Service to Customers. Salespeople provide a wide range of services, including handling of complaints, returning damaged merchandise, providing samples, suggesting business opportunities, and developing recommendations on how the customer can promote products purchased from the salesperson.

If necessary, sales people may even occasionally work at the customer's business. For example, a salesperson selling fishing tackle may arrange an in-store demonstration of a manufacturer's products and offer to repair fishing reels as a service to the retailer's customers.

Furthermore, a manufacturer may have its salespeople sell to distributors or wholesalers. Then the manufacturer's representative may make sales calls with the distributor's salespeople to aid them in selling and servicing the distributor's customers.

3. Sells to Current and New Customers. The acquisition of new accounts is the lifeblood of a business; it brings new revenues into the company. This important job must be done if a salesperson's territory is to grow.

While new accounts are crucial, salespeople also strive to increase the sales volume of their present customers by encouraging them to purchase additional items within the same product line along with any new product offerings.

4. Helps Customers Resell Products to Their Customers. A major part of many sales jobs is for the salesperson to help wholesalers and retailers resell the products that they have purchased. The salesperson helps wholesale customers sell products to retail customers and helps retail customers sell products to consumers.

Consider the Quaker Oats salesperson selling a product to grocery wholesalers. Not only must the wholesaler be contacted, but also grocery retailers must be called on, sales made, and orders written up and sent to the wholesaler. In turn, the wholesaler sells and delivers the products to the retailers. The Quaker Oats salesperson also develops promotional programs to help the retailer sell the firm's products. These programs involve supplying advertising materials, putting on store demonstrations, and setting up product displays.

5. Helps Customers Use Products after Purchase. The salesperson's job is not over after the sale is made. Often customers must be shown how to obtain the full benefit from the product. For example, after a customer buys an IBM computer system, technical specialists help the buyer learn how to operate the equipment.

6. Builds Goodwill with Customers. A selling job is people oriented, entailing face-to-face contact with the customer. Many sales are based, to some extent, on friendship and trust. The salesperson needs to develop a personal, friendly, businesslike relationship with everyone who may influence a buying decision. This is an ongoing part of the salesperson's job, and requires integrity, high ethical standards, and a sincere interest in satisfying customers' needs.

7. Provides Company with Market Information. Salespeople provide information to their companies on such topics as competitors' activities, customers' reactions to new products, complaints about products or policies, market opportunities, and their own job activities. This information is so important for many companies that their salespeople are required to send in weekly or monthly reports on the activities of the firm's competition in their territory. Salespeople are a vital part of their employers' information retrieval system.

When combined, and properly carried out, these seven sales job activities produce a successful sales performance. An example of how a salesperson integrates these activities helps to better understand the sales job. See the accompanying box, "A typical day for a Xerox salesperson."

A Typical Day for a Xerox Salesperson

You are responsible for your sales coverage, time, and budget. Help is available and you'll have plenty of marketing and service support; but you're expected to work independently, without constant direction.

Your day is devoted primarily to customer contact. Potential customers may phone the branch and ask to see a Xerox representative. More likely, however, you will acquire customers by making appointments or by visiting businesses to meet the decision makers, discuss their needs, and offer solutions to their problems. As part of your position, you'll make product presentations, either at the Xerox branch office or at the customer's office. You will also spend a fair amount of time on the telephone, following up leads, arranging appointments, and speaking with managers in a variety of businesses and organizations.

In working with customers, you'll need to solve a number of problems. What Xerox product best fits the customer's needs? How do Xerox products compare with the competition? Should the machine be purchased or leased? What's the total cash outlay—and per copy cost—for the machine and its service? How should the product be financed? Where should the machine be placed for maximum efficiency? What training is needed for employees? How can Xerox products meet future office needs?

You'll also be engaged in a number of customer support activities, such as expediting product deliveries, checking credit, writing proposals, and training customer employees in the use of the product. You might also refer customers to other Xerox sales organizations and make joint calls with representatives from these organizations.

Each day will bring you new challenges to face and problems to solve. Your days will be busy and interesting.[4]

Is a Sales Career Right for You?

It may be too early in your life to determine if you really want to be a salesperson. The balance of this book will aid you in investigating sales as a career. Your search for a career, any career, begins with *you*. In considering a sales career, be honest and realistic with yourself. Ask yourself questions such as:

- What are my past accomplishments?
- What are my future goals?
- Do I want to have the responsibility of a sales job?
- Do I mind travel? How much travel is acceptable?
- How much freedom do I want in the job?
- Do I have the personality characteristics for the job?

Your answers to these questions can help you analyze the various types of sales jobs and establish criteria for evaluating job openings. You should determine the industries, types of products or services, and specific companies in which you have an interest.

College placement offices, libraries, and business periodicals offer a wealth of information on companies as well as sales positions in them. Conversations with friends and acquaintances who are involved in selling, or have been in sales can give you realistic insight into what challenges, rewards, and disadvantages the sales vocation offers. To better prepare yourself to obtain a sales job, you must understand what companies look for in their salespeople.

A Sales Manager's View of the Recruit

The following discussion of what sales managers consider when hiring a salesperson is based on a summary of a talk given by a sales manager to a sales class. It is reasonably representative of what companies look for when hiring salespeople.

> We look for outstanding applicants who are mature and intelligent. They should be able to handle themselves well in the interview, demonstrating good interpersonal skills. They should have a well-thought-out career plan and be able to discuss it rationally. They should have a friendly, pleasing personality. A clean, neat appearance is a must. They should have a positive attitude, be willing to work hard, be ambitious, and demonstrate a good degree of interest in the employer's business field. They should have good grades and other personal, school, and business accomplishments. Finally, they should have clear goals and objectives in life. The more common characteristics upon which applicants for our company are judged are (1) appearance, (2) self-expression, (3) maturity, (4) personality, (5) experience, (6) enthusiasm, and (7) interest in the job.

People often consider a sales career because they have heard that a person can earn a good salary selling. They think anyone can sell. These people have really not considered all of the facts. As you are beginning to see, a sales job has high rewards because it also has many important responsibilities. Companies do not pay high salaries for nothing. As you will see in this book, a sales career involves great challenges which require hard work by qualified individuals. Let us review the characteristics of a successful salesperson.

Success in Selling—What Does It Take?

Throughout this book you will read comments from salespeople about their jobs. In order to answer the question, "What makes a salesperson successful?" I asked them what they felt was required of them to be successful salespeople. The eight most frequently mentioned characteristics were: (1) love of their job; (2) willingness to work hard; (3) need to achieve success; (4) optimistic outlook; (5) knowledge of their job: (6) careful use of selling time; (7) ability to listen to customers; and (8) customer service. Each of these characteristics is described more fully below.

Love of Selling

The successful salesperson is an individual who loves selling, finds it exciting, and is strongly convinced that the product being sold offers something of great value. Prudential Life Insurance salesman George Morris states it best by saying, "To be successful you need a very deep commitment to your product and what it will do."[5*] In selling her Amway products, Bernice Hansen emphasizes that she "has wonderful products that everyone needs. . . . If you believe in what you are doing as strongly as I do, you have the self-confidence to be successful."[6]

To be sure, a love of selling itself is one characteristic of successful salespeople. Irving Rousso, who made a salary of $547,875 selling for the Russ Togs Corporation, says, "I'm still hungry and don't ask me why. I just know that it still gives me a thrill and a chill every time I get a reorder."[7] Other salespeople quoted throughout this book make similar comments about how their enthusiasm for their work helps them to be successful. This eagerness to do their job results in hard work.

Willingness to Work Hard

Successful salespeople will tell you that even though they enjoy it, selling requires long hours of hard work, day in and day out, to reach their personal goals. This usually means working at night to plan the next day's activities and working on many Saturdays and sometimes Sundays.

A ten-to-twelve hour work day is common. It is their love of work

---

* A profile of George Morris appears in Chapter 10.

and their need for success that apparently motivates some salespeople to make this personal sacrifice. Matt Suffoletto of IBM says, "If you would make each sales call, presentation, or proposal as if it were the single event from which you will gain quota attainment, recognition, or promotion, you will always be miles in front of your competition."[8] Underlying a tolerance for hard work, there is often a desire for success in life.

Need to Achieve

Each of us has a desire to be successful; yet some individuals seem to have a much higher desire for success. Successful salespeople have, as part of their personality, a strong work ethic and a high need to strive for success. If people love their work, are willing to work hard, and have a strong desire to achieve success, do you think they will be successful? I believe you would say yes to that question.

Steve Gibson of U.S. Steel* finds "being second best is not good enough. I am personally challenged to be my customers' best steel representative. I want to excel. I've found that asking myself the simple question "Did I do my best?" at the end of each business day is sufficient."[9] "Second is not good enough," "Go beyond the call of duty," and "Make that second effort," are frequent comments of successful salespeople.

The need to achieve involves persistence. Consider former president Calvin Coolidge's following comments:

Nothing in this world can take the place of *persistence*. Talent will not. Nothing is more common than unsuccessful men with talent. Genius will not. Unsuccessful genius is almost a proverb. Education will not. The world is full of educated derelicts. Persistence and determination alone are omnipotent. The slogan "press on" has solved and always will solve the problems of the human race.

The enthusiastic person who is willing to work hard in pursuit of a goal must be optimistic!

Have an Optimistic Outlook

All of the salespeople I know credit a positive attitude toward their companies, products, customers, themselves, and life as major reasons for their success. Successful salespeople are enthusiastic, confident, and constantly think of themselves as successful. Sure, salespeople have times when things do not go as they wish. Yet their positive mental attitude helps them to overcome periodic problems. They continually look for methods to improve their attitude.

---

* A profile of Steve Gibson appears in Chapter 13.

One method of maintaining a positive self-image is illustrated in the credo of Elbert Hubbard. At the age of 35, Hubbard retired as a highly successful soap salesman. He went on to become successful as a magazine publisher, a marketer of books, furniture, and a direct mail specialist. Elbert Hubbard's business credo was as follows:

I believe in myself.

I believe in the goods I sell.

I believe in the firm for whom I work.

I believe in my colleagues and helpers.

I believe in American Business Methods.

I believe in producers, creators, manufacturers, distributors, and in all industrial workers of the world who have a job, and hold it down.

I believe that Truth is an asset.

I believe in good cheer and in good health, and I recognize the fact that the first requisite in success is not to achieve the dollar, but to confer a benefit, and that the reward will come automatically and usually as a matter of course.

I believe in sunshine, fresh air, spinach, applesauce, laughter, buttermilk, babies, bombazine, and chiffon, always remembering that the greatest word in the English language is *sufficiency*.

I believe that when I make a sale, I make a friend.

And I believe that when I part with a man, I must do it in such a way that when he sees me again, he will be glad and so will I.

I believe in the hands that work, and the brains that think, and in the hearts that love.

Amen, and Amen.

Although Mr. Hubbard's philosophy may sound a bit old-fashioned, it all boils down to:

■ Believing in yourself.

■ Thinking of yourself as a success.

■ Being enthusiastic when helping buyers—be service oriented.

■ Being positive in your outlook on life and the job.

In no other career is the need to think positively more important than in sales. As a salesperson you should examine your inner self, commonly referred to as your self-concept, and make sure you have a positive, enthusiastic attitude toward yourself, your work, and your customers. As Figure 1–4 illustrates, do not be afraid to fail.

Optimism and hard work are building blocks for success. In addition, top salespeople believe job and product knowledge are also necessary if you wish to be successful in a sales career.

Figure 1–4

Don't Be Afraid To Fail

You've failed
many times,
although you may not
remember.
You fell down
the first time
you tried to walk.
You almost drowned
the first time
you tried to
swim, didn't you?
Did you hit the
ball the first time
you swung a bat?
Heavy hitters,
the ones who hit the
most home runs,
also strike
out a lot.
R. H. Macy
failed seven
times before his
store in New York
caught on.
English novelist
John Creasey got
753 rejection slips
before he published
564 books.
Babe Ruth struck out
1,330 times,
but he also hit
714 home runs.
Don't worry about
failure.
Worry about the
chances you miss
when you don't
even try.

Be Knowledgeable

Successful salespeople place a great deal of emphasis on being thoroughly knowledgeable on all aspects of their business. This helps them to project a professional image and to build customer confidence.

When you read Mike Impink's profile at the beginning of Chapter 2, consider the product and customer knowledge he must have to sell $21 million of Alcoa aluminum products to developmental engineers, production managers, and corporate officers. The comments later in the book from salespeople representing such companies as Prudential Insurance, Century 21 Realtors, and Upjohn Pharmaceuticals discuss the need to be informed. Take, for example, Steve Gibson of U.S. Steel who says:

I am forever amazed by the volume of knowledge required in our business. The way I've found to keep ahead is by designating a time each week for reading and education. I routinely read the *Houston Business Journal,* *American Metal Market, Wall Street Journal,* and various other important periodicals. I also keep current on U.S. Steel's advertising campaigns and review product literature to help plan for my sales calls. To supplement my education, I am a member of the American Institute of Steel Engineers and participate as a steel fellow for the American Iron and Steel Institute.[10]

As products and services become more complex, companies place even greater emphasis on training their salespeople, and salespeople on training themselves. It is no wonder that corporate recruiters seek above-average individuals to fill their entry-level sales positions.

This knowledge characteristic also includes awareness of the most up-to-date ideas concerning selling skills. Successful salespeople are experts at developing and presenting talks that sell their products. They are constantly educating themselves on methods of better determining customers' needs and of effectively communicating the benefit of their products in order to satisfy those needs.

Salespeople read selling books and magazine articles on selling, and attend sales training courses to learn how to sell their products better. This knowledge is incorporated into their sales presentation, which is rehearsed until it sounds like a natural conversation between seller and buyer. Another characteristic that is found in good salespeople is the careful use of time.

Value Time

Since there is only so much time in the day for contacting customers and there are so many demands on their time, successful salespeople value time and use it wisely by carefully planning their day's activities. Effective time management is a must. What customer will be called upon, what product is to be presented, and how to go about presenting it must be planned carefully.

Ask Questions and Then Listen to Uncover Customer Needs

Joe Gandolfo, who sold over *one billion dollars* of life insurance in a single year, has a sign on his office wall that reads: "God gave you two ears and one mouth, and He meant for you to do twice as much listening as talking."[11]

Good salespeople are good listeners. They ask questions to uncover prospects' needs and then listen as prospects answer the questions and state their needs. Then they show how their products' benefits will fulfill these needs. The ability to identify and meet customer needs separates the successful salesperson from the average salesperson. To meet customers' needs successfully, you have to provide service.

Serve Your Customer

The most important of all these characteristics for establishing a lasting sales relationship with a customer is to be willing to provide service. Customers must believe that you care about them and their welfare. Successful salespeople respect their customers, treat them fairly, honestly like them, and develop a good working relationship with them much like a partnership. They provide outstanding service to each.

These factors help them to earn the respect of their customers and to be considered professional businesspeople with high ethics. Steve Gibson of U.S. Steel says, "I've found the Golden Rule of 'Do unto others . . . always to be a basis of earning respect."[12]

Summary of Major Selling Issues

Personal selling is an old and honorable profession. It is responsible for helping to improve this country's standard of living and providing benefits to individual buyers through the purchase of products. Thousands of people have chosen a sales career because of the availability of sales jobs, the personal freedom it provides, its challenge, the multitude of opportunities for success, and its nonfinancial and financial rewards.

The salesperson's job requires the planning, organization, and execution of activities that increase sales and profits. These involve selling to new customers, obtaining reorders, selling new products, helping customers find new uses for present products, helping customers use products properly, and suggesting ways wholesalers and retailers can sell to their customers.

A person can become a successful salesperson through company and personal training and by the proper application of this knowledge in the development of skills and abilities for benefiting customers. It is also important to believe in the product or service being sold, work hard, want to succeed, and maintain a positive outlook toward both selling and oneself. In addition, a successful salesperson should be knowledgeable, should be able to plan, and should use selling time wisely. It is also important to be a good listener, and provide service to customers.

The remainder of the book will expand on these topics to provide you with the background either to improve your present selling ability or to help you decide if a sales career is the right one for you.

Review and Discussion Questions

1. Chapter 1 profiled Matt Suffoletto of IBM who commented on job rewards and opportunities of a sales career. Relate his comments

to the book's description of job opportunities, a sales career path, and the rewards of the salesperson.

2. The term *salesperson* refers to many types of sales jobs. What are the major types of sales jobs available?

3. Chapter 1 described characteristics of several successful salespeople currently selling goods and services for national companies. Describe those characteristics and then discuss whether or not those same characteristics are also needed for success in other types of jobs.

4. People choose a particular career for many reasons. What are the five reasons someone might choose a sales career?

5. What is meant by the term *career path*? What are the various jobs to which a salesperson might be promoted in his company?

6. A salesperson manages a sales territory. A territory manager must perform numerous activities. What are seven important activities performed in the territory?

Projects

1. Interview one or more salespeople and write a brief report on what they like and dislike about their jobs; why they chose a sales career; what activities they perform; and what they believe it takes to succeed in selling their products.

2. Contact your college placement office and report on what they believe firms who are recruiting people for sales positions look for in applicants.

Case

Susan Sheppard

Susan Sheppard comes from a small Texas town. Her family had such a low income that they could not afford to help out with her college expenses, so she worked as a school intramurals track and softball coordinator and later as a dormitory counselor. Susan majored in marketing at Texas A&M University, graduated third in her class with a 3.89 grade point average and was treasurer of the 1,000-member Marketing Society. She has a pleasant personality but would not be described as "outgoing." Her faculty advisor wanted her to go on to graduate school. However, while Susan liked school, she felt it was time to earn a salary which would provide her enough money to "live a little."

In her last semester she was offered three jobs, one with a bank paying $800 a month, another with a retail department store paying $1,000 monthly, and one from Burroughs, where she was told she would earn $15,000 the first year and over $25,000 the second year. Susan did not really feel that she could sell, especially since she would start off in Houston selling desk adding machines for six months. She would be going door to door contacting small businesses selling desk adding machines. This was part of the initial training program. After one year she was then to move into selling small computer systems to banks. Here she would be on a $1,000-a-month straight salary and commission. Susan had never sold anything and could not imagine being able to sell enough computers so that she could earn $13,000 in commissions.

Questions:

1. If you were Susan, which job would you take? Why?
2. How would you describe Susan Sheppard?
3. Which job do you feel she should take or should she continue to look for another job?

2

Where Personal Selling
Fits into the Firm

**Learning
objectives**

1. To discuss the role of personal selling in the firm and the firm's marketing effort.

2. To illustrate how the firm's product, price, distribution, and promotion efforts are coordinated for maximum sales success.

3. To explain the relationship of the salesperson's objectives and quotas to the corporate and marketing objectives.

4. To show why sales objectives are important.

**Key Terms
for Selling**

Marketing

Marketing concept

Marketing mix

Product

Price

Distribution

Promotion

Personal selling

Advertising

Publicity

Sales promotion

Sales objectives

Sales quotas

Strategies

Tactics

Profile

Mike Impink
Alcoa

My name is Mike Impink, and I am a sales representative with the Aluminum Company of America. I have worked for Alcoa as a sales representative in three different assignments since graduating from Lehigh University in 1977 with an MBA degree.

My career began with an intensive training program approximately 12 weeks long, and included a tour of Alcoa's manufacturing facilities. I have moved through three progressively more responsible sales assignments over the past four years, and I look forward to the opportunity to move into sales management, marketing, or product management.

My role as a sales representative is complex and involves the responsibility for total annual sales of approximately $21 million. My job is to work with customers and prospects to help them improve their products, lower their costs, and increase the efficiency of their manufacturing processes. I work with and sell to developmental engineers, production managers, and corporate officers, as well as buyers and purchasing agents. I evaluate each aspect of my customer's business and develop persuasive recommendations for the use of aluminum. I negotiate contracts, assist in making credit arrangements, and suggest proper packaging and delivery methods.

Alcoa is known for its effective and innovative industrial marketing. In large measure, this reputation results from the kind of people who represent the company—people who are first and foremost professional in their ability to identify and solve customer problems.

I have found three sales techniques to be critical to a successful sales effort. First, you must bring creativity and innovation to solving the customer's problems. In addition, you must be willing to take risks in developing your approach to selling. If you are not willing to try new approaches, you will not achieve real personal and professional growth. Finally, and most important, you must add persistence to both of the above. Rarely is success easily achieved. Thus you must persevere, because even if you are creative and do take risks, you will have to overcome seemingly unlimited hurdles. You will find persistence to be critical.

"Each year," one national sales manager said, "our corporate marketing group gives us a selling program for existing and new products, and I am instructed which months in the year to have my salespeople place special effort on products with our customers. We are given product, competitive, and market information, along with sales presentation materials. This information is used to develop sales plans and presentations for our customers.

"We hold sales meetings to present this program to all of our field sales personnel. As the sales force begins to sell a product, our national product advertising, sampling, and couponing begins. This process results in a coordinated marketing effort aimed at selling a single product both to consumers and to our retail customers all over America. Sales quotas are established for each salesperson for each product we are selling in a particular sales period (such as for a two-month period). Salespeople who reach their quotas earn bonus money and sales contest prizes as well as corporate recognition of their selling ability."

This sales manager's comments show that a firm's sales force is but one part of its total marketing effort. This chapter introduces you to the purpose and components of a firm's marketing efforts, along with the role and importance of the sales force in a firm's total marketing effort. The chapter ends with a discussion of sales objectives and quotas to illustrate their importance to the firm and their salespeople.

Marketing Sells a Firm's Products and Services

What does a business firm do in our economy? Reduced to basics, businesses have two major functions: *production* of products or services and *marketing* those products and services.

To be successful in today's competitive marketplace, people in business realize that they must first determine people's needs, and then produce goods and services to satisfy them. A company, whether it is General Motors or a small retailer, is in business to create want-satisfying products and services for its customers. In today's competitive business environment, the success of products and services is determined by the consumers who buy them. Goods and services that do not satisfy consumers will be forced from the market, since consumers will not buy them.

If you asked the general public what the term *marketing* means, many would say *selling*. Selling, in turn, usually implies advertising and personal selling to the public. Yet the act of selling is only one part of a firm's marketing activities.

The role of the marketing function in a business is basically to generate sales or revenues for the company. The firm's customers exchange something of value (such as money, credit, or other goods) for the firm's goods and services. Thus, marketing is an *exchange* process. **Marketing** can be defined as the business and individual activities designed to create profitable exchanges between buyer and seller in order to satisfy the buyer's needs. These activities involve the development, pricing, promotion, and distribution of want-satisfying goods and services to consumers and industrial users. Marketing activities are therefore very important both to the individual company and to our economy as a whole. This has not always been the case.

Business Has Changed over the Years

American business has gone through many changes of philosophy and direction. To a large extent these changes were brought about by the ultimate realization that the "consumer is king." However, this has not always been the viewpoint of business. Several major nonconsumer marketing phases existed prior to the emergence of today's consumer-oriented attitude.

Production-Oriented Stage Was First.   Before the Great Depression of the 1930s a common saying in industry was, "Build a better mousetrap, and the world will beat a path to your door." Companies were basically production-oriented. "We know what people want—they want our product"; or, "I like this product and so will others" were phrases often used by corporate presidents.

In those early days, few firms had marketing departments, and many did not even have a formal sales department. An engineer would develop a product, have the production department make it, and then simply put it in the catalog and wait for people to order. Production and engineering shaped the company's objectives and planning. Products were sold at a price determined by production and financial executives. Henry Ford, for example, said that customers could have any color automobile they wanted as long as it was black. The automobile was a new, exciting product, needed by consumers. America bought what was produced.

Next Came the Sales-Oriented Stage.   By the early 1940s, it became clear that the attitude and needs of the consumer had changed. The military requirements of World War II created a shortage of goods and services. This wartime deprivation resulted in a strong consumer demand when the war was over.

A few years after the war, consumers had many products to choose from and firms found they had to go to the consumer, instead of waiting for consumers to buy. Companies still produced goods with little regard for the consumer's needs. However, the use of personal selling and advertising began to be recognized as important selling methods. In the postwar era firms placed most of their emphasis on advertising their product, expecting their salespeople to contact customers and take their orders.

Salespeople, armed with very unsophisticated selling techniques, were asked to contact potential customers, show them their products, and take their orders. Training for salespeople consisted mainly of providing them with product knowledge. They had to rely on natural ability for developing and giving sales presentations. Very few companies recognized the value of training their salespeople on selling techniques. However, as the 1950s approached, businesses found that they had to become market oriented rather than sales oriented.

Market-Oriented Stage: The Now Generation. Today's marketing philosophy is market or customer oriented. No longer do companies manufacture a product and give it to salespeople to sell without first considering the customer. Firms developed complementary goals of both achieving a profitable sales volume *and* satisfying their customers. Marketing, rather than selling, became the focus of business sales activities. In the 1950s companies began to carefully examine consumer needs, and concentrated on developing products which both satisfied these needs and earned profits.

Providing customer satisfaction, while allowing the organization to achieve its goals, is the major thrust of this **marketing concept.** You can see the marketing concept being used by many companies. Charles Revson, late president of Revlon, said, "In the factory we make cosmetics, and in the drugstore we sell hope." Revlon finds out what customers want and then creates products to satisfy these wants. Firms also incorporate the consumer-oriented or marketing concept into their advertising. Burger King advertises, "Have it your way," while United Airlines states, "You're the boss."

Customers represent the beginning and the end of a firm's marketing process. "What do customers want?" "Can we satisfy customer's wants at a profit?" and "Are our customers satisfied with our products?" are three important questions asked by industry today. Firms examine their customers' needs, then use several marketing elements to show customers how their products will satisfy their needs. Skillful use of these *marketing elements* is what separates today's leading firms from those of little market share.

Essentials of a Firm's Marketing Effort

The essentials of a firm's marketing effort are their ability (1) to determine the needs of their customers and (2) to create and maintain an effective marketing mix which satisfies the needs of their customers. A firm's **marketing mix** consists of four main elements—product, price, distribution or place, and promotion—used by a marketing manager to market goods and services. It is the marketing manager's responsibility to determine how best to use each of these elements in the firm's marketing efforts.

Product. A **product** refers to a good or service. Today, firms spend enormous amounts of time and money creating the products they sell. They carefully research what customers want before developing a product. Consideration is given to the product itself, and its package design, trademarks, warranties, and service policies.

Research and development and strategies for selling new products are major activities of the corporate marketing department. Typically, sales personnel have very little input on what products should be produced. Their involvement in selling the product begins after the product has been produced.*

Price. Corporate management also determines each product's initial **price.** This process involves establishing each product's normal price and possible special discount prices. Since product price is often critical to customers, it is an important part of the marketing mix.

Companies develop varied pricing techniques and methods for their salespeople to use. For example, General Motors, Chrysler, and Ford have offered consumers cash rebates to increase automobile sales. Companies such as Quaker Oats, Kraft, and Lever Brothers send out discount coupons to consumers, and offer special price reductions to retailers on their products so that retailers will reduce their prices. Some salespeople use offers of price reductions in their sales presentations to entice the retailer to purchase large quantities of the product. Getting large shipments to retailers and other types of customers leads to another element of the marketing mix.

Distribution. The marketing manager also determines the best method of distributing the product. It is important to have the product available to customers in a convenient and accessible location.

Several examples of **distribution** channels for consumer and industrial products are shown in Figure 2–1. The manufacturer of consumer products may have its salespeople selling directly to the household consumer. Most consumer product manufacturers, however, sell directly to resellers—retailers or wholesalers. Two main distribution channels for manufacturers of industrial products are selling directly to the industrial user, such as another manufacturer, or selling to a wholesaler, who in turn sells to another manufacturer.

Promotion. The **promotional** element of the marketing mix is designed to increase company sales by communicating product

---

* Product, price, and distribution are discussed further in Chapter 5.

Figure 2–1 Examples of Distribution Channels for Consumer and Industrial Products

Consumer products

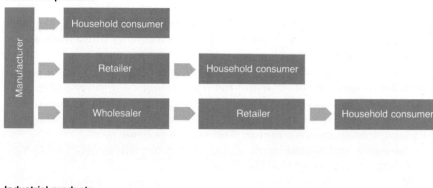

Industrial products

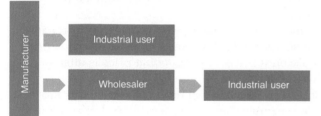

information to potential customers. The four basic parts of firm's promotional effort are: (1) **personal selling,** (2) **advertising,** (3) **publicity,** and (4) **sales promotion.** These are briefly explained in Figure 2–2. As you see, the company's sales force is one segment of the firm's promotional effort.

In addition to informing people about a product's existence, promotion also is used to educate consumers about the product's features, advantages, and benefits; tell them where to buy it; and make them aware of its price versus value. The question arises as to "What is the best promotional element to use in selling a product?" This decision is made only after consideration of the type of product and the customers who will buy it.

The marketing manager determines what proportion of the firm's budget will be allocated to each product and how much emphasis on each of the promotional variables will be given to each product. IBM, for example, allocates more of its promotional budget to the sales force as part of its promotional effort than to the other three variables, as do most companies selling industrial products. Major brewers (Anheuser Busch, Miller, and Schlitz), like most consumer goods producers, spend more money on advertising than on their personal selling effort. No matter what promotional variables are used, they must be coordinated

Figure 2–2 Promotion Activities

Personal selling   Personal communication of information to persuade a prospective customer to buy a product or service which satisfies that individual's needs.

Advertising   Nonpersonal communication of information paid for by an identified sponsor such as an individual or an organization. Modes of advertising include television, radio, direct mail, catalogs, newspaper, and outdoor advertising such as billboards.

Publicity   Nonpersonal communications of information that is not paid for by an individual or organization. Information appears in media such as television, radio, and newspaper.

Sales promotion   Involves activities or materials used to create sales for the goods or services. The two types of sales promotion are consumer and trade sales promotion. Consumer sales promotion includes free samples, coupons, contests, and demonstrations to consumers. Trade sales promotion encourages wholesalers and retailers to purchase and to sell aggressively using devices such as sales contests, displays, special purchase prices, and free merchandise.

with other marketing mix decisions, including price and distribution. The following example will illustrate the importance of this coordination.

The original marketing of the Timex watch is an excellent example of how a firm determines consumer's needs and then develops a marketing mix for selling their product. Timex used five essential elements in their marketing plan. First, *product:* Timex recognized that a large market existed for a low-cost, functional watch. Second, *price:* low production costs made possible a low-priced, quality watch. The third element was *distribution:* they made the watch available through an innovative distribution system that largely excluded the traditional jewelry store channel in favor of mass merchandisers, drugstores, and grocery stores. Fourth, they used *nonpersonal promotion:* television advertising made potential customers aware of the watch and its advantages. Fifth, *personal promotion,* or aggressive personal selling at the wholesale and retail levels convinced buyers to purchase and display Timex watches. Timex's marketing plan has made the company very successful!

Role of the Sales Force in the Firm's Promotional Efforts

The use of salespeople to promote a company's products is a necessity in today's competitive marketplace. In terms of the cost effectiveness, many companies consider the sales force their best promotional tool. Companies have found that their customers want to be contacted by supplier representatives. For customers, the salesperson is the company. The salesperson provides the customer with product information and service and is the link between the company and its customers. The salesperson manages a territory, and is responsible to the company for reaching assigned job objectives.

Sales Force Objectives

The basic **objectives** of salespeople are to make profitable sales to customers and potential customers and to transmit information received from the firm's customers back to the firm. Given the general marketing and promotion plan, the sales manager's job is to coordinate the activities of the sales force in support of each product or group of products.

Typically, the sales force is urged to increase the company's total sales. They do so by increasing sales of particular products by specified dollar amounts or units. Once their sales objectives and quotas are established by corporate management, top field sales management develops strategies and tactics to attain them. Individual salespeople's quotas are derived from the quotas given to the entire sales force. The **sales quota** is the specific quantitative share of the portion of work assigned to the sales group or individual toward which that group's or person's effort is directed. A salesperson may be given a quota of making six sales calls each day and increasing sales by 10 percent for the coming year. The strategies and tactics mentioned above are designed to aid the salesperson in achieving these quotas.

Sales Force Strategies

Strategies are plans that have been made to enable the sales force to reach its sales quotas. The number of salespeople to employ and which products to promote during a sales period are examples of strategies. The **tactics** used to implement these strategies are the specific "how to's" of reaching objectives. For example, "what materials can we furnish our salespeople to help them develop a quality sales presentation?" This can include product samples and visual aids.

The sales manager considers the quotas for the sales force and then decides how much time and money salespeople should spend on selling the specific products sold to customers in the various markets served by the firm. Figure 2–3 is an example of how a consumer goods company allocates its salespeople's time by developing a 1984 sales promotion calendar. In April 1983, advertising, promotion, product, and sales personnel in the firm's marketing department determined which of their products they would promote in 1984. Also determined were the months of the year each product would be emphasized through promotion and sales force activities. They decided that March was the best time to introduce a new product (product N). It was determined that some

Figure 2–3 1984 Sales Promotion Calendar

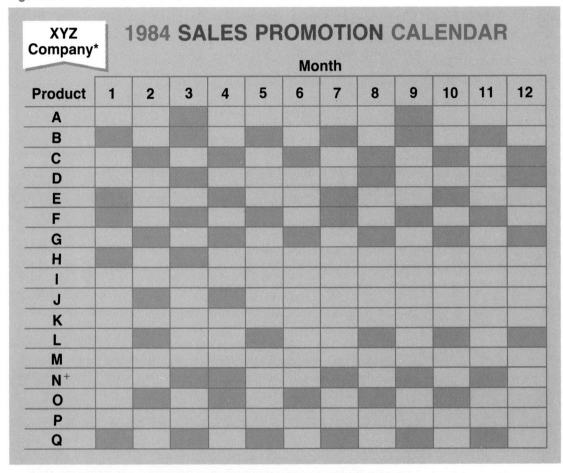

* Company name changed and actual yearly sales program reduced at company request.
† New product introduction.

products (such as products B, F, G, O, and Q) should receive heavier promotional efforts than others. In contrast, other products (such as products, I, K, M, and P) will receive no promotional efforts for 1984.

At sales meetings, field sales personnel for this company are told which products to emphasize for the coming sales period. They are given sales quotas on each product. As the sales force begins to place special sales efforts on a given product, other promotional efforts are simultaneously begun (such as television advertising, mailing samples, and cents-off coupons to consumer). This sequencing provides the company with a coordinated and concentrated selling effort.

Evaluation of Sales Performance

At the end of the sales period, sales personnel are evaluated on their performance. Corporate management asks two questions: "Did you meet your sales quotas?" and "Why or why not?"

Why Use Sales Quotas?

Sales quotas are an important device for motivating and evaluating a salesperson's performance. Companies use sales quotas for planning, evaluation, establishing standards of performance, and as an aid in determining compensation.

The Process of Setting Sales Quotas

The extent to which company sales quotas are reached traditionally has determined the degree of an organization's success. If sales quotas are reached or exceeded, the firm is successful.

Typically, the corporate president or board of directors establish the general company goals of improving—let's say—return-on-investment (ROI). Functional areas of the firm, such as production, research and development, and marketing, are asked to improve their ROI. As a result, marketing's objectives might be to increase sales 6 percent while production is asked to reduce the cost of manufacturing the product.

Each of the organization's sales regions is given a sales quota equivalent to increasing total sales 6 percent, and the objective of reducing costs per sales call. They are also asked to determine if overall sales cost can be reduced. In turn, each sales district is given a sales quota of increasing sales by 6 percent, raising the district's order/sales call ratio by increasing selling effectiveness through improved on-the-job training, and reevaluating the profitability of each territory in the district to see whether changes should be made.

At the bottom of this vertical objective-setting process are the salespeople. Each might be asked to increase sales by 6 percent, increase the order/call ratio by 20 percent, and open two new accounts monthly.

This objective-setting process is a formalized, sequential process in which each group and each person within the group is given specific quotas and time parameters for accomplishing them. By assigning each of these sales groups and the individuals within them specific quotas toward which their efforts will be directed, a company maximizes the probability of obtaining the overall organizational goals of increasing ROI and of using the firm's resources efficiently.

To illustrate how objectives and quotas are actually established by a corporation with several operating divisions, examine Figure 2–4. The

Figure 2–4 Procter & Gamble Consumer Products Sales Organization

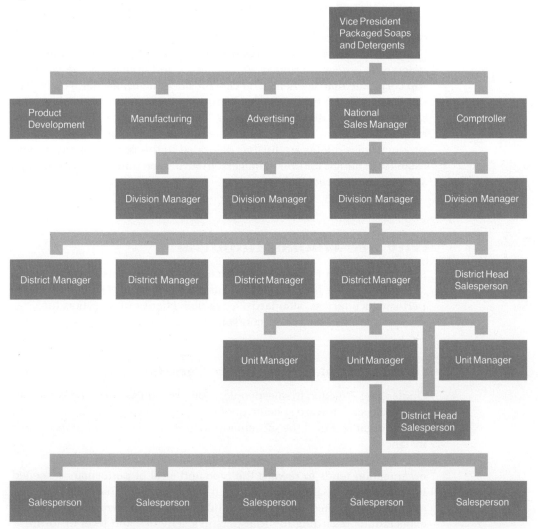

Source: Courtesy of The Procter & Gamble Company.

Procter & Gamble Consumer Products Organization has seven product category divisions: (1) packaged soap and detergents, (2) bar soap and household cleaning products, (3) food products, (4) health and beauty care, (5) personal care, (6) paper products, and (7) coffee products. Each division has its own functional specialists (manufacturing, advertising, etc.) and its own sales force. Seven different P&G salespeople, representing the different product groups, call on the same customers—for example, a large retail grocery chain. Each product category has a sales organization, structured like the one shown in Figure 2–4. The district head salesperson's position is occupied by an individual who is being trained to become a unit manager. The trainee works in the district sales manager's office and aids the unit manager in carrying out recruiting, training, and evaluation programs.

In this division the vice president in charge of packaged soaps and detergents is given performance objectives and quotas for the year by top corporate management. The vice president delegates these objectives downward to the national sales manager, who in turn establishes sales quotas with each divisional manager. These quotas usually take the form of reaching a total sales figure for each product line and individual product. Sales quotas are further delegated to the district manager, who establishes quotas for unit managers. In turn, each unit manager develops sales quotas for each salesperson.

Why are Quotas Important?

Sales quotas are of major importance because they establish the "end state" or "bottom line" sought by management. Quotas serve to provide performance targets, standards, a possible change of direction for salespeople's behavior, and control.

Quotas Provide Performance Targets

Quotas give direction to salespeople. A salesperson's efforts and resources can be directed toward specific quotas or targets designated as important by the organization—the aforementioned 6 percent sales increase, for instance.

Quotas also provide "incentives" for salespeople. Because the organization tends to reward the type and level of performance needed to reach quotas, salespeople typically are rewarded financially for attaining designated sales quotas. Such quotas represent management's expectations regarding the salesperson's activities and level of future accomplishment.

Quotas Provide Standards

Quotas provide means for determining how well a salesperson is performing. Management compares assigned quotas to actual sales. Here, quotas become the primary basis for evaluating the performance of both sales groups (i.e., regions or districts) and individual salespeople. The attainment of quotas also is used to determine the results of such things as sales contests, pay increases, and job promotion for sales personnel.

Quotas Provide Change of Direction

Quotas can serve to redirect the salesperson's activities. Procter & Gamble, for example, will emphasize only a few products during a two-month sales period. At the beginning of each period, sales meetings are held to present the products to be heavily promoted by salespeople. Specific sales quotas and selling techniques are discussed. While they will willingly sell any of their products, salespeople typically concentrate on selling those products which have been assigned quotas. For the next sales period, different products may be emphasized. By placing sales quotas on specific products, management can direct a salesperson's selling activities.

Quotas Provide Control

Since quotas serve to guide or direct the behavior of salespeople, they are a "control device" in that they are used to evaluate individuals— just as grades are used to evaluate students. A salesperson joining a company enters into an authority relationship with her superior. The sales manager has the formal power to require behavior that the salesperson might not otherwise consider and the right to exact punishment for noncompliance. The salesperson's acknowledgment of the manager's authority gives the organization a means of influencing or controlling the salesperson's activities.

Quotas serve as an indirect supervisory technique. The manager has the authority to require the salesperson to perform at a reasonable level. To increase performance, a sales manager may ask a salesperson to average 10 customer sales calls each day. This requirement indirectly monitors the salesperson's activities. Quotas for total sales volume and individual product sales volume also exist. The salesperson, therefore, concentrates on selling these products and reaching quotas.

Summary of Major Selling Issues

Most people today associate marketing with selling. Yet the act of selling is only one part of the overall marketing activities of the firm. The task of providing products that satisfy consumer wants forms the basis for our current marketing system. Marketing is an exchange process between buyers and sellers, the purpose of which is to satisfy the buyer's needs and wants through the purchase of the seller's products.

This "marketing concept" evolved over the years, developing as American business matured. Initially, American business was production oriented, basically assuming that people would buy whatever was efficiently produced. This concept gradually evolved into a sales-oriented approach in which firms generally felt that an effective sales approach would stimulate consumer demand for a product. The marketing-oriented philosophy of today focuses on a firm's desire to increase sales while anticipating and satisfying consumer needs. Progressive businesses today are much more consumer oriented than those of the past.

The marketing mix consists of four variables—product, price, distribution, and promotion. The product variable encompasses the physical attributes of the product. Pricing involves the marketing manager in establishing each product's price as well as overall pricing policies. Getting that product to the right place at the right time is the distribution variable. The promotion variable is concerned with increasing demand through communicating information to potential customers via personal selling, advertising, publicity, and sales promotion.

Firms must carefully consider the role of the sales force in their promotional program or promotional aspect of the marketing mix. A firm has to decide if a sales force is a viable direct marketing tool for them, and if so, what types of selling activities will optimally promote their product. When a sales force is chosen as a promotional tool, a firm must decide on such factors as territorial design and assignment, modes of performance evaluation, and a suitable form of salesperson compensation, and the training of selling techniques.

The basic objectives of salespeople are to make profitable sales to customers and potential customers, and also to transmit information received from customers back to the firm. Sales force performance is often evaluated on attainment of general and specific sales objectives and quotas. A quota is a portion of work assigned to an individual or group which serves as a guide for goals to be accomplished and as a means of evaluating how completely they are accomplished. Objectives, including both quantitative and qualitative goals, are broader than quotas. A firm's success often depends on how well it meets its objectives. Objectives are usually set in a formalized process in which each person is given goals to meet within a certain period.

Objectives are important to management because they basically establish the job goals salespeople are expected to attain. Objectives serve to provide performance targets which give salespeople direction on how well they are performing, and also provide standards for evaluating their performance. Objectives can also provide guidance or direction in the behavior of salespeople, telling them which products to sell at different times of the year.

Review and Discussion Questions

1. Discuss the role of personal selling as it relates to a firm's marketing effort.

2. Explain the difference between the production, sales, and marketing stage in the evolution of marketing management.
3. Discuss the four elements of a firm's marketing mix. Give several examples of how companies today have developed a marketing mix to compete in their industry.
4. Assume that the XYZ company has hired you. One of the first things you are asked is what do you believe is the relationship between the sales quota your manager gives you and sales objectives expected of the entire sales force. What would you say?
5. What type of coordination is needed between the firm's sales force and its advertising department in order to have a coordinated selling effort?

Project

Visit a local company and determine the marketing mix it uses in selling its products or services. Determine what the company expects of its salespeople and how the company helps them sell its products and services.

Cases

2–1 The Xerox Corporation

In 1974 Xerox held an 86 percent market share of the multibillion dollar copy industry. The beginning of 1980 found their market share had slipped to 54 percent. Why?

For years Xerox had concentrated its efforts on bigger and better copiers, applying the advance in technology to increase copier speed and quality. They concentrated on the middle to high-priced copiers. Xerox ignored the low-cost coated-paper copiers developed by three companies—Japan's Ricoh and Savin and Nashua in the United States. These companies introduced less expensive, efficient, plain-paper copiers targeted at customers wanting low-volume, low-speed machines. This equipment account for 40 percent of copier sales worldwide. At the same time, Xerox was trying to counteract IBM's entry into the medium-volume segment.

Xerox is not unlike many companies, expecially market leaders. Their competitors develop a marketing mix which, when successful, can cause the market leader to experience loss of sales.

Question:
What should Xerox do in order to increase sales?

2–2 Change in Sales Strategy: AT&T

In 1977, AT&T began what would be the largest change in history for a corporate organization. It was estimated that three to five years would be needed before the entire reorganization could be completed. The Bell system has historically considered its mission to be providing telephone service, tying the nation together in a reliable and economical network. With 1977 revenues of $36.5 billion, Bell ranked fourth among corporations and was easily the largest in terms of assets, with $94 billion. AT&T set in motion a change that would transform the firm from a regulated utility into a fiercely competitive supplier of all forms of communications systems, including computerized services. Management decided to become marketing-oriented rather than production-oriented. The big change began when the company announced the creation of three new executive vice presidential posts: business services, residential services, and network services. This was the company's first substantial effort to structure itself along the lines of its major customer market segments.

The change in AT&T's corporation offices necessitated changes in the firm's marketing effort. First, the marketing department was restructured in terms of AT&T's major markets. Marketing managers began to concentrate on anticipating customer needs rather than simply reacting to market development, as they had often done in the past. For the first time, AT&T began to make market analyses, segmenting business customers into more than 50 industry classifications, studying each segment to determine needs, and developing services that provided individualized solutions to customers' problems.

Marketing managers now make formal product requests based on these studies, describing the general characteristics of the products or services they think are needed. Then a product manager takes over to make sure the market research is translated into new products. The product managers carry out analyses to determine whether there will be enough demand for a new product or service to make a profit on it. If it proves out, they oversee its development. Once the new product is in the field, the product manager serves as the head of a team of functional specialists in such areas as repair, installation, and accounting. All of this attention to costs is a history-making phenomenon at Ma Bell.

AT&T decided to reorganize its sales force strictly along industry lines. Account executives were assigned to various markets, which were finely segmented according to the federal government's Standard Industrial Classification (a breakdown of industrial markets by type), and the account executives were held responsible for all customers in that particular industry. Individual account executives were supposed to win the customers' trust, penetrate and control their decision making, and even involve themselves in the customers' business planning to anticipate their needs. This kind of "system selling" is a far cry from the traditional role of an AT&T salesperson, which was hardly more than being an order taker. Now the account executives will be judged solely on the amount of revenues brought in and on how much was spent to generate that revenue. In short, "system selling" is now the key to the AT&T marketing strategy. Salespeople became order-getters and, in assuming that new role, greatly elevated the importance of personal selling in the firm's marketing efforts.

Questions:

1. Why did AT&T change their organizational structure and sales strategy?
2. When AT&T changed their sales strategy, their salespeople also changed? How?

Why and How People Buy

Salespeople are trained to emphasize the benefits of their product or service. The idea is to "sell" the buyer with a positive approach. Often, however, sales are made by eliminating the negatives.

Most buyers operate out of three basic fears: The product won't do what the salesman says it will do; the product is not worth the price; others will think I used poor judgment.

How do you convert negatives to positives? First, you have to recognize these fears at work. Then administer the antidotes:

The product won't perform— demonstrate, show pictures or slides, provide case histories, leave samples if practical.

Not worth the price—reemphasize benefits and economies.

What others will think—this is the subtlest fear, but the most insidious. Offer support through testimonials and recommendations. If necessary, put words in the buyer's mouth—supply arguments that he can use to defend his position.

Preparation for Successful Selling

3

The Psychology of Selling: Why People Buy

Learning Objectives

1. To emphasize the importance of relating a product's benefits to the customer's needs instead of only stressing features and advantages in the sales presentation.

2. To illustrate techniques on how to determine a customer's needs.

3. To present factors which influence the consumer's buying decision.

4. To begin to stimulate ideas on methods for selling.

Key Terms for Selling

Black box

Stimulus-response

Needs

Wants

Maslow's need hierarchy

Economic need

Conscious need level

Preconscious need level

Unconscious need level

Benefit selling

FAB selling technique

Feature

Advantage

Benefit

Perception

Selective perception

Selective distortion

Selective retention

Learning

Attitudes

Belief

Personality

Self-concept

Real self

Self-image

Looking-glass self

Ideal self

Routine decision making

Limited decision making

Extensive decision making

Need arousal

Collection of information

Information evaluation

Purchase decision

Purchase satisfaction

Purchase dissonance

Profile

Jim Mobley
General Mills

After graduating from Southern Methodist University in Dallas, Texas, Jim Mobley began his sales career in 1968 as a Dallas area sales representative for General Mills, Inc., Grocery Products Sales Division. Over the years Jim has advanced through several different sales positions within General Mills to his present assignment of district sales manager. He is responsible for six account managers and for the sale of approximately 3,000,000 cases annually.

"General Mills salespeople," says Jim, "are involved in selling approximately 200 different consumer food products and sizes directly to grocery wholesalers, who in turn supply the retail grocery industry. These salespeople then contact individual food retailers to persuade them to purchase and promote General Mills products. To aid its salespeople in their selling effort, the company allows them to offer promotional price allowances and merchandising aids to their customer. Massive promotional campaigns involving advertising, couponing, and free samples are also directed towards the retailer's customers. Salespeople use these incentives and information in their sales presentation to help them make the sale.

" 'Why our customers buy' is sometimes complicated by the fact that our customers normally stock a certain maximum number of products. The grocery industry operates on a very small per-unit net profit and is restricted by both warehouse and retail shelf space. In the majority of our sales of new items to accounts, we're not only selling the new product but we must offer the account guidance in what similar product should be deleted. We also must show them where the new product fits into their product mix and where it is to be placed on the retail grocery shelf.

"It is important that we make our presentations in a professional manner with documentation on potential benefits such as sales and profits. We make it as easy as possible for an account to consider and purchase our products. For example, we may sell a product using test market results, volume potential for the account, and anticipated customer demand for the product. We then lay out a merchandising plan for the new product which covers media support, couponing, consumer programs, and introductory price discounts. Market share information will show the account what products are weak and if a product must be eliminated from the retailer's shelf, and what products warrant deletion.

Hopefully these products are not ours, but from time to time a weak product of ours sometimes falls into this group.

"Using good business rationale will add credibility to your sales presentations and build customer rapport and trust. Giving your buyer this type of credible information will build stronger presentations in the future as well as maintain the oh-so-valuable customer rapport. We deal with the same buyers day in and day out, and it is very important in our industry that we build the rapport and trust that is necessary for continually successful sales presentations.

"As you can see, a sales career offers an opportunity to be competitive and can be an exciting and challenging career. I personally have found sales to be rewarding, an excellent opportunity for growth within the company. Sales provides the opportunity to be challenged on a daily basis. These are things which are not found in all career avenues."

Joe Gandolfo has been reported to have sold more life insurance than any other person in the world. His sales average has been over $800 million each year. In 1975 he sold an incredible $1 billion worth of insurance policies.

Joe's philosophy of selling is that "selling is 98 percent understanding human beings and two percent product knowledge." Do not let that statement mislead you, for Joe holds the Charter Life Underwriter (CLU) designation as a member of the American College of Life Underwriters. He is extremely knowledgeable about insurance, tax shelters, and pension plans. In fact, he spends several hours a day studying recent changes on pensions and taxation. *"But,"* Joe says, *"I still maintain that it's not product knowledge but understanding of human beings that makes a salesman effective."*[1]

Joe Gandolfo's philosophy toward selling is shared by all successful salespeople. In order to sell, you need to understand people's needs and behavior. Corporations spend millions of dollars each year training their salespeople how to determine a prospect's buying needs, what factors influence these needs, and how to convert this information into the development of a sales presentation.

Part II of this book examines major areas of selling knowledge that salespeople should possess in order to develop a successful sales presentation. This chapter examines 'why' and 'how' an individual buys.

There are numerous influences on 'why' people buy one product rather than another. We will discuss these reasons and apply them to the various steps in the consumer's "buying process." This chapter presents a number of selling techniques which will later aid you with your sales presentation.

Why People Buy—The Black Box Approach

The question of why people buy has interested salespeople for many years. Salespeople know that some customers buy their product after the presentation, yet wonder what thought process resulted in the decision to buy or not to buy. Prospective buyers are usually exposed to various types of sales presentations. In some manner a person internalizes or considers this information and then makes a buying decision.[2] This process of "internalization" is referred to as a **black box** because we cannot see into the buyer's mind—meaning that the salesperson can apply the stimuli (a sales presentation) and observe the behavior of the prospect, but obviously cannot witness the prospect's actual decision-making process.

Figure 3–1 Stimulus-Response Model of Buyer Behavior

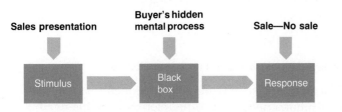

The classic model of buyer behavior shown in Figure 3–1 is called a **stimulus-response** model. A stimulus (sales presentation) is applied resulting in a response (purchase decision).[3] This model assumes that prospects will respond in some predictable manner to the sales presentation. Unfortunately, it does not tell us 'why' they buy the product or not. This information is concealed in the "black box."

Salespeople seek to understand as much as they can about the mental processes that yield the prospects' responses. We do know:

■ That people buy for both practical and psychological (emotional) reasons.

■ Methods salespeople can use to aid themselves in determining the prospects' thoughts during the sales presentations.

■ Many of the factors buyers consider in making a purchase decision.

This chapter introduces you to these three important topics. Each topic emphasizes the salesperson's need to understand people's behavior.

Psychological Influences on Buying

Since personal selling requires an understanding of human behavior, each salesperson must be concerned with a prospective customer's motivations, perceptions, learning, attitudes, and personality. Further, the salesperson should know how each type of behavior might influence a customer's purchase decision.

Motivation to Buy Must Be There

Human beings are motivated by needs and wants. These needs and wants build up inside, causing people to desire to buy a product—a new car or a new duplicating machine. People's **needs** result from a "lack of something desirable." **Wants** are "needs learned by the person." For example, people need transportation, but some want a Cadillac, while others prefer a Ford Mustang.

This example illustrates that both practical reasons (the need for transportation) and emotional or psychological reasons (the desire for the prestige of owning a Cadillac) influence the buying decision. Different individuals have different reasons for wanting to buy. The salesperson must determine a prospect's needs and then match the product's benefits to the particular needs and wants of that prospect.

Maslow's Need Hierarchy Provides Clues

Years ago, psychologist Abraham H. Maslow developed a widely accepted categorization of human needs which he referred to as his **need hierarchy.** Maslow based his hierarchy of needs on several major assumptions. First, all individuals have in common certain basic needs that are the origins of their motivation. Second, these needs are hierarchical, in that one level of need satisfaction must be met before an individual progresses to the next level. Third, an unsatisfied need serves as a motivator. Fourth, once a need has been satisfied, it no longer acts as a motivator.

Maslow proposed five basic levels of needs as shown in Figure 3–2, and defined them as:

Level 1   *Physiological needs* are necessary to maintain health and normal well-being, including food, drink, clothing, and shelter. Sales example: Newlyweds contact a realtor about buying their first home.

Level 2   *Safety needs* are desires for factors that give a safe and secure environment and freedom from danger, such as health and home insurance or deadbolt locks for the doors of one's house. Sales example: An elderly person enters a retail store asking about a security system for a house.

Figure 3–2 Maslow's Need Hierarchy Provides Clues to Prospect's Needs

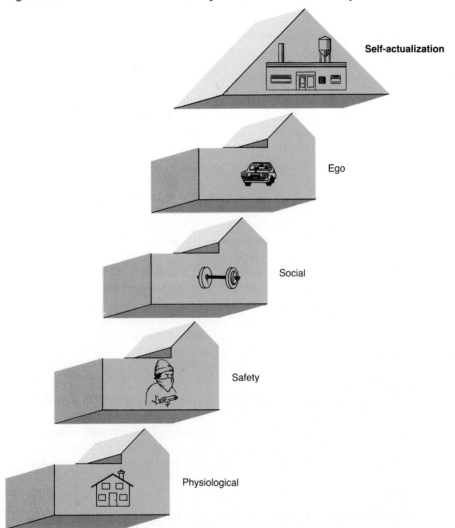

Level 3 *Social needs* include a feeling of belonging, love, and acceptance from others. Sales example: A person walks into a health spa.

Level 4 *Ego needs* are truly individual needs including self-esteem, personal reputation, and status. Fulfillment of esteem needs gives the individual a feeling of personal worth and self-confidence. Sales example: A new college graduate goes to buy a new sports car.

Level 5 *Self-actualization* needs relate to the desire to attain one's full potential in life and work.[4] Sales example: A person wanting to open a business goes to a bank to discuss a commercial loan.

Maslow's research examined an individual's personal needs. These needs can influence a person's buying decision and provide clues as to why someone would buy. As a salesperson, you should recognize that people have needs and that unmet needs will motivate them to buy your product. Certainly it is sometimes difficult to determine the particular type of need people expect to fulfill by purchasing a product. However, we do know that most individuals are concerned about their economic need.

Economic Needs: The Most Bang for the Buck

Economic needs are the buyer's need to purchase the most satisfying product for the money. Economic needs include not only price, but also quality (performance, dependability, durability), convenience of buying, and service. Some people's purchases are based primarily on economic need. However, most people consider the economic implications of all of their purchases along with other reasons for buying.

Many salespeople mistakenly assume that people base their buying decision solely on price. This is not always correct. A higher product price relative to competing goods can often be offset by such factors as service, quality, better performance, friendliness of the salesperson, or convenience of purchase.

Whatever a person's need might be, it is important for a salesperson to uncover it. Once you determine the individual's need, you are better prepared to develop your sales presentation in a manner relating your product's benefits to that particular need. This is not always easy to do, since people themselves may not be fully aware of their needs.

Awareness of Needs: Some Are Unsure

You have seen that people purchase products to satisfy various needs. Often, however, these needs are developed over such a long period of time that they may not be fully conscious of their reasons for buying or not buying a product. The buying decision can be complicated by their level of awareness of their needs. Three degrees or levels of need awareness have been identified—conscious, preconscious, and unconscious.[5]

At the 'first level,' the **conscious level,** buyers are fully aware of their needs. These are the easiest people to sell to because they know what products they want and are willing to talk about their needs. A customer might say to the salesperson, "I'd like to buy a new car and I want a Cadillac, loaded with accessories. What can you show me?"

At the 'second level,' the **preconscious level,** buyers may not be fully aware of their needs. Needs may not be fully developed in the conscious mind. They know what general type of product they want, but may not wish to discuss it with you fully. For example, a buyer may want to buy a certain product because of a strong 'ego' need, yet be hesitant about telling you so. If you don't make a sale, and ask why, this buyer may present false reasons (such as saying your price is too high), rather than revealing the real motivation. Falsification is much easier than stating the true reasons for not buying your product, thus getting into a long conversation with you, arguing with you, or telling you that your product is unsatisfactory. You must avoid this 'brush-off' and determine a buyer's real needs first and then relate your product's benefits to these needs.

At the third level, the **unconscious level,** people do not know why they buy a product, only that they do buy. When people say, "I really don't know what I want to buy," it may be true. Their buying motives might have been developed in early childhood and may have been repressed. In this case, the salesperson needs to determine which needs are influential. Often this can be accomplished by skillful questioning to draw out prospective buyers' unconscious needs. An awareness of the types of needs that buyers may have will allow you to present your product as a vehicle for the satisfaction of those needs. Several methods of presenting a product's benefits are available.

A *FAB*ulous Approach to Buyer Need Satisfaction

Possibly the most powerful selling technique used by successful salespeople today is **benefit selling.** In benefit selling the salesperson relates a product's benefits to the customer's needs, using the product's features and advantages as support. This technique is often referred to as the *FAB* **selling technique** (*F*eature, *A*dvantage, and *B*enefit). These key terms are defined as follows:

■ A product **feature** is 'any *physical characteristic* of a product.'

■ A product **advantage** is 'the *performance characteristic* of a product that describes how it can be used or will help the buyer.'

■ A product **benefit** is 'a favorable *result* the buyer receives from the product because of a particular feature or advantage that has the ability to satisfy a buyer's need.'

The Product's Features: So What?

All products have feature or 'characteristics.' The following are examples:

size	quantity
color	price
taste	shape
quality	ingredients
delivery	packaging
terms	flavor

Descriptions of a product's features answer the question, "What is it?" Typically, when used by themselves in the sales presentation, features have little persuasive power since buyers are interested in specific benefits rather than features.

When discussing a product's features *alone,* imagine the customer is thinking, "So what? So your product has this shape or quality; how does it perform and how will it benefit me?" This situation warrants discussion of the product's advantages as they relate directly to the buyer's needs.

The Product's Advantages: Prove It!

Once a product feature is presented to the customer, the salesperson normally begins to discuss the advantages provided by that product's physical characteristics. This is much better than discussing only its features. Chances of making a sale are increased by describing the product's advantages, how a product can be used, or how it will help the buyer. Examples of product advantages follow:

It is the fastest-selling soap on the market.

You can store more information and retrieve it more rapidly with our computer.

This machine will copy on both sides of the page instead of only one.

How does the prospective customer know that your claims for a product are true? Imagine a prospect thinking, "Prove it!" You have to be prepared to substantiate any claims you make.

Companies typically train their salespeople thoroughly on the product's physical and performance characteristics. A salesperson may have excellent knowledge of the product, yet be unable to describe it in terms which allow the prospect to visualize the benefits of purchasing it. This is because many salespeople present only a product's features and advantages, leaving the buyer to imagine its benefits.

While your chances of making a sale increase when you discuss both the features and the advantages of your product, you must learn how to stress product benefits which are important to the prospect in your presentation. Once you have mastered this selling technique, your sales will increase.

The Product's Benefits Sell It

People are interested in what the product will do for them. Benefit selling appeals to the customer's personal motives by answering the question, "What's in it for me?" In your presentation you should stress how the prospect will benefit from the purchase rather than the features and advantages of your product.

To illustrate this idea of buying benefits instead of only features or advantages, consider four items: (1) a diamond ring, (2) camera film, (3) STP motor oil, and (4) movie tickets. Do people buy these products or services for their features or advantages? No, people buy the product's benefits such as:

Two-carat diamond ring—image of success, investment, or to please wife.

Camera film—memories of places, friends, and family.

STP motor oil—engine protection, car investment, or peace of mind.

Movie tickets—entertainment, escape from reality, or relaxation.

As you can see, people are buying benefits, not a product's features or advantages. These benefits can be both practical, such as an investment, and psychological, such as an image of success. The salesperson needs to consider benefits to answer the prospect's question, "What's in it for me?"

Example: Vacuum cleaner salesperson to householder: "This vacuum cleaner's high speed motor (feature) works twice as fast (advantage) with less effort (advantage), saving you 15 to 30 minutes in cleaning time (benefit) and the aches and pains of pushing a heavy machine (benefit)."

Notice that the benefit specifically states favorable results of buying the vacuum cleaner, answering the buyer's question, "What's in it for *me?*" You can see the benefits are specific statements, not generalizations. Instead of just saying, "This vacuum cleaner will save you time," you also say, "you will save 15 to 30 minutes"

Notice that a benefit can result in a further benefit to the prospect. For example, by saving cleaning time (a benefit) you reduce the aches and pains of pushing a heavier machine (a benefit of a benefit). Examples of product benefits include:

time savings

increased sales

cost reductions

more customers
 drawn into
 retail store

elimination of
 out-of-stock
 merchandise

greater profit

Not only are benefits important, but the order in which you introduce product benefits during your presentation, along with its features and advantages, is also necessary to plan.

Order Can Be Important

Some salespeople prefer to state the 'benefit' first and then state that the 'feature' or 'advantage' makes that 'benefit' possible, such as, "The king-size Tide will bring you *additional profits* (benefits) because it is the *fastest selling size* (advantage)." In this example, the advantage supports the statement of derived customer benefits.

While stating the benefit first is the preferable method, you do not always have to discuss the three parts of the FAB formula in any particular order.

Example: Air conditioning salesperson to customer: "This air conditioner has a high energy efficiency rating (feature) *that will save you 10 percent on your energy costs* (benefit) because it uses less electricity (advantage)."

Example: Sporting goods salesperson to customer: "With this ball, you'll get an extra 10 to 20 yards on your drives (advantage) *helping to reduce your score* (benefit) because of its new solid core (feature)."

Example: Salesperson to buyer of grocery store health and beauty aids buyer: *"You can increase your store traffic by 10 to 20 percent* (benefit) *and build your sales volume by at least 5 percent* (benefit) by advertising and reducing the price (feature) of Prell's economy size in your next Wednesday ad."

New salespeople are frequently not accustomed to using feature, advantage, and benefit phrases. To aid in making their use a regular part of your sales conversation, a standardized *FAB sequence* can be used as follows:

The . . . (feature) . . . means you . . . (advantage) . . . the real benefit to you being . . . (benefit). . . .

This FAB sequence allows you to easily remember to state the product's benefit in a natural, conversational manner. For example, *"The* new solid core center of the Gunshot Golf Ball *means you* will have an extra 10 to 20 yards on your drives, *with the real benefit to you being* a lower score." You can substitute virtually any features,

Figure 3–3 Examples of Features, Advantages, and Benefits

Features	Advantages	Benefits
Nationally advertised consumer product	Will sell more product	Will make you high profit
Air conditioner with high energy rating efficiency	Uses less electricity	Saves 10 percent energy costs
Product made of stainless steel	Will not rust	Reduces your replacement costs
Supermarket computer system with the IBM 3651 Store Controller	Can store more information and retrieve it rapidly by supervising up to 24 grocery check-out scanners and terminals and look up prices on up to 22,000 items	Provides greater accuracy, register balancing, store ordering, inventory management
Five percent interest on money in bank checking account	Earns interest which would not normally be received	Gives you one extra bag of groceries each month

advantages, and benefits between these transition phrases to develop FAB sequences. Several sequences can be used one after another to emphasize your product's benefits.

Figure 3–3 presents five examples of features, advantages, and benefits of products. The first column lists features or product characteristics such as size, shape, performance and maintenance data. The second column shows advantages that arise from respective features. These are the performance characteristics, or what the product will do. The third column contains benefits to the customer of these features and advantages. For each major feature of your product you should develop the resulting advantage and benefit and incorporate these into your sales presentation, as will be discussed more fully in Chapter 8.

Why should you emphasize benefits? There are two reasons. First, they fulfill a person's needs or solve a problem. That is what buyers want to know about. Second, sell to more people. Stressing benefits in your presentation, rather than features or advantages, will bring you success.

Given that people make a buying decision based on whether they believe a product's benefits will satisfy their needs, how can you uncover a buyer's needs?

How to Determine Important Buying Needs—A Key of Success

Your initial task when first meeting the customer is to differentiate between important buying needs and those of lesser or no importance. Figure 3–4 illustrates the concept that buyers have both important needs

Figure 3–4   Seller Matches Buyer's Important Needs to Product's Benefits and Emphasizes in Sales Presentation

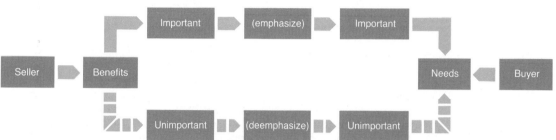

and needs that are not major reasons for buying a product (relatively unimportant buying needs).

You should determine buyers' important needs and concentrate on emphasizing product benefits that will satisfy these needs. Benefits that would satisfy buyers' unimportant needs should be deemphasized in the sales presentation. If, for example, buyers say that price is important, but you determine that they can afford your product, and are also interested in purchasing a stylish, good-quality product, then emphasize the style and quality of your product.

Elmer Wheeler, a famous sales speaker, said "Sell the sizzle, not the steak!" Wheeler is saying that people buy for reasons other than what the product will actually do or its price. They have both practical and psychological or emotional reasons for buying. Customers may not buy the product to solve the rational need that the salesperson perceives to be important. They may buy to satisfy an emotional need not so easily recognized. It is important to understand this sales concept and to learn to determine the buyer's important buying needs. A list of some of the most common psychological buying needs includes:

fear	love of family
vanity (keep up with the Joneses)	personal pleasure
	desire to succeed
desire for gain or prevention of loss	comfort or luxury
	self-preservation
security	
curiosity	

It is up to you to determine which buying needs are most important to the customer. How can you do this? Several methods are frequently used to uncover important needs:

Ask questions: Questions can often bring out needs that the prospect would not reveal or does not know exist. The salesperson asks, "Is a quiet ceiling fan important to

	you?" "Yes, it is," says the buyer. "If I could provide you with the quietest ceiling fan on the market, would you be interested?"
Observe:	Look at prospects, study their surroundings. Experienced salespeople can determine a great deal about people by observing such things as the way they dress, or where they live and work.
Listen:	Prospects may drop leading remarks like, "I wish I had a television like this one."
Talk to others:	Ask others about a prospect's needs. For instance, ask an office manager's secretary about the manager's satisfaction with a copy machine.
Combination:	A skillful salesperson may talk to others, listen to a prospect, probe with questions and make careful observations—all in an effort to uncover the prospect's needs.

Once the major buying need is determined, you are ready to relate the person's needs to your product's benefits. Like the television camera that transmits images to the television receiver, buyers picture desired products in their minds. Before the picture is focused clearly, buyers often need to be "turned on and tuned in." Once you find their real reasons for wanting to buy a particular type of product, or identify major problems that they want to solve, you have uncovered the key to selling to them.

Uncovering these important buying needs is like pushing a button that turns on a machine. You have just pushed the customer's "hot button." You have awakened a need, and customers realize that you understand their problems. *Basically, this is what selling is all about—determining needs and skillfully relating your product's benefits to show how its purchase will fulfill customers' needs.*

This is not always an easy task. As we have seen, people have a multitude of different needs, and may not truly understand or see their unconscious needs or problems. In this situation, your challenge is to convert customers' apparently unconscious needs into recognized and understood needs. Several of the later chapters in this book are devoted to selling techniques aimed at uncovering or "smoking out" buyer needs. Getting buyers to realize their needs enables them to focus on your sales presentation to determine if your product will meet these needs. Once buyers experience a need, their perceptions of your product become important.

Your Buyer's Perception

Why would two people have the same need but buy different products? Likewise, why might the same individual at different times view your product in diverse ways? The answers to both of these questions involves how the person perceives your product.

Perception is the process by which a person selects, organizes, and interprets information. The buyer receives the salesperson's product information through the senses: sight, hearing, touch, taste, and smell. These senses act as filtering devices through which information must pass before it can be used.

As the definition indicates, perception has three components. Each plays a part in determining buyers' responses to you and to your sales presentation. Buyers often receive large amounts of information in a short period of time, and typically perceive and use only a small amount of it. Some information is ignored or quickly forgotten because of the difficulty of retaining large amounts of information. This process is known as **selective exposure**, because only a portion of the information an individual is exposed to is selected to be organized, interpreted, and allowed to be exposed to our awareness.

Why does some information reach a buyer's consciousness while other information does not? First, the salesperson may not present the information in a manner which assures its proper reception. For example, there may be too much information given at one time. This causes confusion, and the buyer tunes you out. In some cases, information may be haphazardly presented, causing the buyer to receive it in an unorganized manner.

A sales presentation which appeals to the buyer's five senses helps to penetrate perceptual barriers. It also enhances understanding and reception of the information as you present it. Selling techniques such as asking questions, using visual aids, and demonstrating a product, can force buyers to participate in the presentation. This helps you determine if they understand your information.

Second, buyers will tend to allow information to reach consciousness if it relates to needs they recognize and wish to fulfill. If, for example, someone is giving you reasons for purchasing life insurance, and you do not perceive a need for it, there is a good chance that your mind will allow very little of this information to be perceived. However, if you need life insurance, chances are you will listen carefully to the salesperson. If you are uncertain about something, you will ask questions to increase your understanding.

A buyer's perceptual process also may result in **selective distortion,** or the altering of information. It frequently occurs when information is received which is inconsistent with a person's beliefs and attitudes. When buyers listen to a sales presentation on a product which they perceive to be of low quality, they may mentally alter the information to coincide with present beliefs and attitudes, thereby reinforcing themselves. Should buyers believe that the product is of high quality, even when it is not, they may change any negative information about the product into positive information. This distortion can substantially lessen the intended *effect* of a salesperson attempting to compare a product to the product currently used by the individual.

Selective retention also can influence perception. Here buyers may remember only information that supports their attitudes and beliefs, forgetting whatever does not. After a salesperson leaves, buyers may forget the product's advantages stressed by the salesperson because they are not consistent with their beliefs and attitudes.

These perceptions help explain why a buyer may or may not buy. The buyer's perceptional process acts as a filter by determining what part of the sales message is heard, how it is interpreted, and what product information is retained. Therefore, two different sales messages given by two different salespeople, even though they concern very similar products, can be received differently. A buyer can tune-out one of the sales presentations and tune-in the other, and purchase the perceived product.

While you cannot control a buyer's perceptions, you can often influence and change them. To be successful, you must understand that perceptual barriers can arise during your presentation. You must learn to recognize when they occur and be able to overcome them.

Buyer Perceptions, Attitudes, and Beliefs Are Learned

You make a sales presentation concerning your product's features, advantages, and benefits. Your goal is to provide information that makes your buyer knowledgeable enough to make an educated purchase decision. However, a person's perceptual process may prevent your information from being fully utilized by the buyer. Understanding how people develop their perceptions can help you be more successful in selling.

Perceptions are learned. People develop their perceptions through experience. This is why **learning** is defined as "acquiring knowledge or a behavior based upon past experiences."

Successful salespeople must help buyers learn about them and their products. If buyers have learned to trust you, they will listen and have faith in what you say, therefore increasing your chance of making sales. If your products perform as you claim they will, buyers will repurchase them more readily. If your presentation provides the information necessary to making a decision, your probability of making the sale increases. Product knowledge influences the buyer's attitude and beliefs about your product.

A person's **attitudes** are "learned predispositions toward something." These feelings can be favorable or unfavorable. If a person is neutral toward the product or has no knowledge of the product, no attitude is said to exist. A buyer's attitude is shaped by past and present experience.

Creating a positive attitude is important, but it alone will not result in your making the sale. To sell to someone, you also must convert the buyer's attitude into a belief. A **belief** is "a state of mind in which trust or confidence is placed in something or someone." The buyer must believe your product will fulfill a need or solve a problem. A favorable attitude toward one product rather than another comes from a belief that one of them is better.

Also, a buyer must believe you are the best person from whom to buy. If you are not trusted as the best source, people will not buy from you. Assume, for example, that someone decides to buy a 19-inch, portable, XL-100 RCA color television. Three RCA dealers are in the trading area and each dealer offers to sell an XL-100 at approximately the same price. Chances are the purchaser will buy from the salesperson believed to be the best, even though there is no reason not to trust the other two dealers.

If buyers' perceptions create favorable attitudes leading them to believe that your product is best for them and that they should buy from you—you make sales. Often, however, people may not know you or your product. Your job is to provide information about your product which allows buyers to form positive attitudes and beliefs. Should their perception, attitudes, and beliefs be negative, distorted, or incorrect, you must change them. As a salesperson you spend much of your time creating or changing people's learned attitudes and beliefs about your product. This is the most difficult challenge a salesperson faces.

Example of a Buyer's Misperceptions

Assume, as an example, that a woman is shopping for a ceiling fan for her home. The three main features of the product she is interested in are price, quality, and style. While shopping around, she had seen two brands, the Hunter and the Economy brand. The information she received on these two brands has caused her to conclude that all ceiling fans are basically alike. Each brand seems to offer the same features and advantages. Because of this attitude, she has formed the belief that she should purchase a low-price fan, in this case the Economy ceiling fan. Cost is the key factor influencing this purchase decision.

She decides to stop at one more store which sells Casa Blanca fans. She asks the salesperson to see some lower-priced fans. These fans turn out to be more expensive than either the Hunter or Economy models. Noting their prices, she says to the salesperson, "That's not what I had in mind." She walks away as the salesperson says, "Thanks for coming by."

What should the salesperson have done? When the customer walked into the store, the salesperson knew her general need was for a ceiling fan. However, the customer had wrongly assumed that all brands are alike. It was the salesperson's job to first ask the customer "fact-finding" questions such as, "Where will you use the fan?" "What color do you have in mind?" "Is there a particular style you are interested in?" "What features are you looking for?" "What price range would you like to see?" These questions allow the salesperson to determine the customer's specific needs, her attitudes and beliefs about ceiling fans.

Learning the answers to these questions enables the salesperson to explain the benefits of the Casa Blanca fan as compared to the Hunter and Economy brands. The salesperson can show that fans have different features, advantages, and benefits, and why there are price differences among the three fans. The buyer then can make a decision as to which ceiling fan best suits her specific needs. Knowledge of a buyer's learned attitudes and beliefs can "make sales"; with this information a salesperson can alter the buyer's perceptions or reinforce them when presenting the benefits of his product.

The Buyer's Personality Should Be Considered

People's personalities can also affect buying behavior by influencing the types of products that fulfill their particular needs. **Personality** can be viewed as "the individual's distinguishing character traits, attitudes, or habits." While it is difficult to know exactly how personality affects buying behavior, it is generally believed that personality does have some influence on a person's perceptions, attitudes, and beliefs and thus on buying behavior.

Self-Concept

One of the best ways to examine personality is to consider a buyer's **self-concept,** the view of the self.[6] Internal or personal self-evaluation may influence a buyer's attitude toward the products desired or not desired. Some theorists believe that people buy products that match their self-concept.

According to the self-concept theory, buyers possess four images:

1. The **real self**—people as they actually are.
2. The **self-image**—how people see themselves.
3. The **ideal self**—what people would like to be.
4. The **looking-glass self**—how people think others regard them.

As a salesperson you should attempt to understand the buyer's self-concept, for it may be the key to understanding the buyer's attitudes and beliefs. For example, if a man is apparently unsatisfied with his self-image, he might be sold through appeals to his ideal self-image. You might compliment him by saying, "Mr. Buyer, it is obvious that the people in your community think very highly of you. They know you as an ideal family man and good provider for your family [looking-glass self]. Your purchase of this life insurance policy will provide your family the security you want for them [ideal self]." This appeal is targeted at the looking-glass self and the ideal self. Success in sales is often closely linked to the salesperson's knowledge of the buyer's self-concept, rather than the buyer's real self.

Selling Based upon Personality

While it is important to know a buyer's self-concept, you should also attempt to uncover any additional aspects of the prospect's personality that might influence a decision to buy so that you can further adjust your sales approach. Take, for example, a person you recognize as well-organized, emotionally controlled, and very rational in making a decision. You also find this prospect to be difficult to get to know, opinionated, and extremely cautious over the purchase decision. How do you deal with this type of personality?

First, it is most important that you recognize people as individuals, each having somewhat different past experiences. Second, you want to customize your presentation to the individual by considering attitudes, beliefs, and personality. For the person described above, you might need to use a well-planned sales presentation based on facts. Certainly you should be patient, developing trust only after numerous "soft-sell" calls, and never critizing the competing product currently being used. Do not push for the order. Once having become your customer, believing in *you* and *your* product, the buyer will no longer buy from your competitor.

Conversely, with the prospect who is characterized as friendly, outgoing, disorganized, prone to rapid, emotional buying decisions, you may be more aggressive. Be careful of using too many facts and details on this type of person, because this may actually lose the sale. With people who respond to emotional appeals, a salesperson should discuss only the benefits of buying the product. Benefits appealing to the ego can be used effectively in your sales presentation. If you are at first unsuccessful, make several more attempts to close the sale. Be sure to make routine sales calls on people with this type of personality. They listen to each salesperson, and may switch from product to product. Figure 3–5 further illustrates the idea that you should consider each buyer's personality during the sales call.

Certainly it is difficult to assign all of your customers into personality categories, as is done in Figure 3–5. However, it is important to study

Figure 3–5 Example of Selling to People with Different Personalities

Dominant people are extremely competitive. They are ambitious, tough, aggressive, manipulative, overbearing, closed-minded, anti-intellectual, insensitive, and status-conscious. They are fiercely independent and individualistic. Taking orders, accepting advice, or following procedures is a kind of defeat for them. They tend to distrust others; dominant people know that they will do anything to win and assume that others want to take advantage of them.	**Detached people** distrust others and feel uncomfortable with them, particularly with those who try to dominate or get close. They do not understand emotions and try to avoid them. They are shy, aloof, impersonal, uncommunicative, and generally like order and predictability. They are independent and want to be alone, but do not want to flaunt authority. They are open-minded about such impersonal issues as facts and logic, and they pride themselves on their objectivity.	**Dependent people** really need other people's love, acceptance, approval, and understanding. They are warm, friendly, sincerely interested in other people, and want to be helpful. They are happy being part of a group, are good listeners, and are cooperative and compliant. Dependent people go along with others' ideas because they want to be liked. They constantly ask for reassurance. Their insecurity makes them easy to exploit; they are loyal to people who do not deserve it.
The close: Direct and forceful. Never seem to demand surrender. Lay out the facts, then appeal to his decisiveness and independence.	*The close: Low-pressure and logical. Detached people hate to be pushed. Instead, show that the most logical action is to buy now.*	*The close: Forceful but friendly. Dependent people are indecisive and do not mind being pushed by people they trust.*

Source: Reprinted by permission from *Sales & Marketing Management* Magazine. Copyright © 1978.

the particular personality characteristics of each customer in order to treat them as unique individuals. For example, do not make the mistake of being pushy with all of your customers with a dependent personality. Instead, study your customer's reactions to the way you do things. After a number of calls, you will in time be able to make sales based upon a customer's personality.

You Can Classify Buying Situations

Some people may appear to make up their minds quickly and easily either to buy or not to buy. This is not always the case. The quickness

Figure 3-6   The Three Classes of Buying Situations

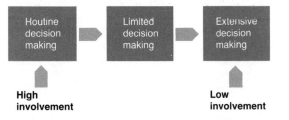

and ease of deciding which product to buy typically depends upon the type of buying situation. Purchasing a gallon of milk is quite different from buying an automobile. People have more difficulty in selecting, organizing, and interpreting information in purchasing an automobile. Also, their attitudes and beliefs toward the automobile may not be well formed.

True, a few people have the type of personality (and resources) which allow them to quickly purchase an expensive product like an automobile, but this is unusual. When purchasing some types of products, most people carefully compare competing brands. They talk to salespeople. As information is collected, attitudes and beliefs are formed toward each product. People must decide which product has the most desirable features, advantages, and benefits. When considering several brands, people may seek information on each. The more information collected, the greater difficulty they may have in deciding which product to buy.

Purchase decisions can usually be classified as to the difficulty involved in deciding which product to buy. The purchase decision can be viewed as a problem-solving activity falling into one of the three classifications shown in Figure 3–6. These situations are routine decision making, limited decision making, and extensive decision making.

Some Decisions Are Routine

Many products are repeatedly purchased. People are in the habit of buying a particular product. They give little thought or time to the routine purchase; they fully realize the product's benefits. These are called low-involvement goods because they involve a routine buying decision. People's attitudes and beliefs toward the product are already formed and are usually very positive. Cigarettes, cold drinks, beer, and many grocery items are often purchased through **routine decision making.**

For your customer currently making a routine purchase decision, you should reinforce the point that this is a correct buying decision. It is important for you to have the product in stock. If you do not have it, the customer may go to another supplier.

For someone not currently using your product, your challenge is to change this person's product loyalty or normal buying habits. The features, advantages, and benefits of your product should be directly compared to the buyer's preferred brand. Of course, not all purchase decisions are routine.

Some Decisions Are Limited

When buyers are unfamiliar with a particular brand of product, they seek more information in making a purchase decision. In this case, there is **limited decision making**—a moderate level of actual buyer involvement in the decision. The general qualities of goods in the product class are known to the buyer. However, buyers are not familiar with each brand's features, advantages, and benefits. For example, they may perceive that Xerox, 3M, and Canon copiers are the same in performance.

These buyers have more involvement in buying decisions in terms of shopping time, money, and potential dissatisfaction with the purchase than in the routine purchase decision. They seek information to aid them in making the correct decision. A sales presentation should be developed that provides buyers with the necessary knowledge to make brand comparisons and to increase their confidence that the purchase of your product is the correct decision. Occasionally, the purchase of some products requires prospective buyers to go one step further and apply extensive decision making.

Some Decisions Are Extensive

Buyers seeking to purchase products such as insurance, a home, or an automobile can be described as being highly involved in making the buying decision. They may be unfamiliar with a specific brand or type of a product and have difficulty in making the purchase decision. This kind of purchase requires more of an investment in time and money than does the limited decision. This situation demands **extensive decision making** and problem-solving activities.

In making extensive decisions, buyers believe that much more is at stake relative to other buying decisions. They may become frustrated during the decision-making process, especially if a large amount of information is available. They may become confused, not knowing what product features they are interested in because of unfamiliarity with the products. Buying an automobile or a life insurance policy, for example, entail potentially confusing purchase decisions.

You should determine all possible reasons why buyers are interested in a product. Then, in a simple, straightforward manner, present only enough information to allow the buyer to make a decision. At this time, product comparisons can be made, if necessary. You can also help the buyer evaluate alternative products.

In summary, it becomes your job to *provide buyers with product*

Figure 3–7 Five-Step Model of Buying Process

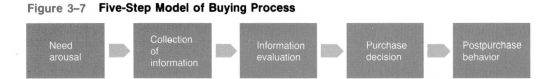

*knowledge that allows them to develop favorable personal **attitudes** toward your product. These attitudes will result in positive **beliefs** that your products fulfill their needs.* Determining the type of decision process a buyer is engaged in is critical to you as a salesperson.

View Buyers as Decision Makers

Buyers, whether private consumers or industrial purchasing agents, are constantly exposed to information about various products. Manufacturers use newspaper, radio, and television advertising, direct-mail offers, and salespeople to stimulate people to buy their products. What steps do people go through in making a purchase decision?

Typically, the buying decision involves the five basic steps shown in Figure 3–7. Buyers recognize a need, collect information provided by the salesperson, evaluate that information, decide to buy, and after the purchase determine whether they are satisfied with the purchase. This sequence reveals that several things occur before and after the purchase, all of which should be considered by the salesperson.

Need Arousal

As you remember from the first part of this chapter, buyers may experience a need themselves, or the need can be triggered by the salesperson (**need arousal**). It could be psychological, social, or economic; it could be a need for safety, for self-actualization, or ego fulfillment. It is important to determine a person's needs in order to know what product information to provide. This information should relate the product's benefits to the person's needs.

Collection of Information

If buyers know which product will satisfy a need, they will buy quickly. The salesperson may need only to approach them; they already want to buy the product.

However, when buyers are faced with limited or extensive problem solving, they may want to **collect a great deal of information** about the product. They might visit several retail stores, contact several potential suppliers. They may talk with a number of salespeople about a product's price, advantages, size, and warranty before making a decision.

Information Evaluation

A person's **evaluation of product information** determines what will be purchased. After mentally processing all the information about products that will satisfy a need—and this may or may not include your product—a buyer matches this information with needs, attitudes, and beliefs, as discussed earlier, in making a decision. Only then will a **purchase decision** be made.

This evaluation process includes rating preferences on factors such as price, quality, and brand reputation. Attitudes on different products are based on either psychological or rational reasons.

At this stage, a salesperson can be very effective. Providing information that matches product features, advantages, and benefits with a buyer's needs, attitudes, and beliefs, will increase the chances of a favorable evaluation of a product. So the salesperson is charged with the responsibility of uncovering the person's needs, attitudes, and beliefs early in the discussion so as to match the product with the person's needs.

One way to get such information is to determine not only needs, beliefs, and attitudes, but also the type of information a person needs before making a decision. Here are examples of questions you need to know the answers to:

- What product attributes are important in this decision—price, quality, service?
- Of these, what are *most* important?
- What are the prospect's attitudes toward your products?
- What are the prospect's attitudes toward your competitors' products?
- What level of satisfaction is expected from buying the product?

This type of questioning not only tells you about the customer's needs but also involves the customer in the presentation and may convey the idea that you are truly interested in his or her needs. This attitude towards you is in itself enough to create positive attitudes about your product.

Armed with this knowledge about the customer, the salesperson is in a better position to provide the information necessary for a decision and also to help the customer evaluate that information in favor of your product. The information should be provided simply, clearly, and straightforwardly. It should seek to correct any negative information or impressions about your product. Matching information with a customer's needs may enable you to:

Alter the person's beliefs about your product, for example, by convincing the customer that your product is priced higher than the competition because it is a "quality" product.

Alter the person's beliefs about your competitor's products.

Change the amount of importance a person attaches to a particular product attribute, for example, by getting the customer to consider quality and service rather than price alone.

Bring out unnoticed attributes of your product.

Change the search for the "ideal" product into a more realistic pursuit, such as by substituting a $100,000 home for a $200,000 home, or showing a man whose height is six foot ten inches a mid-sized car rather than a compact.

A company has no better promotional device than having its sales force help their prospects and customers to evaluate products on the market—and not merely their own. The two-way communication between buyer and seller is exceptionally effective in providing the information needed to make the sale on the one hand, and to evaluate the product on the other. Salespeople provide knowledge to aid people in their decision-making process. In many respects, salespeople can be viewed as teachers (professors, if you will) who provide helpful information.

Purchase Decision

Is the sale made, once the prospect states an intention to buy? No. You should not consider the sale final until the contract is signed, or you have the buyer's money, because there is still a chance for a change of mind. Even after a customer has selected a product, purchase intentions can be changed by four basic factors. These are:

1. The attitude of others, such as a spouse, friend, or boss. Consideration should be given to both the intensity of another person's attitude and the level of motivation the buyer has to comply with or to resist this other person's attitude.
2. The perceived risk of buying the product—will it give a return on the money?
3. Uncontrollable circumstances, such as not being able to finance the purchase of a house or to pass the physical examination for a large life insurance policy.
4. The salesperson's actions after the decision has been reached; sometimes it is unwise to continue to talk about a product after this point; something could change the customer's mind.

The third factor, uncontrollable circumstances, is self-explanatory. However, how can attitudes of others influence a sale? A man may want to buy a dark, conservative business suit, whereas his wife wants him to buy a sport coat and slacks. The buyer's original favorable attitude toward the business suit may have been changed by his wife. A wife's strong disapproval can quite possibly change his mind. In industrial selling, others in the buyer's firm can influence the sale. Be sure and tell your story.

Since buyers may not always be sure that they will be satisfied with a purchase, they may perceive a risk, may experience tension and anxiety after buying your product. Haven't we all asked ourselves, "Have I made the correct decision?" The levels of tension and anxiety people experience are related to their perceptions of and attitudes to the products they have had to choose from. Uncertainty about differences between your product and those of your competitors can create anxiety, especially if both products' benefits appear to very similar, or if your product is more expensive yet promises better benefits. This is especially true for products involving limited or extensive decisions. Prospects might see little difference between products, or may like them all—and thus can fairly easily change their minds several times before buying.

Finally, many sales have been lost when, after a buyer has said, "I will buy," the salesperson continues to talk. Additional information sometimes causes buyers to change their minds. It is important to finalize the sale as quickly as possible after the buyer makes a decision. Once the prospect decides, stop talking, pack up your bag, and leave.

Postpurchase

No, the decision process does *not* end with the purchase—not for the buyer at least! A product, once purchased, yields certain levels of satisfaction and dissatisfaction. **Purchase satisfaction** comes from receiving benefits expected, or greater than expected, from a product. If buyers' experiences from the use of a product exceed expectations, they are said to be satisfied, but if experiences are below expectations, the customer is said to be dissatisfied.

The buyer can experience **dissonance** after the product's purchase. Dissonance causes tension over whether the right decision was made in buying the product. Some people refer to this as buyer's remorse. Dissonance increases with the importance of the decision and the difficulty of choosing between products. Should dissonance occur, buyers may get rid of a product by returning it, or by selling it to someone else. Alternatively, they may seek assurance from the salesperson or friends that the product is a good one and that they made the correct purchase decision (positively reinforcing themselves).

You can help the buyer to be satisfied with the product and lower the level of dissonance in several ways. First, if necessary, show the buyer how to use the product properly. Second, be realistic in your claims made for the product. Exaggerated claims may create dissatisfaction. Third, continually reinforce buyers' decisions by reminding them how well the product actually performs and fulfills their needs. Remember, in some situations buyers can return the product to the seller after purchase. This cancels your sale and hurts your chances of making future sales to this customer.

In summary, you should seek to sell a product that satisfies the buyer's needs. In doing so, remember the sale is made only when the actual purchase is complete, and that you should continue to reinforce the buyer's attitudes about the product at all times, even after the sale. This practice reduces the perceived risk of making a bad buy, which allows buyers to listen to and trust your sales message even though some of your proposals may be out of line with their purchase plans. It also can reduce the buyers' post-purchase dissonance. Buyers who have developed a trust in your product claims believe that you will help them properly use the product.

To Buy or Not to Buy— A Choice Decision

Salespeople realize that people buy a product because of a need, and that needs can be complex due to the influence of perceptions, attitudes, beliefs, and personality. Furthermore, perceptions, attitudes, and beliefs may differ from one purchase situation to another. How, then, is it possible to state in simple terms why people buy one product and not another?

No, salespeople do not have to be psychologists to understand human behavior. Nor do they need to understand the material covered in the courses taken by a psychology major. Furthermore, the average salesperson cannot be expected to know all that is involved in the psychological and practical processes that a buyer goes through in making a purchase decision.

What the salesperson *does* need to understand are the various factors that can influence the buying decision, the fact that buyers actually examine various factors that can influence these decisions, that buyers actually go through various steps in making these decisions, and how to develop a sales presentation that persuades buyers to purchase the product in order to satisfy needs. To do this, the salesperson should consider the following questions before developing a sales presentation.

■ What type of product is desired?

■ What type of buying situation is it?

■ How will the product be used?

■ Who is involved in the buying decision?

■ What practical factors may influence the buyer's decision?

■ What psychological factors may influence the buyer's decision?

■ What are the buyer's important buying needs?

Again, it seems necessary to know a great deal about a person's attitudes and beliefs to answer these questions. Can this be made simpler? Yes. Simply stated, "to buy or not to buy" is a choice decision. The person's choice takes one of two forms. First, a person has the choice of buying a product or not. Second, the choice can be between competing products. The question salespeople should ask themselves is, "How can I convince a person to choose my product?" The answer to this question involves four things, each of which is necessary to making the sale. People will buy if:

1. They perceive a need or problem.
2. They desire to fulfill a need or solve a problem.
3. They decide there is a high probability that your product will fulfill their needs or solve their problems better than your competitor's products.
4. They believe they should buy from you.

What do you do if you know your product can reduce your prospect's manufacturing costs, saving the firm $5,000 a year, for a cost of $4,000, and the prospect says, "No thanks, I like my present equipment"? This buyer does not perceive a need, and will not buy. Suppose you make your point about reducing operating costs, but for some reason the prospect is not interested in reducing costs? Chances are, this person will not buy no matter how persuasively you present your product's benefits—because high costs are not seen as an important problem.

Furthermore, even customers who want to solve a problem, but do not like your product, are certainly not going to buy. But if you have convinced them, if they want to solve a problem, and if they perceive your product as solving this problem, the question is still: "Will these customers buy from you?" They will, if they believe you represent the best supplier. If they would rather buy from another supplier, you have lost the sale. Your job is to provide the necessary information so that customer's say yes to each of these four questions.

Summary of Major Selling Issues

As a salesperson, you should be knowledgeable about factors which influence your buyer's purchase decision. This knowledge, which helps to increase the salesperson's self-confidence and the buyer's confidence in the salesperson, can be obtained through training and practice.

A firm's marketing effort involves various efforts to create exchanges to satisfy the buyer's needs and wants. The salesperson should understand the characteristics of their market (consumer or industrial), and how these characteristics relate to the buyer's behavior in order to better serve and sell to their customers.

The individual goes through various steps or stages in the three buying situations of routine decision making, limited problem solving, and extensive problem solving. You should uncover who is involved in the buying decision and the main factors which influence the decision. These factors include various psychological and practical buying influences.

Psychological factors include the buyer's motives, perceptions, learning, attitudes, beliefs, and personality—all of which influence the individual's needs and result in a search for information on what products to buy to satisfy them. The information is evaluated, resulting in the decision to buy or not to buy. These same two factors influence whether the buyer is satisfied or dissatisfied with the product.

Salespeople should realize that all prospects will not buy their products, at least not all of the time, due to the many factors influencing their buying decisions. You need to be able to uncover buyers' needs and provide the knowledge that allows them to develop personal attitudes toward the product that result in positive beliefs that your products fulfill their needs.

Uncovering prospects' needs is often difficult, since they may be reluctant to tell you their true needs or may not really know what and why they want to buy. You can usually feel confident that people buy for reasons such as to satisfy a need, fulfill a desire, and obtain a value. To determine these important buying needs, you can ask questions, observe prospects, listen to them, and talk to their associates about their needs.

Review and Discussion Questions

1. What three types of buying situations may the buyer be in when contacted by a salesperson? Briefly describe each type.
2. What are the psychological factors which may influence the prospect's buying decision?
3. While you do not have to be a psychologist or understand exactly how the buyer's "black box" works, you do need to uncover the buyer's motives for buying.
   A. What techniques can be used to uncover the buyer's motives?
   B. The prospect's intention to buy can be influenced by several things. What information does the salesperson need to obtain concerning the prospect's buying intentions before developing a sales presentation?

Figure 4–4 What Nonverbal Signals Are These Buyers Giving to You?

1. When you mention your price, this purchasing agent tilts her head back, raises her hands and her body posture becomes rigid. What nonverbal signals is she communicating and how would you move on with the sale?

2. As you explain your sales features, this buyer looks away, clasps his hands and crosses his legs away from you. What nonverbal signals is he communicating and how would you move on with the sale?

3. As you explain the quality of your product, this company president opens his arms and leans toward you. What nonverbal signals is he communicating and how would you move on with the sale?

Reproduced from the sales training course "The Languages of Selling," by Gerhard Gschwandtner & Associates, Falmouth, VA 22401.

Answers to Figure 4-4

1. Your buyer is sending red signals. That means you are facing nearly insurmountable barriers. You've got to stop what you are doing, express understanding, and redirect your approach.

2. This buyer is sending yellow signals that warn you to exercise caution. Your own words and gestures must be aimed at relaxing the buyer or he may soon communicate red signals.

3. This buyer is sending green signals that say: everything is "go." With no obstacles to your selling strategy, simply move on to the close.

The buyer was sending Joe signals that he likes doing business with people he knows. He did not want to get down to business immediately. He wanted to visit for a while. There was never any true communication established between Jackson and Jones, causing Jones to misread the customer and incorrectly handle the situation.

Salespeople, as illustrated in the above example, often lose a sale after failing to recognize communication barriers between buyer and seller. The main reasons communication breaks down in the sales situation are:

Differences in Perception. If the buyer and seller do not share a common understanding of information contained in the presentation, communication will break down. The closer a buyer's and seller's perceptions, attitudes, and beliefs, the stronger communication will be between them.

Buyer Does Not Recognize a Need for Product. Communication barriers exist if the salesperson is unable to convince the buyer of a need, and/or that the salesperson represents the best supplier to buy from.

Selling Pressure. There is a fine line between what is acceptable sales pressure and enthusiasm and what the buyer perceives as a high-pressure sales technique. A pushy, arrogant selling style can quickly cause the prospect to erect a communication barrier.

Information Overload. You may present the buyer with an excess of information. This overload may cause confusion, perhaps offense, and the buyer will stop listening to you. The engineer making a presentation to a buyer who is not an engineer may concentrate on the technical aspects of a product, while the buyer only wants a small amount of information.

Disorganized Sales Presentation. Sales presentations that seem unorganized to the buyer tend to cause frustration, even anger. Buyers commonly expect you to understand their needs or problems and to customize your sales presentation to their individual situation. If you fail to do this, communication can break down.

Distractions. When a buyer receives a telephone call or someone walks into the office, distractions occur. A buyer's thoughts may become sidetracked, and it may be difficult to regain attention and interest.

Poor Listening. At times the buyer may not actually be listening to you. This often occurs if you do all or most of the talking, not allowing the buyer to participate in the conversation.

The seven barriers to communications listed above are certainly not the only ones which may occur. Mainly, it is important to understand that communication barriers can exist. As in the example of Joe Jones, the buyer may actually need the product and the salesperson may have excellent product knowledge and believe that a good sales presentation was made, yet because of communication barriers, the buyer rejects the salesperson and the product. As a salesperson, you must constantly seek ways of recognizing and overcoming communication barriers, and getting back to identifying and satisfying buyer needs through persuasive communications.

Master Persuasive Communication and the Force Is with You

In order to become a better communicator, you need to consider two major elements of communication. First, you should always strive to improve the message you deliver in the sales presentation. You need to be a capable encoder. Second, you need to improve your ability to determine what the buyer is actually communicating to you. Therefore, you also need to be a good listener or decoder. A good sales communicator knows how to effectively encode *and* decode during a presentation.

Salespeople want to be good communicators in order to persuade people to purchase their products. **Persuasion** means the ability to change a person's belief, position, or course of action. The more effective you are at communicating, the greater are your chances of being successful at persuasion.

The chapters on the selling process will go into greater detail on specific persuasion techniques. For now, let's review several general factors to consider in developing persuasive communications. These factors relate to several components of the simple communication model discussed earlier: feedback, empathy, simplicity, listening, attitude, and proof statements.

Feedback Guides Your Presentation

You need to learn how to generate feedback to determine whether your listener has received your intended message. Feedback does not refer to just any type of listening behavior by the buyer, but to a recognizable response from the buyer. A shake of the head, a frown, or an effort to say something are all signals to the salesperson. If the salesperson fails to notice or respond to these signals, no feedback can occur, which means faulty or incomplete communication. A salesperson's observation of feedback is akin to an auto racer's glances at his tachometer. Both aid in ascertaining a receiver's response.

Often feedback must be sought openly because the prospect will not always give it voluntarily. By interjecting into the presentation questions that require the customer to give a particular response, you can stimulate feedback. Questioning, sometimes called probing, allows the salesperson to determine the buyer's attitude toward the sales presentation.

Fisk Telephone Systems, Inc., included this type of feedback in their sales training sessions. Fisk sales trainers suggested to their salespeople that they use questions in their presentations. Some of these questions were:

Do you think you are paying too much for your telecommunications equipment?

Are you happy with the service now being provided to you?

Are you happy with the equipment your present supplier has installed for your company?

These questions were intended to draw negative responses from the customers concerning their relationship with their present supplier. They provided the Fisk salespeople with a method of determining how the prospect felt about the competitor. These responses allow the salesperson to discuss the specific features, advantages, and benefits of Fisk products relative to the products presently used by the prospect. Thus in planning your presentation, it is important to predetermine when and what feedback-producing questions to ask. One way of creating positive feedback is through empathy.

Empathy Puts You in Your Customer's Shoes

Empathy is the ability to identify and understand the other person's feelings, ideas, and situation. As a salesperson, you need to be interested in what the buyer is saying, not just in giving your sales presentation. Many of the barriers to communication mentioned earlier can be overcome when you place yourself in the buyer's shoes. Empathy is saying to a prospect, "I'm here to help you," or asking, "Tell me your problems and needs so I can help *you.*" Empathy is also evidenced by a salesperson's display of sincerity and interest in the buyer's situation.

This may mean acknowledging from time to time that a prospect may not truly need your product. Take, for example, the Scott Paper Company salesperson who finds that the customer still has 90 percent of the paper towels purchased three months ago. There is no reason to sell this customer more paper towels. It is time to help the customer sell the paper towels now on hand by suggesting displays, price reductions, and formats for newspaper advertisements. It is wise always to adopt your customer's point of view in order to meet the customer's needs best.

Keep It Simple, You Silver-Tongued Devil

The new salesperson was sitting in a customer's office waiting for the buyer. Her boss was with her. As they heard the buyer come into the office, the sales manager said, "Remember, a **KISS** for him." No, he

Figure 4–5

Twenty Questions

Communication. It's more than just a word. It's a delicate exercise in which you want to provide information to the buyer, but not too much! You want to befriend him, but not too much! And you want to question him, probe him, but not too much!

Too many questions become an interrogation. However, everyone likes to be asked what they think, especially concerning subjects important to them. So try and phrase your questions as if you're having a conversation with the buyer. Because that's exactly what you're doing.

When you become an especially good questioner, you'll be able to put your answers into the buyer's mouth and lead him down the path to the order: "Doesn't your business thrive on services such as this? ... Wouldn't you say that's a savings well worth considering? ... Isn't your company fighting to hold on to its market share? Then couldn't you use our product at this time? How many can I sign you up for?"

Speaking of Selling, © 1980, Sales Builders Division of S&MM.

was not saying to give the buyer a kiss, but to use the old selling philosophy of *Keep it simple, salesperson.*

The story is told of a little old lady who went into a hardware store. The clerk greeted her and offered her some help. She replied that she was looking for a heater. So the clerk said, "Gee, are you lucky! We've got a big sale on these heaters, and a tremendous selection. Let me show you." So after maybe 30 or 45 minutes of discussing duothermic controls, heat induction, and all the factors involved with how a heater operates, including the features and advantages of each of the 12 models, he turned to the little old lady and said, "Now, do you have any questions?" To which she replied, "Yes, just one, Sonny. Which one of these things will keep a little old lady warm?"

How Can You Simplify the Following Statements?

1. A mass of concentrated earthly material perennially rotating in its axis will not accumulate an accretion of bryophytic vegetation.

2. Individuals who are perforce constrained to be domiciled in vitreous structures of patent frangibility should on no account employ petrous formations as projectiles.

3. A superabundance of talent skilled in the preparation of gastronomic concoctions will impair the quality of a certain potable solution made by immersing a gallinaceous bird in ebullient Adam's ale.

Answers:

1. A rolling stone gathers no moss. 2. People who live in glass houses shouldn't throw stones. 3. Too many cooks spoil the broth.

An overcomplex, technical presentation can and should be avoided when it is unnecessary. You should use words and materials that can be understood easily by the buyer. The skilled salesperson can make a prospect feel comfortable with a new product or complex technology through the subtle use of nontechnical information and a respectful attitude.

Creating Mutual Trust Develops Friendship

Salespeople who develop a mutual trust relationship with their customers cannot help being successful. This type of relationship eventually results in high "source credibility" and even friendship. The buyer realized that in the past he was not sold products that failed to perform to expectations; the products were worth their price; and the salesperson did everything promised. Building mutual trust is very important to effective long-run communication.

Listening Clues You In

Salespeople often believe that their job is to talk rather than listen. If they will both talk *and* listen, their persuasive powers will increase.

Since people can listen (about 400 words per minute) roughly twice as fast as the average rate of speech, it is understandable that a person's mind may wander while listening to a salesperson's presentation. To keep the buyer **listening** to you, ask questions, get the buyer involved in the conversation. Once you ask a question—listen. Carefully listen to what is being said to you. One writer suggests five "Guides for Listening":

1. Avoid making value judgements.
2. Listen to the full story.
3. Recognize feelings and emotions.
4. Restate the buyer's position (summarize for clarity).
5. Question with care.[6]

Another writer developed "Ten Commandments for Good Listening." Notice that "stop talking" is both the first and last commandment. These commandments are as follows:

1. Stop talking.
2. Put the speaker at ease.
3. Show the speaker you want to listen.
4. Remove distractions.
5. Empathize with the speaker.
6. Be patient.
7. Hold your temper.
8. Go easy on argument and criticism.
9. Ask questions.
10. Stop talking.[7]

It is sometimes difficult, especially for the novice salesperson, to stay calm when a prospect displays favorable signs. The novice may continue to talk on and on about a particular situation or problem. The salesperson must *learn to listen.* Listening implies sincerity and respect. It is a key to sales success.

> His thoughts were slow,
>   His words were few,
> And never made to glisten.
>   But he was a joy
> Wherever he went.
>   You should have heard him listen.
>
> *Author Unknown*

Your Attitude Makes the Difference

While a variety of methods and techniques exist in selling, truly effective sales persuasion is based on the salesperson's attitude toward the sales job and his customers. The most important element of this attitude is the salesperson's degree of interest and enthusiasm in helping people to fulfill their needs. This is the foundation for building effective communication techniques. **Enthusiasm** is a condition in which an individual is filled with excitement toward something. "Excitement" does not mean an aggressive attitude, but rather a positive view toward solving the customers' problems.

You need to sell yourself *on* yourself and *on* being a salesperson. The highly successful salesperson goes all out in helping customers. You should strive to make the buyer feel "important." Show the buyer that you are there solely as a problem solver. You can do this by developing methods of expressing true interest such as asking questions, instead of talking at the buyer. This type of attitude will in turn benefit you by allowing you to look at the sales situation from the buyer's viewpoint (empathy).

Salespeople who have established **credibility** with their customers through continued empathy, willingness to listen to specific needs, and continual enthusiasm toward their work and their customers' business can make claims that their customers treat as "gospel" in some cases. Enthusiasm combined with proof statements greatly improve a salesperson's persuasive ability.

Proof Statements Make You Believable

Salespeople have known for years that the use of highly credible sources can improve persuasiveness of the sales presentation message. **Proof statements** are statements that substantiate claims made by the salesperson. Pharmaceutical companies often quote research studies done by outstanding physicians at prestigious medical schools to validate claims of product benefits. These proof statements add high credibility to a sales message.

Salespeople sometimes quote acknowledged experts in a field on the use of the products. By demonstrating that other customers or respected individuals use the products, they encourage customer belief in the validity of information presented in a sales presentation. People place greater confidence in a trustworthy objective source (particularly one not associated with the salesperson's firm) and are therefore more receptive to what is said by the salesperson.

Summary of Major Selling Issues

Communication is operationally defined as transmission of verbal and nonverbal information and understanding between salesperson and prospect. Modes of communication commonly used in a sales presentation are: words, gestures, visual aids, and nonverbal communications.

A model of the communication process is composed of a sender (encoder) who transmits a specific message via some media to a receiver (decoder) who responds to that message. The effectiveness of this communication process can be hampered by noise which distorts the message as it travels to the receiver. A sender (encoder) can judge the effectiveness of a message and media choice by monitoring the feedback from the receiver.

Barriers can exist or develop which hinder or prevent constructive communication during a sales presentation. These barriers may relate to the perceptional differences between the sender and receiver, outside distractions, or how sales information is conveyed. Regardless of their source, these barriers must be recognized and either overcome or eliminated if communication is to be effected.

Nonverbal communication has emerged as a critical component of the overall communication process within the past ten or fifteen years. Recognition of nonverbal communication is essential for sales success in today's business environment. Awareness of the prospect's territorial space, a firm and confident handshake, and accurate interpretation of the language of body and limb positioning can be a tremendous aid to a salesperson's success.

A salesperson's overall persuasive power can be enhanced through the development of several key characteristics. The salesperson who creates a relationship based on mutual trust with a customer by displaying true empathy (desire to understand customer's situation and environment), a willing ear (more listening, less talking), and a positive attitude of enthusiastic pursuit of lasting solutions to that customer's needs and problems, greatly increases the likelihood of making that sale—not just in the short run, but over the long haul.

Review and Discussion Questions

1. Draw the salesperson-buyer communication process. Describe each step in the process. Why is two-way communication important in this process?
2. This chapter outlined several forms of nonverbal communication.
   A. Give an example of a salesperson making a good first impression through the proper use of an introductory handshake.
   B. What signals should the salesperson look for from a buyer's "body language." Give several examples of these signals.
3. A salesperson may spend hours developing a sales presentation and yet the buyer still does not buy. One reason for losing a sale is

that the salesperson and the buyer do not communicate. What barriers to communication may be present between seller and buyer during a sales presentation?

4. When two people are talking, they want the listener to understand what they are saying. They both want to be effective communicators. The same is true of the salesperson who wants the buyer to listen to a sales presentation. What can the salesperson do to help ensure that the buyer is listening?

5. You arrive at the industrial purchasing agent's office on time. This is your first meeting. After you have waited 5 minutes, the agent's secretary says, "She will see you." After the initial greeting, she asks you to sit down. For each of the three following situations determine:

A. What nonverbal signals is she communicating?

B. How would you respond nonverbally?

C. What would you say to her?

(1) She sits down behind her desk. She is sitting straight up in her chair. She clasps her hands together and with little expression on her face says, "What can I do for you?"

(2) She sits down behind her desk. She moves slightly backwards in her chair, crosses her arms, and while looking around the room says, "What can I do for you?"

(3) She sits down behind her desk. She moves slightly forward in her chair, seems hurried, yet relaxed toward your presence. Her arms are uncrossed. She looks you squarely in the eye, and with a pleasant look on her face says, "What can I do for you?"

6. In each of the following selling situations determine:

A. What nonverbal signals is the buyer communicating?

B. How would you respond nonverbally?

C. What would you say?

(1) The buyer seems happy to see you. Because you have been calling on him for several years, the two of you have become business friends. In the middle of your presentation, you notice the buyer slowly lean back in his chair. As you continue to talk a puzzled look comes over his face.

(2) As you begin the main part of your presentation, the buyer reaches for the telephone and says, "Keep going, I need to tell my secretary something."

(3) As a salesperson with only six months experience, you are somewhat nervous about calling on an important buyer who has been a purchasing agent for almost 20 years. Three minutes after you have begun your presentation, he rapidly raises his arms straight up into the air and slowly clasps his hands behind his head. He leans so far back in his chair that you think he is going to fall backward on the floor.

At the same time, he crosses his legs away from you and slowly closes his eyes. You keep on talking. Slowly the buyer opens his eyes, uncrosses his legs, and sits up in his chair. He leans forward, placing his elbows on the desk top, seemingly propping his head up with his hands. He seems relaxed as he says, "Let me see what you have here." He reaches his hand out for you to give him the presentation materials you have developed for him.

(4) At the end of your presentation, the buyer leans forward, his arms open, and smiles as he says, "You really don't expect me to buy that piece of junk, do you?"

Project

The use of questions by the salesperson is an effective method of obtaining feedback from a buyer. This statement applies to conversation between two people. For the next two days, try using questions in your conversations with other people and report on your results. These questions should reflect an interest in the person you are conversing with and the topic being discussed. Use of the second person tense (you, your . . .) should increase feedback, and create an atmosphere of trust.

For example, questions such as, "What do you mean?" "What do you think?" or "How does that sound?" can be used by you in your conversation to have other people participate and to help you to determine how they feel toward your topic of conversation.

Asking people's opinions can also result in a positive response, since they may feel flattered that you care about their opinion. Questions can also help you guide the direction of topics discussed in your conversation. Try to determine people's reactions to your questions and report on your findings in class.

Cases

4–1 Skaggs Manufacturing

John Andrews arrived promptly for his 10:00 A.M. meeting with Martha Gillespie, the buyer for Skaggs Manufacturing. At 10:15, when Ms. Gillespie hadn't arrived, John asked her secretary if she was out of the office for the morning. The secretary smiled and said, "She'll probably be a few minutes late." John resented this delay and was convinced that Gillespie had forgotten the appointment.

Finally, at 10:20 Gillespie entered her office, walked over to John, said hello and promptly excused herself to talk to the secretary about a tennis game scheduled for that afternoon. Ten minutes later, Gillespie led John into her office. At the same time, a competing salesperson entered the office for a 10:30 appointment. With the door open, Gillespie asked John, "What's new today?" As John began to talk, Gillespie began reading letters on her desk and signing them. Shortly after that, the telephone began to ring, whereupon Gillespie talked to her husband for 10 minutes.

As she hung up, Gillespie looked at John and suddenly realized his frustration. She promptly buzzed her secretary and said, "Hold all calls." She got up and shut the door. John again began his presentation when Gillespie leaned backward in her chair, pulled her golf shoes out of a desk drawer and began to brush them.

About that time, the secretary entered the office and said, "Martha, your 10:30 appointment is about to leave. What should I tell him?" "Tell him to wait, I need to see him." Then she said, "John, I wish we had more time. Look, I think I have enough of your product to last until your next visit. I'll see you then. Thanks for coming by."

John quickly rose to his feet, did not shake hands, said "OK," and left.

Questions:

1. What nonverbal cues did the salesperson, John Andrews, experience when contacting Martha Gillespie?
2. If you were John, how would you have handled the situation?

4–2 Lanier Dictaphone (A)

Judy Allison, the Lanier Dictaphone saleswoman in Alabama, entered the office of Bill Taylor, purchasing agent for a large manufacturing firm. Two weeks earlier, she had made her first sales call and had left a demonstrater dictaphone for Taylor to have executives of the company try out. The previous evening Taylor had called Judy and asked her to see him so that he could give her an order. After the initial "hellos," the conversation went like this:

Buyer:	Judy, thanks for coming by today. Our executives really liked your equipment. Here is an order for four dictaphones. When can you deliver them?
Salesperson:	Is tomorrow too soon?
Buyer:	That is perfect. Leave them with Joyce, my secretary. Joyce, [*Bill says over the intercom*], Judy will deliver the dictaphones tomorrow and go ahead and take them to Sally, Anne, and Sherri. Women sure understand the use of modern equipment!
Salesperson:	Bill, thanks for your help.
Buyer:	Forget it Judy, I wish I could have helped more. Your dictaphones can reduce the number of secretaries in the typing pool, resulting in big savings to our company.

Salesperson: You're right; many of my customers are going to them for that very reason.

Buyer: I know, but some executives still feel people cannot be replaced by machines.

Question:

Analyze and describe the conversation between Judy and Bill. What should Judy do now?

|5

So, What Do I Need to Know?

Learning objectives

1. To discuss the major body of knowledge needed for increased sales success.
2. To illustrate how this knowledge can be used during the sales presentation.
3. To show how sales aids are used by people selling consumer goods.

Key Terms for Selling

Sales training

National advertising

Retail advertising

Cooperative advertising

Trade advertising

Industrial advertising

Direct-mail advertising

Consumer sales promotion

Trade sales promotion

Point-of-purchase displays

Shelf positioning

Shelf facings

SAMI data

Premiums

Contests and sweepstakes

Consumer premiums

Dealer premiums

Price

List price

Net price

Zone price

FOB shipping point

FOB destination

Noncumulative quantity discount

Cumulative quantity discount

Cash discounts

Trade discounts

Consumer discounts

Markup

Gross profit

Net profit

Profile

Patrick E. Kamlowsky
Hughes Tool

My name is Patrick E. Kamlowsky. I am a sales technician for the Hughes Tool Company. Hughes Tool is acknowledged as the world leader in rock bit manufacturing. Hughes rock bits (a replaceable part which performs the job of drilling or boring into the earth for oil or gas wells) are found wherever man's search for oil and gas takes him.

I began working for Hughes Tool upon graduation from Wheeling College, in Wheeling, West Virginia, in November, 1978, with a bachelor of arts degree. I had no previous oil field experience, and indeed, had never seen a drilling rig. After completion of a thorough initial training program, I was assigned responsibility for sales coverage of all drilling operations within a specific geographic area. In covering my territory I have daily contact with petroleum engineers and drilling foremen from both large producers, like Exxon U.S.A., and smaller, independent oil producers, such as Martin Exploration.

Since the "oil patch" operates constantly 365 days a year, I am on 24-hour call to aid my customers in any manner possible. My personal reward on many jobs is not merely selling a rock bit, but observing its use in aiding a driller in cutting costs per foot, which can run into tens of thousands of dollars.

Today's oil and gas drilling operations are highly technical in nature. Intimate product knowledge is an essential asset for selling. It is used in fulfilling the Hughes' philosophy of assisting the exploration firm in drilling in a safe and cost-effective manner. It is my responsibility to update the drill site foreman or engineer on current developments in drill bit design, and help minimize the drilling cost per foot.

Product knowledge on rock bits is not obtained solely through rote memorization. It is primarily gained through detailed observation of the use, function, and performance of rock bits in actual field drilling work under adverse operating conditions. Proper interpretation of oil field operating results allows me to make valid, useful recommendations on appropriate drilling procedures and the type of rock bit to use. Improper drilling procedure or use of the wrong bit type can substantially increase the cost of drilling an oil or gas well. Though the cost of a rock bit is a comparatively small portion of the total capital outlay made in drilling an oil or gas well, the selection of a proper rock bit is, in my opinion, essential to a successful, cost-efficient drilling operation."

The Gillette Company introduced a new line of skin care products—
Aapri—with a $17.4 million advertising and promotion campaign.
Network television advertisements of Aapri were seen by approximately
97 percent of its target market (women aged 18–49) at least twelve times
during the year. These commercials were shown during both day-time
and prime-time television viewing hours.

Aapri appeared in full-color, two-page advertisements in such national
magazines as: *Cosmopolitan, People, Glamour, Redbook, McCalls,* and
Good Housekeeping. The combined monthly circulation of these target
market periodicals is 163 million copies. Gillette mailed out 15 million
⅝ ounce free Aapri samples at a cost of $4.1 million. Prepriced (.79¢)
samples were made available through in-store retail promotional
displays.

Four million dollars of the introductory budget went into retail trade-
off invoice allowances, early-buy allowances, and co-op advertisements.
Placement allowances also were available on counter and floorstand
displays, which included consumer brochures.[1]

Gillette salespeople used this information in promoting the Aapri line
to wholesale and retail trade customers when the products were initially
introduced. This type of information can build the confidence of a
hesitant buyer by showing that a company is fully behind a new, untried
product. The salesperson needs to learn of and keep current on
information concerning the company, product, distribution, promotion,
pricing, competition, industry trends, and the economy. This chapter
examines areas of information that are essential to the success of all
salespeople.

Where'd You Learn That: Sources of Sales Knowledge

Knowledge for selling is obtained in two ways. First, most companies
provide some form of formal sales training. This information is taught
through preliminary training programs and sales meetings. Second, the
salesperson learns by being on the job. Experience is surely the best
teacher for the beginning salesperson.

Sales training is the effort put forth by an employer to provide the
opportunity for the salesperson to receive job-related attitudes, concepts,
rules, and skills that result in improved performance in the selling
environment.

John H. Patterson, founder of the National Cash Register Company and known as the "father of sales training," used to say, "At NCR our salesmen never stop learning."[2] This philosophy is the reason that successful companies thoroughly train new salespeople and maintain ongoing training programs for their experienced sales personnel.

Companies are interested in training primarily to increase sales volume, salesperson productivity, and profitability. This emphasis on sales training for *results* has been expressed by the chairman and chief executive officer of U.S. Steel:

> We support training and development activities to get results. . . . We're interested in the specific things that provide greater rewards to the employee, increased return to the stockholder, and enable reinvestment of sales revenue to meet the growing needs of the business. In other words, [we're interested in] those things which affect the 'bottom line.'[3]

Like many professional careers, selling is a skill that can truly be developed only through *experience*. Sales knowledge obtained through education, reading, formalized sales training and word-of-mouth is helpful in enhancing overall sales ability, but actual experience is the critical source of sales knowledge. Some sales managers will hire only experienced people to fill entry-level selling slots. Indeed, some corporations will not allow people to fill marketing staff positions unless they have had field sales experience with the company or a major competitor.

Sales experience makes for a better salesperson by: showing how buyers perceive a product or product line; revealing unrecognized or undervalued product benefits or shortcomings; voicing a multitude of unanticipated protests and objections; showing a great number of prospect moods and attitudes over a short period of time; generally, providing a challenge that makes selling a skill never to be truly mastered, only improved. No author or sales trainer can simulate the almost infinite variety of situations that a salesperson will confront over the span of a career. Authors and trainers can provide only general guidelines as a framework for action. Actual selling experience alone gives a person direct feedback on how to function in a specific selling situation.

The sales knowledge gained through periodic sales training and actual experience benefits not only the salesperson but also the firm and its customers.

Why Salespeople Require Knowledge

A knowledgeable salesperson will be able to provide better service to customers. Knowledge based on experience should result in increased sales. However, there are also two other important reasons for the salesperson to have selling knowledge. These are (1) to increase the salesperson's self-confidence, and (2) to build the buyer's confidence in the salesperson. These reasons are, for the salesperson, *the* major reasons for acquiring sales knowledge.

Knowledge Increases Confidence in Salespeople

Salespeople who are calling on, for example, computer systems engineers, university professors, or aerospace experts may be at a disadvantage. In many cases they will have less education and experience than their prospects in their fields of expertise. Imagine yourself making a sales call on Dr. Michael DeBakey, the distinguished heart surgeon. Can you educate him in the use of your company's synthetic heart valves? Not really, but you can offer your help in supplying product information from your firm's medical department. This personal service, your product knowledge, and his specific needs are what will make the sale for you. Knowledge about your company, its market, and your buyer will enable you to acquire confidence in yourself, ultimately resulting in increased sales.

. . . And in Buyers

Furthermore, prospects and customers want to do business with salespeople who know their business and the products they sell. When a prospect has confidence in the salesperson's expertise, a sales presentation becomes more acceptable and believable to the prospect. You should strive to be "the" expert on all aspects of your product. Knowledge of your product and its uses will also allow you to confidently answer questions and field objections raised by prospects. You can explain better how a product suits a customer's needs. But product knowledge alone may not be enough to convince every buyer.

Know Your Firm

Knowledge of your firm can sometimes aid you in projecting an "expert" image to the prospect. Company knowledge includes information of the history, policies, procedures, distribution systems, promotional activities, and pricing practices that have guided the firm to its present status. The type and extent of company knowledge to be used depends on the company, its product lines, and the industry. In general, consumer goods salespeople require little information about the technical nature of their products; however, selling high-technology products (computers, complex machinery, etc.) to highly knowledgeable industrial buyers requires extensive knowledge.

General Company Information

All salespeople need to be aware of the background and present operating policies of their company. These policies are your guidelines, and you must understand them to do your job effectively. Information on company growth, policies, procedures, production and service facilities may often be of use in your sales presentation. Here are four examples:

Company Growth and Accomplishment. Knowledge of your firm's development since its origin provides you with promotional material and builds your confidence in your company.

An IBM office products salesperson might say to a buyer,

> In 1952, IBM placed its first commercial electronic computer on the market. That year our sales were $342 million. Currently, our sales are projected to be over $30 billion. IBM has reached these high sales figures because our advanced, technological office equipment and information processors are the best available at any price. This IBM 'Star Trek I' system I am showing you is the most advanced piece on equipment on the market today. It is five years ahead of any other computer!

Policies and Procedures. To give good service, you should be able to tell a customer: how an order is processed; how long it takes for orders to be filled; your firm's returned goods policy; how to open a new account; and what to do in the event of a shipping error. If you handle these situations quickly and fairly, your buyer will gain confidence in you and your firm.

Production Facilities. Many companies require their new salespeople to tour their production facilities to give them a first-hand look at the company's operations. This is a good opportunity to gain product knowledge. For example, the Bigelow-Sanford Carpet Company salesperson can say, "When I was visiting our production plant, I viewed each step of the carpet production process. The research and development department allowed us to watch comparison tests between our carpets and competitor's carpets. Our carpets did everything but fly . . . but they are working on that!"

Service Facilities. Many companies have both service facilities and service representatives to help their customers. Being able to say, "We can have a service representative here the same day you call our service center," strengthens a sales presentation, especially if service is important for the customer (as it is in the office copier and computer industries).

Know Your Product

Knowledge about your company's products and those of your competitors is a major component of sales knowledge. You should become an expert on your company's products. You should understand how they are produced, and their level of quality. This type of product knowledge is important to the buyer.

Your product knowledge may include such technical details as:

Performance data.

Physical size and characteristics.

How the product operates.

Specific features, advantages, and benefits of the product.

How well the product is selling in the marketplace.

Many companies have their new salespeople work in a manufacturing plant (for example, on the assembly line), or in the warehouse (filling orders and receiving stock). This hands-on experience may cost the salesperson a lot of sweat and sore muscles for a couple of weeks or months, but the payoff is a world of product knowledge and help in future selling that could not be earned in any other way. U.S. Steel, for example, has its new salespeople spend several weeks in a production plant. Often new salespeople in the oil and gas industry find themselves roughnecking and driving trucks during the first few months on the job. Also, a sales representative for McKesson Chemical is apt to spend the first two or three weeks on the job in a warehouse unloading freight cars and flatbed trucks and filling 55-gallon drums with various liquid chemicals.

Much can be learned at periodic company sales meetings. At sales meetings a consumer goods manufacturer may concentrate on developing sales presentations for the products to receive special emphasis during the company sales period. Company advertising programs, price discounts, and promotional allowances for these products are discussed. Although little time is spent on the technical aspects of consumer products, much time is devoted to discussing the marketing mix for these products (product type, promotion, distribution, and price).

Sales managers for technical products might spend as much as 75 percent of a sales meeting discussing product information. The remaining time might be allotted to sales techniques.

In many cases, distributors of low-priced, high-volume products (food retailers, for instance) or users of high-priced "critical components" (tires for autos) are equally or more concerned with how quickly and by what means they will receive a product. This involves a very important kind of information: knowledge of your firm's channels of distribution.

A Little Knowledge of Distribution Can Go a Long Way

It is essential to understand the channel of distribution used by your company to move its products to the final consumer. Knowledge of each channel member is also vital. Wholesalers and retailers often stock thousands of products, and each may have hundreds of salespeople, like you, from a multitude of companies calling on its buyers. You should know as much about each channel member as possible. Some important information you will need is:

- Likes and dislikes of each channel member's customers.
- Product lines and assortment each one carries.
- When each member sees salespeople.
- Their distribution, promotion, and pricing policies.
- What and how much of a product, each has purchased in the past.

While most of your channel members will have similar policies concerning salespeople, you should keep abreast of the differences between them.

Conflict and Cooperation in Distribution Channels

A trade channel can be ideally viewed as a group of firms acting together to move goods from the manufacturer to users. Yet power struggles do exist in distribution channels. Wholesalers may resist buying a new product until it is actually demanded by their retail customers. Supermarket retailers may already have 12 different brands of hand soap, toothpaste, or cookies. Why should they buy another brand that comes in three sizes? If they were to buy this new product, would a present product need to be dropped?

What about the large retailer, such as Sears or Safeway, that typically demands special favors such as products built to specifications, lower prices, and special delivery from the manufacturer? The manufacturer selling to mass merchandisers who discount their products may find it difficult to convince nondiscounters, like Sears, to help sell these products.

These are just a few examples of the type of channel conflicts you may have to face. If the problem turns into a stalemate, the channel member affected by the problem may be forced to take an alternative course of action. If wholesalers will not cooperate as the manufacturer wishes, the manufacturer may sell only to retailers. If a manufacturer will not cooperate with a wholesaler or retailer, that wholesaler or retailer may begin manufacturing its own ''house brand'' products.

These alternative solutions can be costly to both parties involved in terms of lost sales, or the additional costs incurred. Both manufacturers and middlemen can promote a spirit of cooperation by establishing policies and taking actions to benefit their channel counterparts.

Cooperation from the Manufacturer. The manufacturer should enable its salespeople to offer their middlemen:

A reasonable assortment of products, properly designed, reasonably priced, and available in the quantities requested.

Deletion of individual products from the product line when needed.

A fair or proportionate amount of advertising for new products (when applicable) to build product demand.

A pledge to honor service guarantees and to refund or replace damaged merchandise.

Regular sales call schedule on middlemen.

Reasonable estimates of quantities of product to stock or order.

Useful market information.

By treating each middleman as a partner rather than an adversary, and considering their viewpoints, you can reduce channel conflicts for the manufacturer.

Cooperation from the Middlemen. Likewise, wholesalers and retailers should consider the manufacturer's point of view. Often a manufacturer has spent years developing a product, and is prepared to spend millions of promotional dollars to introduce the product to the market. Failure by middlemen to stock a new product, or in some cases to carry adequate quantities of a new product, can jeopardize the tremendous investment in time, capital and human resources that the manufacturer has made.

What can the middlemen do to cooperate with the manufacturer? They can:

Give careful consideration to the sales proposal of a manufacturer's salesperson, especially those representing large suppliers.

Provide their employees with essential product information.

Carry an adequate supply of a product.

Properly display and price products to avoid consumer confusion.

Advertise and promote as agreed upon with manufacturer's salesperson.

Honor manufacturer's warranties and coupons.

Pay bills on time.

While periodic channel conflicts are almost unavoidable, cooperation between channel members is important for efficient movement of goods from manufacturer to end user. Although they may seem fairly obvious, the actions and policies suggested here are important to stress. They can aid channel members in avoiding costly conflicts, thereby furthering the efficient diffusion of industrial and consumer goods.

In many cases, the manufacturer or middleman's sales representative is the medium through which such channel smoothing policies are administered. In this important function, effective salespeople can benefit

117 So, What Do I Need to Know?

not only employers and customers, but also themselves. Channel cooperation aids salespeople by increasing sales revenue and maintaining long-run supplier-relationships. Another help comes from advertising.

Advertising Aids Salespeople

Personal selling, advertising, publicity, and sales promotion are the main ingredients of a firm's promotional effort. Companies sometimes coordinate these three promotional tools in a promotional campaign. A sales force may be asked by the corporate marketing manager to concentrate on selling product A for the months of April and May. Meanwhile, product A is simultaneously promoted on television and in magazines, and direct mail samples or cents-off coupons for product A are being sent to consumers.

Keeping abreast of your company's advertising and sales promotion activities is a must. By incorporating this data into your sales

Figure 5–1   Example of Advertising and Sales Promotion Information Salesperson Tells Buyer

1. Massive sampling and couponing
   - There will be a blanketing of the top 300 markets with 4.4 oz. sample plus eight-cents-off coupon. Your market is included.
   - There will be a 75 percent coverage of homes in the top one hundred markets. Your market is included.
2. Heavy advertising
   - Nighttime network TV.
   - Daytime network TV.
   - Saturation spot TV.
   - Newspapers.
   - The total network and spot advertising will reach 85 percent of all homes in the United States five times each week, based on a four-week average. This means that, in four weeks, "Fresh Mouth" will have attained 150 million home impressions—130,000,000 of these will be against women.
   - There will be half-page, two-color inserts in local newspapers in 50 markets, including yours. This is more than 20 million circulation. Scheduled to tie in with saturation sampling is a couponing program.
   - Fifteen million dollars will be spent on promotion to ensure consumer acceptance.
3. TV advertising theme—the salesperson would show pictures or drawings of the advertisements.
   - The commercial with POWER to sell!
   - "POWER to kill mouth odor—POWER to kill germs—POWER to give FRESH MOUTH."
   - The commercial shows a young male, about twenty years of age, walking up to a young girl, saying, "Hi, Susan!" They kiss and she says, "My, you have a fresh mouth. Bill!" He looks at the camera with a smile and says, "It works!" The announcer closes the commercial by saying "FRESH MOUTH—it has the POWER!"
4. Display materials
   - Shelf display tag.
   - Small floor stand for end-of-aisle display—holds two dozen 12 oz. bottles.
   - Large floor stand—holds four dozen 12 oz. bottles.

presentation, you can provide your customers with a world of information that they probably knew little about, and that could secure you the sale. Figure 5–1 illustrates the type of advertising and sales promotion you would use when making a sales presentation for a mouthwash called Fresh Mouth. Suppose Fresh Mouth was a new product and had just emerged from the test market. As a lead-in to the information in Figure 5–1, you might say:

> Mr. Buyer, Fresh Mouth was a proven success in our Eastern test markets. "Fresh Mouth" had a 9.8 percent market share only nine months after the start of advertising. Laboratory tests proved that the Fresh Mouth formula is superior to that of the leading competition. Consumer panels significantly preferred Fresh Mouth to leading competing brands. There was a repurchase rate of 50 percent after sampling. The trade (retailers) gave enthusiastic support in the test market areas.

[Now you would discuss the information contained in Figure 5–1.]

Types of Advertising Differ

The development and timing of an advertising campaign for a product or service is handled by a firm's advertising department or by an outside advertising agency. The result of this effort is the television commercial, radio spot, print media (newspaper or magazine), or other form of advertisement (billboard, transit placard, etc.). Following the development of the actual ad, the firm itself must establish and coordinate a plan for tying in sales force efforts with the new ad campaign. There are five basic types of advertising programs that a company can use: national, retail, trade, industrial, and direct-mail advertising.

National Advertising. A **national advertising program** is designed to reach all users of the product, whether consumers or industrial buyers. These ads are shown across the country. In some cases, national advertisers may restrict their expenditures to the "top 100" markets. "Top 100" refers to the 100 largest major metropolitan areas where most of the U.S. population is concentrated. Therefore, the advertiser gets more punch per ad dollar. Giant marketing companies like Procter & Gamble, IBM, Ford, Holiday Inn, and Coca-Cola commonly use national advertising.

Retail Advertising. **Retail advertising** is used by a retailer to reach customers within its geographic trading area. Local supermarkets and department stores regularly advertise nationally distributed branded products. National-brand advertising may be totally paid for by the retailer, or its costs may be partially picked up by the manufacturer.

Cooperative or **"co-op" advertising** refers to advertising conducted by the retailer with cost paid for by the manufacturer or shared by the manufacturer and retailer. It is obviously an attractive selling aid for the salesperson to be able to give the buyer an "advertising allowance" to promote a firm's goods.

Figure 5–2 shows an advertising agreement between a retailer and a manufacturer. The agreement provides for:

The duration (time period) of the advertisement.

The product(s) to be advertised.

The amount of money to be paid to the retailer for advertising purposes (based on amount and sizes of product purchased).

The type of advertising agreed upon.

Proof by the retailer, that the product has actually been advertised as agreed (a copy of the advertisement).

Cooperative advertising follows a fairly simple cycle. After agreeing upon the size of the order, you (the salesperson) and your buyer complete the advertising agreement and you both sign it. You then give the buyer a copy of the signed agreement. On your next sales visit the retailer gives you a copy of the advertisement. Again, both of you sign the bottom of the agreement, and you send the signed agreement and advertisement to the appropriate company personnel. In response, your office sends you the reimbursement check, and on your next sales call you give the check to the buyer. The cycle is ended.

An advertising agreement, skillfully employed, can be an effective selling tool. The salesperson with a positive attitude toward making the sale will already have an advertising agreement filled out before seeing a retail buyer. Based on past sales and future sales potential, and using this advertising money, the salesperson can present a "suggested order" for the buyer. After discussing the information in Figure 5–2 the salesperson might close the sale by saying:

Considering the size of your store, your past purchases, and the promotional campaign my company has suggested for Fresh Mouth, I suggest you buy 12 dozen of the 24 oz. size, 14 dozen of the 18 oz., 24 dozen of the 12 oz. size, and 12 dozen of the 6 oz. size. Let's reduce the price of the 18 oz. size and advertise it. I will build you a display over on that wall and pay $54 of your advertising cost. (The salesperson hands the filled out contract to the buyer.)

Generally, national and retail advertising is aimed at the final consumers of a product. But not all advertising is directed toward consumers. Trade and industrial advertising are aimed at other members in the channel of distribution, and other manufacturers.

Trade Advertising. **Trade advertising** is undertaken by the manufacturer and is directed toward the wholesaler or retailer. Such an advertisement appears in trade magazines serving only the wholesaler or retailer. Figure 5–3 is an example of a manufacturer (Schering) advertising to retail pharmacies in the popular trade magazine *American Druggist*.

Figure 5–2

BACTERIA FIGHTERS INCORPORATED

**Advertising Agreement
between
Bacteria Fighters Inc.
and
the Undersigned Account**

1. APPLICABILITY: This agreement provides for special advertising services on **Fresh Mouth.**

2. AVAILABILITY: This agreement is available on proportionally equal terms to all competing accounts who purchase **Fresh Mouth** during the period December 1, 1983, to January 31, 1984, on one order with split shipments acceptable straight stock purchases of the 6 Fl. Oz., 12 Fl. Oz., 15 Fl. Oz., 24 Fl. Oz. (1 Pt. 4 Fl. Oz. Marked Weight) sizes may be applied to the total advertising fund.

3. AMOUNT OF EARNINGS AVAILABLE:

	No. of Dozens Purchased		Adv. Allowance Rate per Dozen		Total Fund
Fresh Mouth 24 Fl. Oz. Size	_____	×	40¢	=	_____
Fresh Mouth 18 Fl. Oz. Size	_____	×	30¢	=	_____
Fresh Mouth 12 Fl. Oz. Size	_____	×	20¢	=	_____
Fresh Mouth 6 Fl. Oz. Size	_____	×	10¢	=	_____
			TOTAL FUND	=	_____

4. ADVERTISING SERVICES REQUIRED: Account agrees to advertise **Fresh Mouth** in print and/or radio and/or television at least once during the period January 31, 1984, to April 30, 1984, subject to the following terms and conditions:

   a. For the purpose of this agreement the term "print" means newspapers and/or other print media having a circulation of not less than 3,000.

   b. Radio and/or television advertising is also acceptable under this agreement.

   c. Advertising must include retail price, and/or number of Bonus Trading Stamps, and/or other special consumer incentive.

   d. Any advertising furnished under this agreement shall not be considered as advertising furnished under any other agreement.

5. RATES OF PAYMENT: Subject to the maximum fund available. **B.F. Inc.** will pay to accounts the allowances as set forth in #3 above for Account's print and/or radio and/or television advertising of any size(s) **Fresh Mouth.**

6. CERTIFICATION AND PAYMENT:

   a. Print Media—Payment for newspaper and other print media features will be made after receipt by **Fresh Mouth** of a properly executed certificate of performance accompanied by newspaper advertising tear sheets or copies of other print media used, together with an affidavit indicating the date, method and extent of circulation.

   b. Radio and/or Television—Payment for radio and/or television features will be made after receipt by **B.F. Inc.** of a properly executed certificate of performance and Account's statement certifying the number, date, time and type of radio and/or television features run, accompanied by affidavits from an authorized representative of the station(s), or other satisfactory proof, that such announcements were so broadcast over said station(s).

7. CANCELLATION: Any funds for which payment has not been applied by June 30, 1984, shall be cancelled and **B.F. Inc.** shall have no further liability to account with respect thereto. No amount claimed to be due hereunder is to be deducted from any invoice.

8. TERMINATION: This agreement may be terminated at any time by either party on fifteen (15) days' written notice.

9. MODIFICATION: **B.F. Inc.** representatives are not authorized to modify or waive any provisions of this agreement.

Figure 5–2 *(concluded)*

Bacteria Fighters Inc.

_____	_____
B.F. Inc. Representative's Signature	Print Account's Name

_____	_____	_____
Region	Unit No.	Account's Signature

Date _____ , 198___

_____
Advertising As

_____
Street Address

_____ | _____
City | State

- -

CERTIFICATE OF PERFORMANCE

This is to certify that we have accepted delivery of the goods and have performed the services required under the **B.F. Inc.** agreement dated _____ and are entitled to $_____ Total.

_____ | _____
Dealer's Name | IBM No.

_____
B.F. Inc. Representative's Signature

_____
Dealer's Signature

Date _____ , 198___

Industrial Advertising. **Industrial advertising** is aimed at individuals and organizations who purchase products for use in manufacturing other products. General Electric may advertise small electric motors in magazines read by buyers employed by firms such as Whirlpool or Sears.

Direct-Mail Advertising. Advertisements mailed directly to the consumer or industrial user can be an effective method of exposing these users to a product, or act as a reminder that the product is available to meet a specific need. Often, trial samples or coupons accompany the direct-mail piece.

Direct-mail advertising can solicit a response from a current user of a product. For example, the user may be asked to fill out and mail in a questionnaire. In return, the manufacturer sends the user a sample of the product, or information about the product.

Why Spend Money on Advertising?

Table 5–1 lists the 10 U.S. companies that spent most on advertising in 1982. Why would a company spend so many millions on advertising? Companies advertise because they hope to:

- Increase overall sales as well as sales of a specific product.
- Pave the way for their salespeople by building product and/or company recognition.

Figure 5–3 Example of Various Discounts for Retailers

4. In the following statements, write down each idea that is a benefit:
    A. Counselor talking to student:
       "In order to improve your science grade, Susie, you must establish better study habits."
    B. Construction supervisor talking to a worker:
       "That job will be a great deal easier, Joe, and you won't be as tired when you go home nights, if you use that little truck over there."
    C. Father talking to his son:
       "You will make a lot of friends, Johnny, and be respected at school if you learn how to play the piano."
    D. Banker talking to customer:
       "If you open this special checking account, Ms. Brown, paying your bills will be much easier."

5. In the following statements, determine what parts of the statements are features, advantages, or benefits.
    A. Hardware sales representative to homeowner:
       "Blade changing is quick and easy with this saw, because it has a push-button blade release."
    B. Consumer sales representative to grocery store buyer:
       "The king-size package of Tide will bring in additional profits because it is the fastest growing, most economical size."
    C. Clothing salesperson to customer:
       "For long wear and savings on your clothing costs, you can't beat these slacks. All the seams are double-stitched and the material is 100 percent Dacron."

6. Indicate which of the following statements are a feature, advantage, or benefit? Write your answer on a sheet of paper.
    A. "Made of pure vinyl."
    B. "Lasts twice as long as competing brands."
    C. "It's quick-frozen at 30° below zero."
    D. "Available in small, medium, and large sizes."
    E. "New."
    F. "No unpleasant aftertaste."
    G. "Saves time, work, and money."
    H. "Approved by underwriters' laboratory."
    I. "Gives 20% more miles to the gallon."
    J. "Contains XR-10."
    K. "Baked fresh daily."
    L. "Includes a one-year guarantee on parts and labor."
    M. "Is packed 48 units or eight 6-packs to the case."
    N. "Guaranteed to increase your sales by 10%."
    O. "Adds variety to your meal planning."

7. Consider the following information:

   The DESKTOP XEROX 2300 copier is a versatile model that delivers the first copy in six seconds. It is also the lowest-priced new Xerox copier available. The 2300 is designed as a general purpose office copier and occupies less than half the top of a standard desk. The new unit copies on a full range of office materials as large as 8½ by 14 inches. A special feature is its ability to reproduce 5½ by 8½-inch billing statements from the same tray used for letter-size or legal-size paper. Selling price of the 2300 will be as low as $3,495 and rentals as low as $60 a month on a two-year contract without a copy allowance.

   What are the features, advantages, and benefits of the "Desktop Xerox 2300 copier? What are additional benefits of the copier? List two additional features, advantages, and benefits that a Xerox salesperson could use in presenting the new copier to a prospective buyer.

8. Several features of a car are listed below in capital letters. Match each feature with its corresponding benefit(s):

   A. Low hoodline:
      (1) Better visibility.
      (2) Economy.
      (3) Quick startup.
   B. Tinted glass:
      (1) Reflects sunlight.
      (2) Reduces eye strain.
      (3) Reduces glare from sun.
   C. Rear window defroster:
      (1) Clears rear windshield, and thus reduces the danger of driving on a cold foggy day.
      (2) Rear windshield can be deiced or defogged automatically so you do not have to do it yourself.
      (3) Increases the cost of the car by $250.
   D. Whitewall tires:
      (1) Provide better handling and a more stable ride.
      (2) More appealing to see.
      (3) Increases the "life" of your tires.

9. In order to convince your customers that your product's benefits are important, you must show how your product benefits will meet their needs. Suppose your customer says: "I need some kind of gadget that will get me out of bed in the morning." Check the statement below which best relates your product feature, the G.E. clock radio's snooze alarm, to this customer's need:

A. "Ms. Jones, this G.E. radio has a snooze alarm which is very easy to operate. See, all you do is set this button and off it goes. . . ."

B. "Ms. Jones, the G.E. radio is the newest radio on the market. It carries a one-year guarantee and you can trade in your present radio and receive a substantial cut in the price.

C. "Ms. Jones, since you say you have trouble getting up in the morning, you want an alarm system that will make sure you wake up. Now, G.E.'s snooze alarm will wake you up no matter how often you shut the alarm off. You see, the alarm goes off every seven minutes until you switch off the special 'early bird' knob."

10. A salesperson says: "You expect a pencil sharpener to be durable. Our sharpener is durable because it's constructed with titanium steel bearings. Because of these bearings, our sharpener will not jam up on you and will last a long time."
    A. In the above example, the "titanium steel bearings" are a:
       (1) Benefit.
       (2) Feature.
       (3) Need.
       (4) Advantage.
    B. "Will not jam up on you" and "Will last a long time" are:
       (1) Benefits.
       (2) Features.
       (3) Needs.
       (4) Advantages.
    C. In the statement "Will not jam up on you" the salesperson has:
       (1) Converted a product feature into an advantage.
       (2) Converted benefits into a product feature.
       (3) Related a product feature to the customer's need via benefits.
       (4) Numbers (1) and (2) are correct.
       (5) Numbers (1) and (3) are correct.
    D. The statement "Will last a long time" is a:
       (1) Benefit.
       (2) Feature.
       (3) Need.
       (4) Advantage.

11. For each of the following products, determine a potential benefit based upon their advantages.

	Product	Feature	Advantage
A.	Pioneer stereo turntable	Direct-drive turntable	More dependable, fewer moving parts
B.	Tab	Only 1 calorie per 16 oz.	Will not increase your body weight when you drink it
C.	BIC erasable ink pen	Erasable ink	Can erase mistakes
D.	Ceiling fan	Hangs from ceiling, high efficiency	Out of the way, uses less electricity
E.	Mattel's Intellivision video game	3-dimensional display	More realistic
F.	Sheer panty hose	No dark patches	Looks like real skin
G.	Drilling an oil well	One of our engineers for the entire job	Better service
H.	Volkswagen Rabbit automobile	Small, light weight	Good gas mileage
I.	Hefty trash bags	2-ply	Puncture proof, can overstuff it

12. As a salesperson for Procter & Gamble's soap division, you have been asked by your sales manager to determine the features, advantages, and benefits for Tide detergent and discuss the use of Tide's benefits in a sales presentation at your next sales meeting. You have determined the following four features of Tide. Listed underneath each feature are your ideas of factors which might be of interest to retail grocery buyers. For each, determine the benefit you would emphasize.

A. #1 Selling detergent:
   (1) Best traffic-pulling detergent.
   (2) Great brand loyalty.
   (3) High percent of market share.

B. Four sizes:
   (1) Increase your total detergent sales.
   (2) Boxes are standard sizes.
   (3) Case cost is the same.

C. Heaviest manufacturer-advertised detergent:
   (1) Continue to attract new customers to your store.
   (2) More customers remember this brand's advertising.
   (3) Produces high repeat business.

D. Distinctive, colorful package:
   (1) Speeds shopping—easy for shoppers to locate on shelves.
   (2) High visual impact stimulates impulse purchases when on special display.
   (3) Familiar package design easy to recognize in store ads.

Projects

1. Keep a diary of your purchases for two weeks. Select five or more of the products you purchased during that period and write a short

report on why you purchased each product and what you feel are the features, advantages, and benefits of each product.
2. This week examine the television advertisements of three different products or services and report on the features, advantages, and benefits used in the commercial to persuade people to buy each product.

Cases

3–1 Economy Ceiling Fans, Inc.

As a salesperson for Economy Ceiling Fans, you have been asked to research and determine your customers' attitudes and beliefs toward your brand of ceiling fans. With this information you will determine if your company has the correct product line and suggest selling points for the company's salespeople when discussing fans with customers who come into their chain of retail stores.

You decide to hold an open house in one of your typical stores located in an upper-income neighborhood on a Sunday and advertise your special prices and a wine and cheese party and a seafood buffet celebrating your first anniversary. During that time you ask everyone to be seated, thank them for coming, and ask them to discuss their attitudes towards your company and ceiling fans in general.

Some people felt that ceiling fans should be shopped for without considering brands but, once a brand is selected they go to the stores carrying that particular brand and buy from the store with the best price. Most people had collected information on fans from personal sources (such as friends) commercial sources (such as advertising, salespeople, company literature) and public sources (such as consumer rating organizations). Sixty percent had narrowed their choice to fans from Hunter, Casa Blanca, and Economy, and they seemed to look for three things in a ceiling fan: price, quality, and style.

Question:

Given this information on why people buy ceiling fans, what should salespeople be instructed to do when a customer enters their store?

3–2 McDonald's Ford Dealership

The used car salesman for McDonald's Ford, John Alexander, approaches a 25- to 27-year-old female, June Miller, in the car lot and says:

	Can I help you?
Buyer:	20,000 miles on this one—I'll bet a little old lady owned this lemon! What was it, really, before you set it back?
Salesman:	That is the actual mileage. Hi, I'm John Alexander and you are. . . . [*he waits for reply*].

Buyer: June Miller.

Salesman: June, what can I help you with?

Buyer: Oh, I don't know. Something that runs and will get me around.

Salesman: Do you travel out of town or just drive back and forth to work?

Buyer: I drive everywhere! I'm even getting in a car pool with my boss.

Salesman: Good mileage is important then.

Buyer: Sure is. [*She walks over and looks at a full-size, four-door Ford LTD.*] Say, I like this one! $6,500! You have to be kidding.

Salesman: Do you need that much room?

Buyer: Not really, there is just me.

Salesman: June, are you saying you need a car which is dependable, gets good gas mileage, not too big and not too expensive?

Buyer: How did you guess:

Salesman: Follow me . . . [*he shows her 5 cars he considers have what she said. Then he asks:*] which one of these do you like?"

Buyer: Well, they are OK, but I really don't like them. Thanks for your time. I'll shop around a little more. Give me your card and I'll get back to you later.

Questions:

1. Describe the situation and the buyer's apparent needs.
2. What should the salesman do now that the buyer has said "no" to the cars he has shown June and she is about to leave the car lot?

4

Communication and Persuasion: It's Not All Talk

Learning Objectives

1. To present and discuss the salesperson-buyer communication process.
2. To discuss and illustrate the importance of using nonverbal communications when selling.
3. To review barriers to effective sales communications.
4. To introduce ways of developing persuasive communications.

Key Terms for Selling

Communication

Source

Encoding process

Message

Medium

Decoding process

Receiver

Feedback

Noise

Nonverbal communication

Territorial space

Intimate space

Personal space

Social space

Public space

Acceptance signals

Caution signals

Disagreement signals

Persuasion

Empathy

KISS

Listening

Enthusiasm

Source credibility

Proof statements

Profile

Kim Allen
McNeil

Kim Allen is a territory manager with the McNeil Consumer Products Company, a division of Johnson & Johnson, (hereafter CPC). She received her bachelor's degree in food marketing from St. Joseph's University in Philadelphia, Pennsylvania. McNeil Consumer Products Company manufactures the Tylenol product line of aspirin substitutes, which includes Adult Strength, Pediatric, Co-tylenol, and Sine-Aid.

Kim says, "My primary responsibility is to manage the sales of McNeil CPC products through food, drug mass merchandiser, and other trade channels in my assigned territory which covers Philadelphia and its northern suburbs. In fulfilling this responsibility my main objectives are to maximize sales of my products and their various sizes to customers, check for maximum retail shelf inventories, and sell point-of-purchase displays to food and drug stores, while simultaneously meeting my sales quota and regularly submitting reports of activities to my district manager."

"Immediate assumption of responsibility and the opportunity to sell the number one analgesic product on the market sold me on McNeil CPC. Of all the firms I interviewed with while still in college, McNeil CPC was the only one which offered a good deal of responsibility from the first day on the job. McNeil is a people-oriented company. The sales force is always rewarded for a job well done.

"McNeil CPC's training program trained me in all aspects of selling, including preparation of sales presentations. The most valuable technique I derived from these selling seminars is listening. The stereotyped salesperson unfortunately seems to be an extremely aggressive, uncaring individual. Conversely, the most successful salespeople owe much of their success to actually listening to determine what the customer's need is before attempting to satisfy that need.

"Selling Tylenol per se is not difficult. The main sales objective is to maintain its number one position in the market through high volume sales. This is the challenging part of my job."

Amos Skaggs, purchasing agent, stands as a salesperson enters his office. "Hi, Mr. Skaggs," he says, offering his hand. Mr. Skaggs returns a limp, one-second handshake and sits down behind his desk. He begins to open his afternoon mail, almost as though no one else was in the room.

The salesperson sits down and begins his canned sales talk by saying, "Mr. Skaggs, I'm here to show you how your company can lower manufacturing costs by 10 percent." Mr. Skaggs lays his mail down on his desk, leans back in his chair, crosses his arms, and with a growl says: "I'm glad to hear that. You know something, young fellow, pretty soon it won't cost us anything to manufacture our products." "Why is that?" he mumbles, meekly looking down to the floor. "Well, you are the ninth person I've seen today who has offered to save us 10 percent of our costs."

Mr. Skaggs stands up, leans over the table and while peering over his glasses says slowly, "I believe I've heard enough sales pitches for one day." The initially enthusiastic salesperson now apologetically says, "If this is not a good time for you, sir, I can come back at a later date."

In this imaginary sales call, buyer and seller communicated both verbal and nonverbal messages. Here, nonverbal messages conveyed both parties' attitudes better than the actual verbal exchange. The salesperson's negative reactions served to increase Mr. Skaggs's hostile attitude. He could sense the salesperson did not understand his problem and was there to sell him something, not solve his problem. This impression caused a rapid breakdown in communication. The end result, as in this case, is usually NO SALE.

While there may be many other factors which are crucial to sales success, the ability to communicate effectively is certainly of prime importance. In order to convincingly convey this important sales skill, this chapter directly applies a basic communication model to the buyer-seller interaction. Afterward, several factors influencing communication, along with a number of possible barriers to effective communication, are described. The often ignored, though always critical topic of nonverbal communications (remember Amos Skaggs) is also examined in some depth. The balance of this chapter relates some techniques which can be used to improve sales communications.

Communication: It Takes Two

Communication, in a sales context, is the act of transmitting verbal and nonverbal information and understanding between seller and buyer. This definition presents communication as a process of sending and

receiving messages with some type of response expected between the seller and the buyer.

Communication during the sales presentation takes many forms. Ideas and attitudes can be effectively communicated by media other than just language. Actually, in a normal two-person conversation less than 35 percent of the social meaning utilizes verbal components. Said another way, much of the social meaning of what is said in a conversation is conveyed nonverbally.

Research has found that face-to-face communication is composed of *verbal, vocal,* and *facial* communication messages. One equation presents the total impact of communicated messages as equal to 7 percent verbal plus 38 percent vocal plus 55 percent facial.[1] If one recognizes these findings as a reasonable approximation of the total communicative process, then uninformed salespeople are actually ignoring a major part of the communication process that occurs during buyer-seller interaction. We can say that how the sales message is given can often be as important to making the sale as what is said. Thus, nonverbal communications can be very important in communication between buyer and seller. An awareness of nonverbal communication can be a valuable tool in successfully making a sale.

Vocal communication includes such factors as voice quality, pitch, pause, and inflection. Radio newscaster Paul Harvey is famous for "how" he broadcasts the news. His vocal pauses and inflections are masterfully used to obtain and hold the attention of his radio audience. A salesperson's use of vocal factors can aid in sales presentation, too. Along with verbal, vocal, and facial communication, a number of other elements are also involved in sales communications.

Salesperson-Buyer Communication Process Requires Feedback

A basic communication model which depicts how the salesperson-buyer communication process works is shown in Figure 4–1. Basically, communication takes place when a "sender" transmits a "message" through some type of "medium" to a "receiver" who responds to that message. Figure 4–1 presents a model which contains eight major communications elements. Each of these elements is defined below.

Source.   The "source" of the communication (also called the communicator); in our case the salesperson.

Encoding Process.   The conversion by the salesperson of ideas and concepts into the language and materials used in the sales presentation.

Message.   The information is conveyed in the sales presentation.

Medium.   The form of communication used in the sales presentation

Figure 4–1   Salesperson-Buyer Communication Process

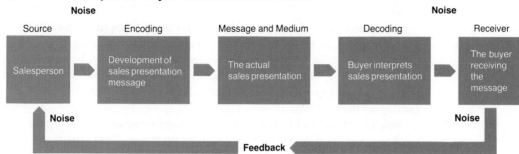

and discussion; most frequently words, visual materials, and body language.

Decoding Process.   Receipt and translation (interpretation) of the information by the receiver (prospective buyer).

Receiver.   The person the communication is intended for; in our case the prospect or buyer.

Feedback.   Reaction to the communication as transmitted to the sender. This reaction may be verbal or nonverbal.

Noise.   Factors that distort communications between buyer and seller. Noise includes barriers to communications, which will be discussed later.

This model portrays the communication process. A salesperson should know how to develop a sales presentation (encode) so that the buyer obtains maximum understanding of the message (decoding). Communication media that most effectively communicate a specific sales message should be used. Clear verbal discussion, employment of visual aids such as pictures or diagrams, and development of models or samples of the actual product are several types of media a salesperson might use in communicating a particular sales message.

One-way communication occurs when the salesperson talks and the buyer only listens. The salesperson needs a response or feedback from the buyer to know if communication is taking place. Does the buyer understand the message? Once feedback or interaction and understanding between buyer and seller exists in a communication process, two-way communication has been established.

Two-way communication is essential to you to make the sale. The buyer must understand your message's information in order to make a buying decision. Two-way communication gives the salesperson the ability to present a product's benefits, instantly receive buyer reactions, and answer questions. Buyers usually react both verbally and nonverbally to your presentation.

Nonverbal Communication: Watch for It

Recognition and analysis of nonverbal communication in sales transactions is relatively new. Only in the past ten to fifteen years has the subject been formally examined in any detail. The presence and use of nonverbal communication, however, have been acknowledged for many years. In the early 1900s Sigmund Freud noted that people cannot keep a secret, even if they do not speak. A person's gestures and actions reveal hidden feelings about something.[2]

People communicate nonverbally in several ways. Four major **nonverbal communication** channels are: the physical space between buyer and seller, appearance, handshake, and body movements.

Concept of Space

The concept of **territorial space** refers to the area around the self a person will not allow another person to enter without consent. Early experiments in territorial space dealt with animals. These experiments determined that higher-status members of a group are often afforded a freedom of movement that is less available to those of lower status.[3] This idea has been applied to socially acceptable distances of space that human beings keep between themselves in certain situations. Territorial space can easily be related to the selling situation.

Space considerations are important to salespeople because violations of territorial space without customer consent may set off the customer's defense mechanisms and create a barrier to communications. A person (buyer) has four types of main distances to consider—intimate (up to two feet); personal (two to four feet); social (four to twelve); and public (greater than twelve feet).

Intimate space of up to two feet, or about arm's length, is the most sensitive zone, since it is reserved for very close friends and loved ones. To enter intimate space in the buyer-seller relationship, for some prospects, could be socially unacceptable—possibly offensive.

During the presentation a salesperson should carefully listen and look for signs that indicate the buyer feels uncomfortable, perhaps that the salesperson is too close. A buyer may deduce from such closeness that the salesperson is attempting to dominate or overpower the buyer. This feeling can result in resistance to the salesperson. If such uneasiness is detected, the salesperson should move back, reassuring the customer.

Personal space is the closest zone a stranger or business acquaintance is normally allowed to enter. Even in this zone, a prospect may be uncomfortable. Barriers, such as a desk, are often used to reduce the threat implied when someone enters this zone.

Social space is the area normally used for a sales presentation. Again, the buyer often uses a desk to maintain a distance of four feet or more

between buyer and seller. Standing while facing a seated prospect may communicate to the buyer that the salesperson seems too dominating. Thus the salesperson should normally stay seated in order to convey a relaxed manner.

A salesperson should consider beginning a presentation in the middle of the social distance zone, six to eight feet, in order to avoid the prospect's erecting negative mental barriers. This is especially true if the salesperson is not a friend of the prospect.

Public space is often used by the salesperson making a presentation to a group of people. It is similar to the distance between teacher and student in a classroom. People are at ease and thus easy to communicate with at this distance, since they do not feel threatened by the salesperson.

Space Threats. The "territorial imperative" causes people to feel that they should defend their space or territory. The salesperson who pulls up a chair too close, takes over all or part of the prospect's desk, leans on or over the desk, or touches objects on the desk runs the risk of invading a prospect's territory. Be careful not to create defensive barriers. However, should you sense a friendliness between yourself and the prospect, use territorial space to your benefit.

Space Invasion. The prospect who allows you to enter or invade personal and even intimate space is saying, "Come on into my space, let's be friends." Now you can use space to your advantage.

In most offices, the salesperson sits directly across the desk from the prospect. The prospect controls the space arrangement. This is one kind of defensive barrier, allowing the prospect to control much of the conversation. Often seating is prearranged and it could be a space threat if you moved your chair when calling upon a prospect for the first time.

However, if you have a choice between a chair across the desk or beside the desk, take the latter seat as shown in Figure 4–2. Sitting at the side lowers the desk communication barrier. If you are friends with the buyer, move your chair to the side of the desk yourself. This helps create a friendly, cooperative environment between you and the buyer.

Communications through Appearance and the Handshake

Other common methods of nonverbal communications are signals conveyed by a person's physical appearance and handshake. Once territorial space has been established, general appearance would be the next medium of nonverbal communication conveyed to a customer by a salesperson. Appearance not only conveys information such as age, sex, height, weight, race, and physical characteristics, but also provides a great deal of data on personality. Hairstyle is one of the first things a buyer notices about a salesperson.

Figure 4–2   Office Arrangements and Territorial Space

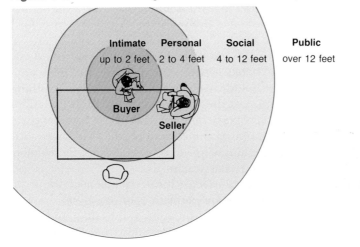

Intimate — up to 2 feet
Personal — 2 to 4 feet
Social — 4 to 12 feet
Public — over 12 feet

Buyer

Seller

Style Hair Carefully.   Hairstyle has traditionally been an important factor in evaluating personal appearance. Although the longer hairstyles for men, which emerged in the late 1960s, have gained increased acceptance, longer hair has traditionally been associated with a liberal outlook on life and thus could affect the customer's attitude toward a product. Today's male salespeople might possibly best consider what type of customer they will be calling on and adjust their hairstyles accordingly. This is equally true for the female salesperson.

Though recently decreasing somewhat in popularity, male facial hair is still worn by some male salespeople. For several decades, American males did not sport beards and moustaches to any great extent, but that trend reversed in the 1960s and 70s. A research study in the early 1970s asked people their opinion of facial hair and came up with two very different opinions. One group felt that bearded men are perceived as more sensitive, more masculine, more intelligent, and warmer than clean-shaven men. The other group felt that men with beards are perceived as more deviant, radical, independent, and introverted.[4]

Salespeople should carefully consider their grooming and its impact on customer's perceptions. Some companies ask their salesmen to be clean shaven and wear conservative haircuts. And their saleswomen are asked to choose a simple, businesslike, shoulder-length hair style. Other companies leave grooming up to each individual. Your grooming objective is to eliminate communication barriers. It could be your grooming which causes you to convey a favorable first impression. Should your company not have a policy on grooming, examine your customer's grooming before deciding upon your own.

Dress as a Professional.   Wardrobe has always been a major determinant of sales success, and today it is emphasized as never before. A variety of books and articles have been written on proper dress for business people. Two of the most popular books on the subject are *Dress for Success* (for men) and *The Woman's Dress for Success Book,* both by John Molloy. These books espouse the doctrine that male and female sales representatives should wear conservative, "serious" clothing that projects professionalism, just the right amount of authority, and a desire to please the customer. Sporty clothing is believed to accentuate sales aggressiveness, placing a purchasing agent on the defensive, and resulting in lost sales. Too "feminine" or frivolous clothing for women could project a poor image of a saleswoman.

Molloy believes that decision rules exist for every major clothing item and accessory, but that these are derivatives of one basic commandment—dress in a simple, elegant style. Xerox, IBM, and other large companies have incorporated Molloy's ideas into their sales training and daily policies. Although they do not have a formal dress code, these firms encourage sales personnel to wear dark, conservative clothing. This practice is designed to project a conservative, stable corporate image to both customers and the general public.

The nonverbal messages that salespeople emit through appearance should be positive in all sales situations. Characteristics of the buyer, cultural aspects of a sales territory, and the type of product being sold are all determinants of mode of dress. In considering these aspects you should create a business wardrobe that will send positive, nonverbal messages in every sales situation. Once you have determined your appropriate dress and hairstyle, the next nonverbal communication channel to consider is your contact with a prospect through your handshake.

Shake Hands Firmly and Look'em in the Eye.   The handshake is said to have been evolved as a gesture of peace between warriors. By joining hands, two warriors were unable to bear arms against one another (assuming that a shield and not a weapon was held in the left hand).

Today a handshake is the most common way for two people to touch one another in a business situation, and some people feel that it can be a very revealing gesture. A firm handshake is more intense and is indicative of greater liking and warmer feelings. A prolonged handshake is more intimate than a brief one, and could conceivably cause the customer discomfort, especially in a sales call on a new prospect. A loosely clasped, cold, or limp handshake is usually interpreted as indicating aloofness and unwillingness to become involved. This "cold fish" handshake is also perceived as being unaffectionate and unfriendly.

General rules for a successful handshake are these: do not extend your hand first. Allow your customer to initiate the gesture. Maintain

Figure 4–3 Five Main Nonverbal Body Movement Communication Channels

| Body angle | Face | Hands | Arms | Legs |

eye contact with your customer during the handshake, gripping the hand firmly. These actions will allow you to initially establish an atmosphere of honesty and mutual respect, starting the presentation in a positive manner.

Body Language Gives You Clues

From birth, people learn to communicate their needs, likes, and dislikes through nonverbal means. The salesperson can learn much from a prospect's raised eyebrow, a smile, a touch, a scowl, or reluctance to make eye contact during a sales presentation. The prospect can communicate with you literally without uttering a word. An ability to interpret these signals can be an invaluable tool to the successful sales professional. In conjunction with interpretation of body language, skillful use and control of the salesperson's own physical actions, gestures, and overall body position can also be helpful.

The buyer can send nonverbal signals via five communication modes, as shown in Figure 4–3. They are the body angle, facial expression, arm movement or position, hand movements or position, and leg position. Likewise, these modes can generally send three basic types of messages: (1) acceptance, (2) caution, and (3) disagreement.

Acceptance signals indicate that your buyer is favorably inclined towards you and your presentation. These signals give you the "green light" to proceed. While this may not end in a sale, at the very least the prospect is saying, "I am willing to listen." What you are saying is both acceptable and interesting. Some common acceptance signals are:

Body angle—leaning forward or upright at attention.

Face—smiling, pleasant expression, relaxed, eyes examining visual aids, direct eye contact, positive voice tones.

Arms—relaxed and generally open.

Hands—relaxed and generally open, perhaps performing business

calculations on paper, holding on as you attempt to withdraw a product sample or sales materials, firm handshake.

Legs—crossed and pointed toward you or uncrossed.

Salespeople frequently rely only on facial expressions as indicators of acceptance. This practice may be misleading, since buyers may consciously control their facial expressions. You should scan each of the five key body areas to verify your interpretation of facial signals. A buyer who increases eye contact, maintains a relaxed position, and exhibits positive facial expressions is giving you excellent acceptance signals.

Acceptance signals indicate that buyers perceive that they may have a need that your product might meet. You have obtained their attention and interest. You are free to continue with your planned sales presentation.

Caution signals should alert you that buyers are either neutral or skeptical toward what you are saying. Caution signals are indicated by:

Body angle—leaning away from you.

Face—puzzled, little or no expression, averted eyes or little eye contact, neutral or questioning voice tone, saying little, and then only asking a few questions.

Arms—crossed, tense.

Hands—moving, fidgeting with something, clasped, weak handshake.

Legs—moving, crossed away from you.

Caution signals are very important for you to recognize and adjust to for two main reasons. First, they indicate blocked communications. Buyers' perceptions, attitudes, and beliefs regarding your presentation may cause them to be skeptical, judgmental, or uninterested in your product. They may not recognize that they need your product or that it can benefit them. Even though you may have their attention, they show very little interest in or desire for your product.

Second, if caution signals are not properly handled, they may evolve into disagreement signals, creating a breakdown in communication and making a sale very difficult to make. Proper handling of caution signals requires that you:

- Adjust to the situation by slowing up or departing from your planned presentation.
- Use open-ended questions to encourage your buyers to talk and express their attitudes and beliefs. "Have you ever been interested in improving efficiency of your workers?" or "What do you think about this benefit?" are examples of open-ended questions.
- Carefully listen to what buyers say and respond directly.
- Project acceptance signals yourself. Be positive, enthusiastic, and smile.

Remember, you are glad to be there to help buyers satisfy their needs. Refrain from projecting caution signals even if a buyer does so. If you project a positive image in this situation, there is greater probability that you will change a caution light to a green one and make the sale.

Your objective in using these techniques is to change the caution signal to the green, go-ahead signal. If you continue to receive caution signals, you should proceed carefully with your presentation. Be realistic, alert to the possibility that the buyer may begin to believe your product is not truly beneficial and begin sending disagreement or "red light" signals.

Disagreement signals tell you immediately to stop your planned presentation and quickly adjust to the situation. Disagreement, or red light signals, indicate you are dealing with a person who is becoming completely uninterested in your product. Anger or hostility may develop if you continue your presentation. Your continuation can cause a buyer to feel an unacceptable level of sales pressure resulting in a complete communication breakdown. Disagreement signals may be indicated by:

Body angle—retracted shoulders, leaning away from you, moving the entire body back from you or wanting to move away.

Face—tense, showing anger, wrinkled face and brow, very little eye contact, negative voice tones, may become suddenly silent.

Arms—tense, crossed over chest.

Hands—motions of rejection or disapproval, tense and clenched, weak handshake.

Legs—crossed and away from you.

You should handle disagreement signals, as you do caution signals, by using open-ended questions, and projecting acceptance signals yourself. There are four additional techniques to use. First, stop your planned presentation. There is no use in continuing until you have changed disagreement signals into caution or acceptance signals. Second, temporarily reduce or eliminate any pressure on the person to buy or to participate in the conversation. Let the buyer relax as you slowly move back to selling. Third, let your buyer know you are aware that something upsetting has occurred. Show that you know that you are there to help, not to sell at any cost. Finally, you may wish to use direct questions to determine a buyer's attitudes and beliefs such as, "What do you think of . . . ?" or ". . . Have I said something you do not agree with?"

Body Guidelines.   Over a period of time, you should know customers well enough to have a good understanding of the meaning of their body movements. Although a prospect may say "no" to making a purchase, body movements may indicate uncertainty. As Richard Dreyfuss says

in *The Goodbye Girl*, "Your lips say *no, no, no,* but your eyes say *yes, yes, yes!*" This phrase sometimes holds true for selling.

The interpretation of most body language is obvious. However, you should be cautious in interpreting an isolated gesture, such as assuming that very little eye contact means the prospect is displeased with what you are saying. Instead, concentrate on nonverbal cues that are part of a cluster or pattern. Let's say your prospect begins staring at the wall. That is a clue that may mean nothing. You continue your talk. Now the prospect leans back in the chair. That is another clue. By itself it may be meaningless, but in conjunction with the first clue, it begins to take on meaning. Now you see the prospect turn away from you, legs crossed, brow wrinkled. You now have a cluster of clues, all forming a pattern. Now it is time to adjust or change your presentation. Figure 4–4 relates some common nonverbal signals that buyers may give you.

To recapitulate, nonverbal communication is well worth considering in selling. A salesperson ought to:

- Be able to recognize nonverbal signals.
- Be able to interpret them correctly.
- Be prepared to alter a selling strategy by slowing, changing, or stopping a planned presentation.
- Respond nonverbally and verbally to a buyer's nonverbal signals.

Effective communication is essential in making a sale. Nonverbal communication signals are an important part of the total communications process between buyer and seller. Professional salespeople seek to learn and understand nonverbal communication as a way of increasing their sales success.

Barriers to Communication

Like the high hurdler, a salesperson often must overcome a multitude of obstacles. These obstacles are more aptly called "barriers to communication." Consider this example:

Salesperson Joe Jones heard that the XYZ Company buyer, Jake Jackson, was displeased with the company's present supplier. Joe had analyzed XYZ's operation and knew that his product could save the company thousands of dollars a year. Imagine Joe's surprise when Jackson terminated the visit quickly with no sale and no mention of a future appointment.

Joe told his boss about the interview. "Jackson kept asking me where I went to school, whether I wanted coffee, and how I liked selling, while I was trying to explain to him the features, advantages, and benefits of our product. Suddenly, Jackson stopped the interview." Joe asked the boss, "What did I do wrong? I know he needed our product."[5]

- Give salespeople additional selling information to use in their sales presentations.
- Develop leads for their salespeople (through mail-ins, ad response, etc.).
- Increase cooperation from middlemen (through co-op advertising, and promotional campaigns).
- Help educate the customer about the company's products.
- Inform prospects that a product is on the market and where to buy it.
- Aid in reducing cognitive dissonance over the purchase.
- Create sales or presell customers between a salesperson's calls.

Advertising serves a variety of purposes, depending on the nature of a product or industry. The majority of the ten top advertisers listed in Table 5–1 are well-known manufacturers of consumer goods. This indicates that more advertising dollars are lavished on consumer items. However, as industrial advertising has more specified channels of communication (such as trade periodicals, and trade shows) and a smaller number of potential customers, advertising costs tend to be lower. In either case, advertising, carefully employed, can benefit both a firm and its sales force. Sales promotion is another potential aid to a company and its sales force.

Sales Promotion Generates Sales for You

Sales promotion involves activities or materials other than personal selling, advertising, and publicity used to create sales for goods or services. Sales promotion can be divided into consumer and trade sales promotion. **Consumer sales promotion** includes free samples, coupons,

Table 5–1 Top 10 U.S. Advertisers

Rank	Company Name	Total Advertising Dollars 1982 (in millions)
1	Procter & Gamble Co.	$726.1
2	Sears Roebuck & Co.	631.2
3	General Motors Corp.	549.0
4	R. J. Reynolds Industries	530.3
5	Phillip Morris, Inc.	501.7
6	General Foods Corp.	429.1
7	AT&T	373.6
8	K-Mart Corp.	365.3
9	Nabisco Brands	335.2
10	American Home Products	325.4

Source: *Advertising Age*, September 5, 1983, p. 1.

"*I don't know who you are.*
I don't know your company.
I don't know your company's product.
I don't know what your company stands for.
I don't know your company's customers.
I don't know your company's record.
I don't know your company's reputation.
Now—what was it you wanted to sell me?"

MORAL: Sales start **before** your salesman calls—with **business** publication advertising.

McGRAW-HILL MAGAZINES
BUSINESS • PROFESSIONAL • TECHNICAL

contests, and demonstrations to consumers. **Trade sales promotion** encourages resellers to purchase and aggressively sell a manufacturer's products by offering incentives like sales contests, displays, special purchase prices, and free merchandise (for example: buy 10 cases of a product and get an eleventh free).

The company's promotional efforts can be a useful sales tool for an enterprising salesperson. Sales promotion offers may prove to the retailer or wholesaler that the selling firm will actively assist in creating consumer demand. This in turn improves the salesperson's probability of making the sale. Some of the more popular sales promotion items, which we will briefly discuss, are: point-of-purchase displays, shelf positioning, premiums, contests, and sweepstakes, and consumer premiums.

Point-of-Purchase Displays: Get'em Out There

Point-of-purchase (POP) displays allow a product to be easily seen and purchased. A product POP display may include photographs, banners, drawings, coupons, a giant-sized product carton, aisle dumps, and counter or floor stands. POP displays greatly increase product sales. It is up to the salesperson to obtain the retailer's cooperation to allow the use of the POP display in the store.

Figure 5–4 shows a Del Monte's salesperson making a giant display of canned food products. People are attracted to displays. They catch the customer's attention and make products easy to purchase, which results in increased product sales.

Figure 5–4

Del Monte's prominence in the supermarket begins with consumer demand for quality products with the trusted red and green label and is fostered by an experienced nationwide sales force adept at promoting special programs in each local area.

Photo courtesy of R. J. Reynolds Industries, Inc.

Get the Buyer Interested!

Kathyleen Paynter of Campbell Soup believes that a large part of her job involves getting retailers to promote her products in their stores. Kathyleen says:

Aside from basic selling skills, I think two very important selling aids are enthusiasm and imagination to get the buyer interested in the sale. Using imaginative selling ideas will get the buyer's attention and make him interested in the sale. Dare to do something different or 'crazy' to get his attention. If applicable, sampling your product—in my case, out of a thermos—is a great way to get even the busiest buyer to talk with you.

Here are some unusual selling ideas I've had success with:

- I once made a cookie shaped like the V-8 trademark to sell a 50-case display, advertisement and feature of V-8 products.
- I made a 6½ foot Chunky Soup Robot out of excess point-of-sale material to sell a large Chunky Soup display.
- I helped a product manager win a Caribbean cruise by designing a Soup'n'Celery tie-in display, and dressing up as a can of soup and getting his wife to dress as a stalk of celery.

The use of unusual display pieces and costumes gets the store personnel and customers interested in a display and, therefore, increases sales and that helps everyone.

Shelf Positioning Is Important to Your Success

Another important sales stimulator you can use is the shelf positioning of your products. **Shelf positioning** refers to the physical placement of the product within the retailer's store. **Shelf facings** are the number of individual products placed beside each other on the shelf. You should determine where a store's customers can easily find and examine your company's products, and place your products in that space or position with as many shelf-facings as the store will allow. Figure 5–5 shows how a Campbell's Soup salesman has effectively obtained excellent shelf positioning and multiple shelf facings in a retail grocery outlet.

The major obstacle you must face when attempting to obtain shelf space for your products is limited space. A retail store has only a fixed amount of display space—and thousands of products to stock. You are competing for shelf space with other salespeople, and with the retailer's own brands.

Figure 5–5

This Campbell's salesperson obtained excellent shelf positioning and shelf facings

Photo Courtesy of Campbell Soup Company

It is often up to the salesperson to sell the store manager on purchasing different sizes of a particular product. Also, the salesperson may want a product displayed at several locations in the store. A Johnson & Johnson salesperson may want his J&J baby powder and baby shampoo displayed with both baby products and adult toiletries.

SAMI Data Helps Get You Shelf Space. SAMI **(Selling Areas—Marketing, Inc.)** is a company that supplies sales data to manufacturers who sell through retail food stores. This data shows manufacturers the movement of products to retail food stores from warehouses of wholesalers in 36 major television market areas containing about 75 percent of national food sales. These warehouses contract to provide SAMI with this information every four weeks on computer cards or tapes. This service provides manufacturers who sell to warehouses with sales data both for their brands and for those of their competitors.

Manufacturers, in turn, relay this information to their salespeople to aid them in promoting certain products to their retail buyers, and to improve shelf positioning for their products. The Quaker Oats Company is one of many food companies who provide their salespeople with SAMI information.

Suppose a Quaker salesperson finds that a supermarket has 100 feet of shelf space allocated to dog food, and that Quaker Kel-L-Ration Kibbles-'n'Bits has 5 feet of this shelf space. In checking his SAMI data, the salesperson finds that Kibbles'n'Bits has a 10 percent market share in the retailer's trading area. Given this discrepancy, the Quaker salesperson now has a logical reason as to why the store buyer should allow an increase in shelf space for this product from 5 to 10 feet. Such a move could increase Kibbles'n'Bits sales in that store, benefiting both the retailer and Quaker.

Premiums

The premium has come a long way from being just a trinket in a Cracker Jacks box. Today it is a major marketing tool. In 1984, American businesses will spend well over $10 billion on consumer and trade premiums and incentives.[4] Premiums create sales.

A **premium** is an article of merchandise offered as an incentive to the user to take some action. The premium may act as an incentive to buy, to sample the product, come into the retail store, or simply stir up interest so the user will request further information. Premiums serve a number of purposes: to permit consumer sampling of a new product; to introduce a new product; to encourage point-of-purchase displays; and to boost sales of slow products. Figure 5–6 presents the three major categories of premiums: (1) contests and sweepstakes, (2) consumer premiums, and (3) dealer premiums.

Contests and Sweepstakes Are Fun. Contests and sweepstakes are popular premium offers. Coca-Cola, for example, offered consumers the chance to win up to $1,000 by completing the phrase "Coke, The Real Thing" with words found under Coke, Tab, and Sprite bottle caps marked with the number "1." General Mills once offered a one-week family vacation in Nashville, Tennessee, plus $5000 to consumers who redeemed 10 cents off coupons on the back of boxes of Golden Grahams Cereal.

Figure 5–7 shows a sweepstakes offer which helped the Quaker Oats sales force get their retail grocery customers to buy extra amounts of Cap'n Crunch cereal. The Quaker salesperson used this sales aid to show a buyer how his sales of Cap'n Crunch cereal would increase because of the sweepstakes offered to children, and the "25 cents off" coupon offered to consumers.

Consumer Premiums Get Cooperation. The widest variety of premiums are those directed at consumers. When a company has offered a premium for a product, its salespeople can use that premium in their sales presentations for two reasons. First, the premium can be used to help make the sale. Second, the premium can be used to urge the customer to buy a larger than normal quantity of the product. Six types of **consumer premiums** commonly used by companies are shown in Figure 5–6.

The consumer can 'mail in' for a premium, or receive the premium (a direct premium) when the product is purchased. The third type of

Figure 5–6   Examples of Premiums

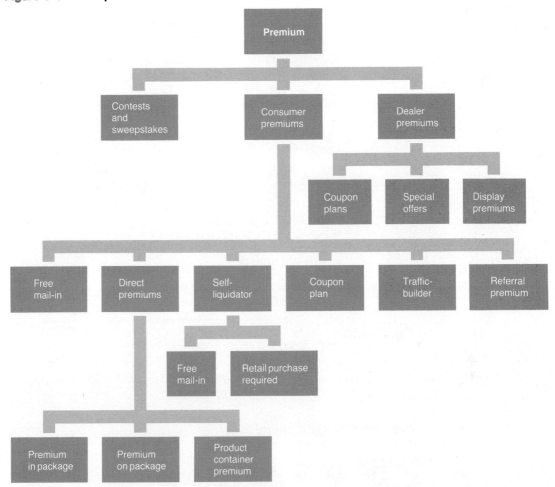

consumer premiums are called self-liquidators. These are an offer to sell a second product, usually at a reduced cost, when the consumer sends in proof of purchase of buying a first product. The salesperson says to the buyer, "This month we have a self-liquidator with Gillette Foamy Shave Cream. Your customer buys Foamy and sends in your sales receipt and for $1 they will receive a Gillette Trac II shaver and blades. This should increase your normal sales 10 percent." In another instance, Gillette has attached razors to cans of Foamy, making it a direct premium.

Coupon plans, the fourth type of consumer premium, require the buyer to save each coupon received from the purchase of a product and trade in accumulated coupons for merchandise. For example, the Betty Crocker Coupon program promotes Gold Medal Flour, Wheaties,

Figure 5–7

Courtesy of the Quaker Oats
Company

and Bisquick. Coupons taken from packages of these goods can be exchanged for silver-plated flatware.

Free products offered to customers who come in to see a product demonstration are called traffic-builders. For example, an appliance dealer might offer a plastic laundry basket to homeowners who come into the store to examine a line of washers and dryers. An auto dealership may give a free U.S. road map to individuals who test-drive a new model of automobile.

Many people believe that the best form of advertising is a satisfied customer. This type of customer can positively influence someone else's attitude toward a product. The referral premium plan works this way: You have sold your product to Ms. Young. She liked it. You ask her for the names of one or more friends who have seen the product and might be prospective buyers. You offer her an attractive premium if any of her friends or neighbors buys your product.

If carefully designed and administered, consumer premiums can benefit all parties involved—consumer, wholesaler, retailer, sponsoring firm, *and* salesperson. Premiums also work when directed at distributors.

Dealer Premiums.   Premiums are usually consumer-oriented. Yet many companies also offer premiums to middlemen. There are three principal types of **dealer premiums** in use today:

1. The *coupon plan* offers the dealer a choice of items from a catalog in return for coupons included with purchases of the manufacturer's products.
2. The *special deal* is a "one-shot" premium tied to the purchase of products.
3. The *display premium* allows the retailer who buys a product to get and keep a store display. The salesperson tells the buyer, "With your purchase of 20 dozen assorted toothbrushes you will receive free this beautiful, high-quality display rack worth $50. You can place it on this shelf and it will hold all of your various brands of toothbrushes."

The grocery, drug and toiletries, and automotive supply industries are several major users of dealer premiums.

Although promotional devices are often extremely effective selling aids, customers are still to a great extent concerned with unit price, quantity discounts, and credit terms. Therefore, these are key areas of selling knowledge.

What's It Worth? Pricing Your Product

An important part of a comprehensive marketing strategy for a product is establishing its price. **Price** refers to the value or worth of a product that attracts the buyer to exchange money or something of value for the product or service. A product has some want-satisfying attributes for which the prospect is willing to exchange something of value. The person's wants assign a value to the item offered for sale. For instance, a golfer who wants to purchase a dozen golf balls has already conceived some estimated measure of the product's value. Of course, the sporting goods store may have set a price higher than his estimate. This could diminish want somewhat, depending on the difference between the two. Should the golfer then find the same brand of golf balls on sale at a discount store, at a price more in line with a preconceived idea of the product's value, the want may be strong enough to stimulate purchase of the product.

Many companies offer their customers various types of discounts from their normal price to entice them to buy. These discounts become an important part of the firm's marketing effort. They are usually developed at the corporate level by the firm's marketing managers. Immediately before the sales period when the product's promotion begins, the sales force is informed of special discounts they may offer their customers. This discount information becomes an important part of their sales presentation. It is extremely important for salespeople to familiarize themselves with the company's price, discount, and credit policies so that they can use them to competitive advantage, as well as enhance their professional image in the eyes of the buyer.

Types of Prices

While a firm may engage in any number of pricing practices, all companies have a list price, net price, and prices based on transportation terms. Five of the more commonly quoted types of prices are defined as follows:

List price—the standard price charged to customers.

Net price—price after allowance for all discounts.

Zone price—price based on geographical location or zone of customers.

FOB shipping point—FOB (free on board) means the buyer pays transportation charges on the goods—title to goods passes to customer when they are loaded on shipping vehicles.

FOB destination—seller pays all shipping costs.

These prices are established by the company. The salesperson is not normally involved in pricing the product. This type of pricing allows the salesperson to quote prices according to company guidelines.

Selling the same quantity of like products at different prices to two different industrial users or resellers is illegal. Laws such as the Robinson-Patman Act of 1936 forbid price discrimination in *interstate* commerce which will injure competition. While the law does not apply to sales within a state (intrastate sales), a majority of states have similar laws.

A company can justify different prices if it can prove to the courts that its price differentials do not substantially reduce competition. Often companies can justify price differentials by showing the courts one of two things. First, take the case of one customer buying more of a product than another. For the customer purchasing larger quantities, a firm can manufacture and market the products at a lower cost. These lower costs are passed on to the customer in the form of reduced prices. Second, price differentials can be justified when a company must lower prices to meet competition. Thus, if justified, companies can offer their customers different prices. They typically do this through discounts.

Discounts Lower the Price

Discounts are a reduction in price from the list price. In developing a program to sell a product line over a specified period of time, marketing managers consider discounts along with the advertising and personal selling efforts engaged in by the firm. The main types of discounts allowed to buyers are quantity, cash, trade, and consumer discounts.

Quantity Discounts: Buy More, Pay Less.   Quantity discounts result from the manufacturer's saving in production costs because it can produce large quantities of the product. These savings are passed on to customers who buy in large quantities using discounts. Quantity discounts can either be noncumulative or cumulative.

One-time reductions in prices are **noncumulative quantity discounts,** and are commonly used in the sale of both consumer and industrial goods. The Kimberly-Clark salesperson might offer the buyer of Kleenex a 15 percent price reduction on the purchase of one boxcar load of Kleenex. The Colgate salesperson may be able to offer the retailer free two dozen of the king-size Colgate toothpaste for every twelve dozen purchased.

The salesperson is expected to use these discounts as inducements for the retailer to buy in large quantities. The sales goal is to get the customer to display and locally advertise the product at a price lower than normal. Ideally, the retailer's selling price should reflect the price reduction allowed because of the quantity discount.

Cumulative quantity discounts are discounts received for buying a certain amount of a product over a stated period of time, such as one year. Again, these discounts reflect savings in manufacturing and marketing costs.

To receive a 10 percent discount, a buyer may have to purchase 12,000 units of the product. Under the cumulative discount, the buyer would not be required to purchase the 12,000 units at the same time. As long as the agreed-upon amount is purchased within the specified time, the 10 percent discount on each purchase applies. A cumulative discount allows the buyer to purchase the products as needed rather than in a single order.

Cash Discounts: Get the Customer to Pay on Time.   Cash **discounts** are earned by buyers who pay bills within a stated period of time. For example, if the customer purchases $10,000 worth of goods on June 1 and the cash discount is "2/10 net 30," the customer pays $9,800 instead of $10,000. "2 /10 net 30" can be translated into a 2 percent discount if the bill is completely paid within 10 days of the sale. If the payment is not made within 10 days, the full $10,000 is due in 30 days. The salesperson might ask the buyer to reduce the price of the product to its net invoice costs and advertise it. The buyer's gross profit would be the 2 percent cash discount.

Trade Discounts Get Middlemen's Attention. The manufacturer may reduce prices to middlemen to compensate them for the services they perform. This is a **trade discount.** The trade discount is usually stated as a percentage off of the list retail price. A wholesaler may be offered a 50 percent discount and the retailer a 40 percent discount off the list price. The wholesaler's price to its retail customers is 10 percent above its cost or 40 percent off the list price. The wholesaler earns 10 percent gross profit on sales to retail customers. Middlemen are still eligible to earn the quantity and cash discounts.

Consumer Discounts Increase Sales. **Consumer discounts** are one-time price reductions passed on from the manufacturer to the middlemen or directly to the consumer. "Cents-off" product labels are price reductions passed directly to the consumer. A package marked 15 cents off each product or $1.80 a dozen uses a consumer discount.

The manufacturer expects middlemen to reduce the price from their normal price. A mass merchandiser might normally sell a product with a list price of $2.50 for $1.98. The manufacturer would want their salespeople to persuade the retailer to price the product 15 cents lower than the $1.98, or at a price of $1.83.

Cents-off coupons which the consumer brings to the retail store are another example of a temporary price discount. In both the cents-off and coupon examples, the manufacturer is insuring that the price reduction is passed on to the consumer. This is done because the middlemen may not have promoted the product or reduced the price, keeping the quantity or off-invoice savings for themselves. An offer of a cents-off product label and coupons are used by the salesperson to sell larger quantities to customers. A summary of discounts, and examples of each, is provided in Figure 5–8.

Markup Represents Gross Profit

Markup refers to the dollar amount added to the cost of the product to get its selling price. Markup is often expressed as a percentage, and represents gross profit, 'not' net profit. **Gross profit** is the money available to cover the costs of marketing the product, operating the business, and profit. **Net profit** is the money remaining after the costs of marketing and operating the business are paid.

Figure 5–9 presents an example of markup based on a product's selling price for each channel-of-distribution member. Each channel member

Figure 5–8   Types and Examples of Discounts

Types of Discounts	Discount Examples

Quantity discount
  Noncumulative
  (one time offer)
	Buy 11 dozen get 1 dozen free.
	20 percent off on all purchases
	$5 off-invoice for each floor-stand
	  purchase.

Cumulative
  (yearly purchases)
	5 percent discount with purchase of
	  8,000 units.
	8 percent discount with purchase of
	  10,000 units.
	10 percent discount with purchase of
	  12,000 units.

Cash discounts	2/10 end-of-month. 2/10 net 30.
Trade discounts	40 percent off to retailers. 50 percent off to wholesalers.
Consumer discounts	15 cents off regular price marked on product's package. 10 cents off coupon.

has a different percentage markup. The product that costs the manufacturer $3 to produce eventually costs the consumer $12. The manufacturer's selling price represents the wholesaler's cost. Price markups enable the wholesaler to pay business operating costs, to cover the product's cost, and to make a profit. The wholesaler's selling price of $6 becomes the retailer's cost. In turn, the retailer marks the product up to cover its cost, and the associated costs of doing business (such as stocking the product and allocation of "fixed costs" per square foot), and to maintain a desired level of profit.

The percentage markup can be based on either the product's selling price or its cost. It is important to know which method of determining markup is to be used. Using the manufacturer's cost of $3, markup of $2, and selling price of $5 shown in Figure 5–9, the methods of determining percentage markup can have different results as shown below:

$$\text{Percentage markup on selling price} = \frac{\text{amount added to cost}}{\text{selling price}} = \frac{\$2.00}{\$5.00} = 40 \text{ percent}$$

$$\text{Percentage markup on cost} = \frac{\text{amount added to cost}}{\text{cost}} = \frac{\$2.00}{\$3.00} = 66.6 \text{ percent}$$

Figure 5–9   Example of Markup on Selling Price in Channel of Distribution

Manufacturer	Wholesaler	Retailer
$3.00 = Cost to manufacturer	$5.00 = Cost from manufacturer	$6.00 = Cost from wholesaler
+ 2.00 = Markup (40 percent)	+ 1.00 = Markup (16.6 percent)	+ 6.00 = Markup (50 percent)
$5.00 = Selling price	$6.00 = Selling price	$12.00 = Selling price

In general, middlemen want to buy goods at low prices and establish selling prices at a competitive level which will allow for a reasonable profit. Such objectives result in retailers having different markups on different goods. For example, a retailer may have markups of 10 percent on groceries, 30 percent on cameras, and 50 percent on houseware items. Too, based on type of store (discount—high volume; specialty— low volume; department—high service), markups may vary greatly depending on volume of sales and degree of service rendered.

In preparing the sales presentation for an individual customer, the salesperson should consider all of the various discounts available to suggest a promotional plan for the retailer. For example, the Chlor-Trimeton advertisement shown in Figure 5–3 illustrates several of the various discounts a retailer can receive with the purchase of this decongestant. The Schering salesperson can use these discounts in the sales presentation by suggesting that the retailer advertise the product at a reduced price and place the promotional display by each of the store's cash registers.

Be Creative in Your Pricing Techniques

Salespeople often use creative pricing techniques when selling to retailers and helping them to resell the products they have purchased. Take for example the RCA salesperson who presented a retailer his $100 promotional discount and suggested the retailer purchase 30 units and sell an $800 color television for $599. The salesperson pointed out that the retailer would still make the normal 50 percent markup as shown in Figure 5–10. The retailer said no, since even though the percentage gross profit (markup) would be the same, the actual dollar return would be too low. (Compare "Normal Cost and Profit" box with "Salesperson's First Suggestion" in Figure 5–10.)

The salesperson wasn't finished yet, however. After leaving the store briefly to visit a local appliance retailer who agreed to sell 30 ceiling fans (at a retail price of $99) for $50 each, the salesperson returned with a second suggestion. Advertise the televisions for $799 and offer a "free" ceiling fan with each purchase. As shown in Figure 5–10, the retailer would make a higher percentage markup of 56 percent and

Figure 5–10 Examples of Creative Pricing

Normal cost and profit	
$800	= Television retail price
−400	= Normal cost
$400	= Markup (400/800 = 50 percent of retail price)

Deal cost and profit	
$400	= Normal cost
−100	= Promotional allowance
$300	= Deal Cost

Salesperson's first suggestion:	
$599	= Promotional selling price
−300	= Deal cost
$299	= Markup (299/599 = 50 percent of selling price)

Salesperson's second suggestion:	
$799	= advertised price
−350	= total cost ($300 deal cost plus $50 fan)
$450	= markup (450/800 = 56 percent of selling price)

receive more actual cash—$450. The retailer agreed, and all 30 television sets were sold in a single weekend! The salesperson used this same creative pricing technique for six other customers in different cities. The moral of this story is to look for new, creative ways to sell your product. If you combine a little extra effort with a little ingenuity, any sale is possible.

Customer Credit: Get'em to Pay on Time

It is often the salesperson's responsibility to open up new accounts, see that customers pay on time, and collect overdue bills. Table 5–2 shows an example of a salesperson's customers accounts receivable and aged trial balance. Five customers are 30 days or more past due on paying their account balances.

The next time the salesperson calls, Jones Lumber and Hardware Unlimited may be required to pay at least their 90-day balance before any more products can be ordered. Otherwise, it is quite possible that friction could develop. The salesperson's credit department may prohibit further sales to overdue customers.

Table 5–2 Example of a Salesperson's Customers Accounts Receivable and Aged Trial Balance

Territory Number	Customer Number	Customer Name	Total Balance	Current Balance	30 Days	60 Days	90 Days	Sales to Date
043	00035	Ace Hardware	943.65	943.65				5628.11
043	00605	Jones Lumber	584.54	247.78	85.55	154.30	96.91	626.76
043	01426	ABC Fix-it	1103.69	377.04	435.14	291.51		1434.17
043	39782	Hardware Unlimited	2932.59	743.04	846.50	773.44	569.61	3387.99
043	04568	McNeal Supplies	72.02		72.02			952.81
043	04569	Building Supplies	400.41	392.37	8.04			1422.82
		Territory total or grand total	6036.90	2703.88	1447.25	1219.25	666.52	13,452.66

The salesperson should know the company's credit policies and be provided a statement of the customer's accounts receivable. Given this information, this salesperson can be prepared when the buyer from Jones Lumber says:

> Jill, send me $300 worth of your product.

Salesperson: Mr. Jones, you will have it next Friday. Would you have your bookkeeper make out a check for $336.76? I'll send it in with your order.

The $336.76 is the total past due amount owed by Jones Lumber to the salesperson's company as shown in Table 5–2. The salesperson can get in a tough spot between serving her customer and her company. However, she must avoid bad-debt losses, and should politely get straight to the point with customers who are not paying their bills.

The sale is not complete until the product is paid for. If it is not paid for, both the salesperson and the company lose. The salesperson must know the customer's past and future ability to pay. Credit and payment cooperation between salesperson and customer results in better service to the customer and profitable sales for the salesperson.

Know Your Competition, Industry, and Economy

Today's successful salespeople understand their *competitors'* products, policies, and practices just as well as they do their own. It is quite common for a buyer to ask a salesperson, "How does your product compare to the one I'm presently using?" If unable to confidently answer such a question, a salesperson will lose ground in the selling race. A salesperson needs to be prepared to discuss product features, advantages, and benefits, in comparison to those of other products, and confidently show why the salesperson's product will fulfill the buyer's needs better than competitive products.

One method to obtain information on competitors is through advertisements. From the advertising of a competitor, Joe Mitchell, a salesperson representing a large business machines firm, developed a chart for comparing the sales points of his various machines against those of the competition. Joe does not do this for fun, nor does he name the competitive equipment on the chart. Instead, he just calls them "Machine A, Machine B, Machine C," etc. When he finds a claimed benefit in one of the other machines which his product does not have, he works to find a better benefit to balance it off. "Maybe the chart isn't always useful," Joe says, "but it certainly has prepared me to face a customer. I know just what other machines have, and what they do not have, that my prospect might be interested in. I know the principal sales arguments that will be used in selling these machines and also the benefits I must bring up to offset and surpass competition.

"Many times a prospect will mention an advertisment of another company and ask about some statement or other," Joe goes on to say. "Because I've studied those ads and taken the time to find out what's behind the claims, I can give an honest answer and also can point out how my machine has the same feature or quality, and then offer additional benefits. Of course, I never run down a competitor's product. I just try to run ahead of it."

The salesperson selling industrial goods and the industrial buyer work for different companies, but are both in the same industry. The industrial buyer often seeks information from salespeople on the *industry* itself, and how economic trends might influence the industry *and* both of their companies. Thus, the salesperson should be well informed on the industry and the economy. The salesperson can get this type of information from the company, newspapers, television, radio, the *Wall Street Journal,* industrial and trade periodicals, and magazines such as *Business Week* and *U.S. News and World Report.* The salesperson who is well informed will generally be more successful than the poorly informed salesperson.

Summary of Major Selling Issues

Company knowledge includes information on a firm's history, development policies, procedures, products, distribution, promotion, and pricing. A salesperson should also be knowledgeable about the competition, the firm's industry, and the economy. This type of knowledge can even be used as an aid in improving one's self-concept. A high degree of such knowledge helps the salesperson to build a positive self-image and to feel thoroughly prepared to interact with customers.

Wholesalers and retailers stock thousands of products, often making it difficult for them to support any one manufacturer's products as wanted by the manufacturer. This situation may result in conflicts between members of the channel of distribution. To reduce these conflicts and aid middlemen in selling its products, manufacturers offer assistance in advertising, sales promotion aids, and pricing allowances. In addition, many manufacturers spend millions of dollars to compel consumers and industrial buyers to purchase from the middlemen and the manufacturer.

National, retail, trade, industrial, and direct-mail advertising are used to create demand for products and can be used as a powerful selling tool for the salesperson to use in the sales presentation. Sales promotion activities and materials are another potential selling tool for the salesperson to use in selling consumer and industrial buyers. Samples, coupons, contests, premiums, demonstrations, and displays are effective sales promotion techniques which can be employed to help sell merchandise.

Price, discounts, and credit policies are additional facts the salesperson should be able to discuss confidently with customers. Each day the salesperson is involved in informing or answering questions posed by customers in these three areas. Customers always want to know the salesperson's list and net price, and if there are any transportation charges. Discounts (whether quantity, cash, trade, or consumer) represent important buying incentives offered by the manufacturer to the buyer. The buyer will want to know the terms of payment. The salesperson will need to understand company credit policies in order to open new accounts, see that customers pay on time, and collect overdue bills.

Review and Discussion Questions

1. A salesperson's knowledge needs to extend into many areas such as: general company knowledge, product knowledge, knowledge of upcoming advertising and promotional campaigns, knowledge about company price, discount, and credit policies, and knowledge about the competition, the industry, and the economy. These are all vital for sales success. For each of the above mentioned categories, explain how a salesperson's knowledge can lay the groundwork for success selling.

2. How do salespeople generally acquire their sales knowledge?

3. At times a manufacturer may experience conflicts between itself and members of its channel of distribution. What types of conflicts may arise? Why? What type of cooperation is needed on the part of the manufacturer to reduce channel conflict? From middlemen?

4. Explain how a salesperson's knowledge can be converted into selling points to be used in the sales presentation. Give two examples.

5. A salesperson should have a good understanding of the competition, customers and everything connected with his company. Why, however, should a salesperson take the time to be up-to-date on facts about the economy and his industry?

6. What is the difference between a product's shelf positioning and its shelf facing? How can a salesperson maximize both shelf positioning and shelf facings? Why is it important to do this?

7. What is meant by the term SAMI? How can a salesperson use SAMI information to advantage in a sales presentation?

8. Companies use numerous types of premiums in their efforts to

market their products. Why? What types of premiums do they use? How can a salesperson use a premium offer in a sales presentation to a reseller?

9. Many companies offer their customers various types of discounts from their normal, or list, price to entice them to buy. Discuss the main types of discounts which can be offered. Should the salesperson mention a discount at the first, middle, or last of a sales presentation? Why?

10. It costs a company $6 to manufacture a product which it sold for $10 to a wholesaler who in turn sold it to a retailer for $12. A customer of the retailer bought it for $24. What was the markup on selling price for each member of this product's channel of distribution?

11. Determine the markup of a product which cost your customer $1, with the following potential suggested resell prices of: $1.25, $1.50, $2.00. How much profit would the reseller make selling your product at each of the three suggested resell prices?

12. What are the major types of advertising a manufacturer might use to promote its products? How can a salesperson use information about the company's advertising in his sales presentation?

13. Before firms, such as General Foods and Quaker Oats, introduce a new consumer product nationally, they frequently first place the product in a test market to see how it will sell. How can a salesperson use test information in a sales presentation?

14. Assume you sell hardware supplies to grocery, drug, and hardware retailers. Tomorrow, December 15, you plan to call on the ACE Hardware chain—your largest customer. To reach your sales quota for this year, you must get a large order. You know they will buy something, however you want them to purchase an extra amount. Furthermore, you know they are 120 days overdue on paying what you shipped them months ago and your company's credit manager will not ship them more merchandise until they pay their bill. How would you handle the sales call? Include in your answer where you would bring up the overdue bill problem in your sales presentation. Also include what you would do if the buyer said, "I haven't paid for my last order yet! How can I buy from you today?"

15. What is cooperative advertising? Explain the steps involved.

16. Why do companies advertise?

17. Consumer sales promotion and trade sales promotion try to increase sales to consumers, and resellers, respectively. Listed below are several promotional techniques. Classify each as a consumer or trade promotional technique, and give an example for each. Can any of the promotions be used for both consumers and the trade?

A. coupons on or inside packages

B. free installation (premium)
C. displays
D. sales contests
E. drawings for gifts
F. demonstrations
G. samples
H. special pricing (buy 3, get 1 free)
I. sweepstakes

18. List and define five commonly quoted types of prices.

19. Following are examples of several different types of discounts. In each situation: *(a)* explain what type of discount is being used, *(b)* determine by what percentage the *cost* of the product has been reduced, and the savings per unit, and *(c)* answer all other questions asked for each situation.

A. Bustwell Inc., a regional business computer sales firm, is attempting to sell a convenience store chain (Gas 'N' Go) a new computer operated gasoline pump meter. The device will help reduce gasoline theft, give an extremely accurate record of each sale, and aid in determining when Gas 'N' Go should order more gasoline. Mr. Gas, of the convenience chain, seems interested in your initial proposal but believes the price may be too high. The cost of each computer is $1,000, but you could sell Mr. Gas 50 computers for $45,000. The Gas 'N' Go chain owns 43 stores, and is building eight more, which will open in about one month.

B. The Storage Bin Warehouse in your territory has reported a number of break-ins in the past three months. As a salesperson for No-Doubt Security Products, you believe your extensive line of alarm systems and locks could greatly benefit the warehouse. You make an appointment with the manager at the Storage Bin for early next week. During your preparation for the sales call, you discover that the warehouse at present uses poor quality locks and has no security system. You plan to offer the manager a security package consisting of 150 Sure-Bolt dead locks (for his 150 private storage rooms) at a price of $10 each, and a new alarm system costing $5,000. The terms of the sale are 2/10 net 30. How would the total cost change if the terms of the alarm system alone were changed to 5/10 net 30 (and the locks remained 2/10 net 30)? What is the cost of the security package if the Storage Bin takes 25 days to pay for the purchase?

C. You are a salesperson for Madcap Arcade Games, selling video games and pinball machines. A local business wants to open an arcade, and would like to buy a new game about every 2 weeks. A new game costs $3,000. You can offer a 5 percent discount (in the form of an end-of-year rebate) if at least 25

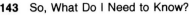

games are purchased from you during the next one-year period. What will the discount (in dollars) now be?

D.   The XYZ company is having its year-end sales push. As a salesperson for XYZ, a manufacturer of consumer goods like toothpaste, shampoo, and razor blades, you have been instructed to give a "buy eleven get one free" discount to half of your accounts. The remainder of your accounts, because of their small volume, are to be offered 10 percent off on all purchases. Compare the two situations. Who is getting the better deal?

Project

To complete this project you will need to visit two places. First, visit your local library. Examine magazines, such as the *American Druggist, Journal of the American Medical Association, Purchasing, Sales and Marketing Management,* and report on the type of promotions companies are offering their customers. Second, visit local retailers, such as a supermarket, and report on merchandising techniques being used to promote individual products. Once you have collected information on several products, pick one product and describe how this information could become part of a sales presentation.

Cases

5–1 Claire Cosmetics

Jane Thompson has recently been hired by a national cosmetics manufacturer. She has just graduated from college. Having had no previous work experience, she has always felt nervous about making sales presentations. Her large customers make her especially nervous. However, for the one month she had been in her territory Jane was really only taking orders, which took off much of the pressure, and the salespeople whom Jane replaced did an excellent job and customers seemed to accept Jane because of this.

In today's mail Jane receives information on products the company wants the sales force to emphasize next month. She is instructed to review the material and come to next week's sales meeting prepared to discuss the information. Of the four products to concentrate on, one product will receive special emphasis.

Claire Super Hold hair spray will have the following sales promotion aids and price allowances.

Floor stand containing 12 eight-ounce and 36 twelve-ounce sizes.

Counter display containing 6 eight ounce and 6 twelve-ounce sizes.

$1 floor stand and counter display off-invoice allowance.

10 percent co-op advertising allowance, requiring proof of advertising.

10 percent off-invoice discount for each dozen of each size purchased.

The eight-ounce size has a suggested retail price of $1.39 and has a normal invoice cost of 83 cents or $9.96 a dozen. The more popular 12-ounce size retails for $1.99 and costs $1.19 each or $14.28 a dozen. Jane knows that she, like each salesperson, will be called upon at the meeting to give her ideas on how to sell this product in front of the 10 salespeople in her district. Her boss will be there and, it is rumored, the national sales manager will be in the area and may attend. This really makes her nervous.

Questions:

1. What can Jane do to prepare herself for the meeting to reduce her nervousness?   *pratice*
2. If you were attending the meeting what ideas would you present?
   Benefits

5–2 McBath Feminine Apparel

Getting a new, improved product into a chain of stores that has never carried her line of ladies' apparel is a new experience for Lynn Morris. Lynn has just been promoted to key account sales representative for McBath Feminine Apparel in the past month.

She has worked for McBath since graduating from college three years earlier. As a novice salesperson in a large metropolitan market, she had inherited a sales territory where virtually all of the major department stores in her area carried the popular McBath line. By displaying a service attitude, Lynn kept all her original accounts, and even managed to help several of these outlets increase their sales of her McBath products, but she was never really given the opportunity to sell to new accounts.

Now, she has accepted the key account (a key account is one that generates a large volume of sales for the company) sales position in another region of the country. Further, she has been given the responsibility of selling to a large chain of department stores (Federale) that has never carried McBath products. Vice president of marketing at McBath, Maurice Leverett, is counting heavily on adding the Federale chain because James McBath, the company's hard-driving president, is intent on continuing McBath's rapid sales growth.

Lynn firmly believes that her products are the best on the market. She is concerned, however, about the sales interview she has scheduled with the chief purchasing agent at Federale, Mary Bruce. Despite McBath's high quality image, and its reputation for having a dependable, hard-working sales force, Mary Bruce has turned down other McBath salespeople several times over the past six years saying: "We already stock four manufacturer's undergarments and lingerie. We are quite happy with the lines we now carry and with the service their salespeople provide us. Besides, we only have so much floor space to devote to bras (McBath's major item) and we don't want to confuse our customers with another line."

Lynn has decided to make her company's new display system her major selling point for several reasons:

■ Several high-ranking McBath executives (including vice president of marketing Leverette) are strong backers of the new display and want it in all retail outlets.

■ The stores currently using the display for test marketing purposes have shown an increase in sales for McBath products of 50 percent.

■ Federale will not have to set aside very much space for the new system, and it can be installed, stocked, and ready for use in less than one hour.

■ The display will increase shopping convenience, by allowing shoppers easy access to the well-known, trusted line of McBath products with the aid of clear, soft-shell plastic packaging and easy-to-understand sizing.

■ A new advertising campaign will start in a few weeks and will emphasize the revolutionary display. Other promotions, such as coupons and special introductory sales will also be tried.

Questions:
1. Lynn believes a good presentation will be critical for her to sell Ms. Bruce the new display. How should she structure her presentation? What are the key selling points she should discuss?
2. Assume you are Maurice Leverett (vice president of marketing for McBath). Give an example of each of the four major types of discounts, discussed in this chapter, you could have your salespeople use to aid them in getting the new display into retail stores. What type of discount do you think will be the most effective? The least effective? Explain your reasoning.
3. How can Lynn use quantity (cumulative and noncumulative), cash, trade, and consumer discounts to her advantage?

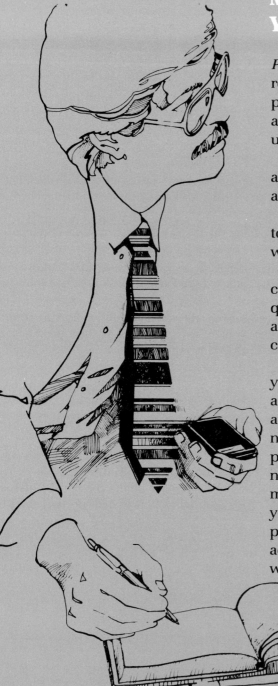

Making the Sale before You Make the Call

Planning. All that time-consuming reading, studying, note-taking, and practicing. It's homework, and not always fun. But like most homework, it usually pays off, especially if you . . .

Study the prospect . . . know in advance his needs and wants, problems and concerns.

Study the product . . . be prepared to match its features to those needs and wants.

Anticipate objections . . . few sales calls sail smoothly. Imagine what questions might be raised, what answers are appropriate, and how flexible you can be. Try to visualize the presentation.

Stay informed . . . be prepared to use your knowledge of the buyer's company and industry. The prospect will appreciate your preparation. Read newspapers and trade journals. Talk to people in the industry. Review your notes and old call reports. Talk to your manager, your colleagues. Smooth out your presentation. Practice. Rehearse. It probably will take more time than the actual sales call itself. And it will be well worth it.

The Dynamics of Selling

|6

Find Your Prospect—Then Plan Your Sales Call

 Learning Objectives

1. To establish the ten steps of the sales process.
2. To convey the importance of sales prospecting.
3. To illustrate how to make an appointment with the prospect.
4. To present the four elements of sales call planning.

Key Terms for Selling

Sales process

Prospect

Prospecting

Lead

Qualified prospect

Cold canvas method

Endless chain method

Exhibitions and
   demonstrations

Center of influence
   method

Direct mail prospecting

Telephone prospecting

Telemarketing

Observation method

Sales planning

Sales call objective

Customer profile

Customer benefit plan

Sales presentation

Profile

Vikki Morrison
Century 21

In 1980, Vikki Morrison handled sales of real estate worth slightly over 9 million dollars, and was honored as the top salesperson out of Century 21's 65,000 independent agents. Working out of her office in Huntington Beach, California, Vikki collected $253,589 in commissions before paying her broker's share of these fees. By May of the following year she had already sold an additional $5.2 million worth of residential real estate, well on her way to achieving her goal of selling $12 million.

Vikki strongly believes in effective sales prospecting. "Prospecting for business is the only way you can obtain clientele," says Vikki. "Every person you meet is a potential client; everyone, from your dry cleaner and your grocer, to local gas station owners, as well as my individual geographical residential areas I call a "farm." In my field I contact a household on a once-a-month basis in hopes of establishing face-to-face contact, and a chance to chat with the homeowner." Vikki often knocks on doors of some 400 homes each month.

"After four or five contacts with the same individuals, and hopefully, a positive response, I actually build a relationship with these people, based on friendship. I don't discuss selling real estate with them unless they bring up the subject. We are friends. We discuss everything else and I especially enjoy learning about their different talents and hobbies. There are some very unique people in the world if you take the time to find out about them.

"I plan each day in advance. I have a daytimer that I follow religiously. I go into my farm with 3 x 5 cards containing each person's name, address, and any other pertinent information about them. I have been doing it for so long that if someone from my farm telephones and says, "Hi, this is Sally Jones," I can immediately picture her house and the street on which she lives. I can usually recall the names of her children and sometimes even that of her dog. I provide a number of services for these people throughout the year, and when they decide to sell their homes, they many times call me.

"Selling, to me, is the lifeblood of our economy. Salespeople lead the way for all forms of business. I love selling real estate, but I could sell anything I believe in."

"Planned sales calls are a must" says U.S. Steel salesman Steve Gibson. "I begin my planning by carefully examining the account's situation and what product they will probably need. Then I review the latest trade journals for his industry's current trends. With this information I develop several sales presentation scenarios with potential questions and answers that the customer may wish me to discuss.

"While it is important to plan the presentation, you must be prepared to be flexible and anticipate the need to change your plan. A sales call must be fluid and dynamic based upon your customer's actual situation and needs at the time of the call which is difficult to plan."

The first two parts of this book give you much of the background a salesperson needs for making an actual presentation. You can be the most knowledgeable person on topics such as buyer behavior, competitors, and product information, yet still have difficulty being a successful salesperson unless you are thoroughly prepared for each part of the sales call. Part 3 of this book examines the various elements of the sales process and sales presentation.

Vikki Morrison has introduced you to the importance of prospects and methods to obtain an appointment with the prospect. Later in this chapter, Steve Gibson's remarks on planning the sales call will be closely examined in a discussion of the four steps in planning. Let's begin by explaining what is meant by the sales process.

The Sales Process

The **sales process** refers to a sequential series of actions by the salesperson that leads toward the customer taking a desired action and ends with a follow-up to ensure purchase satisfaction. This desired action by a prospect is usually buying, and certainly that is the most important action. Such desired actions can also include advertising, displaying, or reducing the price of the product.

Although many factors may influence how a salesperson makes a presentation in any one situation, there does exist a logical, sequential series of actions that, if followed, can greatly increase the chances of making a sale. This selling process involves ten basic steps as briefly listed in Figure 6–1. Each of these steps will be discussed in greater detail in the following chapters. Steps three through nine compose the sales presentation itself. Before a sales presentation can be attempted, several important preparatory activities should be carried out.

Figure 6–1 Steps in the Selling Process

Step 1. Prospecting:
Locating and qualifying prospects.

Step 2. Preapproach:
Obtaining interview, determining sales call objective, developing customer profile, customer benefit program, and sales presentation strategies.

Step 3. Approach:
Meeting prospect and beginning customized sales presentation.

Step 4. Presentation:
Further uncovering needs, relating product benefits to needs using demonstration, dramatization, visuals, and proof statements.

Step 5. Trial Close:
Asking prospect's *opinion* during and after presentation.

Step 6. Objections:
Uncovering objections.

Step 7. Meet Objections:
Satisfactorily answering objections.

Step 8. Trial Close:
Asking prospect's *opinion* after overcoming each objection and immediately before the close.

Step 9. Close:
Bringing prospect to the logical conclusion to buy.

Step 10. Follow-up:
Servicing customer after the sale.

Steps before the Sales Presentation

As indicated in Figure 6–2, a successful salesperson is involved in prospecting, obtaining an appointment with the prospect, and planning the sales interview prior to ever actually meeting with the prospect.

Figure 6–2 Steps before the Sales Presentation

Prospecting ▷ Obtaining an appointment ▷ Preapproach planning

Like a successful lawyer, the salesperson does a great amount of background work before meeting the judge—the prospect. One rule of thumb states that a good sales process involves 20 percent presentation, 40 percent preparation, and 40 percent follow-up, especially when selling large accounts. As in most professions, success in selling often requires as much or more preparation before and between calls than is involved in actually making the calls themselves.

Prospecting—Lifeblood of Selling

Prospecting is the first step in the selling process. A **prospect** is a qualified person or business that has the potential to buy your product or service. **Prospecting** is the lifeblood of sales because it identifies potential customers. There are two reasons that a salesperson must look constantly for new prospects: (1) to increase sales, and (2) to replace customers that will be lost over time.

A prospect should not be confused with a "lead." The name of a person or business who might be a prospect is referred to as a **lead.** A lead can also be referred to as a "suspect," indicating the person or business is suspected of being a prospect. Once the lead has been "qualified," the lead becomes a prospect. You can ask yourself seven questions to determine if an individual or business is **qualified** to buy:

1. Does this individual or business *need* my services or products?
2. Does this individual or business *perceive* a *need* or *problem* that may be satisfied by my product or service?
3. Does the individual or business have a sincere *desire* to fulfill this need or solve this problem?
4. Can this person's desire to fulfill needs or solve problems be converted into a *belief* that my product is needed?
5. Does this individual or business have the *financial resources* to pay?
6. Does the individual have the *authority* to buy?
7. Will this potential prospect's purchase be large enough to be *profitable?*

The majority of salespeople operate in single sales territories containing customers, prospects, and leads. Although locating leads and qualifying prospects are important activities for all salespeople, those selling products directly to the consumer, such as life insurance, automobiles, or real estate rely more heavily on prospecting than their industrial and retail store counterparts. Yet prospecting is also important to the latter.

Take, for example, Matt Suffoletto's (IBM) comments on prospecting:

Prospecting is the process of acquiring basic demographic knowledge of potential customers for your product. Lists are available from many vendors which break down businesses in a given geography by industry, revenue, and number of employees. These lists can provide an approach to mass marketing, via either mailings or telephone canvassing. That canvassing is either done by the salesperson or through an administrative sales support person. No matter who performs the canvass or how it is done, it is an important element in increasing sales productivity. The next step of qualifying the potential customer is often included in the prospecting process. Qualification is a means of quickly determining two facts. First, is there potential need for your product and second, is the prospect capable of making a purchase decision? Specifically, does he or she have the decision authority and the financial ability to acquire your product?

Where to Find Prospects

Sources of prospects can be many and varied or few and similar, depending on the service or product provided by the salesperson. Basically, these sources can be categorized as follows:

- Personal acquaintances.
- "Bird dogs," who are people who know about area residents, such as a real estate salesperson, bank clerk, gas station attendant, etc.
- Newspaper leads.
- Lists and directories, such as the telephone directory.
- Old accounts.

Naturally, persons selling different services and products might not use the same sources for prospects. A salesperson of oil field pipe supplies would most likely make extensive use of various industry directories in a search for names of drilling companies. A life insurance salesperson could, and should, use personal acquaintances, "bird dogs," and old accounts as sources of prospects. A pharmaceutical salesperson would scan the local newspaper looking for announcements of new physicians, hospital, medical office, and clinical laboratory openings, whereas a sales representative for a company such as General Foods or Quaker Oats would watch for announcements of the construction of new grocery stores and shopping centers.

Top real estate salesperson Vikki Morrison feels that prospecting, which for her means knowing people in her neighborhood, has greatly aided her in becoming a successful salesperson. She strives to become her prospect's friend.

"In my area, most of the people I see are wives—and any woman who tried to farm in this tract in high heels and a dress, dripping with jewelry, would never make it," she believes. "I'm not trying to impress anybody. These people either know me or they know about me from the neighbors. I'm no threat—especially in my tennies and polyester pants and CENTURY 21 T-shirt!" she laughs. [See Figure 6–3.]

"Usually, I never meet the husband until the actual listing—then he wants to meet me to find out if I really know what I'm doing in real estate. As far as he's concerned, I'm just a friend of his wife's." "These are the people I care about," she explains. "If someone needs a plumber or babysitter or a dentist, they call me. If I need a closing gift and someone on the block does creative things, I call them. We're all in this together!"

Figure 6–3

Top producer Vikki Morrison visits with Coco J. Weisinger during her recent visit to her neighborhood farm in Huntington Beach, Calif. Vikki says her usual attire— casual right down to the tennis shoes—is nonthreatening to housewives.

Courtesy of Century 21

Planning a Prospecting Strategy

Prospecting, like other sales activities, is a skill which can be constantly improved by a dedicated salesperson. Some salespeople charge themselves with finding X number of prospects per week. Indeed, Burroughs Corp. (a large manufacturer of computers and other types of business equipment) asks its sales force to allocate a portion of each working day to finding and contacting several new prospects. A successful salesperson continually evaluates prospecting methods, comparing results and records with the mode of prospecting used, in pursuit of a prospecting strategy that will result in the most effective contact rate.

Prospecting Methods

The actual method by which a salesperson obtains prospects may vary. Several of the more popular prospecting methods, as shown in Figure 6–4, are the cold canvas method, the endless chain method, group prospecting, public exhibitions and demonstrations, finding and getting the help of centers of influence, direct mail, telephone prospecting telemarketing, and observation.

The Cold Canvas Method. The **cold canvas prospecting method** is based on the law of averages. For example, if past experience reveals that one person out of ten will buy a product, then 50 sales calls could result in five sales. Thus the salesperson contacts as many leads as possible, recognizing that a certain percentage of people approached will buy. There is normally no knowledge about the individual or

Figure 6–4 **Methods of Prospecting for Customers**

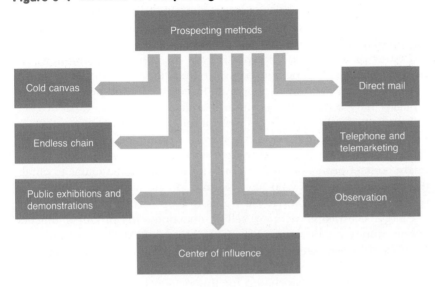

business called upon. This form of prospecting relies solely on the volume of "cold" calls made.

The door-to-door and the telephone salesperson both employ cold canvas prospectors. For example, each summer the Southwestern Company hires college students to sell their medical books, children's books, and Bibles. These salespeople go into a town and knock on the door of every person living on each block they work, often contacting up to 50 people each day. They frequently ask people if they know of others who might like to purchase their products.

Endless Chain. One popular method of obtaining prospects is the **endless chain referral method.** After every sale (or contact with a person), the salesperson asks the customer for a list of several friends who might also be interested in the product. The salesperson then approaches these prospects, attempts to sell to them, and also asks them for the names of potential prospects. The salesperson says, "Ms. Jones, whom of your friends can you recommend for me to contact?" Ideally, this procedure provides the salesperson with a constant supply of prospects. The endless chain is widely used in the sale of such services as insurance and products such as Tupperware and Avon cosmetics.

Public Exhibitions and Demonstrations. **Exhibitions and demonstrations** frequently take place at trade shows, and other types of special interest gatherings. Many times, related firms will sponsor a booth at such shows, and staff it with one or more salespeople. As people walk up to the booth to examine the products, a salesperson has only a few minutes to qualify leads, get their names and addresses so as to later contact them at their homes or offices for demonstrations. Although salesperson-buyer contact is usually brief, this type of gathering does give a salesperson extensive contact with a large number of potential buyers over a fairly brief period of time.

Center of Influence.   Prospecting via the **center of influence method** involves finding and cultivating people in a community or territory who are willing to cooperate in helping to find prospects. They typically have a particular position that gives them some form of influence over other people, as well as information that allows the salesperson to identify good prospects. For example, a person who graduates from a college and begins work for a local real estate firm might contact professors and administrators at his alma mater to obtain the names of teachers who have taken a job at another university and will be moving out of town. He wants to help them sell their homes.

Clergy, salespeople who are selling noncompeting products, officers of community organizations like the Chamber of Commerce, and members of organizations such as the Lions Club or a country club are other individuals who may function as a center of influence. Be sure to show your appreciation for this person's assistance. Keeping such influential persons informed on the outcome of your contact with the prospect helps to secure future aid.

Direct Mail.   In cases where there are a large number of prospects for a product, **direct mail** can sometimes be effectively used to contact individuals and businesses. Direct-mail advertisements have the advantage of contacting large numbers of people, who may be spread across an extended geographical area, at a relatively low cost as compared to using salespeople. People who request more information from the company can subsequently be contacted by a salesperson.

Telephone Prospecting.   Like direct mailing, use of **telephone prospecting** to contact a large number of prospects across a vast area can be far less costly than the use of a canvassing sales force, though usually more costly than mailouts.

This person-to-person contact afforded by the telephone allows for interaction on the part of the lead and caller enabling a lead to be quickly qualified or rejected. Salespeople can even contact their local Bell System affiliate for aid in incorporating the telephone into their sales program. Figure 6–5 illustrates how the Bell Telemarketing program can be used to increase sales and prospect for new accounts.

One example of telephone prospecting is the aluminum siding salesperson who telephones a lead and asks two questions that quickly determine if that person is or is not a prospect. The questions are:

Telephone Salesperson: "Sir, how old is your home?"
Lead: "One year old."
Telephone Salesperson: "Is your home brick or wood?"

Figure 6–5

Courtesy of AT&T Long Lines

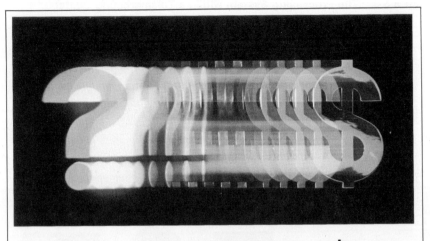

To turn more inquiries into sales, move faster.

If you're not set up to follow through at once on an inquiry—on a coupon, a letter, a phone call—you're in danger of losing your prospect.

The fastest response is through the Bell network, the world's largest and most advanced information management system.

Since you already have access to the network, there's no problem reaching your prospect. But how you handle your response is also crucial.

Properly done, with a Bell Telemarketing program, it can prove decisive in building sales and adding active new accounts.

Bell's program for handling inquiries can show you how to organize and plan for effective use of the phone. Your salespeople learn techniques to screen the inquiry, and so eliminate unnecessary in-person visits. And they learn tested, proven techniques for producing sales by phone.

Bell can discuss programs and services (such as WATS and 800 Service) and help you select what is best suited to your needs.

All you have to do is call now 800-821-2121, toll free. In Missouri, call 800-892-2121.

800-821-2121

See how easy it is to put our knowledge to work for you.

The knowledge business

Lead:	"Brick!"
Telephone Salesperson:	"Since you do not need siding, would you recommend we contact any of your neighbors or friends who can use a high-quality siding at a competitive price?" [Endless chain technique]

Telemarketing: The Salesperson's Assistant. The biggest sales buzzword of the 1980s is **telemarketing.** Telemarketing is a marketing communication system using telecommunication technology and trained personnel to conduct planned, measurable marketing activities directed at targeted groups of consumers.[1]

Figure 6–6 The Processing System within a Telemarketing Center

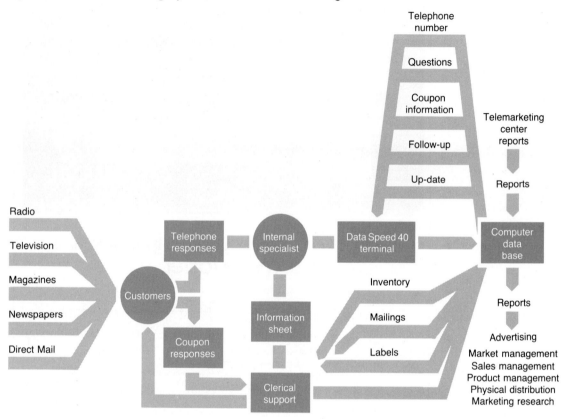

The internal processes of a telemarketing center are shown in Figure 6–6. Many firms initiate their telemarketing venture by featuring an 800 number in some advertisement. In print ads a coupon may be made available for the reader to use. When the coupon response or a telephone call comes in to the center, a trained specialist calls the respondent (in the case of coupons) or answers the in-coming call. The telemarketing center specialist fulfills the request and, in many cases, determines whether the customer has sufficient potential to warrant a face-to-face sales call.

From thousands of such contacts with the public, a firm can develop a valuable data base that produces many informational reports. Many *Fortune* 500 companies, a few of which are discussed below, use telemarketing centers in this way. Figure 6–7 describes some of their informational reports.

Examples of Firms Using Telemarketing.   The B. F. Goodrich Chemical Group uses a telemarketing center for order taking, customer

Figure 6–7 Reports from a Telemarketing Center to Other Marketing Groups within the Firm

Advertising	*Physical Distribution*
Inquiries per advertisement	Consumers' orders
Profiles of respondents	Distributors' orders
Sales conversion rates per advertisement	Tracing & dispatching
	Shipment requirements
	Inventory requirements
	Product return needs
	Customer service needs

Market Management	*Product Management*
Segment analyses	Sales per product
Marginal account identification	Questions & complaints
	Consumer profiles

Marketing Research	*Sales Management*
Demographic data	Lead qualification
Image and attitude	Marginal account status
Forecasting data	

service, and information dissemination. When customers call, a center specialist brings up the customer's file on a data terminal screen, records the order, checks inventory and, when necessary, talks with production and shipping to schedule the shipment. Field sales personnel are also provided current inventory data and estimated arrival times. High-volume accounts are scheduled for field visits, thereby increasing the number and quality of contacts between B. F. Goodrich and its best customers.

The Fotomat Company is another successful adopter of telemarketing. They introduced a new product—videotape sales and rentals—through their media advertising, which featured an 800 number to encourage call-in orders. They closely coordinated their distribution activities with the telemarketing system and have realized cost savings and improved customer service.

The 3M Company relies on a telemarketing center to assist customers with equipment trouble. After calling 3M's 800 number, the customer describes the problem to a skilled technician with access to an on-line computer system. On more than 30 percent of the calls, 3M has found, the equipment difficulty can be solved in minutes without having to dispatch a service technician. This has improved customer service activities and provided a valuable service at a very reasonable cost to 3M.

Westinghouse Credit Corporation uses telemarketing to qualify leads and develop good prospects for field salespeople. Calls are made from the telemarketing center to determine interest, verify mailing information, and transmit leads to branch offices. Results are used for planning future distribution needs such as volumes and locations.

The publication of an 800 number on packages, information sheets, and sale displays invites a two-way information exchange between customers and the telemarketing centers for Procter & Gamble and Johnson & Johnson. This exchange not only facilitates effective distribution activities but also encourages the use of a familiar channel for future or repeat sales. Clairol and Scott's also offer follow-up services for their hair-tinting products and lawn products, respectively.

The Observation Method. Of course, a salesperson can often find prospects by constantly **observing** what is happening in the sales area. Office furniture, computer, and copier salespeople look for new business construction in their territories. New families moving into town are excellent leads for real estate and insurance salespeople. No matter what prospecting method used, it is always important to keep your eyes and ears open for information on who needs your product.

What Is the Best Prospecting Method?

Like many other components of the selling process, prospecting methods should be chosen in light of the major factors defining a particular selling situation. As in most other optional situations discussed in this text, there is *no one* optimal mode of prospecting to fit all situations. Generalizations can be made, however, regarding the criteria used in choosing an optimal prospecting method for a particular selling situation. Three criteria which should be used in developing the "best" prospecting method for you should have you:

1. *Customize* or choose a prospecting method which fits the specific needs of your individual firm. Do not copy another company's method.
2. Concentrate on *high potential* customers first, leaving for later prospects of lower potential.
3. Always *call back* on prospects who did not buy. With new products, do not restrict yourself to present customers only. A business may not have purchased your present products because they did not fit their present needs; however, your new product may be exactly what they need.

Always keep knocking on your customer's doors in order to help them solve their problems through the purchase of your product.

Successful Selling Secrets: Vikki Morrison

"There are no secrets to successful selling. There is only hard work from 7:00 in the morning to 10:00 at night. The biggest secret is total honesty at all times, with all parties. You should act with integrity and treat clients with the same respect you want from them.

"Never call clients with anything but calm assurance in your voice, because if they feel you are panicked, they will become panicked. Your walk, speech, mannerisms, and eye-to-eye contact say more about you than you'll ever know, so practice all forms of your presentation every day in every way. I suppose a secret is to save the best house for last. I just try to do the best job for the client, even when it means turning them over to another agent who would have a more suitable property in a different area."

Vikki does not work "alone"; she uses her available resources in selling. A computer terminal in Vikki's office gives her up-to-date information on Century 21's listing and analysis of proposed transactions. She personally employs three assistants to help her keep up with the listings and shoppers. Vikki knows the value of the real estate in her area and can give free market analysis with less than one hour's notice.

"An important part of my job is providing customers personal service via constant follow-up, before the appointment, during, and after the sale. I have periodic follow-ups to see how they like their new home or investments. Anniversary flowers and cards on their birthday are a specialty of mine. I try to eliminate any and all of their buying fears when I can, and be available to reassure them.

"I sell on emotional appeal. No matter what the facts, most people still buy based on emotion. The trigger for someone's emotional side can be quite varied. For example, for some men, their families are their hot button; for others, the greed appeal of a good deal is more important. Every person is different and should be handled as the very important individual that they are.

"Another factor in my selling is that I care about my clients. They know it, I know it, and they feel it when I'm working with them and long after the escrow is closed. These people are my good friends and we have fun together."

Obtaining the Sales Interview

Given a satisfactory method of sales prospecting and an understanding of the psychology of buying, a key factor in the selling process that has yet to be addressed is actually obtaining a sales interview. Although cold calling (approaching a prospect without prior notice) is quite suitable in a number of selling situations, industrial buyers and some other types of individuals may have neither the time nor the desire to consult with a sales representative who has not first secured an appointment.

The Benefits of Appointment Making

The practice of making an appointment before calling on a prospect can save a salesperson literally hours in time wasted in traveling and waiting to see someone who is busy or even absent. When an appointment is made, a buyer knows you are coming. People are normally in a more receptive mood when they expect someone than when an unfamiliar salesperson "pops in." Appointment making is often associated with a serious, professional image, and is sometimes taken as an outward gesture of respect toward a prospect.

From the salesperson's point of view, an appointment provides a time set aside for the buyer to listen to a sales presentation. This is important, since adequate time to explain a proposition improves the chance of making the sale. In addition, a list of appointments aids a salesperson in optimally allocating each day's selling time. Appointments can be arranged by telephone or by contacting the prospect's office personally.

Telephone Appointment. For obvious reasons of time and cost, the telephone is often used to make sales appointments. Though seemingly a simple task, obtaining an appointment over the telephone is frequently not easy to do. Business executives are generally busy and their time is scarce. However, there are a number of practices which can aid in successfully making an appointment over the telephone:

- Plan and write down what you will say. This will help you organize and concisely present your message.
- Clearly identify yourself and your company.
- State the purpose of your call and briefly outline how the prospect may benefit from the interview.
- Prepare a brief sales message, stressing product benefits over features. Present only enough information to stimulate interest.
- Do not take "no" for an answer. You should be persistent even if there is a negative reaction to the call.

Ask for an interview so that you can further explain product benefits.

Phrase your appointment request as a question. Your prospect should be given a choice, such as: "Would nine or one o'clock Tuesday be better for you?"

Successful use of the telephone in appointment scheduling requires an organized, clear message that will capture interest quickly. Before you dial a prospect's number, you should mentally or physically sketch out exactly what you plan to say. While on the telephone you should get to the point quickly (as you may have only a minute), disclosing just enough information to stimulate the prospect's interest. For example:

> Mr. West, this is Sally Irwin of On-Line Computer Company calling you from Birmingham, Alabama. Businessmen such as yourself are saving the costs of rental or purchase of computer systems, while receiving the same benefits they get from the computer they presently have. May I explain how they are doing this on Tuesday at nine o'clock in the morning or would one o'clock in the afternoon be preferable?

One method for obtaining an appointment with anyone in the world is for you to have someone else make it for you. Now, that sounds simple enough, doesn't it? However, I do not mean just have anyone make the appointment. It should be a satisfied customer. Say, "Listen, you must have a couple of people who could use my product. Would you mind telling me who they are? I'd like you to call them up and say I'm on my way over?" Or, "Would you just call them up and ask them if they would meet with me?" This simple technique frequently works. In some situations an opportunity to make an appointment personally arises or is necessitated by circumstance.

Personally Making the Appointment.   Many business executives are constantly bombarded with an unending procession of interorganizational memos, correspondence, reports, forms, and *salespeople*. In order to use their time optimally, many executives establish policies to aid them in determining whom to see, what to read, and so on. They maintain gatekeepers (secretaries, receptionists, or other subordinates) who execute established time-use policies by acting as filters for all correspondence, telephone messages, and people seeking entry to the executive suite. Successful navigation of this filtration system often requires a professional salesperson who: (1) is determined to see the executive and believes it can be done; (2) develops friends within the firm (many times including the gatekeepers); and (3) optimizes time by calling only on those individuals who make or participate in the purchase decision.

Believe in Yourself.   As a salesperson you should believe that you can obtain interviews because you have a good offer for your prospects. You can develop confidence in yourself by knowing your products and by knowing your prospects; their business and their needs. Speak and carry yourself as though you expect to get in to see the prospect. Instead of saying, "May I see Ms. Vickery?" you say, while handing the secretary your card, "Could you please tell Ms. Vickery that Mr. Baker from XYZ Corporation is here?"

Develop Friends in the Prospect's Firm. Successful salespeople know that people within the prospect's firm can often indirectly help in arranging for an interview and influence buyers to purchase a product. A successful Cadillac salesperson states:

> To do business with the boss, you must sell yourself to everyone on his staff. I sincerely like people—so it came naturally to me. I treat secretaries and chauffeurs as equals and friends. Ditto for switchboard operators and maids. I regularly sent small gifts to them all. An outstanding investment.
>
> The little people are great allies. They can't buy the product. But they can kill the sale. Who needs influential enemies? The champ doesn't want anyone standing behind him throwing rocks.
>
> In many cases, all you do is treat people decently—an act that sets you apart from 70 percent of your competitors.[2]

Matt Suffoletto, the IBM sales representative profiled in Chapter 1, says it another way:

> I have observed one common distinction of successful salespeople. They not only call on the normal chain of people within the customer's organization, but they have periodic contact with higher level decision-makers to communicate the added value which their products and services have provided. This concept when exercised judiciously, can have a tremendous impact on your effectiveness.

Respect, trust and friendship are three key elements in any salesperson's success. Timing is also important.

Call at the Right Time on the Right Person. Both gatekeepers and busy executives appreciate salespeople who do not waste their time. Using past sales call records or by calling the prospect's receptionist, a salesperson can determine when the prospect prefers to receive visitors. Direct questions such as asking the receptionist, "Does Mr. Smith purchase your firm's office supplies?" or "Whom should I see concerning the purchase of office supplies?" can be used to determine whom to see.

Do Not Waste Time Waiting. Once you have asked the receptionist if the prospect can see you today, you should: (1) determine how long you will have to wait, and if you can afford to wait that length of time: (2) be productive while waiting by reviewing how you will make the sales presentation to the prospect; and (3) once an acceptable amount of waiting time has passed, tell the receptionist, "I have another appointment and must leave in a moment." When politely approached, the receptionist will usually attempt to get you in. If still unable to enter the office, you can ask for an appointment as follows: "Will you please see if I can get an appointment for 10 on Tuesday?" If this request does not result in an immediate interview, it implies the establishment of another interview time. If you establish a positive relationship with a prospect and with gatekeeper(s), waiting time will normally decrease while your priority will increase.

Customer Sales Planning—The Preapproach

Once the prospect has been located and qualified, the salesperson is ready to plan the sales interview. To illustrate why **planning** is important, let's first review an actual sales call using disguised names.

Dan Roberts was a salesperson for University Press, a publisher of college textbooks. He called on professors at colleges and universities to show his press's new books, and to remind them of the backlist of older books. Dan entered the office of Elizabeth Johnston, a professor at a school in his territory. The conversation went like this:

Salesperson: Hello, Professor Johnson? [Pronouncing the name incorrectly.]

Buyer: Yes, I am Professor Johnston. Can I help you?

Salesperson: I'm Dan Roberts, with University Press.

Buyer: I'm off to class. I can see you during my office hours.

Salesperson: Office hours. Oh, well, I wanted to talk to you about our new salesmanship book. Do you teach a course on selling?

Buyer: [abruptly] That's my favorite subject. Who is the author?

Salesperson: Oh, I'm not sure, let me check my catalog. Yes, here it is, it's . . . Johnston. Say, that is you!

Dan Roberts was certainly unprepared for the call. He did not know how to pronounce Professor Johnston's name; he did not find out the professor's office hours; he was not aware that the professor taught the course in selling; and he did not know his product. He was really embarrassed to find out that the professor had written the very book he was promoting. The one thing Dan did do correctly was to have an objective for the call—to visit with professors who teach good sales procedure. However, he should have looked at the school's class schedule to determine who was teaching the course and at what time. Dan's lack of preparation implied to Professor Johnston that he was not a good salesperson, and that he did not regard the call as worthy of preparation. These shortcomings got Dan off to a bad start with Professor Johnston.

Matt Suffoletto of IBM: Planning the Sales Call

"The sales call is still the key to most sales efforts, and planning a sales call is the foundation of a successful sale. You would never consider going on a long distance trip without looking at a roadmap. Similarly, you should plan what you want to accomplish on a sales call, and later measure yourself against that plan.

"If I were to ask you to describe the best salesperson you have ever encountered, you would probably respond that he or she was convincing and impressive. You can prepare yourself to be both convincing and impressive. First, you must know your product and more importantly, the product's application for your customer. Second, you must know your customer. You can gain a wealth of background knowledge about your customer's business from such sources as corporate annual reports, *Dunn & Bradstreet* directories, and the local Chamber of Commerce. Overall, planning shows up and pays off in increased sales when you do your homework."

Reasons for Planning the Sales Call

While salespeople would say there are numerous reasons for planning the sales call, four of the most frequently mentioned reasons are these: planning aids in building confidence; it develops an atmosphere of good will between the buyer and seller; it reflects professionalism; and it generally increases sales. Each of these claims is certainly worthy of consideration.

Builds Self-Confidence. If you are to give a speech before a large group of people, you tend to be nervous. This nervousness can be greatly reduced and your self-confidence increased simply by planning what you will say and practicing your talk. The same is true in making a sales presentation. By carefully planning your presentation, you will have increased confidence in yourself and your ability as a salesperson. This is why planning the sales call is especially important.

Develops an Atmosphere of Goodwill. The salesperson who understands a customer's needs and is prepared to discuss how a product will benefit the prospect is appreciated and respected by the buyer. Knowledge of a prospect and concern for the prospect's needs demonstrates a sincere interest in a prospect which is generally rewarded with an attitude of good will on the part of the prospect. This goodwill gradually aids in building the buyer's confidence and results in a belief that the salesperson can be trusted to fulfill obligations.

Creates Professionalism. Good business relationships are built on your knowledge of your company, your industry, and your customers' needs. Show prospects that you are calling on them to help solve their problems or satisfy their needs. These factors are the mark of a professional salesperson who uses specialized knowledge in an ethical manner to aid customers.

Increases Sales. A confident salesperson who is well prepared to discuss how products will solve particular needs will always be more successful than the unprepared salesperson. Careful planning ensures that you have diagnosed a situation and have a remedy for your customer's problem. Planning assures that a sales presentation is well thought out and will be appropriately presented.

Like other beneficial presales call activities, planning is most effective (and time efficient) when done logically and methodically. Some salespeople try what they consider to be "planning," later discarding the process because "it took too much time." In many cases, these individuals were not aware of the basic elements of sales planning.

Computer Information with Your Bacon and Eggs

Tomorrow's traveling salesperson will start the day by hooking a portable computer-printer-plotter combination to the motel-room telephone. While he shaves and showers, or has breakfast in bed, the computer will receive from the home office the newest sales leads that came in the day before, along with special messages put on the system by the sales manager such as price changes, advice on how to counter a new competitive product that will debut that week, and improvements made in the delivery schedule that would be a strong selling point.

The printer will also churn out the leads the salesperson is scheduled to call on that day, including a profile of the prospect's product application, interfaces with the company, and buying potential. A recap of the salesperson's last visit, and his comments, along with any problems the prospect may be having, will also be printed. The plotter will provide a map of the territory he will cover, with information on the location of each call, travel time, and an estimate of the time he should spend based upon each account's buying potential.

The computer will also remind him that tomorrow is the manager's birthday and that he has switched from cigars to pipes.[3]

Elements of Sales Call Planning

Figure 6–8 depicts the four facets for consideration in **sales planning.** These facets are: (1) determining the sales call objective; (2) developing or reviewing the customer profile; (3) development of a customer benefit plan; and (4) the development of the individual sales presentation based upon the sales call objective, customer profile, and customer benefit plan.

Figure 6–8   Steps in Planning the Sales Call

| Determination of sales call objective | Development of customer profile | Development of customer benefits | Development of sales presentation |

Always Have a Sales Call Objective.   A salesperson should meet with a prospect or customer with an objective in mind. The **sales call objective** should be: (1) specific, (2) measurable, and (3) directly beneficial to the customer. For example, the Colgate salesperson might have objectives of checking all merchandise and having the customer make a routine reorder on merchandise and sell promotional quantities of Colgate toothpaste.

The Colgate salesperson might call on a chain store manager with the multiple objectives of: making sure that Colgate products are placed where they will sell most rapidly; replenishing the store's stock of Colgate products so that customers will not leave the store disgruntled due to stockouts; and aiding the manager in deciding how much "promotional" Colgate toothpaste and Rapid Shave shaving cream should be displayed.

Industrial salespeople develop similar objectives to determine if their present customers need to reorder and also sell new products. A sales call plan, such as shown in Figure 6–9, can be used as a guide for determining the appropriate strategy to use in contacting each customer.

Customer Profile Provides Insight.   As much relevant information as possible should be reviewed regarding the firm, the buyer, and the individuals who influence the buying decision before a sales call is made in order to properly develop a customized presentation. The material discussed in Chapters 3 and 13 concerning the various factors on why the buyer buys should also be considered by the salesperson at this time. A **customer profile** should tell you:

Who makes the buying decisions in the organization—an individual or committee?

What is the buyer's background? The background of the buyer's company? The buyer's expectations of you?

What are the desired business terms and needs of the account, such as delivery, credit, technical service?

Figure 6–9

Customer Sales Call Planner

1. Name: _____
   Address: _____
2. Type of business: _____
   Name of buyer: _____
3. People who influence buying decision or aid in using or selling our
   product: _____
4. Buying hours and best time to see buyer: _____
5. Receptionist's name: _____
6. Buyer's profile: _____
7. Sales call objectives: _____
8. What are customer's important buying needs? _____
9. Sales presentation
   A. Sales approach: _____
   B. Features, advantages, benefits: _____
   C. Method of demonstrating FAB: _____
   D. How to relate benefits to customer's needs: _____
   E. Trial close to use: _____
   F. Anticipated objections: _____
   G. Trial close to use: _____
   H. How to close this customer: _____
   I. Hard or soft close: _____
10. Sales made—product use/promotional plan agreed upon: _____
    _____
11. Post sales call comments (reason did-did not buy; what to do on next call;
    follow-up promised): _____

What competitors successfully do business with the account? Why?

What are the purchasing policies and practices of the account? For example, does the customer buy special price offer promotions, or only see salespeople on Tuesday and Thursday?

What is the past history of the account? For example, past purchases of our products, inventory turnover, profit per shelf foot, our brand's volume sales growth, payment practices, and attitude toward resale prices.

You can determine this information from a review of records on the company or through personal contact with the company.

Customer Benefit Plan: What It's All About! Beginning with your sales call objectives and what you know or have learned about your prospect, you are now ready to develop your **customer benefit plan.** The customer benefit plan contains the nucleus of the information you will use in your sales presentation; thus it should be developed to the best of your ability. Creating a customer benefit plan can be approached as a four-step process:

Step 1: Select the "features, advantages, and *benefits*" of your product to present to your prospect. This addresses the issue of "why" your product should be purchased. The main reason your product should be purchased by your prospect is that its benefits fulfill certain needs or solve certain problems. Carefully determine the benefits you wish to present.

Step 2: Develop your "marketing plan." If selling to a wholesaler or retailer, your marketing plan should include how, once they buy your product, they will sell your product to their customers. An effective marketing plan would include your suggestions on how a retailer, for example, should promote the product through displays, advertising, proper shelf-space and positioning, and pricing. For an end-user of the product, such as the company who buys your manufacturing equipment, computer, or photocopier, you should develop a program showing how your product can be most effectively used or coordinated with existing equipment.

Step 3: Develop your "business proposition" which includes items such as your price, percent markup, forecasted profit per-square foot of shelf-space, return-on-investment, and payment plan. Value analysis is an example of a business proposition for an industrial product.

Step 4: Develop a "suggested purchase order" based upon your customer benefit plan. A proper presentation of your analysis of customer needs and your product's ability to fulfill these needs, along with a satisfactory business proposition and marketing plan should allow you to justify to the prospect how much of your product to purchase. This suggestion may also have to include, depending upon the nature of your product, such things as what to buy, how much to buy, the assortment to buy, and when to ship the product to the customer.

Visual aids should be developed to effectively communicate the information developed in these four steps. The visuals should be organized in the order you will discuss them. Your next step is to plan all aspects of the sales presentation itself.

The Sales Presentation Is Where It All Comes Together. It is now time to plan your **sales presentation** from beginning to end. This process involves developing the seven steps of the sales presentation described earlier in Table 6–1. These are the approach, presentation, and trial close method to uncover objections, ways to overcome objections, additional trial closes, and the close of the sales presentation. Each of these steps will be discussed in detail in the following chapters.

Figure 6–10 **A Sequence of Events to Complete in Developing a Sales Presentation**

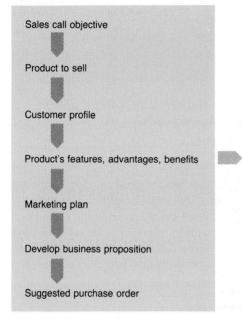

Figure 6–10 summarizes the procedures and steps relevant to planning a sales presentation. First you should develop your sales call objective by determining which product or products you will be presenting to your prospect. Based upon your call objective and what you know about your prospect (customer profile), you determine which specific product benefits to present, a market plan for your prospect, the business proposition you will discuss with the prospect, and your suggestion of what and how much the prospect should buy. This information is sequenced as you wish to present it. Visuals aids and demonstrations can be developed to help you create an informative and persuasive sales presentation. As was mentioned earlier, the *last step* in planning your sales call is the development and rehearsal of your sales presentation.

In developing the sales presentation it is helpful to think in terms of leading the prospect through five steps or phases that many salespeople believe make up a purchase decision. These are referred to as the prospect's mental steps.

The Prospect's Mental Steps

In making a sales presentation, you need to quickly obtain the prospect's full attention, develop interest in your product, create a desire to fulfill a need, establish the prospect's conviction the product will fill the need,

Figure 6–11 The Prospect's Five Mental Steps in Buying

and finally get action by having the prospect actually purchase the product. These steps occur in the following order.

Attention

From the first moment you begin to talk, you should quickly capture and maintain the prospect's attention. This may be difficult at times because of distractions, pressing demands on the prospect's time, or simply lack of interest. You should carefully plan what to say and how to say it. Since attention getters have only temporary effect, you must be ready to quickly move to Step 2, sustaining the prospect's interest.

Interest

Before meeting with prospects, you should determine their important buying motives. These can be used in capturing their interest. If not, you may have to determine them at the first of your presentation by asking questions. Prospects enter the interest stage if they listen to and enter into a discussion with you. You should quickly strive to link your product's benefits to prospects' needs. If this link is completed, prospects usually express a desire for the product.

Desire

Using the FAB formula (Chapter 3), you should strive to bring prospects from lukewarm interest to a boiling desire for your product. Desire is created when prospects expresses a wish or wanting for a product like yours.

To better determine if the product should be purchased, prospects may have questions for you and may present objections to your product. You should anticipate prospects' objections and provide information to maintain their desire.

Conviction

While prospects may desire a product, they still have to be convinced that your product is the best for their needs and that you are the best supplier of the product. In the conviction step you strive to develop a strong *belief* that the product is best suited to prospects' specific needs. Conviction is established when no doubts remain about purchasing the product from you.

Purchase or Action

Once the prospect is convinced, you must plan the most appropriate method of asking the prospect to buy or act. If each of the preceding steps have been carried out correctly, closing the sale is the easiest step in the sales presentation.

Overview of the Sales Process

We have briefly discussed the various steps in the selling process, reviewed the sales presentation, and examined the five mental steps a prospect moves through toward purchasing a product. Each step will be examined in more depth later, along with methods and techniques that successful salespeople use to lead the prospect to make the correct purchase decision. Figure 6–12 presents an overview of the selling process and gives corresponding examples of the prospect's mental stages and questions that may be posed at various points during the presentation.

You see that the approach is used to get the prospect's attention and interest by having the prospect recognize a need or problem, and stating a wish to fulfill the need or solve the problem. The presentation constantly maintains interest in the information you present and generates desires for the product.

Uncovering and answering the prospect's questions and revealing and meeting or overcoming objections results in more intense desire. This desire is transformed into the conviction that your product can fulfill the prospect's needs or solve problems. Once you have determined the prospect is in the conviction stage, you are ready for the close.

Summary of Major Selling Issues

The sales process involves a series of actions beginning with prospecting for customers. The sales presentation is the major element of this process. Before making the presentation, the salesperson must find prospects to contact, obtain appointments, and plan the entire sales presentation.

Prospecting involves locating and qualifying the individuals or businesses that have the potential to buy a product. A person or business who might be a prospect is a *lead*. Questions that are used to determine if someone is qualified are: "Is there a real need?" "Is the prospect

Figure 6–12   The Selling Process and Examples of Prospect's Mental Thoughts and Questions

Steps in the Selling Process	Prospect's Mental Steps	Prospect's Potential Verbal and Mental Questions
1. Prospecting Salesperson locates and qualifies prospects. 2. Preapproach Salesperson obtains interview, determines sales call objective, develops customer profile, customer benefit program and selling strategies. Customer's needs are determined.		
3. Approach Salesperson meets prospect and begins individualized sales presentation. Needs are further uncovered.	*Attention* due to arousal of potential need or problem. *Interest* due to recognized need or problem and the desire to fulfill the need or solve the problem.	Should I see salesperson? Should I continue to listen, interact, devote much time to a salesperson? What's in it for me?
4. Presentation Salesperson relates product benefits to needs using demonstration, dramatizations, visuals, and proof statements.	*Interest* in information which provides knowledge and influences perceptions and attitude. *Desire* begins to develop based upon information evaluation of product features, advantages, and benefits. This is due to forming positive attitudes toward product that it may fulfill need or solve problem. Positive attitudes brought about by knowledge obtained from presentation.	Is the salesperson prepared? Are my needs understood? Is the seller interested in my needs? Should I continue to listen and interact? So what? (to statements about features) Prove it! (to statements about advantages) Are the benefits of this product the best to fulfill my needs?
5. Trial Close Salesperson asks prospect's opinion on benefits during and after presentation.	*Desire* continues based upon information evaluation.	
6. Objections Salesperson uncovers objections.	*Desire* continues based upon information evaluation.	Do I understand the salesperson's marketing plan and business position. I need more information to make a decision. Can you meet my conditions?
7. Meet Objections Salesperson satisfactorily answers objections.	*Desire* begins to be transformed into belief. *Conviction* established due to belief product and salesperson can solve needs or problems better than competitive products. Appears ready to buy.	Let me see the reaction when I give the salesperson a hard time. I have a minor—major objection to what you are saying. Is something nonverbal being communicated? Did I get a reasonable answer to my objection?

Figure 6–12 *(concluded)*

Steps in the Selling Process	Prospect's Mental Steps	Prospect's Potential Verbal and Mental Questions
8. Trial Close Salesperson uses another trial close to see if objections have been overcome, or if presentation went smoothly before the close, to determine if the prospect is ready to buy.	*Conviction* becomes stronger.	Can I believe and trust this person? Should I reveal my real concerns?
9. Close Salesperson has determined prospect is ready to buy and now asks for the order.	*Action* (purchase) occurs based upon positive beliefs that the product will fulfill needs or solve problems.	I am asked to make a buying decision now. If I buy and I am dissatisfied, what can I do? Will I receive after-the-sale service as promised? What are my expectations towards this purchase? Why don't you ask me to buy? Ask one more time and I'll buy.
10. Follow-Up Salesperson provides customer service after the sale.	Satisfaction—Dissatisfaction	Did the product meet my expectations? Am I experiencing dissonance? How is the service associated with this product? Should I buy again from this salesperson?

aware of that need?'' ''Is there a desire to fulfill the need?'' ''Does the prospect believe a certain product can be of benefit?'' ''Does the prospect have the finances and authority to buy?'' and ''Are potential sales large enough to be profitable to me?''

Several of the more popular prospecting methods are cold canvas and endless chain methods, public exhibitions and demonstrations, locating centers of influence, direct mailouts, telephone and observation prospecting. To obtain a continual supply of prospects, the salesperson should develop a prospecting method suitable for each situation.

Once a lead has been located and qualified as a prospect, the salesperson can make an appointment with that prospect by telephone or in person. At times it is difficult to arrange an appointment, so the salesperson must develop ways of getting to see the prospect. One of the best ways to see the prospect is to develop friends within the prospect's firm who can help arrange for an interview. Believing in yourself and feeling that you have a product needed by the prospect is important.

The importance of careful planning of the sales call cannot be overemphasized. Plan your sales call in order to build your self-confidence, to develop good will between yourself and your prospect, to create an image of professionalism in the prospect's mind, and of course, to increase your sales. In planning the sales call, the salesperson should determine the objective for contacting the prospect, develop or review the customer's profile, develop a customer benefit plan, and finally, create an individualized sales presentation. Once these are accomplished, you are ready to meet the prospect.

Review and Discussion Questions

1. Century 21 saleswoman Vikki Morrison was profiled in Chapter 6. Discuss what Vikki said about the importance of prospecting and methods she uses.

2. What is the difference between a lead and a prospect? What should you, as a salesperson, do to "qualify" a potential customer?

3. This chapter termed prospecting, the "lifeblood of selling."
   A. Where do salespeople find prospects?
   B. List and briefly explain seven prospecting methods discussed in this chapter. Can you think of any other ways to find prospects?

4. What are the elements to consider when planning a sales call? Explain each.

5. An important part of planning a sales call is the development of a customer benefit plan. First, what are the major components of the customer benefit plan? Second, what is the difference in developing a customer benefit plan for a General Foods' salesperson selling consumer products versus being an industrial salesperson for a company such as IBM?

6. Many salespeople feel a prospect goes through several mental steps in making a decision to purchase a product. Discuss each of these steps.

7. Outline and discuss the sequence of events involved in developing a sales presentation.

8. Some salespeople feel a person should not be asked to buy a product until the prospect's mind has entered the conviction step of the mental process. Why?

9. What is the difference, if any, between the selling process and the sales presentation?

10. First, define the term *the selling process*. Second, list the major steps in the selling process on the left side of a page of paper. Third, beside each step of the selling process write the corresponding mental step a prospect should be experiencing.

11. Below are 13 situations commonly faced by salespeople. For each situation, determine which mental buying stage your prospect is experiencing. Give your reason "why" you feel the prospect is that stage.
    A. "Come on in, I can only visit with you for about 5 minutes."
    B. "That sounds good, but how can I be sure it will do what you say it will!"
    C. "Yes, I see your copier can make 20 copies a minute and copy on both sides of the page. Big deal!"
    D. The buyer thinks, "Will the purchase of this equipment help my standing with my boss?"
    E. "I didn't know there were products like this on the market."
    F. The buyer thinks, "I'm not sure if I should listen or not."
    G. "I wish my equipment could do what yours does."
    H. "Well, that sounds good, but I'm not sure."
    I. "What kind of great deal do you have for me today?"
    J. "When can you ship it?"
    K. You discuss your business proposition with your buyer and you get a favorable nonverbal response.
    L. "I like what you have to say. Your deal sounds good. But I'd better check with my other suppliers first."
    M. You have completed your presentation. The buyer has said almost nothing to you, including asking no questions and giving no objections. You wonder if you should close.

12. Assume you have started your own business to manufacture and market a product line selling for between $5,000 and $10,000. Your primary customers appear to be small retailers. How would you uncover leads and convert them into prospects without personally contacting them?

13. Think of a product sold through one of your local supermarkets. Assume you had recently been hired by the product's manufacturer to contact the store's buyer to purchase a promotional quantity of your product and to arrange for display and advertising. What information do you need for planning your sales call and what features, advantages, and benefits would you consider appropriate to use in your sales presentation?

14. Assume you had determined that John Firestone, vice president of Pierce Chemicals, was a prospect for your paper and metal containers. You decide to call Mr. Firestone to see if he can see you this week. When his secretary answers the telephone, you say, "May I speak to Mr. Firestone, please," to which she says, "What is it you wish to talk to him about?" How would you answer her question? Now what would you say if you were told, "I'm sorry, but Mr. Firestone is too busy to talk with you"?

15. You are a new salesperson. Next week your regional sales manager

will be in town to check on the progress you have made in searching for new clients for your line of industrial chemicals. You have learned that Big Industries, Inc., a high technology company, is in need of a supplier of your product. Also, a friend has told you about twelve local manufacturing firms that could possibly use your product. The sales potential of each of these firms is about one-tenth that of Big Industries. Knowing that your sales manager expects results, explain:

A.   How you will qualify each lead (assuming the 12 smaller firms are similar).

B.   After you have obtained interviews, develop a customer benefit plan for each case.

Projects

1.   Contact several salespeople in your community and ask them to discuss their prospecting system, plus the steps they go through in planning their sales call. Write a short paper on your results and be prepared to discuss it in class.

2.   Ask a buyer for a business in your community what salespeople should do when calling on a buyer. Find out if the salespeople this buyer sees are prepared for each sales call. Ask why or why not something is purchased. Do salespeople use the FAB as discussed in this chapter? Does the buyer think privately, "So what?" "Prove it!" and "What's in it for me?" Finally, ask what superiors expect of a buyer in the buyer's dealings with salespeople.

Cases

6–1   Lanier Dictaphone (B)

You work for the Lanier Dictaphone Equipment Corporation selling recording equipment. Imagine yourself as just entering the lobby and reception room of a small manufacturing company. You hand the receptionist your business card and ask to see the purchasing agent. "What is this in reference to?" the secretary asks, as two other salespeople approach.

Question:

Which of the following alternatives would you use and why?

A.   Give a quick explanation of your equipment, ask whether the secretary has heard of your company, or used your equipment, and again ask to see the purchasing agent.

B. "I would like to discuss our dictating equipment."
C. "I sell dictating equipment designed to save your company money and provide greater efficiency. Companies like yours really like our products. Could you help me get in to see your purchasing agent?"
D. Give a complete presentation and demonstration.

6–2   Ms. Hansen's Mental Steps in Buying Your Product

Picture yourself as a Procter & Gamble salesperson who plans to call upon Ms. Hansen, a buyer for your largest independent grocery store. Your sales call objective is to convince Ms. Hansen that she should buy your "family" size of Tide detergent. Her store now carries the three smaller sizes. You have developed a marketing plan that you feel will help convince her that she is losing sales and profits by not stocking Tide's family size.

You enter the grocery store, check your present merchandise, and quickly develop a suggested order. As Ms. Hansen walks down the aisle toward you, she appears to be in her normal grumpy mood. After your greeting and handshake, your conversation goes like this:

Salesperson: Your sales are really up! I've checked your stock in the warehouse and on your shelf. This is what it looks like you need. [You discuss sales of each of your products and their various sizes, suggesting a quantity she should purchase based upon her past sales and present inventory.]

Buyer: Ok, that looks good. Go ahead and ship it.

Salesperson: Thank you. Say, Ms. Hansen, you've said before that the shortage of shelf space prevents you from stocking our family size Tide— though you admit you may be losing some sales as a result. If we could determine how much volume you're missing, I think you'd be willing to *make* space for it, wouldn't you?

Buyer: Yes, but I don't see how that can be done.

Salesperson: Well, I'd like to suggest a test—a weekend display of all four sizes of Tide.

Buyer: What do you mean?

Salesperson: My thought was to run all sizes at regular shelf price without any ad support. This would give us a "pure" test. Six cases of each size should let us compare sales of the various sizes and see what you're missing by regularly stocking only the smaller sizes. I think the additional sales and profits you'll get on the family size will convince you to start stocking it on a regular basis. What do you think?

Buyer: Well, maybe.

Questions:

1. Examine each of the things you said to Ms. Hansen, stating what part of the customer benefit plan each of your comments is concerned with.
2. What are the features, advantages, and benefits you have in your sales presentation?
3. Examine each of Ms. Hansen's replies to you, stating which of the mental buying steps she is in at that particular time during your sales presentation.
4. At the end of your conversation, Ms. Hansen said, "Well, maybe." Which of the following should you do now?
   A. Continue to explain your features, advantages, and benefits.
   B. Ask a trial close question.
   C. Ask for the order.
   D. Back off and try again on the next sales call.
   E. Wait for Ms. Hansen to say "OK, ship it."

6–3   Machinery Lubricants, Inc.

Ralph Jackson sells industrial lubricants to manufacturing plants. The lubricants are used to lubricate the plant's machinery. Tomorrow, Ralph plans to call upon the purchasing agent for Acme Manufacturing Company.

For the last two years, Ralph has been selling Acme Hydraulic Oil 65 in drums. Ralph's sales call objective is to persuade Acme to switch from purchasing his oil in drums to a bulk oil system. Last year Acme bought approximately 364 drums or 20,000 gallons at a cost of $1.39 a gallon or $27,800. A deposit of $20 was made for each drum. Traditionally, many drums are lost and from one to two gallons of oil may be left in each drum when returned by customers. This is a loss to the company.

Ralph wants to sell Acme two 3,000-gallon storage tanks for a cost of $1,700. He has arranged with Pump Supply Company to install the tanks for $1,095. Thus the total cost of the system will be $2,795. This system reduces the cost of the oil from $1.39 to $1.25 per gallon, which will allow it to pay for itself over time. Other advantages include having fewer orders to process each year, a reduction in storage space, and less handling of the oil by workers.

Question:

If you were Ralph, how would you plan the sales call?

7

Select Your Presentation Method, Then Open It Strategically

Learning Objectives

1. To discuss four sales presentation methods.

2. To explain the importance of a salesperson using an approach to open the sales presentation and provide examples of approaches which open with statements, questions, and demonstrations.

3. To illustrate why the approach should have a theme which is related to the presentation and the prospect's important buying motives.

4. To present four types of questioning techniques for use throughout the presentation.

Key Terms for Selling

Memorized presentation

Formula presentation

Need-satisfaction presentation

Problem-solution presentation

Introductory approach

Complimentary approach

Referral approach

Premium approach

Product approach

Showmanship approach

Customer benefit approach

Curiosity approach

Opinion approach

Shock approach

Multiple question approach (SPIN)

Direct question

Nondirective question

Rephrasing question

Redirect question

Profile

Gary Grant
NCR

Gary Grant is currently district sales manager in Indianapolis, Indiana, for the Financial Systems Division of NCR. Prior to joining NCR in 1976 Gary earned his bachelor's degree in computer science and his masters degree in business administration from the University of Georgia in 1971. Upon completion of his MBA studies Gary joined a data processing services corporation, becoming manager of Electronic Funds Transfer System. Later he joined a financial institution as vice president of operations.

With respect to his career with NCR Gary states, "Throughout my sales career with NCR, whether it was in my assignment in New York City with one account, or my assignment in Chicago with multiple large financial customers to my current duties as district sales manager in Indianapolis where I call on small savings and loans to large commercial banks, the basics in selling are the same. I must (1) qualify the prospect, (2) make a thorough survey, (3) develop professional product and system sales presentations, (4) provide for customer demonstrations, (5) prepare proposals, (6) get the order.

"To make sure I have everyone's attention, generate interest, and provide transition, the presentation opening is very important. Since we rarely close a sale in just one call, we use one method of opening our sales call on the first call on the prospect and another method of opening the presentation on the second call. In the initial call we ask the prospect numerous questions to help uncover needs. I then get permission to do a survey of the prospect's present operation, problems, and needs.

"In the second call, my approach to opening any sales presentation is to state the reason for the presentation. I restate the problems I have found during my survey and interviews. Restating of the problem is critical as all decision makers attending the presentation may not be aware of each and every problem. Next I indicate that if this problem is not solved what conseqences the customer might expect if the decisions are delayed. And finally I try to convince the customer I have a solution. It is important here that I convince the customer my solution will be beneficial. With a good approach I should capture my audience and create the desire to listen and move into the actual presentation. Without a good approach I might as well pack my bags and move on because I will not grab the opportunity and therefore lose the order."

"The presentation is my tool to tell my story," says Gary Grant of NCR. "The battle for the order begins during preparation and rehearsal. Without planning the proper approach and gaining the all important prospects' subconcious attitude of, 'Yes, I want to listen to Gary's presentation,' my presentation will fall on deaf ears and consequently . . . a lost order.

"In planning the presentation my attitude is a major element. I must constantly be aware that I am the expert and that the customer is looking to me for solutions.

"For each presentation, knowledge of the customers' requirements, my product lines, and my competitions' product lines are essential. Developing the presentation depends on the problems and solution required. For example, if I am proposing a bank teller terminal, I will research product features that might increase teller efficiency and put on the presentation myself, one-on-one, with the customer using flip charts in a note book highlighting my terminal's advantages. When I am proposing large computer systems that are highly technical and significant dollar sales in the millions, a team approach is required in order to truly evaluate the software, hardware, maintenance, financing, and corporate support involved in the solution. This type of presentation can take days or weeks to prepare with many customer visits and will generally last one to two hours."

Salespeople, sales trainers, and sales managers agree that the most challenging, rewarding, and enjoyable aspect of the buyer-seller interaction is the sales presentation. An effective presentation completely and clearly explains all aspects of a salesperson's proposition as it relates to a buyer's needs. Surprisingly, or perhaps not so surprisingly, attaining this objective is not as easy as you might think. Few successful salespeople will claim that they had little trouble developing a good presentation, or mastering the art of giving the sales presentation. How then can you, as a novice, develop a sales presentation which will improve your chances of making the sale?

You must select a sales presentation method as NCR's Gary Grant suggests according to: your prior knowledge of the customer, your sales call objective, and your customer benefit plan. You are now ready to begin developing your sales presentation. The particular sales presentation method you have selected will make an excellent framework to build your specific presentation on. The sales opener, or approach, is the first major part of the sales presentation.

This chapter discusses four sales presentation methods. The reasons successful salespeople develop special approaches for the sales interview are examined next along with objectives of the approach, several types of approaches, and applied examples of each type of approach. Matching the proper approach to the situation, and how to handle a prospect that shows little or no interest are then reviewed. The chapter begins by examining a question frequently pondered by new salespeople—"Do I have the right to present my product to a prospect?"

The Right to Approach

You have the right (or duty) to present your product if you can show that it will definitely benefit the prospect. In essence, you have to prove that *you* are worthy of the prospect's time and serious attention. You may earn the right to this attention in a number of ways:

■ By exhibiting specific product or business knowledge.

■ By expressing a sincere desire to solve a buyer's problem and satisfy a need.

■ By stating or implying that your product will save money or increase the firm's profit margin.

■ By displaying a service attitude.

Basically, prospects want to know how you and your product will benefit *them* and *the companies* they represent. Your sales approach should initially establish and thereafter concentrate on your product's key benefits for each prospect.

This strategy is especially important during the approach stage of a presentation because it aids in securing the prospect's interest in you and your product. At this point you, at the very least, want this unspoken reaction from the prospect: "Well, I'd better hear this salesperson out, I may hear something that will be of use to me." Now that you have justified your right to sell to a prospect, you must determine just how to present your product.

Sales Presentation Methods—Select One Carefully

The sales presentation involves a persuasive vocal and visual explanation of a business proposition. While there are many ways of making a presentation, only four will be discussed here. These four methods are presented to highlight the alternatives available to help you sell your products.

As shown on the continuum in Figure 7–1, these four sales

Figure 7–1   The Structure of Sales Presentations

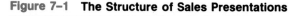

Structured	Semi-structured	Unstructured	Customized
Memorized selling	Formula selling	Need satisfaction selling	Problem- solution selling

presentation methods are the (1) memorized or stimulus-response, (2) formula, (3) need-satisfaction, and (4) problem-solving selling methods. The basic difference in the four methods concerns what percentage of the conversation is controlled by the salesperson. In the more structured memorized and formula selling techniques, the salesperson normally requires a monopoly on the conversation, while the less structured methods allow for a much greater degree of buyer-seller interaction in which both parties participate equally in the conversation.

Memorized Sales Presentation

The **memorized presentation** is based on either of two assumptions: that a prospect's needs can be stimulated by direct exposure to the product, via the sales presentation, or that these needs have already been stimulated because the prospect has made the effort to seek out the product. In either case, the salesperson's role is to develop this initial stimulus into an affirmative response to an eventual purchase request.

The salesperson does 80 to 90 percent of the talking during a memorized sales presentation, only occasionally allowing the prospect to respond to predetermined questions. Notably, the salesperson does not attempt to determine the prospect's needs during the interview, but just gives the same canned sales talk to all prospects. Since no attempt is being made at this point to learn what goes on in the consumer's mind (remember the black box), the salesperson concentrates on discussing the product and its benefits, concluding the pitch with a purchase request. It is hoped that a convincing presentation of product benefits (stimulus) will cause the prospect to buy (response).

National Cash Register Co. (now NCR Corp.) pioneered the use of canned sales presentations. An analysis of the sales approaches of some of its top salespeople done during the 1920s revealed to NCR that they were saying basically the same things. The firm proceeded to prepare a series of standardized sales presentations based on the findings of

Figure 7–2 Example of a Memorized Sales Presentation and Participation Time by the Customer and Salesperson

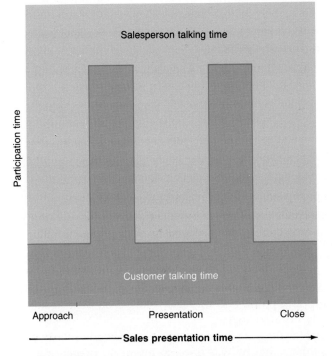

Source: Adapted from G. M. Grikscheit, H. C. Cash, and W. J. E. Crissy, *Handbook of Selling: Psychological, Managerial, and Marketing Bases* (New York: John Wiley & Sons, 1981).

their sales approach analysis, ultimately requiring its sales force to memorize these approaches for use during sales calls. The method worked quite well for NCR, and was later adopted by a number of other firms. Canned sales presentations are still in use today, mainly in telephone and door-to-door selling.

Despite its impersonal aura, the canned or memorized sales presentation has a number of distinct advantages:

It ensures that the salesperson will give a well-planned presentation and that the same information will be discussed by all of the company's salespeople.

It both aids and lends confidence to the inexperienced salesperson.

It is effective when selling time is short, as in door-to-door or telephone selling.

It is effective when the product is a nontechnical one, such as books, cooking utensils, and cosmetics.

As may be apparent, the stimulus-response method has several major drawbacks:

It presents features, advantages and benefits which may not be important to the buyer;

It allows for little prospect participation;

It is impractical to use when selling technical products which require prospect input and discussion;

It proceeds quickly through the sales presentation to the close, requiring the salesperson to close or ask for the order several times which may be interpreted by the prospect as high-pressure selling.

The story is told of the new salesperson who was halfway through a canned presentation when the prospect had to answer the telephone. When the prospect finished the telephone conversation, the salesperson had forgotten the stopping point, and therefore started all over again. The prospect naturally became angry.

In telling of his early selling experiences, consumer goods salesman John Anderson remembers that he was once so intent on presenting his memorized presentation that halfway through it the prospect yelled, "Enough, John, I've been waiting for you to see me, I'm ready to buy. I know all about your products." John was so intent on giving his canned presentation, and listening to himself talk, that he did not recognize the prospect's buying signals.

The point can be made that for some selling situations a highly structured presentation can be used successfully. Its advantages and disadvantages should be examined to determine if it is appropriate for your prospects and your types of products.

Some situations may seem partially appropriate for the memorized approach, but require a more personal touch. Such circumstances warrant the examination of formula selling.

The Formula Presentation

The **formula presentation,** often referred to as the "persuasive selling presentation," is akin to the stimulus-response method: it is based on the assumption that similar prospects in similar situations can be approached with similar presentations. However, in order for the

Figure 7–3 Dyno Electric Cart Memorized Presentation

Situation: You are calling on a purchasing manager to try to elicit an order for some electric cars (like a golf cart) to be used at a plant for transportation in and around the buildings and grounds. The major benefit you wish to emphasize in your presentation is that these carts "save time" so you incorporate this concept into your approach. For this product you are able to use the memorized stimulus-response presentation.[1]

Salesperson: Hello, Mr. Pride, my name is Karen Nordstrom and I'd like to talk with you about how to save your company executive's time. By the way, thanks for taking time to talk with me.

Buyer: What's on your mind?

Salesperson: As a busy executive, you know time is a valuable commodity. Nearly everyone would like to have a few extra minutes each day and that is the business I'm in, selling time. While I can't actually sell you time, I do have a product that is the next best thing . . . a Dyno electric cart—a real time-saver for your executives.

Buyer: Yeah, well, sure everyone would like to have extra time. However, I don't think we need any golf carts. [First objection.]

Salesperson: Dyno electric cart is more than a golf cart. It is an electric car designed for use in industrial plants. It has been engineered to give comfortable, rapid transportation in warehouses, plants, and across open areas.

Buyer: They probably cost too much for us to use. [Positive buying signal phrased as an objection.]

Salesperson: First of all, they only cost $2,200 each. With their five-year normal life that is only $400 per year plus a few cents electricity and a few dollars for maintenance. Under normal use and care, these carts only require about $100 of service in their five-year life. Thus, for about $50 a month you can save your key people a lot of time. [Creative pricing—show photographs of carts in use.]

Buyer: It would be nice to save time, but I don't think managment would go for the idea. [Third objection, but still showing interest.]

Salesperson: That is exactly why I am here. Your executives will appreciate what you have done for them. You will look good in their eyes if you give them an opportunity to look at a product that will save time and energy. Saving time is only part of our story. Dyno cars also save energy and thus keep you sharper toward the end of the day. Would you want a demonstration today or Tuesday? [Alternative close.]

Buyer: How long would your demonstration take? (positive buying signal).

Salesperson: I only need one hour. When would it be convenient for me to bring the car in for your executives to try out?

Buyer: There really isn't any good time. [Objection.]

Salesperson: That's true. Therefore, the sooner we get to show you a Dyno car, the sooner your management group can see its benefits. How about next Tuesday? I could be here at 8:00 and we could go over this item just before your weekly management group meeting. I know you usually have a meeting Tuesdays at 9:00 because I tried to call on you a few weeks ago and your secretary told me you were in the weekly management meeting. [Close of the sale.]

Buyer: Well, we could do it then.

Salesperson: Fine, I'll be here. Your executives will really be happy! [Positive reinforcement.]

formula method to apply, the salesperson must first know something about the prospective buyer. The salesperson follows a less structured, general outline in making a presentation, allowing more flexibility and less direction.

The salesperson generally controls the conversation during the sales talk, especially at the beginning. Figure 7–4 illustrates how a salesperson should take charge during a formula selling situation. For example, the salesperson might make a sales opener (approach), discuss the product's features, advantages, and benefits, and then start to solicit comments from the buyer through the use of trial closes, answering questions, and handling objections. At the end of the participation curve, the salesperson regains control over the discussion, and moves in to close the sale.

The formula selling approach obtains its name from the salesperson using the attention, interest, desire, and action (AIDA) procedure of developing and giving the sales presentation. We earlier added "conviction" to the procedure because the prospect may want or desire

Figure 7–4 Example of a Formula Sales Presentation and Participation Time by the Customer and Salesperson

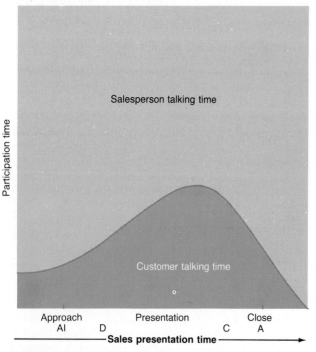

Source: Adapted from G. M. Grikscheit, H. C. Cash, and W. J. E. Crissy, *Handbook of Selling: Psychological, Managerial, and Marketing Bases* (New York: John Wiley & Sons, 1981).

the product, yet not be convinced this is the best product or the best salesperson from which to buy.

Straight rebuy and modified rebuy situations, especially with consumer goods, lend themselves to this method. Many prospects or customers are going to buy because they are familiar with the salesperson's company. The question is, "How can a salesperson for Quaker Oats, Revlon, Gillette, Procter & Gamble, or any other well-known manufacturer develop a presentation that will convince a customer to purchase promotional quantities of a product, participate in a local advertising campaign, or stock a new untried product?"

Formula selling can be a very effective method for calling on customers who are currently buying, and prospects about whose operation the salesperson has learned a great deal. In such situations, formula selling offers a number of significant advantages:

It insures that all information is presented in a logical manner.

It allows for a reasonable amount of buyer-seller interaction.

It allows for smooth handling of *anticipated* questions and objections.

When executed in a smooth, conversational manner, the formula method of selling has no major flaws, as long as the salesperson has correctly identified the prospect's needs and wants. The Procter & Gamble formula sales presentation given as an example in Figure 7–5 can be given to any retailer who is not selling all available sizes of Tide (or of any other product). In this situation a formula approach is used in calling on a customer the salesperson has sold to previously. If, on the other hand, the salesperson had not known a customer's needs and used this Tide presentation, chances are customer objections would arise early in the presentation—as they sometimes do with the stimulus-response sales presentation method. Still, the formula technique is not adaptable to a number of complex selling situations. This requires still another sales presentation.

The Need Satisfaction Presentation

The **need satisfaction presentation** is different from the stimulus-response and the formalized approaches in that it is designed as a relatively flexible, "interactive" sales presentation. It is the most challenging and creative form of selling.

The salesperson will typically start the presentation with a probing question like: "What are you looking for in investment property?" or, "What type of computer needs does your company have?" This opening brings up a discussion of the prospect's needs, and also gives the salesperson an opportunity to determine whether any of the products being offered might be beneficial. When something the prospect has said is not understood by the salesperson, it can be clarified by a question

Figure 7-5   Example of a Formula Approach Sales Presentation

Formula Steps	Buyer-Seller Roles	Sales Presentation
Summarize the situation for *attention* and *interest*	*Salesperson:*	Ms. Hanson, you've said before that the shortage of shelf space prevents you from stocking our family-size Tide—though you admit you may be losing some sales as a result. If we could determine *how much* volume you're missing, I think you'd be willing to *make* space for it, wouldn't you? [Trial close.]
State your marketing plan for *interest*	*Buyer:*	Yes, but I don't see how that can be done.
	Salesperson:	Well, I'd like to suggest a test—a weekend display of all four sizes of Tide.
	Buyer:	What do you mean?
Explain your marketing plan for *interest* and *desire*	*Salesperson:*	My thought was to run all sizes at regular shelf price *without* any ad support. This would give us a "pure" test. Six cases of each size should let us compare sales of the various sizes and see what you're missing by regularly stocking only the smaller sizes. I think the additional sales and profits you'll get on the family size will convince you to start stocking it on a regular basis. [Reinforce key benefits.] What do you think? [Trial close.]
Buyer appears in *conviction* stage	*Buyer:*	Well, maybe. [Positive reaction to trial close.]
Suggest an easy next step *action*	*Salesperson:*	May I enter the six cases of family size Tide in the order book now? [Close.]

or by restating what the buyer has said. The need satisfaction format is especially suited to the sale of industrial and technical goods with stringent specifications and high price tags.

Often, as shown in Figure 7–6, the first 50 to 60 percent of conversation time (referred to as the *need development* phase) is devoted to a discussion of the buyer's needs. Once aware of the prospect's needs (the *need awareness* phase), the salesperson begins to take control of the conversation by restating the prospect's needs to clarify the situation. During the last stage of the presentation, the *need fulfillment* phase, the salesperson shows how the product will satisfy mutually agreed-upon needs. As you can see in Figure 7–7, the salesperson selling the Dyno Electric Cart begins the interview with the prospect by using a planned series of questions to uncover problems and to determine whether the prospect is interested in solving them.[2]

Should you have to come back a second time to see the prospect,

Figure 7–6 Example of a Need Satisfaction Sales Presentation and Participation Time by the Customer and Salesperson

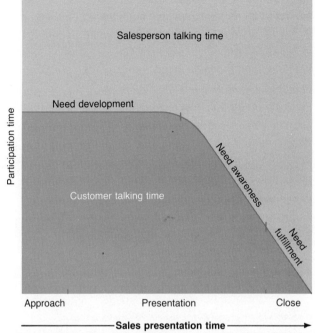

Source: Adapted from G. M. Grikscheit, H. C. Cash, and W. J. E. Crissy, *Handbook of Selling: Psychological, Managerial, and Marketing Bases* (New York: John Wiley & Sons, 1981).

as is often the case in selling industrial products, you would use the formula sales presentation method in calling on the same prospect. You might begin with a benefit statement such as:

"Mr. Pride, when we talked last week you were interested in saving your executives time and energy in getting to and from your plant, and you felt the Dyno Electric Cart could do this for you." (You could pause and let him answer or say, "Is that correct?").

From the buyer's response to your question, you can quickly determine what to do. If an objection is raised, you can respond to it. If more information is asked for, you can provide it. If what you have said about your product has pleased the buyer, you simply ask for the order.

You should be cautious when uncovering a prospect's needs. Too many questions can alienate the prospect. Remember, many prospects do not want to initially open up to salespeople. Actually, some salespeople are uncomfortable with the need-satisfaction approach because they feel less in control of the selling situation than with a canned or formula presentation. A good point to remember is that you

Figure 7–7 Example of a Need Satisfaction Presentation

Salesperson: Mr. Pride you really have a large manufacturing facility. How large is it?

Buyer: We have approximately 50 acres under-roof, with our main production building being almost 25 acres under one roof. There are a total of six buildings used for production.

Salesperson: How far is it from your executive's offices here to your plant area? It looks like it must be two miles over to there.

Buyer: Well, it does, but it's only one mile.

Salesperson: How do your executives get over to the plant area?

Buyer: They walk over through our underground tunnel. Some walk on the road when we have good weather.

Salesperson: When they get to the plant area, how do they get around in the plant?

Buyer: Well, they walk or catch a ride on one of the small tractors the workers use in the plant.

Salesperson: Have your executives ever complained about their having to do all of that walking?

Buyer: All of the time!

Salesperson: What is it they don't like about their long walks?

Buyer: Well, I hear everything from "It wears out my shoe leather," to "It's hard on my pace-maker." The main complaints are the time it takes them and that some of the older executives are exhausted by the time they get back to their offices. Many people need to go over to the plant but don't.

Salesperson: It sounds as if your executives would have an interest in reducing their travel time and not having to exert so much energy. By doing so, doesn't it seem they would get to the plant as they need to, saving them time and energy and the company money?

Buyer: I guess so.

Salesperson: Mr. Pride, on the average how much salary would you say your executives make an hour?

Buyer: Maybe $20 an hour.

Salesperson: If I could show you how you can save your executive's time in getting to and from your plant, would you be interested?

Buyer: Yes, I would. [Now the salesperson moves into the presentation.]

are not a performer on a stage, but that rather, your job is to meet your prospect's needs—not your own. Eventually, you can learn to anticipate customer reactions to this presentation method and learn to welcome the challenge of the interaction between you and the buyer.

The Problem-Solution Presentation

In selling highly complex or technical products such as insurance, industrial equipment, accounting systems, office equipment, and computers, salespeople are often required to make several sales calls in order to develop a detailed analysis of a prospect's needs. After completing this analysis, the salesperson arrives at a solution to the prospect's problems and usually uses both a written analysis and an oral presentation. The **problem-solution presentation** usually consists of six steps:

1. Convincing the prospect to allow the salesperson to conduct the analysis.

2. Actually making the analysis.
3. Buyer and seller mutually agreeing upon the problems and determining that the buyer wants to solve them.
4. Preparing the proposal for a solution to the prospect's needs.
5. Preparing the sales presentation based upon the analysis and proposal.
6. Making the sales presentation.

The problem-solution presentation is a flexible, customized approach involving an in-depth study of a prospective buyer's needs, and requiring a well-planned presentation. The salesperson may find it necessary to present the proposal to a group of individuals. In some cases, a *selling team* may be required for the presentation of a technical, high-dollar investment solution to a problem. The salesperson may lead the interview, allowing team members to present information in their areas of expertise (such as computer software or financial analysis). Team selling requires an immense amount of coordinated interaction between sales, financial, and technical areas, offering a true challenge to the salesperson with managerial aspirations.

Step 3 cannot be overemphasized, for it is important to determine whether you and the prospect share the same perceptions of the buyer's needs and problems. You should be wary of saying, "My survey has shown these problems, and this is what I suggest you need to buy." Instead, you should develop a question approach to determine if the prospect believes them to be real and important problems. Once both of you agree upon the problems and you determine that the buyer is interested in solving them, you may proceed with your presentation.

Matt Suffoleto of IBM Uses the Problem-Solution Presentation Method

"A successful salesperson has expertise in the products he or she sells, as well as an in-depth knowledge of the customer's business. The salesperson often makes recommendations which alter the mainstream of the customer's business process. Recognizing the requirement for business skills, IBM provides training in both the technical aspects of our products, as well as their industrial application.

"My territory consists of manufacturing customers; hence I pride myself in understanding concepts such as inventory control, time phased requirements planning, and shop floor control. Typically, I work with customer user department and data processing people to do application surveys, and detailed justification analysis. After

(continued)

the background work is completed, I make proposals and presentations to educate the chain of decision makers on the IBM recommendations.

"Selling involves the transformation of the features of your product into benefits for the customer. The principal vehicles for that communication are the sales call, formal presentations, and proposals. The larger the magnitude of the sale, the more time and effort is spent on presentations and proposals. A proposal may range from a simple one page letter and attachment with prices, terms, and conditions, to multi-volume binders with detailed information on the product, including its use, detailed justification, implementation schedules, and contracts. The wide range of comprehensiveness implies an equal range in time commitment of the salesperson.

"Very few sales are made in a single call. At the first sales call the salesperson generally searches for additional information that needs to be brought back, analysis that needs to be done, or questions to be answered. These are opportunities to demonstrate responsiveness to the customer. Getting back to the customer in a very timely and professional manner is a way to build trust and confidence into a business relationship."

Which is the Best Presentation Method?

Each of the four sales presentations methods can be the best one when the method is properly matched with the *situation*. For example, the stimulus-response method can be used where time is short and the product is simple. Formula selling is effective in repeat purchases or when you know or have already determined the needs of the prospect. The need-satisfaction method is most appropriate where information needs to be first gathered from the prospect as is often the case in selling industrial products. Finally, the problem-solving presentation is excellent for selling high-cost technical products or services, and especially for system selling involving several sales calls and a business proposition. To help improve sales, the salesperson should understand and be able to use each method based upon each situation.

The Approach—Opening the Sales Presentation

Raleigh Johnson had spent days qualifying the prospect, arranging for an appointment, planning every aspect of the sales presentation and in the first 60 seconds of the sales presentation realized his chance of selling was excellent. He was quickly able to determine the prospect's needs and evoke attention and interest in his product because of the technique he used to begin the sales interview.

A buyer's reactions to the salesperson in the early minutes of the sales presentation are critical to a successful sale. This short time period is so important that it is treated as an individual step in selling referred to as the approach. Part of any approach is the prospect's first impression of you.

The First Impression of You Is Critical to Success

When you first meet your prospect, the initial impression you make is based on appearances. If this impression is favorable, your prospect is more likely to listen to you, but if it is not favorable, your prospect may erect communcation barriers that can be difficult to overcome.

The first impression is centered upon the image projected by your (1) appearance, and (2) attitude. Here are some suggestions on making a favorable first impression.

- Wear business clothes that are suitable and fairly conservative.
- Be neat in dress and grooming.
- Refrain from smoking, chewing gum, or drinking when in your prospect's office.
- Keep an erect posture to project confidence.
- Leave all unnecessary materials outside the office (overcoat, umbrella, or newspaper).
- If possible, sit down. Should the prospect not offer a chair, ask, "May I sit here?"
- Be enthusiastic and positive toward the interview.
- Smile, always smile! (Try and be sincere with your smile; it will aid you in being enthusiastic and positive toward your prospect.)
- Do not apologize for taking the prospect's time.
- Do not imply that you were just passing by and that the sales call was not planned.
- Maintain eye contact with the prospect.
- If the prospect offers to shake hands do so with a firm, positive grip, while continuing to maintain eye contact.
- If possible, before the interview, learn how to pronounce your prospect's name correctly, and use it throughout the interview. Should the prospect introduce you to other people, remember their names by using the five ways to remember names shown in Figure 7–8.

Figure 7-8 Five Ways to Remember Prospect's Name

1. Be sure to hear the person's name and use it, "It's good to meet you, Mr. Firestone."
2. Spell it out in your mind, or if it is an unusual name, ask the person to spell the name.
3. Relate the name to something you are familiar with, such as relating the name Firestone to Firestone automobile tires.
4. Use the name in the conversation.
5. Repeat the name at the end of the conversation, such as "Goodbye, Mr. Firestone."

Like an actor, the salesperson must learn how to project and maintain a positive, confident, and enthusiastic first impression no matter what mood the prospect is in when first encountering salesperson.

The Situational Approach

The situation you face will determine what approach technique you should use to begin your sales presentation. The situation is dictated by a number of variables, which only you can truly identify. Some of the more common situational variables are:

- The type of *product* you are selling.
- Whether this is a *repeat call* on the same person.
- Your degree of knowledge about the *customer's needs*.
- The *time* you have in which to make your sales presentation.
- Whether the customer *is aware of a problem.*
- Your sales call *objective*.
- The *type of approach* you believe will be well received by the customer.
- Your *customer benefit plan.*

These factors must be examined and assigned a degree of importance before you ever step into your customer's office. This approach selection process can greatly aid you in making a satisfactory impression.

Approach Techniques and Objectives.   Approach techniques can be grouped into three general categories: (1) opening with a statement; (2) opening with a demonstration; and (3) opening with a question or questions.

Your choice of approach technique depends upon which of the four sales presentation methods you have selected based upon your situation and sales presentation plan. Figure 7-9 presents one way of determining which approach technique to use. Using questions in a sales approach is feasible with any of the four presentation methods, whereas statements and demonstrations typically should be reserved for either the stimulus-response or formula sales presentation methods. Because of their customer-oriented nature, the need-satisfaction and problem-solving sales presentation methods should always employ questions at the outset.

Figure 7–9 The Approach Technique to Use for Each of the Four Sales Presentation Methods

Sales Presentation Methods	Approach Techniques		
	Statement	Demonstration	Questions
Memorized ("canned")	✓	✓	✓
Formula (persuasive selling)	✓	✓	✓
Need-satisfaction			✓
Problem-solving			✓

The following three sections will review each of these approach techniques, giving examples to increase understanding of their use and particular beneficial aspects.

Both the "statement" and "demonstration" approach techniques have three basic objectives. The objectives are:

1. To capture the *attention* of the prospect.
2. To stimulate the prospect's *interest*.
3. To provide a *transition* into the sales presentation.

You should imagine the prospect silently asking three questions: (1) "Shall I see this person?" (2) "Shall I listen, talk with, and devote more time to this person?" and (3) "What's in it for *me?*" The answers to these questions will help determine the outcome of the sale. If you choose to use either of these two approaches, you should create a statement or demonstration approach which will cause the prospect to say yes to each of these three questions.

The sales approach can be a frightening, lonely, heart-stopping experience. It can easily lead to ego-bruising rejection. Your challenge is to move the prospect from an often cold, indifferent, or sometimes even hostile frame of mind to an aroused excitement about the product. By quickly obtaining the prospect's attention and interest, the conversation can make a smooth transition into the presentation which greatly improves the probability of making the sale by allowing you to quickly lead into the sales presentation.

The use of questions in your approach should have the following objectives:

1. To *uncover* the needs or problems *important* to the prospect.
2. To determine if the prospect wishes to *fulfill* these needs or *solve* these problems.
3. To have the prospect *tell you* about these needs or problems, and the intention to do something about them.

Figure 7–10 The Approach Leads Quickly into the Sales Presentation

Approach ▶ Sales presentation

Since people buy to fulfill needs or solve problems, the use of questions in your approach is preferable to the use of statements or demonstrations. Questions allow you to uncover needs, whereas statements and demonstrations are used when you assume you already know the prospect's needs. However, all three approach techniques can be used by the salesperson in the proper situation.

Openings with Statements

Opening statements can be effective if properly planned, especially if the salesperson has been able to uncover the prospect's needs before entering the office. Four statement approaches frequently used are the: (1) introductory approach; (2) complimentary approach; (3) referral approach; and (4) premium approach.

Introductory Approach.   The **introductory approach** is the most common and the least powerful because it does little to capture the prospect's attention and interest. It opens with the salesperson's name and business: "Hello, Ms. Crompton, my name is John Gladstone, representing the Pierce Chemical Company."

The introductory approach is needed when meeting a prospect for the first time. In most cases, though, the introductory approach should be used in conjunction with another approach. This additional approach could quite easily be the complimentary approach.

Complimentary Approach.   Everyone likes a compliment. If the **complimentary approach** is sincere, it can be an effective beginning to a sales interview.

> "Ms. Rosenberg, you certainly have a thriving restaurant business. I have enjoyed eating many lunches here. You know, I have several products that could make your business even better and make things easier for you and your employees."

> "Mr. Davidson, I was just visiting with your boss who commented that you were doing a good job in keeping the company's printing costs down. I have a couple of ideas which may help you further reduce your costs!"

Sometimes a suitable compliment is not in order, or just cannot be generated. Another way to get the buyer's attention is to mention a mutual acquaintance as a reference.

Referral Approach.   The use of another person's name can be effective if the prospect respects that person. It is important to remember, however that the **referral approach** can have a negative effect if the prospect does not like the person.

> "Ms. Rosenburg, my name is Carlos Ramirez, with the Restaurant Supply Corporation. When I talked to your brother last week, he

wanted me to give you the opportunity to see our line of paper products for your restaurant."

"Hello, Mr. Gillespie—Linda Crawford suggested that I contact you concerning our new Xerox table copier."

One salesperson tells of asking the customer to tape-record a brief introduction to a friend. When calling on the friend, the salesperson placed the recorder on the desk and said, "Amos McDonald has a message for you, Ms. James . . . let's listen."

Few people can obtain a reference for every prospect they intend to contact (this may be especially true for a beginning salesperson). Even if you don't know "all the right people," you can still get on track by offering the buyer something for nothing—a premium.

Premium Approach.   Everyone likes to receive something free. When appropriate you can use free samples and novelty items as a **premium approach.**

> Early in the morning of her first day on a new campus, one textbook salesperson makes a practice of leaving a dozen doughnuts in the faculty lounge with her card stapled to the box. She claims that prospects actually come looking for her!

> "Mr. Jones, here is a beautiful desk calendar with your name engraved on it. Each month I will place a new calendar in the holder which, by the way, will feature one of our products. This month's calendar, for example, features our lubricating oil."

> "Ms. Rogers, this high-quality Fuller hair brush is yours, free, for just giving me five minutes of your time."

> "Ms. McCall [*handing her the product to examine*] I want to leave samples for you, your cosmetic representatives, and your best customers of Revlon's newest addition to our perfume line."

Creative use of premiums can be an effective sales approach. Demonstrations can also leave a favorable impression with a prospect.

Demonstration Openings

Openings using demonstrations and dramatics can be effective, because of their ability to force the prospect into participating in the interview. Of the two methods discussed here, the product approach is more frequently used by itself or in combination with statements and questions.

Product Approach.   The salesperson places the product on the counter or hands it to the customer, saying nothing. The salesperson waits for the prospect to begin the conversation. The **product approach** is useful if the product is new, unique, colorful, or if it is an existing product that has been noticeably changed.

If, for example, Pepsi-Cola completely changed the shape of its bottle and label, the salesperson would simply hand the new product to the retail buyer and wait for a reaction. In marketing a new pocket calculator for college students, the Texas Instruments salesperson might simply lay the product on the buyer's desk and wait. It is possible to effectively combine the product approach with the showmanship approach.

Showmanship Approach. The **showmanship approach** involves doing something unusual to catch the prospect's attention and interest. This should be done carefully so that the approach does not backfire, which can happen if the demonstration does not work or is so flamboyant as to be inappropriate for the situation.

"Ms. Rosenburg, our paper plates are the strongest on the market, making them drip-free, a quality your customers will appreciate." [*The salesperson places a paper plate on her lap and pours cooking grease or motor oil onto it while speaking to the prospect.*]

As she hands the buyer a plate from a new line of china, she lets it drop onto the floor. It does not break. While picking it up, she says, "Our new breakthrough in treating quality china will revolutionize the industry. Your customers, especially new brides, will love this feature. Don't you think so?

The salesperson selling Super Glue would repeat the television advertisement for the prospect. In the prospect's office, the salesperson glues two objects together, such as a broken handle back onto a coffee cup, waits one minute, hands the cup to the buyer for a test, and then begins the sales presentation. The mended cup can be left with the buyer as a gift and a reminder.

The life insurance salesperson hands the prospect a bunch of daisies saying, "Steve, when you're pushing daisies, what will your family be doing?" [This might be too tactless to use on anyone except a close friend, but you get the picture.]

A Successful Saleswoman's Approach

Sheila Fisher, a middle-aged widow, lived in California for 25 years before returning to her native England three years ago. She wanted to move back to California and wanted a home of her own. She had some cash available for a down payment, but her income was fixed and she was not sure what she could make if she went back to work as a hair stylist. However, she did know what she did not want. "I don't want exotic financing," Sheila told Vikki Morrison, Century 21's top salesperson. "I want to keep my life simple. I don't want to get in a situation where, in three years, I'll have to sell."

This encounter was their first face-to-face meeting. Vikki has a formula for such situations. In a previous telephone conversation, she had gotten a rough idea of what Ms. Fisher wanted: A three-bedroom home with a formal dining room and assumable financing that will keep her monthly payments at or below $600 after a $50,000 down payment.

Before the meeting, Vikki had combed the multiple listing book for condominiums that matched Fisher's needs and compiled a list of addresses. If she had viewed the home before, she simply called the owners to warn them she would be dropping in. If she hadn't visited the home Vikki put it on the list of homes to screen before Ms. Fisher's arrival.

By the time the two women met, Vikki had mapped out a tour of five homes, building up to a spacious condominium with a $144,000 price tag that the realtor thought was the best of the lot. But she didn't really expect to sell any of them that day.

"This is our getting-acquainted day," Vikki told Sheila as she turned into traffic on busy Golden West Avenue. "So be very blunt, very up-front. That's the only way I can learn your tastes. Okay?"

Ms. Fisher agreed. She had already decided that she liked Vikki Morrison, the fourth real estate agent whom she had consulted.

"I think she's listening to me," she confided in Vikki's absence. "I think she understands."

Opening with Questions

Questions are the most common openers because they allow the salesperson to better determine the prospect's needs, and force the prospect to participate in the sales interview. Only questions that the salesperson knows from experience and preplanning will receive a positive reaction from the buyer should be used, since a negative reaction would be hard to overcome.

Like opening statements, opening questions can be synthesized to suit a number of selling situations. In the following sections, several basic questioning approaches will be introduced. This listing is by no means exclusive, but serves only to introduce the reader to a smattering of questioning frameworks. With experience, a salesperson can develop a knack for determining what question to ask what prospect.

Customer Benefit Approach.   Using this approach, the salesperson asks a question that implies that the product will benefit the prospect. If it is their initial meeting the salesperson can include both his (her) and the company's name.

"Hi, I'm Charles Foster of ABC Shipping and Storage Company! Mr. McDaniel, would you be interested in a new storage and shipping container that will reduce your transfer costs by 10 to 20 percent?"

"Would you be interested in saving 20 percent on the purchase of our IBM typewriters?"

"Ms. Johnson, did you know that several thousand companies—like yours—have saved 10 to 20 percent on their manufacturing cost as described in this *Newsweek* article? (continue, not waiting for a response) They did it by installing our computerized assembly system! Is that of interest to you?"

Your **customer benefit approach** statement should be carefully construction so as to anticipate the buyer's response. However, you should always be prepared for the unexpected, as when the salesperson said, "This office machine will pay for itself in no time at all." "Fine," the buyer said. "As soon as it does, send it to us."

A customer benefit approach can also be implemented through the use of a direct statement of product benefits. While the customer benefit approach begins with a question, it can be used with a statement showing how the product can benefit the prospect. The three customer benefit questions shown earlier can be converted into benefit statements.

"Mr. McDaniel, I want to talk with you about our new storage and shipping container which will reduce your costs by 10 to 20 percent."

"I'm here to show you how to save 20 percent on the purchase of our IBM typewriters."

"Ms. Johnson, several thousand companies—like yours—have saved 10 to 20 percent on their manufacturing cost by installing our computerized assembly system! I'd like fifteen minutes of your time to show you how we can reduce your manufacturing costs."

Benefit statements are useful in situations where you are aware of the prospect's or customer's critical needs and know you have a short time to make your presentation. However, to assure a positive atmosphere, statements can be followed by a short question . . . "Is that of interest to you?" . . . to help insure that the benefits are important to the buyer. Even if you know of the buyer's interest, a positive response . . . "Yes" . . . to your question is a commitment; the buyer will listen to your presentation because of the possible benefits offered by your product.

Furthermore, you can use the buyer's response to this question as a reference point, something to refer to, throughout your presentation. Continuation of an earlier example will illustrate the use of a reference point.

"Mr. McDaniel, earlier you mentioned your interest in reducing your shipping cost. The [Now mention your product's feature.] enables you to [Now discuss your product's advantages.] And the benefit to you is the reduction of manufacturing costs."

Sometimes salespeople have to prepare an approach that temporarily baffles a prospect. One of the more common ways of baffling entails the exploitation of human curiosity.

Curiosity Approach. The salesperson asks a question or does something to make the prospect **curious** about the product or service. For example, a salesperson for Richard D. Irwin, Inc., the company that publishes this text, might say,

"Do you know why college professors such as yourself have made this [as she hands the book to the prospect] the best-selling book about how to sell on the market?"

"Do you know why a recent *Newsweek* article described our new computerized assembly system as revolutionary?" [The salesperson briefly displays the *Newsweek* issue, then puts it away before the customer can request to look at the article. Interrupting a sales presentation by urging a prospect to review an article would lose the prospect's attention for the rest of the interview.]

One manufacturer's salesperson sent a telegram to a customer saying, "Tomorrow is the big day for you and your company." When the salesperson arrived for the interview, the prospect could not wait to find out what the salesperson's message meant.

In calling on a male buyer who liked to smoke cigars, a consumer goods saleswoman set a cigar box on the buyer's desk. After some chat, the buyer said, "What's in the box?" The saleswoman handed the box to the buyer and said, "Open it." Inside was one of her products which she wanted to sell him. After he bought, she gave him the cigars. Selling can be fun, especially if the salesperson enjoys being creative.

Opinion Approach. People are usually flattered when asked their **opinion** on a subject. Most prospects are happy to discuss their needs if asked correctly. Here are some examples:

"I'm new at this business, so I wonder if you could help me? My company says our Model 100 copier is the best product on the market for the money. What do you think?"

"Mr. Jackson, I've been trying to sell you for months on using our products. What is your honest opinion about our line of electric motors?"

This technique is especially good for the new salesperson because it shows that you value the buyer's opinion. Opinion questioning also shows that you are not going to attempt to challenge a potential buyer's expertise by spouting a memorized pitch.

Shock Approach. As its title implies, the **shock approach** uses a question designed to make the prospect think seriously about a subject related to the salesperson's product. For example:

> "Did you know that you have a 20 percent chance of having a heart attack this year?" (Life insurance.)

> "Did you know that home burglary, according to the FBI, has increased this year by 15 percent over last year?" (Alarm system.)

> "Shoplifting costs store owners millions of dollars each year! Did you know that there is a good chance you have a shoplifter in your store right now?" (Store cameras and mirrors.)

This type of question must be used carefully, as some prospects may feel you are merely trying to pressure them into a purchase by making alarming remarks.

Multiple Question Approach (SPIN). In many selling situations it is wise to use questions to determine the prospect's needs. A series of questions can be an effective sales interview opener. Multiple questions force the prospect to immediately participate in the sales interview, and quickly develop two-way communication. Carefully listening to the prospect's needs will aid in determining what features, advantages, and benefits to use in the sales presentation itself.

A relatively new method of using multiple questions is the **SPIN approach,** which involves using a series of four types of questions in a specific sequence.[3] SPIN stands for: (1) *S*ituation, (2) *P*roblem, (3) *I*mplication, and (4) *N*eed-payoff questions. Since SPIN requires questions to be asked in their proper sequence, its steps will be carefully described in the following four sections.

Step 1. *Situation* questions. Ask about the prospect's general situation as it relates to your product.

Industrial examples:	Dyno Electric Cart salesperson to purchasing agent: "How large are your manufacturing plant facilities?"
	IBM typewriter salesperson to purchasing agent: "How many secretaries do you have in your company?"
Consumer examples:	Real estate salesperson to prospect: "How many people do you have in your family?"
	Appliance salesperson selling a microwave oven to prospect: "Do you like to cook?" "Do you and your family eat out much?"

As the name of this question implies, the salesperson first asks a "situation" question that helps provide a general understanding of the buyer's needs. Situation questioning allows the salesperson to move smoothly into questions on specific problem areas. Also, beginning an approach using specific questions may make the prospect uncomfortable and unwilling to talk to you about problems, and may even deny them. These are warm-up questions enabling you to get a better understanding of the prospect's business.

Step 2. *Problem questions.* Ask about specific problems, dissatisfactions, or difficulties perceived by the prospect relative to your situation question.

Industrial examples: Dyno Electric Cart salesperson to purchasing agent: "Have your executives ever complained about having to do so much walking in and around the plant?"

IBM typewriter salesperson to purchasing agent: "Do your Royal typewriters do all that your secretaries want them to do?" (You may have previously asked the secretaries this question and know that they are dissatisfied.)

Consumer examples: Real estate salesperson to prospect: "Has your family grown so that you need more space?"

Appliance salesperson selling microwave oven to prospect, "Are you happy with your present oven?" "Are there times when you must quickly prepare meals?"

Problem questions should be asked early in the presentation to bring out the needs or problems of the prospect. Your goal is to have the prospect admit, "Yes, I do have a problem."

To maximize your chance of making the sale, you must determine which of the prospect's needs or problems are important (explicit needs) and which are unimportant. The more explicit needs you can discover, the more vividly you can relate your products' benefits to areas the prospect is actually interested in, and thus, the higher your probability of making the sale.

An important or explicit need or problem is recognized as such by the prospect. There is a desire to fulfill the need or solve the problem. Problem questions are useful in developing explicit needs.

If the prospect should state a specific need after your situation or problem questions, do not move directly into your sales presentation.

Continue with the next two steps to increase your chance of making the sale. A prospect may sometimes not appreciate all the ramifications of a problem.

Step 3. *I*mplication questions. Ask about the implications of the prospect's problems or how a problem affects various related operational aspects of a home, life, or business.

Industrial examples: Dyno Electric Cart salesperson to purchasing agent: "It sounds as if your executives would have an interest in reducing their travel time and not having to exert so much energy in transit. Doesn't it seem that if they could do so, they would get to the plant as quickly as they need to, saving themselves time and energy, and the company money?"

IBM typewriter salesperson to purchasing agent: "Does this problem mean your secretaries are not as efficient as they should be, thus increasing your costs per page typed?"

Consumer examples: Real estate salesperson to prospect: "So with the new baby and your needing a room as an office in your home, what problems does your present residence create for you?"

Appliance salesperson to prospect: "With both of you working, does your present kitchen oven mean . . . inconvenience for you?" ". . . that you have to eat out more than you want to?" ". . . that you have to eat junk foods instead of well-balanced meals?"

Implication questions seek to help the prospect realize the true dimensions of a problem. The phrasing of the question is important in getting the prospect to discuss problems or areas for improvement, and fixes them in the prospect's mind. In this situation, the prospect is personally motivated to fulfill this need or solve this problem.

If possible attach a "bottom line" figure to the implication question. You want the prospect to state, or agree with you, that the implications of the problem are causing such things as: production slowdowns of one percent resulting in increased costs of 25 cents per unit; increased reproduction costs of one cent per copy; loss of customers; or hiring added personnel to make service calls costing an extra $500 a week.

You use this hard data later in your discussion of the business proposition. Using the prospect's data you can show how your product can influence his costs, productivity, or customers.

Step 4. *N*eed-payoff questions. Ask if the prospect has an important, explicit need.

Industrial examples: Dyno Electric Cart salesperson to purchasing agent: "If I could show you how you can solve your executive's problems in getting to and from your plant, and at the same time save your company money, would you have an interest?

IBM office products salesperson to purchasing agent: "Would you be interested in a method to improve your secretaries' efficiency at a lower cost than you now incur?"

Consumer examples: Real estate salesperson to prospect: "If I could show you how to cover your space problems at the same cost per square foot, would you be interested?

Appliance salesperson to prospect: "Do you need a convenient way to prepare well-balanced, nutritious meals at home?"

Phrasing the need-payoff question is the same as opening with a benefit statement. However, in using the SPIN approach, the prospect defines the need. If the prospect responds positively to the need-payoff questions, you know this is an important (explicit) need. You may have to repeat the P-I-N questions to fully develop all of the prospect's important needs.

The Procter & Gamble, Tide, sales presentation shown in Figure 7–5 is an example of using the P-I-N approach for a customer with whom you are very familiar. Let's say your customer says yes to your need-payoff question: "If we could determine how much volume you're missing, I think you'd be willing to make space for the large size, wouldn't you?" Then you move directly into your brief sales presentation.

If the answer is No, you know that this is not an important need. Start over again by asking *P*roblem, *I*mplication, and *N*eed-payoff questions to determine important needs.

Product Not Mentioned in SPIN Approach. As you see from the SPIN examples, the product is not mentioned in the approach. This allows you to develop the prospect's need without revealing exactly what you are selling. When a salesperson first walks into the buyer's office and says, "I want to talk about Product X," the chances of a negative response greatly increase because the buyer does not perceive a need for the product. SPIN questions allow you to better determine the buyer's needs before you begin your presentation.

The Use of Questions Results in Sales Success

Since this is the first chapter in which you have been exposed to the use of questioning techniques, and since properly questioning your prospect or customer is so important to your sales success, you should now be exposed to the many uses and types of questions.

Asking questions, sometimes called probes, is an excellent technique for: (1) obtaining information from the prospect, (2) developing two-way communication, and (3) increasing prospect participation.

When using questions in selling, you need to know or to be able to anticipate the answer you want to your question. Once you know the answer you want, you can develop the question. This procedure can apply to requesting information you do not have, and to confirming information you already know.

An ideal question is one a prospect is willing and able to answer. Only questions which can help make the sale should be asked, so use questions sparingly and wisely.

Why would asking a question get the prospect's attention? Because to give an answer a prospect must think about the topic to some extent. There are four basic categories of questions which can be used at any point during your presentation. These categories are: (1) direct, (2) nondirective, (3) rephrasing, and (4) redirect questions.

The Direct Question

The **"direct" question** can be answered with very few words. A simple yes or no will answer most direct questions. They are especially useful in moving a customer toward a specific topic. Examples the salesperson might use are: "Mr. Berger, are you interested in saving 20 percent on your manufacturing costs?" or, "Reducing manufacturing costs are important, aren't they?" You should be able to anticipate a yes response from these questions.

Never phrase the direct question as a direct negative-no question. A *direct negative-no question* is any question that can be answered in a manner that cuts you completely off. The retail salesperson says, "May I help you?" and the reply usually is, "No, I'm just looking." It's like hanging up the telephone on you. You are completely cut off.

Other types of direct questions ask "what kind" or "how many?" These questions also ask for a limited, short answer from the prospect. The implication and need-payoff questions used in SPIN are examples of direct questions used for the approach.

However, the answer to a direct question does not really tell you much, because there is little feedback involved. You may need more information to determine the buyer's needs and problems, especially if you could not find them out before making the sales call. Nondirective questioning can aid you in your quest for information.

The Nondirective Question

To open up two-way communication, the salesperson can use an open-ended or **nondirective question** by beginning the question with one of six words: Who, what, where, when, how, and why. Examples include:

■ Who will use this product?

■ What features are you looking for in a product like this?

■ Where will you use this product?

■ When will you need the product?

■ How often will you use the product?

■ Why do you need or want to buy this type of product?

One word questions such as "Oh?" or "Really?" can also be useful in some situations. One-word questions should be said so that the tone increases or is emphasized: "Oh?!" This prompts the customer to continue talking. Try it—it works.

To practice using the open-ended questioning technique, ask a friend a question—any question—beginning with one of these six words, or use a one-word question, and see what answer you get. Chances are, the response will consist of several sentences. In a selling situation, this type of response allows the salesperson to better determine the prospect's needs.

The purpose of using a nondirective question is to obtain unknown or additional information, and to draw out clues to hidden or future needs and problems and to leave the situation open for free discussion of what is on the customer's mind. Situation and implication questions are examples of the nondirective question.

The Rephrasing Question

The third type of question is called a **rephrasing question.** At times, the prospect's meaning is not clearly stated. In this situation, if appropriate, the salesperson might say:

Are you saying that price is the most important thing you are interested in? (sincerely, not too aggressively)

Then what you are saying is, if I can improve the delivery time you would be interested in buying?

This form of restatement allows for clarification of meaning and determination of the prospect's needs. If the prospect answers yes to the second question, you would work out a way to improve delivery. Should no be the answer to the delivery question, you know delivery time is not an important buying motive, and can continue to probe for the true problem.

The Redirect Question

The fourth type of question is the **redirect question.** This is used to "redirect" the prospect to selling points which both parties agree upon. There are always areas of agreement between buyer and seller even if the prospect is opposed to purchasing the product. The redirect question is an excellent alternative or backup opener. An example will clarify the concept of redirective questioning.

Imagine you walk into a prospect's office, introduce yourself, and get this response, "I'm sorry, but there is no use in us talking. We are satisfied with our present suppliers. Thanks for coming by." Respond by replacing your planned opener with a redirecting question. You might say:

We do agree that having a supplier that can reduce your costs is important.

You will agree that manufacturers must use the most cost efficient equipment to stay competitive these days, wouldn't you?

Wouldn't you agree that you need to continually find new ways to increase your company's sales?

Using a redirect question moves the conversation from a negative position to a positive or neutral one, while reestablishing communications between two people. The ability to redirect a seemingly terminated conversation through the use of a well-placed question may impress the prospect simply by showing that you are not a run-of-the-mill order taker, but a professional salesperson who sincerely believes in the beneficial qualities of your product.

Three Rules for Using Questions

The first rule is to use only questions that you can anticipate the answer to or that will not lead you into a situation from which you cannot escape. While questions are a powerful selling technique, they can easily backfire on you.

The second rule in using a question is to pause or wait after submitting a question to allow the prospect time to respond to it. Waiting for an answer to a well-planned question is sometimes an excruciating process—seconds may seem like minutes. A salesperson must allow the prospect time to consider the question, and hope for a response. Failing to allow a prospect enough time defeats the major purpose of questioning, which is to establish two-way communication between the prospect and the salesperson.

The third rule is to listen. Many salespeople are so intent on talking that they forget to listen to what the prospect says (or disregard his nonverbal signals). Salespeople need to listen consciously to prospects so that they can ask intelligent, meaningful questions that will aid both themselves and their prospects in determining what needs and problems exist and how to solve them. Prospects appreciate a good listener and view a willingness to listen as an indication that the salesperson is truly interested in their situation.

Keep Quiet and Get the Order

Dennis DeMaria, Branch Manager, Westvaco, Folcroft, PA says "One of the biggest single weapons you as a salesperson can use in getting an order from a customer or prospect is keeping quiet and patiently waiting for the buyer to answer your questions. A general rule in the selling profession is that the person who asks the questions is the person who has control of the interview. The information obtained from asking questions is the necessary ammunition you use to find the buyer's likes, dislikes, hot buttons and areas to avoid. This valuable information also informs the salesperson whether the customer is ready to buy or whether he or she should continue selling.

"Experience has shown that salespeople *do* ask questions but they forget the most important part of this sales principle: *after you ask a question you must be patient, don't talk and let the buyer answer.* It does not matter how long it takes for the buyer to respond, keep quiet and wait for the answer. Remember, the first person to speak after a question has been asked, loses."[4]

He Is Still Not Listening?

What happens when you give your best opening approach, and as you continue to talk you realize your prospect is not listening? What about prospects who open mail, who fold their arms while looking at the wall or seem to be looking beyond you into the hallway, or who even make telephone calls in your presence?

This is the time to use one of your alternative openers which will tune him into your message. The prospect must be forced to participate in the talk by using either the question or demonstration approach. By handing the person something, showing him something, or asking a question, attention can be briefly recaptured, no matter how indifferent a prospect is to your presence.

If you can overcome such preoccupation or indifference in the early minutes of your interview by quickly capturing the prospect's attention and interest, the probability of your making a sale will greatly improve. This is why the approach is so important to the success of a sales call.

It is crucial that you never become flustered or confused when a communication problem arises during your approach. As was mentioned earlier, the salesperson who can deftly capture another person's imagination earns the right to a prospect's full attention and interest. Your prospect should not be handled as an adversary, for in that type of situation you will seldom, if ever, gain the sale.

You Need to Be Flexible on Your Approach

Picture yourself as a salesperson getting ready to come face-to-face with an important prospect, Ellen Myerson. You have planned exactly what to say in the sales presentation; but how can you be sure to get Ms. Myerson to listen to your sales presentation? You realize she is busy and may be indifferent to your being in the office; she probably is preoccupied with her own business-related situation and several of your competitors may already have seen her today.

You have planned to open your presentation with a statement on how successful your memory typewriter has been in helping secretaries save time and eliminate errors in their typing. When you enter the office, Ms. Myerson comments on how efficient her secretaries are and how they produce error-free work. From her remarks, you quickly determine that your planned statement approach is inappropriate. What do you do now?

You might begin by remarking how lucky she is to have such conscientious secretaries, and then proceed into the SPIN question approach, first asking questions to determine general problems that she may have, and then using further questions to uncover specific problem areas she might like to solve. Once you have determined specific problems, you could ascertain whether they are important enough for her to want to solve them in the near future. If so, you can make a statement which summarizes how your product's benefits will solve her critical needs, and test for a positive response. A positive response will allow you to conditionally move into your sales presentation.

You should always be prepared to change any part of your sales presentation to meet the particular characteristics of a specific selling situation or environment.

Summary of Major Selling Issues

Prospects want to talk with you when they believe that you will directly benefit them. Your knowledge of your product, and an appreciation of your prospects and their situation should aid you in developing a presentation which is keyed to your prospects and their needs and problems.

Depending on your product type, the number of sales calls that you have to make each day, and the type of prospects that you are calling on, you can develop a sales presentation. Simpler products which may be applicable to a number of prospects can be presented using a memorized or formula type of presentation, while more complex, customer-specific items require a need-satisfaction or problem-solution type of presentation. Having decided upon a basic mode of sales presentation, you are ready to concentrate on developing a sales approach.

As the first real step in your sales presentation, your approach is an extremely critical factor. To assure your prospects' attention and interest during a memorized or formula mode of presentation, you may want to use a statement or demonstration approach. In more technically oriented situations where you and the prospects must agree upon needs and problems, a questioning approach (SPIN, for instance) is in order. Generally, in developing your approach you should imagine your prospects asking themselves: "Do I have time to listen, talk with, or devote to this person?" "What's in it for me?"

Words alone will not assure you a hearing. The first impression that you make on a prospect can negate your otherwise positive and sincere opening. To assure a favorable impression in most selling situations, you should generally dress conservatively, be well groomed, and act as though you are truly glad to meet this person.

Your approach statement should be especially designed for each prospect. You can choose to open with a statement, question, or demonstration by using any one of many techniques. Several alternative approaches should be held in readiness should you feel the need to alter your plans for a specific situation.

Carefully phrased questions are extremely useful at any point in a sales presentation. Questions should display a sincere interest in prospects and their situations. Skillfully handled questions employed in a sales approach can wrest a prospects' attention from distractions, centering it on you and your presentation. Questions can generally be of use in determining prospect wants and needs, and thereby increasing prospect participation in the sales presentation. Four basic types of questions discussed in this chapter are direct, nondirective, rephrasing, and redirect questions.

In using questions, you should be sure to ask the type of questions which you can anticipate the answer to. Also, remember to allow prospects time to completely answer the question and be sure to listen carefully to their answers for a guide as to how well you are progressing toward selling to them. Should you determine that your prospect is not listening to you, do something to recapture attention. Techniques such as offering something, standing up, or asking questions can refocus the prospect's attention long enough for you to move back into your presentation.

Review and Discussion Questions

1. What are the four sales presentation methods discussed in this chapter? Briefly explain each method. Be sure to include any similarities and differences in your answer.
2. Explain the reasons for using questions when making a sales presentation. Discuss the rules for questioning that should be followed by the salesperson when using questions.
3. What are three general categories of the approach? Give an example of each.
4. What is SPIN? Give an example of a salesperson using SPIN.
5. In each of the following instances determine if a direct, nondirective, rephrasing or redirect question is being used. Also, discuss each of the four types of questions.
   A. "Now let's see if I have this right, you are looking for a high quality product and price is no object?"
   B. "What type of clothes are you looking for?"
   C. "Are you interested in Model 101 or Model 921?"
   D. "Well, I can appreciate your beliefs, but you would agree that price is not the only thing to consider when buying a copier, wouldn't you?"
   E. "When would you like to have your new Xerox 9000 installed?"
   F. "Are you saying that *where* you go for vacation is more important than the cost of getting there?"
   G. "You would agree that saving time is important to a busy executive like yourself, wouldn't you?"
6. Which of the following approaches do you think is the best? Why?
   A. "Ms. Jones, in the past you've made it a practice to reduce the facings on heavy-duty household detergents in the winter months because of slower movement."

B. "Mr. Brown, you'll recall that last time I was in, you expressed concern over the fact that your store labor was running higher than the industry average of 8 percent of sales."

C. "Hi! I'm Jeanette Smith of Procter & Gamble, and I'd like to talk to you about Cheer. How's it selling?

7. Assume you are a salesperson for NCR (the National Cash Register Corporation) and you want to sell the owner/manager (Mr. Johnson) of a large independent supermarket your computerized customer check-out system. You have just met Mr. Johnson inside the front door of the supermarket, and after your initial introduction the conversation goes as follows:

Salesperson: Mr. Johnson, your customers are really backed up at your cash registers aren't they?

Buyer: Yeah, it's a real problem.

Salesperson: Do your checkers ever make mistakes when they are in a rush?

Buyer: They sure do!

Salesperson: Have you ever thought about shortening check-out time while reducing checker errors?

Buyer: Yes, but those methods are too expensive!

Salesperson: Does your supermarket generate over $1 million in sales each month?

Buyer: Oh, yes—why?

Salesperson: Would you be interested in discussing a method of decreasing customer check out time 100 percent and greatly lessening the number of errors made by your checkers, if I can show you that the costs of solving your problems will be more than offset by your savings?

A. Using the framework of the SPIN approach technique determine whether each of the above questions asked by the salesperson is a situation, problem, implication, or need-payoff question.

B. If Mr. Johnson says yes to your last question, what should you do next?

C. If Mr. Johnson says no to your last question, what should you do next?

8. As a salesman for Gatti's Electric Company, Cliff Defee is interested in selling John Bonham more of his portable electric generators. John is a construction foreman for a firm specializing in building large buildings such as shopping centers, office buildings and manufacturing plants. He is currently using three of Cliff's newest models. Cliff has just learned John will be building a new manufacturing plant. As Cliff examines the specifications for the new plant he feels John will require several additional generators. Two types of approaches Cliff might make are depicted in the following situations:

Situation A

Salesperson:	I see you got the Jonesville job.
Buyer:	Sure did.
Salesperson:	Are the specs ok?
Buyer:	Yes.
Salesperson:	Will you need more machines?
Buyer:	Yes, but not yours!

Situation B

Salesperson:	I understand you have three of our electric sets.
Buyer:	Yes I do.
Salesperson:	I'm sure you'll need additional units on your next job.
Buyer:	You're right, I will.
Salesperson:	Well, I've gone over your plant specifications and put together products just like you need.
Buyer:	What I don't *need* are any of your lousy generators.
Salesperson:	Well, that's impossible. It's a brand new design.
Buyer:	Sorry, I've got to go.

Questions:

(1) Briefly describe both approaches in situation A and B. In both situations Cliff finds himself in a tough spot. What should he do now?

(2) What type of approach could Cliff have made that would have allowed him to uncover John's dissatisfaction? Would the approach you are suggesting also be appropriate if John had been satisfied with the generators?

9. This is a cold call on the warehouse manager for Coats Western Wear, a retailer with four stores. You know most of the manager's work consists of deliveries from the warehouse to the four stores. Based on your past experience, you suspect that the volume of shipments to the warehouse fluctuates, with certain seasons of the year being extremely busy.

   As a salesperson for Hercules Shelfing, you want to sell the manager your heavy-duty gauge steel shelfing for use in the warehouse. Since this is a relatively small sale, you decide to go in cold, relying only on your questioning ability to uncover potential problems and make the prospect aware of them.

   You are now face-to-face with the warehouse manager. You have introduced yourself and after some small talk you feel it is time to begin your approach. Which of the following questions would serve your purpose best?

   A. Have you had any recent storage problems?

B. How do you take care of your extra storage need during your busy seasons such as Christmas?
C. Can you tell me a little about your storage problems?

Projects

1. Television advertisements are constructed to quickly capture the viewer's attention and interest in order to sell a product or service. Examine at least five commercials and report on the method each one used to get your attention, stimulate your interest, and move you from this attention-interest phase into discussing the product. Determine whether the first few seconds of the commercial related to the product's features, advantages, or benefits, and if so, how? You may wish to use a tape recorder.

2. Assume that you are scheduled for a 30-minute job interview next week with a representative of a company you are really interested in working for. How would you prepare for the interview, and what could you do during the first few minutes of the interview to get the recruiter interested in hiring you? Can you see any differences between this interview situation and the environment of a salesperson making a sales call on a prospect?

3. Assume you are a salesperson selling a consumer item, such as a wristwatch. Without any preparation, make a sales presentation to a friend. If possible, record your sales presentation on a tape recorder. Analyze the recording and determine the approximate conversation time of your prospect. On the basis of your analysis, which of the four sales presentation methods discussed in Chapter 7 did you use? How early in the sales presentation did your prospect begin to give you objections?

Cases

7-1   The Thompson Company

Before making a cold call on the Thompson Company, you did some research on the account. Barbara Thompson is both president and chief purchasing officer. In this dual capacity she is often so rushed that she is normally impatient with salespeople. She is known for her habit of quickly turning down the salesperson, and shutting off the discussion by turning and walking away. In looking over Ms. Thompson's operation, you notice that the inefficient metal shelving she is using in her warehouse is starting to collapse. Warehouse employees have attempted to remedy the situation by building wooden shelves and reinforcing the weakened metal shelves with lumber. They have also begun stacking boxes on the floor requiring much more space.

You recognize the importance of getting off to a fast start with Ms.

Thompson. You must capture her attention and interest quickly or she may not talk with you.

Question:

1. Which of the following attention-getters would you choose:
    A. "Ms. Thompson, I'd like to show you how Hercules shelving can save you both time and money."
    B. "Ms. Thompson, can you spare a few moments of your time to talk about new shelving for your warehouse?"
    C. "Ms. Thompson, how would you like to double your storage space?"

7–2   The Copy Corporation

Assume you are contacting the purchasing agent for office supplies of a large chain of retail department stores. After hearing that the company is opening 10 new stores, you determine they will need a copier for each store. Three months earlier you had sold this purchasing agent a lease agreement on two of your larger machines. The buyer wanted to try your machines in the company's new stores. If they liked them, you would get the account. Unknown to you, one of the machines was not working properly, causing the purchasing agent to be pressured by a store manager to replace it immediately. As you walk into the purchasing agent's office, you say:

Salesperson: I understand you are opening 10 new stores in the next six months.

Buyer: I don't know who told you, but you seem to know!

Salesperson: If you'll let me know when you want a copier at each store, I'll arrange for it to be there!

Buyer: Look, I don't want anymore of your lousy copiers! When the leases expire, I want you here to pick them up or I'll throw them out in the street! I've got a meeting now. I want to see you in three months.

Questions:

1. Describe this situation, commenting on what the salesperson did correctly and what was done incorrectly.
2. Develop another approach the salesperson could use to uncover the problems experienced by the purchasing agent.

7–3   Electronic Office Security Corporation

Ann Saroyan is a salesperson for the Electric Office Security Corporation. She sells industrial security systems that detect intruders and activate an alarm. When Ann first began selling, she used to make brief opening remarks to her prospects and then move quickly into her presentation. While this resulted in selling many of her security systems, she felt there must be a better method.

Ann began to analyze the reasons prospects would not buy. Her conclusion was that even after her presentation, prospects still did not feel they needed a security alarm system. She decided to develop a multiple-question approach which would allow her to determine the prospect's attitude toward a need for a security system. If the prospect does not initially feel a need for her product, she wants her approach to help convince the prospect of a need for a security system.

Ann developed and carefully rehearsed her new sales presentation. Her first sales call using her multiple-question approach was with a large accounting firm. She asked the receptionist who she should see and was referred to Joe Bell. After she waited 20 minutes, Mr. Bell asked her to come into his office. The conversation went like this:

Salesperson:	This is a beautiful old building, Mr. Bell, have you been here long?
Buyer:	About ten years. Before we moved here we were in one of those ugly glass and concrete towers. Now, you wanted to talk to me about office security.
Salesperson:	Yes, Mr. Bell. Tell me, do you have a burglar alarm system at present?
Buyer:	No we don't. We've never had a break-in here.
Salesperson:	I see. Could you tell me what's the most valuable item in your building?
Buyer:	Probably the computer.
Salesperson:	And is it fairly small?
Buyer:	Yes, amazingly, it's not much bigger than a typewriter.
Salesperson:	Would it be difficult to run your business without it—if it was stolen for example?
Buyer:	Oh yes, that would be quite awkward.
Salesperson:	Could you tell me a bit more about the problem you would face without your computer?
Buyer:	It would be inconvenient in the short term for our accounts and records people, but I suppose we could manage until our insurance gave us a replacement.
Salesperson:	But without a computer wouldn't your billing to customers suffer?
Buyer:	Not if we got the replacement quickly.
Salesperson:	You said the computer itself is insured. Do you happen to know if the software—the programs, your customer files—is insured too?
Buyer:	I don't believe so, our insurance covers the equipment only.

Salesperson:	And do you keep back-up records somewhere else—in the bank for example?
Buyer:	No we don't.
Salesperson:	Mr. Bell, in my experience, software isn't left behind after a theft. Wouldn't it be a very serious problem to you if that software was taken?
Buyer:	Yes, you're right, I suppose. Redevelopment would certainly cost a lot, the original programs were very expensive.
Salesperson:	And ever worse, because software development can take a long time, wouldn't that hold up your billing to customers?
Buyer:	We could always do that manually.
Salesperson:	What effect would that have on your processing costs?
Buyer:	I see your point. It would certainly be expensive to run a manual system as well as being inconvenient.
Salesperson:	And if you lost your software wouldn't it also make it harder to process customer orders?
Buyer:	Yes, I don't have much contact with that part of the business, but without order processing and stock control I'm sure we would grind to a halt in a matter of days.
Salesperson:	Are there any other items in the building which would be hard to replace if stolen?
Buyer:	Some of the furnishings. I would hate to lose this antique clock for example. In fact most of our furnishings would be very hard to replace in the same style.
Salesperson:	So if you lost them wouldn't it hurt the character of your office?
Buyer:	Yes, it would be damaging. We've built a gracious, civilized image here and without it we would be like dozens of other people in our business, the glass and concrete image.
Salesperson:	This may sound like an odd question, but how many doors do you have at ground level?
Buyer:	Let me see . . . uh . . . six.
Salesperson:	And ground level windows?
Buyer:	About ten or a dozen.
Salesperson:	So there's 16 or 18 points where a thief could break in, compared with one or two points in the average glass and concrete office. Doesn't that concern you?
Buyer:	Put that way it does. I suppose we're not very secure.

Questions:

1. Did the dialogue between buyer and seller seem natural to you?
2. Did the the salesperson use too many questions in her approach?
3. Analyze each of the salesperson's questions and state whether it is a situation, problem, implication, or need payoff type of question.

4. Analyze each of the buyer's responses to the salesperson's questions and state what type of need the salesperson's question uncovered. Was it an implied or minor need response or was it an explicit or important need response? Why?
5. How would you improve upon this salesperson's approach?
6. After the buyer's last statement which of the following would you do?
   A. Move into the presentation.
   B. Ask a problem question.
   C. Ask a need payoff question.
   D. Ask for an appointment to fully discuss your system.

8

Elements of Making a Great Presentation

Learning Objectives

1. To present the purpose and essential steps of the sales presentation.
2. To discuss the six elements of the sales presentation mix.
3. To review difficulties which may arise during the sales presentation.
4. To emphasize the need to properly diagnose the prospect in order to determine how to design the sales presentation.

Key Terms for Selling

Sales presentation mix	Metaphor
Logical reasoning	Analogy
Suggestive propositions	Proof statements
Prestige suggestion	Visuals
Autosuggestion	Dramatization
Direct suggestion	Demonstration
Indirect suggestion	Trial close
Counter suggestion	Interruptions
Paul Harvey dialogue	Competition
Simile	Detailed comparison

Profile

Linda M. Slaby-Baker
Quaker Oats

Graduating with a degree in nutrition from the University of Houston and working as a dietary supervisor for Hermann Hospital; as a food intern for the catering department of the Braesword Marriott Hotel; and as an order clerk for the produce department of the Fleming Foods Supermarket chain while in college, provided me with the academic and practical background for my professional career in the food industry. I began at Quaker Oats Company as a sales representative. After one year I was promoted to my current position of account supervisor.

As an account supervisor, my major areas of responsibility is Safeway Division in Houston. Safeway's Houston Division currently has 95 stores. The majority of these stores are in the Houston and Austin area. My responsibilities for Safeway include selling new and existing products, processing orders through Quaker's distribution center to Safeway's warehouse, being considered part of the merchandising team for the Safeway stores, and servicing the 95 individual stores.

Probably the most demanding part of my job is selling new products, and convincing Safeway to purchase more of my present products. To do this I must work hard on the preparation of a good sales presentation. This takes a number of hours to research facts and figures, analyze the information, and formulate a smooth, concise sales delivery.

It is important to incorporate into the presentation information of interest to each individual buyer. You must understand what features and benefits will interest your buyer, so you can direct your sales presentation in that angle. I once called on a buyer for an account of thirty stores who wanted only information on sales of my new items in his competitor's stores. My present buyers want information on merchandising deal support, statistical market information, and percentage of growth in the product category.

The most important thing to keep in mind during a presentation is to relax. Buyers must have confidence in your sales ability before they will accept your products. Your delivery should reflect calmness and self-confidence. Grocery buyers try to intimidate you with their vast knowledge of the industry. Often they will make demands that they know are impossible just to see how far you will go. The important thing to remember is do your homework and know your resources. If you are unable to answer all the buyer's questions, at least know where you can get the answers.

"Your presentation," says Linda Slaby-Baker, "should be a give-and-take of mutually beneficial information between you and your buyer. Probe your buyer with questions and then let him talk. Asking questions invites the buyer into your presentation and you quickly learn what he wants to hear. Buyers are human; they love to give their viewpoints. Ask the buyer for his input into the structuring of trade deals, the spending of advertising dollars, or how to increase the sales on a slow product.

"Visual aids bring life to your presentations. Visuals take the buyer's mind off you and on a graph, a chart, an advertisement, or a sample. Samples of the product are a must in consumer product presentation. Always leave a sample for the buyer to try.

"In my presentations, I use a number of bar graphs to illustrate the sales growth of products and indexing charts to illustrate shares of the market. Since I am in a business where the products are edible, I bring samples for my buyers to taste. To sell a new syrup, I brought in a small toaster and heated up some frozen waffles. I poured the syrup over the warm waffles and the buyer sampled the product in his office. The result was, I sold the syrup."

This chapter discusses the elements of the presentation. We begin with examining the purpose and essential steps in the presentation. Next, we review and expand upon presentation techniques used by salespeople such as Linda Slaby-Baker of the Quaker Oats Company. We end the chapter discussing the importance of the proper use of trial closes and difficulties which may arise in the presentation, along with the need to design your presentation around an individual situation and buyer.

The Purpose of the Presentation

Certainly the main goal of your presentation is to sell your product to your customer. However, we know that a prospective buyer considers many things before making a decision on which product to buy. As we have seen, the approach or first few minutes of the interview should be constructed to do such things as determine the prospect's need, capture attention and interest, while allowing for a smooth transition into the presentation.

The presentation itself is a continuation of the approach. What then should be the purpose of the presentation? Basically, the purpose of the presentation is to provide *knowledge* via the features, advantages, and benefits of your product, your marketing plan and business proposal. This allows the buyer to develop positive personal *attitudes* towards your product. The attitudes result in *desire* (or *need*) for the type of product you are selling. Your job, as a salesperson, is to convert that need into a want, and into the *belief* that your specific product is the best product to fulfill a certain need. Furthermore, you must convince the buyer that not only is your product the best but also you are the best source to buy from. When this occurs, your prospect has moved into the *conviction* stage of the mental buying process.

A real need is established, the buyer wants to fulfill that need, and there is a high probability your product is best for the purpose. This results in your making a sale, as shown in Figure 8–1. Whether to buy or not is a "choice decision," and you have provided the necessary information so that the customer chooses to buy from you.

An Example. Let us assume, for example, you are a salesperson for IBM and you wish to sell a company ten of your new memory electric typewriters costing $5,000 each. The prospect's company is at present using your competitor's electric typewriters which cost $3,000 each. How should you conceptualize the prospect's thought processes regarding whether to buy or not buy from you (as shown in Figure 8–1) in order to develop your presentation?

First, you should realize that the prospect has certain attitudes toward present equipment (typewriters). The prospect's job performance is

Figure 8–1 The Five Purposes of the Presentation

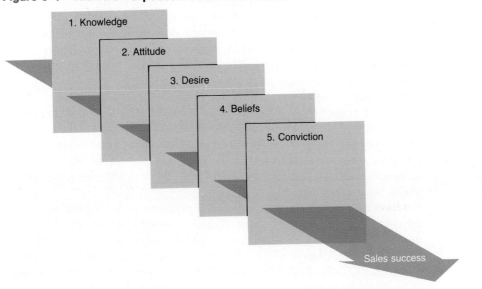

1. Knowledge
2. Attitude
3. Desire
4. Beliefs
5. Conviction

Sales success

judged according to the management of certain responsibilities. Thus improving the performance of company employees is important. However, the prospect knows nothing about you, your product, or your product's benefits. The prospect may feel that IBM products are good, high-quality products, but expensive. However, you cannot be sure about the buyer's present attitudes.

You should develop a SPIN approach to determine the buyer's attitudes toward typewriters in general and the memory typewriter specifically. Once you have gone through each of the four SPIN questions, and you feel more information about your product is in order, you begin your presentation.

You present the product information you feel will allow the buyer to develop a positive attitude toward your product. Next, using possibly a value analysis type of proposal, you show how a memory typewriter can increase a secretary's efficiency, reduce costs per item typed, and pay for itself in one year, using a return-on-investment technique. A positive reaction from your prospect indicates that the desire stage of the mental buying process has been reached. There is a need for some brand of memory typewriter.

Now you show why your IBM memory typewriter is the best solution to the buyer's need and show that you will provide service after the sale. A positive response on these two items now indicates that the prospect believes your product is best and that the "conviction" stage has been reached. The prospect wants to buy the IBM memory typewriter.

Up to this point, you have discussed your product's features, advantages, and benefits, your marketing plan, and your business proposition. You have *not* asked the prospect to buy. Rather, you have developed a presentation to lead the prospect through four of the five mental buying steps: the attention, interest, desire, and conviction steps. It may take you five minutes, two hours, or several weeks of repeat calls to move the prospect into the conviction stage.

You should realize that you must move the prospect into the conviction stage before a sale is made. So hold off asking the prospect to buy until the conviction stage. Otherwise, this usually results in objections and failure to listen to your whole story, thus fewer sales. The sales presentation has seven major steps. Each step is taken in order to logically and sequentially move the prospect into the conviction stage of the buying process.

When a person buys something, did you ever stop to think what is actually being purchased? Is the customer really buying your product? Not really. What is actually being bought is a mental picture of the future in which your product helps to fulfill some expectation. The buyer has mentally conceived of certain needs. Your presentation must create mental images which move your prospect into the conviction stage.

Figure 8–2 Three Essential Steps within the Presentation

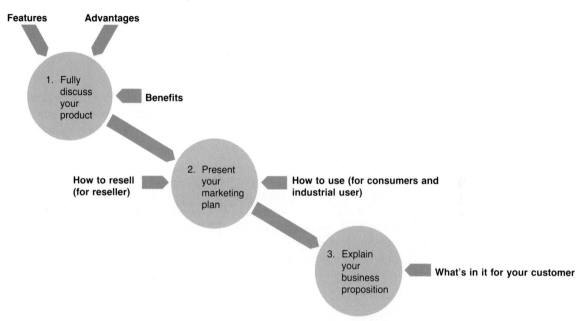

Three Essential Steps within the Presentation

No matter which of the four sales presentation methods you use, your presentation should follow the three essential steps shown in Figure 8–2.* These are:

Step 1:   Fully discuss the features, advantages, and *benefits* of your product. Tell your whole story.

Step 2:   Present your marketing plan. For your wholesalers and retailers, this is your suggestion on how they should *resell* the product. For end users, it is your suggestion on how they can *use* the product.

Step 3:   Explain your business proposition. This step relates the *value* of your product to its *cost*. It should be discussed last, since you always want to present your product's benefits and marketing plan relative to your product's price.

Ideally, information in each of these steps should be presented in such a manner as to create a visual picture in the prospect's mind of the benefits of the purchase. To do this, you should use persuasive communication and participation techniques, proof statements, visual

---
* These three steps are discussed in Chapter 6 under the topic "Customer Benefit Plan."

aids, dramatization, and demonstrations in your talk as you move through each of the three steps.

The Sales Presentation Mix

Salespeople sell different products in many different ways but all use six broad classes of presentation elements to some degree in their presentations to provide information in a meaningful way to the prospect or customer. For this reason, I refer to these elements as the *presentation mix*.

The **sales presentation mix** refers to the elements the salesperson assembles to sell to prospects and customers. While all elements should be part of the presentation, it is up to the individual to determine the extent to which each element is emphasized. This determination should be primarily based upon the sales call objective, customer profile, and customer benefit plan. Let's now examine each of these six elements, as shown in Figure 8–3.

Figure 8–3 **The Salesperson's Presentation Mix**

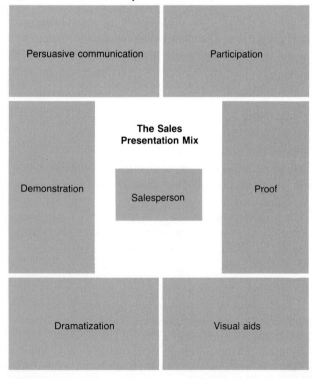

Persuasive Communications

To be a successful salesperson, do you need to be a smooth talker? No, but you do need to consider and use factors that aid in clearly communicating your message. As shown in Table 8–1, sales managers in 44 major manufacturing firms ranked three factors (enthusiasm, persuasiveness, verbal skill) as important attributes for salespeople. Enthusiasm was ranked most important, with high persuasiveness and high verbal skill ranking fourth and sixth, respectively.

In Chapter 4 we discussed seven factors which, if used, will help you to be a better communicator. The factors related to:

1. Using questions.
2. Having empathy.
3. Keeping the message simple.
4. Creating mutual trust.
5. Listening.
6. Having a positive attitude and enthusiasm.
7. Being believable.

Additional persuasive factors to consider in the presentation are logical reasoning, persuasive suggestions, a sense of fun, personalized relationships, trust, body language, a controlled presentation, diplomacy, and the "Paul Harvey dialogue" or conversation style.

Logical Reasoning. The application of logic through reasoning is an effective persuasive technique which appeals to prospects' common sense by requiring them to think about the proposition and to compare

Table 8–1 Sales Manager's Ranking of Characteristics for Salespeople

	Attribute	1 (10)	2 (9)	3 (8)	4 (7)	5 (6)	6 (5)	7 (4)	8 (3)	9 (2)	10 (1)	Total Points
1.	Enthusiasm	16	5	8	5	1	5	—	1	—	—	338
2.	Well organized	6	8	11	3	5	5	1	2	—	—	304
3.	Obvious ambition	8	6	5	7	4	3	2	3	3	—	285
4.	High persuasiveness	2	10	3	1	10	4	5	3	1	2	254
5.	General sales experience	3	2	4	6	6	2	8	8	5	4	226
6.	High verbal skill	2	3	3	6	2	7	7	6	4	1	215
7.	Specific sales experience	2	4	2	8	6	1	5	4	4	5	214
8.	Highly recommended	1	—	1	4	3	3	7	2	7	2	149
9.	Follows instructions	—	2	—	3	4	4	2	9	9	8	142
10.	Sociability	—	1	1	2	—	7	6	6	8	10	134

*Rank Assigned by Respondents**

* The top numeral in each column is the ranking given by executives, with 1 being most important and 10 least important. Numbers in parentheses are point ratings assigned to each rank. Numbers in the table show the number of respondents who assigned each rank to each attribute.

Source: Stan Moss, "What Sales Executives Look For in New Salespeople," *Sales and Marketing Management* (March 1978), p. 47.

alternative solutions to problems. It can have excellent results when applied to selling computers, heavy equipment, and communication systems. This is especially so when selling complicated proposals involving comparative cost data, when price versus benefits must be judged, and when the product is a radically new concept.

Logical reasoning involves a presentation constructed around three parts: a major premise, a minor premise, and a conclusion. Here is an example:

1. Major premise: All manufacturers wish to reduce costs and increase efficiency.
2. Minor premise: My equipment will reduce your costs and increase your efficiency.
3. Conclusion: Therefore you should buy my equipment.

If presented exactly in the straightforward manner as above, the logical formula may be too blunt; the prospect may raise defense. However, you can develop the framework or outline of the presentation to first determine if the prospect is interested in reducing costs and increasing manufacturing efficiency. If so, then a value analysis can be presented showing the benefits of your product over other alternatives. Information such as performance data, costs, service, and delivery information can be presented in a persuasive manner using various elements of the presentation mix.

Persuasion through Suggestion.   Suggestion, like logical reasoning, can be effectively used to persuade prospects. The skilled use of suggestions can arouse attention, interest, desire, conviction, and action. Types of suggestions which may be considered for incorporation into the presentation are:

1. **Suggestive propositions** imply that the prospect should act now, such as, "Shouldn't you go ahead and buy now before the price goes up next month? Prospects often like to postpone their buying decisions so the suggestive approach can help overcome this problem.
2. **Prestige suggestions** are used to get the prospect to visualize using products that famous people, companies, or someone the prospect might trust uses, such as, "The National Professional Engineers' Association has endorsed our equipment. That's the reason several hundred of the *Fortune* 500 manufacturers are using our products. This elite group of manufacturers are finding the equipment is further helping them to increase their profits, sales, and market share. Is this of interest to you?"
3. **Autosuggestion** attempts to have prospects imagining themselves using the product. Television advertisements frequently use this form of suggestion. The salesperson visualizes the product, saying, "Just

imagine how this equipment will look and operate in your store. Your employees will perform much better and will thank you."

4. The **direct suggestion** is widely used by professional salespeople in all industry because it does not "tell," but suggests they buy, which does not offend the buyer. Such a suggestion might go thus: "Based upon our survey of your needs I suggest you purchase. . . ." or "Lets consider this: we ship you three train carloads of Whirlpool washers and dryers of the following colors and models. . . ."

5. The **indirect suggestion** can be used at various times for some prospects when it is better not to be direct in suggesting a recommended course of action. Indirect suggestions help instill in prospects' minds factors such as doubt about a competitor's products or desire for your product which makes it seem as if it is their idea: "Should you buy 50 or 75 dozen 12 oz. Revlon hairspray for your promotion?" or, "Have you talked with anyone who has used that product?"

6. The **counter suggestion** is used to get an opposite response from the prospect: "Do you really want such a high quality product?" Often the buyer will begin expanding on why a high quality product is needed. This is an especially effective technique to include in the presentation if you have already determined the prospect wants a high-quality product.

Make the Presentation Fun.　Selling is fun, not a battle between the prospect and salesperson, so loosen up and enjoy the presentation. This is easy to do, once you realize that you believe in yourself and what your are selling—so sound like it! Have the *right mental attitude* and you can be successful.

Personalize Your Relationship.　When I worked for a large national industrial manufacturer, my sales manager taught me to personalize my presentation. He would say, "Charles, you are enthusiastic, you believe in yourself, your products, your company, and you give a very good presentation. To improve, however, you need to personalize your relationship with each of your customers. In some manner let them know during your presentation that you have their best interests at heart. He would always say, "Show 'em that you love 'em."

I came up with the short phrase, "You have me." Once I incorporated this into my presentation at the appropriate time, I saw a significant increase in my total sales and sales to customer call ratio by saying something like: "You are not only buying my products but also me. You have me on call 24 hours a day to help you in any way I can."

Yes, it does sound somewhat corny, but it helped show my customers that I cared for them and they could believe in me. This helped to build trust between us. You might choose a different way, yet it is important to tell and show them that you are looking out for their interests.

Building Trust.   Two of the best and easiest ways to build your persuasive powers with prospects is to be *honest* and *do what you say* you will. This results in building trust which increases sales. Most professional buyers have elephant-like memories which can be used to your advantage if you follow through after the sale and do what you said you would do when presenting your proposal.

Honesty is always the best policy and is an effective way to build trust. The salesperson should never claim more than the product can actually accomplish. If the product does not live up to expectations, then apologize, return the product for credit, or trade the product for another product. This is extremely important in obtaining repeat sales. This builds trust; the next time the prospect is reluctant to buy, then you say, "Haven't I always taken care of you? Trust me, this product is what you need. I guarantee it!"

Use Your Own Body Language.   Just as you watch for buying signals from a prospect, so too the prospect watches your facial expressions and body movements. The salesperson's own nonverbal communications should project a positive image to the prospect, one that shows you know what your are talking about and understand the buyer's needs. Your customer will think, I can trust this person.

The best nonverbal selling technique to use is the smile. As my sales manager said, "It's often not what you say but how you say it and you can say almost anything to anyone if you do it with a smile. So practice your facial expressions and smile—always smile."

Control the Presentation.   In making the presentation, you always need to be able to direct the conversation as planned in order to lead the prospect through your presentation and proposal. The salesperson is often faced with how to maintain control and what to do should the prospect take control of the conversation. For example, what do you do if the prospect likes to talk about hobbies, attacks your company or products for poor service or credit mix-ups, or is a kidder and likes to poke fun at your products, which he might call "dogs"?

When this happens, the salesperson should stay with a planned presentation if at all possible. If there is some complaint, this should be addressed first. If the prospect likes to talk about other things, then do so only for a brief period. When the prospect's attention and interest are hard to maintain, questions or some manner of getting participation in the presentation are the two best methods to rechannel the conversation.

Be sure to keep control of the visual aids and any materials you use in your presentation. New salespeople often make the mistake of handing prospects their catalog, price list, or brochures showing several products. When buyers are looking through all of this information, chances are they are not listening to you. Too much informatin can cause frustration and they will not buy. So hold on to your product materials with one hand and discuss the points of information you wish to present while prospects look and listen to you.

Be a Diplomat.   All salespeople will face the situation where the prospects feel they are right, or know it all, and the salesperson has different opinions. For example, the salesperson may have previously sold the prospect's company a machine which is always breaking down due to its operator, not the piece of equipment, yet the salesperson's company gets the blame. What to do?

The salesperson has to be a diplomat in cases where tempers rise and prospects are wrong, but feel they are correct and will not change their opinions. Retreat may be the best option; otherwise, you run the risk of destroying the relationship. If you challenge the prospect, you could win the battle only to lose the war. This is a decision the salesperson must make based upon the individual situation.

Use the Paul Harvey Dialogue.   Paul Harvey has the most listened-to radio news broadcast in America because of what he says and how he says it. Listen to him yourself. Then use the **Paul Harvey dialogue.** Construct your presentation to incorporate his excellent methods of speech, delivery, and particularly how he ''builds'' suspense into his stories. With these techniques, your talk comes alive, rather than sounding like a dull, monotone, memorized presentation.

Consider, for example, Mr. Harvey's story of Dr. Pemberton's Pick-Me-Up. Notice how masterfully he tells his story. Salespeople who can incorporate Mr. Harvey's speech techniques better capture their prospect's attention and interest.

Dr. Pemberton's Pick-Me-Up

In the first place, Dr. Pemberton wasn't even a doctor. But who'd trust a product called ''Mr. Pemberton's Triplex Liver Pills?''

No one.

Therefore he called it ''Dr. Pemberton's Globe of Flower Cough Syrup'' and ''Dr. Pemberton's Extract of Styllinger Blood Medicine.''

But if Dr. Pemberton wasn't a doctor, he also wasn't a quack. He merely lived in an era, right after the Civil War, when the corner druggist knew as much about medicines as the national drug manufacturers. And that's just what John Pemberton was. A corner druggist.

It was sometime after moving his business from Columbus to Atlanta—some while after ''Dr. Pemberton's Indian Queen Hair Dye''—that this obscure Georgia Pharmacist started fiddling with a basement brew you'll want to know about.

(continued)

Most patent medicines in those days contained alcohol. None of that in John Pemberton's new concoction. In fact, according to some, he was trying to effect a headache cure . . . or perhaps a hangover cure for the other patent medicines.

John experimented with the extracts of fruits and nuts and leaves, but that was for taste. If he was going to cure a headache he'd need, perhaps, a stimulant? Yes. Caffeine. And an analgesic. Some say . . . cocaine.

Now it was all over but the selling. But John, who had spent most of his time developing this new pick-me-up, would need financial help. So, during the summer of 1886, Dr. Pemberton took a jug of the reddish-brown syrup to Jacobs Pharmacy, one of the most reputable in Atlanta.

What was in it, the manager wanted to know?

Dr. Pemberton explained that it was a secret but the manager should try some. Just mix with water and drink.

Well, Jacobs bought Pemberton's potion . . . advertised it, too . . . but sales were slow. Apparently Georgians were quite free of aches and pains that summer. That's when fate stumbled in.

The story goes that a customer came into the pharmacy one morning with a hangover. The clerk remembered Dr. Pemberton's syrup and went to mix some. He was new on the job, not yet acquainted with the procedure . . . and used carbonated water by mistake.

His mistake is still in the recipe today. Any cocaine in the original creation has long since been eliminated, so it may or may not cure your headache. The other ingredients remain basically the same.

Dr. Pemberton, the master of cures, could not cure himself. His health failed soon after that last discovery. The little business he built around it could have been bought for less than two thousand dollars when he died.

So the country druggist never shared the pot of gold at the end of what is now a rainbow of lights as wide as the world—spelling out . . . Coca-Cola![1]

Simile, Metaphor, and Analogy. As shown by Paul Harvey's dialogue example, words can be used as selling tools. Similes, metaphors, analogies, pauses, silence, and changes in the rate of speaking, tone, and pitch can be extremely effective methods of gaining prospects' attention and capturing their interest in a proposal.

A **simile** is a comparison statement using the words *like* or *as* such as, "Our glue holds like cement." A **metaphor** is much like a simile, but does not use the words *like* or *as* when comparing one object to another.

The **analogy** compares two different situations which have something in common such as, "our 'Sun Screen' for your home will stop the sun's heat and glare before it hits your window. It's like having a shade tree in front of your window without blocking the view." Remember to talk the prospect's language by using familiar terminology and buzz words in a conversational tone.

Participation Is Essential to Success

The second major part of the presentation involves techniques for getting the prospect to participate in the presentation. Four ways to induce participation is through the use of:

1. Questions.
2. Product use.
3. Visuals.
4. Demonstrations.

We have already discussed the use of questions and will discuss the use of visuals and demonstrations later, so let's briefly consider having prospects actually use the product:

- If you are selling stereos, let them see, hear, feel them!
- If you are selling food, let them see, smell, taste it!
- If you are selling clothes, let them feel and wear them!

By letting prospects use the product, you can appeal to their senses of sight, sound, touch, and smell. The presentation should be developed to appeal to the senses, since people often buy because of emotional needs and the senses are keys to developing emotional appeals.

Proof Statements Build Believability

Prospects often say to themselves, Before I buy, you must *prove it!* Prove it is a thought everyone has from time to time. Salespeople must therefore prove they will do what they promise to do, such as helping to make product displays when the merchandise arrives. Usually, prove it means proving to a prospect during a presentation that the product's benefits and the salesperson's proposal are legitimate.

Because salespeople often have a reputation for exaggeration, prospects are at times skeptical of the salesperson's claims. By incorporating **proof statements** into the presentation, the salesperson can increase the prospect's confidence and trust that product claims are accurate. Several useful proof techniques are customers' past sales figures, the guarantee, testimonials, company proof results, and independent research results.

Past Sales Help Predict the Future. Customers' past sales proof statements are frequently used by the salesperson when contacting present customers. Customers keep records of their past purchases from each of their suppliers which can be used by the salesperson to suggest what quantities, of which products, to purchase. For example, the Colgate salesperson would check a customer's present inventory of all products carried; determine the number of products sold in a month; subtract inventory from forecasted sales and suggest the customer purchase that amount. It is difficult for buyers to refuse to buy when presentations are based on their own sales records. If they are offered a price discount and promotional allowances, they might purchase three to ten times the normal amount (a promotional purchase).

Assume, for example, that a food store normally carries 10 dozen of the king size Colgate toothpaste in inventory with 3 dozen on the shelf, and sells approximately 20 dozen a month. The salesperson would produce the buyer's past sales record and simply say, "You should buy 7 to 10 dozen king size Colgate toothpaste." If offering promotional allowances, the salesperson might say:

> The Colgate king size is your most profitable and best-selling item. You normally sell 20 dozen Colgate king size each month with a 30 percent gross profit. With our 15 percent price reduction, this month only, and our advertising allowances, I suggest, based upon your normal sales, that you buy either 80 to 100 dozen, reduce the price 15 percent, display it, and advertise the discount in your newspaper specials. This will attract people to your store and help increase store sales and allow you to make your normal profit.

The salesperson now stops talking to see the buyer's reaction. A suggested order plus an alternative on the quantity to purchase have been proposed. Does that quantity seem high to you? It may be high, just right, or low, but it is the buyer's decision. The salesperson is saying, given your past sales and with my customer benefit plan I believe you can sell X amount. The Colgate salesperson (like comparable consumer goods salespeople) might suggest purchases not only of toothpaste but of all Colgate products. That same sales call could involve multiple presentations of several products which have promotional allowances, plus the recommendation of the purchase of ten or more items based upon present inventories and the previous months's sales.

The Guarantee. The guarantee is a powerful proof technique because it assures prospects that if they are dissatisfied with their purchase, the salesperson or the company will stand behind a product. The manufacturer has certain product warranties which the retail salesperson can use in a presentation.

Furthermore, the consumer goods salesperson selling to retailers may say, "I'll guarantee this product will sell for you. If not, we can return what you do not sell." The industrial salesperson may explain the equipment's warranties and service policies and state, "This is the best equipment for your situation that you can buy. If after you have used it for three months and you are not 100 percent satisfied, I will return it for you."

Testimonials.　Use of testimonials in the presentation as proof of the product's features, advantages, and benefits is an excellent method to build trust and confidence. Today we see manufacturers effectively advertising their consumer products using testimonials, such as Roger Staubach, the ex-Dallas Cowboys football star, asking people, "How do you spell relief?" Professional buyers, however, are impressed by testimonials from prominent people and experts as to a product's features, advantages, and benefits.

Company Proof Results.　Companies routinely furnish data concerning their products. Consumer goods salespeople can use sales data, such as test market information and current sales data. Industrial salespeople use performance data and facts based upon company research as proof of their products' performance.

A consumer goods manufacturer gave its salespeople test market sales information to use in their presentation on a new product which was being introduced nationally. Using this information, a salesperson might say:

> Our new product will begin to sell as soon as you put it on your shelf. The product was a success in our eastern test market. It had 9.8 percent market share only nine months after the start of advertising. Laboratory tests proved our formula superior to that of the leading competition in our consumer product tests. There was a high repurchase rate of 50 percent after sampling. This means increased sales and profits for you.

Independent Research Results.　Proof furnished by reputable sources outside the company usually have more credibility than company-generated data. Pharmaceutical salespeople frequently report to physicians' medical research findings on their products which are published in leading medical journals by medical research authorities.

"On a typical day," says Sandra Snow of the Upjohn Company, "I see as many physicians as possible and initiate a discussion with them about one of our products that will have importance to them in their fields of medicine. I attempt to point out advantages that our drugs have in various states, by using third-party documentation published in current medical journals and texts. The information has much more meaning to a physician who knows that it is not me or the Upjohn Company that has shown our drug to have an advantage, but rather a group of researchers who have conducted a scientific study. All of the material that we give to the physician has previously been approved for our use by the Food and Drug Administration."

Publications such as *Road Test Magazine, Consumer Reports,* newspaper stories, and governmental reports, such as the Environmental Protection Agency publications, may contain information the salesperson can use in the presentation. For a proof statement referring to independent research results to be most effective, it is important it should contain: (1) a restatement of the benefit before proving it, (2) the proof source and relevant facts or figures about the product, and (3) expansion of the benefit. Consider the following example of a salesperson's proof statement:

> I'm sure that you want a radio that's really going to sell and be profitable for you (benefit restatement). Figures in *Consumer Guide* and *Consumer Sales* magazine indicate that the Sony XL 100 radios, although the newest on the market, are the third largest in sales (source and facts). Therefore, when you handle the Sony XL line, you'll find that your radio sales and profits will increase, and you will see more customers coming into your store (benefit expansion).

Proof statements should be incorporated into the presentation. They provide a logical answer to the buyer's challenge to "prove it!" Quite often proof statements can be presented through the use of visual aids.

The Visual Presentation—Show and Tell

In giving a sales presentation, the salesperson does two things. You *show* and *tell* the prospect about a proposal. You *tell* using persuasive communications, participation techniques, and proof statements. You *show* by using visual aids.

People retain approximately 10 percent of what they hear, but 50 percent of what they see. Consequently, you have five times the chance of making a lasting impression with an illustrated sales presentation rather than with words alone.

Visuals are most effective when you believe in them and have woven them into the message of your sales presentation. You use them to:

- Increase retention.
- Reinforce message.
- Reduce misunderstanding.
- Create a unique and lasting impression.
- Show your buyer you are a professional.

The visual presentation ("showing") incorporates the three remaining elements of the presentation mix shown in Figure 8–4 which are: (1) visual aids, (2) dramatization, and (3) demonstration. Certainly there is

Figure 8–4 The Show Elements of the Sales Presentation

some overlap between the three, for a demonstration does use visuals and can be considered to have some dramatics. Let's examine each of the elements to consider how they can be used separately or combined into a selling presentation.

Visual Aids Help Tell the Story

Visuals, or visual aids, refer to devices that appeal chiefly to the prospect's vision with the intent of producing mental images of the product's features, advantages, and benefits. Many companies routinely supply their salespeople visuals for their products. Some of the common visuals are:

The product itself.

Charts and graphics illustrating product features and advantages such as performance and sales data.

Photographs of the product and its uses.

Models of the products, especially for large, bulky products.

Audiovisual equipment such as films, slides, and tape cassettes.

Sales manuals and product catalogs.

Order forms.

Figure 8–5 is an illustration of an Uarco Business Forms salesperson making a video-slide presentation to company executives. Many sales organizations supply their salespeople with video equipment to show things such as examples of their advertisements or their products in operation.

Most visual aids are carried in the salesperson's bag. The sales bag should be checked before each sales call to insure all visuals necessary for the presentation are organized in the sales bag in such a manner

Figure 8–5   A Saleswoman Making a Slide Presentation for Uarco Business Forms

to allow the salesperson to easily reach into the bag and pull out needed visuals. Only new, top-quality, professionally developed visuals should be used. Tattered, torn, or smudged visuals should be routinely discarded. The best visual aid is your showing the buyer the actual product.

Quaker Oats salesperson Linda Slaby-Baker illustrates in Figure 8–6 the use of visual aids when calling on customers. After planning her sales call, she packs her sales bag, enthusiastically greets her buyer, and begins her sales presentation. Her visual aids consist of the product itself, visuals she has created tailored to this particular buyer, and visuals furnished to her by Quaker Oats. The use of visuals allows Linda to give her sales presentation in a persuasive manner. As you see in Figure 8–6, Linda uses different visuals, different body positions, and different conversational techniques to actively bring her buyer into their conversation. This provides her sales presentation with a dramatic element which greatly improves her probability of making the sale.

Dramatization Improves Your Chances

Dramatics refers to talking or presenting the product in a striking, showy, or extravagant manner. Thus, salesmanship can involve **dramatization** or theatrical presentation of products. However, dramatics should be incorporated into the presentation only when you are 100 percent sure that the dramatics can be carried out acceptably. This was not considered by the salesperson who set the buyer's trash can on fire. The salesperson had difficulty extinguishing the fire with his new fire extinguisher and ran the buyer out of the room because of extensive smoke. However, if carried out correctly, dramatics can be very effective. One of the best methods of developing ideas for the dramatization of a product is to watch television commercials. Products are presented using visuals, many are demonstrated, and certainly most are dramatized. Take, for example, the following television advertisements.

"We challenged the competition . . . and they ran!" says the Heinz tomato ketchup advertisement. Two national brands of ketchup and Heinz Ketchup are poured into a paper coffee filter held up by a tea strainer. The competition's ketchup begins to drip, then runs through the filter. The Heinz ketchup does not drip or run, indicating the high quality of the Heinz ketchup relative to their competition.

Bounty paper towel advertisement shows coffee spilled and shows how quickly the product absorbs the coffee relative to the competitive paper towel.

The STP motor oil additive advertisement shows a person dipping one screwdriver into STP motor oil additive and another screwdriver into a plain motor oil. The person can pick up and hold with two fingers the end of the screwdriver covered with plain motor oil. The screwdriver covered with STP motor oil additive slips out of the fingers indicating STP provides better lubrication for an automobile engine.

You can use your dramatic demonstration to set you apart from the many, many salespeople buyers see each day. Buyers, such as industrial purchasing agents, like to see you, for they know you will have an informative and often entertaining sales presentation. One salesperson known for his effective presentations was George Wynn. George was an industrial salesperson for Exxon U.S.A. responsible for the sales of machine lubricating oils and greases in Dayton, Cincinnati, and Columbus, Ohio.

One group of products sold by George consisted of oils and greases sold to the food processing industry. These lubricants had to be approved by the Federal Food and Drug Administration for "incidental food contact." One of the products sold was a lubricating grease, Carum 280. George ordered a number of one-pound cans for customer samples. As George started his sales presentation of these FDA approved products, he would take one of the cans from his sample case, open it, and spread this grease on a slice of bread also removed from his sample case. After taking a bite of the bread spread with the grease, he then offered a

Figure 8–6 Quaker Oats Saleswoman Linda Slaby-Baker Illustrates the Use of Visual Aids

Linda reviews call plan before seeing buyer.

Products and sales aids placed in and arranged in her sales bag.

Enters buyer's office.

Greets buyer with firm handshake, smile, eye contact.

Begins presentation using products and sales aids in bag.

Developed her own sales aids customized to her buyer.

Shows facts, figures, reasons to buy.

Linda uses company sales aids to get buyer involved in presentation.

bite to the buyer. The buyer generally refused the offer. However, in the mind of the buyer, this dramatic demonstration set George's presentation apart from others. It helped prove to the buyer the product was safe to use in a food processing plant.

Another dramatic demonstration used by George involved lubricating greases used by the steel industry. Greases that are resistant to high temperatures are desirable for most applications in the steel industry. Exxon developed a line of temperature-resistant greases which made use of a new thickener that held the oil in suspension better than competitive products. In order to demonstrate this product attribute, George used a pie tin held at a 45° angle centered over a small lighted alcohol lamp. A small glob of the Exxon grease as well as globs of several better-known competitors were placed on the pie tin. As the pie tin was heated, the oil separated from each of the competitive greases and ran down the pie tin. The oil did not separate from the Exxon product, thus dramatically demonstrating the high temperature resistance of this steel mill grease when compared to the leading competitive products.

Demonstrations Prove It!

One of the best ways to convince a prospect that a product is needed is to show the merits of the product through a **demonstration,** as did George Wynn. If a picture is worth a thousand words, then a demonstration is worth a thousand pictures. Therefore, it is best to show the product, if possible, and to actually have the prospect use it. If this is not feasible, then pictures, models, motion pictures, or slides are the next best alternative. Whatever the salesperson is attempting to sell, the prospect should be able to see it.

Psychological studies have shown that people receive 87 percent of their information on the outside world through their eyes and only 13 percent through the other four senses. What this says to the salesperson is to make a product visible. Also let the prospect feel, see, hear, smell, and use the product. The dynamic demonstration appeals to human senses by telling, showing, and creating buyer-seller interaction.

Demonstrations are part of the dramatization and fun of your presentation. Do not underestimate their ability to make sales for you, no matter how simple they may appear. For example, a glass company some years ago came out with a shatterproof glass. This was not standard equipment in automobiles then, as it is now. They had their salesmen going around the country trying to sell this shatterproof glass. One of the salespeople completely outsold the rest of the sales force. When they had their convention, they said, "Joe, how come you sell so much glass?" He replied, "Well, what I've been doing is taking little chunks of glass and a ball peen hammer along with me on my sales calls. I take the little chunk of glass and I hit it with the hammer. This shows that it's shatterproof. It splinters, but doesn't shatter and fall all over the ground. This has been helping me to sell a lot of glass.''

So the next year they equipped everyone of their salespeople with a little ball peen hammer and little chunks of glass. But an interesting thing happened. Joe still far outsold the rest of the sales force in his sales. So, when the convention came around again the next year, they asked, ''Joe, how is it you're selling so much? You told us what you did last year. What are you doing different?'' He replied, ''Well, this year, I gave the glass *and* the hammer to the customer and let *him* hit it.'' You see, the first year he had dramatization in his demonstration. The second year Joe had dramatization and participation in his demonstration. Again, it's often not what you say but how you say it which makes the sale for you.

A Demonstration Checklist. There are seven points to keep in mind as you prepare your demonstration. These points are shown in Figure 8–7. First, is the demonstration really needed and appropriate for your prospects? Certainly every sale does not need a demonstration nor will all products lend themselves to a demonstration.

If the demonstration is appropriate, what is its objective? What should the demonstration accomplish? Next, you should be sure you have properly planned and organized the demonstration. It is important to rehearse it so that the demonstration flows smoothly and appears to be natural. Take your time in talking and going through your demonstration so as to make it look easy. Remember, if you, the expert, cannot operate the machine, for example, imagine how difficult it will be for the prospect.

The only way to insure a smooth demonstration is to practice. Yet there is always the possibility that the demonstration will not go as planned or will backfire no matter how simple it may be. You need to

Figure 8–7

Sales Demonstration Checklist

- ☑ Is the demonstration *needed* and *appropriate?*
- ☑ Have I developed a specific demonstration *objective?*
- ☑ Have I properly *planned* and *organized* the demonstration?
- ☑ Have I rehearsed to the point that the demonstration *flows smoothly* and appears to be *natural?*
- ☑ What is the probability the demonstration will *go as planned?*
- ☑ What is the probability the demonstration will *backfire?*
- ☑ Does my demonstration present my product in an *ethical* and *professional* manner?

be prepared for this. An example was an ex-student of mine who was demonstrating his new Kodak slide projector. Two bulbs in a row burned out as he demonstrated the product to a buyer for a large discount chain. He anticipated what could go wrong and always carried extra parts in his sales bag. When the first bulb went out, he began talking of how easy it was to exchange bulbs, and when the second one blew, he said "I want to show you that again," with a smile. He always carried two spare bulbs, but now he carries three.

Lastly, you should make sure your demonstration presents the product in an ethical and professional manner. You do not want to misrepresent the product or proposal. A complex product, such as a large computer system, can be presented as simple to install with a few start-up problems, yet the buyer may find the computer system difficult to get into operation.

Get Participation in Your Demonstration.   By getting the prospect to participate in the demonstration, you can be assured that not only have you obtained a buyer's attention but that you can also direct it where you want it. It also helps the prospect visualize owning and operating the product. The successful demonstration aids in reducing buying uncertainties and thus resistance to its purchase. The salesperson can have the prospect do four things to have a successful demonstration:

1. Let the prospect do something simple.
2. Let the prospect work an important feature.
3. Let the prospect do something routine, frequently repeated.
4. Ask the prospect questions throughout the demonstration.

First, get the prospect to do something which is simple, easy to do with a low probability of foul-up. Second, in planning the demonstration, select the main features you will stress in the interview and allow the prospect to participate on the feature that relates most to an important buying motive. Again, you need to keep it simple.

A third way to have a successful demonstration is to get the prospect to do something with the product that is frequently done. Finally, be sure to get feedback from the prospect throughout the demonstration by asking questions or pausing in your conversation. This is extremely important as it will:

Determine the prospect's attitude toward the product.
Allow you to progress in the demonstration or wait and answer any
    questions or address any objections.
Aid in getting the prospect into the positive yes mood.
Set the stage for the close of the sale.

Little agreements lead to the big agreement to say yes. Be sure to phrase the questions in a positive manner, such as, "That is really easy

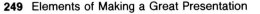

to operate, isn't it?'' instead of, ''This isn't hard to operate, is it?'' They ask the same thing, yet the response to the first question is positive instead of negative. The best questions force the prospect to mentally place the product in use, such as the question phrased, ''Do you feel this feature could increase your employee's production?'' The answer yes, commits the buyer to the idea that the feature will increase employee production. Remember, it is often not what you say, but how you say it.

Reasons for Using Visual Aids, Dramatics, and Demonstrations

As we have seen, visual aids, dramatics, and demonstrations are important to the salesperson's success in selling a prospect. The reasons for using them are that they:

- Capture attention and interest.
- Create two-way communications.
- Involve the prospect through participation.
- Afford a more complete, clearer explanation of products.
- Increase a salesperson's persuasion powers by obtaining positive commitments on a product's single feature, advantage, or benefit.

Guidelines for Using Visual Aids, Dramatics, and Demonstrations

While visual aids, dramatics, and demonstrations are important, their proper use is critical if they are to be effective. When using them, you should consider:

- First rehearsing by practicing in front of a mirror, on a tape recorder, and to a friend. Once you are ready to make your presentation, first see your less important prospects. This allows you to refine the presentation further before contacting your large accounts.
- Customizing them to the sales call objective, prospect's customer profile, and customer benefit plan, concentrating on the prospect's important buying motives and using appropriate multiple appeals to sight, touch, hearing, and smell.
- Making them *simple, clear,* and *straightforward.*
- Being sure to *control* the demonstration in order not to let the prospect take from you your selling aids. It can be disastrous to have the prospect not listen or pass up major selling points you wished to present.
- Making them *true to life.*

■ Encouraging *prospect participation*.

■ Incorporating *trial closes* (questions) after showing or demonstrating a major feature, advantage, or benefit in order to determine if it is believed and important to the prospect.

The Trial Close—A Major Step in the Sales Presentation

The **trial close** is one of the best selling techniques that you can use in your sales presentation. It is used to check the "pulse" or attitude of your prospect toward your sales presentation. The trial close should be used at the following four important times:

1. After making a *strong selling point* in the presentation.
2. After the *presentation*.
3. After answering an *objection*.
4. *Immediately before* you move to *close* the sale.

The trial close allows you to determine: (1) whether the prospect likes your product's feature, advantage, or benefit (the strong selling point); (2) whether you have successfully answered the objection; (3) whether any objections remain; and (4) whether the prospect is ready for you to close the sale. It is a powerful technique to induce two-way communication (feedback) and participation from your prospect.

If, for example, the prospect says little while you make your presentation, and if you get a no answer when you come to the close, you may find it difficult to change the prospect's mind. You have not learned the real reasons why the prospect says no. So to help avoid this, salespeople use the trial close to determine the prospect's attitude toward the product throughout the presentation.

The trial close asks for the prospect's *opinion*, not a decision to buy. It is a direct question which can be answered with very few words.* Examples of a trial close are:

"How does that sound to you?"

"Are these the features you are looking for?"

"Is this what you are interested in?"

"That's great—isn't it?"

"I think that's important—don't you?"

If the prospect responds favorably to your trial close, then you know that you are in agreement or that you have satisfactorily answered an objection. Thus the prospect may be ready to buy. However, if you get

---

* See Chapter 7 for other uses and examples of direct questions.

a negative response, you know not to close. Either you have not answered some objection or the prospect is not interested in the feature, advantage, or benefit you are discussing. This type of feedback allows you to better uncover what your prospect thinks about your product's potential for satisfying needs.

Sell Sequence

One way to remember to incorporate a trial close into your presentation is the use of the *Sell Sequence*. Each letter of the word "sell" stands for a sequence of things to do and say in order to stress benefits important to the customer.

S	**E**	**L**	**L**
Show feature	*Explain* advantage	*Lead* into benefit	*Let* customer talk

By remembering the word "sell," you can remember to *show the feature, explain the advantage, lead into the benefit, and then let customer talk by asking a question about the benefit (trial close).*

Example: Industrial salesperson to industrial purchasing agent: "This equipment is made of stainless steel (feature) which means it won't rust (advantage). The real benefit is that it reduces your replacement costs; thus saving you money! (benefit) That's what you're interested in—right!? (trial close)

Example: Beecham salesperson to consumer goods buyer: "Beecham will spend an extra one million dollars in the next two months advertising Cling Free fabric softener (feature). Plus, you can take advantage of this month's $1.20 per dozen price reduction (feature). This means you will sell 15 to 20 percent more Cling Free in the next two months (advantage), thus making you higher profits and pulling more customers into your store (benefits). How does that sound!? (trial close)

Once you attempt your trial close, carefully listen to what the customer says and watch for nonverbal signals to determine if what you have said has made an impact. If you get a positive response to your trial close, consider asking the customer to buy at once.

Remember, the trial close does not ask the customer to buy or make any type of purchase decision. It asks only for an "opinion." The trial close is a trial question to determine the customer's opinion towards the salespersons' proposition in order to know if it is time to close the sale. Thus its main purpose is to induce feedback from the buyer.

The Ideal Presentation

In the ideal presentation, your approach technique quickly captures your prospect's interest and immediately gets signals that the prospect has a need for your product and is ready to listen. The ideal prospect is friendly, polite, relaxed, will not allow anyone to interrupt you, asks questions, and participates in your demonstration as you had planned. This allows you to move skillfully through your presentation.

The ideal customer cheerfully and positively answers each of your questions, allowing you to anticipate just the correct moment to ask for the order. You are completely relaxed and sure of yourself when you come to the close. The customer says "Yes," and enthusiastically thanks you for your valuable time. Several weeks later, you receive a copy of the letter your customer wrote your company's president glowing with praise for your professionalism and sincere concern for the customer.

Be Prepared for Presentation Difficulties

Yes, a few sales presentations go somewhat like that, yet most have one or more hurdles you should be prepared for. While certainly not all of the difficulties you might face can be discussed here, three main problems which are possible to encounter during your sales presentation are interruptions; how to handle the discussion of competition; and the necessity oftentimes of making the presentation in a less than ideal situation.

How to Handle Interruptions

It is quite common for **interruptions** to occur during the presentation. The secretary comes into the office or the telephone rings, distracting the prospect. What should you do?

First, you should determine if the discussion that interrupted your presentation is personal or confidential. If so, by gesture or voice you can offer to leave the room—which is always appreciated by the prospect. While waiting, you should regroup your thoughts and mentally review how you will move back into the presentation. Once the discussion is over, you can:

1. Wait quietly and patiently until you have completely regained the prospect's attention.
2. Briefly restate the selling points which had interested the prospect, as, for example, "We were discussing your needs for a product such

as ours and you seemed especially interested in knowing about our service, delivery, and installation. Is that right?''

3. Do something to increase the prospect's participation, such as showing the product, using other visuals, or asking questions. Watch closely to determine if you have regained the prospect's interest.

4. If interest is regained, you can move deeper into the presentation.

Should You Discuss Your Competition?

Competition is something all salespeople must contend with every day. If you are selling a product, you must compete with others selling comparable products. How should you handle competition? Basically, you should keep in mind four considerations: (1) do not refer to a competitor unless absolutely necessary; (2) acknowledge your competitor only briefly; (3) make a detailed comparison of your product and that of your competitor; and (4) whether or not to discuss competition depends upon the situation.

Do Not Refer to Competition. First of all, you can lessen any surprises the buyer may present by properly planning for the sales call. In developing your customer profile, chances are you will find out what competing products are being used, and your prospect's attitude toward your products and those of your competitors. Based upon your findings, the presentation can be developed without specifically referring to competition.

Acknowledge Competition and Drop It. Many salespeople feel their competition should not be discussed unless the prospect brings it up. Then acknowledge competition only briefly and return to your product. "Yes, I am familiar with that product's features. In fact, the last three of my customers were using that product and have switched over to ours. May I tell you why?''

Here you do not knock competition, but acknowledge it and in a positive manner move the prospect's attention back to your products. If the prospect continues to bring up a competing product, you should determine the prospect's attitude toward it. You might ask, "What do you think about the Burroughs B1900 computer system?" The answer will help you mentally determine how you can prove that your product offers the prospect more benefits than your competitor's product.

Make a Detailed Comparison. At times it is necessary and appropriate to make a **detailed comparison** of your product to a competing one, especially for industrial products. If products are very similar, then you emphasize your company's service, guarantees, and what you personally do for customers.

If your product has features that are lacking in a competitor's product, then refer to these advantages, possibly indirectly. "Our product is the only one on the market with this feature! Is this important to you?''

Ask the question and wait for the response. A "Yes" answer brings you one step closer to the sale.

Often the prospect can use both your product and that of a competitor. For example, a pharmaceutical salesperson is selling an antibiotic which functions like penicillin, as well as killing bacteria resistant to penicillin. However, it costs 20 times more than penicillin. This salesperson would say, "Yes, Dr. Jones, penicillin is the drug of choice for . . . disease. But do you have patients for whom penicillin is not effective?" "Yes I do," says the doctor. "Then for those patients I want you to consider my product because . . . ."

Competition Discussion Based on the Situation.   Whether or not you should discuss competition depends on the individual prospect, which is the most sensible approach. Based upon your selling philosophy and your knowledge of the prospect, you choose how to deal with competition. If ever in doubt, due to insufficient prospect knowledge, it is best not to discuss competition.

Be Professional

No matter how you discuss competition with your prospect, you should always remember to act as a professional. If you are going to discuss competition, talk only about information you personally know is accurate, be straightforward and honest, not belittling and discourteous.

Your prospect may like both the competitor's products and yours. A loyalty to the competitor may have been built up over the years; by knocking competition, you may insult and alienate your prospect. However, the advantages and disadvantages of a competitive product can be pointed out acceptably if done in a professional manner. One salesperson relates this story:

> Several customers I called upon were very loyal to my competitors; however just as many were loyal to my company. I will always remember the president of a chain of retail stores flew 500 miles to be at one of our salesmen's retirement dinners. In his talk he noted how some 30 years ago, when he opened his first store, this salesperson extended him company credit and made him a personal loan which helped him get started.

It would be very difficult for a competing salesperson to sell to this loyal customer. When contacting customers, especially those buying competitive products, it is very important to uncover why they use competitive products before discussing competition in the presentation.

When the Presentation Takes Place

The ideal presentation takes place in a quiet room with only the salesperson and the prospect and no interruptions. However, at times

Figure 8–8 Examples of Less than Ideal Presentation Situations

Courtesy of Atlantic Richfield Company

Courtesy of Wallace Business Forms

the salesperson may meet the prospect somewhere other than a private office and feel the need to make the presentation under less than ideal conditions.

Figure 8–8 shows an Atlantic Richfield salesperson talking with the customer in front of his filling station, and a Wallace Business Forms salesperson making a presentation somewhere in the prospect's business. For short presentations, a stand-up situation may be adequate; however, when making a longer presentation you may want to ask the prospect, "Could we go back to your office?" or make another appointment.

Diagnose the Prospect to Determine Your Sales Presentation

You have seen that in contacting prospects you should be prepared for various situations. That is why selling is so challenging and why companies reward their salespeople so well.

In order to further emphasize the need for mental preparation before meeting prospects, examples of selling strategies for different types of prospects are presented in Figure 8–9. Imagine yourself making a sales call on each type. How would you handle them?

Summary of Major Selling Issues

The sales presentation is a persuasive vocal and visual explanation of a proposition. While there are numerous methods for making a sales

Figure 8–9 Examples of Selling Strategies for Different Types of Prospects

Your Prospect	*Selling Strategies*
The silent prospect	Determine if this is "the silent type" of personality or if the prospect is indifferent and does not want to talk. Ask questions that will unfreeze the prospect. Take it slow. If necessary, move to personal activities; talk about family, amusements, and then slowly move into business.
The indifferent prospect	Do your homework. Personalize the presentation by using facts, proofs, benefits, along with visual aids and demonstrations. You must get the prospect into the act on a personal level.
The skeptical prospect	Use facts and proofs and be specific. Use demonstrations, samples, and let the prospect try out the product.
The no-time prospect	Many prospects are extremely busy, so based on profiles, select one major feature, relate it to a benefit in an effort to get attention and interest so as to allow you more time.
The hot-head prospect	Some prospects are excitable and like to argue; so relax, smile, and let the prospect blow off steam. You may want to postpone the interview if the prospect does not relax. Keep a friend, do not make an enemy by being pushy.
The indecisive prospect	Keep the prospect from getting away by creating a sense of urgency—"Buy now, not later because . . . ." Do not present too many facts which will cause further confusion. Keep it simple. Close, close, close!
The know-it-all prospect	Expert, opinionated, and closed-minded prospects should be complimented and recognized for their knowledge. Use questions to ask for their opinion; do not tell them. Talk very little and get them to help educate you on your products. Let them talk themselves into buying.

presentation, the four common ones are the stimulus-response, formula, need-satisfaction, and problem-solution selling methods. Each method can be effective if used for the proper situation.

In developing your presentation, you should consider which elements of the sales presentation mix you will use for each prospect. The proper use of persuasive communication techniques, methods to develop prospect participation, proof statements, visual aids, dramatization, and demonstrations can greatly increase your chance of illustrating to your prospect how your products will satisfy his needs.

As we know, it is often not what we say but how we say it that results in making the sale. Persuasive communication techniques, such as questioning, listening, logical reasoning, suggestion, and the use of trial closes help to uncover needs, to communicate effectively, and to pull the prospect into the conversation.

Proof statements are especially useful in showing your prospect that what you are saying is true and that you can be trusted. When challenged, "Prove It!" do so by incorporating in your presentation facts on a customer's past sales, guaranteeing the product will work or sell, testimonials, company and independent research results.

In order to both show and tell, visuals need to be properly designed to illustrate features, advantages, and benefits of your products through the use of graphics, dramatization, and demonstration. This allows you to capture your prospect's attention and interest, create two-way communication and participation, express your proposition in a clearer, more complete manner, and make more sales. Careful attention to the development and rehearsal of the presentation is needed to insure it is carried out smoothly and naturally.

At any time you should be prepared for the unexpected, such as a demonstration which breaks down, interruptions, the prospect's questions about the competition, or the necessity of making your presentation in a less than ideal place, such as the aisle of a retail store or in the warehouse.

The presentation part of the overall sales presentation is the heart of the sale. It is where you develop the desire, conviction, and action. By giving an effective presentation, you will have fewer objections to your proposition, which makes for a easier close of the sale.

Let me conclude in this way: If you want to be a real professional in selling, you need to acquire, or create for yourself, materials that will help you get your message across and get others to believe it. If you try to sell without using the components of the sales presentation mix, you are losing sales not because of what you say but how you are saying it. Exhibits, facts, statistics, examples, analogies, testimonials, and samples should be part of your repertoire. Without them you are not really equipped to do a professional job of selling.

Review and Discussion Questions

1. You plan to give a demonstration of the Dyno Electric Cart to the purchasing agent of a company having a manufacturing plant which covers 200 acres. Which of the following is the best technique for your demonstration? Why?

   A. Let your prospect drive the cart.

   B. You drive the cart and have the prospect ride so you can discuss the cart's benefits.

   C. Leave a demonstrator and check back the next week to see how many the prospect will buy.

2. In contacting a purchasing agent for your Dyno Electric Carts you plan to use your 10-page visual "presenter" to guide the prospect through your benefit story. This selling aid is in a binder form and contains photographs of your cart in action, along with its various color options, guarantee, and testimonials. Should you:

   A. Hand over the binder? Why?

   B. Hold it yourself? Why?

3. Assume you were half-way through your presentation when your prospect had to answer the telephone. The call lasts five minutes. What would you do?

4. Discuss the various elements of the sales presentation mix and indicate why you need to use visuals during your presentation.

5. Fully explain how a trial close can be beneficial to a salesperson. What is the difference between a trial close and actually asking for the order?

6. Occasionally, you will find that even though customers are interested in a product benefit, they doubt that your product can provide it. Imagine that you are a mill salesperson for Mohawk Carpets. You are introducing a new line of carpets. You have just told your customer that because of Mohawk's synthetic fibers, your carpets will not fade even if exposed to direct sunlight. Your customer then says: "That sounds great, but I don't know. I've had too many customers complaining about fading."

   A. As you can see, the customer who doubts whether your carpet will resist fading is questioning a:

     (1) Need.

     (2) Product benefit.

     (3) Product feature.

   B. The carpet's ability to resist fading is:

     (1) Important to the customer.

     (2) Of no interest to the customer.

In response to the above remark, the salesperson offers proof as follows:

"I understand your concern, but a carpet made of synthetic fibers will not fade. A recent study conducted by the Home Research Institute and reported in the *Home Digest* proves that synthetic fibers hold their colors much better than natural fibers. And since Mohawk's carpets are made with synthetic fibers, you'll never hear any complaints about these carpets fading."

C. Examine each sentence in the above remarks and state if it is:
   (1) An expansion of the benefit.
   (2) A restatement of the benefit.
   (3) A proof of the benefit.

7. In your proof statement that proves the benefit, you should cite your proof source, in addition to relevant facts or figures about your product. Which of the following is a correct "proof of a benefit"?
   A. "Well, an article in last month's *Appliance Report* stated that the Williams blender is more durable than the other top ten brands."
   B. "You'll get ten percent longer use from the Hanig razor."
   C. *"Marathon* is the most widely read magazine among those with incomes over $25,000 per year."
   D. "Figures in *Marathon* magazine indicate that your sales in general will increase if you stock Majestic housewares in your store."

8. Examine the following conversation.

   Customer: "What you say is important, all right, but how do I know that these chairs will take wear and tear the way you say they will?"

   Salesperson: "The durability of a chair is an important factor to consider. That's why the Crest chairs have reinforced plastic webbing seats. *Furniture Dealers Weekly* states that plastic webbing of the type used in Crest chairs is 32 percent more effective in preventing sagging chair seats than fabric webbing. This means that your chairs will last longer, and will take the wear and tear that your customers require."

   A. Examine each sentence in the above remarks and state if it is:
      (1) An expansion of the benefit.
      (2) A restatement of the benefit.
      (3) A proof of the benefit.

9. After a two-hour drive to see an important new prospect, you stop at a local coffee shop for a bite to eat. As you are looking over your presentation charts, the coffee spills on about half a dozen of them. You don't have substitute presentation charts with you. What should you do?
   A. Phone the prospect and say that you'd like to make another appointment. Say that something came up.
   B. Go ahead and keep the appointment. At the start of your presentation, tell the prospect about the coffee spill and apologize for it.
   C. Go ahead with your presentation. But don't make excuses. The coffee stains are barely noticeable if you're not on the lookout for them.

Projects

1. What is the one thing in this world on which you are an expert? Yourself! Develop a presentation on yourself for a sales job with a company of your choice. Relate this assignment to each of the ten steps in "the selling process."
2. Visit several retail stores in your community, such as an appliance, bicycle, or sporting goods store, and report on the demonstration techniques, if any, which were used to sell to you. Suggest ways you would have presented the product.
3. Report on one television advertisement which used each of the following: proof statement, demonstration, unusual visual aids, and dramatization.
4. In your library are magazines in which companies advertise their products to their retail and wholesale customers, along with informing them of their current price discounts. Find three or more of the advertisements containing current price discounts offered by manufacturers to wholesalers and/or retailers. How might you use this information in a sales presentation?

Cases

8–1   Dyno Electro Cart Company

You are planning a call back on Mr. Pride and the president of his company to sell them several of your electric carts. (See Figure 7–3 in Chapter 7.) The company's manufacturing plant covers some 200 acres and you have sold many companies smaller than this one up to 10 carts. Since Mr. Pride is allowing you to meet with his company's president and maybe other executives, you know he is interested in your carts.

You are determined to make a spellbinding presentation of your product's benefits which will make use of visual aids and a demonstration of the cart itself. Mr. Pride raised several objections on your last presentation which may be brought up again by other executives (see Figure 7–3). Your challenge is to develop a dramatic, convincing presentation.

Questions:

1. You plan to give a "live" demonstration of the cart to show how effective it is to move around the plant. Which of the following is the best technique for the demonstration?
    A. Get Mr. Pride and the president involved by letting them drive the cart.
    B. You drive letting them ride so they will listen more carefully to you.
    C. Leave a demonstrator and check back the next week to see how many they will buy.

2. You are also planning to use your 10 page visual "presenter" to guide them through your benefit story. This selling aid is in a binder form and contains photographs of your cart in action, along with its various color option, guarantee, and testimonials. Should you:

   A. Get Mr. Pride to participate by letting him hold it?

   B. Handle it yourself, let him watch and listen while you turn the pages and tell your story?

8–2 Fresh Mouth: Selling a New Mouthwash

As a salesperson for Hygiene Incorporated, you have been sent the following information on a new product you are shortly to begin to sell. Using this information how would you develop your presentation?

The Product. The product is a new mouthwash or oral antiseptic called "Fresh Mouth." The trademark is the name in longhand with a pair of red female lips substituting for the letter "O" in "mouth." The product is a red liquid packaged in a new, uniquely shaped bottle. It is produced by Hygiene Incorporated (HI), a corporation that has an established niche in the toiletries and hygiene products market.

Fresh Mouth is available in a full line of four sizes:

6 oz.—The perfect trial and travel size!

12 oz.—Second largest dollar-producing size!

18 oz.—Accounts for 41 percent of consumer sales!

24 oz.—The fastest growing segment in the mouthwash market!

The *most* important goal is to gain multiple size distribution, and it is thought that going in with all four sizes at one time will aid in achieving this objective. As with other markets, there is size loyalty as well as brand loyalty in the mouthwash business. It was reported in a recent Nielsen study that 18 percent of shoppers not finding the particular size of a brand they wished to purchase did not make any purchase at all. Our experience shows we can expect 40 percent better movement in accounts where we have multiple sizes on the shelf.

Test Market. A proven success in the eastern markets, Fresh Mouth had a 9.8 percent market share only nine months after the start of advertising. Laboratory tests proved that the Fresh Mouth formula is superior to that of the leading competition. It was significantly preferred to competition in consumer product tests. There was a high repurchase rate of 50 percent after sampling. The trade gave enthusiastic support in the test market areas.

National Introduction. Fresh Mouth is now ready for national introduction to your market with the following unbeatable introductory program:

1. Massive sampling and couponing
   - There will be a blanketing of the top 300 markets with 4.4 oz. sample plus eight cents off coupon. Your market is included.
   - There will be a 75 percent coverage of homes in the top one hundred markets. Your market is included.
2. Heavy advertising
   - Nighttime network TV
   - Daytime network TV
   - Saturation spot TV
   - Newspapers
   - The total network and spot advertising will reach 85 percent of all homes in the U.S. five times each week, based on a four-week average. This means that, in four weeks, Fresh Mouth will have attained 150,000,000 home impressions—130,000,000 of these will be against women.
   - There will be half-page, two-color inserts in local newspapers in fifty markets, including yours. This is more than 20,000,000 circulation. Scheduled to tie in with saturation sampling is a couponing program.
   - Fifteen million dollars will be spent on promotion to ensure consumer acceptance.
3. TV advertising theme
   - The commercial with POWER to sell!
   - "POWER to kill mouth odor—POWER to kill germs—POWER to give FRESH MOUTH."
   - The commercial shows a young male, about twenty years of age, walking up to a young girl, saying, "Hi, Susan!" They kiss and she says, "My, you have a fresh mouth, Bill!" He looks at the camera with a smile and says, "It works!" The announcer closes the commercial by saying "FRESH MOUTH—it has the POWER!"
4. Display materials
   - Shelf display tag
   - Small floor stand for end-of-aisle display—holds two dozen 12 oz. bottles.
   - Large floor stand—holds four dozen 12 oz. bottles.

Introductory pricing. The introductory deal is designed to ensure that acceptance of Fresh Mouth by each account will be a shoo-in. The basis of the deal is off-invoice allowances (i.e., price reductions) used in the test markets. In addition, we are offering an advertising allowance which requires only one advertisement as proof of running the ad and a 3 percent quantity discount on all orders of any size will offer the best introductory deal we have ever had. Please note that the 12 and 18 oz. sizes are packed one dozen bulk, the 6 oz. size is packed two dozen to a case, and the 24 oz. size is packed one-half dozen to a case. On the 24 oz. size only half-dozen orders will be honored, with a $1 off-invoice allowance and a 20¢ per dozen advertising allowance for an invoice cost of $3.41 per case. One order can be applied to the introductory allowances. A split shipment is acceptable. For example, the retailer may order fifty dozen and have thirty-five dozen shipped now and fifteen dozen shipped no later than thirty days after the first shipment. Terms are 2 percent—twenty days—net thirty days from date of shipment. The form shown in Exhibit 1 on page 264 is a copy of the ''deal sheet'' for you to develop a recommended promotional plan for each of your customers.

Pertinent Retail Data

Retail Cost and Available Gross Profit Information	6 oz.	12 oz.	18 oz.	24 oz.
Suggested retail selling price	.99	1.09	1.39	1.69
Regular retail value per dozen	11.88	13.08	16.68	20.28
Regular cost per dozen	6.98	7.68	9.79	11.90
Regular profit per dozen: Dollars	4.90	5.40	6.89	8.37
Percent	41.20	41.20	41.30	41.30
Special allowance per dozen	.60	1.05	1.50	2.00
Special cost per dozen	6.37	6.63	8.29	9.90
Special profit per dozen: Dollars	5.51	6.45	8.39	10.38
Percent	46.30	49.30	50.30	51.20
Least unit cost, excluding 2% cash discount	53.1¢	55.2¢	69.1¢	82.5¢
Advertising allowances per dozen	.60	1.05	1.50	2.00

Salespeople's Incentives. Each salesperson has approximately 200 accounts of various sizes and types, such as grocery and discount retail stores. The company is offering you a bonus for each size sold as follows:

Size	Bonus per Dozen
24 oz.	75¢
18 oz.	50¢
12 oz.	35¢
6 oz.	25¢

Plus, for each account that purchases a minimum order of one dozen of each size, a bonus of $5 dollars is paid. If, for example, all 200 accounts purchased a minimum order of all sizes, the salesperson would earn a $1,370 cash bonus.

Exhibit 1   Introducing "Fresh Mouth" Oral Antiseptic

Account Name: _____

		Allowances Available			
Size	Suggested Order	Promotion Allowance per Dozen	Fund	Advertising Allowance per Dozen	Fund
24 oz.	_____	$2.00	$_____	$.40	$_____
18 oz.	_____	1.50	$_____	.30	$_____
12 oz.	_____	1.05	$_____	.20	$_____
6 oz.	_____	.60	$_____	.10	$_____
		Total promotion fund	$_____	Total advertising fund	$_____

Recommended Promotional Plan

	24 oz.	18 oz.	12 oz.	6 oz.
Suggested order	_____	_____	_____	_____
Least unit cost	_____	_____	_____	_____
Suggested ad price	_____	_____	_____	_____
Suggested ad date	_____	_____	_____	_____
Suggested promotion	_____	_____	_____	_____

_____
_____
_____
_____

The Situation.   You are a new salesperson for HI. The account you will first sell is a large independent grocery store called the Harris Food Store. Mr. Ronnie Harris is the buyer. Based on the store's size, past sales of your products, and the sales quota you are assigned, you feel Harris could buy three dozen of the 6 oz.; fifteen dozen of the 18 oz.; six dozen of the 12 oz.; and three dozen of the 24 oz. size. However, you feel that if he will display, advertise, and discount the price, he should be able to sell twice that amount. So that will be your suggested order to Harris.

Questions:
1. If Harris purchases what you recommend, what will be your cash bonus?
2. Why should Harris buy from you?
3. What objections might Harris be expected to raise?
4. Develop a sales presentation to sell Harris your suggested order.

8–3   Major Oil, Inc.

Ralph Jackson sells industrial lubricants to manufacturing plants. The lubricants are used for the plants' machinery. He is calling upon Jeff Sager, a purchasing agent for Acme Manufacturing Company. Jeff presently buys Ralph's Hydraulic Oil 65 in drums. Ralph's sales call objective is to persuade Jeff to switch from purchasing his oil in drums to a bulk oil system. The secretary has just admitted him to Jeff's office.

Salesman: Hello Jeff.

Customer: Well if it's not Ralph Jackson, my lube oil salesman. How is everything over at Major Oil these days?

Salesman: Fine! We're adding to our warehouse so we won't be quite as crowded. Say, I know you like to fly and I was reading this magazine about the old Piper Tri-Pacer.

Customer: Yeah! I do enjoy flying and fooling with old airplanes. I just got back this weekend from a fly-in over at Centerville.

Salesman: You don't say; what type planes did they have?

Customer: They had a large bunch of homebuilts. You know—many pilots that build their own planes may spend from 5 to 15 years just building their plane.

Salesman: Would you like to build your own plane someday?

Customer: Yes, I would but you know this job takes so much time and with my schedule here and some travel, I don't know if I'll ever get time to start on a plane, much less finish one.

Salesman: Well, I don't know that I can save you that much time, but I can save the people in the plant time as well as reducing your cost of Hydraulic Oil 65. Also, I may even save your office some time and expense by not having to place so many orders.

You know we visited a couple of weeks ago about the possibility of your buying Hydraulic Oil 65 in bulk and thus reducing the costs per gallon by buying larger quantities each time you order. In addition, you will save tying your money up in the $20 drum deposit or even losing the deposit by losing or damaging the empty drum.

Customer: Sounds like this is fixing to cost us some money.

Salesman: Well, we might have to spend a little money to save a larger amount, plus make it easier and quicker in the plant. Do you know exactly what you are paying for Hydraulic Oil 65 now?

Customer: I think it's about a buck forty a gallon.

Salesman: That's close. Your delivered cost is $1.39 per gallon, not counting drum deposit. You used approximately 20,000 gallons of Hydraulic Oil 65 last year at a total cost of $27,800.

Customer: Between what I pay at the gas station and what we pay here I see why Major Oil is getting bigger and richer all the time. How much money *can* you save us?

Salesman: Well, we just try to get by and make ends meet. However, I can save your company more than $2800 per year on oil costs alone.

This case was developed by Professor George Wynn, Assistant Professor of Marketing, University of Arkansas at Fayetteville © 1983.

Customer: That sounds awful big. How are you going to do that?

Salesman: I am going to show you how you can purchase oil in bulk, save 14¢ per gallon on each gallon you buy (14¢ times 20,000 gallons equals $2800) and totally eliminate handling those drums and having your money tied up in deposits. Last year you purchased about 364 drums and I'll bet you did not get all these drums back to us.

Customer: I know we damaged some drums and I imagine we furnished some trash barrels for our employees if the truth were known. I wonder how much total deposit we pay?

Salesman: Yeah probably. The total deposit on those drums was $7280. Are you and your company totally satisfied with the performance of Hydraulic Oil 65?

Customer: We seem to be. I have heard nothing to the contrary and our bearing supplier, Timken, says that the oil is doing a first class job. You know this savings sounds good in theory, but will it really work? Besides, where will we put a big bulk system?

Salesman: Jeff, I've already checked pretty thoroughly into what the total equipment and installation will cost. Here's a picture of the installation we made over at the Foundry and Machine Shop. We put the installation aboveground to save the expense of digging holes for the tanks. This cover shown here in the picture protects the pump and motor from the weather, and the pipe into the shop goes underground. There's a control switch for the pump motor mounted inside the building right alongside the nozzle outlet. It looks pretty good, doesn't it?

Customer: Certainly does Ralph, but what about the cost here?

Salesman: We can get two new 3000-gallon tanks delivered here for a cost of $1700.00 from our tank supplier. This is about $120.00 less than what you could buy them for. Our quantity purchases of tanks give us a little better price and we'll be glad to pass these savings on to you. I have checked with Pump Supply Company and they have in stock the pump and motor with flexible coupling and built-in pump relief valve, just what we need for handling this oil, and the cost is $475.00. The control switch, pipe, pipe fittings, inside hose, and nozzle come to $120.00, and the fellow who does our installation work has given me a commitment to do all the installation work for $500.00, including furnishing the blocks to make the tank supports.

This totals $2795, so lets round off to $2800. And at a savings of 14¢ per gallon, based on your present usage of 20,000 gallons per year, this would be completely paid off in about 12 months, during which time you'd be paying $1.25 per gallon for your oil rather than the $1.39 you're now paying. How does this sound to you, Jeff?

Customer: That sounds pretty good to me, Ralph. Didn't you all have a write-up of this nature in a recent issue of your company magazine?

Salesman: We sure did. It was in the March issue. Here it is right here. The situation was a little different but the basic idea is the same. Our company has been able to use this idea to considerable advantage and over the past three years I personally have set up six installations of this type. Do you have any questions regarding the plan I've outlined?

Customer: Just one thing—you know we're short on space out back of the warehouse. Have you thought about where we might locate an installation of this type?

Salesman: Yes, I have, Jeff. You'll recall one of our earlier conversations where you were telling me about your plans to clean up that old scrap pile back near the corner of the warehouse. That would be an ideal location, and we could then locate the control switch, filling hose, and nozzle right on the inside at the end of the assembly line so the units could be given their initial oil fill just before they come off the assembly line. How would that fit into your plans?

Customer: That's a good idea, Ralph. That way we can get that junk pile cleaned up, replace it with a decent looking installation, and then make our initial oil fill the last step in our assembly procedure.

Salesman: Do you have any other questions, Jeff?

Customer: No, I believe I've got the whole picture now.

Salesman: Good. Now, just to sum up our thinking, Jeff, the total cost of installation will be about $3000.00. Immediately upon completion of the installation, and when you receive your first transport truck load shipment of Hydraulic Oil 65, instead of being billed a $1.39 per gallon, as you are now paying for barrel deliveries, you will be billed $1.25 per gallon. I'll work with Bill Smith, the plant superintendent, and I'll handle all the outside contacts so that we can get the installation in with little turmoil.

Customer: That sounds good to me. When can we get started on the installation?

Salesman: Tomorrow! I'll bring a contract for you to run through your people and get signed and it should take about three to four weeks after the contract is signed.

Customer: Good. What do I need to do right now?

Salesman: If you'll arrange to get the junk cleaned out of the corner, then we'll be all ready to go. I'll order the equipment and get it moving so we can be set to go in about four weeks. What would be the best time to see you tomorrow?

Customer: Anytime will be okay with me, Ralph.

Salesman: Swell, Jeff. Thanks for your help and I know you're going to be pleased with this new installation and also save some real money. See you tomorrow.

Questions:

1. Evaluate Ralph's sales presentation. Include in your answer comments on his approach, presentation, use of trial closes, handling of objections, and his close.
2. How would you develop visual materials to illustrate Ralph's sales presentation, including the arithmetic.
3. Now that Ralph has sold Jeff, what should Ralph now do?

9

Objections Are Your Friends

Profile

Bruce Scagel
Scott Paper

Bruce Scagel received his bachelor's degree in English from Washington and Jefferson College, and did graduate work in business at Syracuse University.

His career with Scott Paper began in 1976 as a consumer products sales representative in Jacksonville, Florida. Bruce says, "I served in various levels of field sales before assuming my current position as assistant marketing personnel manager at corporate headquarters in Philadelphia, Pennsylvania. I began my career in a sales position because it offered opportunities for rapid advancement as well as a variety of interesting and challenging activities.

"My philosophy of selling incorporates traditional sales techniques with personal approaches. I believe it's initially necessary to learn as much as possible about each customer, the objectives, challenges, and the particular problems he or she faces. By addressing these objectives and challenges with specific products and services, the salesperson enhances opportunity for success."

Ask Bruce what he believes are the key factors for sales success, and he will stress four points. "First, know your customers and their operations. I believe it's necessary to know as much about my customers as possible, including their needs and objectives—how they operate and who their key people are before attempting the sale. Consistency and follow-through make up the second key selling point. Generally, the most respected and successful salesperson is the one who is consistent in dealing with the customer, and who follows through on commitment and promises. Third, you must lose your fear of failure. One of the greatest impediments to successful selling is fearing that the buyer will not buy. In my career, I've been most successful when I've been well prepared and confident. However, I am also aware that I will not make every sale. Accept the results and move on to the next project. Fourth, to be successful you must ask questions. Through questioning, the salesperson can identify the buyer's needs, objectives, and primary challenges. Timely questioning can keep a sale alive when the buyer appears to be losing interest in the product or service being offered. My observations have been that many inexperienced salespeople find this aspect of the sale the most difficult to master because they fear that they will lose control of the presentation. In fact, conversation is one of the most appropriate means to lead the buyer to the desired conclusions."

Scott Paper Company salesman Bruce Scagel has a positive philosophy regarding sales objections: "During the sale, objections are often raised, and the manner in which the salesperson responds often constitutes the difference between success and failure. The salesperson should resist being defensive or put off by objections; rather he or she should address them confidently, keeping in mind that they're fundamental to the sale. It's been said that the selling process doesn't begin until the buyer raises an objection. For the most part I would agree.

"Objections are often raised for the following reasons: the buyers want to avoid a decision; they are operating with misinformation; they want or need more information or they simply want reassurance. In each case, the salesperson who listens closely and attempts to understand the buyer's needs and objectives can respond appropriately."

This chapter expands on Bruce's comments, and also discusses how to meet objections, techniques to use in overcoming objections, and how to proceed after an objection has been addressed.

Welcome Objections!

When a prospect first gives an objection, *smile,* because that's when you start earning your salary. You want to receive personal satisfaction from your job and at the same time increase your salary—right? Well, both will occur as soon as you learn to accept objections as a challenge which, when handled correctly, will benefit both your prospect and yourself. The more effectively you can meet customers' needs and solve their problems, the more successful you will be in sales. If you *fear* objections, you will *fumble* your response, often causing you to *fail.*

Remember, while people do want to buy, they *do not* want to be taken advantage of. Buyers who cannot see how your offering will fulfill their needs ask questions and raise objections. If you cannot effectively answer the questions or meet the objections, you will not make the sale. It is *your* fault, not the buyer's fault, that the sale was not made, if you sincerely believe your offering fulfills a need but the prospect still will not buy. The salesperson who can overcome objections when they are raised, and smoothly move back into a presentation can expect to succeed.

When Do Prospects Object?

The prospect may object at any time during your sales call—from introduction to close. Imagine walking into a retail store (as once happened to me), carrying a sales bag, and the buyer yells out, "Oh no, not another salesman. I don't even want to see you, let alone buy from you!" What do you say?

I said, "I understand. I'm not here to sell you anything, only check your stock, help you stock your shelves, and return any old or damaged merchandise for a refund." As I turned to walk away, the buyer said, "Come on back here, I want to talk to you."

If I had simply said "OK" and left, I would not have made that sale. I knew that I could benefit that customer, and my response and attitude showed it. The point is to always be ready to handle a prospect's objections, whether at the approach, during the presentation, after a trial close, after you have already met a previous objection, or during the close of the sale.

Who Is the Toughest Prospect?

You will find the toughest prospects to be those who do not say anything. You do not know if they are interested in your product, bored with you, or just being polite. You would love to have an objection from them. Sales resistance is much better than indifference.

Second toughest are those who agree with everything you say but who are not really listening. They like people, like to visit with them, but are really not thinking of buying. In the retail situation, they may say they are looking, but talk with you mainly for the conversation. An industrial buyer who may need a break from the routine may say, "Sure, I'll talk with you. Let's have a cup of coffee. . . ." Sometimes buyers on company time, whose job it is to see salespeople, will speak with you but without any real intention to buy.

What Are Objections?

Interestingly enough, prospects who present objections are often more easily sold on your product. They are interested enough to object; they want to know what you have to offer.

Opposition or resistance to the request of the salesperson is labeled a **sales objection.** Sales objections should be welcomed because they show prospect interest and aid in determining what stage the prospect has reached in the buying cycle—attention, interest, desire, conviction, or readiness to close. As with other subjects, sales objections can be conveniently classified.

Four Major Categories of Objections

You will hear prospects object to various things in many different ways. Most objections salespeople encounter can be placed into the four categories shown in Figure 9–1. Know how you will handle each situation before it occurs. An advance decision on how you will handle these types of objections will help you become a better salesperson by improving your image as a problem solver.

Figure 9–1   Four Major Categories of Objections

| Hidden objections | Stalling objections | No-need objections | Money objections |

The Hidden Objection

Prospects who ask trivial, unimportant questions or conceal their feelings beneath a veil of silence have **hidden objections.** They are unwilling to discuss their true objections to a product because they may feel they are not your business; they are afraid objections will offend you; or they simply may not feel your sales call is worthy of full attention.

Such prospects may even carry on a good conversation with you without ever revealing their true feelings. You have to ask questions and carefully listen to know what questions to ask in order to smoke out their real objections to your product. Learning how to determine what questions to ask a prospect and how to ask them are skills developed by conscious effort over a long period of time. Your ability to ask probing questions will improve with each sales call if you consciously try to develop this ability.

Smoke Out Hidden Objections.   With prospects who are unwilling to discuss their objections or who may not know why they are reluctant to buy, you need to be prepared to "smoke out" objections by asking questions. You must do what you can to get the objections out in the open. Consider the following questions:

"What would it take to convince you?"

"What causes you to say that?"

"Let's consider this, suppose my product would . . . [do what prospect wants] . . . then you would want to consider it, wouldn't you?"

"Come on now, tell me, what's really on your mind?"

Uncovering hidden objections is not always easy. You should observe the prospect's tone of voice, facial expressions, and physical movements. Pay close attention to what the prospect is saying. You may have to "read between the lines" occasionally to find the buyer's true objections. All of these factors will help you discover whether objections are real or simply an excuse to cover a hidden objection.

Prospects may not consciously know what their real objections are. Sometimes they will claim that the price of a product is too high. In reality, they may be reluctant to spend money on anything. If you attempt to show that your price is competitive, the real objection will remain unanswered and no sale will result. Remember, you cannot convince anyone to buy until you understand what a prospect needs to be convinced of.

If, after answering all of the apparent questions, the prospect is still not sold, you might attempt to subtly uncover the hidden objection. You might simply ask the prospect what the real objection is. Direct inquiry should be used as a last resort because it may indirectly amount to calling the prospect a liar, but if it is used carefully, it may enable the salesperson to bring out the prospect's true objection. Smoking out hidden objections is a selling art form that is developed over time by skillful salespeople. Its successful use can greatly increase your sales. This approach should be used carefully, but if it enables the salesperson to uncover a hidden objection, then it will have served its purpose.

The Stalling Objection

When your prospect says, "I'll think it over. . . ." or, "I'll be ready to buy on your next visit," you must determine if the statement is the truth or if it is a smoke screen designed to get rid of you. This **stalling** tactic is a common type of objection.

What you discovered when developing your customer profile and customer benefit plan will aid you in determining how to handle this type of objection. Suppose that before seeing a certain retail customer you had checked the supply of your merchandise in both the store's stockroom and on the retail shelf and this occurs:

Buyer: I have enough merchandise for now. Thanks for coming by.

Salesperson: Ms. Marcher, you have 50 cases in the warehouse and on display. You sell 50 cases each month, right?

You have forced her hand. This buyer will either have to order more merchandise from you or tell you why she is allowing her supply of the product to dwindle.

One of the toughest stalls to overcome arises when selling a new consumer product. Retail buyers are generally reluctant to stock consumer goods which customers have not yet asked for, even new goods produced by large, established consumer product manufacturers. The following excerpt is taken from a sales call made by an experienced consumer goods salesperson on a reluctant retail buyer. This excerpt begins with an interruption made by the buyer during a presentation of a new brand of toothpaste:

Buyer: Well, it sounds good, but I have seven brands and 21 different sizes of toothpaste now. There is just no place to put it. [A false objection—smoke screen.]

Salesperson: Suppose you had 100 customers walk right down the aisle and ask for Colgate 100 Toothpaste. Could you find room then?

Buyer: Well, maybe. But I'll wait until then. [The real objection.]

Salesperson: If this were a barber shop and you did not have your barber pole outside, people wouldn't come in because they wouldn't know it was a barber shop, would they?

Buyer: Probably not.

Salesperson: The same logic applies to Colgate 100. When people see it, they will buy it. You would agree that our other heavily advertised products sell for you, right? [Trial close.]

Buyer: Yeah, they do, all right. [Positive response, now reenter your selling sequence.]

The salesperson eliminated the stall in this case through a logical analogy.

A third common stall is the alibi that your prospect has to get approval from someone else, such as a boss, buying committee, purchasing agent, or home office. Since the buyer's attitude toward purchasing your product will influence the firm's buying decision, it is important you determine the buyer's attitude toward your product.

When the buyer stalls by saying, "I will have to get approval from my boss," you can counter by saying, "If you had the authority, you would go ahead with the purchase, wouldn't you?" If the answer is "yes," chances are the buyer will exert a positive influence on the firm's buying decision. If not, then you must uncover the real objections. Otherwise, chances are you will not make the sale.

Two additional responses to the "I've got to think it over" stall are: "What are some of the issues you have to think about?" Or you may directly focus on the prospect's stall by saying, "Would you share with me some of the things that are holding you back?"

Another effective response to "I've got to talk to my boss," is: "Of course you do. What are some of the things you would talk about?" This allows you to agree with the reluctant prospect. You are now on the buyer's side. It helps encourage the buyer to talk and to trust you. This "empathy" response ("Of course you do.") puts you in the other person's position.

Sometimes the prospect will not answer your question. Instead, the response is, "Oh, I just need to get an opinion." You can follow up

450
275

175

with a multiple choice question such as: "Would you be exploring whether this is a good purchase in comparison with a competitor's product or would you be wondering about the financing?" This helps display an attitude of genuine caring.

As with any response to an objection, be sure to communicate a positive attitude. Do not get demanding, defensive, or hostile. Otherwise, your nonverbal expressions may signal a defensive attitude, reinforcing the prospect's defenses.

Your goal in dealing with a stall is to help prospects realistically examine reasons for and against buying now. If you are absolutely sure it is not in their best interest to buy now, tell them so. They will respect you for it. You will feel better about yourself. The next time you see these customers, they will be much more trusting and open with you.

However, the main thing to remember is not to be satisfied with a false objection or a stall. Tactfully pursue the issue until you have unearthed the buyer's true feelings about your product. If this does not work, (1) then you should present the benefits of using your product now; (2) if there is a special price deal, mention it now; and (3) if there is a penalty or delay, mention it. Bring out any or all of your main selling benefits now and keep on selling!

The No-Need Objection

The prospect says, "Sounds good, I really like what you had to say, and I know you have a good product, but I'm not interested now. Our present product . . . [or supply or merchandise] . . . works well. We will stay with it." Standing up to conclude the interview, the prospect says, "Thanks very much for coming by." This type of objection can disarm an unwary salesperson.

The **no-need objection** is widely used because it politely gets rid of the salesperson. Some salespeople actually bring it upon themselves by making a poor sales presentation. They allow prospects to sit and listen to a sales pitch, without getting them to participate by showing them true concern and asking them questions. Therefore, as soon as the presentation is over, prospects can quickly say, "Sounds good, but . . ." In essence, they are saying no, making it very difficult for the salesperson to continue the call. While not always a valid objection, the no-need response strongly implies the end of a sales call.

The no-need objection is especially tricky because it may also include a hidden objection and/or a stall. If your presentation was indeed a solo performance or a monologue, your prospect might very well be indifferent to you and your product, having tuned you out halfway through the second act. Aside from departing with a whimpered "Thanks for your time," you might attempt to resurrect your presentation by asking questions.

The Money Objection

The **money objection** encompasses several forms of economic excuses: "I have no money"; "I don't have that much money"; "It costs too much"; or the ever-popular "Your price is too high." These objections are simple for the buyer to say, especially in a recessionary economy.

Often prospects will want to know the price of your product before you can begin your presentation, and will not want you to explain how the product's benefits will outweigh its costs. Price is a real consideration and must be discussed, but it is risky to discuss product price until it can be compared to product benefits. If you successfully postpone the price discussion, you must eventually come back to it, because your prospect will seldom forget it. Some prospects are so preoccupied with price that they will give minimal attention to your presentation until the topic reemerges. Others will falsely present price as their main objection to your product, concealing the true objection.

By observing nonverbal signals, asking questions, listening, and positively responding to the price question when it arises, you can easily handle price-oriented objections.

Many salespeople think that offering the lowest price gives them a greater chance of sales success. Generally, this supposition is not valid. Once you realize this, you will become even more successful. You might even state that your product is *not* the least expensive one available because of its benefits and advantages, and the satisfaction it provides. Once you convey this concept to your buyer, price becomes a secondary factor which usually can be dealt with successfully.

Do not be afraid of price as an objection; be ready for it and welcome it. Quote the price and go right on selling. It is usually the inexperienced salesperson who blows this often minor objection into a major one. If the price objection does become major (as shown in Figure 9–2), prospects can become excited and overreact to your price. The end result is the loss of the sale. If prospects overreact, slow down the conversation; let them talk it out and slowly begin to present product benefits as related to cost.

Handle Objections as They Arise

At times, situations will arise in which you feel it is best to postpone your answer to an objection. When the objection raised will be covered later in your presentation, or when you are building up to that point, it is best to pass over it for the time. As a general rule, however, it is best to meet objections as they arise because postponement may result in a negative mental picture or reaction such as the following:

Figure 9–2 **Price Seems to Have Excited This Buyer!**

"Your Price". . .

"Is"

"How". . .

"High!?"

The prospect may stop listening until you address the objection.

The prospect may feel you are trying to hide something.

You also feel it's a problem.

You cannot answer because you do not know how to deal with this objection or you do not know the answer to the objection.

It may appear that you are not interested in the prospect's opinion.

The objection could be the only thing left before closing the sale. So meet the objection, determine if you have satisfied the prospect, use another trial close to uncover other objections, and, if there are no more objections, move toward closing the sale.

Figure 9–3 Techniques for Meeting Objections

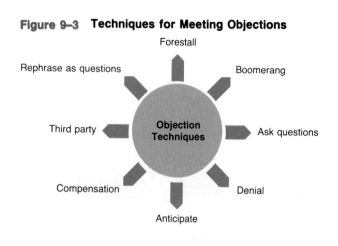

Techniques for Meeting Objections

Having uncovered all objections, a salesperson must answer them to the satisfaction of the prospect. Naturally, different situations will require different techniques, but there are several techniques, as shown in Figure 9–3, the salesperson can apply in most situations.

- Rephrase an objection as a question.
- Forestalling objection.
- Boomerang the objection.
- Ask questions regarding the objection.
- Direct denial of the objection.
- Anticipating the objection.
- Compensation for the objection.
- Obtaining a third-party answer to the objection.

Rephrase an Objection as a Question

Since it is easier to answer a question than to overcome an objection, you should rephrase an objection as a question when you can do so naturally. Most objections can be easily rephrased. Figure 9–4 presents examples of several possible procedures for rephrasing an objection as a question. Each procedure, except the objection based on a bad previous experience with the product by the prospect, has the same first three steps: (1) acknowledging the prospect's viewpoint, (2) rephrasing the objection into a question, and (3) obtaining agreement on the question. Here is an example.

Buyer:	I don't know—your price is higher than the others' are.
Salesperson:	I can appreciate that. You want to know what particular benefits my product has that make it worth its slightly higher price. [or "What you're saying is that you want to get the best product for your money."] Is that correct?
Buyer:	Yes, that's right.

Now discuss product benefits versus price. Once you have done so, attempt trial close by asking for the prospect's viewpoint to see if you have overcome the objection.

Salesperson:	Do you see how the benefits of this product make it worth the price?

A variation of this sequence is Scott Paper Company's Bruce Scagel's "Feel-Felt-Found" method in which he first acknowledges the prospect's viewpoint, saying:

"John, I understand how you *feel*. Bill at XYZ store *felt* the same way, but he *found* after reviewing our total program of products and services, that he would profit by buying now."

Bruce refers to rephrasing the objection as a question as his "Isolate and Gain Commitment" method. He gives as an example:

Mary, as I understand it, your only objection to our program is the following . . . If I can solve this problem, then I'll assume that you will be prepared to accept our program.

Bruce knows he can solve the problem or he would not have asked the question. When Mary says "Yes," he has isolated the main problem. He is not handling an objection, rather he is answering a question. He now shows her how to overcome the problem and then continues his selling. If Mary says "No," Bruce knows he has not isolated her main

Figure 9–4 Examples of Rephrasing Objections as a Question

Facts Are Incorrect	*Facts Are Incomplete*	*Facts Are Correct*	*Based on Bad Personal Experience*
1. Acknowledge viewpoint.	1. Acknowledge viewpoint.	1. Acknowledge viewpoint.	1. Thank prospect for telling you.
2. Rephrase objection.	2. Rephrase objection.	2. Rephrase objection.	2. Acknowledge viewpoint.
3. Obtain agreement.	3. Obtain agreement.	3. Obtain agreement.	3. Rephrase objection.
4. Answer question providing information supported by proof—third party.	4. Answer question by providing the complete facts.	4. Answer question, outweigh with benefits.	4. Obtain agreement.
5. Ask for present viewpoint.	5. Ask for present viewpoint.	5. Ask for present viewpoint.	5. Answer question.
6. Move back into selling sequence.	6. Move back into selling sequence.	6. Move back into selling sequence.	6. Move back into selling sequence.

objection. He now must start over in his attempt to uncover her objections. He might say, "Well, I guess I misunderstood. Exactly what is the question?" And now, when Mary responds, it will usually come back as a question. "Well, the question was about. . . ." You see, what you need to do is to get the customer involved and find out what is going on internally. You can do this with the proper use of questions.

Forestalling Objections Is Sometimes Necessary

Often the prospect may skip ahead of you in your sales presentation by asking questions which you plan to address later in your presentation. If you judge that the objection will be handled to your prospect's satisfaction by your customary method, and that your prospect is truly willing to wait until that later time in the presentation, you can politely **forestall the objection.** Five examples of forestalling objections are:

Prospect: Your price is too high.

Salesperson: In just a minute I'll show you why this product is reasonably priced, based on the savings you will receive compared to what you are presently doing. That's what you're interested in, savings, right?

or

Salesperson: Well, it may sound like a lot of money. But let's consider the final price when we know which model you need. OK?

or

Salesperson: There are several ways we can handle your costs. Let's discuss them in just a minute. First, I want to show you. . . .

or

Salesperson: I'm glad you brought that up (or I was hoping you would want to know that) because we want to carefully examine the cost in just a minute.

or

Salesperson: High? Why, in a minute I'll show you why it's the best buy on the market. In fact, I'll bet you a Coke that you will believe it's a great deal for your company!

Tactfully used, forestalling can leave you in control of the presentation. Normally you should respond to the objection immediately. However, occasionally it is not appropriate to address the objection. This is usually true of the price objection. Price is the primary objection you would want to forestall if you have not had the opportunity to discuss the benefits of your product. If you have fully discussed your product, then you should always immediately respond to the price objection.

Send It Back with the Boomerang Method

You should be ready at any time to turn an objection into a reason to buy. By convincing the prospect that an objection is in fact a benefit, you will have turned the buyer immediately in favor of your product. This is the very heart of the **boomerang method.** Take, for example, the wholesale drug salesperson, working for a firm like McKesson and Robbins, who wants to sell a pharmacist a new type of container for prescription medicines. Handling the container, the prospect says:

Prospect: They look nice, but I don't like them as well as my others. The tops seem hard to remove.

Salesperson: Yes, they are hard to remove. We designed them so that children couldn't get into the medicine. Isn't that a great safety measure? [trial close]

or the industrial equipment salesperson unaware that a customer is extremely dissatisfied with a present product:

Prospect: I have been using your portable generators, and do not want to use them anymore.

Salesperson: Why?

Prospect: Well, the fuses kept blowing out and causing delays in completing this project! So get out of here and take your worthless generators with you.

Salesperson: [*with a smile*] Thank you for telling me. Say, you know you and our company's design engineers have a lot in common.

Prospect: Oh yeah! I'll bet! [*sarcastically*]

Salesperson: Suppose you were chief engineer in charge of manufacturing our generators. What would you do if valued customers—like yourself—said your generators had problems?

Prospect: I'd throw them in the trash.

Salesperson: Come on, what would you really do? [*with a smile*]

Prospect: Well, I would fix it.

Salesperson: That's why I said you and our design engineers have a lot in common. They acted on your suggestion.

[Comment: You have used reverse psychology. Now the prospect is listening, giving you time to explain your product's new features and to offer to repair the old units. You are ready to sell more products, if possible.]

Another example is the industrial salesperson who responded to the prospect's high price objection by saying, "Well, that's the very reason you should buy it." The prospect was caught off guard and quickly asked, "What do you mean?" "Well," said the salesperson, "for just 10 percent more you can buy the type of equipment you really want and need. It is dependable, along with being safe and simple to operate.

Your production will increase so that very quickly you have paid back the price differential." The prospect said, "Well, I hadn't thought of it quite like that. I guess I'll buy it after all."

Boomeranging an objection requires good timing and quick thinking. Experience in a particular selling field, knowledge of your prospect's needs, a positive attitude, and a willingness to stand up to the objection are necessary attributes for successful use of this technique.

Ask Questions to Smoke Out Objections

Intelligent questioning can impress a prospect in several ways. Technical questions show a prospect that a salesperson "knows the business." Questions relating to a prospect's particular business show that a salesperson is concerned more with the prospect's needs than with just making a sale. Finally, people who **ask intelligent, well thought-out questions,** whether they know much about their product, the prospect's business, or life in general, often receive admiration. Buyers are impressed with the sales professional who knows what to ask and when to ask it! Examples of questions are:

Prospect: This house is not as nice as the one someone else showed us yesterday.
Salesperson: Would you tell me why?

or

Prospect: This product does not have the . . . [feature].
Salesperson: If it did have the . . . [feature], would you be interested?

[Comment: The above example is an excellent questioning technique to determine if the objection is a smoke screen, a major or minor objection, or a practical or psychological objection. If the prospect says "no" to the response you know the feature was not important.]

or

Prospect: I don't like your price.
Salesperson: Will you base your decision on price or on the product offered you . . . at a fair price?

[Comment: If the prospect says "price," you show how benefits outweigh costs. If the decision is said to be based upon the product, you have eliminated the price objection.]

Five-Question Sequence Method of Overcoming Objections. We have seen that buyers bring up objections for numerous reasons. From time to time all salespeople can sense that a buyer is not going to buy. As you gain sales experience, you will be able to feel it yourself. It may be the buyer's facial expressions or a tone of voice that tips you off. When this occurs you need to quickly find out why a prospect doesn't want to buy. For doing this, consider the use of a preplanned series of questions as shown in Figure 9–5.

Let's assume you have finished your presentation. You try to close the sale and you can plainly see the buyer is not willing to go any further in the conversation. What do you do? Consider using the following **five-question sequence.**

First, use this question, "There must be some good reason why you're hesitating to go ahead now. Do you mind if I ask what it is?" When the reason is stated, or even if it is an objection, you should immediately double-check the objection with one more question by using question number two in the series: "In addition to that, is there any other reason for not going ahead?" The buyer may give the real reason for not buying, or may give the original objection. No matter what is said, you have set up a condition for buying.

Now you use question number three, which is a "just supposing" question. "Just supposing you could . . . then you'd want to go ahead?" If the answer is yes, then you discuss how you can do what is needed. If you get a negative response, then you use question number four which is, "Then there must be some other reason. May I ask what it is?" Respond with question number two again. Then ask, "Just supposing . . . you'd want to go ahead?" Should you get another negative response, then use question number five, by saying, "What would it take to convince you?"

What often happens now will surprise you. For the buyer will often say, "Oh, I don't know, I guess I'm convinced. Go ahead and ship it to me." Or you might be asked to go back over some part of your presentation. The important thing is that this series of questions keeps the conversation going and gets the real objections out in the open, which helps increase your sales. Now let's role-play this (imagine you are the salesperson):

Figure 9–5 Five-Question Sequence Method of Overcoming Objections

Question 1: There must be some good reason why you're hesitating to go ahead now. Do you mind if I ask what it is?

Question 2: In addition to that, is there any other reason for not going ahead?

Question 3: Just supposing you could convince yourself that. . . . Then you'd want to go ahead with it? (If positive response, go back to selling; if negative response, go to question 4.)

Question 4: Then there must be some other reason. May I ask what it is? (After response move back to question 2. Can go directly to question 5 or complete the sequence 1 or 2 more times before going to question 5.)

Question 5: What would it take to convince you?

Salesperson:	Should we ship this out to you this week or next?
Buyer:	Neither; see me on your next trip. I'll have to think about it.
Salesperson:	You know, there must be some very good reason why you're hesitating to go ahead now. Would you mind if I asked what it is?" [Question 1]
Buyer:	Too much money.
Salesperson:	Too much money. Well, you know, I appreciate the fact that you want to get the most for your money. In addition to the money, is there any other reason for not going ahead? [Question 2]
Buyer:	No.
Salesperson:	Well, just supposing then, that you could convince yourself that your savings from this machine would pay for itself in just a few months. And that we could fit it into your budget. Then you'd want to go ahead with it? [Question 3]
Buyer:	Yes, I would.

Now you go back to selling by discussing the return on investment and affordable payment terms. You went from the first objection to the "double-check" question ("In addition to the money, is there any other reason for not going ahead?"). Then you used the "just supposing" question. You met the condition, the machine's cost. Then you went to the "convince" question. The buyer said, "Yes," so you can keep on selling. Now let's role-play as if the buyer had said "no." (Again, you are the salesperson.)

Buyer:	No, I wouldn't go ahead.
Salesperson:	Well, then there must be some other reason why you're hesitating to go ahead now. Do you mind if I ask what it is? [Question 4]
Buyer:	It takes too much time to train my employees on the use of the machine.
Salesperson:	Well, you know, I appreciate that. Time is money. In addition to the time, is there any other reason for not going ahead? [Question 2]
Buyer:	Not really.
Salesperson:	Just supposing that you could convince yourself that this machine would actually save your employees time so they could do other things, you'd find the money then, wouldn't you? [Question 3]
Buyer:	I'm not sure. [Another potential negative response]
Salesperson:	Money and time are important to you, right?
Buyer:	Yes they are.
Salesperson:	What would it take for me to convince you this machine will save you time and money? [Question 5]

Now you have to get a response. The buyer has to set the condition. You as the salesperson are always in control. The buyer is answering the questions. Remember, you want to help the person to buy. When you get an objection, you are being told what you have to do in order to make the sale happen. So do not fear objections, welcome them.

Direct Denial Should Be Used Tactfully

You will often be faced with objections that are incomplete or incorrect. You should acknowledge the prospect's viewpoint, then answer the question by providing the complete or correct facts.

Prospect: No, I'm not going to buy any of your lawn mowers for my store. The Bigs-Weaver salesperson said they break down after a few months.

Salesperson: Well, I can understand. No one would buy mowers that don't hold up. Is that the only reason you won't buy?

Prospect: Yes, it is, and that's enough!

Salesperson: That BW salesperson was not aware of the facts, I'm afraid. My company produces the finest lawn mowers in the industry. In fact, we are so sure of our quality that we have a new three-year guarantee on all parts and labor. [*pause*]

Prospect: I didn't know that. [positive buying signal]

Salesperson: Are you interested in selling your customers quality lawn mowers like these? [trial close]

Prospect: Yes, I am. [appears that you have overcome the objection]

Salesperson: Well, I'd like to sell you one hundred lawn mowers. If even one breaks down, call me and I'll personally come over and repair it. [close]

As you see by this example, you do not say, "Well, you fathead, why do you say a thing like that?" Here tact is critical in using a direct denial. A smart or huffy response can serve to alienate your prospect. However, a **direct denial** based upon facts, logic, and politeness can be effective in overcoming the objective.

If I say to you, "You're wrong. Let me tell you why," what happens to your mind? It closes! So if I tell you that you are wrong and this closes your mind, what would I have to tell you to open your mind? That you are right! But if what you said was indeed wrong, do I tell you it was right? No, instead, do as the example illustrated by saying, "You know, you're right to be concerned about this. Let me explain." You have made the buyer right and kept the buyer's mind open. Also, you could say, "You know, my best customer had those small feelings until I explained that. . . ." You have not made the customer wrong, but right.

Anticipating Objections Comes with Experience

It is better to forestall or overcome objections before they arise. The sales presentation can be developed to directly address **anticipated**

objections. Take a manufacturer's salesperson selling exterior house paint who learns that a not-too-ethical competitor has been telling retail dealers that this paint starts to chip and peel after six months.

Realizing the predicament, this salesperson develops a presentation that very quickly points out, "Three independent testing laboratories have shown that this paint will not chip or peel for eight years after application." The salesperson has forestalled or answered the objection before it is raised by using a proof statement. This technique can also prevent a negative mood from entering into the buyer-seller dialogue.

Another way to anticipate objections is to bring disadvantages out before the prospect does. Many products have flaws, and these come up sometimes as you are trying to make a sale. If you know of an objection that comes up consistently, you ought to bring it up. Because if you bring it up first, you don't have to defend it.

On the other hand, a customer who brings up an objection feels compelled to defend that objection. For example, you might be showing real estate property. En route to the location, you say, "You know, before we get out there, I just want to mention a couple of things. You're going to notice that it needs a little paint in a few places, and there are a couple of shingles on the roof I noticed the other day that you may have to replace." When you arrive, your customer may take a look and say, "Well, those shingles aren't so bad . . . and I can see . . . we're going to paint it anyway." Yet if you reached the house without a little prior warning of small defects, those would be the first things a customer would notice.

A third way of using an anticipated objection is to brag about it and turn it into a sales benefit. You might say, "I want to mention something important before we go any further. Our price is a high one because as you are beginning to see, it is quality merchandise, and we're proud of the fact that we put this price on it. This allows us to build in the quality that we know has to go in it to give you the service and type of product which will fulfill your needs. Our customers are happy when they buy it from us, because we're able to stand behind our product."

You have taken all the sting out of the price objection because you have brought it up yourself. It is difficult for a buyer to come back and say, "It's too high," because you have already mentioned that. So there are times when you can anticipate objections and use them to your advantage.

Compensation or Counterbalance Method

Sometimes a prospect's objection is valid, and calls for the **compensation method** in overcoming objections. Several reasons for buying must exist to justify or compensate for a negative aspect of making a purchase. For example, a higher product price can be justified by benefits such as better service or higher performance. In the following example, it is true that the prospect can make more profit on each unit of a competing product. You must develop a technique to show how your product has benefits which will bring the prospect more profit in the long run.

Prospect: I can make five percent more profit with the Stainless line of cookware and it is quality merchandise.

Salesperson: Yes, you are right. The Stainless cookware is quality merchandise. However, you can have an exclusive distributorship on the Supreme cookware line, and still have high quality merchandise. You don't have to worry about Supreme being discounted by nearby competitors as you do with Stainless. This will be the only store in town carrying Supreme.

If the advantages you present to counterbalance the objection are important to the buyer, you now have an opportunity to make the sale.

Let a Third Party Answer

An effective technique to use in responding to an objection is to answer it by referring to a third party and using someone else's experience as your proof or testimony. A wide range of proof statements are used by salespeople today. You might respond to a question in this way: "I'm glad you asked. Here is what our research has shown. . . ." or, "EPA tests have shown. . . ." or, "You know, my best customer brought that point up before making the purchase . . . but was completely satisfied." These are examples of several basic proof statement formats.

Secondary data or experience, especially that from a reliable or reputable source, can be especially successful with the expert or skeptical prospect. If after hearing secondary testimony, the prospect was still unsure about the product, one successful equipment salesperson would ask the buyer to directly contact a current user:

Salesperson: I still haven't answered your entire question, have I?

Buyer: Not really.

Salesperson: Let's do this. Here is a list of several people presently using our product. I want you to call them up *right now* and ask them that same question. I'll pay for the call.

A salesperson should use this version of the third-party technique only when certain that the prospect is still unsatisfied with how an objection has been handled, and that positive proof will probably clinch the sale. This dramatic technique allows the salesperson to really impress a prospect. It also shows a flattering willingness to go to great lengths to validate a claim.

Basic Points to Consider in Meeting Objections

No matter what type of objections are raised by the prospect, there are certain basic points to consider in meeting objections. You should learn to anticipate objections, consider objections as opportunities, be positive toward objections, and understand objections before you attempt to overcome them.

Anticipate Objections

Plan for objections that might be raised by your presentation. Consider not only the reasons prospects should buy but also why they should not buy. Structure your presentation so as to minimize the disadvantages of your product. Be sure not to discuss disadvantages unless prospects bring them up in the conversation.

After each sales call, review the prospect's objections. Divide them into major and minor objections. Then develop ways of overcoming them. Your planning for and rehearsal of overcoming objections will allow you to respond to them in a natural and positive manner.

Consider Objections as Opportunities

Objections should be welcomed. They indicate prospects' willingness to discuss your product. They are interested enough in your presentation to talk with you.

Objections help you understand what prospects are thinking. They provide clues to prospects' needs. Only bring objections into the discussion once you are able to overcome them.

Be Positive

When you respond to an objection, use positive body language, such as a smile. Strive to respond in a manner that gets your prospect to be friendly and to stay in a positive mood. Do not take the objection personally. You should never treat the objection with hostility. Take the objection in stride by responding respectfully, and showing sincere interest in your prospect's opinion.

At times the prospect may raise objections based upon incorrect information. Politely deny objections which are not true. Be realistic; all products have drawbacks, even yours. If a competitor's product has a feature yours does not have, point out the overriding benefits of your product.

Understand Objections

When customers give you an objection, they are doing one of three things, as shown in Figure 9–6. They are either requesting more

Figure 9–6 What Does a Prospect Mean by an Objection?

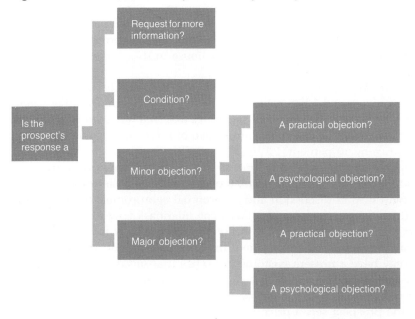

information, setting a condition, or giving you a genuine objection.

Request for Information.   Many times prospects appear to be making objections whey they are actually making a request for more information. That is why it is important to listen. If prospects request more information, chances are they are in the conviction stage. You have created a desire; they want the product, but they are not convinced you have the best product or that you are the best supplier of that product. If you feel that this is or may be the case—supply the information that has been indirectly requested.

A Condition.   At times, prospects may raise an objection which turns into a **condition of the sale.** They are saying, "If you can meet my request, I'll buy" or, "Under certain conditions I will buy from you."

If you sense that the objection is a condition, you must quickly determine if you can help the prospect meet the condition. If you cannot, then politely close the interview. Take the following real estate example:

Prospect: It's a nice house, but the price is too high. I can't afford a $1,000 a month house payment. [You do not know if this is an objection or condition.]

Salesperson: I know what you mean [acknowledging the prospect's viewpoint]. If you don't mind my asking, what is your monthly salary?

Prospect: My take-home pay is $1,400 a month.

In this case, the prospect has set a condition on the purchase which cannot realistically be met by the salesperson; it is not an objection. Attempting to continue the exchange by bargaining would have wasted time and possibly angered the prospect. Now that the prospect's income is known, the salesperson can show a house in the prospect's price range.

Negotiation Can Overcome a Condition.   Often conditions are stated by the prospect which can be overcome through **negotiation** between buyer and seller. Prospects may say things like, "I'll buy your equipment if you can deliver it in one month instead of three" or, "If you'll reduce your price by 10 percent, I'll buy."

If you determine that this type of statement is a condition rather than an objection, through negotiation you may be able to make the sale with further discussion and an eventual compromise between you and the buyer. In the example above, you might ask your manufacturing plant if the equipment can be shipped to the prospect in two months instead of three. This arrangement may be acceptable to the prospect. You may have a present customer who has that piece of equipment but is not using it. You might arrange for the prospect to lease it from your customer for three months.

If the prospect sets a price condition, saying, "I will buy your typewriter only if you reduce your price 10 percent," you might determine if your company will reduce the price if the buyer is willing to purchase a larger quantity of typewriters. Consider this actual example. As a state agency, Texas A&M University purchases much of its office equipment on a bid system. The Lanier Business Products salesperson could not sell the Texas A&M Marketing Department a word processor because the cost of a single machine was too high for that department's budget. The department wanted the machine; however, they could not afford it. Instead of giving up, the salesperson went to other departments in the university and found a need for a total of 16 machines (at a price of $4,000 per word processor less than the price of one machine). Lanier could substantially lower the price because of the large number of machines purchased. The salesperson determined that price was a condition, found a way to overcome the condition, and made the sale. Through initiation and inquiry, a potentially lost sale was turned into a multiple victory beneficial to all parties concerned.

Now there are two broad categories of objections. One of them is called "hopeless." A hopeless objection is one that can not be solved or answered. Examples of a hopeless objection would be "I already have one," "I'm bankrupt," "I'd like to buy your life insurance, but the doctor only gives me 30 days to live." So there are objections you could call hopeless. You can not overcome them.

If your prospect does not buy and no condition exists or the objection is not hopeless, it is your fault you did not make the sale

because you could not provide information to show how your offering would suit the buyer's needs.

The second category is the objection which can be answered. It is a "true" objection. The true objection has two types: the major and the minor objection.

You've Got to Do Better than That

In a recent issue of *Purchasing Magazine,* a leading expert on negotiation explained that there are seven magic words that drive salespeople crazy. They are: *"You've got to do better than that."*

The author, Dr. Chester L. Karrass, says that the uninhibited use of this crunch technique ultimately results in false economy because sellers soon learn to add 10 percent to bids in order to have something to shave later when the crunch comes.

Personal Selling Power collected responses from selected readers who have handled the crunch technique with success.[1] They used answers like:

1. I understand that you want a lower price, and we will be more than happy to lower it to the level you have in mind. Let's review the options that you'd like to cut from our proposal, so we can meet your needs.

2. We are building a product up to a quality, not down to a price. A lower price would prevent us from staying in business and serving your needs later on.

3. Yes, we can do better than that if you agree to give us a larger order.

4. It was my understanding that we were discussing the sale of our product and not the sale of our business.

5. I appreciate your sense of humor—how much better can you get than rock-bottom? You see, our policy is to quote the best price first. We have built our reputation on high quality and integrity—it's the best policy.

6. I'd be glad to give you the names of two customers so you can find out how much they paid for our product. And you'll see it's exactly the same as we are asking you to pay. We could not develop our reputation without being fair to everyone.

7. I appreciate the opportunity to do a better selling job. Obviously, you must have a reason for looking exclusively on the dollar side of our proposal. Let's review the value that you'll be receiving. . . ."

Major or Minor Objection.   Once you determine that the prospect has raised a true objection, you need to determine its importance. If it is of little or no importance, then quickly address it and return to selling. Be careful not to provide a long response or blow a minor objection up into a major discussion item. The minor objection is often a defense mechanism of little actual importance to the prospect. Concentrate on objections directly related to the prospect's important buying motives.

Practical or Psychological Objection.   Objections, minor or major, can be **practical** (overt) or **psychological** (hidden) in nature. Figure 9–7 gives some examples. A real objection is tangible, such as a high price. If this is a real objection, and the prospect says so, you can show that your product is of high quality and worth the price, or you might suggest removing some optional features and reducing the price. As long as the prospect clearly states the real objection to purchasing the product, you should be able to answer the objection.

However, prospects will not always be so agreeable as to clearly state their objections openly. Rather, they will often give some excuse as to why they are not ready to make a purchase, concealing real objections. Usually the prospect will not purchase the product until those hidden objections are rectified. It is up to you to uncover a prospect's hidden objections and eliminate them satisfactorily.

Figure 9–7 Examples of Objections

Practical	Psychological
Price	Resistance to spending money
Not what is needed	
Has overstock of your or competitor's products	Resistance to domination
	Predetermined beliefs
Delivery schedules	Negative image of salespeople
	Dislike of making buying decision

After Meeting the Objection— What to Do?

Your prospect has raised an objection which you have answered and overcome, now what? First, as shown in Figure 9–8, use a trial close, then be prepared to either move back into your presentation or to close the sale.

First, Use a Trial Close

After meeting an objection at any time during the interview, you need to know if you have overcome the objection. If you have not overcome

Figure 9–8 Procedure to Follow When Objection is Raised by Prospect

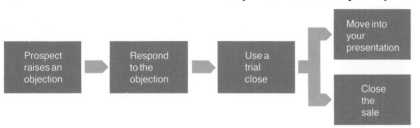

it, your prospect may bring it up again. Whether it resurfaces or not, if your prospect believes that an objection was important, your failure to handle it, or mishandling of it, will probably cost you the sale. Ideally, all objections raised should be met before closing the sale. So the first thing to do after responding to the objection is to use a trial close to determine if you have overcome the objection. Next, you either move back into your presentation or close the sale.

Move Back into Your Presentation

Once you are satisfied that you have answered and overcome an objection, you need to make a smooth transition back into your presentation. Continue your presentation where you left off.

Move to Close Your Sale

If you have completely finished your presentation when the prospect raised an objection and the prospect's response to your trial close indicates you have overcome an objection, your next move is to close the sale. If the objection was raised during your close, then it is time for you to close again.

If You Cannot Overcome the Objection

Should you be unable to overcome an objection or close a sale because of an objection, you should be prepared to move back into your presentation and concentrate on new or previously discussed features, advantages, and benefits of your product. If you have determined that the objection raised by your prospect is a major one which you cannot overcome, admit it and show how your product's benefits outweigh this disadvantage.

If you are 100 percent sure that you cannot overcome the objection and that the prospect is not going to buy, you should go ahead and close. *Always ask for the order.* Never be afraid to ask your prospect to buy. It never hurts to ask. It is the buyer who says no, not you.

Someone else may walk into the prospect's office after you with a product similar to yours. Your competitor may also be unable to overcome this person's objection, but may get the sale nonetheless, just by asking for it!

Summary of Major Selling Issues

People want to buy but they do not want to be taken advantage of, so they often ask questions or raise objections during a sales presentation. Your responsibility is to be prepared to logically and clearly respond to your prospect's objections whenever they arise, whether during your approach or when you move to close the sale.

Sales objections indicate a prospect's opposition or resistance to the request of the salesperson. Basic points to consider in meeting objections are to anticipate them, welcome them as opportunities, respond warmly and positively to them, make sure you understand them, rephrase them as questions when possible, be prepared to smoke out hidden objections, and handle them as they arise.

Before you can successfully meet objections you need to first determine if the prospect's response to your statement or close is a request for more information, a condition of the sale, or an objection. If it is a real objection, determine whether it is minor or major. Respond to it using a trial close, and if you have successfully answered it then continue your presentation based upon where you are in the sales presentation. For example, if you are still in the presentation, then move back into your selling sequence. If you have completed the presentation, move to your close. If you are in the close and the prospect voices an objection, then you must decide whether to use another close or move back into the presentation and discuss additional benefits.

You should be aware of and plan for objections. Objections may be classified as hidden, stalling, no-need, and money objections. Develop several techniques to help you overcome each of these types of objections, such as forestalling the objection, turning the objection into a benefit, asking questions to smoke out hidden objections, denying the objection if appropriate, illustrating how product benefits outweigh the objection drawbacks, or developing proof statements which answer the objection.

Welcome your prospects' objections. They will help you determine if you are on the right track or guide you to uncovering what prospects' needs actually are, and if they believe your product will fulfill those needs. Valid objections should be viewed as beneficial for you and the customer. A true objection reveals the customer's need, allowing a salesperson to demonstrate how a product can meet that need. Objections can also show up inadequacies in a salesperson's presentation or product knowledge. Finally, objections make selling a skill which a person can constantly improve. Over time, a dedicated salesperson can learn how to handle every conceivable product objection—tactfully, honestly, and to the customer's benefit.

Review and Discussion Questions

1. Name each major category of objections and give one or more examples of a technique for meeting the objection. Choose a different technique for each objection category.
2. Most prospects will ask about a salesperson's products or raise an objection. Discuss objections, including in your answer such things as: (a) what they are, (b) when a prospect might raise an objection, and (c) what the basic points to consider when responding to an objection are.
3. At times a salesperson may wish to rephrase objections as questions. What is the procedure one should follow to rephrase an objection as a question?
4. Before successfully meeting objections, a salesperson should first be clear about the objection. Discuss the factors that need to be determined to be sure you understand the objection.
5. Assume you are a salesperson and your prospect raises an objection to buying your product. What should be your attitude toward this situation?
6. Halfway through your sales presentation, your prospect stops you and says, "That sounds like a great deal and you certainly have a good product, but I'm not interested now; maybe later." What should you do?
7. Assume you are a salesperson for the Japan Computer Corporation. You have finished our computer presentation, and the purchasing agent for Gulf Oil says, "Well, that sounds real good and you do have the lowest price I have ever heard of for a computer system. In fact, it's $200,000 less than the other bids. But we have decided to stay with IBM, mainly because $200,000 on a $1,000,000 computer system is not that much money to us." Let's further assume that you also know that other than the price, IBM has significant advantages in all areas over your product. What would you do?
8. Using your knowledge of negotiation, which of these methods would be the best way to handle a prospective new car purchaser and why? A customer has told you she is only looking, prices are too high, and she cannot afford a new automobile at this time.
   A. Agree with her, then proceed to the next available customer.
   B. Show the customer a cheaper model of the same car.

    C.   Explain to the customer how payments can be tailored to fit almost anyone's budget.

    D.   Ask her why she is wasting her time looking at new cars.

9.   When a customer is not receptive to your product, you will very often find that there is some objection. Listed below are several situations in which the customer has an objection to a product.

    A.   The customer assumes he must buy the whole set of books. However, partial purchases are permitted.

    B.   The customer does not like the color and it's the only color your product comes in.

    C.   The customer doesn't want to invest in a new set of books because he doesn't want to lose money on his old one. You have not yet told him about your trade-in deal.

In which of the above situations does the objection arise from a misunderstanding or lack of knowledge on the customer's part? In which situation(s) does the product fail to offer a benefit that the customer considers important?

10. Consider the following two situations and then answer the questions which follow them:

Situation A

Customer:	I don't think I could sell your stoves here. Having to clean these ovens . . . no, I'm sorry; my customers want convenience and they can afford to pay for it.
Salesperson:	Then you think that your customers would find it inconvenient or bothersome to have to clean the Master oven?
Customer:	They sure would.
Salesperson:	That's just why the Master oven is fully automatic; it cleans itself at the push of a button. So you see, your customers will get convenience when they buy the Master oven.

Situation B

Customer:	But I'll never get them off the shelf. My customers aren't millionaires, you know!
Salesperson:	Then you think our toasters are too expensive?"
Customer:	Yes, definitely.
Salesperson:	But look at it this way: although the Tri-X is a little more expensive than some of the other models, you can be sure your customers will get a dependable toaster, one that will not overheat and short out. Moreover, the Tri-X comes with a one-year guarantee and that's a longer guarantee than any other manufacturer offers.

Refer to the preceding situations:

A.   In Situation A, the customer is objecting to the product because:

(1)   There is some misunderstanding about it.

       (2)   The product fails to offer a benefit which the customer feels is important.

  B.   Compared with Situation B, Situation A shows a customer objection that is:

       (1)   Difficult to answers.

       (2)   Easy to answer.

  C.   In both Situation A and Situation B, the salesperson responds to the customer's objection by *first:*

       (1)   Answering the objection directly.

       (2)   Offering agreement.

       (3)   Restating the objection in question form.

  D.   Restating an objection in question form before handling it is important for a number of reasons:

       (1)   It helps to clarify the objection.

       (2)   It shows that you are interested in, and attentive to, the customer's needs and problems.

       (3)   Both (1) and (2) are important reasons.

       (4)   Both (1) and (2) are not important reasons.

  E.   However, nothing you say in a restatement should imply agreement with the objection, since this will only make the objection appear more important to the customer. Which of the following phrases might you use in restating an objection?

       (1)   "Are you saying . . . ?"

       (2)   "Exactly! That's just what I was going to bring up next. . . ."

       (3)   "I agree, that is a problem. . . ."

       (4)   "If I understand you, then. . . ."

       (5)   "In other words. . . ."

       (6)   "Then you feel that. . . ."

  F.   The salesperson in Situation B knows that the cost of a product cannot be reduced even though the customer objects to it. To handle this difficult objection, the salesperson minimizes it in the customer's mind by:

       (1)   Answering it directly.

       (2)   Offering agreement with the objection.

       (3)   Stressing other relevant benefits of his product.

11.   A relatively easy-to-answer objection can result from:

  A.   The customer's misunderstanding.

  B.   The failure of a product to provide a benefit of interest to the customer.

  C.   Your failure to provide the customer with all necessary information.

12.   A more difficult-to-answer objection results from:

  A.   A lack of information on the customer's part.

B. The customer's misunderstanding.

C. The failure of your product to provide a benefit of interest to the customer.

13. When you restate the objection in question form, your objective is to:

A. Clarify the customer's remark.

B. Imply that you agree with the objection.

C. Indicate that you are interested in the customer's need or problem.

14. You will restate the objection in question form whenever you encounter:

A. An easy-to-answer objection.

B. A difficult-to-answer objection.

15. Which response is best when you get the customer reply, "I'd like to think it over?"

A. Give all the benefits of using the product now.

B. If there is a penalty for delaying, mention it now.

C. If there is a special price deal available, mention it now.

D. None of the above is appropriate.

E. Depending upon the circumstances, all three choices are appropriate.

16. Cliff Jamison sells business forms and he's regarded as a top-notch salesperson. He works hard, plans ahead and exhibits self-confidence. On this day he was making his first presentation to a prospective new client, the California Steel Company.

"Ladies and gentlemen," said Jamison, "our forms are of the very highest quality yet they are priced below those of our competitors. I know you are a large user of business forms and that you use a wide variety of them. Whatever your need for business forms, I assure you that we can supply them. And our forms are noted for their durability. They can be run through your machines at 60 per minute and they'll perform perfectly."

"Perfectly, Mr. Jamison?" asked the California Steel executive. "Didn't you have some trouble at Ogden's last year?"

"Oh," replied Jamison, "that wasn't the fault of our forms. They had a stupid operator who didn't follow instructions. I assure you that if our instructions are followed precisely you will have no trouble whatever.

"Furthermore, we keep a large inventory of our forms so that you need never worry about delays. A phone call to our office is all that is necessary to insure prompt delivery to your plant of precisely the forms you need. I hope, therefore, that I can be favored with your order. . . ." Did Jamison handle this situation correctly? Why?

17. One of your customers, Margaret Port, has referred you to a friend who needs your Hercules Shelving for a storage warehouse. Margaret recently purchased your heavy-duty, 18-guage steel shelving and is very pleased with it. She said, "This will be an easy sale for you. My friend really needs shelving and I told him about yours."

Margaret's information is correct and your presentation to her friend goes smoothly. The customer has asked numerous questions and seems ready to buy. Just before you ask for the order, the customer says, "Looks like your product is exactly what I need. I'd like to think this over. Could you call me next week?" Which of the following would you do? Why?

A. Follow the suggestion and call next week.
B. Go ahead and ask for the order.
C. Ask questions about the reason for the delay.

Projects

1. A national sales company is at your school wishing to hire salespeople. What are some objections such a company might have toward hiring you? How would you overcome them during a job interview?

2. Visit three different types of business (such as a grocery store, hardware store, and stereo shop) and pick out one product from each business. If you were that store's buyer, think of the major objections or questions you would ask a product salesperson if you were asked to buy a large quantity and promote it. Now, as that salesperson, how would you overcome those objections?

Cases

9–1 Handy Dan

As you drive up into the parking lot of one of your best distributors of your home building supplies, you recall how only two years ago they purchased the largest opening order you ever sold. Last year their sales doubled and this year you hope to sell them over $100,000 worth.

As you wait, the receptionist informs you that since your last visit your buyer, John Smalley, was fired and another buyer was transferred in to take his place. John and you had become reasonably good friends over the past two years and you hated to see him go.

As you enter the new buyer's office, she askes you to have a seat and then says: "I've got some bad news for you. I'm considering switching suppliers. Your prices are too high."

Questions:

1. Under these circumstances the best way to react to this objection would be:
   A. "It's certainly a good idea to compare prices, because price is always an important consideration. When you add up all the benefits we offer, however, I think you'll find that our prices—over the long haul—are actually lower than the competition's."
   B. "Would you mind telling me exactly why you're considering this move?"
   C. "Gee, I'm really surprised at this move. After all, we were the ones who originally got you interested in handling home building supplies. Our service has been good, and most importantly, you've derived excellent profits from our line."
2. Why did you not choose the other two alternatives?

9–2   Ace Building Supplies

This is your fourth call on Ace Building Supplies to get them to begin carrying and selling your home building supplies to local builders. Joe Newland, the buyer, has given you every indication that he likes your products.

During the call, Joe reaffirms his liking for your products and attempts to end the interview by standing up saying: "We'll be ready to do business with you in three months—right after this slow season ends. Stop by then and we'll definitely place an order with you."

Questions:

1. Under these circumstances, which one of the following would you do? Why?
   A. Call back in three months to get the order as suggested.
   B. Try to get a firm commitment or order now.
   C. Telephone Joe in a month (rather than make a personal visit) and try to get the order.
2. Why did you not choose the other two alternatives?

9–3   Get Your Junk Merchandise out of My Store

As Kit Utterback walked up to Joan Adams, the cosmetic buyer of Foley's Department Stores, she noticed Joan seemed very upset. The conversation went like this:

Joan: That new make-up of yours is separating in the bottles. We can't and won't sell junk like that. I always thought Revlon made quality products.

Kit: Joan, you know we make the highest quality products in the industry but . . .

Joan: But nothing, take all of that junk of yours off of my shelves and out of the warehouse. Give me a credit for it. I'm switching to Max Factor products.

Joan turned and walked off, leaving Kit standing there not knowing what to say. Kit went to the warehouse to examine the merchandise. While she was in the warehouse the warehouse manager apologized to Kit for leaving the merchandise in the sun on the loading docks. Kit asked if Joan knew about this. "Yes," was the reply, "but there is no talking to her these days. She was turned down for a promotion and she is taking it out on everyone. Her cousin went to work for Max Factor and Joan is changing over to all of their products."

Question:

What should Kit do?

9–4 Electric Generator Corporation (B)

George Wynn is a salesperson for EGC whose primary responsibility is to contact engineers in charge of the construction of commercial buildings. One such engineer is Don Snyder who is in charge of building the new Texas A&M University College of Business Administration facility. Don's Houston-based engineering firm had purchased three new EGI portable generators for use on this project. George had learned that Don's company will build four more buildings on the A&M campus and he felt Don might buy more machines.

Salesperson: Don, I understand you have three of our new model electric generators.

Buyer: Yeah, you're not kidding.

Salesperson: I'm sure you'll need additional units on these new jobs.

Buyer: Yeah, we sure will.

Salesperson: I've gone over the building's proposed floor plans and put together the type of products you need.

Buyer: They buy down in Houston, you need to see them!

Salesperson: I was just in there yesterday and they said it was up to you.

Buyer: Well young man, I'm busy today.

Salesperson: Can I see you tomorrow?

Buyer: No need, I don't want any more of your lousy generators!

Salesperson: What do you mean, that is our most modern design?

Buyer: Those so called "new" fuses of yours are exploding after five minutes' use. The auto-transformer starter won't start . . . did you see the lights dim, that's another fuse blowing.

Question:

George has a great deal of pressure on him to sell the new EGI. Don's business represents a big and important sale, both now and in the future. If you were George what would you do?

9–5 Vacuum Cleaner Inc.

Jane Dowdy, a salesperson for Sani-Sweep Vacuum Cleaner, feels that a customer's attitude toward her product generally falls into one of three categories: acceptance, indifference, or rejection. First, if a customer is satisfied with a present product, or feels no need for a product of her type, the customer's attitude toward her product is likely to be one of indifference. When this occurs, Jane likes to directly probe her customer to uncover areas of possible dissatisfaction with the competitor's product. Second, if the customer seems to agree with her benefit statements and displays no adverse feelings toward her product, the customer's attitude is likely to be one of acceptance. Jane quickly introduces additional benefits and makes a trial close. Third, if the customer is not receptive to Jane's benefit statements and appears to have doubts or reservations about the product, the response is to make an objection. For this customer Jane prefers to restate the objection as a question.

Before deciding upon the approach (or strategy) to use in a sales interview, Jane determines the customer's attitude toward her product. She must discover the attitude by means of what is said in response to her benefit statements about the product. At the end of her work day, Jane reviewed three situations which she had encountered. The conversations went like this:

Situation 1

Salesperson: Our Sani-Sweep is the first vacuum cleaner of its kind to run on flashlight batteries.

Customer: Say, that sounds like a good deal.

Situation 2

Salesperson: Our Sani-Sweep is the first vacuum cleaner of its kind to run on flashlight batteries.

Customer: Oh, that's dandy. So, I'm running to the store buying new batteries every week.

Situation 3

Salesperson: Our Sani-Sweep is the first vacuum cleaner of its kind to run on flashlight batteries.

Customer: Well, that's nice, but our floors are covered by that new type of tile that never needs vacuuming.

Questions:

1. For each situation, was the customer's attitude one of acceptance, indifference, or objection?
2. For each situation, how should Jane respond to the customer? Why? Give specific examples of how you would respond.

10

Close, Close, Close

Learning Objectives

1. To explain the essentials of closing a sale.
2. To discuss the timing of a close.
3. To present examples of several closing techniques.
4. To stress the importance of flexibility, and closing based on the situation.

Key Terms for Selling

Closing

Buying signal

Alternative choice close

Assumptive close

Compliment close

Summary of benefits close

Continuous-yes close

Minor-points close

T-account close

Standing-room-only close

Profile

George W. Morris
Prudential Life Insurance

Realizing my interest was in a career of selling, I interviewed with companies in many industries while a student at the University of Oklahoma. When I interviewed with the general agent of the Massachusetts Mutual Insurance Company in Oklahoma City prior to graduation, I become very fascinated about the opportunities the insurance business offered. The Mass Mutual was not then operating in Amarillo, my home town, and a friend suggested I talk to the manager of the Prudential Life Insurance Company for Fort Worth and the West Texas area. It appeared to me that I wanted to be associated with a major, reputable company, so while studying for final exams, I was simultaneously preparing to learn the Prudential Dollar Guide Presentation. I received my degree on June 11, 1950, and signed my contract the next day to start in the insurance business.

Mr. McCelvey, my first manager with Prudential, used to say the development of a sales presentation was simply "fixing" the prospect's problems and helping him accomplish his objectives. Thirty-one years later in the insurance business, I couldn't agree more! The sales presentation is the ability of the agent to build extremely close, personal relationships with people, learn about their objectives, desires, concerns and commitments, and help them accomplish these. If everything has been done to develop the sales presentation properly, the "closing" of the sale is simply the next logical sequence.

To be successful in an insurance career a person needs a very deep commitment to the product of life insurance and what it will do. The insurance business will test a person's "metal" and this abiding faith will be needed in times of discouragement and frustration. As you experience death claims and see what the product can and does do for families, corporations, partnerships, trusts, and other entities, uniquely, the faith and commitment to the product are sure to come. This develops the philosophy of "you're not only in the insurance business, the insurance business is in you!"

A person who is interested in an insurance career should first overcome the negatives sometimes attached to the life insurance business. These negatives, however, are more than offset, in my opinion, by the limitless opportunity for a large income, ultimate respect and admiration from your clientele, complete independence to pursue your career as you feel best, and not dependent upon the political whims of your superior but based totally on your capabilities and commitment.

"My company," said one executive, "had done business for many years with a firm which helped us merchandise our industrial products. I persuaded our advertising manager to have another firm also submit a proposal on how to best handle our products. Both suppliers received enthusiastic consideration on their proposals from our executives, and submitted competitive bids on price."

"The salesman for the new company had every reason," the executive went on to say, "to believe he would receive our business and so did I. However, our advertising manager felt the company should stay with the old firm because of the chance we would take by adopting something new. It was too risky for him. He knew what to expect from the old company." This executive had not discussed this concern with the newcomer's salesman during his presentation. The salesman failed to overcome and thus make the sale. He probably never found out why he lost the order.[1]

The point of the above example is that successful salespeople do not give a presentation and then ask for the order. Successful salespeople develop selling techniques which aid them in developing a natural instinct, sensitivity, and timing for when and how to close each buyer. This chapter wraps up our discussion of the main elements of the sales presentation. We will begin by discussing when to close, showing examples of buying signals, and discussing what makes a good closer. Next is a discussion of the number of times you should attempt to close a sale, along with some problems associated with closing. Eight closing techniques are presented, followed by an explanation of the importance of being prepared to close several times based upon the situation.

When Should I Pop the Question?

Closing is the process of helping people make a decision that will benefit them. You help people make that decision by asking them to buy. As successful salespeople know, there are no magic phrases and techniques to use in closing a sale. It is simply the end result of your presentation. As insurance agent George Morris says, "If everything has been done to properly develop a sales presentation, the closing of the sale is simply the next step in a logical sequence.''

Although it seems obvious, some salespeople forget that prospects know that the salesperson is there to sell them something. So, as soon as the two meet, the prospect's mind may already have progressed beyond the major portion of the salesperson's presentation. At times, the prospect may be ready to make the buying decision very early in the interview.

So when should you attempt to close a sale? Simply, *when the prospect is ready!* More specifically, when the prospect is in the "conviction stage" of the mental buying process. A buyer can enter the conviction stage at virtually any time during the sales presentation. As shown in Figure 10–1, you might ask someone to buy as early as the approach stage or as late as another day. Ninety-nine percent of the time, however, the close comes after the presentation. An ability to read a prospect's buying signals correctly can aid a salesperson in deciding when and how to close a sale.

Reading Buying Signals

After prospects have gone through each stage of the mental buying process and are ready to buy, they will often give you some type of signal. A **buying signal** refers to anything prospects say or do to indicate that they are ready to buy. Buying signals hint that prospects are in

Figure 10–1 Close When the Prospect Is Ready

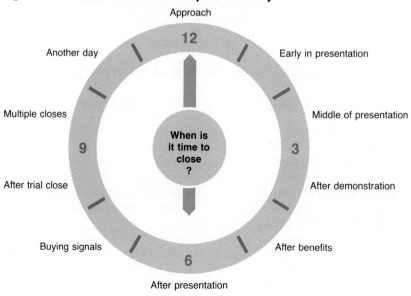

the conviction stage of the buying process. Several ways in which buyers may signal that they are ready to buy are as follows. The prospect:

■ *Asks questions*—"How much is it?" "When is the earliest I can receive it?" "What are your service and return goods policies?" At times, you may wish to respond to a buying signal question with another question, as shown in Figure 10–2. This helps you better determine your prospect's thoughts and needs. If your question is answered positively, the prospect is showing a high interest level and you are close to closing the sale.

■ *Asks another person's opinion*—The executive calls someone on the telephone and says, "Come in here a minute; I have something to ask you." Or the wife turns to her husband and says, "What do you think about it?"

■ *Relaxes and becomes friendly*—Once the prospect decides to purchase a product, the pressure of the buying situation is eliminated. A state of visible anxiety changes to one of refreshed relaxation because your new customer believes you are now a friend.

■ *Pulls out an order form*—If, as you are talking, your prospect pulls out an order form, it is time to move toward your close.

■ *Carefully examines merchandise*—When a prospect begins to carefully scrutinize your product or seems to be contemplating the purchase, this may be an indirect request for prompting. Given these indications, you should attempt a trial close: "What do you think about. . . ?" Should you obtain a positive response to this question, move on to close the sale.

A buyer may send verbal or nonverbal buying signals at any time before or during your sales presentation (remember Figure 10–1). The accurate interpretation of buying signals should prompt you to attempt

Figure 10–2 Examples of Answering a Prospect's Buying Signal Question with a Question

Buyer Says:	Salesperson Replies:
Can I get it in yellow?	Do you want it in yellow?
What's your price?	In what quantity?
What kind of terms do you offer?	What kind of terms do you want?
When can you make delivery?	When do you want delivery?
How big a copier should I get?	How big do you need?
Can I get this special price on an order I place now and next month?	Would you like to split your shipment?
Do you carry 8, 12, 36, and 54-foot pipe?	Are those the sizes you commonly use?
How large an order do I need to place to receive your best price?	How big an order do you have in mind?
Do you have the Model 6400 in stock?	Is that the one you like best?

a trial close. In beginning your trial close, summarize the major selling points desired by your prospect. If you receive a positive response to your trial close, you can move on to wrap up the sale. A negative response should result in a return to your presentation. In any case, a successful trial close can save you and your prospect valuable time, while a thwarted trial close will allow you to assess your selling situation.

What Makes a Good Closer?

In every sales force there are individuals who seem to be better than others at closing sales. Some rationalize this difference of abilities by saying, "It comes naturally to some people," or, "They've just got what it takes." Well, what does it take to be a good closer?

Good closers, most important, have a strong desire to close each sale. They have a positive attitude about their product's ability to benefit the prospect. They know their customers and tailor their presentations to meet each one's specific needs.

Good closers spend time in preparing for each sales call. They take the time to carefully ascertain the needs of their prospects and customers by observing, asking intelligent questions, and most of all earnestly listening to them.

The successful salesperson does not stop on the prospect's first no. If a customer says no, determine the nature of the objection and then move back into the presentation. After discussing information relative to overcoming the objection, use a trial close to determine if you have overcome the objection, and then determine if there are other objections. If resistance continues, remain positive and remember that every time you attempt to close, you get closer to making the sale. Additionally, always ask for the order and then shut up.

Ask for the Order and Shut Up!

No matter when or how you close, remember that when you ask for the order it is very important to be silent. Do not say a single word. If you say something—anything—you increase your probability of losing the sale.

You must put the prospect in a position of having to: (1) make a decision; (2) speak first; and (3) respond to close. If you say anything after your close, you take the pressure off the prospect to make that decision.

Imagine this situation. The salesperson has finished his presentation and says, "Would you want this delivery in two or four weeks?" The average salesperson cannot wait over ten seconds for the prospect's reply without saying something like, "I can deliver it anytime," or beginning to talk again about the product. This destroys the "closing moment." The prospect does not have to make the decision. There is time to think of reasons not to buy. By keeping quiet for a few seconds, the prospect can again escape making the decision.

All individuals experience the urge to say "no," even when they are not sure of what you are selling or may actually want what you are proposing. At times, everyone is hesitant in making a decision. To help the prospect make the decision, you must maintain silence after the close.

The professional salesperson "asks for the order and shuts up." The professional can stay quiet all day if necessary. Rarely will the silence last over thirty seconds. During that time do not say anything or make a distracting gesture; merely project positive nonverbal signs. Otherwise, you will lessen your chances of making the sale. This is the time to mentally prepare your responses to the prospect's reaction.

It sounds simple, yet it is not. Your stomach may churn. Your nerves make you want to move. You catch yourself with a serious look on your face, instead of a positive one. You may look away from the buyer. Most of all, you want to talk in order to relieve the uncomfortable feeling that grows as the silence continues. Finally, the prospect will say something. Now you can respond to the reaction to your close.

You should constantly practice asking your closing question, shutting up for thirty seconds, and then responding. This will develop your skill and courage to close.

Get the Order and Get Out!

Talking can also lose the sale for you after the prospect has said yes. An exception would be if you are asking the customer for names of other prospects. Once this is done, however, you should leave. It is best to get the order and get out.

In continuing to talk, you may give information that changes the buyer's mind. So ask for the order and remain silent until the buyer responds. If you succeed, finalize the sale and leave.

How Many Times Should You Close?

Courtesy and common sense imply a reasonable limit to the number of closes attempted by a salesperson at any one sitting. However, salespeople are calling on customers and prospects to sell their products.

In order to sell, you must be able to use multiple closes. The fact is, as the chapter title indicates, three closes is a minimum for successful salespeople. Three to five well-executed closes should not offend a prospect. Attempting several closes in one call challenges a salesperson to employ wit, charm, and personality in a creative manner. So always take at least three strikes before you count yourself out of the sale.

Closing under Fire

To effectively close more sales, you should never take the first no from the prospect to mean an absolute refusal to buy. Instead, you must be able to "close under fire." In other words, you must be able to ask a prospect who may be in a bad mood or may even appear hostile toward you, to buy.

Take the experience of a consumer goods salesperson who suggested that a large drug wholesaler should buy a six-month supply of the company's entire line of merchandise. Outraged, the purchasing agent threw the order book across the room. The salesperson explained to the furious buyer that the company had doubled its promotional spending in the buyer's area and that it would be wise to stock up because of an upcoming increase in sales. The salesperson calmly picked up the order book, smiled, and handed it to the buyer saying, "Did you want to buy more?"

The buyer laughed and said, "What do you honestly believe is a reasonable amount to buy?" This was a buying signal that the prospect would buy, but in a lesser quantity. They settled on an increased order of a two-month supply over the amount of merchandise normally purchased. This example illustrates why it is very important for the salesperson to react calmly to an occasional hostile situation.

Difficulties with Closing

Closing the sale should be the easiest part of the presentation. It serves as a natural wrap-up to your sales presentation because you are now solidifying the details of the purchase agreement. Yet salespeople sometimes have difficulty closing the sale for a number of reasons.

One reason salespeople may fail to close a sale and get an order is that they are not confident of their ability to close. Perhaps some earlier failure to make a sale has brought about this mental block. They may give their presentation and stop short of asking for the order. Obviously, the seller must overcome this fear of closing to become successful.

Second, salespeople often determine on their own that the prospect does not need the quantity, or type, of merchandise or that the prospect simply should not buy. So they do not ask the prospect to buy. The salesperson should remember that "it is the prospect's decision and responsibility whether or not to buy." Do not make that decision for the prospect.

Finally, the salesperson may not have worked hard enough in developing a customer profile and customer benefit plan—resulting in a poor presentation! Many times a poorly prepared presentation will fall apart before the salesperson's very eyes. Like a Boy Scout, it is important to be prepared and develop a well-planned, well-rehearsed presentation.

Essentials of Closing Sales

While there are numerous factors to consider in closing the sale, the following are essential if you wish to improve your chances.

- Be sure your prospect understands what you are saying.
- Always present a complete story to insure understanding.
- Tailor your close to each prospect. Eighty percent of your customers will respond to a "standard" close. It is the other 20 percent you need to be prepared for. You should be prepared to give the "expert" the facts requested, to give the egotist praise, to lead the indecisive prospect, and to slow down for the slow thinker.
- Everything you do and say should take into consideration the customer's point of view.
- Never stop at the first "no."
- Learn to recognize buying signals.
- Before you close, attempt a trial close.
- After asking for the order—shut up.
- Set high goals for yourself and develop a personal committment to reach your goals.
- Develop and maintain a positive, confident, and enthusiastic attitude toward yourself, your products, your prospects, and your close.

Twelve Steps to a Successful Closing

Before we discuss specific techniques on how to ask for the order or close the sale, you need to remember that you will greatly increase the number of sales you are able to close by following 12 simple steps. These steps are:

Step 1: Think *success!*

Step 2: *Plan* your sales call.

Step 3: Confirm your prospect's *needs* in the approach.

Step 4: Give a *great* presentation.

Step 5: Use *trial closes* during and after your presentation.

Step 6: Smoke out a prospect's *real* objections.

Step 7: *Overcome* these real objections.

Step 8: Use a *trial close* after overcoming each objection.

Step 9: Summarize *benefits* as related to buyer's *needs*.

Step 10: Use a *trial close* to confirm step 9.

Step 11: Ask for the *order* and then *shut up*.

Step 12: Leave the door *open!* Act as a professional.

As you see from these 12 steps, a successful close is the end result of a series of steps you have gone through before you ask for the order. As Figure 10–3 states, "closing is not one giant step."

Should you not make the sale, always remember to act as a professional salesperson and be courteous and appreciative of the opportunity to present your product to the prospect. This allows the door to be open when you come back another time. Thus, Step 12 cannot be overlooked—always remember to leave the door open!

Too often salespeople believe there is some mystical art to closing a sale. Some believe that if they say the right words in the appropriate manner, the prospect will buy. They concentrate on developing tricky closing techniques and often are extremely pushy with prospects in hopes of pressuring them into purchasing. Certainly, salespeople need to learn alternative closing techniques. However, what is most needed is a thorough understanding of the entire selling process and of the critical role that closing plays in that process.

A memorized presentation and a hurriedly presented product will not be nearly as successful as the skillful use of the 12 steps to a successful close. A close look at the 12 steps will illustrate that a lot of hard work, planning, and skillful execution of your plan occur before you reach Step 11 and ask for the order. The point is that if salespeople understand how each of the 12 steps applies to them and their customers, and if they are capable of performing each step, they will earn the right to close.

In fact, many times the close will occur automatically because it has become the easiest part of the sales presentation. Often the prospect will close for the salesperson, saying: "That sounds great, I'd like to buy that." All that the salesperson has to do is finalize the details, and write up the order. Often, though, the prospect will be undecided on the product after the presentation, so the skillful salesperson should develop a number of closing techniques.

Prepare Several Closing Techniques

To be able to successfully close more sales, you need to be able to determine your prospect's situation, understand the prospect's attitude

Figure 10–3

Closing Is Not One Giant Step

Too many salesmen regard the close as a separate and distinct part of the sales call. "I've discussed benefits and features, answered some objections, handled price, and now it's time to close."

Chronologically, of course, the "close" does come at the end. But you should have been closing right along.

Closing is the natural outgrowth of the sales presentation. If the rest of the sales call has been a success, closing should simply mean working out terms and signing the order.

What about the salesman who says, "I always have trouble closing. Everything's fine until it's time to close the sale." Chances are, there's no basis for the sale. "Everything's fine …" may merely be a way of saying, "I stated my case and he listened. At least he never told me to pack up and go."

Speaking of Selling © 1980, Sales Builders Division of S&MM.

toward your presentation, and be prepared to instantly select a closing technique from several techniques you know based upon your prospect. For example, suppose you had profiled the prospect as having a big ego, so you planned to use the "compliment" closing technique (to be discussed shortly). You find the prospect is eager to buy but undecided about which model or the number of products to buy, so you switch to using your "standing room only" closing technique. By changing to a closing technique that fits the situation, you can speed up the sale and still keep your customer satisfied.

Successful salespeople should be able to adapt their planned presentation to any prospect or any situation that may arise. Some salespeople have five to ten closing techniques, each designed for a specific type of situation. The following are eight of the more commonly used closing techniques:

- Alternative choice close
- Assumptive close
- Compliment close
- Summary of benefits close
- Continuous-yes close
- Minor-points close
- T-Account of balance sheet close
- Standing room only close

Whatever product is being sold, whether an industrial or consumer product, these closing techniques can be used to ask your prospect for the order. (See Figure 10–4.)

The Alternative Choice Close Is an Old Favorite

The **alternative choice close** was popularized in the 1930s as the story spread of the Walgreen Drug Company's purchase of 800 dozen eggs at a special price. A sales trainer named Elmer Wheeler suggested to the Walgreen clerks that when a customer asked for a malted milk at a Walgreen fountain, the clerk should say, "Do you want one egg or two?" Customers had not even thought of eggs in their malteds. Now they were faced with the choice of *how many* eggs—not whether or not they wanted an egg. Within one week all 800 dozen of the eggs were sold at a profit. Two examples of the alternative close are:

Which do you prefer—one or two neckties to go with your suit?
Would you prefer the Xerox 6200 or 6400 copier?

As you see, the alternative choice does not give the prospect a choice of buying or not buying, but asks which one or how many items they

Figure 10–4 Techniques for Closing the Sale

want to buy. It says, "You are going to buy, so let's settle the details on what you will purchase." Buying nothing at all is not an option.

Take for example the salesperson who says: "Would you prefer the Xerox 6200 or 6400?" This question: (1) assumes the customer has a desire to buy one of the copiers; (2) assumes the customer will buy; and (3) allows the customer to have a preference. If the customer prefers the Xerox 6400, you know the prospect is ready to buy, so you begin your close. A customer who says, "I'm not sure," is still in the desire stage, so you continue to discuss product benefits. However, you see that the customer likes both machines. Should the prospect appear to be indecisive, you can ask: "Is there something you are unsure of?" This question probes to find out why your prospect is not ready to choose.

If used correctly, the alternative choice close is a very effective closing technique. It provides a choice between something and something, never between something and nothing. By presenting a choice, you either receive a yes decision or uncover objections, which if successfully met will allow you to come closer to making the sale.

The Assumptive Close

With the **assumptive close,** the salesperson assumes the prospect will buy. Statements can be made such as, "I'll call your order in tonight," or, "I'll have this shipped to you tomorrow." If the prospect does not say anything, you can assume your suggested order has been accepted.

Many times the salesperson who has called on a customer for a long time can fill out the order form, hand it to the customer, and say, "This is what I'm going to send you," or, "This is what I believe you need this month." Many salespeople have earned the trust of their customers to such an extent that the salesperson orders for them. Here the assumptive close is especially effective.

The Compliment Close Inflates the Ego

Everyone likes to receive compliments. The **compliment close** is especially effective when you are talking with a prospect who is a self-styled expert, who has a big ego, or who is in a bad mood. Would-be experts and egotistical prospects both value their own opinion. By complimenting them, you get them to listen and respond favorably to your presentation. The prospect with a low ego, low self-esteem, or one who finds it difficult to come to a decision will also respond favorably to a compliment. Here is an example of a housewares salesperson closing a sale with a grocery retail buyer:

Salesperson: "It is obvious you know a great deal about the grocery business. You have every square foot of your store making a good profit. Ms. Stevenson, our products will also provide you with a good profit margin. In fact, our profit will exceed your store's average profit-per-square-foot. And they sell like hotcakes. This added benefit of high turnover will further increase your profits—which you have said is important to you." [He pauses and when there is no response continues.] "Given the number of customers coming into your store, and our expected sales of these products due to normal turnover, along with our marketing plan, *I suggest you buy. . . .*" [He states the products and their quantities.] "This will provide you with sufficient quantities to meet your customers' demands for the next two months, plus provide you the profit you expect out of your products." [Now he waits for the response or again asks for the order using the alternative choice or assumptive close.]

All buyers appreciate your recognition of their better points. Conscientious merchants take pride in their ways of doing business; customers coming into the retail clothing store take pride in their appearance; people considering life insurance take pride in looking after their families. So compliment prospects relative to something which will benefit them as you attempt to close the sale. Remember, always make your compliment an honest one. No matter how trusting you may think most people are, nearly anyone can detect insincerity in a compliment. When a compliment is not in order, you may choose to summarize the benefits of your product for a specific customer.

The Summary of Benefits Close Is Most Popular

During the sales presentation it is important to remember the main features, advantages, and benefits of interest to the prospect in order to use them successfully during the close. Summarize these benefits in a positive manner so that the prospect agrees with what you are saying; then ask for the order.

Here is an example of a salesperson using the **summary of benefits close** on a prospect. Assume that the salesperson knows that the prospect likes the product's profit margin, delivery schedule, and credit terms.

Salesperson: "Ms. Stevenson, you say you like our profit margin, fast delivery, and credit policy. Is that right? [Summary and trial close.]

Prospect: "Yes, I do, Chuck."

Salesperson: "With the number of customers coming into your store and our expected sales of the products due to normal turnover, along with our marketing plan, *I suggest you buy. . . .*" [He states the products and their quantities.] "This will provide you sufficient qualities to meet customer demand for the next two months, plus provide you with the profit you expect from your products. I can have the order to you early next week." [Now he waits for her response or again asks for the order using the alternative choice or assumptive close.]

You can easily adapt the *FAB* statements, discussed in Chapter 3, for your "summary" close. The vacuum cleaner salesperson might say, "As we have discussed, this vacuum cleaner's high speed motor [feature] works twice as fast [advantage] with less effort [advantage], saving you 15 to 30 minutes in cleaning time [benefit] and the aches and pains of pushing a heavy machine [benefit of benefit]. Would you want the Deluxe or the Ambassador model?"

The sporting goods salesperson might say, "As we have said, this ball will give you an extra 10 to 20 yards on your drive [advantage], helping to reduce your score [benefit] because of its new solid core [feature]. Will a dozen be enough?" The air conditioning salesperson could say, "This air conditioner has a high efficiency rating [feature] that will save you 10 percent on your energy costs [benefit] because it uses less electricity [advantage]. Would you want it delivered this week or do you prefer next week?

The summary close is favored by industrial product manufacturers like Xerox. Cindy Kerns, who is profiled in Chapter 15, says the major closing technique taught at the Xerox Training Center consists of the three basic steps of the summary close, which are: (1) determine the key product benefits which interest the prospect during the presentation, (2) summarize these benefits, and (3) make a proposal. The summary of benefits technique is useful when you need a simple, straightforward close, rather than a close aimed at a specific prospect's personality.

The Continuous-Yes Close Generates Positive Responses

The **continuous-yes close** is like the summary close. However, instead of summarizing product benefits, the salesperson develops a series of benefit questions which the prospect must answer.

Salesperson:	Ms. Stevenson, you have said you like our quality products, right?
Prospect:	Yes, that's right.
Salesperson:	And you like our fast delivery?
Prospect:	Yes, I do.
Salesperson:	You also like our profit margin and credit terms?
Prospect:	That's correct.
Salesperson:	Ms. Stevenson, our quality products, fast delivery, profit margin, and good credit terms will provide you with an excellent profit. With the large number of customers you have coming into your store. . . . [Salesperson completes the close as done in the summary of benefits close.]

In this example of the continuous-yes close, the salesperson recognized four product benefits that the prospect liked: (1) the product's quality, (2) fast delivery, (3) profit margin, and (4) favorable credit terms. After the presentation, three questions were used to give the prospect the opportunity to agree that she was impressed with each of the four product benefits. By stacking these positive questions, the salesperson kept the prospect continually saying, ''Yes, I like that benefit.''

The prospect has now placed herself in a positive frame of mind. Her positive stance toward the product makes it very likely that she will continue to say ''yes'' when asked to buy.

You should realize, of course, that some prospects may want to be ''cute,'' and relish the thought of seeing the look of surprise on your face when, after they agree to all of your product benefit statements (yes . . . yes . . . yes), they respond to your order request with an unexpected no. Also, some more suspicious prospects may view your continuous-yes close as trickery or as an insult to their intelligence rather than as an aid to them in making a purchase decision. In either case, your calm handling of the situation will reflect a sales professionalism that will both surprise the trickster and impress the suspicious person.

The Minor-Points Close Is Not Threatening

It is sometimes much easier for a prospect to concede several minor points about a product than to make a sweeping decision on whether to buy or not to buy. Big decisions are often difficult for some buyers to make. By getting the prospect to make decisions on a product's minor points, you can subtly lead into the decision to buy.

The **minor-points close** is similar to the alternative choice close. The alternative choice close asks the prospect to make a choice between two products. To some people, this represents a high-risk decision which they may prefer not to make. Whereas the minor-points close asks the prospect to make a low-risk decision on a minor, usually low-cost element of a single product such as delivery dates, optimal features, color, size, payment terms, or order quantity. Single or multiple product element choices may be presented to the prospect. The stereo salesperson says, "Would you prefer the single or multiple record changer for your stereo system?" The Lanier Business Products salesperson asks, "Are you interested in buying or leasing our equipment?" The automobile salesperson asks, "Would you like your car to be air-conditioned?"

This close is widely used when prospects have difficulty in making a decision or when they are not in the mood to buy. It also can be effectively used as a second close. If, for example, the prospect says no to your first close because of difficulty in deciding whether or not to buy, you can close on minor points.

The T-Account or Balance Sheet Close Was Ben Franklin's Favorite

The **T-account close** is based upon the process people go through when they make a decision. Some sales trainers refer to it as the Benjamin Franklin close. In his *Poor Richard's Almanac* Benjamin said . . . "You know, I believe most of my life is going to be made up of making decisions about things. I want to make as many good ones as I possibly can." So in deciding on a course of action, his technique was to take pencil and paper and draw a line down the center of the paper. On one side, he put all the noes and on the other side he put all the yeses. Now if there were more noes than yeses, he would not do something. If yeses outweighed the noes, then he felt it was a good thing to do; this was the correct decision.

This is actually the process a customer goes through when making a buying decision, weighing the noes against the yeses. So at times, it may be a good idea to use this technique. Yeses, and noes, debits and credits, or to act and not to act are common column headings used today. For example, on a sheet of paper the salesperson draws a large T, placing "to act" (asset) on the left side and "not to act" (liability) on the right side (debit and credit in accounting terms). The salesperson reviews the presentation with the prospect, listing the positive features, advantages, and benefits the prospect likes on the left side, and all negative points on the right. This is designed to show the product's benefits outweigh its liabilities, and to lead the prospect to conclude that now is the time to buy. If prospects make their own lists, the balance sheet close can be quite convincing. Here is an example:

Salesperson: Ms. Stevenson, here's a pad of paper and a pencil. Bear with me a minute and let's review what we have just talked about. Could you please draw a large *T* on the page and write "To Act" at the top on the left and "Not to Act" on the right. Now, you said you liked our fast delivery. Is that right?

Prospect: Yes.

Salesperson:	OK, please write down "fast delivery" in the To Act column. Great! You were impressed with our profit margin and credit terms. Is that right?
Prospect:	Yes.
Salesperson:	OK, how about writing that down in the left-hand column? Now is there anything that could be improved?
Prospect:	Yes, don't you remember? I feel you have a narrow assortment with only one style of broom and one style of mop. [Objection.]
Salesperson:	Well, write that down in the right-hand column. Is that everything?

TO ACT	NOT TO ACT
fast delivery good profit good credit	narrow assortment

Prospect:	Yes.
Salesperson:	Ms. Stevenson, which in your opinion outweighs the other—the reason to act or not to act? [A trial close.]
Prospect:	Well, the To Act column does. But it seems I need a better assortment of products. [Same objection again.]
Salesperson:	We have found that assortment is not important to most people. A broom and mop are pretty much a broom and mop. They want a good quality product that looks good and will hold up under continuous use. Customers like our products' looks and quality. Aren't these good-looking products? [Trial close showing broom and mop.]
Prospect:	Look OK to me. [Positive response—she didn't bring up assortment so assume you have overcome objection.]
Salesperson:	Ms. Stevenson, I can offer you a quality product, fast delivery, excellent profit, and good credit terms. I'd like to suggest this. You buy one dozen mops and one dozen brooms for each of your 210 stores. However let's consider this first! The XYZ chain found our mops had excellent drawing power when advertised. Their sales of buckets and floor waxes doubled. Each store sold an average of 12 mops. [He pauses, listens, and notices her reaction.] You can do the same thing!
Prospect:	I'd have to contact the Johnson Wax's salesperson and I really don't have the time. [A positive buying signal.]
Salesperson:	Ms. Stevenson, let me help. I'll call Johnson's and get them to contact you. Also, I'll go by and see your advertising manager to schedule the ads. OK? [Assumptive close.]
Prospect:	OK, go ahead, but this stuff had better sell.
Salesperson:	[*smiling*] Customers will flock to your stores [He's building a picture in her mind.] looking for mops, polish, and buckets. Say, that reminds me, you will need a dozen buckets for each store. [Continuous-yes, keep talking.] I'll write up the order [Assumptive.]

Some salespeople recommend that the columns of the T-account be reversed so that the Not to Act column is on the left and the To Act column is on the right. This allows the salesperson first to discuss the reasons not to buy, followed by the reasons to buy, ending the presentation on the positive side. This is a decision that can be made by the salesperson based upon preference.

Modified T-Account or Balance Sheet Close. Some salespeople modify the T-account close by only listing reasons to act in one column. They do not want to remind the prospect of any negative reasons not to buy as they attempt to close the sale. This is very similar to the continuous-yes close. The only difference is that the product benefits are written on a piece of paper.

This is a very powerful sales tool because prospects are mentally considering reasons to buy and not to buy anyway. You may just as well get the reasons out in the open so you can participate and be a part of the decision-making process.

While this close can be used anytime, it is especially useful as one of your secondary or backup closes. For example, if the summary close did not make the sale, go on to your next close, the T-account close. You see, a contrary idea in the mind of the prospect is like steam under pressure, that is, explosive. So when you remove the pressure from the steam by getting an objection out in the open, opposition vaporizes. An objection often becomes a minor one or goes away. Remember, however,if the customer says, "Well, I'm going to buy it," do not say, "Well, let's first take a look at the reasons not to buy." Go ahead and finalize the sale.

The Standing-Room-Only Close Gets Action

What happens if someone tells you that you cannot have something that you have an interest in or would like to have? You instantly want it! When you face an indecisive prospect or if you want to have the prospect purchase a larger quantity, indicate that if they do not act now they may *not* be able to buy in the future. To get the prospect to act at once, you can use the **standing-room-only close:**

"I'm not sure if I have your size. Would you want them if I have them in stock?"

"My customers have been buying all we can produce. I'm not sure if I have any left to sell you."

"Well, I know you are thinking of ordering X amount but we really need to order . . . (a larger amount) . . . because we now have it in stock and I don't think we will be able to keep up with demand and fill your summer order."

"The cost of this equipment will increase 10 percent next week. Can I ship it today or do you want to pay the higher price?"

For the right product, person, and situation, this is an excellent close. Both retail and industrial salespeople can use this technique to get the prospect so excited they cannot wait to buy. However, it should only be used in complete honesty. Prospects realize that factors such as labor strikes, weather, transportation, inflation, and inventory shortages could make it difficult to buy in the future. You can do them a favor by getting them to buy now using the standing-room-only close.

Prepare a Multiple Close Sequence

By keeping several difficult closes ready to aid you in any situation, you will put yourself in a better position to close more sales. Also the use of a multiple close sequence, combined with methods to overcome objections, will greatly enhance your chance of making a sale.

For example, you could begin with a summary close. Assuming the buyer says no, you could rephrase the objection, and then use an alternative close. If again the buyer says no, you could then use the five-question sequence method for overcoming objections, cycling through it two or three times.*

Figure 10–5 gives an example of multiple closes incorporating techniques to overcome objections. The successful closing of the sale often requires both methods to overcome objections and closing techniques.

Close Based on the Situation

Since different closing techniques work best for certain situations, salespeople often identify the common objections they encounter and develop specific approaches to closing designed to overcome these objections. Table 10–1 lists some of the ways in which different closing techniques can be used to meet objections.

Assume for example that a buyer has a predetermined belief that a competitor's product is what is needed. The salesperson could use the T-account approach to show how a product's benefits are greater than those of a competitor. In developing your sales presentation, you should review your customer profile and develop your main closing technique, along with several alternatives. By being prepared for each sales call, you will experience an increase in your confidence and enthusiasm which will result in a more positive selling attitude so that you can both help your customer, and reach your personal goals.

---

* See Chapter 9 for correct procedures on overcoming objections.

Figure 10–5 Example of Multiple Closes Incorporating Techniques for Overcoming Objections

Salesperson:	So we have found that the Octron bulb is going to reduce your storage space requirements for your replacement stock. It offers a higher color output for your designers reducing their eye fatigue and shadowing. [Summary benefits.] Should I arrange for delivery within the week?
Buyer:	Well, those are all good points, but I'm still not prepared to buy. It's too costly.
Salesperson:	What you're saying is "You want to know what particular benefits my product has that make it worth its slightly higher price?" Is that correct?
Buyer:	Yes, I guess so.
Salesperson:	Earlier we saw that considering the extended life of the lamps and their energy savings you can actually save $375 each year by replacing your present lamps with GE Watt-Misers. This shows that you actually save money using our product. Right? [Trial close.]
Buyer:	Yes, I guess you're right.
Salesperson:	Great! Do you prefer installation this weekend or after regular business hours next week? [Alternative close.]
Buyer:	Neither. I need to think about it more.
Salesperson:	There must be some good reason why you're hesitating to go ahead now. Do you mind if I ask what it is? [Question 1 in sequence.]
Buyer:	I don't think I can afford relamping all at one time.
Salesperson:	In addition to that, is there another reason for not going ahead? [Question 2 in sequence.]
Buyer:	No.
Salesperson:	Just supposing, you could convince yourself that group relamping is less expensive than spot replacing . . . then you'd want to go ahead with it? [Question 3.]
Buyer:	I guess so.
Salesperson:	Group relamping is not an absolute necessity; however, it does allow you to realize immediate energy savings on all of your fixtures. It actually saves you much of the labor costs of spot replacement because the lamps are installed with "production line" efficiency. See what I mean? [Trial close.]
Buyer:	Yes, I do.
Salesperson:	Would you like installation at night or on the weekend? [Alternative close.]
Buyer:	I'd still like to think about it.
Salesperson:	There must be another reason why you're hesitating to go ahead now. Do you mind if I ask what it is? [Question 1.]
Buyer:	We just don't have the money now to make that kind of investment.
Salesperson:	In addition to that, is there any other reason for not going ahead? [Question 2.]
Buyer:	No. My supervisor just will not let me buy anything.
Salesperson:	You agree you could save money for your company on this purchase—right?
Buyer:	Yes.
Salesperson:	How about calling your supervisor now and asking about how much money we can save him in addition to reducing your storage space and eye fatigue of your employees? Maybe both of us could visit your supervisor.

Table 10–1 Closing Techniques Based upon Situation

	Approach to Closing								
Situation	Alternative	Compliment	Summary	Continuous-Yes	Minor-Points	Assumptive	T-Account	Standing Room Only	Why
Customer is indecisive	X		X	X	X		X	X	Forces a decision
Customer is expert or egotist		X					X		Lets "expert" make the decision
Customer is hostile		X		X					Positive strokes
Customer is a friend						X			You take care of the small things
Customer has predetermined beliefs							X		Benefits outweigh disbeliefs
Customer is greedy, wants a deal								X	Buy now

Research Reinforces Book's Sales Success Strategies

This chapter ends the discussion on the parts of the sales presentation. While it is difficult to summarize all of the sales success strategies you should use, which are discussed throughout the book, one research report reinforces several of the key procedures that will improve your sales performance.

The research sought to examine two key questions all salespeople frequently ask themselves: What makes one sales call a success and another a failure? Do salespeople make common mistakes that prevent success?

To answer questions such as these, Xerox Learning Systems, a subsidiary of the Xerox Corporation, enlisted a team of observers to monitor and analyze more than 500 personal sales calls of 24 different sales organizations. The product and services sold ranged from computers to industrial refuse disposal.

Mike Radick, the Xerox senior development specialist overseeing the study, states that the average successful sales call observed was 33 minutes long. During that call, the salesperson asked 13.6 questions and described 6.4 product benefits and 7.7 product features. Meanwhile, the customer described 2.2 different needs, raised 1.0 objections, made 2.8 statements of acceptance, and asked 7.7 questions.

The observers noted that it does not appear to matter whether the salesperson is 28 or 48 years old, is male or female, or has 2 or 20 years' experience. What matters is the ability to use certain skills and avoid common errors. The following are six common mistakes that the researchers found prevented successful sales calls:

Tells Instead of Sells; Doesn't Ask Enough Questions.   The salesperson does most of the talking. Instead of asking questions to determine a customer's interest, the salesperson charges ahead and rattles off product benefits. This forces the customer into the passive role of listening to details that may not be of any interest. As a result, the customer becomes increasingly irritated.

For example, a person selling a computerized payroll system may tell a customer how much clerical time can be saved by using this service. However, if clerical time is not a concern, then the customer has no interest in learning about ways to reduce time spent on payroll processing. On the other hand, the same customer may have a high need for more accurate recordkeeping and be extremely interested in the computerized reports the system can generate.

Over-Controls the Call; Asks Too Many Closed-End Questions. This sales dialogue resembles an interrogation, and the customer has limited opportunities to express needs. The over-controlling salesperson steers the conversation to subjects the salesperson wants to talk about without regard to the customer. When the customer does talk, the salesperson often fails to listen or respond, or doesn't acknowledge the importance of what the customer says. As a result, the customer is alienated, and the sales call fails.

Doesn't Respond to Customer Needs with Benefits.   Instead, the salesperson leaves it up to the customer to infer how those features will satisfy his or her needs. Consider the customer who needs a high-speed machine. The salesperson responds with information about heat tolerance, but doesn't link that to the rate at which the equipment can turn out the customer's product. As a result, the customer becomes confused, loses interest, and the call fails.

The research shows a direct relationship between the result of a call and the number of different benefits given in response to customer needs; the more need-related benefits cited, the greater the probability of success.

Doesn't Recognize Needs; Gives Benefits Prematurely.   For example, a customer discussing telephone equipment mentions that some clients complain that the line is always busy. The salesperson points out the benefits of his answering service, but the customer responds that busy lines are not very important since people are likely to call back. In this case, the customer is not concerned enough to want to solve the problem.

Doesn't Recognize or Handle Negative Attitudes Effectively.   The salesperson fails to recognize customer statements of objection (opposition), indifference (no need), or skepticism (doubts). What isn't dealt with effectively remains on the customer's mind, and, left with a negative attitude, the customer will not make a commitment. The research also shows that customer skepticism, indifference, and objection are three different attitudes. Each has a different effect on the call, and each requires a different strategy for selling success.

Makes Weak Closing Statements; Doesn't Recognize When or How to Close. In one extreme case that was observed, the customer tried to close the sale on a positive note, but the salesperson failed to recognize the cue and continued selling until the customer lost interest. The lesson in this is that successful salespeople are alert to closing opportunities throughout the call.

The most powerful way to close a sales call involves a summary of the benefits which interested the customer. Success was achieved in three out of every four calls that included this closing technique.

Keys to Improved Selling

How is the bridge from average to successful salesperson made? Xerox found it involves learning and using each of the following skills:

- Ask questions to gather information and uncover needs.
- Recognize when a customer has a real need and how the benefits of the product or service can satisfy it.
- Establish a balanced dialogue with customers.
- Recognize and handle negative customer attitudes promptly and directly.
- Use a benefit summary and an action plan requiring commitment when closing.[2]

Learning and using these five selling skills, plus others emphasized throughout the book, in combination with your own natural ability and positive mental attitude will allow you to be a successful, professional salesperson.

Summary of Major Selling Issues

Closing is the process of helping people make decisions that will benefit them. You help people make those decisions by asking them to buy. The close of the sale is the next logical sequence after your presentation. At this time you finalize the details of the sale (earlier your prospect has been convinced to buy). You should constantly be looking and listening for buying signals from your prospect in order to know when to close. It is time to close the sale anytime the prospect is ready, whether at the beginning or at the end of your presentation.

As you prepare to close the sale, be sure you have presented a complete story on your proposition and that your prospect completely understands what you have presented. Tailor your close to each prospect's personality and see the situation from the prospect's viewpoint. You should remember that you may make your presentation and close too early, causing the prospect to say no instead of "I don't understand your proposition and I don't want to be taken advantage of." This is why you should never take the first no. It is another reason why you should use a trial close immediately before you close. But no matter when or how to close, do so in a positive, confident, and enthusiastic manner in order to better serve your prospect and help you reach your personal goals. Learn and abide by the 12 steps to a successful closing.

Plan and rehearse closing techniques for each prospect. Develop closing techniques which are natural for yourself or consider using or adopting closes such as the alternative, compliment, summary, continuous-yes, minor decision, assumption, T-account, or the standing-room-only close. Be sure to consider the situation you face and be ready to switch from your planned close should your prospect's situation be different than you had anticipated.

A good closer has a strong desire to close each sale. Rarely, if ever, should you accept the first no as the final answer. If you work in a professional manner, you should be able to close a minimum of three to five times.

Do not become upset or unnerved if a problem creeps up when you are ready to close. Keep a cool head, determine any objections, overcome them, and try to close again—you can't make a sale until you ask for the order! Remember to take at least three strikes before you count yourself out of the sale.

Review and Discussion Questions

1. Explain the term *close* as it relates to the sales presentation. Include in your answer a discussion of when to close, the meaning and examples of buying signals, and a discussion of the use of multiple closes.
2. What are the essential elements a salesperson should consider in closing a prospect?
3. Why are some people better at closing a sale than other people? Is it luck?
4. Explain the importance of not accepting the first no and thus using multiple closes even under hostile circumstances.
5. Discuss five closing techniques and give examples of each technique.
6. A salesperson should use a closing technique which is simple and straightforward, and should ask the prospect only to buy rather than do something in addition to buying. In which of the following examples, if any, is the salesperson suggesting something to the buyer which is actually a close, rather than something the buyer has to do in addition to buying?

A. "If you have no objection, I'll go out to the warehouse now to see about reserving space for this new item."

B. "To get this promotion off right, we should notify each of your store managers. I've already prepared a bulletin for them. Should *I* arrange to have a copy sent to each manager, or do *you* want to do it?"

C. "To get this promotion off right, we should notify each of your store managers. I've already prepared a bulletin for them. On my way out, I can drop it off with the secretary."

D. "We should contact the warehouse manager about reserving a space for this new item. Do you want to do it now or after I've left?"

7. Buying signals come in numerous forms. When you receive a buying signal, you should stop your presentation and move in for the close of your sale. For each of the following seven situations, choose the appropriate response to your prospect's buying signal which leads most directly to a close.

A. "Can I get it in blue?" Your answer should be: (1) "Yes," (2) "Do you want it in blue?" or (3) "It comes in three colors, including blue."

B. "What's your price?" Your answer should be: (1) "In what quantity?" (2) To quote a specific price, or (3) "In which grade?"

C. "What kind of terms do you offer?" Your answer should be: (1) To provide specific terms, (2) "Terms would have to be arranged," or (3) "What kind of terms do you want?"

D. "How big an order do I have to place to get your best price?" Your answer should be: (1) A schedule of quantity prices, (2) A specific-sized order, or (3) "What size order do you want to place?"

E. "When will you have a new model?" Your answer should be: (1) A specific date, (2) "Do you want our newest model?" or (3) "This is our newest model."

F. "What would be the smallest trial order I could place with you?" Your answer should be: (1) A specific quantity, (2) "How small an order do you want?" or (3) A variety of order sizes.

G. "When could you make delivery?" Your answer should be: (1) "That depends on the size of your order. What order size do you have in mind?" (2) A specific delivery date, or (3) "When do you want delivery?"

8. Which of the following is the most frequently committed sin in closing? Why?

A. Asking for the order too early.

B. Not structuring the presentation toward a closing.

C. Not asking for the order.

9. In the appropriate circumstances, do you agree that a good closing

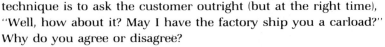

technique is to ask the customer outright (but at the right time), "Well, how about it? May I have the factory ship you a carload?" Why do you agree or disagree?

10. After completing a presentation that has included all of your product's features, advantages, and benefits, you should not delay in asking the customer, "How much of the product do you wish to order?" Is this statement true or false? Why?

11. Each visual aid you use during your presentation can be designed to allow the customer to say yes to your main selling points. What should your visual aids include to allow you to gauge customer interest and help to move to the close? What are several examples?

12. "Now, let's review what we've talked about. We've agreed that the Mohawk's secondary backing and special latex glue make the carpet more durable and contribute to better appearance. In addition, you felt that our direct-to-customer delivery system would save you a lot of money and time. Shall I send you our wall sample display or would you be interested in stocking some 9 by 12's?"

   A. The salesperson's closing statement above helps to ensure customer acceptance by doing which of the following:
      1. Summarizing benefits the customer agreed were important.
      2. Giving an alternative.
      3. Assuming that agreement has been reached.
   B. The salesperson ends the closing statement by:
      1. Asking if the customer has any other questions.
      2. Asking if the product will meet the customers' requirements.
      3. Requesting a commitment from the customer.

13. "Assuming agreement has been reached" reflects the kind of attitude you should project when making a closing statement. When you make a close, nothing you say should reflect doubt, hesitation, or uncertainty. Which of the following salesperson's remarks assume agreement?
   A. "If you feel that Munson is really what you want. . . ."
   B. "Let me leave you two today and deliver the rest next week. . . ."
   C. "Well, if you purchase. . . ."
   D. "Well, it looks as if maybe. . . ."
   E. "We've agreed that. . . ."
   F. "When you purchase the X-7100. . . ."
   G. "Why don't you try a couple, if you like. . . ."

14. A good rule is "Get the order and get out." Do you agree? Why?

15. The real estate salesperson is out showing the property to a couple who look at the house and say, "Gee, this is great. They've taken good care of this place and the rugs and drapes just go perfectly.

Do you think they'd be willing to leave the rugs and drapes?" What should the salesperson do or say? Why?

Projects

1. Assume you are interviewing for a sales job and there are only five minutes remaining. You are very interested in the job and you know if the company is interested in hiring you they will invite you for a visit to their local distribution center and have you work with one of their salespeople for one day. What are several closing techniques you could use to ask for the visit? Give examples of each.

2. Visit several retail stores or manufacturing plants in your local area and ask their purchasing agents what they like and do not like about the close of the sale when they are contacted by salespeople. See if they have already made up their minds to buy or not to buy before the salesperson closes the sale. Ask them how they feel a salesperson should ideally ask for their business.

3. Develop a buyer-seller written script with a minimum of four closes. Use different closing techniques and methods to overcome the objections. Be prepared to role-play your script in class.

Cases

10–1 Skaggs Omega

Skaggs Omega, a large chain of supermarkets, has mailed you an inquiry on hardware items. They specifically wanted to know about your hammers, screwdrivers, and nails. Upon your arrival, you make your presentation to the purchasing agent, Linda Johnson. You start out by stating that you had visited several of their stores. You discuss your revolving retail display which contains an assortment of the three items Johnson had mentioned in her inquiry and relate the displays and advantages and features to benefits for Skaggs.

During your presentation, Johnson has listened but has said very little and has not given you any buying signals. However, it does appear she is interested. She did not object to your price nor did she raise any other objections.

You are approaching the end of your presentation and it is time to close. Actually you have said everything you can think of.

Questions:

1. What is the best way to ask Johnson for the order?
   A. "How do you like our products, Ms. Johnson?"
   B. "What assortment do you prefer, the A or B assortment?"
   C. "Can we go ahead with the order?"

D. "If you'll just okay this order form, Ms. Johnson, we'll have each of your stores receive a display within two weeks."

2. Discuss the remaining alternatives ranking them from good to bad and state what you feel would happen if a salesperson responded in that manner.

10–2   Central Hardware Supply

Sam Gillespie, owner of Central Hardware Supply, was referred to you by a mutual friend. Gillespie had been thinking of dropping two of their product suppliers of home building supplies. "The sale should be guaranteed," your friend had stated.

Your friend's information was correct and your presentation to Gillespie convinces you he will benefit from buying from you. He comments as you conclude your presentation: "Looks like your product will solve our problem. I'd like to think this over, however. Could you call me tomorrow or the next day?"

Questions:

1. The best way to handle this would be to:
   A. Follow his suggestion.
   B. Ignore his request and try a second close.
   C. Probe further. You might ask: "The fact that you have to think this over suggests that I haven't convinced you. Is there something I've omitted or failed to satisfy you with?"
2. What would be your second and third choices? Why?

|11

Winning in the Long Run: Building a Relationship through Service

Learning Objectives

1. To discuss how follow-up and service result in account penetration and improved sales.

2. To present the eight steps involved in increasing your customer's sales.

3. To review the importance of properly handling customer's returned goods requests and complaints in a professional manner.

4. To learn the attitude of several of the top salespeople in the United States toward serving their customers.

Profile

Gary Brown
Richard D. Irwin, Inc.

Photo by Andrew J. Thacker of Photographic Services Unlimited, Inc., Houston, Texas.

My name is Gary Brown and I am a publisher's field representative for Richard D. Irwin, Inc.—the company that published this textbook. I have a B.A. degree in political science and a masters degree in public administration from the University of North Carolina. I have had numerous sales jobs during and since my college career, including three years with the Macmillan Publishing Company.

After working for several years as a management analyst with the City of Raleigh, North Carolina, I joined the Irwin company in 1981 as an outside field representative based in Houston, Texas. I call on 35 colleges in my territory, which requires overnight travel to colleges in College Station, Nacogdoches, San Marcos, San Antonio, Huntsville, Kingsville, Corpus Christi, Edinburg, and Brownsville, Texas.

My company is one of the largest publishers of college textbooks in business and economics. The Irwin books are used in thousands of colleges and universities in the United States and Canada as well as overseas. They are also used in many industrial, governmental, and executive training programs.

Since I have a love for both the college environment and books, selling college textbooks has been a perfect career for me. As a publisher's representative, my sales contact is with professors and instructors who determine which text will be adopted for courses they teach, while the actual book orders come from campus bookstores where students purchase their books. Besides making campus calls, I attend local academic conventions at which the company is exhibiting, and I also conduct market surveys when needed. An important aspect of my job is to build relationships with college professors in my territory and assist in cultivating prospective authors to develop manuscripts for possible publication by our firm. I also provide editorial information to the home office about competing textbooks as well as our own, and help identify new trends in the marketplace. Recently, I won an award from the company for my editorial contributions from the field.

To me, to be successful in college publishing as a salesperson, the most important thing is to make as many sales calls on professors as possible and provide the necessary service and follow-up to all customers. In my mind there is a definite relationship between the number of effective calls made and the total dollar volume generated in a sales territory.

Once the book is adopted, the service and follow-up don't stop. In fact, if you are looking for long-term business, it is at this point that our service really starts. You always want to make sure that professors and instructors have copies of the book they adopted as well as all the supporting materials that accompany the book, like instructor's manuals, solutions manuals, and teaching transparencies. Thus, service and follow-up are two key ingredients in my sales success.

After selling me a life insurance policy, Wayne Bowers, a New York Life Insurance salesman, said "Charles, I'm here to help you in any way I can. Should you have questions about your policy please contact me. This is the beginning of my service to you. As you will see I'm your financial adviser."

Wayne has since sold me another policy, plus reviewed the insurance I can obtain through my university, and suggested some policies I buy from them. When he calls, he always asks how my wife and children are, using their names. If I do not buy from Wayne he acts the same way he would have if I had bought the policy. Could this be why he is so successful?

The often used cliché, "last but not least," applies to this chapter which ends our discussion of the elements of the selling process. Follow-up and service are very important to the success of a salesperson in today's competitive markets. Certainly account servicing is one of the reasons Wayne Bowers has sold well over $1 million of insurance for each of the last 15 years. This chapter discusses: the importance of follow-up and service, ways of keeping your customers, methods of helping them increase their sales, handling customer complaints, and ends by emphasizing the need for you to act as a professional salesperson when servicing your accounts.

Super Salespeople Discuss Service

Providing service after the sale to customers is important, no matter what type of company, product, or service you represent. To illustrate the importance of service to the professional salesperson, three men, each of whom has been referred to as one of America's greatest salespeople, discuss the importance of service in selling real estate, steel, and information systems.

Rich Port built a successful real estate business in Chicago which now consists of 28 offices, 375 salespeople, and generates over $300 million a year in sales. How? Rich explains his success in this manner: "In most fields, a salesperson can offer his customer a product which will have some differences from competitive products. But when we sell a residential property, we're often selling the same product which the buyer can purchase from the real estate office down the street. So in order for us to offer something better, we must give them more service. The key to success in the real estate business is service."[1]

In discussing service, Mike Curto, a retired group vice president of the United States Steel Corporation, says,

> You've got to realize that what we're selling isn't a whole lot different from what our competitor can produce. In steel, we take some iron ore, refine it, and eventually end up with a product of a semifinished nature . . . we have to sell *service*. Our salesman must convince the customer that we're the best in our industry, and that over the long run he's better off doing business with us.
>
> A salesman has to develop a customer's confidence; he must believe that U.S. Steel products are not only equal to what the competition sells, but are the best that can be produced in that particular line. And he better be sure that the products are as good as he says they are, because he's going to be calling back on that customer many times throughout the year.[2]

These two men both stated that their service or product is similar to those offered by the competition. What about a product like computers sold by such companies as IBM, Honeywell, Burroughs, and Amdahl? Francis G. ("Buck") Rogers, vice president of marketing for IBM, believes one of the keys to success at IBM is service. He says,

> IBM means service. With IBM, nothing is successfully sold until it's successfully installed. Now the salesperson goes through the installation phase, including educating the customer, teaching people how the products will actually perform, and showing them how to properly apply the product. Finally, the equipment is delivered; this can be almost a year later. At any rate, that's the installation phase of the sale.
>
> Beyond that, we take it much further. We're dealing with a customer on a continual basis, for example, trying to find new applications to further justify the equipment. At IBM, we're often leasing a fairly expensive piece of equipment, and unless we continue to give the customer the best possible service, always looking out for his best interest, we're taking the risk of losing him.[3]

Based on the statements of these three successful sales-oriented individuals alone, it is easy to see the importance of customer service before, after, and between sales. You should know as much as possible about each of your accounts in order to provide the amount of service necessary to keep your buyers happy.

Account Penetration Is a Secret to Success

Follow-up and service create good will between a salesperson and the customer, which in the long run will increase sales faster relative to the salesperson who does not provide such service. By contacting the customer after the sale to see that the maximum benefit is being derived from the purchase, a salesperson lays the foundation for a positive business relationship.

The ability to work and contact people throughout the account, discussing your products is referred to as *account penetration*. Successful penetration of an account allows you to properly service that account by uncovering its needs and problems. Achieving successful account penetration is dependent on your knowledge of that account's key personnel and their situation. If you do not have a feel for an account's situation, you reduce your chances of maximizing your sales in that account.

Tailor your presentation to meet your buyers' objectives in a manner which will benefit them. By knowing your buyers, their firms, and other key personnel, you are better able to uncover their needs or problems and develop a presentation which fulfills these needs or solves these problems. Account penetration can be determined by:

- Your total and major brand sales growth in an account.
- Distribution of the number of products in a product line, including sizes, used or merchandised by an account.
- Level of cooperation you obtain, such as reduced resale prices, shelf space, advertising and display activity, discussion with their salespeople, and freedom to visit with various people in the account.
- Your reputation as the authority on your type of merchandise for the buyer.

As a general rule, the greater your account penetration, the greater your chances of maximizing sales within the account. Earning the privilege to freely move around in the account allows you to better uncover prospect needs and to discuss your products with people throughout the firm. As people begin to know you and believe that you are there to help them, they allow you to do things which will ultimately increase your sales, such as increasing your shelf space or talking with the users of your industrial equipment in the account's manufacturing facilities. A good sign that you have successfully penetrated an account is when one of your competitors dismally says to another, "Forget that account, it's already sewn up."

Service Can Keep Your Customers

You work days, weeks, even months to convert prospects into customers. What can you do to insure they will continue to buy from you in the future? After landing a major account, there are six factors you ought to consider.

First: Concentrate on improving your account penetration. As discussed earlier, account penetration is critical in uncovering prospect needs or problems, and being able to consistently recommend effective solutions through the purchase of your products. This allows you to demonstrate that you have a customer's best interests at heart and are there to help.

Second: Contact new accounts on a frequent and regular schedule. In determining the frequency of calls you should consider:

Present sales and/or potential future sales to this account.

Number of orders you expect to be placed in a year.

Number of product lines sold to the account.

Complexity, servicing, and redesign requirements of the products purchased by the account.

Since the amount of time spent servicing an account may vary from minutes to hours to days, you should be flexible in developing a call frequency for each of your customers. Typically, you should invest your sales time in direct proportion to the actual or potential sales represented by each account. The most productive number of calls is reached at the point where additional calls do not increase sales to the customer. This relationship of sales volume to sales calls is referred to as the "response function" of the customer to the salesperson's calls.

Third: Handle your customers' complaints promptly. This is an excellent opportunity to prove to your customers that they and their businesses are important to you, and you sincerely care about them. The speed with which you handle even the most trivial complaint will show the value you place on that customer.

Fourth: Always do what you say you will do. Nothing can destroy your relationship with a customer faster than not following through on what you have promised. Promises made and subsequently broken are not tolerated by professional buyers. They have placed their faith (and sometimes reputation) in you by purchasing your products, so you must be faithful to them to insure their future support.

Fifth: Provide service as you would to royalty. "The customer is king" is a popular marketing saying which is especially true in a selling situation. By providing your client with money-saving products and problem-solving ideas, you can become almost indispensable. You are an advisor to listen to rather than an adversary to haggle with. Provide all of the assistance you can. As State Farm Insurance agent Charlotte Cornett says in Figure 11–1, "We're there to help."

Sixth: Show your appreciation. A buyer once told me, "I'm responsible for putting the meat and potatoes on your table," and that was right. Customers contribute to your success, and in return you should show your appreciation. Thank them for their business, do them favors, send them birthday and Christmas cards. Such actions not only inflate the ego; they make people feel appreciated, and show you really care.

Figure 11–1

Courtesy of State Farm Insurance Companies

"With State Farm, you don't call a stranger when you need help."

State Farm agent Charlotte Cornett, Dayton, Ohio.

"When you're insured with State Farm, you call someone you know. When you have a question about your family or personal insurance needs, or you want to report a claim, you call your State Farm agent. We're there to give you personal service.

"That's why so many families come to State Farm and stick with State Farm year after year. The availability of the State Farm agent. Whether it's life, health, home or car insurance—we're there to help."

You'll find the State Farm agent nearest you in your Yellow Pages.

Like a good neighbor, State Farm is there.

State Farm Insurance Companies
Home Offices: Bloomington, Illinois

You Lose a Customer— Keep on Trucking!

All salespeople suffer losses, either through the loss of a sale or an entire account as a competitor takes over. Four things can be done to win back a customer:

1. Visit and Investigate. The first thing to do is to contact the buyer and your friends within the account to determine why the customer did not buy from you. Be sure to get the real reason.
2. Be Professional. If you have completely lost the customer to a competitor, let the customer know you have appreciated past business, that you still value the customer's friendship, and that you are still friendly. Remember to assure this lost account that you are ready to earn future business.
3. Never criticize the competing product your customer has purchased. Don't be unfriendly. If it was a bad decision, let the customer discover it. Sales is never having to say, "I told you so!"
4. Keep Calling. Treat a former customer like a prospect. Continue to make your calls in your normal manner, presenting your product's benefits without directly comparing them to the competition.

Like a professional athlete, a professional salesperson takes defeat gracefully, moving on to the next contest, and performing so well that victories totally overshadow any losses. One method of compensating for the loss of one account is to increase sales to existing accounts.

Increasing Your Customer's Sales

In order to maximize your sales to a customer, you should develop a customer benefit program. This means the account uses in business, or sells to customers, a level of merchandise equal to its maximum sales potential. The salesperson has only two methods to do this:

1. Have present customers buy *more* of a product that they are currently using.
2. Have present customers buy the same products to use for different purposes. A Johnson & Johnson retail sales representative may encourage accounts to stock the firm's baby shampoo in both the infant care *and* adult toiletries sections of their establishments.

It is often not difficult to sell repeat orders; however, to maximize sales in an account, for example with a retailer, you must persuade the customer to consistently promote your product through advertisements, displays, and reduced prices. In order to increase your sales with a customer, the following steps can be taken. Certainly each step cannot be used in all situations, but if followed some or all of them can help increase your sales.

Step 1: Develop an account penetration program. Develop a "master plan" for each of your accounts consisting of specific actions you should take directed toward both developing friends within the account and increasing sales.

Step 2: Examine your distribution. Review the merchandise currently used or carried in inventory. If the account is not using or carrying some of your merchandise, concentrate on improving your distribution. For example, if you have four sizes of a product and the account only carries one or two of them, develop a plan to persuade the customer to carry all four sizes. A general goal may be to have each of your accounts carrying all sizes of your products.

Step 3: Keep merchandise in the warehouse and on the shelf. Never allow the account to run out of stock. "Stockouts" result in lost sales for your firm and your account. Routine calls on your customers will help to avoid stockouts. If the account is critically low on merchandise, telephone in an emergency order. Quick service can maintain, or even increase, your credibility as a sales professional.

Step 4: Fight for shelf space and shelf positioning. If you are selling consumer goods, you should constantly seek to obtain the best shelf space and aisle position. On each sales call, stock the shelf, keep your merchandise clean, and develop merchandising ideas. For example, during a routine visit to a client's store, a consumer goods salesperson found that a product the salesperson represented with a list price of $2.00 was being sold for $1.79. This enterprising salesperson taped a small sign to the shelf showing both prices and discovered later that sales of the product had increased. This device is now routine for all of this salesperson's products.

Step 5: Assist the product's users. If you sell industrial products, you should help users learn to operate your products properly. Make your users aware of product accessories which might aid them in performing a function in a safer, better, or more profitable manner. This type of account servicing can increase both account penetration and sales.

Step 6: Assist retailer's salespeople. To ensure enthusiastic promotion of your firm's products, you must work closely with your account's sales force. Experience indicates that manufacturer's salespeople who cultivate the friendship of the reseller's salespeople and provide them with product knowledge and selling tips are much more likely to be successful than the salesperson who calls only on the account's buyer.

A successful pharmaceutical salesperson suggested to all of the retail salespeople involved in a certain account that as they hand a customer a prescription for an antibiotic they say, "In taking these antibiotics you should also double up on taking your vitamins." Well, most customers were not taking vitamins, so when they said, "I don't have any vitamins," the salesperson would hand them a bottle of vitamins, saying, "I take these myself and highly recommend them to you." Of course, this manufacturer's salesperson had previously given the retail salesperson a sample bottle of vitamins. This sales tip accounted for an increase of over 300 percent in vitamin sales for this reseller.

Step 7: Demonstrate your willingness to help. On each sales call demonstrate your willingness to help the account through your actions. Your actions—not just your words—are what build respect, or distaste, for you. Pull off your coat and dust, mark, stack, and build displays of your merchandise, and return damaged merchandise for credit. Let the buyer know that you are there to help increase retail sales.

Step 8: Obtain customer support. By working hard to help your customers reach their goals through doing the things just discussed, you will find they are willing to help and support you. In essence, you help them; they help you. This type of relationship results in benefits to both you and your customer.

Again, there is no guarantee that doing everything suggested in this or any other text or sales manual will always result in your getting the sale. Conscientious use of sound selling principles *will* increase your likelihood of overall success, though. As mentioned earlier in this chapter, a key characteristic of a sales professional is the ability to accept failure or rejection gracefully, and then quickly to move on to the next objective.

When You Do Not Make the Sale

A group of purchasing agents were asked their biggest gripes about poor sales procedure. One item on their list was this: "They [salespeople] seem to take it personally if they don't get the business, as though you owe them something because they are constantly calling on you."[4]

Although you should try, you cannot always sell everyone as much as you would like to or expect them to place special emphasis on *all* of your products *all* of the time. When you have done the very best you can to persuade prospects or customers to make a purchase, and they still will not buy or do what you wish, remember there is always tomorrow. Act as a professional, adult salesperson, and do not take the buyer's denial personally, but recognize it as a business decision that the buyer must make given the circumstances. Be courteous and cheerful, be grateful for the opportunity to discuss your business proposition. The proper handling of a no sale situation can actually help you build a sound business relationship with your customers by developing a spirit of cooperation.

Return Goods Make You a Hero

One of the best ways to truly help your customers is through the careful examination of the merchandise you have sold them in the past to see if it is old and out-of-date or unsalable due to damage. If any of these conditions exists, the salesperson should cheerfully return them following his company's return goods policies.

Some companies allow you to return any amount of merchandise, whereas other firms have limits on unauthorized returns. A firm may allow no more than $100 of merchandise to be returned at any one time without the company's approval. Some companies require a reciprocal replacement order. Thus if $100 worth of merchandise is returned, the customer must place an order for $100 of new merchandise. You do not want the customer to display or sell damaged goods, so it is in your best interest to return faulty merchandise, an action which aids you in building friendship with each customer.

Handle Complaints Fairly

Customers may be dissatisfied with products for reasons such as:

The product delivered is a different size, color, or model than the one ordered.

The quantity delivered is less than quantity ordered—balance is "backordered" (to be delivered when available).

The product does *not* arrive by the specified date.

Discounts (trade, promotional payment, etc.; see Chapter 5) agreed upon are not rendered by the manufacturer.

The product does not have a feature or perform a function that customer believed it would.

The product is not of specified grade or quality (does not meet agreed upon specifications).

Whenever you determine that the customer's complaint is an honest one, you should make a settlement that is fair to the customer. The slogan "The customer is always right" is a wise adage to follow. Customers may actually be wrong, but if they honestly believe they are right, no amount of haggling or arguing is going to convince them otherwise. A valued account can be lost through temperamental outbursts.

Occasionally a customer will attempt to be dishonest with you, requiring you and your company not to honor a request. I once had a retailer (A) who had purchased some of my firm's merchandise from another retailer (B) who had a "fire sale" and eventually went out of business. Retailer A insisted he purchased it from me and that I return close to $1,000 of damaged goods to my company for full credit. He had actually paid ten cents on the dollar for it at the fire sale. I told Retailer A that I would have to obtain permission from the company to return such a large amount of damaged goods.

That afternoon a competitive salesperson told me that this same Retailer A had asked him to do the same thing. I informed my sales manager of the situation. He investigated the matter and found out about Retailer B who sold most of his merchandise to Retailer A—who happened to be my customer. I went back and confronted Retailer A with this and said it was company policy only to return merchandise that was purchased directly from me. This is a rare situation; yet you must occasionally make similar judgments taking care to consider company policy and customer satisfaction.

Certainly your customer should get the benefit of the doubt. Always have a plan for getting to the bottom of the problem. Some procedures you could follow are:

Obtain as much relevant information from your customer as you can.

Express sincere regret for the problem.

Display a service attitude (a true desire to help).

Review your sales records to make sure the customer purchased the merchandise.

Should you determine that the customer is right, quickly and cheerfully handle the complaint.

Follow up to make sure the customer is satisfied.

Take care of your customers—especially your large accounts. They are difficult to replace and are critical to your success. When you take care of your accounts, they will take care of you.

Build a Professional Reputation

Implied and directly stated throughout this chapter, indeed throughout this text, is the concept of sales professionalism. Sales professionalism directly implies that you are just that—a professional person—due the respect and ready for the responsibilities that accompany the title. In speaking before a large class of marketing students, one sales manager for a large college textbook publishing company continually brought up the concept of sales professionalism. This man directly stated that a professional sales position is not just an 8 to 5 job. It is a professional, responsible, adult position, promising both unlimited opportunity and numerous duties. This veteran publishing sales manager emphasized to these young adults that in the 1980s a sales job is an especially good vocational opportunity because people are looking for "someone we can believe in. Someone who will do what he says—a sales professional."

To be viewed as a professional and respected by your customers and competitors, here are eight important considerations:

- First, be truthful and follow through on what you tell your customer. Do not dispose of your conscience when you start work each day.

- Second, maintain an intimate knowledge of your firm, its products, and your industry. Participate in your company's sales training and take continuing education courses.

- Third, speak well of others, including your company and your competitors.

- Fourth, keep customer information confidential; maintain a professional relationship with each of your accounts.

- Fifth, never take advantage of a customer by using unfair, high-pressure techniques.

- Sixth, be active in community affairs by helping to better your community. For example, live in your territory, be active in your public schools, and join such worthwhile organizations as the Lion's Club or Chamber of Commerce.

- Seventh, think of yourself as a professional and always act as a professional. Have a professional attitude about yourself and customers.

- Eighth, provide service "above and beyond the call of duty." Keep in mind that it is easier to maintain a relationship than to begin one. What was worth going after in the first place is worth preserving. Remember, if you do not pay attention to your customers, they will find someone else who will. The professional salesperson never forgets a customer after the sale.

Here are three examples of salespeople's attitudes on service. One who provides professional service is William Hughes of Westvaco, Inc. One of Hughes's customers related the following incident. "We were going wild trying to find sludge drums that would meet specifications. I spent three days searching for a source, and the lowest quote I got was close to $40 apiece. Hughes spent a week locating them from someone who owed him a favor. We bought them for $8 each."[5]

Matt Suffoletto of IBM says: "Customer service is a key element of marketing. It is a known fact that customers will always select the vendor with the best service record when all else is equal. Further, the customer will often pay a premium for quality service. Another name for service is responsiveness, which you can begin to demonstrate with your first sales call."

The third example of service comes from Irwin's Gary Brown.

"Recently I was involved in a situation where a text we published had a typographical error which would cause a student to get the wrong solution to a problem," says Gary. "After writing a memo to the home office alerting them about the typos, I wrote letters about the typos to professors who used the book in my territory. For the three or so hours of work and several dollars spent on postage and stationery, I'll bet we will hold onto these adoptions, meaning many thousands of dollars to the company. I know for a fact that the professors appreciate this service and attention, and in the long term, when a future textbook decision comes down to my book and the other guy's, they are going to pick mine. After all, would you rather go with a proven product or the unknown?"

Dos and Don'ts for Industrial Salespeople

What does a purchasing agent expect of industrial salespeople? A survey of purchasing agents showed that they expect results. The following list shows some of the specific traits purchasing agents found in their top industrial salespeople. The most important traits in order of importance are:

- Willingness to "go to bat" for the buyer within the supplier's firm.
- Thoroughness and follow-through after the sale.
- Knowledge of the firm's product line.
- Market knowledge and willingness to "keep the buyer posted."
- Imagination in applying one's products to the buyer's needs.
- Knowledge of the buyer's product line.
- Preparation for sales calls.
- Regularity of sales calls.
- Diplomacy in dealing with operating departments.
- Technical education (knowledge of specifications and applications).

The survey also asked purchasing agents what they did not like salespeople to do when calling on them. The results, shown in Figure 11–2, are "The Seven Deadly Sins of Industrial Selling." It is clear that purchasing agents want salespeople to act in a professional manner, to be well trained, to be adequately prepared for each sales call, and to keep the sales call related to *how the salesperson can help the buyer*.

Professional selling starts in the manufacturer's firm. A professional attitude on the part of the manufacturer can reinforce professionalism among its sales force. One such concerned company is B. J. Hughes, a

Figure 11–2   The Seven Deadly Sins of Industrial Selling

1. *Lack of product knowledge.* Salespeople must know their own product lines as well as the buyer's or nothing productive can take place.
2. *Time wasting.* Unannounced sales visits are a nuisance. When salespeople start droning on about golf or grandchildren, more time is wasted.
3. *Poor planning.* Even a routine sales call should be preceded by some homework— maybe to see if it's really necessary.
4. *Pushiness.* This includes prying to find out a competitor's prices, an overwhelming attitude, and backdoor selling.
5. *Lack of dependability.* Failure to stand behind the product, keep communications clear, and honor promises.
6. *Unladylike or ungentlemanly conduct.* "Knocking" competitors, boozing at a business lunch, sloppy dress, and poor taste aren't professional.
7. *Unlimited optimism.* Honesty is preferred to the hallmark of the "Good News Bearers" who will promise anything to get an order. Never promise more than you can deliver.

A few of the more vigorous comments:

■ "They seem to take it personally if they don't get the business; as though you owe them something because they are constantly calling on you."

■ "I don't like it when they blast through the front door like know-it-alls, and put on an unsolicited dog-and-pony show that will guarantee cost saving off in limbo somewhere."

■ "Many salesmen are willing to give you any delivery you want, book an order, and then let you face the results of their 'short quote.'"

■ "They try to sell you, rather than the product."

■ "After the order is won, the honeymoon is over."

■ "Beware the humble pest who is too nice to insult, won't take a hint, won't listen to blunt advice, and is selling a product you neither use nor want to use, yet won't go away."

division of the Hughes Tool Company. The B. J. Hughes company manufactures and sells oil field equipment and services to companies in the oil and gas industry. Figure 11–3 presents Hughes' checklists of *dos* and *don'ts* for their salespeople. By providing these checklists, the company is encouraging them to act in a professional manner.

Figure 11–3 **We Are a Customer-Oriented Company**

Salesman's Checklist of **Do's**	*Salesman's Checklist of* **Don'ts**
1. Know the current products/services and their applications in your area. Look for the new techniques/services your customers want.	1. Never bluff; if you don't know, find out.
	2. Never compromise your own, or anyone else's, morals or principles.
2. Maintain an up-to-date personal call list.	3. Don't be presumptuous—even with friends.
3. Listen attentively to the customer; what he has to say is important.	4. Never criticize a competitor—especially to a customer.
4. Seek out specific problems and the improvements your customers would like to have.	5. Do not take criticisms or turndowns personally—they're seldom meant that way.
5. Keep calls under 5 minutes unless invited to stay.	6. Do not worry or agonize over things that you cannot control or influence. Be concerned more about what you *can* affect.
6. Leave a calling card if the customer is not in.	
7. Identify the individual who makes or influences decisions, and concentrate on him.	7. Do not offend others with profanity; keep it to a minimum.
8. Entertain selectively; your time and your expense account should be investments.	8. Do not allow idle conversation or football, etc., to dominate your sales call. Concentrate on your purpose.
9. Make written notes as reminders.	
10. Plan your work by the week, not by the clock. Plan your use of available time. Plan your sales presentations. Have a purpose.	9. Don't try to match the customer drink for drink when entertaining. Drink only when you want to.
11. Ask for the business on every sales call.	10. Don't be so gung ho that you use high-pressure tactics.
12. Follow through with appropriate action.	11. Never talk your company down—especially to customers. Be proud of it and yourself.
	12. Never smoke in the customer's office unless he is smoking or invites you to smoke.

Source: BJ-Hughes, Inc. Reprinted with permission.

Summary of Major Selling Issues

Providing service to customers is important in all types of selling. Follow-up and service create goodwill between a salesperson and customer which allows the salesperson to penetrate or work throughout the customer's organization. Account penetration helps the salesperson to better service the account and uncover its needs and problems. A service relationship with an account leads to increases in total, and major brand sales, better distribution on all sizes of your products, and customer cooperation in promotion of your products.

To serve your customers best, concentrate on improving your account penetration. Contact each customer on a frequent and regular schedule, making sure you promptly handle all complaints. Be sure you always do what you say you will do, and remember to serve customers as if they were royalty. Finally, always remember to thank all customers sincerely for their business, no matter how large or small, in order to show you appreciate them and their firms.

Should customers begin to buy from a competitor or reduce the level of cooperation they give you, be sure to continue to call upon them in your normal professional manner. In a friendly way, determine why they did not buy from you, and develop new customer benefit plans to recapture their business.

Always strive to help your customers increase their sales of your product or to get the best use from the products you have sold them. In order to persuade a customer to purchase more of your products or use your products in a different manner, develop a sales program to help you maximize your sales to that particular customer. This involves development of an account penetration program; an increase in the number and sizes of products purchased by the customer; maintenance of proper inventory levels in the customer's warehouse and on the shelf; achievement of good shelf space and shelf positioning; clear communication with those who directly sell or use a product; a willingness to assist your wholesale and retail customers' salespeople in any way possible; willingness to help your customers; an overall effort to develop a positive, friendly business relationship with each customer. By doing these eight things, you will increase your ability to help and properly service each of your customers.

Today's professional salesperson is oriented towards service. Follow-up and service after the sale will greatly aid in maximizing your territory's sales and in reaching your personal goals.

Review and Discussion Questions

1. Rich Port, Mike Curto, and Francis Rogers all discussed service in this chapter. What do they feel is important for salespeople to understand about service?

2. What is account penetration? What benefits can a salesperson derive from it?

3. List and briefly explain the factors salespeople should consider to insure that customers will continue to buy from them in the future.

4. What should a salesperson do after losing a customer?

5. A good way for a salesperson to create goodwill is by helping customers to increase their sales. What are the steps the salesperson should go through when attempting to increase customer sales?

6. This chapter discussed several reasons why a salesperson should project a professional image. Why do you think being a sales professional is so important?

7. Return to Figure 11–2, The Seven Deadly Sins of Industrial Selling. Now think of an experience you have had with a salesperson who

displayed a poor sales image. How did the salesperson's attitude affect your purchase decision?

8. You have just learned that one of your customers, Tom's Discount Store, has received a shipment of faulty goods from your warehouse. The total cost of the merchandise is $2,500. Your company has a returned-goods policy that will only allow you to return $500 worth of your product at one time unless a reciprocal order is placed. What would you do?

   A. Call Tom's and tell them you will be out to inspect the shipment in a couple of days.

   B. Ask Tom's to patch up what they can and sell it at a reduce cost in an upcoming clearance sale.

   C. Send the merchandise back to your warehouse and credit Tom's account for the price of the damaged goods.

   D. Get over to Tom's as soon as possible that day, check the shipment to see if there are any undamaged goods that can be put on the shelf, get a replacement order from Tom's manager, and phone in the order immediately.

   E. Call your regional sales manager and ask what to do.

9. As a construction machinery salesperson, you know that equipment malfunctions and breakdowns are costly to your customers. Your firm, however, has an excellent warranty which allows you to replace a broken piece of equipment with one of your demonstrators for a few days while the equipment is being repaired. King Masonry has called you four times in the past three months because the mixer you sold them has broken down. Each time you have cheerfully handled the problem, and in less than two hours they have been able to get back to work. Your company's mixer has traditionally been one of the most dependable on the market, so after the last breakdown you let King Masonry keep the new replacement in hopes of solving any future problems.

   The owner has just called to tell you the new mixer has broken down. He is quite angry and says he may go to another supplier if you cannot get him a replacement immediately.

   A. What should you do?

   B. If you had received a call from another salesperson earlier in the week telling you that King had been misusing the mixer, what would you now do?

Projects

1. Contact the person in charge of the health and beauty aids department of a local supermarket. In your interview with this person, ask questions to determine what service activities salespeople perform in the department. For example, do they build product

displays, put merchandise on the shelves, straighten products on the shelves, and keep a record of how much product is in the store? Also, determine how the department head feels salespeople can best provide service.

2. Contact the person in charge of marketing in a local bank. Report on the role service plays in attracting and retaining bank customers.

Cases

11–1 California Adhesives Corporation

Marilyn Fowler recently became a sales representative for the California Adhesives Corporation, and is to cover the states of Oregon and Washington. After completing a three-week training program, Marilyn was excited about taking on the responsibility of reversing the downward sales trend in her territory which had been without a salesperson for several months.

The previous salesperson had been fired due to poor sales performance, and had not left behind any information regarding accounts. After contacting her first 20 or so customers, Marilyn came to a major conclusion: none of these customers had seen a CAC salesman for six to nine months; they had CAC merchandise which was just not selling, and also had damaged merchandise to return. These customers were generally hostile toward Marilyn because the previous salesperson had used high-pressure tactics to force them to buy, and as one person said, "Your predecessor killed your sales in my business. You said you would provide service and call on me regularly, but I don't care about service. In fact, its OK with me if I never see anyone from your company again. Your competition's products are much better than yours, and their salespeople have been calling in this area for years trying to get my business." Marilyn was beginning to wonder if she had gone to work for the right company.

Questions:

1. If you were Marilyn, what would you do to improve the sales in your territory?
2. How long would your effort take to improve sales and would you *sell* it to your sales manager?

11–2 Sport Shoe Corporation

You are a salesperson for the Sport Shoe Corporation. On arrival at your office you find a letter marked "urgent" on your desk. This letter is from the athletic director of Ball State University, and pertains to the poor quality of basketball shoes you had sold him. The director cited several examples of split soles and poor overall quality as his main complaints. In closing, he mentioned that since the season was drawing near he would be forced to contact the ACME Sport Shoe Company if the situation could not be rectified. What actions on your part would be appropriate? Why?

A. Place a call to the athletic director assuring him of your commitment to service. Promise to be at Ball State at his convenience to rectify the problem.

B. Go by the warehouse and take the athletic director all new shoes and apologize for the delay and poor quality of the merchandise.

C. Write a letter to the athletic director assuring him that SSC sells only high-quality shoes and that this type of problem rarely occurs. Assure him you'll come to his office as soon as possible but if he feels ACME would be a better choice than Sport Shoe he should contact them.

D. Don't worry about the letter because the athletic director seems to have the attitude that he can put pressure on you by threatening to switch companies. Also, the loss in sales of 20–40 pairs of basketball shoes will be a drop in the bucket compared to the valuable sales time you would waste on a piddly account like Ball State.

"How Does the Weather Affect Your Business?"

. . . is a question that can't be answered "yes" or "no."

Yes, you want to engage the buyer in conversation. But not idle conversation. Your goal is to get him talking, to reveal things about himself and his business to you.

"Nice day" is a time filler. Even "Does the weather affect your business?" can be answered "Yep." But "How . . ." or "How much does the weather affect your business?" could open up a stream of conversation about distribution problems, or labor force problems, or maintenance problems, or heating and air conditioning costs, or the terrible blacktop job they did on the parking lot.

It doesn't have to be the weather. Ask about the day's news or an industry development. But ask something that will get the prospect talking, not a question that can be answered "Yep" or "Nope."

Special Selling Topics

12

Retail Selling Is Challenging and Rewarding

Learning Objectives

1. To discuss career opportunities available in retailing and the importance of personal selling.
2. To review the retail sales process.
3. To present examples of retail sales presentations.
4. To explain nine challenging situations in retail selling.

Key Terms for Selling

Retailing	Inducement close
Service approach	Group shopper
Question approach	Substitutions
Product approach	Trading up
Assumptive close	Return goods selling
Physical action close	Price line
Minor point close	Suggestion selling

Profile

Kathleen E. Paynter
Campbell Sales Company

As a sales specialist with the Campbell Sales Company in Philadelphia, Pennsylvania, I started as a sales representative and after eight months was promoted to my present position. My assigned territory consists of approximately 70 grocery stores, chains and independents, and four direct accounts. Some of my responsibilities are to expand and maintain product distribution and product sections, to sell and display Campbell's products, and to er.courage stores to feature and advertise Campbell's products.

Here at Campbell's we use the "Thoroughness Method" of selling, which consists of five basic steps:

1. Prepare for the call.
2. Greet store personnel.
3. Check product distribution.
4. Make a personalized presentation.
5. Follow through with commitments.

I've found that following these basic steps and always asking for the order results in successful sales. Shortcuts lead to sloppy calls and fewer sales.

An important aspect in selling is your appearance. The buyer's initial opinion of you is formed by your appearance, so it's best to make sure the impression is positive. It's not necessary to spend a lot of money on clothes, just make sure they are businesslike, well put together and, especially for women, appropriate for the type of physical tasks you may have to perform. I've found the classic tailored slacks and jacket to be most functional for my work.

One thing never to forget is that you, as a salesperson, are a visitor in your buyer's place of business. The longer you are in sales, the easier this is to forget. Ask their opinions and be sure you make them aware of any changes you would like to make. Trying to *tell* buyers what they need can cause problems. Make suggestions and sell them your ideas with sound reasons.

Selling requires a lot of hard work and preparation. *It's not easy!* Some days will be frustrating, even depressing, and you'll wonder why you're even in sales. But overall, selling is a great challenge and can be exciting as well as a lot of fun. You just have to use your imagination and determination to make each day new and interesting.

Joe Girard is the only salesman listed in the business section of *The Guinness Book of World Records*. Guinness states:

GREATEST SALESMAN. The all-time record for automobile salesmanship in individual units sold is 1,425 in 1973 by Joe Girard of Detroit, Michigan, winner of the Number One Car Salesman title every year since 1966. His commissions in 1975 totaled 191,000.

Joe's success story has appeared in numerous magazines and newspapers as well as on television. What is Joe's secret to success? He says: "I don't have any big secret that nobody else has. I simply sell the world's best product, that's all. I sell Joe Girard! You gotta sell yourself."[1]

Joe puts major emphasis on understanding buyers' needs, qualifying customers, becoming their friend, having customers introduce him to prospects, giving personal service, playing down an automobile's features and advantages while concentrating on benefits. Having made a sale, he shows customers he is thankful for their business and provides all of the service they need to be satisfied with their purchase. These are some of the things which made him the "Number One Car Salesman in the World."[2]

Retail selling, as in Joe Girard's case, can be both challenging and rewarding. This chapter will cover retailing opportunities, the retail sales process, and the "dos and don'ts of retail selling."

What Is Retailing?

Retailing refers 'to any individual or organization that sells its products or services directly to final consumers for their personal, nonbusiness use.'

The distinguishing characteristic of a retail sale is that a retail transaction involves the final consumer—the retail customer.[3] A retail sale may take place over the telephone, through the mail, on a street corner, in a private residence, or in a traditional retail store.

Goods and services sold to final consumers for their personal, nonbusiness use vary from items such as T-shirts and jogging shoes to stocks and bonds, legal services, singing telegrams, and wedding cakes. A person selling panty hose to a department store shopper is engaged in retailing, as is a real estate agent selling a $30,000 house. This chapter will focus mainly on retail transactions which take place in a retail store.

Retail stores account for some $750 billion in sales each year or about 18 percent of all business generated by our nation's economy.[4] The roughly 3 million salespeople associated with retailing are employed by firms as large and diverse as Sears, and Macy's in New York City, which boasts of being the world's largest store, to small "mom and pop" stores.

Although many people unfamiliar with modern retailing might think otherwise, retailing as a career has become very attractive. It is not like it was 100 years ago when the rules in Figure 12–1 were posted.

Financial Rewards Are Excellent

The financial rewards and promotional opportunities for the retail salesperson are excellent. Sure, there are retail firms which pay only the minimum wage, but there are many who pay excellent salaries to qualified people.

As in other forms of professional selling, the financial rewards and promotional opportunities for the retail salesperson are excellent. Your earnings as a retail salesperson can vary depending upon the type of product being sold, the compensation plan you are under (straight salary, salary plus commission, or straight commission), and the organization you are working for.

Figure 12–1 Rules for Retail Clerks in 1882

1. This store must be opened at Sunrise. No mistake. Open 6 o'clock A.M. Summer and Winter. Close about 8:30 or 9 P.M. the year round.

2. Store must be swept—dusted—doors and windows opened—lamps filled, trimmed and chimneys cleaned—counters, base shelves and show cases dusted. Also the coal must be brought in before breakfast, if there is time to do it and attend to all the customers who call.

3. The store is not to be opened on the Sabbath day unless absolutely necessary and then only for a few minutes.

4. Should the store be opened on Sunday the clerks must go in alone and get tobacco for customers in need.

5. The clerk who is in the habit of smoking Spanish Cigars—being shaved at the barbers— going to dancing parties and other places of amusement and being out late at night— will assuredly give his employer reason to be ever suspicious of his integrity and honesty.

6. Clerks are allowed to smoke in the store provided they do not wait on women with a "stogie" in the mouth.

7. Each clerk must pay not less the $5.00 per year to the Church and must attend Sunday School regularly.

8. Men clerks are given one evening a week off for courting and two if they go to prayer meeting.

9. After the 14 hours in the store the leisure hours should be spent mostly in reading.

Source: Reprinted by permission from Delbert J. Duncan, Charles F. Phillips, and Stanley C. Holland, *Modern Retailing Management* (Homewood, Ill.: Richard D. Irwin, 1972), p. 184.

Figure 12–2 illustrates a career path for a large chain of department stores. After completing the initial executive development training program, the individual is given a department to manage, such as women's clothing, and is responsible for training salespeople, and efficiently handling operations. The person next moves to assistant buyer and then to buyer, followed by a promotion to manager of several departments. At this time the individual can elect to stay in store management or move into merchandising.

Along with increased responsibility and authority, promotions within larger retailing companies yield increases in salary. Retail store managers earn salaries ranging from $50 to $150,000 per year, depending on the type of store and compensation program.

Enterprising retail managers may earn bonuses or share in the profits of a store that performs beyond expectations. Successful store managers may eventually move into corporate managerial positions—planning, marketing, training, and expansion schemes for the entire chain!

Figure 12–2 A Possible Retail Career Path

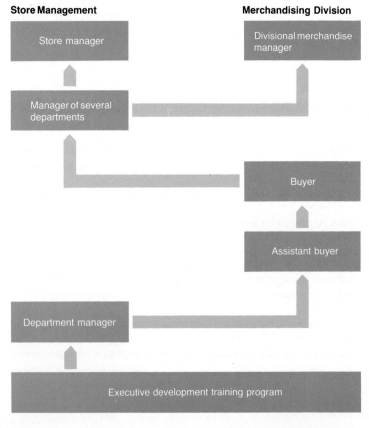

Table 12–1 Compensation of Selected Retail Chief Executives

Company	Compensation
Sears Roebuck & Co.	$1,162,000
Safeway	492,000
K mart Corp.	582,000
J. C. Penney Company, Inc.	866,000
Kroger	1,052,000
F. W. Woolworth Co.	318,000
Great Atlantic & Pacific Tea (A&P)	420,000
Luckey Stores	496,000
American Stores	550,000
Federated Dept. Stores	1,009,000

Source: *Forbes*, June 6, 1983.

Nonfinancial Rewards Are Many

Financial compensation is only one part of the reward you can receive as a retail salesperson. Nonfinancial rewards offered by a retail career are numerous. They include excellent training programs, rapid assumption of responsibility, recognition, opportunity for personal growth and development, travel, and satisfaction from your work.

Retailers Sell like Industrial Salespeople

Fundamental sales principles apply to all types of persuasive situations including retailing. Of course, basic differences do exist between retail and industrial sales, the main difference being that most retailers have their customers come into their particular store to purchase a product or service. However, retailers who sell products such as appliances, carpeting, and building supplies frequently send their salespeople out to call upon customers at their homes. Whether the retail salesperson is selling in the store, over the telephone, or outside the store, the basic selling techniques already discussed can be effectively used when adapted to a particular retailing situation.

The Retail Salesperson's Role

The role of the retail salesperson varies greatly in what is required. Some jobs require the salesperson to act only as an order taker. Other jobs require highly skilled people who can successfully identify and arouse the customers' needs and persuade them to purchase and satisfy those needs. Generally, a retail salesperson is involved, to some extent, in completing transactions, handling customer complaints and merchandise returns, working stock, and personal selling. The following sections will elaborate on each of these four retail sales functions.

Accurately Completing Transactions Is a Must

When a customer is ready to make a purchase, the salesperson must complete the transaction before the sale can be completed. A retail transaction should be handled smoothly and quickly with a great degree of accuracy to avoid frustrating the customer and possibly losing the sale. A good checklist to follow when transacting a sale is listed below:

- Write the sales slip clearly and accurately.
- Accept payment or arrange for credit.
- If change is required, count change accurately, and do not place the money received from the customer in the cash drawer until you have made change.
- When accepting a check or credit card, make sure all forms are signed by the customer.

Many retailing institutions encourage the use of charge accounts by qualified customers. In such an instance you may want to encourage new customers to participate in your store's charge program by asking them to fill out a credit application. Later that day, you could drop these customers a short thank-you card requesting their regular patronage. This type of retail service builds long-lasting relationships between salespeople and their customers.

Handling Complaints Satisfies Customers

The retailer sometimes encounters customers who are not happy with their purchases, and no matter how good a salesperson might be in meeting the needs of the consumer, something can go wrong. The product may be faulty, does not fit, or the customer has decided against the purchase. In general, customers find fault with the product, not themselves.

As in other types of selling, the retail salesperson represents a manufacturer to customers. In the role of representative, the retail salesperson must be courteous and gracious, treating customers as "guests of the house." Such an attitude might be displayed in a willingness to completely answer questions and anticipate customers' needs.

An effective retail salesperson displays an interest in the welfare of each customer. An objective, service attitude is the best approach to take.

Working Stock Is Necessary

Maintaining a variety of neatly displayed items for sale to consumers, and reordering or replacing stock items when depleted is a tedious, time-consuming, but important function of many retail salespeople. The appearance of a store, or a department within a large store, reflects upon the retail salesperson and helps the consumer to develop a good first impression, thereby boosting the retailer's chance for making sales. Working stock also aids a retail salesperson in gaining knowledge of the company's products and their location within the store.

Personal Selling Is Where It's At

Of the four functions of the retail salesperson, personal selling is certainly most important. In most cases, the retail salesperson should consider using the same major parts of the sales presentation used by the industrial salesperson, beginning with the approach. A more detailed explanation of the retail selling process will be discussed next.

Basic Retail Selling Process

The retail sales process puts into action eight basic steps. These are:

1. The approach—involving greeting and determining needs.
2. Presenting the product.
3. Trial close.
4. Uncovering objections.
5. Meeting objections.
6. Trial close.
7. Close.
8. Service after the sale.

Seldom does the retail salesperson have the opportunity to preplan a customized presentation for a single customer. This is why retail selling is challenging. The customer enters the store and you must be prepared to ''show and tell'' about any number of products.

The Approach Is Critical

The approach consists of the activities you engage in to gain your prospects' attention, interest, and willingness to listen to your discussion of a product. Often you already have their attention from the time customers walk in the door looking for assistance. As you walk up to the counter, they say, ''Do you have this or that?''

In other cases, customers do not want immediate assistance. You should never try to force what you have to say on a customer because this may lead to resentment. Only when you have the customer's willing attention should you proceed with your presentation.

In capturing a customer's interest, you should react to nonverbal signs. Nonverbal signs can help you quickly determine whether prospects are willing to listen to what you have to say, and if they want your help. You can learn from these signs what prospects' real objectives are, and if they are seriously considering a purchase.

No matter which type of approach is used, it is important that you greet customers in a warm, friendly manner and make them feel welcome. Treat them as you would treat guests in your home. Be sure to project positive nonverbal signals, such as a smile.

The guiding rule in determining the type of approach to use is to avoid having the customer immediately say no to you. This frequently happens when the salesperson says, "May I help you?" Every shopper has heard "May I help you?" so many times. Though it sounds polite, it is impersonal and allows the customer to reject you. Communication barriers between yourself and the customer are quickly erected.

The Service Approach.   The **service approach** is used to indicate a desire to serve the customer. Do not get in the habit of saying, "Have you been waited on?" "Do you need help?" or, "May I help you?" These can be answered "no." Greet your customers by saying: "Hello! How are you today?" Very likely, you will receive a positive response such as "Hello," "Hi," or "Just fine."

Some salespeople use their names and introduce themselves to customers. Customers sometimes tell you their names in return. Now you are on a first-name basis. Now briefly pause and wait for the customer's next comment. Chances are you will learn what the customer wants.

The Question Approach.   **Questions** can often be an effective approach. At certain times of the year, such as Christmas, it is easy to ask a direct question after the saluation or pause. This question should be a direct, situation-type question, such as "Are you looking for a Christmas gift?"* Someone may be examining a product as you walk up. You might say, "Is this radio for you?" or, "Are you looking for a complete stereo system or speakers?" Customers will usually tell you their needs.

The situation question also should be used to further clarify customers' needs when they tell you the product they are shopping for. The customer says, "Hi. I'm looking for a personal computer." You can respond, "Is it for home or office?" You can continue the use of questions until you determine the customer's needs.

Should the customer say, "I'm not sure what I'm looking for," quickly show a product to establish a reference point. Maybe you have a stereo

---

* Refer to the Chapter 7 discussion of the SPIN approach and the use of questions.

system on sale. Show it and ask, "Is this what you had in mind?" Now most customers will direct you to their real needs.

Watch for buying signals. For example, if they say Yes to the question "Is this what you had in mind?" you may be ready to move towards the close instead of going into a discussion of the product's features, advantages, and benefits.

The Product Approach.   A third approach, the **product approach,** can be used with two types of customers.

1.   The customer who is "just looking."
2.   The customer who has stopped browsing, and is intently scrutinizing a particular group of goods.

An alert salesperson quickly recognizes the mannerisms of the individual who is "just looking." A "looker" usually wanders around aimlessly, avoiding eye contact with the salesperson and keeping a safe distance from retail salespeople. Once the looker stops to examine a product, the salesperson should move in and start talking about the product, giving the customer some information without making it obvious.

In cases where a customer is clearly interested in a product, the salesperson, if possible, can prompt the customer with a question. A person who is peering intently into the window of an auto on a showroom floor might be asked by a salesperson: "Why don't you slide on into it?" (a sports car in this case). To the individual who is carefully examining an article of clothing, a salesperson might say, in a slightly encouraging tone, "Why don't you try it on? The dressing room is right back here."

The Retail Sales Talk Requires Creativity

Following a successful approach in a retail situation is the sales talk or presentation. Customers buy products to meet their needs or solve their problems, and because of the limited amount of time you have to spend with customers, you must use clear, concise, and persuasive language to sell benefits that really mean something to customers. These benefits should be related to the customers' needs and be stated in terms that they understand. The major ways to identify customers' wants, needs, or problems are to ask questions, present alternatives, make suggestions, and use demonstrations.

Ask Those Questions.   The first way to uncover a customers' needs or problems is to ask a revealing question. Suppose that an observant shoe salesperson notices that a customer's shoes are too narrow, causing the leather to stretch out of shape. The customer asks for a pair of shoes in the style selected, stating the size and width. In turn, the salesperson asks, "Do you find your shoes stretching out of shape after a few months of wear?" "Yes . . . most of my shoes tend to do that, and eventually the leather begins to crack.'' The customer had always selected shoes which were too narrow, without realizing it.

In this example, the salesperson discovers a problem that the customer is not even aware of. In many cases a salesperson can learn about customers' problems and needs, which may eventually lead to a sale, through questioning. A salesperson might ask questions such as:

''How will you use this . . . ?''

''Would you be satisfied with . . . ?''

''Do you have trouble with . . . ?''

''Do you always do that . . . ?''

Your use of perceptive questioning in retail sales can aid you in uncovering customer needs, and solving customer problems that otherwise would not have been readily apparent.

Use of Questions in Retail Selling

A retail salesperson in a men's clothing store notices a prospect looking at the sport coats. As the salesperson approaches the customer, he says:

Salesperson: Hello, looking for a suit or sport coat?

Prospect: I'm not really sure what I'm looking for.

Salesperson: Something basic for everyday use or something special?

Prospect: Well, I have to be able to wear it to work.

Salesperson: Where do you work?

Prospect: Oh, I'm a funeral director, but I'm looking for something different—sporty. I sort of like this coat.

Salesperson: Would you like to try that on? [*Puts on a red, white, and blue sports coat.*]

Prospect: Well, it's sporty. What do you think?

Salesperson: Well, you certainly would be sporty. Are you sure this is what you want?

Prospect: Well, I'm not sure. I'm used to dressing so conservatively. Maybe I'd better shop around.

Salesperson: Do you want to be sporty—yet conservative?

Prospect: Yeah, that's it!

Salesperson: I think I have something you'd really like. [*Brings out and tries on a navy blue sport coat.*]

Prospect: This looks sharp!

Salesperson: Step over here and let's select your slacks and shirt. I have a tie that would really set off that blazer!

Present Alternatives. The second way to make a customer aware of a need or problem is to present alternatives. Take for example the customer whose jeans appear to be too short. The salesperson asks: "Do you prefer wearing your jeans so that they just touch the top of your shoes, or would you prefer them to cover the top of your shoe?" The customer replies, "They do seem a little too short, don't they?" The salesperson then recommends that the customer wear preshrunk jeans to avoid the problem of shrinkage due to machine washing and drying. By presenting the customer with a useful alternative, this salesperson tactfully makes the customer aware of a problem, and provides a solution.

Make Suggestions. Another way to point out a need or problem is to make a suggestion. The following example shows this approach. The customer's slacks are obviously too long, causing the bottom of the trousers to wear out. The salesperson asks, "Have you ever tried a 32-inch length slack? The bottom won't drag on the ground and wear out." This salesperson points out the problem to the customer by suggesting a shorter length slack.

Use Demonstrations. The fourth way to point out a need or problem to a retail customer is through demonstration. A shoe store customer insists that she knows what size shoes she wears. The salesperson suggests that the customer should have her feet measured, as shoe size tends to vary with the style of shoe. (Very few customers refuse the request when given this reason.) Once the person's foot is measured, the salesperson shows the size to the customer, who agrees to try on that size shoe.

Demonstrations of products such as televisions, automobiles, stereo systems, appliances, and clothes are commonplace in retail sales because such a demonstration is an excellent way to make the customer aware of needs or problems.

Use the Sell Sequence

No matter whether you use questions, present alternatives, make suggestions, or use demonstrations, it is important to concentrate on emphasizing the benefits of your product. *Show the feature, explain the advantage, lead into the benefit, and let the customer talk by asking a question about the benefit (trial close).*

S	E	L	L
Show feature	*Explain* advantage	*Lead* into benefit	*Let* customer talk

Listen to what your customer says and you will discover the customer's "hot button." Once you determine the customer's needs, match your product's benefits to those needs. Concentrate on discussing benefits that the customer has indicated are important.*

Handling Objections

Because a retail store handles such a large number of products, the retail salesperson must respond to a multitude of objections. Objections should be answered in a way that does not lead to an argument. In some cases this can be accomplished by rephrasing an objection as a question. This and other techniques for overcoming objections (discussed in Chapter 9) can easily be adopted to the retail selling situation.

Some objections are valid. If an objection is a valid one, don't attempt to deny it. You gain status in the eyes of your customer by responding *truthfully* to an objection.

If the objection is invalid, you may choose to deny it or you may ignore the objection if it is not important to make the sale. Since customers usually feel obligated to defend their objections, you may make them mad and lose them if you flatly tell them they are wrong.†

Closing the Sale

Of all the steps in the selling process, closing the sale is often the most difficult for the new retail salesperson, especially when multiple closes are involved.

An experienced retail salesperson senses when a customer is favorably disposed toward a product. Questions a customer asks such as, "How soon could I have this product?" or, "What type of warranty does this item have?" are fairly strong indicators of a willingness to buy. Of course, the customer who approaches a retail sales counter, product in one hand and wallet or credit card in the other, is already sold! In less obvious cases, a trial close can ascertain a customer's readiness to buy.

Types of Closes

While each of the closes discussed in Chapter 10 can be used in a retail situation, there are four closes which are used most frequently in retail selling: the assumptive close, the physical action close, the minor point close, and the inducement close.

---

* See Chapter 3 for a complete discussion of FAB and Chapter 8 on the sell sequence.
† Refer to Chapter 9 for a detailed discussion of handling objections.

The Assumptive Close.   If you have completed your sales talk, have responded to all of your customer's objections, have used a trial close, and have received a positive response, it is fairly obvious that the customer is ready to buy. Going on this **assumption,** it is often best to ask the questions needed to write up the sales ticket such as:

"Shall I go ahead and have this wrapped up for you?"

"May I have your name and address?"

"Will you need help getting this out to your car?"

Customers who are not ready to buy will stop you from finishing the sales slip. If they let you continue, you have made the sale and can go on to your next customer.

The Physical Action Close.   This requires that the salesperson make some **physical action** indicating to the customer an understanding that the sale has taken place. An automobile salesman may hand the customer the keys to a new car. A department store clerk may start wrapping the goods.

Such actions can actually make the decision for a wavering customer. However, this type of close requires finesse and intuition from the salesperson. A premature physical close may make the salesperson appear to be "too pushy."

Closing on a Minor Point.   On product lines in which the customer must make a choice on **minor features** such as color, size, delivery, and terms of the sale, the salesperson may close by asking which of the two characteristics the customer wants such as:

"Would you prefer this in red or blue?"

"Will this be cash or charge?"

Always present a limited number of alternatives to allow the customer a choice between "something" and "something." If only one choice is presented, the customer may respond with, "No." (No to the color, or no to the purchase.) But a choice between alternatives cannot be answered no. Be sure not to present *too many* alternatives, because your customer may become confused.

The Inducement Close.   Assuming you have the authority to offer inducements, a good way to close the sale is to encourage the customer to buy by offering something extra or something free. **Inducements** may be in the form of extended warranties at no charge, a price reduction, a free bonus, free delivery, or free installation.

One stereo salesperson often offers a discount if the customer purchases a stereo combination by saying, "If you purchase this system today, I'll give you a 10 percent discount over what it would cost you to buy each component separately." Often this inducement will convince the customer to cross the line and make the purchase. After all, who can resist the thought of getting something for nothing?

A Retail Salesperson Earns $1.5 Million in Commission

Martin Shafiroff's gross commissions of $1.5 million rank him as possibly the top retail salesperson in the United States. He is reported to sell more securities each year than any other retail stockbroker and is a partner in the investment banking firm of Lehman Brothers Kuhn Loeb Inc. Martin sells investments in securities, real estate, and tax shelters to a variety of people such as professional entertainers, board chairmen and presidents of corporations.

Martin says "product and conviction are only half of my success formula; the other half stresses cold calls and contacts." He strives to convert cold calls into legitimate prospects and turn prospects into accounts—building an investment portfolio for each account. That's the "life blood of my business." Shafiroff says. By carefully planning his day to concentrate *solely* on selling activities, Martin is able to telephone up to sixty clients and prospects each day. By the way, he likes to enter his office before eight in the morning and leave at about seven in the evening.

Martin is a great believer in the use of questions to uncover prospect objections, and he carefully listens to the prospect's response in order to determine his needs. He spends little time on his introduction, only a few minutes on why he called or on an explanation of what he wants the prospect to buy, leaving 70 to 80 percent of his time for asking for the order. Unlike most telephone salespeople who hang up after one no, Martin believes in closing at least three times. He believes the first couple of noes force the prospect into sincerely listening to his investment philosophies and concepts, and lower his defense mechanism.

Martin strongly believes he can help his customers and often must take a strong position. After all, he is selling corporate presidents, who are strong-willed men and women with large egos. He says, "I am very persistent . . . I recall one individual whom I called perhaps fifteen times . . . before he became my customer."

Martin's success revolves around properly planning his time, using multiple closes, determining the prospect's real objection, knowledge of his product, understanding his clients' needs, and many hours of hard work each day.[5]

Follow-Up with Service after the Sale

The sale of high-priced durable goods (cars, appliances, etc.) and intangibles (insurance, stocks and bonds) implies customer contact after the sale.

Proper service and handling of complaints cannot be overemphasized. It is essential for repeat sales. Joe Girard, the world's greatest automobile salesperson, believes one of his secrets to success has been that when the customer comes back with a complaint or needs service, he drops everything and makes sure the customer gets the best service available. He says, "The sales begin 'after' the sale . . . if the customer was good enough to buy from you, then he deserves service."[6]

Customers returning merchandise with a complaint are seldom in a good frame of mind. The salesperson should handle this situation in a calm, diplomatic way. It is the salesperson's responsibility to provide service after the sale. If the customer is not carefully handled, the salesperson will probably lose any chance of making a sale to this buyer in the future. Also, the word could get around, and future sales could be hurt. It is always important to listen to the customer's complaint and ask questions to discover the real problem. How one salesperson quickly resolved a customer's complaint illustrates the proper way to handle a problem after the sale has taken place:

Recently, a friend of mine bought a set of bicycle pedals. After only a few days' use, one of the pedals froze up and would not turn. My friend returned them promptly and demanded a new pair. Without a word, the salesperson looked at the damaged pedal and immediately brought out another pedal. The salesperson then said, "I'm very sorry. If you have any further problem with the replacement set, please come back and I'll be glad to help you." With that, my friend and the salesperson exchanged good-byes and parted company. My friend felt relieved and holds a high opinion of the salesperson and the store. This salesperson kept the door open for future sales by providing service in a cooperative manner.

Challenging Situations in Retail Selling

The examples of retail selling presented so far have been relatively commonplace: one customer interacting with one salesperson for a short period of time. A retail sales situation can be complicated by a number of factors and occurrences. The sections which follow relate several fairly common challenging situations encountered in retail selling.

Selling to Several Customers at the Same Time

A confusing situation may arise when a retail salesperson is required to wait on more than one customer at a time. It is the salesperson's responsibility to attend to as many customers as possible without causing any one of them to be resentful. Often while the salesperson is waiting on a customer who is slow and deliberate in making a decision, another customer, who may be pressed for time, enters the store. The salesperson should offer a greeting or somehow acknowledge the second customer's presence. The salesperson can usually speak to the second customer out of listening range of the first customer. A common greeting is: "Good morning. Someone will be with you soon."

If the first customer is looking at products which the salesperson has displayed, the salesperson may politely take leave of the first customer and attend to the second customer. If the new customer's needs cannot be attended to quickly, the salesperson faces the dilemma of handling both customers at once. The only way to resolve this problem is to move back and forth between each customer. A successful salesperson can effectively wait on several customers at once. It is better to make two sales than to wait on only one customer at a time.

The Group Shopper

Many retail salespeople dread the prospect of waiting on customers who shop in pairs or in larger groups (**group shoppers**) as they believe their efforts to make a sale may thereby be drastically reduced. In such situations, the important thing for the salesperson to do is to identify both the primary decision maker and the person for whom the product is being purchased.

If they are one and the same person, the salesperson has less of a problem. More often than not, the friend or relative is viewed as a "purchase pal," offering the customer a more unbiased view of the situation than a salesperson might. A study conducted analyzing the purchase pal's effects on buyer behavior showed that the presence of a purchase pal increased the likelihood of a sale when the customer was attended to by a salesperson of high expertise.[7]

Substitutions Are Sometimes Necessary

There are two types of situations in which a salesperson may desire to **substitute** one product for another: (1) when the article requested by the customer is in stock, but the salesperson feels it possible to sell another instead, and (2) when the article the customer asks for is out of stock or is not carried in inventory. A substitute product should only be presented when its performance or functional capabilities equal or exceed those of the item requested. The salesperson should be able to make valid claims in relation to the substitute item. The auto tire salesperson may recommend the Uniroyal Fastrak Belted tire because: "For only two dollars more you get 5,000 added miles."

Never should a salesperson present a substitute saying only, "It's just as good." Such a weak statement makes no valid case for a product, and may put a customer on the defensive. In summary, when substituting a product for either of the two cases listed above, the salesperson should quickly present the substitute to the customer, relating it to the product originally requested.

Turning the Customer over to Another Salesperson

Occasionally a salesperson will find it impossible to answer a customer's questions regarding a particular product. In such a case, rather than fabricating an answer, a salesperson should obtain the aid of another employee better versed in the technical aspects of the product in question. The person summoned can be referred to as the manager or as the resident expert on that type of product.

In a recent search for a set of new stereo speakers for my car, I had shopped around, comparing the various brands sold at a variety of specialty stores and general retailers. Most of the salespeople with whom I spoke either knew very little about car stereo speakers, or pushed the top-of-the-line model—to the exclusion of all others.

Shortly after entering one store, I noticed that they had seemed to divide the speakers they carried into two groups. When I asked about the difference between the two types, the salesperson confessed ignorance, but courteously suggested that I might speak to the store owner. As it turned out, the store manager discussed the matter with me, explaining under what circumstances each type of speaker should be used, and I left the store content, having purchased a new set of car stereo speakers.

In retail selling, some salespeople are trained to "turn over" the customer to another salesperson if they feel they cannot make the sale. Salesperson A excuses himself, returns with salesperson B. The introduction may be: "This is Ms. Jones our store manager, who is most familiar with our merchandise," or, "This is Mr. Berry our buyer. He has recently returned from market. He's our expert on. . . ."

Often nonverbal signs are planned to aid in the turnover. Salesperson B slowly takes over the entire presentation. If salesperson A does not get an opportunity, or the hint, to leave, salesperson B slowly moves between the customer and salesperson A. Salesperson A leaves the area. This has proved to be a very successful selling strategy.

The Customer Who Does Not Buy

A retail salesperson often comes into contact with customers who are shopping around at various stores prior to purchasing a particular product. In such cases, the salesperson's objective becomes one of getting the customer to return to the store when a decision has been reached. By pointing out the exclusive benefit of one or two brands of a product, the salesperson avoids confusing the prospect, and may even attempt a few "soft closes." Rather than following the easy way out, and ignoring customers who are shopping around, the professional salesperson attempts to uncover customer needs, to smoke out objections, and to use multiple closes to make a sale which solves a customer's problem or satisfies a need.

Trading up Increases Sales

Often buyers enter the store looking for a product which if purchased would probably not satisfy their needs. After looking, they may not find the ideal product at the low, low price they have in mind, and leave the store.

The salesperson's challenge is to determine such buyers' actual needs, and suggest a product which will truly satisfy them. This activity may result in customers' **trading up,** by suggesting that they purchase:

A higher quality product—a new car instead of a used one; a standard typewriter rather than a portable; a Texas Instruments TI-2500 III with several mathematical functions instead of a calculator with only a few simple functions.

Several products instead of one—slacks and tie to go with a new sport coat; front-end alignment on automobile to go with new tires.

More of the same product—buy two—one to give away, one to keep; buy two pair of jeans instead of one while they are on sale.

Trading up is an effective method of helping both the customer and the salesperson.

Return Goods Selling Is a Must

All retail salespeople have customers **return purchases** from time to time, and when this happens one of four things can typically be done:

1. Refund the customer's money.
2. Credit the customer's charge account (if appropriate).
3. Exchange the product for the same type.
4. Sell the customer another product.

The salesperson should first attempt to sell the customer another product or to exchange the product and if this is not possible, should attempt to credit the customer's account. Cash refunds are a last resort.

On my last birthday my wife gave me a pair of jeans and an umbrella, each valued at $35. She purchased these items from two different stores at which I had never shopped. When I sought to return the gifts, the clerks at both stores cheerfully refunded my money, neither one suggesting that I exchange the item or buy something else.

Why didn't one of the clerks say, "I know your wife would like you to have a nice birthday present. What is it you need in clothing?" With $70 in my pocket, I could have purchased shoes, socks, ties, or could have made a down payment on a sport coat or suit. When I left those two stores, their money was gone forever. If this happens three to five times a year, a store has lost a great deal of sales revenue. A good point to remember is that you can sell at any time—even when the customer is dissatisfied and wants a refund on another item.

Selecting Which Price Line to Show

When several price ranges of merchandise are available to show a customer, the salesperson often becomes perplexed, unable to decide which line of product to show the customer first. Although it may seem rather insulting, an honestly phrased question such as, "What price range do you have in mind?" will ease the uncertainty of this kind of situation. However, the more sensitive, price-conscious customer may be offended by this type of questioning. Also, you do not want to limit the customer to a certain price range unnecessarily.

Some salespeople prefer to show the top-of-the-line product first, hoping that the customer will appreciate the better-quality product, placing value before price. This approach may, however, scare away the price-conscious shopper. Other salespeople prefer to bring out the popular-priced product (moderately priced, best-selling) first, and then move up or down in price according to the customer's reaction.

In stores that carry few **price lines** (a common merchandising policy is to carry three lines), the salesperson may present the customer with a sample of each price range and monitor the response. This procedure allows the customer to choose the particular price range which is most attractive. It is important to clear out unwanted products once the customer has narrowed the selection. It can be confusing to choose between too many products.

Suggestion Selling Is Persuasive

The astute salesperson will generally suggest complementary or related products before the original transaction has been completed. ("Would you like some stockings or polish to go with your new shoes?") The reason merchants stress **suggestion selling** is obvious: it increases the size of sale, adding sales that would otherwise be missed. Once a product has been chosen, the salesperson should suggest additional merchandise that will complement the purchase. Often stores will provide salespeople with a list of products which relate to each other, known as "tie-in" goods. The following example demonstrates the use of tie-in selling.

A customer enters a pet store to purchase a can of fish food.

Salesperson: Hi, Mrs. Smith! How are you today?

Customer: Fine. A can of fish food, please.

Salesperson: Large or medium, Mrs. Smith?

Customer: Oh, medium will do, I guess.

Salesperson: How about a treat food also, freeze dried brine shrimp, tubifex, or some live food?

Customer: No, maybe next time.

Salesperson: Sure, just remember, your fish like a change of diet once in a while, like you and me. How's your filter floss and charcoal situation at home? Do you have enough for this weekend?

Customer: You know, I'm not sure. Better give me a box of charcoal.

Salesperson: That will be $4.08, Mrs. Smith. [*As the customer is handed the bag,*] Have a nice day, and come back soon.

Without the additional sale, Mrs. Smith would have made a purchase of only $1.59. Over the course of a full day, tie-in sales can add substantially to sales.[8]

Two other forms of suggestive selling are: suggesting a larger quantity of the item being purchased, or suggesting some unrelated item. To suggest that the customer buy more at one time, the salesperson might say:

There is a saving in buying three.

Shall I send you the larger one? It's really more economical.

Suggesting an unrelated item generally focuses on products that are either on sale or for some reason are uniquely featured. Items on sale that offer a desirable savings to customers should always be mentioned. In addition, customers should be alerted to newly stocked items. Even if they don't buy at the time, they will know that the store carries the product. Now that you know what you should do in a retail selling situation, you should take note of a few things to avoid in order to be a successful salesperson.

Dos and Don'ts of Retail Selling

There are a multitude of ways to lose sales in retailing. The following list points out a few of the reasons that sales are lost and offers some suggestions on how to avoid them:

■ A lack of enthusiasm. Enthusiasm in a salesperson often generates positive feelings in the customer regarding the salesperson's product. An uncertain customer can be encouraged by an enthusiastic salesperson. Show enthusiasm when talking with the customer.

■ Arguing. This is a deadly sin. Arguing with the customer will only result in a lost sale. Avoid arguing with a customer whenever possible!

■ Vocabulary. Don't talk over your customer's head. Remember to *keep it simple, salesperson*. For example, if you are selling a stereo system, don't talk about the technical aspects, unless the prospect wants to. Talk in words that people understand. Technical words will usually lead to confusion on the part of customers who are not experts. They may get too much information and leave, only to buy from someone else who can explain the product at their level of understanding.

■ Disregarding questions. When customers ask questions, they are looking for answers—don't sidestep issues. If a question is difficult to answer, get help from another salesperson or your manager.

■ Overtalking. Don't confuse this with communication. Communication requires two factors: talking and listening. Overtalking can cause you to miss when customers are saying, "I'm ready to buy." Usually it's best to ask questions first; listen, and then talk.

■ Running down a customer's judgment. *Never* tell customers they are wrong! Such a blatant statement may lead to an argument, and certainly shows a lack of respect for customers. So be a diplomat, politely and delicately showing your prospects your point of view.

■ Don't be repetitive. Customers usually hear your point the first time. After the second or third time, they may walk out on you.

■ Don't keep a customer bottled up. Let your customers speak their minds, so that if they have a comment or complaint, it can come out. Keeping them bottled up through an elaborate sales pitch can lead to frustration on their part. You may never really know their problems, and they may never tell you what they really want or what their real objections are if you don't give them the opportunity to speak.

Example of a Retail Sales Presentation

Customer is looking at a display of Cross gold pens and pencils.

Salesperson: [*giving a big smile*] Hello. My name is _____. Are you looking for a pen and pencil set for yourself or for a gift?

Customer: I'm looking for a graduation gift for my brother, but I'm not necessarily looking for a pen and pencil set.

Salesperson: Is your brother graduating from college or high school?

(continued)

Customer: He is graduating from college this spring.

Salesperson: I can show you quite a few things that would be appropriate gifts. Let's start by taking a look at this elegant Cross pen and pencil set. Don't they look impressive? [Trial close.]

Customer: They look too expensive. Besides, a pen and pencil set doesn't seem like an appropriate gift for a college graduate. [Objection.]

Salesperson: You're right, a Cross pen and pencil set *does* look expensive. [Acknowledge objection.] Just imagine how impressed your brother will be when he opens your gift package and finds these beautiful writing instruments. Even though Cross pen and pencil sets look expensive, they are actually quite reasonably priced, considering the total value you are getting.

Customer: How much does this set cost?

Salesperson: You can buy a Cross pen and pencil set for anywhere from $15 to $300. The one I am showing you is gold-plated and costs only $28. For this modest amount you can purchase a gift for your brother that will be attractive, useful, will last a lifetime, and show him that you truly think he is deserving of the very best. Don't you think that is what a graduation gift should be like? [Trial close.]

Customer: You make it sound pretty good, but frankly I hadn't intended to spend that much money. [Objection.]

Salesperson: Naturally, I can show you something else. However, before I do that, pick up this Cross pen and write your name on this pad of paper. [Demonstration.] Notice that in addition to good looks, Cross pens offer good writing. Cross is widely acclaimed as one of the best ball point pens on the market. It is nicely balanced, has a point that allows the ink to flow on the paper smoothly, and rides over the paper with ease.

Customer: You're right, the pen writes really well. [Positive buying signal.]

Salesperson: Each time your brother writes with this pen he will remember that you gave him this fine writing instrument for graduation. In addition, Cross offers prestige. Many customers tell us that Cross is one of the few pens they have used that is so outstanding that people often comment on it by brand name. Your brother will enjoy having others notice the pen he uses is high in quality.

Customer: You're right. I do tend to notice when someone is using a Cross pen. [Positive buying signal.]

Salesperson: You just can't go wrong with a Cross pen and pencil set for a gift. Shall I wrap it for you? [Close.]

Customer:	It's a hard decision.
Salesperson:	Your brother will be very happy with this gift.
Customer:	Okay. Go ahead and wrap it for me.
Salesperson:	Fine. Would you like me to wrap up another set for you to give yourself? [Suggestion selling.]
Customer:	No, one is enough. Maybe someone will buy one for me someday.[9]

Summary of Major Selling Issues

The retailer is extremely important to the U.S. economy, contributing approximately 18 percent of the nation's total revenue. As a career, retailing offers excellent financial and personal rewards to people who are willing to work hard, have the ability to manage people, and understand the principles of selling.

The retail salesperson's job activities may vary from store to store, yet they usually include making transactions, contacting customers, handling complaints, working stock, and personal selling. The fundamentals of selling discussed in earlier chapters and mentioned in this chapter can be used by the retail salesperson just as they can be used by the industrial salesperson.

In the retail sales presentation, the salesperson should stress product benefits, ask questions, and present alternatives, suggestions, and demonstrations. Objections that are raised by the customer should be handled quickly. Many times questions can be used to smoke out hidden objections. An assumptive, physical action, minor point, or inducement technique can be used to close the sale.

Retail selling is a challenging and demanding vocation that requires finely honed skills to help in handling difficult situations such as selling to several customers at the same time, the group shopper, trading up, or return goods selling. The individual who truly wants to succeed in retailing should begin by learning and practicing good salesmanship techniques.

Review and Discussion Questions

1. Discuss the differences between selling for a retailer versus selling for an industrial firm.
2. What might a typical career path look like for a retail department store?
3. In a retail situation, the *approach* is used to gain the prospect's

attention and interest. Discuss several approaches available to a retail salesperson. Which are the most effective? least effective?

4. What are the four types of closes most often used by a retail salesperson? What are the merits of each?

5. Explain the best method for:
   A. Selling to several customers at one time.
   B. Selling to the group shopper.

6. When a customer comes into a store and asks for a refund, what should the salesperson do?

7. What are some of the things a salesperson should avoid doing? Can you think of others?

8. This chapter discusses the success of Joe Girard in selling automobiles and Martin Shafiroff in selling investments. While each is selling something different, they both feel that several factors help them be successful. What are these factors? Are there factors both men feel are important?

9. Suggestion selling is frequently used in retail selling. Explain what is meant by suggestion selling and give an example of its use.

10. Service after the sale is important in retailing to build repeat sales. Comment on what Joe Girard, the world's greatest automobile salesperson, feels about service.

11. Lynn Madden received four sweaters as gifts this Christmas. One was too small and she is now on her way to Feldman's Department Store to return it. As usual, the store is full of people with complaints about broken merchandise and wanting to return gifts that they can't use. Lynn spots a clerk in the clothing department and asks where she should go for a refund. Annoyed, the busy clerk tells her to go to the window at the back of the store for a refund.
   A. Do you think the clerk did the proper thing?
   B. Analyze the situation and discuss what you believe the clerk should have done.
   C. Explain how Lynn, the clerk, and the store may have all been hurt in this situation.

12. John Black has been looking for a new sport coat for weeks. He has finally found one he really likes at Herb's Haberdashery.

Buyer:	I really like this coat.
Salesperson:	It's one of the best we carry. I think you've made an excellent choice.
Buyer:	I've been looking for quite a while, but I'm not sure this is what I really need.
Salesperson:	I don't think you can go wrong with this coat, Mr. Black. You yourself mentioned that you liked its quality; and it really does show off your good taste.
Buyer:	I am tired of shopping, and it is a good buy . . . OK, I'll take it.

Salesperson: That's wonderful; I'm sure you'll be extremely happy with your decision. Will that be cash or charge?

A. What did the salesperson do correctly in this situation?
B. What opportunities were overlooked?

■ Projects

1. Visit three different types of retailers in your community posing as a customer and report on the selling techniques used by each salesperson you encounter. Comment on what you believe each could have done to improve the sales presentation.
2. Visit a large retailer in your community that trains its employees on the use of selling techniques. Report on their reasons for sales training, how they train, and what they include in their sales training program.
3. Visit a local retailer and ask one of their buyers to describe the return goods policies of three or more of their suppliers. Ask how they handle complaints and returned goods from customers.
4. Visit at least three different types of retailers in your community and ask them how their suppliers' salespeople help them in selling products to customers. Also determine what the retailers believe a salesperson can do to aid them in selling the salesperson's products.

■ Cases

12–1 Bates Lumber and Hardware

Over the course of a typical day, Jim Schmidt probably handles 50 transactions. Jim has been a salesperson for Bates's Lumber and Hardware for six months. Mr. Bates, the owner, has been very pleased with Jim's progress, but is quick to point out his one recurring problem. As Mr. Bates states it, "Jim could sell you a bathtub without a drain plug, but more often than not would charge you the wrong price."

Jim is very outgoing and likable, but unfortunately his arithmetic is very poor. His problems making an accurate transaction manifest themselves in a variety of ways. He has miscopied prices, moved decimals, and often added two and two and come up with five.

"Customers have probably caught all of his larger errors before they make out the check, but it would be impossible for me to estimate the number of 50¢ and $1.00 errors he has made which have gone undetected in the store," said Mr. Bates. He continued, "We used to get very few complaints, but lately our regular customers will make a special effort to tell me that they discovered they were overcharged 10¢ on a bag of nails, or $1.00 on a garden hose the last time they were in the store, and 99 percent of the time, Jim made the sale. And there is no telling how many people he's undercharged. I'm afraid if this continues we may lose many customers, the hardware business is very competitive, you know!''

Jim realizes the problem and has signed up for a continuing education basic math class being taught at the local junior college at night. Mr. Bates is happy that Jim is making an effort to correct his problem and has recently purchased a calculator for Jim to use when making transactions. The past week has gone unusually smoothly for Jim until this morning. Frank Barnes, who is perhaps Bates's largest customer, was in the store to purchase several items for his construction firm. Jim thought he was being very careful, and had used the calculator to arrive at a total of $74.50. Jim told Mr. Barnes the amount, and then it happened—Mr. Barnes went through the roof.

He said a few choice words to Jim and then stormed into Mr. Bates's office, disrupting a personal telephone conversation. Mr. Barnes explained how he had come to discover that he was being overcharged a few cents to a couple of dollars almost every time he had come into the store recently. He felt he was being "cheated and swindled and had been made a fool of." He was disgusted at this treatment after giving Bates almost all his business for the past 15 years. Barnes said, "I came in here myself today to give you one last chance, Bates, but when your salesperson out there overcharged me ten bucks, well that's it! Bates, I thought we had been friends . . . I can't believe what you're trying to pull. If you need to get in touch with me you can call Johnson supply—that's who I'll be doing all my business with from now on!" With that Barnes stormed out of the store.

Questions:
1. If you were Mr. Bates, what would you do to try to salvage Mr. Barnes's business?
2. What would you now do with Jim?
3. Is there anything Jim could do to smooth over relations with Mr. Barnes.
4. Assuming Mr. Bates still wants to keep Jim, is there anything else he can do to help him make sales more accurately?

12-2 Plimpton's Tire Service

Beverly Williams put on the brakes to stop her car. It was a rainy day and the car seemed to slide a few extra feet. When she got home she checked the tires. Sure enough, they were worn almost bare. Have I had these tires this long? Beverly thought to herself. The answer to that question didn't matter. It was obviously time to buy new tires.

Beverly drove her 1966 Mustang to a nearby tire store she had heard advertised many times. She entered the store ready to buy a set of inexpensive, nylon, 4-ply tires. She didn't feel she needed more expensive

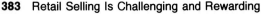

radial tires, because she drove the Mustang only in town, almost exclusively to and from work. While she didn't need a top-of-the-line tire, she did want whitewalls. She thought whitewalls really made her car look better. The conversation went like this:

Buyer: Hello, I'm looking for some new tires.

Salesperson: What type of car?

Buyer: A 66 Mustang. . . . I think the diameter is 14 inches. . . . Oh, I'm looking for an inexpensive tire.

Salesperson: [*Walking over to a display*] These are our cheapest tires.

Buyer: That's a little more than I wanted to spend. [*She pauses, waiting for a reply; getting none, she continues:*] Well, I guess I'll have to shop around.

Questions:

1. Would this salesperson have sold you? Why? *did not say anything about qualities or give of tires (said cheapest)*
2. What did the salesperson do wrong in this case?
3. If you were the salesperson, what would you have done? *given reasonably the cost of the tires could be justified for that price*

12–3 Competition Shoes, Inc.

The ad read, "Competition Shoes—We know what it takes to keep you running." Dave Wilson looked at his running shoes and knew they only had a couple of miles left in them.

Dave had only recently taken up jogging, but he was now addicted to his new hobby and generally ran 15 to 20 miles a week. He realized now that his running shoes were not really very high quality, and now that he was a serious runner he wanted the proper equipment—and that meant better shoes. He decided to see if Competition Shoes had the shoes he needed. That night he went to the store.

Salesperson: Hello, what can I help you with this evening?

Buyer: I am looking for a new pair of running shoes.

Salesperson: Do you have a particular shoe you would like to try on?

Buyer: To be honest with you, I've only been running for three months and I don't know very much about running shoes.

Salesperson: How much do you run a week?

Buyer: I'm up to about 20 miles.

Salesperson: That's a lot of running for a beginner. Do you plan to compete in the future?

Buyer: Well, I started running for the exercise, like so many people do, but I really enjoy running and I would like to prove to myself that I can finish a marathon.

Salesperson: So you would like to compete.

Buyer: Come to think of it, I guess I would.

Salesperson:	Where do you do most of your running, on a track, grass or pavement?
Buyer:	There is a high school track a few blocks from my house, but I have to run on the street to get there and back.
Salesperson:	Mr. Wilson, I have two shoes that I believe will work very well for you [*showing Dave two shoes from the display*]. This Nike shoe is very sturdy and generally holds up well for people who put in as many miles as you do each week. This Big Paw Olympian [*showing Dave the other shoe*] is just as sturdy and has this wide vibration reducing heel. This heel will save your feet and legs a lot of stress. It's especially made for running on hard surfaces.
Buyer:	I'll try the Olympian model on. I'll probaby need a size ten. [*The salesperson gets the shoes, and Dave tries them on.*]
Salesperson:	How do they feel?
Buyer:	Great [*realizing the difference between these shoes and his old pair*], I'll take them.
Salesperson:	That's wonderful, I know they will suit your needs. Now come over here, I want to show you our new, thick, runners socks. With your running schedule, I think you will need three pairs of new socks.

Questions:

1. What did the salesperson do correctly in this situation? Do you think any errors were made?
2. If you were looking for a new pair of running shoes, would you have bought from this salesperson? Why?
3. Do you realize the importance of sales professionalism in a retail situation? How did this salesperson differ from the one in Case 12–2?

13

Selling in the Industrial Setting

 **Learning
Objectives**

1. To examine the characteristics of industrial markets and industrial products.
2. To explain the steps industrial purchasing agents go through in their buying decision.
3. To discuss purchase motives.
4. To illustrate the use of a value analysis and its importance in selling to the industrial buyer.

**Key Terms
for Selling**

Industrial market	Modified rebuy purchase
Derived demand	Gatekeepers
Inelastic demand	Value analysis
Joint demand	Unit cost
New task purchase	Return on investment
Straight rebuy purchase	

Profile

Stephen Gibson
U.S. Steel

Stephen Gibson is a sales representative for U.S. Steel Corporation in Houston, Texas. Before coming to Houston, Steve served in sales capacities in Salt Lake City, Los Angeles, and Memphis. Steve joined the nation's largest steelmaker in 1975 upon graduation from Duke University with a degree in economics. He finds his post with U.S. Steel extremely satisfying and rewarding, and feels it is an excellent opportunity for personal and career growth.

Gibson explains his role with U.S. Steel as follows: "My current sales assignment involves direct solicitation of a diverse group of steel users such as high-technology, oil field related company like Hughes Tool, and a leading manufacturer of air conditioning equipment, the Friedrich Company. In addition, I have numerous smaller company accounts where the purchasing agent is frequently also the president of the firm.

"I find the needs of the individual or group to be solicited can be situational in nature depending on company size and market share, or the individual's responsibility within the organization. I know that customers' motives for buying steel from a specific company differ. Thus, for me to be successful on a sales call, I must identify these motives and create an environment that will motivate buyers to place their steel requirements with United States Steel.

"How do I do this? I attempt to have a well-prepared sales presentation, documented to current market conditions, which pays special attention to the requirements of the buyer's industry and markets. I must be able to show the benefits that will accrue to the company through affiliation with U.S. Steel. I must identify with the buyer and show that as a person he or she is subject to needs, wants, and moods common to all of us. I would hope to establish a relationship based on mutual respect, cooperation, and trust. I would also hope to be perceived as a member of that company's team.

"I have found there are no secrets to success. Hard work and time management mixed with some old-fashioned luck are really the only keys. I do find that some successful people seem to enjoy their work just a little more than others.

"Several years ago as I was preparing for my first sales territory I asked myself what made a good salesman. From my thoughts at that time and subsequent experience, there has evolved a method that I fondly call the "PRECISE" method of salesmanship. *P*lanning your sales call; earning the *r*espect of your customers;

*e*ducating yourself; having *c*onfidence in yourself; having an *i*nquisitive nature (being a problem solver); proper *s*electivity of personal goals and prospects; and possessing an *e*go which pushes you to excell appear to me to be important for being successful in selling.

My method is far from the definition of *precise* as would be indicated in Webster's dictionary. It is only a guide that I find keeps me in tune and on track. I found that blending planning, respect, education, confidence, inquisitive nature, selectivity, and ego works well for me. They yield success."

Bill Hughes, a salesman for Westvaco Corporation, which manufactures corrugated boxes, developed a waterproof corrugated box to replace a wire-bound crate and saved one customer $2,000 a month. Another customer credits Hughes with changing his firm's fiber drum to a corrugated carton for export shipments. The new container is stronger and more waterproof, saving the customer's company $150,000 annually.[1]

This example, along with the accompanying profile of U.S. Steel's Steve Gibson, illustrates the key function of the industrial salesperson. Steve acts as a problem solver for his customers. He is involved in examining the customer's business operation, locating any unnoticed or potential problems, and aiding the buyer in determining methods for solving problems or improving business operations. Clearly, the industrial salesperson has many duties, but by helping the buyer perceive a real need, the salesperson will be better able to explain how his products can benefit the buyer.

This chapter examines the industrial goods market. The demand for industrial products, types of industrial purchases, and the characteristics of industrial products are first discussed. Next, the eight steps in the industrial buying decision are detailed. This is followed by an examination of why purchasing agents buy. Here you will want to thoroughly understand the use of value analysis. It is commonly used in industrial sales presentations.

What's Different about the Industrial Market

The **industrial market,** sometimes called the producer market, is composed of individuals and organizations that purchase products and services to be used in the production of other goods or services which in turn are used in their own business. This includes manufacturers, government customers, and institutional customers. Government customers include city, county, state, and federal agencies. The United States federal government is the largest purchaser or products and services in the world. Institutional customers include public schools, universities, and hospitals.[2]

The basic types of goods and services purchased by buyers in the producer market are shown in Figure 13–1. In addition to raw materials and components, producers purchase facilities (such as buildings), capital equipment, and a wide array of periodic services, such as repair, legal services, and advertising.[3]

Demand for Industrial Products

Three important factors distinguish the demand for industrial products from the demand for consumer goods. When selling in the industrial market, you should consider the influences on the demand for your products and services in order to properly plan your sales presentation. Customer demand for industrial products is (1) derived, (2) inelastic, and (3) joint.

Customers Demand

① **Derived Demand.** The demand for many industrial goods and services is linked directly to consumer demand for other products—it is a **derived demand.** For example, the Whirlpool Corporation buys small electric motors for its refrigerators because consumers purchase the refrigerator; the demand for the motor is based on the demand

Figure 13–1   Classification of Goods and Services in the Industrial Market

   I. Entering goods.
      A. Raw materials.
          1. Farm Products (wheat, cotton, livestock, fruits, and vegetables).
          2. Natural products (fish, lumber, crude petroleum, iron ore).
      B. Manufactured materials and parts.
          1. Component materials (steel, cement, wire, textiles).
          2. Component parts (small motors, tires, castings).
  II. Foundation goods.
      A. Installations.
          1. Buildings and land rights (factories, offices).
          2. Fixed equipment (generators, drill presses, computers, elevators).
      B. Accessory equipment.
          1. Portable or light factory equipment and tools (hand tools, lift trucks).
          2. Office equipment (typewriters, desks).
 III. Facilitating goods.
      A. Supplies.
          1. Operating supplies (lubricants, coal, typing paper, pencils).
          2. Maintenance and repair items (paint, nails, brooms).
      B. Business services.
          1. Maintenance and repair services (window cleaning, typewriter repair).
          2. Business advisory services (legal, management consulting, advertising).

for the refrigerator. People do not buy motors in this case; they buy refrigerators. There would be little demand for refrigerator motors, and other associated components, if no one bought refrigerators.

Other industrial sellers are affected by a change in demand for a particular product. If, for example, the demand for Whirlpool's refrigerators were to decline, the demand for production equipment would decline. Lower demands for steel would result, which would lead to a lower demand for iron ore. A change in a product's demand can set in motion a wave of changes affecting the demand for all firms involved in the product's production.

② **Inelastic Demand.**   The demand for many industrial products is **inelastic.** An increase or decrease in the price of a product will not usually generate a proportionate increase or decrease in sales for that product. The Whirlpool refrigerator has many component parts. The cost of each part represents a fraction of the total cost of producing the refrigerator. Should there be an increase or decrease in the price of a single part, such as the motor, the demand for the appliance would not be significantly influenced. Even if the cost of its motor doubled (assuming it did not represent a large proportion of production costs) and was passed along to the consumer, the refrigerator's sales price would increase by a relatively small amount, having little, if any effect on consumer demand.

③ **Joint Demand.**   The demand for many industrial products is also affected by **joint demand.** Joint demand occurs when two or more products are used together to produce a single product. For example, a firm that manufactures automobiles needs numerous component parts—tires, batteries, steel, glass, etc. These products are demanded jointly.

The salesperson selling products that are demanded jointly must understand the effect of joint demand on the market in general. When a customer purchases a product, there exists an opportunity to sell companion products. An example is the grocery retailer who purchases computerized cash registers. The IBM 3660 Supermarket System shown in Figure 13–2 also requires the purchase of associated items such as a small computer, cash registers, product scanners, and other supplies necessary to operate the equipment in the grocery store.

By now you should realize that industrial goods have three types of demand—derived, inelastic, and joint. By understanding the demand for his product, the salesperson will be better able to sell properly.

Major Types of Industrial Purchases

Industrial purchases are usually one of three general types—new task purchases, straight purchases, or modified rebuy purchases.[4]

The **new task purchase** is made when a product is bought in

Figure 13–2 The IBM 3660 Supermarket System

Courtesy of International
Business Machines Corporation.

conjunction with a job or task not formerly performed by the purchaser. A long period is frequently needed for the salesperson to make this type of sale since the buyer is often cautious, especially when confronted with an expensive product or large quantities of a product. This is the most challenging selling situation, since buyers want to consider all alternative suppliers and may need a great deal of information from each supplier. The salesperson may have to submit a prototype of the product, a price bid, and make several presentations over an extended period of time before the final purchase decision is made. Some examples would be buying capital equipment, construction materials for a new job site, or even an entire plant facility.

major types of industrial purchases

2. The **straight rebuy purchase** is a routine purchase of products bought on a regular basis. This sale normally amounts to no more than casual order taking. Often, buyers will negotiate a blanket purchase order (BPO) agreement, which establishes the price and terms of the sale for a set period of time. Buyers require very little time and information to make their purchase decision. This type of purchase might include continually used raw materials, office supplies, or MRO (maintenance, repair, and operations items such as spare parts for machinery).

3. The **modified rebuy purchase** is somewhat like the straight rebuy purchase procedure. The buyer is seeking a similar product, but wants or needs to negotiate a different set of terms. The buyer may want a lower price, faster delivery, or better quality. For example, a firm that buys oil field drilling bits from a supplier each month (straight rebuy situation) decides it needs a better-quality drilling bit. The firm goes to the same supplier and other suppliers to see whether a better-quality bit is available and at what price (modified rebuy situation). The drilling company still wants drill bits, but is looking for a slightly different product to suit its present needs.

Product Characteristics

Industrial products, like industrial markets, have certain characteristics that a salesperson should consider when selling to buyers of these goods. These product characteristics differ from consumer product characteristics. Industrial products often (1) are technical, (2) require specifications and bids, (3) are complex in their pricing, and (4) are standardized.

Industrial products are often

1. **Technical products.** When compared to consumer goods, industrial sales are more technical in nature. The industrial salesperson must have more product knowledge training than a salesperson of consumer goods. Discussing complex product information with knowledgeable customers, which demands considerable expertise, is essential to success.

2. **Specifications and Bids.** Many industrial goods are bought on the basis of specifications. These specifications may be determined by the

industrial customer, or they may be commonly accepted industry standards. They may be tremendously complex, such as the design of a specialized hydraulic pump, or as simple as stating the particular color to be used.

Bids, based on stated specifications, are usually submitted by several selling firms to the purchasing firm. Each seller bids on a relatively homogeneous similar product. Depending on the buyer's wishes, bids may range from a simple oral quote given over the phone, to a formalized written quotation, to a sealed bid held in the buyer's office and opened on a specific closing date along with all other bids. If the purchasing agent does not want to accept any of the bids, suppliers may be asked to submit second bids. Purchasing firms typically use this system to identify the product's true market price.

If all other factors are equal, the company submitting the lowest bid will win the contract. However, other factors often affect the buying decision. The product's performance and quality level, for example, may be important considerations in the buying decision. Del Monte Corporation may be willing to pay a supplier several cents more per bushel for a higher grade of tomatoes so they can charge a premium price for their canned tomatoes at the retail level.

③ **Complex Pricing.** Because of the technical nature of the product, its inelastic demand characteristic, the buyer's expertise, and the fact that competitive bidding is often involved in the purchase process, pricing in the industrial market can be complex. Final price to the customer can be based on estimates of long-term agreements, present and future labor and material costs, availability of materials, expected salvage value of present equipment, product service agreements, cost-effectiveness of production facilities, and return-on-investment.

A bid under complex pricing may include progress payments whereby the buyer makes periodic payments to the supplier as a down payment, with the remainder paid when the product is delivered; escalator clauses such that should the cost of manufacturing the product increase, the product's price will also increase; specific foreign currency exchange rates; and letters of credit. In addition, the quote will probably include cash terms (the terms for payment explained more fully in Chapter 5), and the delivery terms (also discussed in Chapter 5).

In consideration of the many factors affecting the price of an industrial product, a sales manager may give the company's sales force a range of prices to use in negotiations. You should avoid trying to use low price alone to make a sale. After all, your selling skills will determine your success in the long run.

④ **Standardization.** Many industrial products tend to be relatively homogeneous. When compared to competing products, they often show a high degree of similarity. When a new product or product feature is introduced to the market, its initial advantage may quickly be lost. It is easy for competitors to improve their product slightly and market a similar one. Most of the time the industrial salesperson will be selling products that are very similar to a competitor's products.

Who Makes the Decisions around Here?

Industrial goods have market and product characteristics different from those of consumer goods. Therefore, the buying decision is somewhat different for industrial goods than for consumer goods. The industrial buying process, like the consumer buying process, can be viewed as a series of steps. The eight steps involved in purchasing industrial products are (1) recognition of the problem or need; (2) determination of the characteristics of the needed product; (3) determination of product specifications; (4) search and qualification of potential sources; (5) acquisition and analysis of proposal; (6) selection of supplier(s); (7) establishment of an order routine; and (8) evaluation of product performance.

8 steps involved in purchasing industrial products

Figure 13–3 shows the steps in the industrial buying process, along with each of the three industrial buying situations. For the straight rebuy, steps 2 through 7 can be eliminated. In this situation a need is recognized, such as a low inventory of a product, and the order is automatically processed. The salesperson supplying a product on a straight rebuy basis should contact the customer periodically to check inventory, and to make sure that the order is being quickly processed. This procedure will strengthen a customer's loyalty to and reliance on a seller, indirectly warding off competition. Salespeople should be continually on the alert for the possibility that present customers may reassess their needs and find some problem with a product, and thus seek another supplier. By routinely contacting the customer, the salesperson becomes aware of changes in the buyer's attitude.

In the new task and modified buying situations, several competing

Figure 13–3   Industrial Buying Process and Situations

	Type of Buying Situation		
Steps in Industrial Buying process	New Task	Modified Rebuy	Straight Rebuy
Step 1. Recognition of a problem or need	yes	yes	yes
Step 2. Determination of characteristics of the needed product	yes	yes	no
Step 3. Determination of product specifications	yes	yes	no
Step 4. Search and qualification of potential sources	yes	yes	no
Step 5. Acquisition and analysis of proposal	yes	yes	no
Step 6. Selection of supplier(s)	yes	yes	no
Step 7. Selection of an order routine	yes	yes	no
Step 8. Evaluation of product performance	yes	yes	yes

suppliers' salespeople may be presenting the prospect with information. The salesperson helps to determine the buyer's needs and shows the buyer how they can be fulfilled by a product. The salesperson needs to work closely with everyone who has an influence on the buying decision. When no firm has an initial edge on an industrial order, the salesperson who spends the *right* amount of time with the *right* people often walks away with the order. This person probably spent some time learning *whom* to talk to. Knowing the right people in an organization is vital to a salesperson's existence. With experience, most good salespeople learn whom they need to contact. But how does the beginning salesperson find these influential people? The next section should help provide some answers.

Who Should I Talk To?

Salespeople must locate those people in the buying firm who will influence and make the buying decision. Industrial salespeople may talk with several people about the product before making a sale. For example, a factory worker (the user of the product), the worker's supervisor, the head of the engineering department, the purchasing agent, and the controller may all have some degree of authority in making the purchase decision. Each person should be contacted.

Figure 13–4 illustrates the procedure that one manufacturer has its suppliers follow. The plant engineer who needs a new machine to help in the manufacture of products contacts the company's purchasing agent and explains the problem. The purchasing agent contacts three suppliers and asks that their salespeople contact him. The engineer describes what is needed to each salesperson and asks them to submit bids to the

Figure 13–4 Ten Steps in the Purchase of a Machine

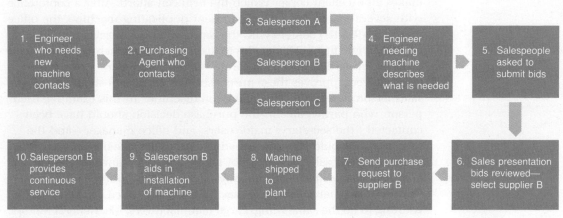

purchasing agent. The salespeople make sales presentations to the purchasing agent and participating engineers, and then submit their bids. Each product is considered and the one best suited for the job is purchased. The machine is shipped to the plant and the salesperson is requested to aid in the installation of the equipment, as well as to help train plant workers on how to use the machine properly. On later sales calls, the salesperson continues to check the machines to make sure they are operating properly, thereby insuring customer satisfaction.

In determining whom to see and how much time to spend with each person, the salesperson should learn who influences the purchase decision and the *strength of each person's influence*. People who may influence the purchase of a product include:

- ■ Initiator—the person proposing to buy or replace the product.
- ■ Deciders—the people who are involved in making the actual decision—such as the plant engineer, purchasing agent, and perhaps someone from top management.
- ■ Influencers—plant engineer, plant workers, and research and development personnel who develop specifications needed for the product.
- ■ Buyers—the purchasing agent.
- ■ Gatekeepers—people who influence where information from salespeople goes and with whom salespeople will be allowed to talk. Receptionists, secretaries, and purchasing agents can be gatekeepers.
- ■ Users—those people that must work with or use the product—for example, plant workers or secretaries.

It is crucial that the salesperson get by the **gatekeepers** and talk to the initiator and to users, influencers, buyers, and deciders. For example, users of a company's copy machine (initiators) may become dissatisfied with its quality of copies. A secretary (influencer) mentions that Xerox makes an excellent copier which the firm can afford. After a conference with several major users of the present duplicating machine, the office manager (decider) confers with the representatives of several competing copy machine firms and decides to lease the Xerox machine. A purchase order is forwarded to the corporate home office where a purchasing agent (buyer) approves these purchases. Which person should the Xerox salesperson have visited in selling the machine? In this example, each person who participates in the purchase decision should have been contacted—the secretary, major users, and office manager—and the salesperson should have explained the product's benefits to each one.

Often a new salesperson is not allowed in the plant nor allowed to talk to people within the company other than the purchasing agent. Hundreds of other salespeople may have already called on the company, wanting to do the same thing. Large manufacturers, like General Motors, have salespeople stop at the receptionist's desk. Whoever the salesperson has asked to see is telephoned. Purchasing agents and other influential individuals will often see only those salespeople who have appointments, or with whom they are well acquainted. A new salesperson calling on G.M. must plan ahead. It will be necessary to call ahead for an appointment, not just drop by.

If a buyer's secretary is reluctant to make an appointment, or if the buyer refuses to establish a meeting time, the salesperson must either give up or use creativity and charm. Sending a reluctant buyer a personalized novelty, such as a small figure of a salesperson holding his sample case along with a note saying: "This salesperson has something which will benefit you" is a creative way of gaining an appointment.

Take another example. After being turned away by a head nurse (gatekeeper), a pharmaceutical salesman put a stethoscope around his neck, obtained a small doctor's bag and proceeded to work his way up to the tenth floor of a large hospital to see the hospital's chief of surgery about a new drug. He told the doctor what he had done and why, and was asked not to do it again. All was not for naught, however, because he arranged to have future conferences with the surgeon in the doctor's lounge upon request. This salesman would not take no for an answer. While you do not want to offend any possible future clients with your persistence, you may be able to open the door on a sale that a gatekeeper tried to keep closed.

Ask yourself, when you do something creative like this, how many others have been stopped by the gatekeeper! Buyers, like all of us, appreciate people who give them special attention, or go out of their way for them, especially if they believe someone understands their needs, sincerely wants to help them, and acts in a professional manner.

Purchasing Agents Are Rational Buyers

When selling to the producer market, the salesperson is dealing with well-trained, knowledgeable, and rational buyers. Industrial purchasing agents in large corporations are often specialists in their jobs. These people are professionals and experts in dealing with professional salespeople.

Purchasing agents carefully examine information presented to them. Quality sales presentations are expected from the salespeople they see. Buying decisions are typically made based on practical, business reasons. Emotional reasons for buying play a less important role in their purchase decisions than in decisions by a consumer. As a result, the time required to make a purchase decision is usually longer than it is in the consumer setting. This is because industrial buyers carefully compare their firm's needs with the features, advantages, and benefits of competing products—a process that takes time.

Why Do Producers Buy?

Buyers in the producer market seek to buy for many reasons. Some of the more common reasons usually evolve from some aspect of the cost and quality of the product. Specific primary buying needs or motives include:

- increasing profits
- Increasing sales
- producing a quality product
- improving the operation's efficiency (resulting in cost reductions)
- helpfulness of the salesperson
- service
- payment
- trade-in allowances
- delivery
- buying a product at the lowest price

As a salesperson, you should determine each buyer's important buying needs if you hope to be successful. You can then develop a sales presentation emphasizing your product's features, advantages, and benefits, and how they can fulfill those needs. one of the best and most often used methods of presenting your product's benefits to the buyer is value analysis.

Value Analysis: A Powerful Selling Tool

Industrial salespeople often include a value analysis in their sales presentation. A **value analysis** determines the best product for the money. It recognizes that a high-priced product may sometimes be a better value than a lower-priced product. Many firms routinely review a value analysis before they decide whether or not to purchase a product.

The value analysis evaluates the product in terms of the buying company's specific needs. It addresses such questions as:

How do your product's features, advantages, and benefits compare to the product currently being used?

Can your product do the same job as your buyer's present product at a lower price?

Does the buyer's current equipment perform better than is required? (Is equipment "too good" for present needs?)

On the other hand, will a higher-priced, better-performing product be more economical in the long run?

A few examples of how value analysis helps solve problems and save customers money are:[5]

One salesperson suggested a change from a high grade of stainless steel being used by a manufacturer to a lower grade. He knew the customer would be able to achieve better machining on the lower grade of stainless steel. The result was a product cost savings exceeding $5,000, plus an improved number of products which could be manufactured.

Detrex Chemical Industries uses chemicals for metal processing. Saving energy is important to Detrex. A salesperson suggested that the firm replace the phosphate surface conditioner currently in use with one that worked at a lower temperature. This saved the company $5,645 in energy costs the first month.

A customer was manufacturing gears by cutting metal blanks in the shop and sending them to another firm for tooth cutting. A company salesperson contracted to do the entire job by showing how this procedure could reduce production costs by 43 percent.

As you can see from these examples, you are often required to analyze the buyer's present operation carefully before suggesting how your product might improve efficiency, enhance the quality or quantity of the product produced, or save money.

In discussing the presentation of a value analysis to a buyer, Patrick Kamlowsky, who sells drilling bits for oil and gas wells for Hughes Tool, said:

It's not as simple as it may appear to make a recommendation and have the oil company adhere to it. You must be thorough in the presentation and present the facts in an objective manner. After all, their money is at stake. The presentation must be logical and based upon those facts which are known; it must be made with as little speculation as possible.

What is difficult is presenting a recommendation to one who has spent thirty or more years in the oil field and has drilled all over the world. I am confronted with the challenge of explaining to this man that the methods which he has employed for years may not be the best application where he is currently drilling. The presentation of the recommendation must therefore be thorough and to the point. When talking to him, I do not imply that his method is outdated or wrong, but that I believe I can help him improve his method. To be successful, I must establish two things very quickly—his respect and my credibility. Showing him my proposal and supporting evidence, and permitting him the time to evaluate it are vital. I don't wish to come on to him too strong, just show him that I genuinely want to help him.*

---

* Patrick Kamlowsky is profiled in Chapter 5.

There are numerous types of value analyses which a salesperson can develop for a prospective buyer. Three types frequently used are: (1) product cost versus true value, (2) unit cost, and (3) return on investment.

value analysis (1) **Compare Product Costs to True Value.** All buyers want to know about costs. The value analysis you develop for a customer should present cost in a simple, straightforward manner. A product's costs are always relative to something else; thus cost must be judged in terms of "value" and results. The base cost of your product should never be the determining factor of the sale. Buying a product solely on the basis of cost could cause a customer to lose money.

Costs should never be discussed until you have the opportunity to compare them to the *value* of a product. In this manner, the customer is able to intelligently compare the true worth of the proposed investment in your product to its true monetary cost. In effect, a good purchase involves more than initial cost; it represents an investment and you must demonstrate that what you sell is a good investment.

Table 13–1 provides an example of how a salesperson might compare the cost of a copier (product X) with that of a competitive copier. The difference between the purchase prices of the two copiers is $305. Product X saves $200 on monthly copy costs, assuming the buyer's firm makes 10,000 copies a month. The buyer receives a savings of two cents per copy. This savings will make up the difference in the initial purchase price in only six weeks. In 15 months, savings on the monthly copy costs will equal the purchase price of product X. Therefore, product X is less expensive, in the long run.

Another example of how a salesperson can show the buyer the true cost of a product is illustrated by the following dialogue between a salesperson for Beechcraft and a buyer.

Salesperson: Mr. Irving, are your key people traveling more than 300 hours a year?

Table 13–1 Example of Cost versus Value of a Small Copier

	Product C	Product X
Initial cost	$2,695	$3,000
Type of paper	Treated paper	Plain paper
Copy speed	12 copies per minute	15 copies per minute
Warm up time	Instant	Instant
Cost of each copy	3¢ a copy	1¢ a copy
Monthly cost (assuming 10,000 copies)	$300	$100

Conclusion: The difference in the purchase price of the two copiers is $305 ($3,000–$2,695). Product X saves $200 on monthly copy costs. The savings on monthly copy costs pays for the higher priced product X in one and one-half months. In 15 months, savings on the monthly copy costs will equal the purchase price of product X.

Buyer: Yes, and much more.

Salesperson: A company airplane could save you some real time and money, especially now that recent federal tax legislation and investment incentives have made the actual costs of ownership the lowest they've been in years. Are you familiar with this new tax legislation?

Buyer: Not really.

Salesperson: Thanks to the major tax reform measures enacted by Congress, business depreciation schedules have been streamlined to permit accelerated write-offs for capital equipment. In the case of business aircraft, the new schedule allows a company to completely write off its investment to a zero residual value in just five years.

In addition, Congress has reduced to five years the length of time required to justify the full 10 percent investment tax credit on airplanes and other major capital investments (while lessening the tax recapture provisions for investments held less than five years). The net result: A direct reduction in corporate income taxes and thus an effective decrease in the real cost of aircraft ownership. For example, let's assume you're considering a jetprop like the Beechcraft King Air F90 shown here. To illustrate the tax benefits of ownership we'll also assume: (1) that your company's taxable income is subject to a 50 percent federal and state tax rate, (2) that the purchase price of your King Air is $1,488,000 (which includes average optional equipment), and (3) that you elect to depreciate the airplane over five years using the new accelerated cost recovery system. Does that sound reasonable?

Buyer: Yes, sounds OK to me.

Salesperson: Here's what your tax savings would look like [*Shows buyer a table*].

Year	Depreciable Base	Depreciation Rate	Depreciation Expense	Tax Savings
1	$1,488,000	15%	$ 223,200	$111,600
2		22	327,360	163,680
3		21	312,480	156,240
4		21	312,480	156,240
5		21	312,480	156,240
Totals		100%	$1,488,000	$744,000

As you can see, the tax savings on depreciation alone are enough to reduce the actual cost of the airplane to half of its original purchase price. And when the added savings of the 10% investment tax credit, the interest expenses on the amount financed, and the various deductible expenses related to operational costs are figured into the total, your capital recovery from tax allowances can reduce the bottom line even more significantly.

What's more, since the biggest share of these savings accrues in the first years of ownership, your cash flow gets plenty of help right up front.

The copier and airplane examples help to illustrate how you can demonstrate to your buyer that your product is a better value than one would think from looking only at its purchase price. Another value analysis technique is to further break down a product's price to its **unit cost.**

Figure 13–5 How Value Analysis Reduces Costs

Weights mounted on a rotor ring were curved to match the ring curve. Did it need this feature? No. Using a straight piece, the cost dropped from 40 cents to 4 cents.

Field coil supports were machined from stock, but the original design blended nicely into a casting operation. The change resulted in lowering the cost from $1.72 to 36 cents each.

This insulating washer was made from laminated phenolic resin and fiber. Machined from individual pieces of material, it cost $1.23. A supplier with specialty equipment now fly-cuts the parts, nesting them on full sheets, at 24 cents each.

Standard nipple and elbow required special machining to fit a totally enclosed motor. Casting a special street "L" with a lug eliminated machining and a special assembly jig. The cost dropped from 63 cents to 38 cents.

An insulator costing $4.56 was originally porcelain, leaded extra heavy. Now molded from polyester and glass, it is lighter and virtually indestructible. New cost: $3.25.

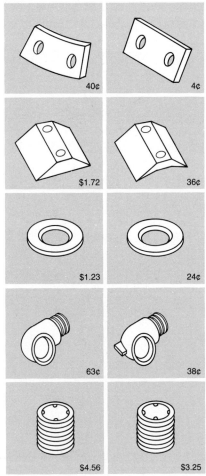

Source: Richard M. Hill and the National Association of Purchasing Management. Used with permission.

Unit Costs Break Price Down.   One method of presenting a product's true value to a buyer is to break the product's total costs into several smaller units. Assume you are selling a computer system that costs $1,000 per month and processes 50,000 transactions each month. The cost per transaction is only 2 cents. Figures 13–5 and 13–6 present six additional examples of how value analysis reduces costs.

Return On Investment Is Listened To.   **Return on investment** refers to an additional sum of money expected from an investment over

Figure 13–6   **A Value-Analyzed Assembly for Directing Steel Cable through an Angle Top**

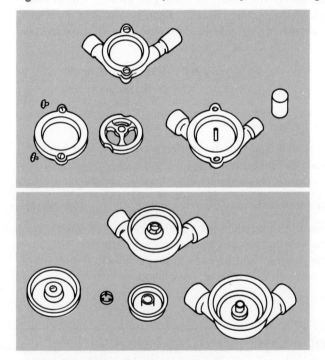

1. Left- and right-hand coupling was eliminated.
2. Cover was changed from brass to plastic.
3. Special tapping operation was eliminated by using only one screw captive to cover. Tapped hole was made concentric with body recess.
4. Pulley was made as screw machine piece rather than a machined casting and made captive to body to simplify field installation.
5. Specialty suppliers with high-speed equipment were used.
6. Cost of unit was reduced 60 percent.

Source: Richard M. Hill and the National Association of Purchasing Management. Used with permission.

and above the original investment. Buyers are very interested in knowing the percentage return on their initial investment. Since the purchase of many industrial products is an investment in that it produces measurable results, you as the salesperson can talk in terms of the percentage return that can be earned by purchasing your product.

Again, assume you are selling computer equipment requiring a $10,000 per month investment. Benefits to the buyer are measured in hours of work saved by employees, plus the resulting salary saving. You first have the buyer agree on an hourly rate, which includes fringe benefit cost; let's say salaries average $5 an hour for employees. The hours saved are then multiplied by this hourly rate to obtain the return on investment. If hours saved amounted to 2,800 per month, this would amount to a savings of $14,000 per month (2,800 hours × $5 hourly rate). You could now develop a table to show the potential return on investment.

Value of hours saved	$14,000 per month
Cost of equipment	−10,000 per month
Profit	4,000 per month
Return on investment ($14,000 ÷ $10,000)	140 percent

Subtracting the $10,000 cost per month from the return of $14,000 per month provides a $4,000 a month profit or a 140 percent return on investment. This can be taken one step further by considering return on investment after taxes, calculated $\dfrac{\$14,000\,(1 - \text{tax rate})}{\$10,000}$. This return on investment presents the buyer with a logical reason to buy. You should remember to let the customer make the cost estimates. The buyer must agree with the figures used for this to be an effective method of demonstrating the real value of buying your product.

Summary of Major Selling Issues

Industrial goods include the raw materials, supplies equipment, and services used in production, as well as finished goods and services intended for the producer, reseller, and government markets. The producer market contains individuals and organizations who purchase products and services for use in the production of other goods or services. Characteristics of the producer market involve derived demand, inelastic demand, and joint demand. Product characteristics are their technical nature, frequent requirements for specifications and bid, complex pricing, and (often) standardization.

The industrial buying decision may be a complex and lengthy process. It usually involves eight basic steps, depending upon whether it is a new task, a modified rebuy, or a straight rebuy situation. It is important for the salesperson to locate the individuals who influence the buying decision and determine the strength of each one's influence in order to allocate the right amount of time and effort to solving a customer's problems. Buyers are concerned about costs and product quality that can result in increased profits and more efficient operations. A value analysis can be used to show the buyer that the salesperson's product is cost efficient.

Review and Discussion Questions

1. Steve Gibson, the salesman from U.S. Steel, was profiled in this chapter. What does Steve believe is important to do in order to be successful in selling steel to his customers?

2. What three types of demand can affect industrial products? Describe each type with an example.

3. Many people within a firm may influence a purchase. Who are these people? Give an example of each "influencer."

4. Value analysis can be an effective sales tool. Define value analysis in your own words, and describe its use in a selling situation.

5. Chart the eight steps in an industrial buying situation.

6. As an industrial salesperson, your job often is to present your product to a company's purchasing agent who makes the decision whether or not to buy your product. Often, this purchasing agent must consider many factors other than your product's merits in coming to a final decision to buy your product. Discuss the major non-product-related factors which may directly influence the purchasing agent's buying decision.

7. Gresham Electric is interested in expanding its sales of small electrical parts to manufacturers of small household appliances. These manufacturers include such companies as General Electric and Westinghouse. Your boss has asked you to study the industrial buying process: (1) recognition of the problem or need; (2) determination of characteristics of the needed product; (3) determination of product specifications; (4) search and qualification of potential sources; (5) acquisition and analysis of proposal; (6) selection of supplier; (7) establishment of an order routine; and (8) evaluation of product performance. What factors affect each step?

8. As a salesperson for the Electric Generator Corporation, you have decided to attempt to sell your EG 600 generator to the Universal Construction Corporation. The EG 600 costs $70,000. You estimate that operating and maintenance costs will average $3,000 a year and that the machine will operate satisfactorily for 10 years. You can

offer a $65,000 price to Universal, if they purchase 10 to 20 machines. Should they purchase over 21 machines their cost would be $58,000 per generator. The generators they are currently using originally cost them $65,000, have a life of seven years, and cost $5,000 each year to operate. As far as you know, their present supplier can not offer them a quantity discount.

A. Develop a value analysis table comparing the two generators.

B. In your presentation, what are the selling points you would stress?

9. You realize as a computer salesperson that the cost of a data processing system is a business-deductible expense. Therefore, the federal income taxes that a business pays to the federal government have to be considered when determining the actual cost of the system to the business. After net profit has been determined, the business must pay the government 48 percent of that net profit. The business keeps the remaining 52 percent.

Assume that you are preparing to make a sales presentation to a small company. You have determined that the business earns approximately $200,000 before taxes. Applying the 48 percent for tax changes, they pay the government $96,000. Their net profit after taxes is $104,000. You want to sell the business a system with an annual invoice cost of $30,000. Your figures show that once the business purchases your system they earn $170,000 before taxes ($200,000 − $30,000 = $170,000).

A. What amount, in tax dollars, would they pay to the government if they buy your system?

B. Compare what the firm would pay the government if they did buy your system, to the amount they would pay the government, if they did not.

C. How much is the company actually paying for your computer system?

Project

Select two similar industrial products made by different manufacturers and compare their features, advantages, and benefits. Select one of the products and state how you would use the information to show a potential buyer its value over the other product. Make sure the product you select is the highest priced product.

Cases

13–1 Electric Generator Corporation

The Electric Generator Corporation was founded in the early 1970s to develop and market electrical products for industrial and commercial markets. Recently the company has developed a new electric generator, the EGI, with a revolutionary design. While its initial cost will be $2,000 higher than any competing generator, reduced maintenance costs will offset the higher purchase price in 18 months. The Electric Generator sales force has been instructed to concentrate all of their effort on selling this new generator as the company feels it has a sales potential of $500 million.

Sandy Hart, their South Texas salesperson, has as her main customer the E. H. Zachary Construction Company of San Antonio, which is the largest nonunion construction firm in the world. Because of the importance of potential Zachary purchases of the EGI (estimated at $1 million), Sandy's boss asks her to take two days off and develop a plan for contacting and selling to Zachary. Monday morning she is expected at the Houston regional sales office to present this plan to her boss, the regional sales manager, and the divisional sales manager. These two people will critique the presentation, and then the four of them will finalize a sales plan which Sandy will present to Zachary's buying committee.

Questions:

1. If you were Sandy, what would be your suggested sales plan?
2. How would a value analysis enter into your presentation?

13–2 Frank's Drilling Service

Frank's Drilling Service specializes in the drilling of oil and gas wells. Scott Atkinson, one of their salesmen, was preparing to contact the drilling engineer at Oilteck, an independent oil company. Scott has learned they are planning to drill approximately 12 new wells in the next six months.

Scott estimates that each oil well will require a drilling depth of approximately 10,000 feet. The drilling service the company is using at present charges 90 cents a foot, plus $1,200 per hour for personnel to operate the equipment. They take about 16 days to drill each well.

Frank's charges $1,200 per hour for personnel and their costs are $1 a foot. Scott believes his drilling crews save customers time and money because they can drill a 10,000 foot well in 12 days.

Questions:

1. Using the above information, develop a value analysis that could be used by Scott to sell to his customer.
2. What are several features, advantages, and benefits Scott should discuss with Oilteck's drilling engineer?

14

Time and Territory Management Is a Key to Success

Profile

Cindy Kerns
Xerox

My name is Cindy Kerns. I am a sales training specialist with Xerox Corporation at their international training center located in Leesburg, Virginia. I received my bachelor's degree in business with a major in marketing from the University of Southern California in 1979. Before assuming my present assignment as a sales trainer, I held various sales assignments with Xerox in Los Angeles.

I have found that a key to success with Xerox is the ability to effectively manage your time. This especially held true for me in my sales assignments where good time and territory management played a major role in my success in my territory.

Effective territory management of any assignment allows you the opportunity to focus on managing the total job. Effective management of a territory requires serious management of the time alloted. For example, a typical sales representative has 168 working hours a month (8 hours a day $\times$ 21 working days in a month). A recent study has shown that out of this 168 working hours per month, only 11 are actually spent in front of the customer selling. Approximately 116 hours per month are spent doing nonselling tasks such as meetings, traveling, lunches, telephone use, proposal writing, etc. The other 41 hours are spent prospecting for business.

A good sales representative will work at turning nonselling hours into actual selling hours spent in front of the customer. One of the ways I found useful in helping me spend more time selling to my customers was to schedule appointments with my accounts beforehand whenever possible. This allowed me to maintain control over the amount of day-to-day activity that I had. It also helps to minimize valuable time spent driving by scheduling my calls as close together as possible. The geography of your territory often requires extensive zoning of your calls in order to avoid wasting valuable time traveling to and from customers' offices.

Waiting time is another valuable commodity in any sales representatives job. A good idea is to utilize the waiting time spent at a customer's location. Such simple tasks as reviewing or writing a proposal, filling out forms and preparing for future sales calls can all be accomplished while waiting to see a customer.

I believe that the most successful sales representatives will take the given fact that they have a limited amount of time to work in a month (168 hours) and then ask themselves, "How can I get as many sales hours in as possible?"

In recalling his early days as a salesman, Shelby H. Carter, Jr., Xerox's senior vice president of sales of U.S. field operations said, "I placed a sign on my car's visor which read, 'Calls are the guts of this business.' We lived in Baltimore," he recalls, "and drove 40 miles every day to get to Annapolis." His wife fixed him a jug of lemonade so he would not have to stop for lunch.

"You've got to make extra calls," he now tells his salesmen, "because 1 more call a day is 5 a week, 20 a month, and 240 calls a year. If you close 10 percent of the people you contact, you have an extra 24 sales a year. You have to be tough on yourself to make that extra call."[1]

Mr. Carter voices the sentiments of sales managers as to the importance of working hard and making extra calls on prospects and customers. The importance of planning your work day and managing your time and territory is very important to your success.

According to a national survey of thousands of salespeople across the nation, managing time and territory is considered the most important factor in carrying out selling duties.[2] Because of such things as the rapidly increasing cost of direct selling, decreasing time for face-to-face customer contact, continued emphasis on profitable sales, and the fact that time is always limited, it is no wonder that many companies are concentrating on improving the way their salespeople manage time and territory.

What Is a Sales Territory?

A **sales territory** comprises a group of customers or a geographical area assigned to a salesperson. The territory may or may not have geographical boundaries. Typically, however, a salesperson is assigned to a geographical area containing present and potential customers.

Why Establish Sales Territories?

Companies develop and use sales territories for numerous reasons. Seven of the more important reasons are discussed below.

To Obtain Thorough Coverage of the Market. With proper coverage of the territories, the company can more nearly reach the sales potential of its markets. The salesperson can analyze the territory and identify and classify customers. At the individual territory level, the salesperson can better meet customers' needs. Division into territories also allows management to easily realign territories as customers and sales increase or decrease.

To Establish Salesperson's Responsibilities. Salespeople act as business managers for their territories. They have the responsibility of maintaining and generating sales volume. Salespeople's job tasks are clearly defined. They know where customers are located and how often they should be called on. They also know what performance goals they are expected to meet. This can have a positive effect on the salesperson's performance and morale.

To Evaluate Performance. Performance can be monitored for each territory. Actual performance data can be collected, analyzed, and compared to expected performance goals. Individual territory performance can be compared to district performance, district performance compared to regional performance, and regional performance compared to the performance of the entire sales force. With computerized reporting systems, the salesperson and a manager can monitor individual territory and customer sales to determine the success of their selling efforts.

To Improve Customer Relations. Customer goodwill and increased sales can be expected when customers receive regular calls. From the customer's viewpoint, the salesperson *is,* for example, Procter & Gamble. The customer looks to the salesperson, not to Procter & Gamble's corporate office, when making purchases. Over the years, some salespeople build up such goodwill with their customers that customers will delay placing their orders because they know the salesperson will be at their business on a certain day or at a specific time of the month. Some salespeople even earn the right to order merchandise for certain of their customers.

To Reduce Sales Expense. Sales territories are designed to avoid duplication of effort so that two or more salespeople are not traveling in the same geographical area. This lowers selling cost and increases company profits. Such benefits as fewer travel miles and fewer overnight trips, plus the contact of productive customers regularly by the same salesperson can improve the firm's sales-cost ratio.

To Allow Better Matching of Salesperson to Customer's Needs. Salespeople can be hired and trained to meet the requirements of the customers in a territory. Research has indicated that the higher the similarity between the customer and the salesperson, the more likely it is that the sales effort will be successful.[3]

Benefit to Salespeople and the Company. Proper territory design can aid in reaching the firm's sales objectives. Thus the company can maximize its sales effort, while the sales force can work in territories that afford them the opportunity to satisfy their personal needs (e.g., good salary).

Why Sales Territories May Not Be Developed. In spite of the stated advantages, there are disadvantages to developing sales territories for some companies such as in the real estate or insurance industry. First, salespeople may be more motivated if they are not restricted by a particular territory and can develop customers wherever they find them. In the chemical industry, for example, salespeople may be allowed to sell to any potential customer. However, after the sale is made, other company salespeople are not allowed to contact that client.

Second, the company may be too small to be concerned with segmenting the market into sales areas. Third, management may not want to take the time, or may not have the know-how for territory development. Fourth, personal friendship may be the basis for attracting customers. For example, life insurance salespeople may first sell policies to their families and friends. However, most companies do establish sales territories.

Elements of Time and Territory Management

For the salesperson, time and territory management (TTM) is a continuous process of planning, executing, and evaluating. The seven key elements involved in this process of time and territory management are shown in Figure 14–1.

Salesperson's Sales Quota

A salesperson is responsible for generating sales in a territory based upon its sales potential. The salesperson's manager typically establishes a total sales quota that each salesperson is expected to reach.

Figure 14–1 **Elements of Time and Territory Management for the Salesperson**

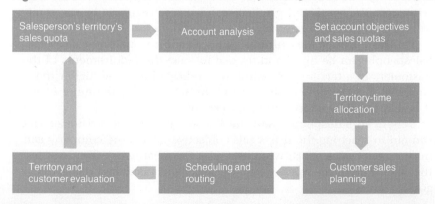

Once this quota is set, it becomes the responsibility of the salesperson to develop territorial sales plans for reaching the quota. While there is no one best planning sequence to follow, Figure 14–1 does present seven factors which should be considered in order to properly manage the territory so as to reach its sales quota.

Account Analysis

Once the salesperson has set a sales goal, it becomes important to analyze each prospect and customer in order to maximize the chances of reaching that goal. First, a salesperson should identify all prospects and present customers, and second, estimate present customers' and prospects' sales potential. This makes it possible to allocate time between customers, to decide what products to emphasize to a specific customer, and how to better plan the sales presentation.

Two general approaches to **analyzing accounts** and thus identifying accounts and their varying levels of sales potential are the undifferentiated selling approach and the account segmentation approach.

The Undifferentiated Selling Approach. An organization may see the accounts in its market as being basically the same. When this happens and selling strategies are designed and applied equally to all accounts, the salesperson is using an **undifferentiated selling** approach. Notice in Figure 14–2 that the salesperson is aiming a single selling strategy at all accounts. The basic assumptions underlying this approach are that the needs of the accounts for a specific product or group of products are similar. Salespeople call on all potential accounts, devoting equal selling time to each of them. The same sales presentation may be used in selling an entire product line. The salesperson feels it can satisfy most customers with a single selling strategy. For example, many door-to-door salespeople use the same selling strategies with each person they contact (stimulus-response sales presentation).

Salespeople whose accounts have homogeneous needs and characteristics may find this approach useful. The undifferentiated selling

Figure 14–2 Undifferentiated Selling Approach

Target accounts

Single selling approach

1

approach has been popular in the past, and some firms still use it. However, many salespeople feel that their accounts have different needs and represent different sales and profit potentials. This makes an account segmentation approach desirable.

The Account Segmentation Approach. Salespeople using the **account segmentation** approach recognize that their territories contain accounts with heterogeneous needs and differing characteristics that require different selling strategies. Consequently, sales objectives, in terms of overall sales and sales of each product, are developed for each customer and prospect. Past sales to the account, new accounts, competition, economic conditions, price and promotion offerings, new products, and salesmanship are among the key elements in the analysis of accounts and territories.

Salespeople classify customers in order to identify the profitable ones. This, in turn, determines where the salesperson's time will be invested. One method of doing this is as follows:

Key account	*a.*	Buys over $200,000 from us annually.
	b.	Loss of this customer would substantially affect the territory's sales and profits.
Unprofitable account	*a.*	Buys less than $1,000 from us annually.
	b.	Little potential to increase purchases above $1,000.
Regular account	*a.*	All other customers.

The unprofitable accounts would not be called upon. The **key accounts** and regular accounts become target customers.

Once the accounts have been broadly classified, categories or types of accounts can be defined in such terms as: extra-large (key), large, medium, and small, which we will refer to as the ELMS system. For example, management may divide the 3,000 accounts in the firm's total marketing into these four basic sales categories, as shown in Table 14–1. As can be seen from the table, there are relatively few extra large or large accounts, but these quite often account for 80 percent of a company's profitable sales even though they represent only 20 percent

Table 14–1 Example of Account Segmentation Based on Yearly Sales

Customer Size	Yearly Sales (actual or potential)	Number of Accounts	Percent
Extra large	over $200,000	100	3.3
Large	$75,000–200,000	500	16.6
Medium	$25,000–75,000	1,000	33.3
Small	$1,000–25,000	1,400	46.6

Table 14–2 **Basic Segmentation of Accounts**

| Account Classification | Customers | | Prospect |
	Sales to Date	Potential Sales	Potential Sales
Extra large			
*L*arge			
*M*edium			
*S*mall			

of the total number of accounts. This is known as the **80/20 principle.** The number of key accounts in an individual territory varies, as does responsibility for them. Even though the key account is in another salesperson's territory, a key account salesperson may call on the "extra-large" customer. Typically this is done because of the account's importance to the company or perhaps the inexperience of the local salesperson.

Accounts can be segmented based on whether the firms are actual customers or prospects. As shown in Table 14–2, actual customers are further segmented on the basis of sales to date and sales potential. Prospects are also segmented into the ELMS classification, and each account's potential sales are estimated.

Multiple Selling Strategies. Figure 14–3 illustrates how multiple selling strategies may be used on the various accounts. Salespeople are aware of the importance of large accounts; in fact, meeting sales objectives often depends on how well products are sold to these customers. As a result, companies often develop their sales force organizational structure to service these accounts incorporating such elements as a key account salesperson to deal with them.

As illustrated in Figure 14–3, selling strategies may vary depending on the account. The bulk of sales force resources (such as personnel, time, samples, and entertainment expenses) should be invested in the

Figure 14–3 **Account Segmentation Approach**

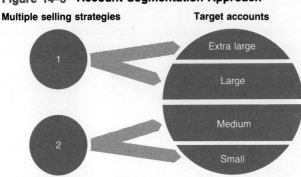

key accounts, and the needs of these large accounts should receive top priority.

Company positioning relative to competition should receive careful consideration. Competitors will also be directing a major selling effort toward these accounts. Thus, salespeople should strive to create the image that their company, its products, and they themselves are uniquely better than what the competition is offering. One way to accomplish this is to spend more time on each sales call and to make more total sales calls during the year, thus providing a problem-solving approach to servicing the accounts.

Selling larger accounts is different than selling medium and small accounts. However, these smaller accounts may generate 20 percent, and sometimes more, of a company's sales and thus should not be ignored.

Multivariable Account Segmentation. Multivariable account segmentation means using more than one criterion to characterize the organization's accounts. This is done because many sales organizations sell to several markets and use many channel members in these markets. Furthermore, different products, product sizes, or product lines may be emphasized to different channel members in the various markets.

Figure 14–4 illustrates how firms might use several variables to segment their accounts. This allows sales personnel to develop plans

Figure 14–4   Multivariable Account Segmentation

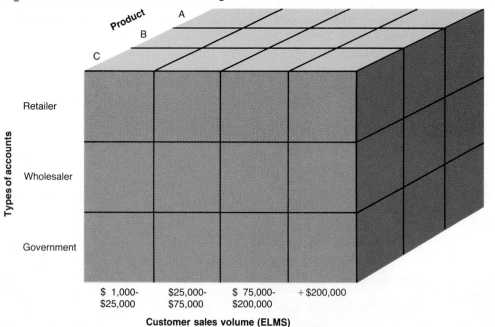

for selling their various products to specific segments of their accounts. For example, different selling strategies might be developed for the extra large and large accounts. There might be different sales plans developed for the retailer, wholesaler, and government accounts. These three types of accounts might be further segmented. Retailers, for instance, could be segmented into mass merchandisers and specialty stores. Furthermore, different products might be emphasized in each account segment. The type of market, environment, account sales potential, and sales volume are major variables for segmenting accounts.

Develop Account Objectives and Sales Quotas

The third element of time and territory management is the development of objectives and sales quotas for individual products for present and potential accounts. Objectives might include increasing product distribution to prospects in the territory or increasing the product assortment purchased by current customers.

Increasing the number of sales calls each day and the number of new accounts obtained for the year are other examples of objectives that can be developed by the salesperson to help meet sales quotas.

Territory-Time Allocation

The fourth element of time and territory management is how salespeople's time is allocated within their territories. Time refers to the time spent by the salesperson in travel around the territory and in actually calling on accounts. There are seven basic factors to consider in time allocation:

1. Number of accounts in the territory;
2. Number of sales calls to be made on customers;
3. Time required for each sales call;
4. Frequency of sales calls on a customer;
5. Travel time around territory;
6. Nonselling time;
7. Return on time invested.

Analysis of accounts in the territory has resulted in the determination of the total number of accounts in the territory and their classification in terms of actual or potential sales. Now, the number of yearly sales calls required, the time required for each sales call, and the intervals between calls should be determined. Usually the frequency of calls will increase as there are increases in (1) sales and/or potential future sales, (2) number of orders placed in a year, (3) number of product lines sold, and (4) complexity, servicing, and redesign requirements of the products.

Since the amount of time spent servicing an account may vary from minutes to hours to days, salespeople should be flexible in developing call frequencies. However, they can establish a minimum number of times each year they want to call on the various classes of accounts. For example, the salesperson determines the frequency of calls for each class of account in the territory, as shown in Table 14–3, where all but the small accounts are contacted once a month.

Typically, the salesperson invests sales time in direct proportion to the actual or potential sales that the account represents. The most productive number of calls is reached at the point where additional calls do not increase sales. This relationship of sales volume to sales calls is the **sales response function** of the customer to the salesperson's calls.

Table 14–3 Account Time Allocation by Salesperson

Customer Size	Calls per Month	Calls per Year	No. of Accounts	=	No. Calls per Year
Extra large	1	12	2		24
Large	1	12	28		336
Medium	1	12	56		672
Small	1 every 3 months	4	78		312
Total			164		1344

Return on Time Invested.   Time is a scarce resource. To be successful, the salesperson should use time effectively to improve territory productivity. In terms of time, costs must also be taken into account, that is, what is the cost both in time and money of an average sales call?

Break-even analysis can be used to determine how much sales volume a salesperson must generate to meet costs in a territory. The difference between cost of goods sold and sales is the gross profit on sales revenue. Gross profit should be large enough to cover selling expenses. A territory's break-even point can be computed in terms of dollars by using the following formula:

$$\text{Break-even point (in dollars)} = \frac{\text{Salesperson's fixed costs}}{\text{Percentage of gross profit}}$$

To illustrate the formula, let us use the values shown here for sales and costs, with gross profit being the difference between sales revenue of a salesperson and costs of goods sold in the territory, expressed as a ratio of gross profit to gross sales in percentage form.

Sales	$200,000
Cost of goods sold	− 140,000
Gross profit	$ 60,000
Gross profit (percentage)	(60,000 ÷ 200,000), or 30 percent

Assume the salesperson's direct costs are as follows:

Salary	$ 20,000
Transportation	4,000
Expenses	5,000
Direct costs	$ 29,000

and substitute in the formula:

$$\text{BEP} = \frac{\$29,000}{.30} = \$96,667$$

If the salesperson sells $96,667 worth of merchandise, it will exactly cover the territory's direct costs. A sales volume of $96,667 means that the salesperson is producing a gross margin of 30 percent, or $29,000. Sales over $96,667 contribute to profit.

Assume that the salesperson works 46 out of 52 weeks (considering time off for vacations, holidays, and illness) or 230 days each year; also assume a five-day week, an eight-hour day in which six calls are made. There are thus 1,840 working hours per year and 1,380 sales calls (230 × 6 calls) made each year in the territory. To determine a salesperson's cost per hour, divide direct costs ($29,000) by yearly hours worked (1,840 hours). The cost per hour equals $15.76. The break-even volume per hour is determined as follows:

$$\begin{matrix} \text{Break-even} \\ \text{volume} \\ \text{per hour} \end{matrix} = \frac{\text{Cost per hour}}{\text{Gross profit percentage}} = \frac{\$15.76}{.30} = \$52.53$$

Thus, the salesperson must sell an average of $52.53 an hour in goods or services to break even in the territory. Carrying this logic a little further, the salesperson must sell an average of $420.24 each day or $70.04 each sales call to break even.

This simple arithmetic shows that a sales territory is a cost- and revenue-generating profit center, and because it is, priorities should be established on account calls in order to maximize territory profits.

The Management of Time. "Time is money" is a popular saying that has direct application to our discussion because of the costs and revenue generated by the individual salesperson. This is particularly evident in the case of the commission salesperson. The salesperson is a territory manager who has the responsibility of managing time wisely in order to maximize territorial profits. Thus, the effective salesperson consistently uses time well. How does the effective salesperson manage time?

Plan by the Day, Week, and Month. Many salespeople develop daily, weekly, and monthly call plans, or general guidelines of customers and geographical areas to be covered. The salesperson may use them to make appointments with customers in advance, to arrange hotel accommodations, etc. Weekly plans are more specific, and include the specific days that customers will be called on. Daily planning starts the night before as the salesperson selects the next day's prospects, determines the time to contact the customer, organizes facts and data, and prepares sales presentation materials. Figure 14–5 is an illustration of a daily plan, and Figure 14–6 shows the location of each account and the sequence of calls.

Qualify the Prospect. The salesperson should be sure that the prospect being called on is qualified to make the purchase decision, and determine whether sales to this account will be large enough to allow for an adequate return on time invested. If not, the prospect should not be called on.

Use Waiting Time. Have you seen salespeople waiting to see buyers? Have you ever noticed their actions? Top salespeople do not read magazines. They work while waiting, studying material about their products, completing call reports, or organizing material for the sales presentation. Also, they quickly determine whether the buyers they are waiting for will be free in a reasonable time. If not, they contact other customers.

Have a Productive Lunchtime. Salespeople often take prospects to lunch. However, the results of one study show that the business lunch does not lead directly to a sale, but to the buyer and seller getting to know one another better, building confidence and trust. In turn, this may lead to sales in the long run.[4]

During a business lunch, salespeople should keep an eye on the clock and not monopolize too much of their buyers' time. They should not have a lunchtime cocktail. While it may seem customary to have a drink at lunch, the salesperson may be less alert in the afternoon as a result. In fact, in some companies a luncheon cocktail is against company policy. A salesperson's lunch alone can be a time to review activities and further

Figure 14–5 Daily Customer Plans

| Hours | Sales Calls | | Service |
	Customers	Prospects	Customers
7:00– 8:00	Go by office pick up order for Jones Hardware		
8:00– 9:00	Travel		
9:00–10:00	Zip Grocery		
10:00–11:00	Ling Television Corp.		
11:00–12:00	Ling Television Corp.		
12:00– 1:00	Lunch and delivery to Jones Hardware		
1:00– 2:00	Texas Instruments		
2:00– 3:00		Ace Equipment	
3:00– 4:00	Travel		
4:00– 5:00			Trailor Mfg.
5:00– 6:00	Plan next day—do paper work		

Figure 14–6 **Example of Daily Customer Plans**

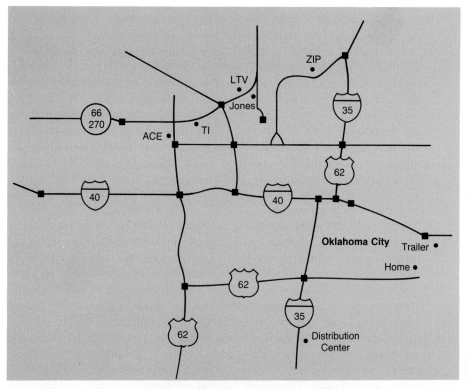

plan for the afternoon. It is a time to relax and start "psyching up" for a productive selling afternoon.

Records and Reports. Records and reports are a written history of sales and of the salesperson's activities. Effective salespeople do their paper work during nonselling times; evenings are best. Many companies take these records and reports into account in the performance evaluation of salespeople. However, paper work should be held to a minimum by the company and kept current by the salesperson.

Customer Sales Planning

The fifth major element of time and territorial managment is developing a sales call objective, a customer profile, and a customer benefit program, including selling strategies for individual customers.* You have a quota to meet, have made your account analysis, have set account objectives, have established the amount of time you will devote to each customer; now you must develop a sales plan for each customer.

---

* Refer to Chapter 6 for further discussion of customer sales planning.

Scheduling and Routing

The sixth element of time and territory management is scheduling sales calls and planning movement around the sales territory.

Scheduling refers to establishing a fixed time (day and hour) for visiting a customer's place of business. **Routing** is the travel pattern used in working a territory. Some sales organizations prefer to determine the formal path or route that their salespeople are to travel when covering their territory. In such cases, management should develop plans that are feasible, flexible, profitable to the company and the individual salesperson, and satisfactory to the customer. In theory, strict formal route designs enable the company to: (1) improve territory coverage; (2) minimize wasted time; and (3) establish communications between management and the sales force in terms of the location and activities of individual salespeople.

In developing route patterns, the management needs to know the salesperson's exact day and time of sales calls for each account, approximate waiting time, sales time, miscellaneous time for contacting people such as the promotional manager, checking inventory, or handling returned merchandise, and travel time between accounts. This task becomes difficult unless territories are small and precisely defined. Most firms allow considerable latitude in routing.

Typically, after finishing a work week, the salesperson fills out a routing report and sends it to the manager. The report states where the salesperson will be working in the future (see Table 14–4). In the example, on Friday, December 16, you are based in Dallas and planning during the week of December 25, to call on accounts in Dallas for two days. Then you plan to work in Waco for a day, spend the night, drive to Fort Worth early the next morning and make calls, and be back home Thursday night. The last day of the week, you again plan to work in Dallas. The weekly route report is sent to your immediate supervisor. In this manner, managment knows where you are and, if necessary, can contact you.

Some firms may ask the salesperson to specify the accounts to be called on and at what times. For example, on Monday, December 26, the salesperson may write, "Dallas, 9 A.M., Texas Instruments; Grand

Table 14–4 Weekly Route Report

Today's Date: December 16		For Week Beginning: December 26
Date	*City*	*Location*
December 26 (Monday)	Dallas	Home
December 27 (Tuesday)	Dallas	Home
December 28 (Wednesday)	Waco	Holiday Inn/South
December 29 (Thursday)	Forth Worth	Home
December 30 (Friday)	Dallas	Home

Prairie, 2 P.M., L.T.V." Thus, management knows where a salesperson will be and which accounts will be visited during a report period. If no overnight travel is necessary to cover a territory, the company may not require any route reports because the salesperson can be contacted at home in the evening.

Territory and Customer Evaluation

Territorial control is the establishment of standards of performance for the individual territory in the form of qualitative and quantitative quotas or goals. Actual performance is compared to these goals for evaluation purposes. This allows the salesperson to see how well territory plans were carried out in meeting performance quotas. If quotas were not met, then new plans must be developed for the territory.

Many companies routinely furnish managers and individual salespeople with reports on the number of times during the year their salespeople have called on each account and the date of the last sales call. Management can monitor the frequency and time intervals between calls for each of their salespeople.

As an example, a national pharmaceutical company supplies its sales force with the "net sales by customer and call report" shown in Table 14–5. The report lists each customer's name, address, and medical specialty. The desired number of monthly calls on a given customer and the actual number of calls to date are noted. Net sales are broken down into last year's sales, the current month's sales, and year-to-date sales. Finally, the date the salesperson last called on each customer is reported.

Using the report, one can see that H. L. Brown is a Houston physician in a general practice. He should be called upon twice a month, and for the four months that have gone by he has been seen eight times to date. He purchased sixty dollars worth of merchandise this month, and his purchases this year are fifty dollars more than they were last year. He was last called on April 20th of the current year. Using this type of information, which might include 200 to 300 customers for each salesperson, management and salespeople can continually review sales call patterns and customer sales to update call frequency and scheduling.

Summary of Major Selling Issues

The way salespeople invest their available sales time may be a critical factor influencing their territory sales. Due to the increasing cost of direct selling, high transportation costs, and the limited resources of time, salespeople have to focus their attention on these factors. Proper management of time and territory is an effective method for the salesperson to maximize territorial sales and profits.

Table 14–5 Net Sales by Customer and Call Frequency: May 1, 1983

| Name | Address | Speciality | Calls | | Net Sales in Dollars | | | | |
| | | | Month | Year-to-Date | Current Month | Year-to-Date | | Entire Last Year | Last Call |
						This Year	Last Year		
H. L. Brown	Houston	GP	2	8	60	350	300	2,000	4–20
Sam Peterson	Galveston	Pediatrics	1	4	0	200	275	1,000	4–18
Susan Gilley	Galveston	GP	1	4	21	75	125	300	4–18
John Bruce	Galveston	GP	0	4	0	1000	750	1,000	3–10
L. J. Heaton	Texas City	GP	2	9	500	2000	1750	5,000	4–19

A sales territory comprises a group of customers or a geographical area assigned to a salesperson. It can be considered a segment out of the company's total market. A salesperson within a territory has to analyze the various segments, estimate sales potential, and develop a marketing mix based on the needs and desires of the marketplace.

Companies develop and use sales territories for a number of reasons. One important reason is to obtain thorough coverage of the market so they can more nearly reach their sales potential. Another reason is to establish a salespeople's responsibilities as they act as territory managers.

Performance can be monitored when territories are established. A territory may also be used to improve customer relations so that customers receive regular calls from their salesperson. This also helps to reduce sales expense as duplication of effort in traveling and customer contacts is avoided. Finally, they allow better matching of salesperson to customer needs and thus they benefit salespeople as well as their company.

There are also disadvantages to developing sales territories. Some salespeople may not be motivated if they feel restricted by a particular territory. Also, a company may be too small to segment its market or management may not want to take time to develop territories.

Time and territory management is a continuous process for a salesperson involving seven key elements. The first major element is the establishment of the territory sales quota. The second element is account analysis which involves identifying present and potential customers and estimating their sales potential. In analyzing these accounts, salespeople may use the undifferentiated selling approach if they view their accounts as basically the same or if the accounts have different characteristics they will use the account segmentation approach.

Developing objectives and sales quotas for individual accounts is the third element. How salespeople's time is allocated in their territories is another key element. Salespeople have to manage their time, plan their schedules, and use all spare time effectively.

The fifth element of time and territorial management is developing a sales call objective, profile, benefit program and selling strategies for individual customers. Salespeople have to find out as much as they can about their customers and maintain records on each one. Once this is done, they can create the proper selling strategies to meet their customers' needs.

Another major element is scheduling the sales calls at specific times and places and routing of salesperson's movement and travel pattern around the territory. Finally, objectives and quotas that were established are used to determine how effectively the salesperson is performing. Actual performance is compared to these standards for evaluation purposes.

Review and Discussion Questions

1. What is a sales territory? Why do firms establish sales territories? Why might sales territories not be developed?
2. Briefly discuss each of the elements of time and territory management and indicate how these seven elements relate to one another.
3. What is the difference between the universal selling approach and the account segmentation approach for analyzing accounts? When might each approach be used?
4. Assume that a sales manager determines that in a given territory each salesperson sells approximately $500,000 yearly. Also, assume that the firm's costs of goods sold are estimated to be 65 percent of sales and that a salesperson's direct costs are $35,000 a year. Each salesperson works 48 weeks a year, eight hours a day, and averages five sales calls per day. Using this information, how much merchandise must each salesperson sell to break even
   A. For the year?
   B. Each day?
   C. Each sales call?
5. What is a key account?
6. What are the factors a salesperson should consider when allocating time?
7. How does an effective salesperson use time?
8. What is the purpose of customer sales planning?
9. Define scheduling. Routing.

Projects

1. Visit a large retailer in your community and ask a buyer or store manager what salespeople do when they make a sales call. Determine the number of times the retailer wants salespeople to visit each month. Are calls from some salespeople preferable to others? If so, why?
2. Contact a salesperson or sales manager and report on each one's philosophy toward managing time and territory. Ask each to calculate how much it costs to contact one prospect and on the average what amount must be sold each day just to break even.

Cases

14–1 Your Selling Day: A Time and Territory Game

Your sales manager is working with you tomorrow only, and you want to call on your customers with the greatest sales potential. See Exhibit 14–1. Because you are on a straight commission, you will also have the opportunity to maximize your income for that day. The area of your territory that you feel should be covered tomorrow contains sixteen customers (see Exhibit 14–2). To determine travel time, allow fifteen minutes for each side of the square. Each sales call takes thirty minutes. You can leave your house at 8:00 A.M. or later. If you take time for lunch, it must be in fifteen minute blocks of time (e.g., fifteen, thirty, forty-five, or sixty minutes). Your last customer cannot be contacted after 4:30 P.M. in order to allow enough sales time. Your customers do not see salespeople after 5:00 P.M. Travel home can be done after 5:00 P.M.

Exhibit 14–1   Customers' Sales Potential

Customer	Sales Potential	Customer	Sales Potential
1	$4,000	9	1,000
2	3,000	10	1,000
3	6,000	11	10,000
4	2,000	12	12,000
5	2,000	13	8,000
6	8,000	14	9,000
7	4,000	15	8,000
8	6,000	16	10,000

Exhibit 14–2   Partial Map of Your Sales Territory

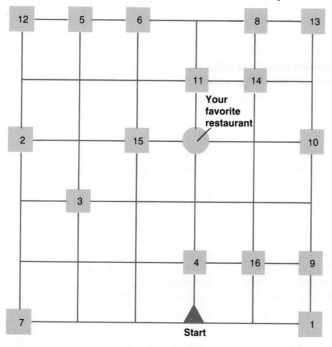

Questions:

1. Develop the route that gives the highest sales potential for the day your boss works with you.
2. For the next day develop the route allowing you to contact the remaining customers in this part of your territory.

14–2 Representative Rubber Company: A Sales Management Learning Exercise

Learning Objectives

1. To gain experience in time management.
2. To learn how to plan a route which meets the requirements of servicing current accounts, developing prospective accounts, and minimizing travel time.

Advance Preparation. Read the Overview, the Representative Rubber Company case, and the Procedure.

Overview. An important ability of successful sales representatives is to know how to efficiently use their time, plan their routes, service accounts, and develop prospective accounts. Conflict often arises between the sales representative and the sales manager in developing time schedules and route plans. This exercise demonstrates how such plans should be developed, and why it is necessary to coordinate such efforts between the sales manager and the sales representative.

The Representative Rubber Case

Company Background. Representative Rubber Company is one of several rubber producing firms in the United States. It produces a full line of tires and tubes along with other rubber products such as hot water bottles, tennis sneakers, industrial rubber products, etc. The firm is divisionalized, and the tire division sells tires and tubes to several thousand independent franchised dealers, as well as through company-owned retail tire stores. The tire division has sales of approximately $300,000,000 in tires, tubes, and repair materials.

Approximately 300 sales representatives are employed to cover the 48 continental states. Hawaii, Alaska, Canada, and Mexico are handled by the firm's international division. Several years before, the firm divided the sales territories of its 300 sales representatives according to the sales volume then coming from each area. That is, sales representatives were assigned to enough counties to give each of them about $1,000,000 in sales.

The Rubber Manufacturers' Association, a trade association to which nearly all tire manufacturers belong, collects annually the tire sales data of each of its members for each county in the United States. These county data are needed for each contributor and distributed to each member. Each member, then, knows his sales and the total industry sales in each county.

Sales Representative's Effective Working Time. Sales representatives are expected to work five days a week. Any sales meetings are held on Saturday mornings, and *need not* be worked into the travel schedule.

Approximately 45 hours, including travel time, are available to a sales representative each week. Occasionally, a sales representative is expected to work more than the average nine hours a day, but is not expected to work more than 45 hours in a week.

All sales representatives live within the confines of their territorial assignment, and are allowed to return home each night.

Prospecting Time. The company has decided that to ensure future business, a minimum of a sales representative's time must be spent on prospecting for new dealers. This involves making calls on competitive accounts, bankers, and others who might either be prospective representative dealers or who would know of such prospects.

Dealer Calls. Current dealers must be called upon at the rate of *two hours per month per $50,000 of annual current business*. This time is spent counting inventory, taking orders, training retail salespeople, helping prepare advertisements, inspecting returned tires, etc.

Data about your territory are given in Exhibits 14–3 through 14–6. In Exhibit 14–3 you will find broad county data on auto registrations, total tire sales in dollars last year, and our firm's sales in each county. Exhibit 14–4 breaks the county sales down into major city and township components and shows the total number of tire dealers in each city. Exhibit 14–5 is a roster of our active accounts and their sales for last

Exhibit 14–3 Selected Territory Data for Representative Rubber Company

County Name	County Auto Registrations	Representative's Current Sales	Total County Tire Sales Last Year
Washington	12,000	$100,000	$ 900,000
Jefferson	11,000	450,000	750,000
Fillmore	10,000	250,000	1,200,000
Arthur	4,000	200,000	260,000

Exhibit 14–4 Estimated Sales by City Last Year, and Dealer Census

County and City	Estimated City Sales	Estimated Number of Dealers	Our Dealers
Washington			
Adamsville	450,000	5	0
Krepston	450,000	4	1
Jefferson			
Jefferson City	450,000	6	4
Wilson	150,000	3	1
Newton	75,000	2	
Ayerville	38,000	3	1
Eaton	37,000	2	1
Fillmore			
Athens	960,000	18	4
Sparta	130,000	4	2
Rhodes	110,000	2	1
Arthur			
Lincoln	260,000	2	1

Exhibit 14–5 Record of Dealer Sales for Last Year in This Territory

Dealer Roster	Estimated Sales
Adamsville	
Krepston	
Pioneer Tire Sales	$100,000
Jefferson City	
Jefferson City Tire	150,000
Main Street Tire & Appliance	100,000
Acme Supply	50,000
Jones and Laughter, Inc.	50,000
Wilson	
American Automotive	60,000
Ayerville	
Ace Recap Company	20,000
Eaton	
Little Accessory Corporation	20,000
Athens	
Athens Supply	50,000
Holsten and Holsten	40,000
Dearborn Tire Company	25,000
North American Auto Supply	15,000
Sparta	
Greek Gifts & Automotive	60,000
Goodbody Tires	15,000
Rhodes	
Rhodes Tire & Appliance	40,000
Lincoln	
J. W. Booth & Sons	200,000

Exhibit 14–6 Map and Mileage Chart for This Territory

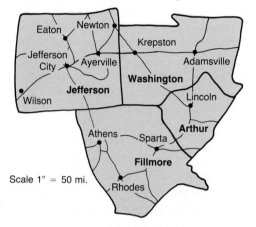

Scale 1″ = 50 mi.

	Adamsville	Athens	Ayerville	Eaton	Jefferson City	Krepston	Lincoln	Newton	Rhodes	Sparta	Wilson
Adamsville	X	215	90	145	115	50	80	90	225	150	170
Athens		X	115	120	90	155	135	155	50	60	145
Ayerville			X	55	25	40	130	40	165	180	80
Eaton				X	30	95	185	90	170	185	85
Jefferson City					X	65	155	65	140	155	55
Krepston						X	90	40	245	160	120
Lincoln							X	130	155	70	210
Newton								X	205	200	120
Rhodes									X	85	195
Sparta										X	195
Wilson											X

year. Finally, Exhibit 14–6 is a map of the territory and a mileage chart for the towns.

Procedure

■ *Step 1.*   Before class, read the Representative Rubber Company case and answer the questions on the page entitled "Criteria for Time and Route Management for Sales Representatives."

■ *Step 2.*   Also, before class, complete the "Routing Form (prepared by Sales Representative)." Be sure to comply with the rules prescribed by the company and to develop the routing schedule over a four-week period. An example of how to fill in the form is shown below the routing schedule.

■ *Step 3.* In class, the administrator will divide the class into groups of three students per group by asking class members to count off by three. Each number 1 is the territorial salesmanager, each number 2 is the sales analyst, and each number 3 is the sales representative in the territory. (5 minutes)

■ *Step 4.* Each group (comprised of a sales manager, a sales analyst, and a sales representative) will meet to develop a four-week routing schedule for the sales representative which meets the rules prescribed by the firm. (20–40 minutes)

■ *Step 5.* Fill in the "Routing Form (prepared by Sales Manager)." All three participants will help in developing the routing schedule; however, the sales manager is in charge and will have final authority in filling out the routing form. (5 minutes)

■ *Step 6.* Complete the form "The Objectives and Criteria, Model, or Framework Used in Sales Representative Routing Procedure."

■ *Step 7.* General class discussion and instructor comments: a) What differences exist among groups in the decisions they reached? Why? b) Were differences between sales representatives' goals and company goals resolved? If so, how? c) From the company's point of view, what is an optimal routing solution for sales representatives? Why?

Criteria for Time and Route Management for Sales Representatives

1. Assume you are a sales representative for Representative Rubber Company. Choose a home town for yourself which takes into consideration where you would like to live and which would be centrally located insofar as covering the territory. Why did you select the town you did? (Note: you should plan to stay overnight sometime during most weeks, but certainly not every night.)

   I would choose to live in _____

   The reason(s) for my choice is(are): _____

   _____

   _____

2. What *criteria* would you use in devising a scheme for dividing your prospecting time among the counties in your territory?

   Criteria:

   A. _____

   B. _____

C. _____

D. _____

E. _____

F. _____

G. _____

H. _____

Which, in your opinion, are the *three most important criteria?*
Why these?

A. _____ B. _____ C. _____

These criteria are the most important because: _____

_____

_____

_____

_____

_____

The Objectives and Criteria, Model, or Framework Used in Sales Representative Routing Procedure

1. The objectives we are trying to achieve for our sales representative routing schedules are:

   (1) _____

   (2) _____

   (3) _____

   (4) _____

2. The criteria, model, framework, and/or approach we are using for achieving these objectives are:

   _____

   _____

   _____

   _____

   _____

3. a. The sales representative is: (circle one)

   (1) very satisfied with the scheduling

   (2) somewhat satisfied with the scheduling

   (3) somewhat dissatisfied with the scheduling

   (4) very dissatisfied with the scheduling

(continued)

b. The reason for his or her satisfaction (or dissatisfaction) is:

_____

_____

_____

4. Describe the interaction which took place in your group in developing your routing decision.

_____

_____

_____

_____

Routing Form   **(prepared by sales representative)**

Week	Monday		Tuesday		Wednesday		Thursday		Friday	
1	Start	Hours	Start	Hours	Start	Hours	Start	Hours	Start	Hours
	End	_____	End	_____	End	_____	End	_____	End	_____
2	Start	Hours	Start	Hours	Start	Hours	Start	Hours	Start	Hours
	End	_____	End	_____	End	_____	End	_____	End	_____
3	Start	Hours	Start	Hours	Start	Hours	Start	Hours	Start	Hours
	End	_____	End	_____	End	_____	End	_____	End	_____
4	Start	Hours	Start	Hours	Start	Hours	Start	Hours	Start	Hours
	End	_____	End	_____	End	_____	End	_____	End	_____

Example:

Monday

	Hours
Start—Jefferson City	
Jefferson City Tire	4
Prospecting	4
Travel	0
End—Jefferson City	8

Routing Form   **(prepared by sales manager)**

Week	Monday		Tuesday		Wednesday		Thursday		Friday	
1	Start	Hours	Start	Hours	Start	Hours	Start	Hours	Start	Hours
	End	———	End	———	End	———	End	———	End	———
2	Start	Hours	Start	Hours	Start	Hours	Start	Hours	Start	Hours
	End	———	End	———	End	———	End	———	End	———
3	Start	Hours	Start	Hours	Start	Hours	Start	Hours	Start	Hours
	End	———	End	———	End	———	End	———	End	———
4	Start	Hours	Start	Hours	Start	Hours	Start	Hours	Start	Hours
	End	———	End	———	End	———	End	———	End	———

Example:

Monday

	Hours
Start—Jefferson City	
Jefferson City Tire	4
Prospecting	4
Travel	0
End—Jefferson City	8

15

Social, Ethical, and Legal Issues in Selling

Learning Objectives

1. To present the concept of social responsibility and reasons why business assumes responsibilities to society.
2. To discuss how managers view the business ethics of industry.
3. To review ethical dealings with salespeople, employers, and customers.
4. To present 10 ways a sales force can act in an ethical manner.

Key Terms for Selling

Social responsibility	Tie-in sale
Ethics	Clayton Act
House account	Exclusive dealership
Robinson-Patman Act	Cooling-off law
Price discrimination	Green River ordinance

Profile

Sandra Snow
Upjohn

After completing my nursing education at Jameson Memorial Hospital in New Castle, Pennsylvania and the University of Pittsburgh, I was a clinical instructor in pediatric nursing at Pittsburgh Children's Hospital and later a head nurse of the pediatrics department of a Florida hospital. Although happy with nursing, I decided to pursue a career in sales because of more opportunities, advancement, and challenge.

Initially my job was calling on the physicians, hospitals, and drug stores in a general sales territory. After 3½ years I was promoted to my present job as a hospital sales specialist responsible for three large hospitals and the University of Miami School of Medicine in Miami, Florida.

As a salesperson, I have responsibility to provide the physician, pharmacist, and nurse with current information about our products. It is imperative that I am knowledgeable not only about our products but also about the disease entities that our drugs treat. I have an obligation to provide this information in an honest and ethical way. Since we may alter the prescribing habits of physicians, it is important that they know not only the benefits of our products, but also the risks. Human health care is not an area where deceptive selling techniques can be used in any way.

I also have an obligation to the company to conduct myself in a professional manner while increasing sales. There is significant government regulation of the pharmaceutical industry and unethical practices by a salesperson reflect not only on that salesperson, but on the company for which he or she works and the industry as a whole.

Having been in sales for six years, I cannot imagine any job offering the same rewards. No two days are the same; the word "boredom" has been eliminated from my vocabulary. I face the challenge of improving selling skills and gaining insights into the concerns, needs and personalities of my customers. And, the job provides constant intellectual stimulation because medicine is advancing and changing so rapidly. Fortunately, I am working for a company that is research-oriented and prides itself on having a knowledgeable sales force. We are constantly learning new things about old drugs, as well as preparing for the introduction of new products.

"Even though it is my job to inform, I feel that we are more effective salespeople if we establish a dialogue with the physician and find out from him his feelings and experiences with our products, rather than being didactic," said Sandra Snow of the Upjohn Company. "It is also important to disseminate this information to pharmacists and nursing personnel via a one-on-one discussion or a continuing education program for a small group. The pharmacist and nurse may not prescribe therapy, but they may pick up both drug toxicity and/or failure."

As you see from Sandra Snow's comments above and from her profile, she is convinced of the need to be honest, ethical, and to act as a professional salesperson. This chapter addresses many of the important social, ethical, and legal issues in selling. We begin by defining the term *social responsibility* and discuss six reasons why firms want their sales personnel to act in a responsible manner. Then we examine ethical issues involved in dealing with salespeople, employers, and customers. We end the chapter by presenting 10 ways a company can help its sales personnel follow ethical selling practices.

The Social Responsibility of Business

Social responsibility in business refers to profitably serving employees and customers in an ethical and lawful manner. This definition involves the individual salesperson, implying that the salesperson is an important resource of the firm and must be treated responsibly, just as it states that a salesperson must treat customers in an ethical manner.

Quite often, corporations are said to operate solely to maximize profits. Certainly profits are important to a firm, just as a grade point average is important to a student. Profit provides the capital to stay in business, to expand, and to compensate for the risks of conducting business. There is a responsibility to make a profit in order to serve society. Imagine what would happen to our society if large corporations, e.g., AT&T, General Motors, did not make a profit and went out of business. Thousands of people and the U.S. Economy would be affected.

Sales managers and salespeople are occasionally accused of obtaining sales in any manner possible. The temptations to make sales at any cost have been curbed both by laws designed to penalize wrongdoers and by the new professionalism of individuals selecting sales as a career. Let's briefly examine why business today should continue to act in a responsible manner and then review how managers view ethics.

Why Assume Social Responsibilities?

There are numerous reasons why a business should assume social responsibilities; six of the major reasons are:

1. It is expected by society.
2. It allows the business to operate better in the long run.
3. It shows community responsibility.
4. Salespeople are company representatives.
5. It minimizes competitors' retaliation.
6. It decreases government intervention.

Social Expectation. Sales managers must understand that they are in business to serve customers profitably but also responsibly. Sales practices must not conflict with the interests of society. As the company grows, it increases its power in the industry and is expected to assume greater social responsibilities. This is the power-responsibility equation.

Better Operations in the Long Run. If the sales force works totally for short-run goals, irresponsible selling practices often result. At the corporate level, executives view the firm as existing to make a profit in the long run, but sales personnel have trouble with this because they typically work in the short run. They have monthly, quarterly, and yearly sales goals that may create pressures to make the sale at any cost. Sales executives must continually monitor their sales units to minimize the temptations to use unethical and illegal sales practices. Pressure on sales personnel must be kept at a reasonable level that allows them to use responsible selling techniques. Extremely high pressure to increase sales can pressure a salesperson to make the sale no matter how. This is especially true if managers openly suggest or overlook unethical sales practices. Sales may increase in the short run, but in time customers will catch on and sales will decrease.

Community Responsibility. Sales managers and their salespeople often participate in community activities and organizations. This includes working with groups such as the Lion's Club, United Fund, Heart Fund, and Little League. Many salespeople are also active in their industry's trade associations.

Salespeople as Company Representatives. Would you want your salespeople giving kickbacks or cheating customers? Certainly not, because the salespeople reflect the image of the company, and, after a time, customers might expect all of the company's salespeople to act in this manner. Buyers could expect kickbacks before doing business with the company. Both actions are costly to the company, and sales managers cannot take the position of "Hear No Evil, See No Evil, Speak No Evil." They must oversee the sales practices of their personnel so that the pressure of reaching sales quotas does not lead to unethical sales practices.

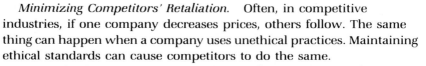

Minimizing Competitors' Retaliation. Often, in competitive industries, if one company decreases prices, others follow. The same thing can happen when a company uses unethical practices. Maintaining ethical standards can cause competitors to do the same.

Decreasing Government Intervention. Sales managers prefer not to have the government intervene in their activities, but over the years the business community has not acted in a totally responsible way. Consequently, government regulation has increased. To make government intervention less necessary, sales managers must develop a code of ethics and help govern their companies' sales practices.

How Managers View Ethics

Ethics are principles of right or good conduct, or a body of such principles, which would affect good and bad business practices. Ethical principles govern the conduct of an individual or group. Over the years a number of surveys have been carried out to determine managers' views of business ethics. In general, they found the following:

■ All managers feel they face ethical problems.
■ Most managers feel they and their employers should be more ethical.
■ Managers are more ethical with their friends than with people they do not know.
■ Even though they want to be more ethical, some managers lower their ethical standards in order to meet job goals.
■ Managers are aware of unethical practices in their industry and company ranging from price discrimination to hiring discrimination.
■ Business ethics can be influenced by an employee's superior and company environment.[1]

The remainder of this chapter discusses some of the possible situations that may arise requiring the sales manager and salespeople to search their consciences. It cannot be all-inclusive, but represents an attempt to give the reader a feel for some of the difficult decisions faced by salespeople.

Ethics in Dealing with Salespeople

Sales managers have both social and ethical responsibilities to their sales personnel. Sales people are a valuable resource; they have been recruited, carefully trained, and given important responsibility. They represent a large financial investment and should be treated in a professional manner. Yet occasionally a company may place their managers and/or salespeople in positions that force them to choose between compromising their personal ethics, or not doing what is required, or leaving the organization. Certainly the choice depends on the magnitude of the situation. At times situations arise in which it is difficult to say whether a sales practice is ethical or unethical. Many sales practices are in the gray area, somewhere between being completely ethical and completely unethical. Four ethical considerations faced by the sales manager are the level of sales pressure to place on a salesperson; decisions concerning a salesperson's territory; whether or not to be honest with the salesperson; and what to do with the salesperson who is ill.

Level of Sales Pressure.   What is an acceptable level of pressure to place on salespeople? Should managers establish performance goals that they know a salesperson has only a 50–50 chance of attaining? Should the manager acknowledge that goals were set too high? If circumstances change in the salesperson's territory—for example, a large customer goes out of business—should the manager lower sales goals?

These are questions all managers must consider. There are no right or wrong answers. Managers are responsible for their groups' goals. There is a natural tendency to place pressure on salespeople so that the managers' goals will be reached. Some managers can motivate their people to produce at high levels without applying pressure, while others place tremendous pressure on their salespeople to attain sales well beyond their quotas. However, managers should set realistic and obtainable goals. They should consider individual territory situations. If this is done fairly, and sales are still down, then pressure may be applied.

Decisions Affecting Territory.   Management makes decisions that affect sales territories, and, in turn, salespeople. For example, the company might increase the number of sales territories, which often necessitates splitting up a single territory. A salesperson has spent years building up the territory to its current sales volume. Customers are taken away. If the salesperson has worked on a commission basis, this would mean a decrease in earnings.

Consider the situation of reducing the number of sales territories. What procedures do you use? Several years ago a large manufacturer of health and beauty aids (shaving cream, toothpaste, shampoo) reduced the number of territories in order to lower selling costs. So, for example, three territories became two. Here is how one of their salespeople described it:

I made my plane reservations to fly from Dallas to Florida to our annual national meeting. Beforehand I was told to bring my records up to date and bring them to the regional office in Dallas. Don't fly, drive to Dallas. I drove from Louisiana to Dallas with my bags packed to go to the national meeting. I walked into the office with my records under my arm. My district and regional managers were there. They told me of the reorganization and said

I was fired. They asked for my car keys. I called my wife, told her what happened and then caught a bus back home. There were five of us in the region that were called in that day. Oh, they gave us a good job recommendation—it's just the way we were treated. Some people had been with the company for five years or more. They didn't go by tenure but where territories were located.

Companies must deal with the individual in a fair and straightforward manner. It would have been better for the managers of these salespeople to go to their home towns and personally explain the changes to them. Instead, they treated the salespeople in an unprofessional manner.

One decision affecting a territory is what to do with extra large customers, sometimes called key accounts. Should they be taken away from the salesperson and made **house accounts?** Here responsibility for contacting the account can be someone from the home office (house) or a key account salesperson. The local salesperson may not get credit for sales to this customer even though located in the salesperson's territory. A salesperson states the problem in this manner?

I've been with the company thirty-five years. When I first began I called on these people who had one grocery store. Today they have 208. The buyer knows me. He buys all of my regular and special greeting cards. They do whatever I ask. I made $12,000 commissions from their sales last year. Now management wants to make it a house account.

Here the salesperson loses money. It is difficult to treat the salesperson fairly in this situation. The company does not want to pay these large commissions and 90 percent of the 208 stores are located out of the salesperson's territory. They should carefully explain this to the salesperson. Instead of taking the full $12,000 away from the salesperson, they could pay a 20 percent commission as a reward for building up the account.

To Tell the Truth?   Should salespeople be told they are not promotable, that they are marginal performers, or that they are being transferred to the poorest territory in the company in hopes that they will be forced to quit? Good judgment must prevail. In general, sales managers prefer to tell the truth.

Do you tell the truth when you fire a salesperson? If a fired employee has tried and has been honest, many sales managers will tell prospective employers that the person quit voluntarily rather than being fired. One manager put it this way: "I feel she can do a good job for another company. I don't want to hurt her future."

The Ill Salesperson.   How much help do you give the alcoholic, drug addicted, or physically or mentally ill salesperson? More and more companies require their salespeople to seek professional help for alcohol or drug abuse. If they honestly try and improve, companies offer support

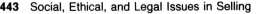

and keep them in the field. Yet there is only so far the company can go. The firm cannot have an intoxicated or "high" salesperson calling on customers. Once the illness begins having a negative effect on business, the salesperson is taken out of the territory. Sick leave and workers' compensation will cover expenses until the salesperson is cured. The manager who shows a sincere, personal interest in helping the ill salesperson can greatly contribute to the person's chances of recovery.

Are These Socially Responsible Actions?

Often it is difficult to determine whether actions are taken by sales executives for profit or social motives.

For example, take the following:

- Training and educational programs for salespeople.
- A company heavily dependent on government contracts hiring minority groups.
- Setting fair sales goals.
- Fairly rewarding salespeople's performance.
- Paying salaries above industry averages.
- Providing extensive medical and life insurance coverage.
- Holding sales meetings in resort areas.

Some people argue that these are responsible acts done unselfishly, while others say that these are good business practices that help maximize a firm's sales and profits. The argument is simply rhetorical. These are examples of good business practices carried out in a responsible manner. No longer can the sales function be carried out in anything other than a manner that is fair to salespeople, customers, and society.

Salespeoples' Ethics in Dealing with Their Employers

Salespeople, as well as sales managers, may occasionally be involved in some of the following:

Misusing Company Assets. The company assets that are most often misused are automobiles, expense accounts, samples, and damaged merchandise credits. All can be used for personal gain or as bribes and kickbacks to customers. For example, a credit for damaged merchandise can be given to a customer when there has been no damage, or valuable product samples can be given to a customer.

Moonlighting.   Salespeople are not closely supervised and, consequently, they may be tempted to take a second job, perhaps on company time. Some salespeople attend college on company time. For example, a salesperson may enroll in an evening MBA program but take off in the early afternoon to prepare for class.

Cheating.   A salesperson may not play fair in contests. If a contest starts in July, the salesperson may not turn in sales orders for the end of June and lump them with July sales. Some might arrange, with or without the customer's permission, to ship merchandise that is not needed or really wanted. The merchandise is held until payment is due and then returned to the company after the contest is over. The salesperson may also overload the customer to win the contest.

Affecting Fellow Salespeople.   Often the unethical practices of one salesperson can affect fellow salespeople. Someone who cheats in winning a contest is taking money and prizes from other salespeople. A salesperson also may not split commissions with fellow employees, or may take customers away from them.

Ethics in Dealing with Customers

Numerous ethical situations may arise in dealing with customers. Some of the more common problems faced include:

Bribes.   A salesperson may attempt to bribe a buyer. Money, gifts, entertainment, and travel opportunities may be offered. At times there is a thin line between good business and the misuse of a bribe or gift. A $10 gift to a $10,000 customer may be merely a gift, but how do we define a $1,000 gift for a $1 million customer? Many companies forbid their buyers to take gifts of any size from salespeople. However, bribery does exist. The U.S. Chamber of Commerce estimates that, of the annual $40 billion "white collar crime," bribes and kickbacks account for $7 billion.[2]

Buyers may ask for cash, merchandise, or travel payment in return for placing an order with the salesperson. Imagine that you are a salesperson working on 5 percent straight commission. The buyer says, "I'm ready to place a $20,000 order for office supplies with you. However, another salesperson has offered to pay my expenses for a weekend in Las Vegas in exchange for my business. You know, $500 tax-free is a lot of money." You quickly calculate that your commission is $1,000. You still make $500. It could be hard to pass up that $500.

Misrepresentation.   In an attempt to make the sale, a salesperson may misrepresent the product, company, company policies, prices, or delivery time. The salesperson may say that the product is of high quality; that it is made by a company that has been in business for one hundred years; that the merchandise can be returned if it is not sold; that the price will not decrease next month; and that there is a two-day delivery time. All or part of these statements could be false. It is hard for the salesperson who routinely calls on customers to get away with such practices, but what about the salesperson who is being transferred, is quitting, or is being fired?

Price Discrimination. Some customers may be given price reductions and promotional allowances and support, while others are not, even though, under certain circumstances, this is in violation of the **Robinson-Patman Act of 1936.** The act does allow sellers to grant what are called quantity discounts to larger buyers based upon savings in the cost of manufacturing, but individual salespeople or managers may practice **price discrimination** to improve sales.

Tie-In Sales. In order to buy a particular line of merchandise, a buyer may be required to buy other products that are not wanted. This is called a **tie-in sale** and is prohibited under the **Clayton Act** when it substantially lessens competition. Yet the individual salesperson or manager can do this. For example, the salesperson of a popular line of cosmetics tells the buyer, "I have a limited supply of the merchandise you want. If all of your twenty-seven stores will display, advertise, and push my total line, I may be able to supply you. That means you'll need to buy ten items you have never purchased before." Is this good business? It's illegal!

Exclusive Dealership. When a contract requires a wholesaler or retailer to purchase products from one manufacturer, it is an **exclusive dealing.** If it tends to lessen competition, it is prohibited under the Clayton Act.

Sales Restrictions. A **Cooling-off** law was passed by the Federal Trade Commission in 1974 allowing customers to back out of a sale involving twenty-five dollars or more within three days. The law covers only sales made door-to-door. It also states that the buyer must receive a written, dated contract and/or receipt of the transaction and be told there is a three-day cancellation period.

Many cities require persons selling directly to consumers to be licensed by the city in which they are doing business if they are not residents, and to pay a license fee. A bond may also be required. These city ordinances are often called **Green River ordinances** because the first legislation of this kind was passed in Green River, Wyoming, in 1933.

Both the cooling-off laws and the Green River Ordinance were passed to protect consumers from salespeople using unethical, high-pressure sales tactics. These statutes, and others, were necessary because a few salespeople used unethical practices in sales transactions.

Conflict of Interest ???

The real estate salesperson assured the young couple that she would work hard to find them the right house. "Consider me your scout," she said. "I'll find you the best house for the least money." The couple was reassured, and on the way home they talked about their good fortune. They had a salesperson working just for them. With prices so high, it was nice to think they had professional help on their side.

The family selling the house felt the same way. They carefully chose the broker because, they observed, with home prices all over the lot these days they hoped a good salesperson might win them several thousand dollars more. They had another reason to choose carefully: At today's prices, the 6 percent sales commission comes to a lot of money. "If we have to pay it," they reasoned, "we're better off paying it to the best salesperson."

It happens all the time, and it can have serious consequences. How can both parties expect the best deal? How can a salesperson promise the seller the most for the money and then make the same promise to the buyer?

In the same vein, how can a salesperson whose commission rises or falls with the price of the house being sold be expected to cut into her own income? Isn't her allegiance totally to the person paying her?

Confusion of this sort has existed in the marketplace for so long that critics are sometimes confounded that regulators haven't made greater efforts to clarify matters.

Two explanations are sometimes offered:

First, it is more a human than a legal problem; even if warned, buyers will continue to assume that salespeople are working solely for them, rather than, as is usual, for the seller who is paying the salesperson a commission.

Second, a good salesperson sometimes can come close to serving the desires of both parties. The point is arguable, but the justification offered is that the salesperson's compromises may be necessary to save a sale from falling through.

A somewhat similar situation exists in the stock market, where many small investors view their stock broker as a confidant and adviser. That relationship can and does exist, of course, but it isn't always so.

What to Do?

Unethical sales practices often originate with management. A manager may not condone them, but has no policy against them. Top management may be strict, but one or more field managers may allow unethical practices. Sales executives must develop social and ethical standards, along with guidelines for their sales personnel to live by. This will help attach a stigma to wrongdoing. With the support of top management, there will be an increased risk of discovery of unethical selling practices because people will not hesitate to divulge instances in which they occur.

Figure 15–1 lists ten ways to keep a sales force on the "straight and narrow." Basically what is shown is the need for firms to create an organizational climate in which unethical sales practices are frowned upon. This is done by top sales executives letting field sales managers

Figure 15–1 10 Ways to Keep Your Sales Force on the Straight and Narrow

1. Get assurance from your board chairman and your president that they expect you to follow both the letter and the spirit of the law.

2. Develop and circulate a sales ethics policy. Seventy-five percent of the companies hit by the SEC in the foreign payoff scandals reported that they had no formal policies on commercial bribery.

3. Set the proper moral climate. John Harris of Booz, Allen & Hamilton suggests that the marketing staffs most likely to commit bribery are in companies in which (1) new ideas are discouraged, (2) "the top person does everything himself," or (3) officers don't attend trade association meetings and feel that "nothing can be learned from the competition." W. Michael Blumenthal, president of Bendix, suggests that because the top manager constantly fields problems "in which the perception of right and wrong is not immediately clear," he must "grasp the nettle of moral judgment—not just once, but every day."

4. Set realistic sales goals. The salesman who is pressured by the need to meet an arbitrary, unfair quota is the one most likely to rationalize his way into a bribery or kickback scheme.

5. Institute controls when needed. For example, don't hesitate to keep close tabs on a salesman whose lifestyle exceeds his known income.

6. Encourage employees to call for help when they face an ethically troublesome sale. "Many of these decisions are close calls," says John C. Taylor III

of Paul, Weiss, Rifkind, Wharton & Garrison, a New York City law firm. "They involve analysis of general corporate policy, complex questions of law and sometimes even of national policy. The employee involved in the negotiations will rarely be sufficiently informed. . . ."

7. Resist a prospectively shady deal. You'll sleep better. Ford Motor exhibitors recently refused to grease a trade union's palm for assembling their booth at a major auto show. A hand-scrawled sign in the vacant space explained why. No one would have noticed the bribe, but people certainly noticed the sign.

8. Meet with your competition if payoffs are an industry problem. Thankfully, no antitrust law ever barred competitors from hammering out a code of ethics.

9. Blow the whistle when you must. Yes, it's the hardest of these suggestions to follow. A *Harvard Business Review* survey reports that four out of seven executives would rather cover up a bribery or price-fixing revelation than suffer the cost and conspicuousness of a prolonged legal battle. So, yes, you'll be bucking convention. You may also risk censure by your peers for "squealing" on the team or damaging the reputation of the company.

10. Keep your perspective. An anonymous author may have had bribery in mind when he said, "Following the path of least resistance is what makes men and rivers crooked."

Source: Reprinted by permission from *Sales & Marketing Management* Magazine. Copyright © 1976.

and their salespeople know that they indulge in such practices at the risk of losing their jobs. Management should set ethical guidelines and follow them. They should police their salespeople, letting it be known that individuals reporting unethical practices are helping their company and, more important, themselves.[3]

Sales managers must help develop and support ethical sales standards. They should publicize these standards and their opposition to unethical sales practices to their subordinate managers and their salespeople. This can be done in sales meetings. Finally, control systems must be established, but an effective control system is difficult to implement. Methods should be established to determine whether salespeople give bribes, falsify reports, or pad expenses. For example, sales made through low bids could be checked to determine whether procedures were correctly followed. Dismissal, demotion, suspension, or reprimand would be possible penalties, e.g., commissions would not be paid on a sale associated with unethical sales practices.

Summary of Major Selling Issues

Social responsibility in business means profitably serving employees and customers in an ethical and lawful manner. Extra costs can accrue because a firm takes socially responsible action, but this is a part of doing business in today's society, and it pays in the long run.

Sales executives must assume socially responsible roles: (1) because this is expected of them by society; (2) in order to operate better in the long run; (3) because of community responsibility; (4) because salespeople are company representatives; (5) to minimize retaliation by competitors; and (6) to decrease government intervention.

Salespeople and managers realize that their business practices should be carried out in an ethical manner. They must be ethical in dealing with their salespeople, their employers, and their customers. Ethical standards and guidelines for sales personnel must be developed, supported, and policed. In the future, ethical selling practices will be even more important to conducting business profitably.

Review and Discussion Questions

1. What is meant by a firm's social responsibility? Why has a sense of social responsibility developed?
2. Why are profits important to a company?
3. Do the following situations represent socially responsible actions by firms:
    A. Creating recreation facilities for sales personnel?
    B. Paying for college courses associated with an MBA program?
    C. Allowing sales personnel to buy company products at a discount?

4. Do managers feel business ethics can be improved? Describe ethical situations sales managers may face in dealing with salespeople.
5. What ethical situations might salespeople have to deal with concerning:
   A. Their employers?
   B. Their customers?
6. How can a company develop policies and procedures to help ensure that their sales force uses ethical sales practices?

Projects

1. Contact your local Better Business Bureau and report on local laws regulating the activities of salespeople.
2. The *Journal of Marketing* has a section entitled "Legal Developments in Marketing." Report on several legal cases found in this section which are related to a firm's personal selling activities.

Cases

15–1   Fancy Frozen Foods*

Last Friday Bill Wilkerson of Fancy Frozen Foods (FFF) was confronted with a situation that now, two days later, he has not resolved successfully. Grady Bryan, a purchasing agent for Smith Supermarket Chains Inc., made it quite apparent to Bill that, if he wanted to retain the company's business in frozen food sales, special action would be necessary. In a telephone conversation, Grady suddenly got onto the subject of his new fishing boat and how much better it would perform with an 80 horsepower, inboard-outboard Evinrude motor. Bill and Grady have been fairly friendly, having done business together for the past four years. However, a conversation of this kind seemed quite out of the ordinary to Bill, especially during a long-distance call for which he was paying. What made Bill quite aware of the direction the conversation was taking was Grady's subtle mention of a competitor, Specialty Frozen Foods, whose territorial sales representative had stopped in to price some outboard motors after lunch with Grady. This alerted Bill to the complicated situation that he was facing. He realized it would take a very tricky strategy to enable his company to retain Smith's exclusive business.

Fancy Frozen Foods

FFF operates in Texas and Louisiana, with Dallas and New Orleans, respectively, being the two largest markets. They carry a complete line

---

* This case was prepared by Bill A. Wilkerson, a salesperson, as a basis for classroom discussion and not to illustrate either effective or ineffective handling of an administrative position. Company names have been changed. Mr. Wilkerson changed jobs two years after he prepared this case.

of frozen foods that they manufacture and wholesale, thereby enabling them to undercut most wholesalers' prices. The company at present employs twenty salespeople. Their territories are divided according to geographic size, thus keeping salespeople's travel time to a minimum. Salespeople are paid a set salary of $12,000 yearly and a commission of 3 percent for everything above a designated quota. Quotas differ by territory. They are set according to the relative potential of each market.

The company has no formal written policy regarding gift giving and entertainment. However, in the past, the president has emphasized that customers may not receive gifts worth more than twenty-five dollars. In addition to this, FFF owns a ranch in West Texas. They invite each of their customers for a three-day vacation, involving hunting and other outdoor activities.

Smith Supermarket Chain

Smith has thirteen supermarkets in Dallas and fifteen outlets in Houston. All of these accounts are currently serviced exclusively by FFF. Grady Bryan, in one of his various duties as warehouse ordering agent in the Dallas area for Smith, is assigned the task of selection of sellers of frozen foods. The thirteen store managers call in their weekly frozen food orders to Grady, who then compiles the orders and calls this one order into Bill Wilkerson of FFF. This type of system is employed to obtain lower prices than would be possible if each individual outlet made its own order. The order is sent to the central warehouse where it is broken down for individual outlets and scheduled for delivery in an efficient fashion.

What to Do?

Bill is confronted with a situation that he obviously had never faced. He has in the past given Grady modest Christmas gifts in line with the president's wishes, and perhaps on occasion has taken Grady to lunch. The company-sponsored hunting trips are another form of entertainment. However, none of these things, at least to Bill, indicated that Bill would be willing to succumb to a suggested bribe of this proportion. The crux of the matter is not that Bill's previous practices have indicated he would be willing to comply with this request, but that Bill's competition has shown a blatant willingness to employ unethical tactics if they will gain Smith's frozen food sales. The question is, should Bill take the chance of losing these thirteen accounts by not offering the bribe, or should he succumb to the bribe and avoid the risk?

Questions:

1. What is the main problem presented in this case?
2. What should Bill do?

15–2 Sports Shirts, Inc.

"I'm glad you came in, Marge. I've been wanting to talk with you." Anne Jackson, sales manager for the southwest region of Sports Togs, Inc., greeted one of her salespeople, Marge Phillips, as she entered the office. The company marketed a line of sports clothing consisting primarily of three styles of running suits.

"What about?" asked Marge.

"You know, since you've been with us, I've always considered you to be one of our top salespeople. You always meet quotas. You always seem to be coming up with new accounts. But I've got a problem that we need to discuss. I got a letter from one of your customers. He claims he couldn't sell the goods you sold him even if he tried all year. And he's also claiming that our running suits aren't worth a dime—that they fall apart soon after the customer buys them. He included some sales data that seemed to point to the fact that he always has a large quantity of our merchandise left at the end of the season. Now, normally, I would just pass this off as a store's sour grapes because of declining sales, but this isn't the first time this has happened. I've received several such letters recently. What do you think the problem might be?"

"I don't see that we really have a problem. I do get complaints about the quality of the merchandise, but that's not my problem. Besides I just concentrate on the profit potential figures for the retailers, and quality seems a secondary consideration in that context. You give me a quota and I meet it. I go in and make my presentation and get the order. I can't help it if they overbuy. What am I supposed to do, refuse to sell them as much as they will take? It's not my fault if they overbuy! I guess I'm just a top-notch salesperson."

The facts certainly indicated that Marge was a good salesperson. Some of her co-workers had said that she could sell snow to the Eskimos. They call her "Load 'em down Marge." In three years with the company, she has already worked her way up to being the top salesperson in the company. Her sales figures are shown in Exhibit 15–1.

The running suits Marge sells are made from one of several combinations of materials and labor that resulted in shirts of different durability. Cost and durability data are summaried in Exhibit 15–2. The company had chosen the second alternative of the three listed.

There had been many complaints about the quality of the running suits that the firm marketed. Seams came apart after only a few washings,

Exhibit 15–1 Sales Data

Year	Quota (000's)	Sales (000's)	New Accounts
1	$400	$450	20
2	440	460	23
3	480	800	30

Exhibit 15–2 Relative Cost of Merchandise

Style Line	Cost		Durability Rating*
	Material	Labor	
A	$1.28	$2.00	5
B	1.45	3.00	10
C	1.95	4.00	20

* The durability rating was basically a measure of the number of washings garments could go through and still look good.

consumers complained. "We sell good running suits, but you can't expect them to last forever," was management's reply.

The manager had other concerns about Marge. However, she was doing such an excellent selling job and was making the company so much money that the manager did not want to have a confrontation. In fact, sales for the entire region had increased 17 percent this year. Much of the increase was due to Marge's influence on the other salespeople. They were applying many of her selling techniques. There were rumors that she was considering buying into a partnership and becoming a manufacturers' agent specializing in high fashion clothing. It would affect sales if Marge left the company. In fact, Jackson was concerned that Marge would hire away the firm's better salespeople.

Jackson remembered when Marge was hired. She had always wanted to sell in the clothing industry, but no one would give her the opportunity. So, upon graduation from college, Marge went to work for a larger department store chain. In two years she moved from managing the women's clothing department in one of the smaller stores to head buyer of women's wear for the entire chain. Marge said she wanted more out of life than a $25,000-a-year job could give. So Jackson hired her on a straight commission of 10 percent on sales up to quota and 15 percent on all sales over quota. This year Marge would earn $98,000 with a sales increase of over 40 percent.

Jackson did not feel Marge had worked less than twelve hours a day since she began. She had always been a "ball of fire." She plowed back much of her earnings into customer goodwill and it appears to have helped her sales. Gifts and entertainment were a large overhead expense item for her. The only expenses the company pays is an amount up to 1 percent of a salesperson's actual sales, and this must go for entertaining. Marge said she spent over $15,000 on her customers. This was in addition to the $4,600 the firm paid.

During the recent year-end performance appraisal session, Jackson was quite surprised when Marge accepted her next year's $1 million sales quota so calmly. Marge said it would be no problem. In fact, she estimated that her sales would increase to between $1.5 and $2 million. When asked why, Marge said a friend of hers was now buyer for the retail chain for which she once worked. The buyer had worked for Marge until she quit to begin working at Sports Togs. Marge recalled discovering that her friend was receiving kickbacks of over $5,000 in cash, merchandise, and vacation trips. Marge said nothing to the chain's management, mainly because she was doing the same thing, which her friend did not know. So Marge was sure she could sell this buyer her entire line of running suits. Further, last year Marge began requiring many of her customers to buy all of the styles and sizes she sold in order to receive the best-selling models.

However, Marge did ask for an additional 1 percent in entertainment expenses. Last summer she had given a party with a live band and professional female and male escorts for buyers. Marge felt this had greatly increased sales and wanted to continue the practice. However, it was quite expensive.

Corporate management had begun to ask about Marge's management capabilities. They felt that if she could train salespeople as well as she sold, she would make a great sales manager.

Questions:

1. How would you describe Marge Phillips' success?
2. Relate Marge's activities to the roles discussed in the chapter.
3. Is she a good salesperson? Do her sales results justify her methods of selling?

You Can't Catch Fish if You Don't Go Fishing

. . . That's what they say. What they don't say is, you can fish every day but you won't catch anything if you fish in your bathtub, or the swimming pool, or a rain puddle.

It's the *quality* of your fishing that really counts. If you're bogged down with unprofitable sales calls, you're wasting your most precious commodity—time!

Are you fishing in the right streams? Ask yourself some of these questions: Where and how can I spend my time most profitably? Do I always have a good reason to call? Am I prepared to say what I must in a reasonably brief time? Do I get right to the point of my call? Do I space my calls out so as to get the maximum order each time? Do I call on certain accounts just because I'm in the neighborhood? Because I like spending time with the buyer? Do I spend a lot of time with unprofitable prospects because I haven't done the proper planning?

Am I realizing the full potential from all, or even most, of my accounts?

Functions of the Sales Manager

16

Planning, Organizing, Staffing of Successful Salespeople

Profile

Martha Hill
Hanes Knitwear

My name is Martha Hill, and I am a regional manager for Hanes Knitwear, a division of Hanes Corporation. After college graduation, I held several sales positions before joining Hanes in 1976; I chose Hanes because of the apparent growth and career potential for me. I began as an entry-level sales person in 1976, and progressed through three promotions to become a regional manager in 1979.

Hanes' underwear business has grown dramatically in recent years, primarily due to changes in sales and marketing strategy. These changes involved a direct sales force with heavy emphasis on retail activities combined with national and local advertising and promotion; the results were dynamic volume and market share gains.

My job as regional sales manager includes responsibility for the hiring, training, and development of seven sales people in addition to analyzing our business and developing sales strategies in order to capitalize on our opportunities. Through many experiences in interviewing and hiring sales people, I value this as one of the most difficult, yet important, aspects of my job. My general philosophy toward selection of candidates is to find the best person for the particular territory, and I systematically screen applicants before, during and after interviews. I use a basic process to find people who are suitable, and I look for characteristics and/or experiences in an applicant's background which will either help to qualify or disqualify the person. I rely heavily on the use of personal interviews because face-to-face selling is exactly what our jobs involve, and the applicant must be able to sell me on hiring him/her in order to be successful at the job.

Orientation of new sales people is another important phase of my job; it is critical to get a new rep started on the right track in order to set the stage for future development. I encourage new reps to ask me their questions, but also to try to learn independently by probing their accounts, consulting their reference materials, and then reporting to me what they have learned. The initiative taken by new reps often indicates their degree of interest and commitment. The application of what they learn is the key to progress, therefore, my training strongly encourages trial of newfound techniques.

"In order for a sales manager to be successful," says sales manager Martha Hill "I believe the person must be flexible, interested in teaching and learning, and must be a versatile communicator. Certainly a manager needs good selling skills, as it is a constant selling situation to persuade sales people to try techniques which will improve their job performance. But the most important skill a manager needs is to be a good listener; a manager must be keenly aware of the attitudes of the sales people and of the accounts. It is a common tendency for sales people and managers to want to talk, dominating a conversation, but much more is learned by listening because a buyer gives the road map to the sale by what he or she says.

Selection of good candidates and thorough orientation of new reps is an essential element of a successful manager's career. The sales team a manager builds is his strength or weakness, consequently the components of that team are crucially important, individually and collectively.

A manager can learn a great deal about interviewing via study and observation, but it is the actual participation and experience of interviewing and hiring that leads to this skill development."

Sales managers, such as Martha Hill, are responsible for planning, organizing, staffing, directing, and controlling their sales forces' activities, strategies, and tactics in order to generate sales that meet corporate objectives. Part 5 of this book examines these five job functions of the sales manager. This chapter discusses the planning, organizing, and staffing functions so important for the success of a sales manager. We begin by considering the transition of a salesperson to sales management.

Transition from Salesperson to Sales Manager

What happens when a salesperson is promoted into a management position? Often, the qualities that make a good sales manager are significantly different from those needed by a salesperson, particularly in terms of attitude toward the job and responsibility.

Salespeople are guided by management, but are basically on their own, not worrying about their peers. They are responsible for their own performance and often feel that they have control over their sales territory. However, the first-level sales manager is responsible not for one, but for eight to twelve sales territories. If a problem develops, for example a decrease in sales, the manager may be tempted to take over the salesperson's job. Instead, the manager should be concerned with developing people who can hurdle problems themselves, and with accomplishing goals through other people, not alone. Instead of having responsibility for $1 million in sales, as a salesperson does, the manager is responsible for $10 million to $20 million, and a regional manager might be responsible for ten times that amount. Managers are thus held responsible for the success of salespeople, and they must be able to work through others to reach their objectives.

Salespeople generally work independently without much interaction with or control by their organization. The job of the sales manager necessitates working closely with many different people—for example, salespeople, superiors, and home office personnel. Managers must realize that they are no longer salespeople, but members of the management team. The sales manager has responsibilities to the company, such as recruiting new salespeople, running an office, visiting important clients, and relaying information to higher management. Although there are many technical skills a sales manager must learn in order to become successful, the first step in the transition from salesperson to sales manager is to understand and accept the differences and the increased responsibilities of the new position.

"At IBM" says Matt Suffoletto, "the typical sales line management career path is generally a series of alternating line and staff positions, each with progressively increasing responsibility. It is our philosophy that before taking the next level of line management responsibility, additional development will be gained through the experience of a staff assignment.

"It is in those staff positions that your horizons are broadened. You begin to work with and see elements of the business other than direct sales. Your concept of available career paths will broaden and your personal preferences will develop as your horizons are expanded in the business."

What is the Salary for Management?

Why do people strive to rise to management positions? One reason is the personal reward of operating and managing an organization. The second reason is its financial reward. A sales job is often a stepping stone to these higher positions; examples of chief executives with sales backgrounds and their salaries are given in Table 16–1. The assumption seems to be that the larger a company's revenues, the heavier the responsibility of the chief executive, and thus the larger the compensation. Salary is usually related to:

- Annual sales volume of units managed.
- Number of salespeople supervised.
- Length of experience in sales.
- Annual sales volume of the firm.

Leaving aside compensation at the top echelons, both corporate and field sales managers typically receive higher salaries than others such as production, advertising, product, or personnel managers at the same organizational level. Moreover, salary is just one part of compensation.

Table 16–1 Salaries of Chief Executives with Sales Background

Company	Yearly Total Remuneration	Company	Yearly Total Remuneration
American Hospital	$1,342,000	Hershey Foods	$ 772,000
Avon Products, Inc.	671,000	Honeywell	1,139,000
Borden	997,000	IBM	1,267,000
Borman's	149,000	Johnson Controls	743,000
CBI Industries	588,000	LTV	2,098,000
Central Soya	304,000	MCA	452,000
Champion International	538,000	National Can	503,000
Clorox	390,000	Petrolane	350,000
Crown Cork & Seal	182,000	Republic Steel	350,000
Diamond International	321,000	J. P. Stevens & Co., Inc.	561,000
Dravo	332,000	Sunbeam	281,000
Fidelity Financial	220,000	Textron	486,000
Foxboro	258,000	Universal Leaf	369,000
Goodyear	1,252,000	Xerox Corporation	651,000

Source: *Forbes*, June 6, 1983.

For example, many firms offer elaborate packages that include extended vacation and holiday periods; pension programs; health, accident, and legal insurance programs; automobiles and compensation for auto expenses; payment of professional association dues; education assistance for themselves and sometimes for their families; financial planning assistance; company airplanes; home and entertainment expenses; and free country club membership. The higher the sales position, the greater the benefits offered.

Overview of the Job

Sales managers are responsible for planning, organizing, staffing, directing, and controlling sales force activities, strategies, and tactics in order to generate sales that meet corporate objectives. They do this through a process called management. Sales managers work with and through individuals and groups in the company, in the sales force, and outside the firm to accomplish their goals. The sales manager's main goal is to achieve the levels of sales volume, profits, and sales growth desired by higher levels of management.

The factor underlying a manager's success in achieving this goal is the ability to influence the behavior of all parties involved. This includes the ability to influence salespeople to do things that they would not do on their own. The manager must be able to recruit good people and provide proper motivation and effective leadership. It is important to remember that the sales manager is held responsible for the success of his salespeople. Consequently, sales managers are performance oriented. They look for ways to make their salespeople more efficient and more effective.

Managerial Skills

It is generally felt that successful managers must have three types of skills—technical, human, and conceptual. These skills can be explained as:

Technical skill	Ability to perform specific tasks; have great depth of knowledge of product; be skilled in all phases of selling.
Human skill	Ability to lead, build morale and effort, motivate, and manage conflict among subordinates.
Conceptual skill	Ability to understand how one's own area of responsibility relates to the total operation of the organization; also, ability to diagnose and assess management problems.

As shown in Figure 16–1, these skills are needed at all management levels. First-line managers, such as the district sales manager, need highly technical skills because they recruit and train salespeople, and they make

Figure 16–1 Managerial Skills and Their Importance at Varying Management Levels

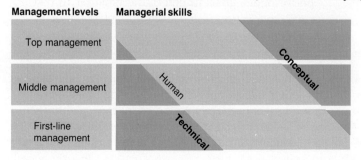

sales calls with their salespeople. The higher the level (such as national sales manager), the better a manager must be able to understand and relate sales management functions to the accomplishment of corporate goals. Human skills are equally important at each managerial level.

A successful sales manager must have excellent "human skills." John D. Rockefeller once stated, "I will pay more for the ability to deal with people than any other ability under the sun."[1] Many feel that the most important skill of a manager—even more important than decisiveness, intelligence, job skills, or knowledge—is the ability to get along with people." In fact, when salespeople were asked what were the important qualifications for the district sales manager's job, leadership was singled out as the most important.

Sales Management Functions

This discussion of the sales manager's functions applies to each of the three basic levels of management. Whether the sales manager is in a top, middle, or first-line managerial position, there are five basic functions to be fulfilled, as indicated in Figure 16-2. These are defined as follows:

Planning	Establishing a broad outline for goals, policies, and procedures that will accomplish the objectives of the organization.
Organizing	Setting up an administrative structure through which work activities are defined, subdivided, and coordinated to accomplish organizational goals.
Staffing	Recruiting, hiring, and training.
Directing	Dealing with people, positively and persuasively, from a leadership position.
Controlling	Comparing actual performance to planned performance goals to determine whether to take corrective action if goals are not achieved, or to continue using the same methods if goals are met.

First-line managers, such as district sales managers who hire salespeople, spend more time directing salespeople than higher-level managers do. In comparison, top-level sales managers spend more time planning and organizing. This can be seen more clearly if we compare the job functions of the corporate sales executive to those of the district sales manager.

Corporate Sales Executive Job Functions

Planning—developing and implementing total organization sales goals, strategies, tactics, and policies.

Organizing—developing the sales structure.

Figure 16–2 Sales Management Functions

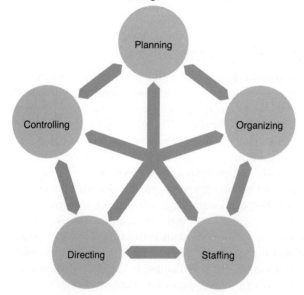

Staffing—promoting and training divisional sales managers.

Directing—developing leadership and motivation strategies for the entire sales organization.

Controlling—evaluating performance of total sales force.

District Sales Manager Job Functions

Planning—developing and implementing specific, individual objectives, strategies, and tactics.

Organizing—developing sales district for effective account coverage.

Staffing—recruiting, hiring, and training salespeople.

Directing—leadership and motivation of the sales district personnel.

Controlling—evaluating individual and sales district performance.

Sales Force Planning

A firm's corporate management, including the national sales manager, develops sales goals for the company. As discussed in Chapter 2, the marketing department is asked to develop plans, strategies, and tactics to allow the company to reach its sales objectives. In turn, the sales force is also asked to develop plans, strategies, and tactics for meeting their sales objectives and quotas. Two important elements of planning are the development of sales forecasts and budgets.

Sales Forecasting

Sales forecasting is one method used to predict a firm's future revenues when planning the company's marketing and sales force activities. Since customer satisfaction is the purpose of every business, it logically follows that the forecast of customer needs should be of primary importance. Forecasting is an integral part of planning that contributes to the overall effectiveness of the organization.

Uses of Sales Forecasts. Sales forecasting involves the prediction of future events that may influence the demand for a firm's goods or services. Total industry sales, total company sales, industry product categories, company product lines, and individual products are major elements that must be taken into account in estimating future demand. These forecasts are made for customer, sales territory, region, division, the entire country, and sometimes world sales. Forecasts are made in terms of short-range (e.g., three to six months), medium-range (e.g., six months to one to two years), and long-range (over two years) demand.

The firm's sales forecast is dependent upon many factors. The planned marketing activities of the firm have a major impact on the level of sales obtained in the marketplace. As shown in Figure 16–3, the firm's marketing plans have an influence on sales forecasts and budgets. Marketing plans can increase sales which, in turn, can increase budgets

Figure 16–3 Planning—Forecasting—Budgeting Sequence

and quotas. From sales forecasts, sales goals are generated for products and product lines, individual salespeople, or company divisions. Typically, sales goals are slightly higher than sales forecasts. Once plans have evolved into sales forecasts, the company develops its sales budgets.

The Sales Manager's Budget

The **sales force budget** is the amount of money available or assigned for a definite period of time, usually one year. It is based on estimates of expenditures during that period of time and proposals for financing the budget. Thus, the budget depends on the sales forecast and the amount of revenue expected to be generated for the organization during that period. The budget for the sales force is a valuable resource that the sales manager reassigns among lower-level managers. Budget funds must be appropriated wisely in order to properly support selling activities that allow sales personnel and the total marketing group to reach performance goals.

Purposes of the Budget. The budget is an extremely important factor in the successful operation of the sales force. Top sales managers spend a great deal of time attempting to convince corporate management to increase the size of their budgets. Budgets are formulated for many reasons, three major ones being planning, coordination, and control.

Planning. Corporations and their functional units develop objectives for future time periods, and budgets determine how these objectives will be met. For example, alternative marketing plans, the probable profit from each plan, and the individual budget for each will be considered before management is able to decide on future marketing programs.

Coordination. The budget is a major management tool for coordinating the activities of all functional areas and subgroups within the total organization. For example, sales must be coordinated with production to ensure that there are enough products to meet demand. The production manager can use sales forecasts and the sales department's marketing plans to determine the necessary production level. Budgeting allows the financial executive to determine the firm's revenues and expenses (e.g., accounts receivable, inventory, raw materials, labor) and enough capital to finance all business operations.

It is important for there to be some flexibility in the budget so that plans may be changed in response to market conditions. Many companies allocate a lump sum dollar amount to their sales managers, allowing the managers to invest in the selling activities dictated by the sales and marketing plans. Thus, each sales group (e.g., division, region, district) has a budget.

Control. Allocation of budgeted funds gives management control over the use of funds. Sales managers estimate their budget needs, are given funds to operate their units, and then are held responsible for reaching their stated goals by effectively using their budgets. As the sales program is implemented and income and expenses are actually generated, results are assessed in terms of the amount budgeted and whether objectives are met.

Methods of Developing Sales Force Budgets. How much money does the sales manager receive to operate the sales force? While there are no fixed financial formulas to use in appropriating funds, there are three general methods of determining how money should be allocated. First, some firms use an arbitrary percentage of sales. Second, other firms may use executive judgment. Third, a few companies estimate the cost of operating each sales force unit, along with costs of each sales program over a specified time period to arrive at a total budget.

In Figure 16–4 some typical costs entailed in operating a sales force are listed. Whichever method is chosen, the actual amount budgeted will be based on the organization's sales forecast, marketing plans, projected profits, top management's perceived importance of the sales force in reaching corporate objectives, and the sales manager's skill in negotiating with superiors. Budgets are often modified several times before the final dollar figures are determined.

Figure 16–4 Sales Force Operating Costs

1. Base salaries.
   A. Management.
   B. Salespeople.
2. Commissions.
3. Other compensation.
   A. Social security.
   B. Retirement plan.
   C. Stock options.
   D. Hospitalization.
4. Special incentives.
5. Office expenses.
6. Product samples.
7. Selling aids.
8. Transportation expenses.
9. Entertainment.
10. Travel.

Budgets Should Be Flexible. It is difficult to allocate exact dollar amounts to the sales group because market conditions may fluctuate. Sales, costs, prices, or the competition's marketing efforts may be higher or lower than expected. The sales force should be able to react to market conditions, and thus the budget should not be fixed in concrete.

> Never ask of money spent
> Where the spender thinks it went.
> Nobody was ever meant
> To remember or invent
> What he did with every cent.
>
> *Robert Frost*

Organizing the Sales Force

Organizing the sales force involves developing an administrative structure through which work activities of all sales personnel are defined, subdivided, and coordinated to accomplish organizational goals. This can further be broken down into the two important parts of design and structure. **Organizational design** is the determination of job tasks to be carried out by employees and groups within the firm, whereas **organizational structure** is the relatively fixed, formally defined relationships of jobs within the firm, as reflected in a company's **organizational chart.**

The Organizational Chart

A company's chart is a graphic representation of its formal structure at a given time. The chart shows: (1) jobs at the various hierarchical levels; (2) specialization of functional areas within the firm; (3) how departments relate to one another; (4) lines of authority or chain of command; and (5) line and staff relationships.

Methods of Organization

Companies can organize themselves using various designs. There is the simple line organization; also there is organization by the various functions of the company, by the geography of their markets; by the type of customers served, and by the products sold. Many firms use some combination of these individual designs. Let's first discuss each of the individual designs and then show how a combination of elements can be used to allow the firm to better serve its customers.

The Line Organization

In the pure **line organization,** the chief executive, usually the president, has complete authority over decision making for the firm. Within the firm there may be no specialists or advisors. There are many small sales firms with this structure. For example, the Compute Corporation is a Texas-based organization that sells used computers. Figure 16–5 shows the firm's line organization. The company was begun by its president, Lewis Stoner, in 1975. He and two salespeople did the selling and bookkeeping. Mr. Stoner buys late-model computers and sells them to companies without a computer of in need of a larger computer. As the business grew, Jake Preston was promoted to vice president of sales as a line assistant and another salesperson was hired. An outside accounting firm maintains the financial records.

Figure 16–5 Compute Corporation's Line Organization

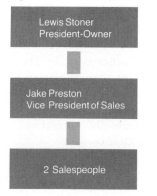

Lewis Stoner
President-Owner

Jake Preston
Vice President of Sales

2 Salespeople

Source: Used with permission of Compute Corporation, Houston, Texas.

The advantages of this type of organization are that it is simple and has low overhead, decisions are made rapidly and communicated quickly, and salespeople tend to feel that they make a major individual contribution to the firm.

In this type of "solo" leadership organization it is difficult to replace key people. In addition, executives may be so busy with the day-to-day operations that little time can be devoted to planning. Also, because everyone is a jack-of-all-trades, lack of specialization can hinder the firm's growth. Finally, growth is difficult unless the number of employees is greatly increased, which would lead to a change in structure—usually to a specialized organizational structure.

Specialized Design

The structure of an organization can be based on a variety of factors such as function, geography, product, customers, or a combination of these factors. It is common for large companies to begin with a functional structure; develop geographical departments; split along product division lines; and end with a customer-focused structure. While a firm may be organized along any one of these lines, typically, a combination of these structural methods is used.

Functional Specialization.   The **functional organization,** sometimes called line and staff organization, is the grouping of work according to its characteristics. It is the most common organizational design. Firms need special expertise so they develop advertising, sales, and marketing research units or departments, and then group all related activities (such as sales and advertising) together, thus introducing specialization into the organizational design. This type of organization is often used by firms that have a smaller number of similar products.

Figure 16–6 **Alarm System Corporation's Functional Organization Design**

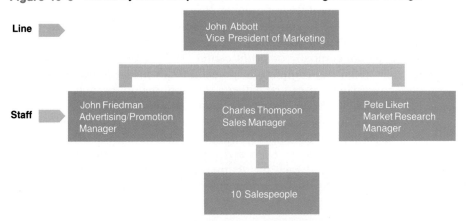

Source: Used with permission of Alarm System, Inc., Kansas City, Missouri.

No single chief executive, no matter how brilliant and dynamic, can effectively handle all of the responsibilities of a relatively large and complex organization. Figure 16–6 shows the functional organizational design of the sales and related units of Alarm System, an industrial and home security firm based in Kansas City, Missouri. Note the difference between this figure and Figure 16–5. The line component of the organization still runs from the chief executive directly down to the salespeople. However, the staff reports directly to the vice president of marketing. The sales manager has staff authority equal to that of the advertising and marketing research managers. However, neither the advertising nor marketing research manager has authority over the salespeople. Persons in staff positions aid the vice president of marketing in marketing planning and operations.

The functional organization structure is suitable when a firm outgrows one type of organization and begins to add specialized positions. For example, as a firm grows, it adds more salespeople to call on an increasing number of customers, to sell a larger number of products or services, and to expand into multiple sales regions or a national market. This design is useful for medium-to-large organizations because it allows them to take advantage of the benefits of specialization.

However, the functional organization structure also involves high overhead because a large number of management positions must be created that are not directly involved in generating income. Such an organization operates more slowly than the line organization, taking longer to respond to changes in the business environment. However, these disadvantages are overshadowed by the advantages.

Geographical Specialization.   Many large corporations are organized on the basis of geographical territory. This type of organization is generally used by companies that have anything other than strictly local distribution of their products. It is also commonly combined with other methods of organization, such as by product or customer. With **geographical specialization,** each territorial unit can be treated virtually as a separate company or profit center. The sales manager of a given territory often has complete responsibility for meeting a unit's sales objectives. The unit can be called a division, region, branch, or district. Let us consider the organizational chart shown in Figure 16–7. Texton Chemical primarily sells industrial chemicals used in the manufacturing of plastics. Texton has three geographical sales divisions. Each division sells the same products. Each division is given the same support by the home office and each has its own performance goals, which are passed down from higher management.

Figure 16–7   Texton Chemical Corporation Geographical Specialization

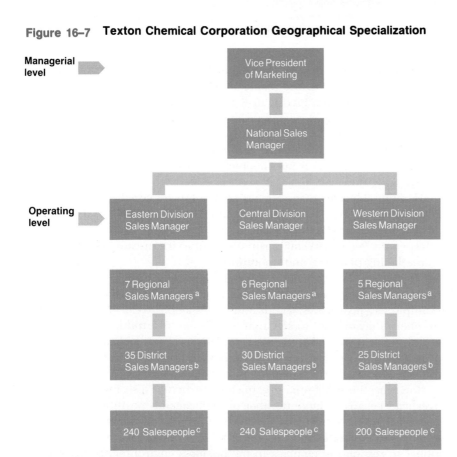

Source: Used with permission of Textron Chemical Corporation, Houston, Texas.

[a] Different number of sales regions due to population differences.

[b] Five district sales managers per region.

[c] Approximately eight salespeople per sales district.

Each of the regional sales managers works at a regional distribution or warehouse center. Although having eighteen regional distribution centers is a costly duplication of facilities, the cost is offset by efficiency. For example, sales managers feel that with this organization there is improvement in (1) control of activities; (2) market coverage; (3) customer service; (4) response to local conditions; and (5) direction of salespeople's efforts in achieving unit goals. Companies selling multiple product lines, with depth of assortment, often organize on the basis of geographical specialization combined with product specialization.

Product Specialization. Another common type of organization in large companies is based on the firm's product. The entire company may be organized by product, with separate sales, advertising, marketing staffs, etc., for each, or some functional units may remain centralized (e.g., advertising) while a separate support staff is created for each product. With the former organization, there would be, for example, a separate sales force and sales management for each product group. These sales divisions are treated as a separate company or profit center, as are geographical divisions. It is quite common for large companies to use a combination of product and geographical departmentalization. In fact, it is difficult to find medium-to-large companies organized solely by product. The Procter & Gamble Toilet Goods organizational chart shown in Chapter 2 is an example of organizing according to **product specialization.**

Product specialization is necessary, or at least useful, when (1) the products are very technical or complex; (2) there are many similar but separate products; (3) products are relatively simple but completely different; (4) product lines are distributed through entirely different trade channels; or (5) different products are sold to similar markets. When any combination of these factors is present, a company should investigate the possibility of product specialization of the sales force.

The advantage of product specialization is that each product receives close attention from the salesperson responsible for selling it. In the case of complex products, the salesperson can master the necessary information to sell the product effectively. The advantages of the organization based on geographical specialization also apply.

The drawbacks of product specialization, similar to those of geographical specialization, are the increased costs of executive personnel, sales personnel, and sales personnel time. A company that is organized by product specialization will often have different sales personnel calling on the same customers trying to sell them different products. Repeated calls by salespeople are costly in time both for the company and for the customer. Thus, if product specialization of the sales force can be avoided, either by hiring a higher caliber of sales personnel or by upgrading the training program, then these steps should be taken; but if not, product specialization should be introduced.

Customer Specialization.   Companies that have several separate and distinct markets that account for major portions of their sales often base their organization on these markets or customers. Firms frequently shift from the product organization structure to one of **customer specialization.** Markets then become the major sales emphasis. Figure 16–8 shows an industrial firm organized in terms of its electronic and aerospace markets. Here the staff positions, e.g., advertising, function for both divisions. Larger firms may create separate divisions with individual staff managers for each.

Many companies, such as Hewlett-Packard, IBM, Xerox, NCR, Burroughs, Gulf Oil, General Foods, and Bell Telephone, have evolved into more market-centered organizations. For example, Bell Telephone has systems salespeople specializing in twenty-six different markets, such as the oil companies. One senior salesperson may be assigned only one account—Exxon, located in Houston. Consequently, that salesperson becomes very knowledgeable about the oil industry and about Exxon's communication systems needs. This is the best method of specialization in use today.

Combination of Design Elements

Many companies organize on the basis of some combination of function, geography, product, or customer design elements. Figure 16–9 illustrates

Figure 16–8   **Electro Corporation Customer Specialization**

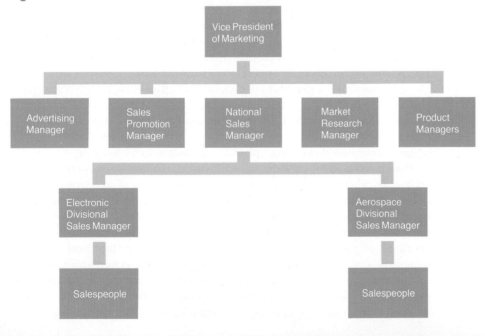

Figure 16–9 **Multiple Design Factors**

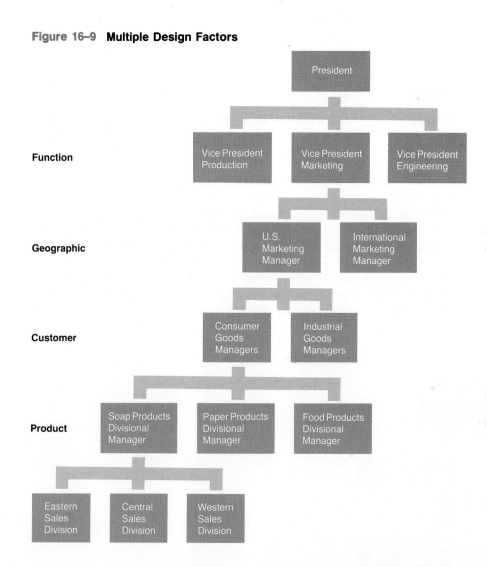

a company with production, marketing, and engineering functional specialists; the firm sells consumer and industrial goods in both U.S. and foreign markets. The consumer goods division sells three categories of products through three geographically organized sales force divisions.

Staffing the Sales Force

Sales force staffing is the entire personnel process of matching the right people to the right sales jobs and placing them in the right sales territory, thereby providing human resources capable of achieving sales force objectives. Staffing involves both manpower planning and employment planning.

Personnel Planning

Sales force **personnel planning** is the process of determining the kind and number of salespeople needed. Personnel planning for the sales force is an outgrowth of corporate, marketing, and sales force objectives. As shown in Figure 16–10, sales force staffing needs are based on the objectives and strategies assigned to the sales force. Determination is based on answers to questions such as: Will we have intensive or sparse coverage of existing and potential customers? Will the sales force be the major element in our promotion mix or the least important part? How many salespeople do we need to accomplish our objectives?

The current sales force is reviewed in order to forecast the total number of salespeople needed to reach sales management's objectives. Individual units, i.e., divisions, regions, or district sales areas, are reviewed to determine their personnel requirements. It is then necessary to determine financial requirements. Sales force plans, as related to

Figure 16–10   Sales Force Personnel Planning Model

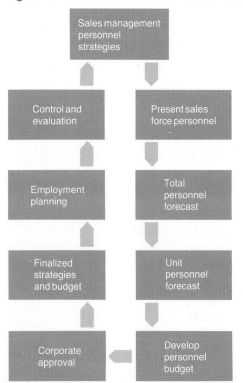

personnel needs, and the sales budget are submitted to the sales manager's superiors for corporate approval. The plans may be accepted or changed. For example, the budget may be reduced, which might result in a reduction of the planned size of the sales force. Once personnel requirements and the budget are finalized, employment planning begins. This entire process is monitored and evaluated to determine whether these requirements are aiding the sales force in reaching objectives.

Job Analysis and Descriptions.   After the number of salespeople to be hired has been decided, it is necessary to determine the type of salesperson to recruit for each sales job. Accordingly, sales managers analyze their salespeople's jobs, develop job descriptions and create job specifications.

A **job analysis** is the definition of a sales position in terms of specific roles or activities to be performed, and the determination of the personal qualifications that are suitable for the job. **Job descriptions** are formal, written statements describing the nature, requirements, and responsibilities (e.g., sales volume, territory, product line, customers, supervisory duties) of a specific sales position. They officially establish what the salesperson will do, how it will be done, and why these duties are to be carried out, as well as indicate the salary range appropriate for the position. Figure 16–11 gives a partial job description for a position selling automotive replacement parts.

This description has five basic parts. The "nature of job" section is

Figure 16–11 Formal Job Description, Transtex Automotive Supply Corporation

Position: Sales representative	Organizational Unit: Replacement parts
Reports to: District manager	Date: (When job was described)

Nature of job
 Responsible for developing new accounts and reaching profitable sales goals in assigned territory.

Principal responsibilities
 Meeting total sales goals for product lines and individual products.
 Maintaining an average of six daily sales calls.
 Maintaining an average of one monthly product presentation to wholesalers.

Dimensions
 Develop strong promotional support from retail and wholesale customers.
 Plan effective territory coverage resulting in high sales-call ratio.
 Informs management of activities by submitting daily and weekly call and sales reports to district manager.

Supervision received
 General and specific tasks are assigned for each sales period. Every two months works with supervisor for a minimum of one day.

Supervision exercised
 None

Used with permission.

a statement of the responsibilities involved. The next section, "principal responsibilities" states the specific end results or performance expected from someone holding the position. They explain how to implement the nature of job section. In the "dimensions" section, job duties are discussed. Finally, there is an explanation of the supervisory responsibilities involved.

Job Specifications. **Job specifications** convert job descriptions into the people qualifications (e.g., abilities, behavior, education, skills) the organization feels are necessary for successful performance of the job involved. Often, specifications for a job are determined by management in compliance with governmental regulations. This includes qualifications for initial employment and for training as a successful salesperson. Increasingly, however, statistical analyses are also being used to assist in generating job specifications. By this means the relation of successful sales performance to certain personal characteristics such as education, specific aptitudes, communication skills, personality type, and experience are statistically determined.

Job Specifications for Successful Salespeople. Sales managers often express frustration over the difficulty of selecting potential salespeople. Typical comments include the following: "What are the characteristics necessary for successful salespeople in my industry and my company? If I knew," states one sales manager, "I'd have fewer staffing problems." "We think we know," says another sales manager. "We hire them. Some do well, others don't." Another manager said: "The company gives us job specifications but they are difficult to use. I have to hire in a short time. I find the best people I can in the job market at that time who have good personality characteristics, background, and potential, and hire them. I don't really use job specifications."

Let us review what little is known about the desirable characteristics that should be included in job specifications. We know the selling job is people oriented. Thus, salespeople must be able to deal with people positively and effectively. Studies of the topic done in the 1960s centered on two basic personality characteristics. The successful salesperson should have the proper empathy and ego drive for a specific type of sales job. Empathy is needed for identifying and understanding the other person's situation. Ego drive is the desire to make the sale, to be able to overcome "no sales" and to continue calling on customers. Other desirable characteristics reported are shown in Figure 16–12. A point can be made that the individual company should determine the job specifications and sales personnel characteristics necessary for successful performance. These should be continually updated. Most sales managers say the minimum components of a successful salesperson are:

1. Education—the individual should be an above-average student.
2. Personality—a good salesperson is achievement oriented, tactful,

Figure 16–12   **Selected Characteristics of Successful Salespeople**

1. High energy levels	8. Good physical appearance
2. High self-confidence	9. Likable
3. Need for material things	10. Self-disciplined
4. Hard working	11. Intelligent
5. Requires little supervision	12. Achievement oriented
6. High perseverance	13. Good communication skills
7. Competitive	

Source: Robert N. McMurry and James S. Arnold, *How To Build A Dynamic Sales Organization* (New York: McGraw-Hill 1968). p. 3; Robert N. McMurry, "The Mystique of Super-Salesmanship," *Harvard Business Review*, March–April 1961, p. 114; David L. Kurtz, "Physical Appearance and Stature: Important Variables in Sales Recruiting," *Personnel Journal*, December 1969, pp. 981–83; John B. Miner, "Personality and Ability Factors in Sales Performance," *Journal of Applied Psychology* 46 (1962), pp. 6–13.

mature, self-confident, a self-starter with a positive outlook on life and a realistic career plan.

3.   Experience—a good salesperson will work hard and go beyond the call of duty; if a recent graduate, this person will have participated in school organizations and developed above-average class projects.

4.   Physical attributes—a good salesperson has a neat appearance, good personal habits, is physically fit, and makes a good first impression.

Guidelines for Job Descriptions and Job Specifications.   Critics of job descriptions and job specifications point out that many are written so unclearly and ambiguously as to be of little actual use in the staffing process. However, companies need to develop useful job descriptions and job specifications. The following list provides suggestions for clarifying job descriptions and specifications:

- Decide upon job objectives and state them in the form of activities (what sales personnel actually do).
- List the tasks required for desired performance.
- Differentiate between routine and critical tasks.
- List alternative methods of performing tasks.
- Specify criteria used to determine whether the job has been performed successfully.
- Specify favorable and unfavorable conditions for the attainment of objectives.
- Specify other general information regarding the job (for example, title, salary, supervisor).
- List work qualifications, education, and/or experience levels required.
- Develop techniques for validating sales job analysis.

Employment Planning

Employment planning refers to the locating, recruiting, evaluation, and hiring of applicants for sales jobs. Recruitment begins with the initiation of a search, i.e., prospecting for applicants. Once all of the activities leading up to and including the actual decision by the applicant to accept or reject the final job are over, the recruitment process ends for the individual applicant. In essence, recruiters are attempting to close sales by getting applicants to accept offers of employment. On the other side, applicants attempt to sell themselves to the prospective employer, while searching for a job that will fulfill their own needs and expectations.

Figure 16–13 illustrates the seven basic steps a recruiter may take in hiring a salesperson. Typically, candidates first complete a job application blank, and undergo an initial interview. If applicants appear to be good candidates, they go through several in-depth interviews. Some companies have applicants work with salespeople to show them what the job is really like. If applicants are married, the manager may also meet with spouses to further explain job requirements.

Tests are frequently given to applicants to determine their intelligence and aptitude for sales jobs. Applicants submit names of people who can provide character references. These are then checked. The final step is the physical examination.

Both the applicant and the sales manager have the option to say no at any of the seven steps in the selection process. During the process

Figure 16–13   **Major Steps in the Sales Personnel Selection Process**

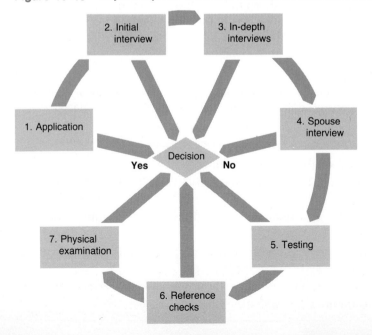

the applicant and the sales manager collect enough information about each other to make this decision.

Legal Framework for Employment.   The sales manager is faced with an increasing number of laws governing employment practices. Although a number of federal agencies are involved, the **Equal Employment Opportunity Commission (EEOC)** is the principal government agency responsible for monitoring discriminatory practices. As such, the EEOC has a major influence on sales force staffing. Changing social values, attitudes toward minorities, women entering the work force, a recognition of the traditional advantages enjoyed by white males, and an increasing number of government regulations necessitated the creation of the commission.

The legislation affecting employment practices ranges from the Constitution itself to more recent laws such as the 1963 Equal Pay Act which specifically prohibits sex discrimination in pay.[2] The provisions of this act were broadened under the 1972 Education Amendments Act which states that ". . . Any employee employed in a bona fide executive, administrative, or professional capacity . . . or in the capacity of outside salesman" is entitled to equal pay. The most far-reaching recent legislation in this context is the Civil Rights Act of 1964, especially Title VII of the act as amended by the Equal Employment Opportunity Act of 1972, which prohibits discrimination based on race, sex, religion, or national origin.

It is important to remember that what might be labeled discrimination is allowed if an employer can show that a given action is "reasonably necessary to the operation of that particular business or enterprise" and thus that employment decisions are based on a "bona fide occupational qualification." Included in this context are such things as age, testing, and inquiries into preemployment background. However, there are few cases in which this argument can stand up against charges of discrimination.

The government has many ways of influencing employment practices. Consequently, the sales manager must have continually updated information on government employment regulations and must have specific guidelines to follow. Very broadly speaking, the equal employment opportunity criteria appear to be based on two questions:

1. Are the employment practices equally applied and do they have the same effect on all potential employees, regardless of race, sex, religion, or national origin?
2. Are the employment practices job related?

A Sales Manager's View of the Recruit

Given the way sales managers train their recruiters, interview sessions, and the post-interview comments of hundreds of students, the following sales manager's view of the recruit and the recruiting process is fairly representative. This particular sales manager had twenty years' experience recruiting for a manufacturer of computer equipment. The following discussion is based on a tape recording of a talk given to a graduate class in sales management.

Is Sales the Right Job for the Applicant?   The search for the sales job begins with the applicant. To obtain any job, applicants must "sell" themselves. If applicants are excited and enthusiastic about the future, recruiters will be too.

Applicants should ask themselves what they are looking for in a job. They should be honest with themselves, and they should be realistic. They need to ask themselves:

What are my past accomplishments and future goals?

Do I want the responsibility of a sales job?

Do I mind travel? How much travel is acceptable?

How much freedom do I want in the job?

Do I have the personality characteristics for the job?

These are questions recruiters attempt to answer about the applicant during the interview.

Job Analysis.   Applicants need to determine which industries, types of products or services, and specific companies they are interested in. Find out what recruiters from different companies may look for in an applicant in order to better prepare yourself.

Recruiters look for outstanding applicants who are mature and intelligent. They should be able to handle themselves well in the interview, demonstrating good interpersonal skills. They should have well-thought-out career plans and be able to discuss them rationally. They should have friendly, pleasing personalities. A clean, neat appearance is a must. They should have positive attitudes, be willing to work hard, be ambitious, and demonstrate a good degree of interest in the employer's business field. They should have good grades and other personal, school, and business accomplishments. Finally, they should have clear goals and objectives in life. The more common characteristics on which applicants for our company are judged are: (1) appearance, (2) self-expression, (3) maturity, (4) personality, (5) experience, (6) enthusiasm, (7) and interest in the job.

The Application Letter.   The application letter introduces the applicant to the prospective employer. It should not totally rehash the information in the resume. It should be neat and personalized. The letter should begin by mentioning the job for which the person is applying. In the next paragraph the applicant should state reasons for being interested in the position and the company. It should indicate knowledge of the company. If currently in school, applicants should

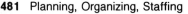

explain how their education qualifies them for the position. The same should be done with school activities and work experience. In the third paragraph the resume can be mentioned, possibly pointing out the relevant factors not previously discussed, e.g., grade point average, honors, graduation date. The last paragraph should positively ask for an interview at a time and place convenient to the company.

The Resume.   The application letter serves to arouse the recruiter's interest and develops the desire to review the resume. Again, neatness is a must. Printed copies may be made with a picture attached. There are many resume formats, but, in general they should contain information such as:

Personal data—including address, birth date.

Job objective.

Education—listing most recent first.

Work experience—listing most recent first.

Activities.

Reference section—stating furnished upon request.

This information summarizes the applicant's life in one to two pages. In a few minutes the recruiter should have a good idea of the applicant's background. Recruiters are busy people. If the resume is mailed and there has not been a response in one to two weeks, the applicant should call and/or write the company.

The Interview.   Applicants should be prepared. They should anticipate interview questions, prepare for them, and practice. Be prepared for questions such as:

What can you tell me about yourself?

Why do you want to be in sales?

What do you know about my company?

Why do you want to work for my company?

What problems have you had and how have you solved them?

Where do you want to be in five years?

Some recruiters may ask the applicant to sell them something, e.g., an ashtray or a pencil. The applicant cannot always prepare for everything. However, the recruiter knows when the applicant is prepared. When being interviewed, it is important to be early in order to review plans for the interview. The recruiter should be addressed by name.

Interview Follow-Up.   A letter immediately following the interview is not always necessary. However, if the recruiter has set a time for notifying the applicant of a decision and if it has passed, a follow-up letter or call is appropriate.

The Second Interview.   An applicant invited for a second interview has passed the first major step in the job search. The recruiter feels that this individual may be what the company seeks in a salesperson. Now, the applicant should really prepare for this visit by doing everything from reviewing information to planning what to wear.

Job Offers.   If a company offers the applicant a job, it is important to respond positively in one of three ways. First, accept the offer and stop interviewing. Second, reject the offer tactfully but give the reasons for your decision; this should be done as soon as possible. Third, request more time to either complete the job search or consider the offer.

No Job Offer.   Should the recruiter feel that there is no match and should not make a job offer, the applicant may write a letter of appreciation for the opportunity to be interviewed. If still interested in the job, the applicant can express hope for future consideration.

Training the Sales Force

Sales training is the effort put forth by an employer to provide the opportunity for the salesperson to acquire job-related attitudes, concepts, rules, and skills that result in improved performance in the selling environment.

John H. Patterson, founder of the National Cash Register Company and known as the "father of sales training," used to say, "At NCR our salesmen never stop learning." This philosophy is the reason that even today successful companies thoroughly train new salespeople and have ongoing training programs for their experienced sales personnel, in which even the most successful salespeople participate.

Basically, sales training is designed to change or reinforce behavior to make salespeople more efficient in achieving their job goals. Salespeople are trained to perform activities they would not normally undertake. In addition, training is used to reinforce currently successful sales practices.

Purposes of Training

Companies are interested in training primarily to increase sales, productivity, and profits. As the chairman and chief executive officer at United States Steel expressed it:

> We support training and development activities to get results. . . . We're interested in specific things that provide greater rewards to the employee, increased return to the stockholder, and enable reinvestment to meet the needs of the business. In other words, [we're interested in] those things which affect the "bottom line." Although you cannot always evaluate training as

readily as some other functions, as people improve their performance it is reflected in on-the-job results as well as all aspects of their lives.[3]

Edward G. Harness, chairman of the board of Procter & Gamble, says: "We grow our own managers, and it starts with finding the right people through an extremely intensive selection process, followed by continuing on-the-job training."[4]

There are specific purposes of training other than improving general sales volume. These tend to relate to the type of training being offered and include:

- Helping salespeople become better managers;
- Orienting the new salesperson to the job;
- Improving knowledge in areas such as product, company, competitors, or selling skills;
- Lowering absenteeism and turnover;
- Positively influencing attitudes in such areas as job satisfaction;
- Lowering selling costs;
- Informing salespeople;
- Obtaining feedback from the salespeople;
- Increasing sales in a particular product or customer category.

Yet the primary purpose of training is to "invest" in the sales organization's most valuable resource—its salespeople. Training is an ongoing process and is the responsibility of the trainee, the trainer, and the organization.

Training Methods

The three basic training methods are discussion, role playing, and on-the-job training.

Discussion.   The discussion approach to sales training can be used in several different ways including case studies and/or small and large discussion groups. Case studies are usually included in presession assignments. At a session, small discussion groups may be formed to further analyze the case and to report the findings to the group. Lectures incorporating discussion and demonstration are the most common and effective method of training. Filmed cases have been shown to be more effective than written cases.

Role Playing.   In **role playing** the trainee acts through the sale of a product or service to a hypothetical buyer. Often the trainee's presentation is videotaped and replayed for critique by a group, the trainee, and the trainer. The role playing procedure is generally some variation of the following:

1. "Define the sales problem." The trainee is told the company is coming out with a new shaving cream.
2. "Establish the situation." The trainee is asked to think about, and then describe, the largest potential account and its buyer.
3. "Cast the characters." The trainer or a trainee is selected to play the buyer.
4. "Brief the participants." Each should learn a role. In addition, the "buyer" may be briefed separately from the salesperson, and given certain specific objections to raise.
5. "Act out the buyer-seller situation." The salesperson goes through a sales presentation with interaction from the buyer.
6. "Discuss, analyze, critique the role playing." This is important to the learning process. If videotaped, the presentation is shown to the group. Trainers often ask the group for their comments first. Then the participants discuss the situation. A critique from the trainer is next. Trainees may be asked to repeat the exercise.

On-the-Job Training. On-the-job training may take several forms. New salespeople may accompany their manager and observe sales calls. At first, the manager makes all of the sales presentations for some period of time. Then, typically, a customer is selected who will be easy to call on, and the trainee makes his first sales presentation with little or no assistance. This is an exciting and important time for the trainee, and the experience must be critiqued in a positive manner in order to establish a good relationship between salesperson and manager.

If a sale was not made, the manager should reassure the salesperson that selling is based on percentages. If the manager maintains a positive attitude, so will the trainee. As Fran Tarkenton, the former Minnesota Vikings quarterback, states, "We're all reinforcing agents and feedback agents for each other, each and every one of us. I'm a great believer in feedback, positive or negative. When something isn't right, tell the performer what and why and how to correct it. And when it's right, deliver the positive reinforcement and positive feedback."

For the experienced salesperson, on-the-job training includes observation by the trainer and curbstone counseling by the sales manager. This way the salesperson gets immediate feedback. When the manager and salesperson leave the customer's office, the manager can critique the sales presentation. If needed, corrections are made. Imagine yourself making six sales presentations in the presence of your manager and having each critiqued. The next day you are prepared to use what you have learned to make more effective sales presentations.

There are many variations in critiquing the salesperson. Some managers prefer to have their salespeople critique themselves. For example, "Judy, that was a very good sales presentation. Can you think of anything that should have been changed or improved upon?" Then, the manager asks whether the trainee would like any help toward becoming more successful, such as more selling aids and samples, or having the manager make the next presentation so that the salesperson can watch and learn.

Where Does Training Take Place?

A salesperson may receive some form of training any place, any time of day or night. Sales training is continuous. In a broad sense, training occurs any time the superior does things such as commenting on a salesperson's reports, talking on the phone to the salesperson, working in the field with the salesperson, or conducting a meeting. The two broad categories of sales training are centralized and decentralized training. Companies often are divided on whether training should be totally centralized, using corporate staff trainers, or whether training should be both centralized and decentralized.

Centralized Training.   Training at a central location is primarily intended for instruction of salespeople from all geographical areas served by the company. Programs typically are held at or close to the home office/manufacturing plant, in a large city, or at a resort. **Centralized training programs** are designed to supplement the basic training done by sales personnel in the field. A survey of selling costs shows that 100 percent of the industrial products managers questioned use their home office as a training site, while 93 percent of the consumer products and 71 percent of service companies used home office sites.

A salesperson may attend a centralized training program when first starting work, after six months to a year of employment, or at stipulated intervals. The new salesperson may initially be trained in the field, then after one year be sent to the home office for training and to tour the firm's manufacturing facilities. There may be further training at the home office every five years.

Centralized training programs usually involve excellent facilities and equipment such as classrooms, videotapes, closed circuit television, and sales laboratories designed for role playing. Trainees get to know each other and corporate executives. Because they are away from home, they can concentrate on learning. Training content can be standardized so that the entire sales force will have a common body of knowledge.

Decentralized Training.   **Decentralized training** may be conducted anywhere; it is the main form of sales force instruction. It can be done in a branch office, in the salesperson's car, at the customer's place of business, in a motel room, or at the salesperson's own home.

There are numerous advantages to decentralized training. For one thing, costs are usually lower. For example, if a branch office is used as the training site, travel costs are less. The sessions are typically shorter, thus saving on motel and meal expenditures. Salespeople's geographical territories are such that often they see one another only during meetings and training programs. Many sales managers feel their salespeople receive as much knowledge and motivation from their peers in informal sessions as they do in regular training. Salespeople can informally discuss their problems in making sales and how they were able to overcome sales resistance. The success stories can particularly benefit the inexperienced salesperson. Of course, these informal talks also occur when salespeople attend centralized training sessions. Finally, supplies, samples, and tools can be provided to take back home after the session.

There are several disadvantages to either type of training. A potential major weakness in decentralized training is that a branch manager may not be an able trainer, which can have a negative effect on the salespeople. On the other hand, centralized training is expensive due to the cost of travel, meals, and facilities. Also, it is expensive for salespeople to be out of their territories, and trainees may not want to be away from their families for a prolonged period of time. Common disadvantages include the fact that salespeople may come to the meeting unprepared, really only wanting to get away from regular work. Trainers understand this, and overcome it by having training sessions that are well prepared, interesting, informative, and that encourage participation. Finally, customer sales may be lost. The cost of lost sales must be offset by increasing productivity and efficiency through the training.

When Does Training Occur?

For new sales personnel, training begins the first day they report to work. Basic company, product, and selling skill information is usually given to the trainee to study. In a recruiting brochure, Procter & Gamble states: "Your training begins the day you join us and will continue throughout your career, regardless of your responsibility or job level."[5] The firm gives its new salespeople a two-day orientation conducted by an immediate supervisor. Company, product, and customer information are presented. Salespeople also receive a company car, equipment, and supplies. After the orientation session, the salespeople call on their customers with their manager. This procedure is not uncommon for those selling consumer goods.

Training does not end with this initial session, but continues throughout the professional salesperson's career. Some firms want their salespeople to be thoroughly trained before they are assigned a sales territory. Conversely, some firms feel that new employees can relate to and retain more from training if they have been in the sales territory for a short period of time.

For example, the computer division of the Burroughs Corporation has a short initial training program for new sales personnel, after which the salesperson is required to sell a certain number of desk calculators.

This gives the individual new to selling some valuable experience. Next, newcomers are sent to school to learn about minicomputers. They then sell minicomputers until a certain level of sales is obtained, and then return to school to be trained on larger computers. After this, salespeople return to their sales territories, and begin to sell. This then is a training, selling, training, selling sequence. The products are technical. Consequently, sales experience and training are alternated, allowing salespeople to progress at their own pace. With this particular company, there is a financial incentive to progress quickly to selling the more expensive computers because salary and commissions may amount to $20,000 the first year of selling calculators, $25,000 the second year of selling minicomputers, and can reach $35,000 by the third year of selling large computer systems.

Companies also provide training for experienced salespeople through periodic sales meetings. Many companies have regular sales meetings once every month or two. In addition, materials are mailed to the homes of sales personnel. Training involves working with a manager in the sales territory. Salespeople also periodically attend training programs at company headquarters.

Who Is Involved in Training?

Typically, there are three basic kinds of sales trainers: corporate staff personnel, regular sales force personnel, and specialists from outside the company.

Figure 16–14 **Basic Sources of Sales Training**

Sales Trainers

Corporate staff trainers	Regular sales force personnel	Outside training specialists

Corporate Staff Trainers. Staff trainers are responsible for the creation, administration, and coordination of a firm's sales management and sales force training and development programs. Typically, the training manager and staff are separate from the personnel department. They have an ongoing relationship with all staff departments and the field organization. The training manager usually reports to someone at the upper corporate level, such as the vice president of sales.

The duties and responsibilities of the training manager can be narrow or broad, depending on the size of the organization and the importance placed on centralized training. The following are some of the major duties:

- The foremost duty of the manager and the manager's staff is to assist sales management in identifying training "needs" and developing programs to meet those needs.
- They organize, coordinate, and schedule the training.
- They determine who will conduct the training and, if needed, provide them with support material.
- The training manager may help evaluate the training and report results to corporate and field management.
- The trainer often coordinates and administers follow-up training.
- The manager prepares an annual budget to meet the goals and needs of each training program.

Sales Force Personnel. Senior sales representatives and district and regional sales managers often are the main trainers of their firm's sales force. These people bring to the training program years of sales experience which leads the trainee to relate quickly to the instructor and to the material being presented. The sales manager possesses power and authority, which aids in getting the sales personnel to cooperate and to exert greater effort in the training sessions. The manager is in a position to train salespeople in the best methods of working and selling. A good rapport between the manager and the sales force can be established if the salesperson sees the trainer as imparting knowledge and teaching skills that will aid the trainee in obtaining personal sales goals.

Neil Salerno, director of marketing for American Motor Inns, Inc., believes very strongly in this system of training. His philosophy is: "Put a new salesman with an old one out in the field for training and in three weeks you have two old salesmen." AMI, which is the largest franchiser of Holiday Inns in the United States, gathers its salespeople from all its properties for week-long training sessions. Salerno says, "We want them to relate to everyone, of course, but salespeople relate more easily to each other than to anyone else."[6]

Management must provide sales force personnel with adequate time, support, and rewards to carry out their training duties. Otherwise, the training personnel may not perform adequately, which can create low morale among salespeople and decrease the effectiveness of the training program. Very often the trainer receives support from the home office personnel (for example, product managers or technical support personnel who discuss product strategies or product information).

The trainer should be not only an effective salesperson but also a competent teacher. A company should use a senior salesperson as a trainer not on the basis of sales ability, but because of effective communications skills. People with both sales and teaching abilities can usually be found, but management must seek them out. An assignment at the corporate level as a trainer can be a step up the career ladder for the salesperson in the field.

Outside Training Specialists. Trainers drawn from outside the company may be consultants specializing in sales training or representatives of programs such as Toastmasters, Dale Carnegie Sales Courses, and the Xerox Sales Learning Programs. Some universities also offer courses for salespeople and sales managers.

Quite often the company will pay all or part of the cost to the salesperson for completing, for example, a college-level sales methods course. One endorsement of such sales training courses came from a vice president of engineering in the Cross Company: "As a result of taking the course, our people have new, positive attitudes toward their jobs, along with a better understanding of the company's goals. They also have a better appreciation of one another's problems, and they show better teamwork in resolving day-to-day situations."

Smaller firms may rely heavily on outside trainers. This practice affords them the type of training they want without the cost of maintaining a training staff. The courses may be standardized or customized for the company. A company should carefully select outside trainers on the basis of individual needs.

Combination of Training Sources. Firms large and small use a combination of the above training sources. A firm may use its sales force personnel to do a large percentage of the training with a sales training director and staff assisting. The latter organize and coordinate training efforts among the staff and trainers. The training director might arrange for a product manager to attend a sales meeting to give technical information and discuss future promotional plans for the product. Firms often hire consultants, such as university professors, to put on in-house seminars dealing with such subjects as the psychological aspects of why industrial buyers purchase goods or selling techniques that can be effective. The firm may also purchase ongoing motivational programs such as the Earl Nightingale motivational phonograph record program. With this program, the salesperson receives a training record every month in the mail or at a sales meeting.

Another method of complementing the training program is through a weekly newsletter. Arnar-Stone Laboratories, a subsidiary of American Hospital Supply Corporation, has one called the *Pharmedia*. It covers topics such as individual sales achievements; tips on refining selling techniques; product knowledge updates; synopses of national, regional, and district sales meetings; new marketing trends; news of interest from all departments; and new operating procedures for the sales representatives. Johnson & Johnson has established a lending library of approximately 800 cassette tapes on subjects such as self-development, sales management, and selling techniques. This sales department library is part of the firm's self-development program for the sales force.[7]

Summary of Major Sales Management Issues

A salesperson who is promoted to sales manager becomes involved in sales planning, organizing, staffing, directing, and controlling sales force activities. This chapter discussed the need to understand how to make sales forecasts and budgets, how to determine the number of salespeople to hire, how to recruit and train salespeople, and the legal aspects of staffing. The sales manager uses this knowledge to achieve the sales volume, profits, and growth desired by higher levels of management. Technical, human, and conceptual skills aid in reaching these goals.

Today, firms design their organizational structure in such a manner as to be able to best serve their customers. Small companies use a simple line organizational design, whereas large firms design specialized structures based upon geography, the products they market, customers, or a combination of these elements.

Sales managers are frequently involved in forecasting their firm's sales. They also are involved in developing budgets and allocating monies to their various sales units, all of which ultimately serve as input into planning and aid in coordinating and controlling sales unit activities.

The contemporary sales manager is knowledgeable in personnel practices involving the recruiting and hiring of salespeople. Government laws need to be considered so that the firm can abide by EEOC guidelines. The staff function involves both personnel planning, or the determination of the kind and number of needed salespeople, and employment planning, which is the locating, recruiting, evaluation, and hiring of applicants for the sales job.

Once the hiring is done, the sales manager becomes involved in training salespeople on things such as product knowledge and selling skills. Training begins immediately, usually taking place in the salesperson's territory and at company training facilities.

As you begin to see, the sales manager is a salesperson first, but also something of a jack-of-all-trades due to the various functions required for the job. The next chapter will discuss directing and controlling functions.

Review and Discussion Questions

1. What is the main "bottom-line" responsibility of a sales manager?
2. Discuss the difference between organizational design and organizational structure. How does design and structure relate to a firm's organizational chart?
3. Discuss the relationship between a firm's marketing plan, sales forecast, and sales force budget.

4. What are the two major elements of the sales manager's staffing function? Discuss each of these elements.
5. In applying for a sales job, what are the important things an applicant should consider doing?

Projects

1. Visit or write to a local Equal Employment Opportunity office and gather current information on the legal aspects of recruiting.
2. Contact one or more sales managers in your community and ask the steps they go through in their recruiting process.

Cases

16–1 New Manhattan Division Sales Manager

Keith Absher is tired and confused. He is sitting quietly at his desk after three long days spent trying to decide how to handle a complex situation that is now his responsibility. His brief sales management experience and his recently completed MBA courses did not seem to provide answers that would allow him to put the situation in order.

As he struggled with alternatives, his mind drifted back over the three-year period in which he had worked with Lauderdale Foods, Inc. It all started when Absher was recruited during his last year at Delta State. He had never really thought favorably about being a salesperson, but the salary was good and a company car was provided. Absher was also planning to get married and it was important to have a job lined up before graduation. So, he accepted the job until something better came along.

After a two-month training period, Absher appeared to be off to a good start. The job involved calling on supermarkets in a three-county area. Lauderdale Foods, Inc. was a large food processing company that marketed more than 150 products nationwide. Although salespersons did not deliver the products or stock the shelves, they were responsible for placing orders through regional warehouses, for picking up damaged merchandise, and for building displays of the company's highly advertised items.

Absher made real progress under the seasoned leadership of his division sales manager, M. B. Wingfield. He grew to appreciate and respect Wingfield on a personal and professional basis. After one year, however, Absher decided that he did not want to remain in field sales for the rest of his life. He made plans that would, hopefully, bring

This case was developed by Gerald Crawford, Professor of Marketing, University of North Alabama, Florence, Alabama. This case represents an actual situation. Copyright © 1980.

opportunities for promotion. The first step was to enroll in a night MBA program at Memphis State University.

Things happened faster than anticipated. After a second year in field sales, he was named assistant division manager when the previous ADM was promoted to division manager in another state. Wingfield again trained Absher in his new managerial role. There were fourteen salespeople in the Memphis Division. All were stable, cooperative, and generally effective in their work. Things went very smoothly and no major problems were encountered.

After his third year with Lauderdale Foods, Absher completed the MBA degree and was immediately promoted to DM in the Manhattan, New York Division. Absher and his family were moved to New York and this is when things began to happen.

When Absher reported to work on Monday morning, he met Guy Carter who was his new boss and regional manager over four other sales divisions in the Metro New York area. Absher also met his new ADM who had just been promoted from a sales territory in the Philadelphia area. Carter chatted with both young managers and briefly brought them up-to-date on the division's strengths and weaknesses. Absher immediately recognized that Carter was certainly a different type of manager than his old boss, Wingfield. Carter appeared to be more direct and businesslike than the people Absher was accustomed to back in Memphis. Carter was really not very helpful. To complicate matters, the new ADM had no background in management and had not worked in this division.

Carter suggested that Absher spend one day working with each of his nineteen salespeople. This would be a good way to orient himself in his new assignment. On Tuesday morning Absher met Mike Beasley at his first call. Beasley was thirty-four years of age and had been with the company ten years. He was short and muscular and wore a hairpiece. In the first call, Beasley spoke with the manager and received permission to rotate the Lauderdale Foods products in the dairy case. While Beasley was busy checking dates and putting things in order, Absher noticed that the store manager had opened Beasley's sample case and had taken several product samples and placed them under his checkout counter. After Beasley completed his work in the dairy case, he wrote up the order and had the store manager enter it into his computer order book. Beasley then proceeded to walk over and very methodically remove the samples from under the counter and put them back in his sample case. He and the manager appeared to say a few harsh words to each other. Later, in the car, Beasley explained that this was not the first time that this had happened and that the manager would "get over it." During the rest of the day several other similar things happened. Absher was not comfortable with the way Beasley handled people even though he had sold a great deal of merchandise during the day.

The next day Absher worked with a highly rated salesperson in the Spanish area. Louis Flores was a handsome young man of Spanish ancestry who frequently spoke to retailers in his native language. In several retail outlets Absher noticed that Flores was "very friendly" with women who worked in the checkout areas and supermarket offices. Although they usually spoke in Spanish, which Absher couldn't understand, it was evident that a good deal of "flirting" was going on. This was against company policy and it did not look very professional. Absher did not say anything about it until he could think it through.

On the third day Absher had arranged to meet George McDonald at his first call. It was a little irritating when McDonald was thirty minutes late. His explanation was that he normally does not make his first call until 9 A.M. anyway. Absher also noted that McDonald took more than one hour for lunch and was ready to end the day thirty minutes before the normal quitting time. McDonald had sold a good deal of merchandise but he surely didn't worry much about company policies. He seemed to do things his own way and this was unusual to Absher.

The new division manager was sitting at his desk thinking through the events of the past three days. Each of the three salespersons that he had worked with were good producers but they handled things in strange ways; they were certainly not like any salespersons he had ever worked with before. It was evident that these people had little respect for company policies and that they had not been trained very well. Absher thought about calling Carter but he knew that it would be a sign of weakness to ask for help so soon. He decided that he would simply have to "confront these salespeople and have an understanding as to what will be expected of them in the future."

Question:

How would you advise Absher to handle these men? Why?

16–2   Automotive Supply Products, Inc.

Two people from the Equal Employment Opportunity Commission (EEOC) have recently completed an audit of Automotive Supply Product's (ASP) sales force personnel files. Of the firm's 550 salespeople, none are female or members of minority groups. This week the company received a recommendation from EEOC that their hiring practices be changed. The report stated that minorities must be hired immediately and moved

---

This case was developed by Teresa Scoggins as a requirement for her MBA at Texas A&M University under the supervision of Professor Charles M. Futrell. The company name and individual names have been changed.

into management within two years. In six months EEOC will visit ASP to follow-up on their recommendations.

Changes in Recruiting Practices

Top management had seen this coming for a long time. Each district manager has always been allowed to recruit and hire his own people. However, it was felt this had to change.

In order to better comply with governmental regulations, and in an effort to centralize employment activities, each region's assistant regional sales manager was given the responsibility of college recruiting. This would allow district managers more time with their salespeople.

The Atlanta Sales Region. Dave Appleby had been with ASP for nine years, and has been the assistant regional sales manager for the last two years. Appleby met with each district manager in the Atlanta region to assure them that he would do his best to screen and select the very best applicants for them to choose from. The district manager would still make the final hiring decision. Appleby also asked each manager how many people he would need and for characteristic preferences for salespeople.

Approximately 80 percent of ASP's sales candidates are recruited from colleges. Each December personnel forecasts are made for the coming year. This includes estimates of both new positions and turnover. On-campus interviewing takes place in March, July, and October resulting in over two hundred students being interviewed each year. Typically four students are usually selected for each opening and undergo an in-depth interview at the local district office. After taking tests and interviewing with office personnel, the four are ranked, with the top candidate asked to work for a day with a local salesperson. That person usually receives the first job offer.

Candidates for the Miami District. Archie Burkett is the sales manager for the Miami district. Burkett is fifty-five years old and has worked for ASP for twenty-five years. During his fifteen years in management, Burkett has gained a reputation for doing a good recruiting job. Several of the people he has hired have been promoted into the New York office. At times Burkett would confess that he had trouble making up his mind on whom to hire. However, he looked for people with ego drive, empathy, and a need to achieve success. It seemed to work for him so he used those three characteristics as a guide. Burkett's own yearly performance appraisal always included his hiring success and costs. In addition, hiring successful people meant better sales for his district which resulted in a higher yearly bonus for Burkett and his salespeople.

When the new personnel selection system was announced, Burkett could see advantages and disadvantages. However, he realized that the move would bring minorities into ASP's sales force. Given twenty-seven years of sales experience, Burkett knew men could do a good job. He was unsure of women. He felt he might find it difficult to train and work with a woman. What would happen if he had to criticize her? He could see her begin crying. Also, what about his yearly bonus? If her sales drop, so does his salary. Burkett remembered the comments of several members of his sales force when two women were hired by a competitor. They said women could not stand the pressure; would not stay out overnight; were not dependable; and would only work for a short time, quitting in order to raise a family. Furthermore one salesperson felt that customers would not like a woman trying to sell them ASPs products. Burkett himself had always felt a woman's place was in the home.

In December Burkett asked for and received approval to hire two new salespeople. His sales had increased so that two new territories could be created. In March, Appleby called Burkett to ask when would be the best time for him to interview three students for the two jobs. Burkett was surprised at having so few to interview. However, Appleby felt these were the best candidates with qualifications well above those of the others. All three applicants were to be interviewed the second week in April. Appleby said he had already mailed all applicants' paper work to Burkett for review.

As Burkett examined the applications he was startled to see that two of the three candidates were women, and he felt very uneasy anticipating his first interview with a female. How should he act? Well, he would worry about that when the time arrived. For now he developed a summary of the three people as shown in Exhibit 16–1. Archie ranked the people in this order Green, Davis, then Glenn.

The Interviews. One applicant was interviewed a day. The interviews took place on Tuesday, Wednesday, and Thursday. As they arrived in the morning, Burkett's secretary met them and administered several tests which took about three hours to complete. Burkett took them to lunch and from approximately 2 to 4 P.M. people in the office interviewed

Exhibit 16–1 Biographical Data on the Candidates

1. Kevin Green. Age 23. Industrial distribution major at the University of Alabama; GPA 2.86; earned 80 percent of money for school working part-time and summers. Played offensive end on Alabama's national championship team under Coach Bear Bryant.

2. Clara Davis. Age 24. Marketing major with BBA and MBA from the University of Florida; GPA 3.85 undergraduate and 4.0 graduate. No work experience. School activities include president of sorority and vice-president of the student body. Likes sports and reading.

3. Susan Glenn. Age 23. Psychology major with 3.56 GPA from Georgia State University; hometown Miami; worked in retail sales for father's small automotive parts store part-time for eight years. No school activities.

them. For the first time Archie asked two salespeople, John Bryant and Larry Billingsley, to also interview the applicants.

John Bryant had been hired by Burkett eight years ago. He and Burkett had become close friends and each year spent one week of their vacation fishing together. Larry Billingsley had been hired by Burkett one year ago. Burkett felt he was bright, hard working, and an excellent salesperson. In fact, Burkett considered Billingsley as top management material. Both Bryant and Billingsley were excited about the opportunity to help recruit. All three candidates would be interviewed and the three men would meet the next week to review all material.

After interviewing Kevin Green, Burkett was excited about hiring him. They had spent almost an hour talking about what it was like to play football at Alabama. Bear Bryant was always Burkett's image of the ideal coach. Even though Green worked in the summers in his father's grocery store, he had a lot of free time to fish. The only drawback to hiring Green was that he might be in the professional football draft.

Wednesday, Burkett interviewed Clara Davis. When Burkett first saw Clara he could not believe it. She was one of the best-looking girls he had ever seen. She had a good firm handshake, constant eye contact, beautiful smile, and a charming personality. Burkett had trouble carrying on a conversation with her. She should be in the movies, not in sales, he thought to himself. She asked pointed questions on training, compensation, and advancement. Davis had broken off her engagement a year ago and decided that she wanted to be in sales management at the corporate level. Davis was astonished that ASP had no female salespeople. However, she left no question in Burkett's mind that if she were offered a job and if she accepted it, she would work night and day to advance quickly in the corporation and Burkett believed her.

The next day Burkett visited with Susan Glenn. He had his back to the door when his secretary and Glenn entered the room. As his secretary introduced Glenn, Burkett turned to shake hands. He was speechless when he saw that Glenn was an attractive, black female. This possibility had never entered Burkett's mind. The interview was shorter than the others. Like Davis, Glenn was personable and witty. She asked several questions about training, advancement, and opportunities for women at ASP. Burkett discussed their three-week training program, compensation, and mentioned that ASP would hire qualified women who had the potential for management positions.

What Decision to Make.   Burkett was glad the interviewing was over. This experience was something he felt he would never forget. The next week he, Bryant, and Billingsley met to discuss the applicants. Appleby was also in town so he was invited.

Exhibit 16–2 shows the categories of psychological traits that the applicants were graded on, based on tests they had taken. Scores were reported in terms of a standard score scale with a mean of 50 and a

Exhibit 16–2 California Psychological Inventory

1. Dominance	10. Good impression
2. Capacity for status	11. Communality
3. Social presence	12. Achievement via conformance
4. Self-acceptance	13. Achievement via independence
5. Sense of well-being	14. Intellectual efficiency
6. Responsibility	15. Psychological mindedness
7. Socialization	16. Flexibility
8. Self-control	17. Femininity
9. Tolerance	

standard deviation of 10. The testing company that graded the tests reported the scores and gave a summary for each person. It appeared to Burkett that each of the candidates had scored basically the same. Based on the test results, Burkett saw very few differences. He told Bryant, Billingsley, and Appleby that the tests made his job more difficult because they did not screen out anyone. On a blackboard, Burkett developed the preferences for the applicants shown in Exhibit 16–3. Burkett was openly upset at the differences in preferences. Even though he felt forced to rank the two women second and third, Burkett did not want to hire either of them. When Appleby said let's hire them all, Burkett left the room. Appleby caught him in the hall and calmly reminded him that, if the firm did not hire qualified minority applicants, it would be guilty of government affirmative action violations.

Exhibit 16–3 Preferences for Applicants

Interviewers' Ranking	Kevin Green	Clara Davis	Susan Glenn
Archie Burkett	1	2	3
John Bryant	2	1	3
Larry Billingsley	3	1	2

Questions:

1. What should Burkett do?
2. How would you rank the applicants?
3. Assuming you could only hire two people, whom would you hire?
4. Discuss personnel practices and laws pertaining to this case.
5. What are the problems in the case, if any? If there are problems, what would you recommend?

17

Motivation, Compensation, and Evaluation of Salespeople

Bob James
American Scientific Products

Profile

My name is Bob James. I'm vice president and southwestern area general manager for American Scientific Products Biomedical division, an operating unit of American Hospital Supply Corporation. From my base in Dallas, I am responsible for some 500 people. They include two area managers, six regional sales managers, about 75 sales representatives and some 420 office, warehouse and distribution personnel.

I grew up in Evanston, Illinois, my corporation's home base. At Marquette University, where I majored in business and philosophy, I was in the Naval ROTC. I planned to be a pilot, but had to give up that dream when I broke my neck on my way to Marine air training.

I was 21, a college graduate and an ex-serviceman. I needed a career. My father said an Evanston company—American Hospital Supply Corporation—looked promising. After talking with American's personnel director, I was hired as a sales trainee. That was in 1958. I've been with American Scientific Products Biomedical division ever since.

The sales rep traditionally has been the backbone of America. Sales is seen as an ideal place to demonstrate your abilities quickly, to differentiate yourself from the crowd.

After working three territories, I was one of the division's top salespeople. But I knew management offered long-term career growth and potentially greater compensation. I could stay with sales and continue developing my territory or I could choose the more varied route of management. I chose management, worked my way up and have been in my present position since 1970.

"A manager's most important job is hiring good people," says Bob James. "I look for someone who cares for others, who listens well and is empathetic—someone I would be proud to bring into my home.

"Salespeople should be incisive and able to respond quickly when someone tries to steer them away from their objective. Honesty is essential. We entrust the corporation's reputation and assets to our salespeople.

"I want salespeople who are self-starters, who constantly strive to improve themselves, who lay plans with short- and long-term goals. To motivate such people, a manager must respond quickly to factors that might deter high-level performance. You need to make sure people are doing all that is necessary to become further entrenched in their accounts. If someone gets sloppy, or needs too much direction, bring such matters to their attention constructively. At the same time, compliment people when they do well.

"In evaluating salespeople, you look at sales performance and how well customers' needs are being met. You also look at a person's flexibility, at how well they implement new ideas within their territories.

"A manager needs these same qualities, and more. They must be able to plan, organize, motivate and control. They should have good people skills. And they should have the drive and self-confidence necessary to be comfortable taking me through their game plans for meeting our objectives.

"In the final analysis, the better people you surround yourself with, the better manager you'll be."

Bob James' comments on what it takes to be a successful sales manager lead us into the important areas of motivating, compensating and evaluating salespeople. Much of a sales manager's job involves these three managerial functions. This chapter discusses the motivation, compensation, and performance evaluation of salespeople. We begin by presenting five factors which can be used to motivate salespeople.

Motivation of the Sales Force

Sales managers are concerned with motivating salespeople at two levels. The first is the motivation of the individual salesperson and the second is the motivation of the entire sales force. At both levels, managers should determine how much motivation is needed if the sales personnel are to successfully accomplish their assigned job goals, and they should determine the methods of motivation that are best for the situation at hand. Finally, they should develop a well-designed motivation program that is coordinated with other sales management activities.

Motivation is a term originally derived from the Latin word *movere,* which means "to move," but it has been expanded to include the various factors by which human behavior is activated. Let us define *motivation* as the arousal, intensity, direction, and persistence of effort directed toward job tasks over a period of time. The sales manager strives to increase the motivation of salespeople toward performing their job activities at a high level through the development of a motivation mix.

The Motivation Mix: Choose Your Ingredients Carefully

What can the sales manager do to motivate salespeople? A review of sales management literature reveals five broad classes of factors, all referred to as the **motivation mix,** used to motivate salespeople, as shown in Figure 17–1.[1] Examples of each factor are as follows:

1. The basic compensation plan.
   Salary.
   Commissions.
   Fringe benefits.
2. Special financial incentives.
   Contests.
   Bonuses.
   Promotion.
3. Nonfinancial rewards.
   Achievement awards.
   Challenging work assignments.
   Psychological rewards.
     Praise.
     Recognition.
4. Leadership techniques.
   Style.
   Personal contact methods (feedback).
   National, regional, district meetings.
   Individual meetings.
   Letters, telephone.
5. Management control procedures.
   Performance evaluation.
   Quotas.
   Reports.

Figure 17–1 Sales Manager's Motivation Mix

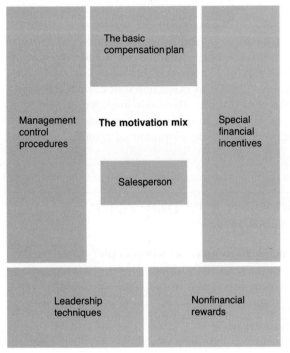

Each of these five factors will be discussed, beginning with compensation.

Methods of Compensating Salespeople

Salespeople are compensated by one of three methods: (1) straight salary, (2) straight commission, or (3) a method using a combination of straight salary and incentives, such as commissions, bonuses, or contests. Each of these compensation methods will be discussed.

Straight Salary

Of all compensation plans, the **straight salary** plan is the simplest. The salesperson is paid a specific dollar amount at regular intervals, usually weekly, semimonthly, or monthly. For example, as shown in Figure 17–2(A), the salesperson earns $12,000 annually regardless of whether that person sells $100,000 or $500,000 in merchandise.

Advantages to the Salesperson. This salary plan can provide a sense of security that a person may require for effective selling because it

Figure 17-2 Examples of Salary Plans

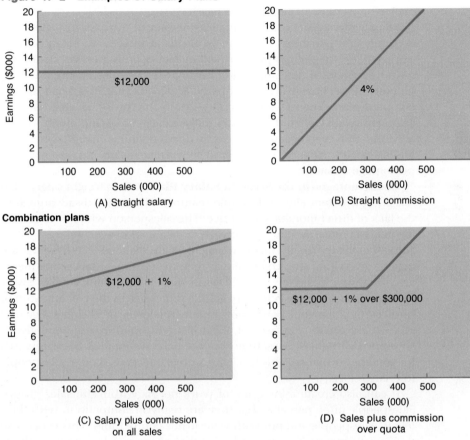

(A) Straight salary

(B) Straight commission

Combination plans

(C) Salary plus commission on all sales

(D) Sales plus commission over quota

ensures a regular income. In theory, pay is independent of sales performance in the short run (a month, three months). However, if performance is low for a prolonged period of time, the company can take corrective action to improve sales or replace the salesperson. High sales performance can be rewarded by a periodic salary increase (every six or twelve months). New recruits and younger salespeople with little sales experience often prefer a compensation plan that gives them a known income.

Advantages to Management. From management's point of view, the plan is simple and economical to administer. Salespeople can be directed toward tasks the company believes are important much more easily than they could if they were on a straight commission plan. Management can direct selling duties which may not immediately result in sales, such as contacting nonproductive accounts or routinely calling on customers who purchase the company's products from a distribution center or wholesaler outside the territory.

Management also usually finds less resistance to reassignments of accounts and personnel transfers with this arrangement. Salespeople are less likely to use high-pressure selling tactics or to overload customers with merchandise that may bring rewards to the salesperson, but not be best for the buyer or the company. Finally, management can project compensation expenses for several years in the future because sales costs are relatively fixed. This can make salary budgeting much more accurate. However, because there is no direct relationship between salary and sales performance, it is difficult to estimate salary expenses as a percentage of sales.

Disadvantages of the Straight Salary Plan. The straight salary plan has several potentially undesirable features. The major disadvantage is the lack of direct monetary incentive. The salesperson who meets certain jog goals is rewarded by an increase in salary. However, salary adjustments are usually made at specified intervals, so that the increase may be given long after the goal was met. In addition, salary adjustments are not always based on specific performance. Often everyone is given the same salary increase or there is little difference in the pay adjustment received by the higher performers and by the lower performers. Because salaries are usually kept secret, even if the top performers were given substantially higher raises, they may not perceive them as being rewards for good performance. This lack of incentive may cause better salespeople to change jobs.

It can also create a lowering of work norms within the sales group. Salespeople often perceive that they are really in competition with their fellow salespeople and not with their firm's competitors. This is because their performance is compared with that of other salespeople in their sales district. They may only want to do an average job and meet or not greatly exceed sales quotas. This arrangement can thus favor the less productive sales people. If not closely supervised, salespeople may accomplish their monthly goals quickly—for example, in three weeks—and not work the rest of the month.

Another problem with the plan is that salary is not distributed in proportion to sales made. One salesperson may sell $500,000 of merchandise and be paid $12,000, while another sells $1 million and also earns $12,000. Also since salaries are a fixed expense of the firm, they cannot be adjusted for downturns in the economy. This can increase direct selling costs as compared to those for other plans. When sales decline, the firm may have to dismiss people. Salespeople who are kept on are often those with the most job tenure and are thus the ones receiving the larger salaries. However, they may not necessarily be the best salespeople. Still another problem of using a straight salary compensation plan is that salespeople may tend to emphasize products that are easiest to sell, especially if this allows them to meet their sales quota.

Many companies increase the number of sales managers to offset these problems. Each manager has fewer salespeople to supervise, helping to ensure that each salesperson is working at maximum capacity. However, this approach usually results primarily in an increase in sales expenses rather than selling effort. The amount of supervision has less effect on performance than the quality of supervision.

When to Use Straight Salary Plans. A straight salary plan is best for jobs in which a high percentage of the work day is devoted to nonselling activities, and for which management finds it cannot effectively evaluate performance. Straight salary can be used effectively for routine selling jobs (selling milk, bread, or beverages), extensive missionary and educational sales (pharmaceutical selling), or sales jobs requiring lengthy presale and postsale service and negotiations (selling technical and complex products). Firms sometimes use this method when the person is in training. For example, some insurance firms pay a salary the first year. After one year the salesperson is placed on a straight commission.

Straight Commission Plans

The **straight commission** plan is a complete incentive compensation plan. If you do not sell anything, you do not earn anything. There are two basic types of commissions plans:

■ Straight commission.

■ Draw against commission.

There are three basic elements of the straight commission plan. First, pay is related directly to a performance unit such as a dollar of sales, a type or amount of product sold, a dollar of profit, type of purchaser, credit terms, or the season of the sales. Second, a percentage rate of commission is attached to the unit. Third, a level at which commissions begin or change is established.

Figure 17–2(B) shows a 4 percent commission on all sales. The salesperson must generate $300,000 in sales to earn the same $12,000 earned by the person under the straight salary plan.

In addition to the single commission plan, multiple commission rates sometimes are used. For example, a 10 percent commission may be paid on the first $100,000 of sales and 12 percent on sales over that amount in the same year. A person who sold $300,000 would receive $34,000 in commissions. When the commission rate increases, it is referred to as a "progressive" commission plan.

On the other hand, some companies use a "regressive" plan by which commission rates decrease as sales increase, such as paying 12 percent on the first $100,000 and 10 percent on sales of that amount. For sales of $300,000 the salesperson would receive $32,000. The regressive system is used to help place an upper limit on a salesperson's earnings in order to encourage top producers to accept management positions if they want to increase their earnings beyond the level attainable in a sales job. In some companies a top salesperson can earn more than a boss.

Drawing Accounts.   One version of the straight line commission plan is known as the drawing account. It combines the incentive of a commission plan with the security of a fixed income. The firm establishes a monetary account for each salesperson. The amount may be based on the individual needs of the salesperson, a base level set by the company, or a base level that takes into consideration the individual salesperson's needs, background, and selling potential.

The salesperson may believe that $1,000 a month is needed to meet base expenditures for that period. Thus at the beginning of the month a draw of $1,000 against commission for that month is given. If sales for a particular month resulted in commissions of $1,100, at the end of the month the company would pay $100 in commissions. Conversely, if commissions earned for that month amounted to only $300, the salesperson would owe the company $700.

Management must monitor each salesperson closely to prevent a negative balance on salary from becoming so large that it is difficult, if not impossible, to repay it. Should the balance become large, the possibility of repayment may be so discouraging that the salesperson might feel compelled to quit the job. Though many firms have contractual agreements calling for repayment of negative balances against a drawing account, collecting an overdraft can be difficult. Some firms use a guaranteed drawing account plan in which the salesperson does not have to pay back overdrafts. Such a plan is actually a salary plus commission.

Advantages of Straight Commission Plans.   Many sales managers believe that the commission plan provides maximum incentive for their salespeople. They know that their earnings are contingent upon selling the firm's products. This expectancy of reward based upon performance should direct salespeople to use their sales time wisely and to perform at maximum capacity. It is the reason many people are attracted to commission sales jobs. Only their own abilities limit their earning potential and no arbitrary earnings decisions can be made by management.

Salespeople often feel that they are in business for themselves. This can be seen as a benefit. If they are fired or leave their employer voluntarily, they can often continue the same business relationship with their customers after taking a job with another company. In addition, more and more people are attracted to part-time commission sales jobs, such as selling real estate or consumer products (e.g., Avon) because of the earning potential. They can call on accounts that they feel are productive, determine their own work schedules, and set their own hours.

Many organizations prefer to use the commission plan because it is simple to administer and selling costs are kept in proportion to sales. This is very important to a new firm that cannot afford to pay a portion of its salespeople a salary if they are not profitably productive, or in case of an economic recession which could cause sales costs to severely affect profits. The firm with limited capital can hire as many salespeople as needed and have no salary costs until sales are made.

Payment is made to the salesperson at the time of the sale, when the order is shipped, or when the order is paid for. For some types of sales, the salesperson may continue to receive payment in the future as long as the product or service is purchased by the customer. Commissions for life insurance policy premiums are an example.

Disadvantages of the Commission Plan.   Straight commission plans have several potential disadvantages. One, particularly for the person who has never sold before, is the uncertainty and insecurity of the plan. The salesperson must sell in order to be paid. This is fine for the company, but may discourage people from seeking sales careers. With some big sales volume items, a long period of time may elapse before a person makes a sale. For example, in commercial real estate it is not uncommon for a person to make only one, two, or three sales a year. These sales often result in large commissions, but the individual must have enough funds to live on between commissions. The uncertainty and insecurity of straight commission sales jobs can lead to high turnover and thus high expenses and sales costs for recruiting, selection, and training of new salespeople.

Often, salespeople on commission develop little loyalty for the company. While feeling that they are in business for themselves can have benefits for salespeople, the company may have difficulty in controlling or channeling salespeople's efforts. Salespeople on commission select their customers and their products, and in a few cases they may use high-pressure techniques to close sales because they will not see their customers again.

Under the straight commission plan, salespeople are much more reluctant to split territories or move from their present territory to another territory. They may have spent time building up a rapport with their customers and do not want to relinquish it. This can pose difficulties for the employer. In addition, with straight commission, service after the sale may be neglected.

The cost of sales may be somewhat greater with a straight commission plan even though a greater sales volume is produced. Salespeople can earn more pay per dollar of sale on straight commission than they can on salary plans. Commissions can fluctuate greatly. In good times, salespeople may earn large commissions, but in an economic recession their earnings may drop drastically through no fault of their own.

Because of the disadvantages of the straight commission plan for employees, sales managers often take for granted a high turnover of sales personnel. Such turnover makes it difficult to build an experienced sales force. Sales managers may hire salespeople quickly, without thorough selection and recruitment, because they realize that if the people do not produce, they will not be with the company for very long. This lack of recruitment, training, and supervision results in an increase in sales costs and loss of potential sales.

The firm using the straight commission plan must work with the salespeople to set realistic sales goals that will allow the salesperson and the firm to meet their objectives. Because performance or sales activities to some extent are dictated by the marketplace and the salesperson's customers, management must reward the behavior or selling activities it seeks from the sales force. For example, different commission rates on different products could be used to deter the salesperson from concentrating on the easy-to-sell, low profit margin items. A lower commission rate could be placed on easy-to-sell products and higher commission rates paid on harder-to-sell products. Bonuses could also be established for the products which the company wants the sales force to concentrate on or a higher commission rate could be placed on these products.

Administrative Problems with the Commission Plan. With today's complex distribution channels and exchange processes, the proper allocation of commissions to salespeople can be a problem. The company must carefully examine the process through which the sales exchange is made to determine their commission compensation policies. Administrative policies must be developed for each of these circumstances to provide proper compensation of sales personnel and to prevent morale problems. For example, if two or more salespeople are involved in a sale, the fair distribution of commissions can be a problem. Should two salespeople put an equal amount of time and effort into the sale, the commission can easily be split on a 50–50 basis. However, if the two salespeople differ in their perception of each person's input, a dispute may arise over the percentage each should earn. One solution is for management to base all commissions that are made by two or more salespeople on the number of sales in which they were involved during that period.

Another potential problem is what to do when there are bad debts. A salesperson may have sold a product or products to a customer who is unable to pay or goes bankrupt. If the salesperson is not directly responsible for the extension of credit to accounts, most firms will not withdraw a commission. The same is true in the case of sales returns.

If a small number of items sold are returned, the company may not deduct money from commissions. However, many firms look at net sales. If, for example, a salesperson sold $11,000 worth of merchandise this month and had returns of $1,000, the company would pay a commission based on sales of $10,000.

Combination Plans

Under a **combination salary plan,** a proportion of the salesperson's total pay is guaranteed while some of it can come from commissions. The most commonly used percentage split is 80 percent base salary and 20 percent incentive. A 70/30 and 60/40 split are the next most common combinations.

Various combinations of salary plus incentives can be used by a company. The more popular plans are the following:

Salary and commission.

Salary and bonus:

   Individual bonus.

   Group bonus.

Salary, commission, and bonus:

   Individual bonus.

   Group bonus.

Figure 17–2C and D illustrate the two popular versions of a combination plan. Figure 17–2C shows earnings of $12,000, plus one percent commission on all sales. Sales of $300,000 earn the salesperson $15,000. Figure 17–2D illustrates a salary plus commission over a sales quota. In this example, the salesperson who sells $300,000 earns one percent on all additional sales. The quota of $300,000 may be based on meeting last year's actual sales or it may represent a sales quota above last year's actual sales.

Bonus: Individual or Group

In addition to combination plans based on salary and commissions, many firms use a bonus system. Bonuses can be used with any basic compensation plan. A **bonus** is something given in addition to what is usually earned by the salesperson. Typically, it is money earned over an extended time period, such as one year.

Across-the-Board Bonus. One type of bonus includes the Christmas or year-end bonus, which is given to all salespeople regardless of their productivity. An equal sum of money may be paid to each salesperson or the bonus may be based on present salary and tenure with the organization. The Upjohn Company pays a Christmas bonus of 1.5

percent of the annual salary to salespeople who have been with the firm for one to two years and 2 percent to those who have been with the firm for two or three years. The percentage may go as high as 8 percent. The bonus is paid on an individual basis and is not related to an employee's performance.

Performance Bonus. The second type of bonus is related to performance. Numerous bonus plans of this type can be devised, but they fall into two general categories according to whether they are awarded on an individual or group basis. Bonuses can be awarded not only on the basis of sales or units sold, but also on the basis of gross profit margins, on sales performance appraisals, on new accounts acquired, on company or geographical sales unit earnings or sales, and on sales of specific products.

A sales region may be given a bonus amount based on its performance as compared to that of other sales regions in the organization. The regional sales manager would then allocate a certain amount to each sales district according to performance. The district manager could distribute the district bonus equally among all salespeople, or use a merit system based on individual performance.

Sales Contests. Another compensation variable for influencing salespeople's performance is the sales contest. **Sales contests** are special sales programs offering salespeople incentives to achieve short-term sales goals. The incentives may include items that indicate recognition of achievement (e.g., certificates, cash, merchandise, or travel).[2] Occasionally contests may run for as long as a year; examples include the insurance or real estate industry's "Million Dollar Club." The incentives are given in addition to regular compensation.

It is estimated that over $4 billion was spent on sales contests in 1983. Of that, industry spent an estimated $2 billion on sales incentives, with 78 percent spent on merchandise awards and 22 percent on incentive travel programs.[3] Up until the late 1960s there was little use of incentive travel programs. However, as corporations attempted to find means of motivating salespeople to top last year's performance, travel was used increasingly to glamorize sales programs. Figure 17–3 illustrates how Harrah's Hotel advertises to attract winners of sales contests to their luxury hotel. Offering merchandise and cash keeps such programs flexible.

The sales contest is an effective incentive method that is used to intensify, direct, and make salespeople more persistent in their work effort over a given period of time. Salespeople will tend to work harder to meet contest goals and thereby earn rewards. Management can direct salespeople to sell specific products or to perform activities they would not normally do through the use of contest incentives. Contests can also cause salespeople to work harder for longer periods of time (persistence) to achieve the contest goals and earn extra rewards. As

Figure 17–3 Sales Contest Winners Go to Harrah's Tahoe

Courtesy of Harrah's Hotels
and Casinos, Reno, Nevada.

one executive in the cosmetic industry stated, "Our incentive program allows us to apply no direct sales pressure while motivating the salespeople, and to reward those who reach company-approved goals. Contests·have helped this company increase sales from $7.8 million to over $31 million in five years."[4]

Contests are used to directly influence several aspects of the salesperson's job, typically, to increase sales volume for a specific product or to find new customers. For example, Crest Communities, a Cincinnati-based real estate firm, sold 1,473 homes in 150 days when offering travel rewards.[5] Another company offered a weekend in Las Vegas to customers and salespeople. It provided the incentive for salespeople to call on noncustomers, and they made sales to fifty dormant accounts in three months. This alone more than paid for the contest. Sara Lee bakery products used a "Top Dough" contest to increase sales.[6] Rockwell International's industrial power tools division uses a T-N-T (Trips 'N Treats) catalog featuring brand-name gifts, and air miles applicable to domestic or international travel.[7]

Sales contests can have several indirect influences on salespeople. Many sales managers feel that these contests, as well as bonuses, can increase the "team spirit" of their sales group, interest in the job, job satisfaction, and can discourage absenteeism and turnover.

The Total Compensation Package

People choose a sales career for both nonfinancial and financial reasons. The salesperson receives numerous forms of financial compensation. Figure 17–4 illustrates the dollar value one company places on its total compensation for the beginning salesperson.

Monthly salary, including fringe benefits, equals $2,428.67, which is $628.67 a month above the base salary of $1,800. In addition, the salesperson participates in an incentive bonus plan, plus ten additional benefits. Thus, it is not surprising that a sales career is attractive to thousands of people.

Nonfinancial Rewards Are Many

Nonfinancial rewards can be very effective in motivating salespeople. The sales manager can reward a salesperson for achieving sales goals with bonuses and other awards. Achievement or recognition awards are commonly presented at sales meetings. While there are usually no financial benefits associated with achievement awards, winning salespeople receive recognition from their managers and fellow salespeople that tends to motivate them to work harder.

Salespeople who do well may be transferred to larger, more challenging sales territories or promoted to key account manager. This recognizes their contribution to the company and serves as further motivation. Furthermore, little personal things such as a sales manager's praise can motivate a salesperson to improve performance.

Figure 17–4 Example of a Company's Salary and Fringe Benefits for a New Representative (based on starting salary of $1,800 per month, with automatic increase to $1,900 on the completion of training)

Starting Salary before Completion of Training (annual):

$21,600.00	($1,800.00/month)—base salary
1,944.00	Company contribution to pension plan for future service only (9 percent)
1,000.00	Company contribution to group health insurance, major medical and life insurance plans
100.00	Telephone allowance
4,500.00	Estimated value of having a car at your disposal
$29,144.00	Total salary
2,428.67	Monthly salary including fringe benefits

Plus an incentive bonus plan determined on relative attainment of sales forecast

Additional benefits that are not measured in dollars, but which contribute materially to your standard of living, as well as to your security and development:

1. Under 5 years, two weeks' vacation; after 5 years, three weeks' vacation; after 15 years, four weeks' vacation; after 25 years, five weeks' vacation.
2. Seven paid holidays.
3. Christmas furlough.
4. Pension plan that is rated as one of the best in the industry.
5. Group health insurance and major medical plan cover not only the Representative but also spouse and unmarried children under 19, and student children to age 26. Continuance of 20 percent of life insurance after retirement at age 60 or later without cost to employee.
6. Liberal sick pay plan.

Total Period Covered

Years of Service	Full Base Pay (weeks)	Half Base Pay (weeks)
Under 5 years	4	12
Over 5 years	8	12
Over 10 years	10	12
Over 15 years	12	12
Over 21 years	16	12

7. New long-term disability plan. LTD provides financial security for you and your family for period of continuous total disability extending beyond the benefits provided under the sick and accident plan or the company workman's compensation supplement.
8. Employees' education fund pays half tuition for approved courses successfully completed, if the Representative is employed less than one year; 75 percent of tuition after one year.
9. Twenty weeks intensive training followed by constant supervision and guidance by district sales manager.
10. Regular reviews of job performance for salary consideration.

It is up to the manager to develop ways of creating a work environment in which performing well is a rewarding experience to the salesperson, even though no pay raise, bonus, or contest is involved. Good job performance should give the salesperson a feeling of accomplishment and satisfaction. Special nonfinancial awards, certificates, medals, and praise are an important part of the manager's motivational mix.

Leadership Is Important to Success

In a recent survey, nearly 500 sales and marketing managers working for some 450 companies of all sizes were asked to rank what they considered the most important factors in managing their firms' sales force. Leadership was ranked first. The second most important factor was the sales manager's ability to motivate salespeople.[8]

Leadership is the process by which the sales manager attempts to influence the activities of salespeople. Figure 17–5 is an illustration of the basic influence process involved in leadership. As shown, the leadership process begins with an intent on the part of person A, followed by an attempt to influence person B, who then reacts in some way that fulfills the intent of person A. An example would be the sales manager attempting to influence each salesperson toward attaining certain performance goals. The manager who possesses the leadership capabilities necessary to influence all salespeople to reach their sales goals will be able to attain the goals assigned to the whole group.

What makes a person a successful leader? How can a potentially successful sales manager be identified? Three major approaches have been explored to answer these questions: the (1) trait approach, (2) behavioral approach, and (3) situational approach.

Trait Approach

Up until forty years ago, most people assumed that leaders were born, not made, and that a person became a leader because of certain personality characteristics. Consequently, researchers attempted to identify the traits that differentiated leaders from followers. According to the **trait leadership approach,** there is a set of characteristics that distinguish successful from unsuccessful leaders. This was the simplest, oldest, and, until the late 1940s, the main method of determining the elements of effective leadership.

This approach asked the question: "What are the traits of successful

Figure 17–5 **Leadership Influence Process**

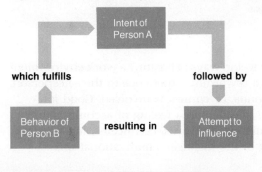

leaders?" Once these traits were determined, it was felt that a firm could hire people who have these characteristics and therefore are effective leaders. A long and growing list of traits have been investigated—for example, a person's physical characteristics, social background, intelligence, and personality. Yet no traits have been established as universally characteristic of successful leaders.

Behavioral Approach

Because the attempt to identify the traits that distinguish leaders was unsuccessful, from the late 1940s to the early 1960s, attention was turned to studying styles of leadership. This meant behavior that could be learned, that was not innate. It was felt that successful leaders may be recognized by their behavior patterns. The **behavioral leadership approach** assumes that effective leaders are distinguished by their particular style of leadership in various situations.

The Ohio State University Studies. In the late 1940s two major studies of leadership were begun at Ohio State University and the University of Michigan. As a result of the work done at Ohio State, two major dimensions of leadership behavior were identified: **initiating structure** and **consideration.**

Initiating structure. This is referred to as a "task-oriented" leadership style because the leader's behavior is aimed at getting the job or task done. A sales manager of this type would:

Emphasize reaching sales goals.

Offer new approaches to selling a prospect.

Criticize poor work.

Assign salespeople to particular tasks.

Consideration. This is a "salesperson-oriented" leadership style. The leader's behavior indicates trust, warmth, respect, and concern for the salesperson's welfare. This kind of leader would:

Be friendly and easily approached.

Back up salespeople in their actions.

Help salespeople with personal problems.

See that salespeople are rewarded for jobs well done.

As shown in Figure 17–6, a leader can be rated in terms of these two leadership styles. Research in this area found no single best leadership style. A combination of the initiating structure and consideration behavior based on the individual situation was found to result in the highest performance. Thus, one sales manager might find the high-high style (high initiating structure-high consideration) successful, whereas another manager might use the same style and be unsuccessful.

Figure 17–6 Leadership Styles: Initiating Structure and Consideration

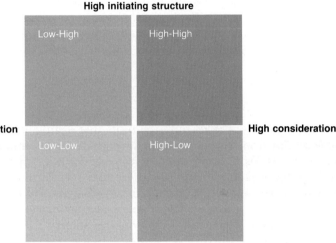

High initiating structure

Low-High | High-High

Low consideration | High consideration

Low-Low | High-Low

Low initiating structure

Furthermore, the manager successfully using the high-high style in one situation may find it ineffective in another situation.

The University of Michigan Studies.   At the University of Michigan, what were called "job-centered" and "employee-centered" leadership styles were studied. These are similar to the initiating structure and consideration styles, respectively, of the Ohio State studies. The results showed that the employee-centered leadership style was best. Both styles actually improved performance; however, a leader using a job-centered style created tensions and pressures that resulted in lower job satisfaction and increased turnover and absenteeism. As with the Ohio State results, it was found that the style of behavior of leaders changes from situation to situation. The leader may be friendly and helpful to subordinates if all is going well, but criticize poor work if performance decreases.

Situational Approach

The trait and behavioral approaches provided the background for the study of leadership in terms of individual situations. The key to a sales manager's effectiveness, according to the **situational approach,** is based on the ability to diagnose a salesperson's situation, and then to select the leadership style that will influence that salesperson to reach the desired performance.

Researchers have identified a number of leadership styles used by sales managers. Four of the basic styles are: (1) an **achievement-oriented** style which involves establishing performance goals that are challenging, while letting salespeople know the manager has confidence that they will achieve goals; (2) a **supportive style** characterized by concern for salespeople's welfare, needs, and well-being; (3) an **instrumental style** involving telling salespeople of what is expected of them—the sales manager is primarily concerned with salespeople performing their tasks effectively so as to allow them to reach their job goals; and (4) a **participative style** in which salespeople take part in setting job goals, and use their own ideas and creativity in accomplishing them.

There are five different styles of participative behavior, shown in Figure 17–7. The behavior at the left is an **autocratic style,** and the behavior at the right is a **democratic style.** Depending on the situation and subordinates, the manager can choose a participative behavior style ranging from highly autocratic to highly democratic. The salesperson has more influence over the job as the sales manager's leadership style

Figure 17–7   Different Participative Styles of Sales Managerial Behavior

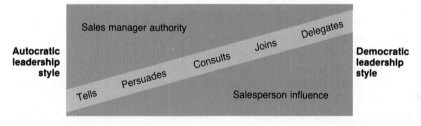

moves to the left. These five participative styles of leadership behavior are described as follows:

- *Telling.*   The sales manager identifies problems and opportunities, makes all decisions, and tells salespeople what to do. A "do it or else" approach is usually used.
- *Persuading.*   As above, the sales manager makes decisions; however, the salesperson's cooperation is sought.
- *Consulting.*   The sales manager presents the problem or situation and asks the salesperson for suggestions on how to act. The sales manager decides what is the most appropriate action.
- *Joining.*   Within the restrictions imposed by superiors, the sales manager is part of the "sales team," and acts as a participant in the decision-making process. The sales manager agrees in advance to support the decision of the group.
- *Delegating.*   The sales manager presents the problem or situation and allows the salesperson to act, giving total support to the salesperson's decision. The success or failure of the action is the responsibility of the salesperson.[9]

Choosing a Leadership Style

While there is no one best way to lead salespeople in all situations, there are leadership techniques that can be used to improve a manager's effectiveness. These are:

- Be familiar with each salesperson's territory, customers, and personal circumstances in order to properly diagnose the person's situation.
- Have the flexibility to be autocratic or democratic when dealing with a salesperson based upon the situation—for example, being democratic with the high-performing salesperson and autocratic with the low performer.
- Clearly show salespeople the path or way to reach their goals.
- Play the role of a coach whose aim is to aid salespeople to reach their personal and territorial goals.
- Develop technical, human, and conceptual skills.

A more specific example of how one chooses a leadership style based on the situation can be seen through this example. A district sales manager (we will call him Bruce) for a large national consumer goods manufacturer, discussed the four styles of leadership he uses in leading his sales group. These four styles are illustrative of some of the situational influences that dictate a particular leadership style.

First, Bruce uses "management by objectives." He develops no more than two yearly objectives for each of his salespeople (such as placing major emphasis on a single product or concentrating on accomplishing certain objectives for a single large account) based on the situation in an individual territory. In this context, Bruce uses instrumental, participative, and achievement-oriented leadership techniques.

Second, Bruce uses "management by THE objective." In all companies there are times when the home office tells the sales force that they are expected to meet certain sales goals. The directive is given to Bruce by upper management and he informs his people that they are expected to reach certain sales goals (such as a 10 percent increase in sales of all sizes of a particular product). He uses instrumental and achievement-oriented leadership techniques in this instance.

Third, Bruce uses "management by motivation." The salespeople doing what is expected of them are given recognition. Having reached a certain level of performance, salespeople become members of an "All Star Team." Letters are also sent to Bruce's boss, Joe, informing him of a salesperson's success. Joe writes personal letters to the salespeople congratulating them on their performance. These are short-term motivators; raises, commissions, and promotions are used as long-term motivators. Supportive and achievement-oriented techniques are applied here.

Fourth, Bruce uses "management by terror." Behavioral researchers have long known that people are motivated not only by a need to achieve, but also by a fear of failure. Twice each year he evaluates performance and continually gives salespeople feedback on their strengths and on where they can improve. Of course, there are times when all managers have to inform people that, unless their performance improves, they should look for another job. This involves instrumental and achievement-oriented techniques.

Only one leadership style is consistently used by Bruce: the achievement-oriented technique. This is typical in sales positions because of the great emphasis placed on performance.

Performance Evaluations Let People Know Where They Stand

Achieving acceptable levels of performance is essential for the organization to stay in business and for the salesperson to reach personal goals. A major part of the manager's job is to lead and motivate salespeople to perform at an acceptable level. At the end of each performance period, such as the end of the year, the manager evaluates each salesperson's performance. This creates a **management control system** which establishes performance goals, evaluates the goals compared to the salesperson's accomplishments and then rewards or penalizes the individual based upon the performance level.[10]

Reasons for Performance Evaluation

In a very general sense, performance evaluations are carried out for three reasons: (1) to appraise a salesperson's past performance; (2) to develop a sales plan to increase the salesperson's future sales; and (3) to motivate salespeople to improve their performance. Sales managers' evaluations provide the basis for numerous decisions on salary, promotions, transfers, demotions, and dismissal.

Appraisal sessions involve giving face-to-face feedback to the salespeople on quality of performance, getting to know each other better, and gaining an understanding of what each person expects from the other.

Who Should Evaluate Salespeople?

The primary evaluator should be the salesperson's immediate superior because this person has direct knowledge about sales performance. The manager has actually worked with the salesperson. In some companies the immediate superior completes the entire evaluation, including

Figure 17–8 Possible Management Input into Salesperson's Performance Evaluation

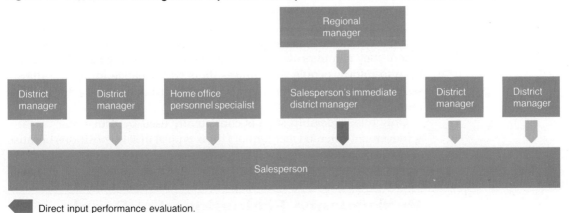

Direct input performance evaluation.

Indirect input performance evaluation.

recommendations for pay raises and promotions. The evaluations and recommendations are sent to the manager's immediate superior for final approval. The manager's superior accepts the recommendations without question. In the majority of organizations several managers evaluate each salesperson. The simplest approach is for the district manager and the regional sales manager to arrive at an evaluation together. The other district managers in the region may also express their opinion when the region's entire management group gets together periodically.

Many companies use the entire region's management group and a home office personnel specialist to evaluate salespeople's work, as shown in Figure 17–8. The specialist presents the home office viewpoint by making sure that the evaluation procedures are followed and that each person is treated fairly.

When Should Salespeople Be Evaluated?

Salespeople should be evaluated at the end of each performance cycle. A performance cycle is a time period related to specific product goals and/or job activities. For example, consumer goods manufacturers typically have certain products they want to emphasize periodically. They may have six performance cycles during the year. Every two months the sales force is given specific sales goals for five to ten different products. It is necessary to compare goals to results after each cycle. In addition, salespeople are monitored monthly in terms of the other products they sell.

These periodic performance evaluations provide the input for semiannual and/or annual performance evaluations. These performance evaluations provide important feedback to both management and salespeople. A minimum of one formal evaluation should be completed yearly for each salesperson.

Performance Criteria

Companies examine their salespeoples' jobs; determine the important parts of the job; and develop performance criteria based upon their findings. These performance criteria serve as the bases for evaluating a salesperson's performance. They are of two types—quantitative and qualitative.

Quantitative Performance Criteria. Of the two categories of performance criteria, the **quantitative criteria** is the best for effectively evaluating performance. This category represents end results or bottom-line objective data, such as:

Sales volume:
- Percentage of increase.
- Market share.
- Quotas obtained.

Average sales calls per day.

New customers obtained.

Gross profit by product, customer, and order size.

Ratio of selling costs to sales.

Sales orders.
- Daily number of orders.
  - Total.
  - By size, customer classification, and product.
- Order to sales call ratio.
- Goods returned.

Qualitative Performance Criteria. Many organizations use **qualitative performance criteria** because they represent the salesperson's major job activities and they indicate why the quantitative measures look as they do. Care should be taken to minimize the evaluator's personal biases and subjectivity in evaluating qualitative performance criteria. Examples of such criteria include:

Sales skills.
- Finding selling points.
- Product knowledge.
- Listening skill.
- Obtaining participation.
- Overcoming objections.
- Closing the sale.

Territory management.

    Planning.

    Use of time.

    Records.

    Customer service.

    Collections.

    Follow-up.

Personal traits.

    Attitude.

    Empathy.

    Human relations skills.

    Team spirit.

    Appearance.

    Motivation.

    Care of car.

    Capacity for self-improvement.

Evaluation Guidelines

Typically, the company sets up procedures for who will do the evaluation and how it will be done. The performance criteria for evaluation have been decided and materials, such as evaluation forms, are available. The following is a basic guideline for an effective performance evaluation.

Both Manager and Salesperson Should Be Prepared for the Interview. The manager should collect all information on the performance of the salesperson. The manager should then contact the salesperson and establish a time and place for the evaluation. The salesperson should be asked to review past performance using the actual evaluation forms, and to review the job description. This takes place before the formal meeting. Quantitative data should be used when possible.

Be Positive. It is extremely important that both manager and salesperson feel that the evaluation is a positive method of helping the salesperson do the job better. The salesperson may feel required to defend rather than explain past performance. Two examples may help to illustrate negative and positive approaches to evaluation:

Manager: Well, Lou, it's that time of the year again.

Salesperson: I'm looking forward to it!

Manager: I didn't have time to review your file, Lou, but I know you really messed up this year on the Goodyear account.

Salesperson: Well?

Manager: Well nothing! I really got chewed out by the regional manager over that.

Salesperson:	Did you look at my total performance? Sales were up 5 percent above the district average.
Manager:	All right, all right, so you're doing OK, but why did you lose the Goodyear account?

The manager is not prepared to talk to Lou. Lou is on the defensive from the very beginning. It is no wonder neither of them looks forward to this confrontation. Compare this negative approach to a performance evaluation to the following positive one.

Manager:	Lou, it is great we can get together and discuss your achievements and your goals.
Salesperson:	I'm looking forward to it!
Manager:	You know I'm pleased with your sales. You're 5 percent above the district average, that's great! You're doing a good job in managing your territory.
Salesperson:	I'm glad you noticed. You know, I often feel I'm out there all by myself.
Manager:	Well, Lou, you're not! Is there anything I can do to help you?
Salesperson:	Well, things are going good.
Manager:	What about the Goodyear account?
Salesperson:	I sure hated to lose them. My competitor got their business with a low price. But they aren't happy with the service or the products. I'll have that account back in my pocket before you know it!
Manager:	I know you will. Lou, we are here today to develop ways to make you the best salesperson in the best district and this is the best district the company has.
Salesperson:	Sounds great to me. What can I do?
Manager:	Did you use the forms I sent you to evaluate your performance?
Salesperson:	Sure did.
Manager:	What did you find out?
Salesperson:	Well, there are a few areas I need to look at.
Manager:	OK, but before we get to those, remember we are here to evaluate your performance in order to help you. You and I will work out a plan for this coming year that will allow you to continue to do the good job that you want to do. How does that sound?
Salesperson:	In other words, ways I can make more money and maybe earn a promotion.
Manager:	That's right. Ways for you to grow and prosper with our company.

These examples point to the need for both people to have a positive attitude toward the evaluation. The manager should believe in the positive effects this talk will have on Lou's future performance and attitude toward his job. The manager has sold Lou on the purpose of their meeting. The evaluation has been prepared for and its purpose agreed upon by both the manager and the salesperson.

Actually Review Performance. Again the manager should be sincere and positive in discussing each of Lou's performance criteria. There will be disagreements. Research has shown that people will tend to evaluate themselves better than their superior does. It is important to:

Freely discuss each performance criterion.

Ask salespeople to discuss their performance.

Ask salespeople to evaluate their own performance.

Give the manager's view of performance.

Finalize the Performance Evaluation.   The manager should now review each performance area with the salesperson. It is preferable to begin by reviewing the high ratings and work down. The salesperson should understand clearly what has been decided upon. If there are disagreements, the manager should explain carefully why the salesperson receives a low evaluation in a particular performance area. Serious differences of opinion can occur when the salesperson does not fully understand what was expected.

Summarize the Total Performance Evaluation.   The salesperson should be told how the manager views past performance. For example: "Susan, you have done above average work this year. You are continuing to improve year after year, and will receive a good raise. If you continue this level of performance, in a few more years you will be ready for a management position."

"Sam, this is the second year in a row your sales have decreased while the district's have increased. This has to change if you are to stay with the company. I don't want to do this, but you have six months to get your territory turned around."

Develop Mutually Agreed on Objectives.   Performance and career objectives can be established now. Both manager and salesperson provide input.

Formalize Evaluation and Objectives.   Immediately after the evaluation session is over, the manager should write a letter to the salesperson restating the results of the performance evaluation and the objectives. A copy is sent to the manager's superior to go into the salesperson's permanent personnel file.

Summary of Major Sales Management Issues

An important challenge of the sales manager is to motivate salespeople using financial and nonfinancial methods. Salary, commissions, contests, bonuses, and travel awards are common financial motivators.

Achievement awards, challenging work assignments, recognition, leadership techniques, and performance evaluation are nonfinancial methods used as motivators.

Today salespeople are paid by several methods but most firms use a combination of salary and financial incentives rather than straight salary or straight commission plans. This provides the salesperson with a guaranteed salary and helps motivate them to reach their sales goals in order to earn commissions and bonuses or to win contests.

The sales manager needs to understand the principles of leadership and apply them to salespeople based upon their individual personalities and territorial situations. It is important to be both people oriented and job oriented toward salespeople in order to help them reach their sales goals. This ultimately helps to reach the manager's goals.

A person's performance is evaluated by comparing their quotas and objectives to their actual sales and job activities to determine their success. The salesperson's immediate manager carries out periodic evaluations each year using both quantitative and qualitative performance criteria.

To effectively evaluate salespeople, managers should develop procedures to assure fair treatment. By being prepared for the interview and having a positive attitude, the salesperson will be receptive to the manager's critique. The manager should evaluate each performance criterion and explain the evaluation to the salesperson. A discussion of the salesperson's past performance concludes the interview.

Future performance quotas and objectives can now be established to serve as goals to reach for the upcoming sales period.

This and the previous chapter have introduced you to the challenging job of a sales manager and concludes the discussion of the fundamentals of selling and sales management.

Review and Discussion Questions

1. What is meant by motivation? What can a sales manager do to motivate salespeople?
2. What are the major methods used to compensate salespeople? Discuss each methods's advantages and disadvantages.
3. Briefly discuss the history and present-day knowledge concerning leadership. What procedures should a sales manager follow in order to be a successful leader?
4. Discuss why salespeople's performance should be evaluated; who should evaluate their performance; when they should be evaluated; and proper procedures for evaluating performance.

<table>
<tr><td>

Project

</td><td>

Visit a sales manager of a local real estate firm and a sales manager of a national corporation and compare how each company goes about motivating their salespeople. Ask each sales manager about the company's leadership style. Finally, determine the performance criteria and procedures each manager uses to evaluate salespeople.

</td></tr>
<tr><td>

Cases

</td><td>

17–1 Surgical Supplies Incorporated

The marketing vice-president for Surgical Supplies Incorporated (SSI), a manufacturer and distributor of medical supplies and equipment, was reviewing the company's method of compensation at the end of 1983. SSI was second in the industry in total sales to American Hospital Supplies. The company's main offices were located in Richmond, Virginia, with plants in Florida, Texas, California, and Michigan. The sales force consisted of over 600 people supervised by sixty sales managers.

SSI had a variety of products that required different levels of selling skills. Their equipment line consisted of such items as X-ray machines, cast saws, therapeutic equipment, prosthesis parts, and dictaphone machines. The medical supplies line included all types of medicines, cast material, bandages, splits, and syringes. To sell both lines the salesperson had to receive a good deal of training. These products were sold to hospitals and to physicians who had their own medical practices.

The Role of the Salespeople.   The salesperson was expected to search for new accounts, service existing accounts, and maintain goodwill between the company and its clients. A typical day might find the salesperson calling on a hospital in the morning. Here, he would check on emergency room needs, the material supplies office, and administrative offices. Afterwards, he might set up a display in the hospital next to the doctor's parking lot. Later, the salesperson might begin making calls on offices located in the immediate area. Usually a salesperson could make several individual calls because the private offices were generally located near the hospitals. A call might be made to introduce new products to the doctor or it might simply be to check with the nurses about replenishing supplies. If the former was the case, a special time might have to be scheduled. Major products often required selling on the weekends.

The products, such as X-ray equipment, could cost as much as $30,000 while other products might not cost more than $10. Generally, the

</td></tr>
</table>

This case was developed by Mr. Rich Knight, under the supervision of Professor Charles M. Futrell. The company name and geographical location have been changed.

individual accounts placed orders for supplies that would last about two weeks. However, hospital accounts, because of the larger storage rooms, normally ordered on a monthly basis. In addition, the hospitals, which had staffs in charge of their inventory, would usually send in their order forms without the help of a salesperson. SSI policy was to check with these people on a regular basis whether they needed any additional help or not. Salespersons were not expected to repair the X-ray machines although they did clean film processors and service other minor problems, such as replacing the special batteries for dictaphones.

Sales Force Compensation. Bill Woodson, a marketing vice president, had brought up the idea of examining the firm's sales force compensation. He believed two areas involving sales personnel needed improvement—sales force turnover and number of sales calls.

Sales managers did some occasional selling, but their primary responsibility was supervision and training of the sales force. Each manager had from nine to eleven salespeople reporting to him. They were paid a straight salary which depended on their length of time with SSI. In addition, a bonus was paid to the sales managers at the end of the year depending on how well their district had done. Salaries for all sales managers averaged $45,200, with a range of $39,500 to $58,500.

The sales personnel were paid a straight salary their first year. SSI management felt that the first year salesperson knew so little about selling and contributed such a small portion to profits relative to experienced sales personnel that a straight salary would benefit them more. These first year salespeople were paid $21,500 in 1983. They are typically placed in smaller territories with relatively lower sales. As they gained experience they were paid a larger base salary which also depended on the length of time they had been with the company. A bonus was received at the end of each year according to their district's performance. The bonus equals .001 percent of sales. Sales this year are expected to be $2,350,000. Sales managers and sales personnel were reimbursed for all expenses incurred while selling. SSI was proud of the fact that most of its sales force had at least bachelor's degrees, with several members having MBAs.

As Woodson looked over the sales personnel compensation policy, he wondered why his turnover rate was so high. It appeared to him that many of the salespeople would get training from SSI and then run off to one of their competitors. He also felt that because the salespeople were unsupervised so much, they often took off early in the afternoon and possibly did not even work on some days. Woodson understood that there would be several people who would try to take advantage of this freedom. However, he believed that there was just not enough incentive to hunt for those extra sales or spend after hours with clients. It appeared to him that the compensation method in use was benefiting only those persons who had been with the firm for some time. He felt there was not enough incentive to keep the really good performers. The aggressive salespersons could earn more in other companies without having to wait. For example, both American Hospital and Stevens Hospital paid a 2 percent commission on sales and a base salary. As Woodson considered what method to use, he looked at a summary of a survey on compensation SSI had just finished compiling. The findings are summarized in Exhibits 17–1 and 17–2.

Afterwards, he went over the three basic compensation plans—straight salary, straight commission, and a combination of salary and incentives. Then he called Bill Jones, SSI's national sales manager, to discuss the possible alternatives.

Exhibit 17–1 Sales Managers' Salaries

Firm	Average Salaries 1983	Range
SSI	$45,200	$39,500–$55,500
American Hospital	$47,100	$39,500–$60,100
Stevens Hospital	$43,200	$35,100–$56,300
Industry Average	$44,100	$32,200–$60,100

Exhibit 17–2 Salespeople's Salaries

Firm	Average Salaries 1983	Range
SSI	$26,200	$21,500–$48,200
American Hospital	$28,500	$22,100–$52,100
Stevens Hospital	$23,400	$18,700–$48,300
Industry Average	$24,100	$18,600–$52,100

Questions:
1. What are the advantages and disadvantages of a straight salary for Surgical Supplies?
2. Is the compensation plan causing a problem? How?
3. What would you do to correct the situation, if anything?

17–2   The Dunn Corporation

Robert Head, the newly appointed sales manager for the Dunn Corporation, had completed a review of the sales force that he inherited. He knew that he had an important decision facing him regarding one of his sales representatives, John Little.

Company Background.   The Dunn Corporation, with headquarters in Tuscaloosa, Alabama, produced and sold asphalt roofing products

This case was developed by Professor James L. Taylor, Department of Management and Marketing, University of Alabama. The company name has been changed.

and other building materials throughout the southeastern United States. The primary market area consisted of the states of Alabama, Tennessee, Georgia, Florida, and Mississippi. There were also selected accounts in Kentucky, Indiana, and South Carolina. Five sales representatives covered the primary marketing area, with each representative having one of the states assigned as a territory. The selected accounts were assigned to the sales representatives at the sales manager's discretion.

Historically, the management of Dunn had pursued a conservative growth strategy with particular emphasis on achieving maximum return on investment. In order to keep costs down, capital expenditures for replacement of worn-out or obsolete equipment were given low priority. This led to a drop in production efficiency at the company's Tuscaloosa plant such that production was unable to keep pace with demand. Thus, from 1975 to 1981, company sales were limited by the availability of the product. However, despite these difficulties, the company had been profitable and had built an excellent reputation in the construction industry for service and quality.

The company had initiated successful capital improvement programs during 1980 and 1981; consequently, the company's production capacity had been greatly increased. No longer would Dunn's sales performance be hindered by lack of product availablity. Robert Head recognized that this increase in production capacity would require some revisions in the sales representative's duties. More time would have to be spent seeking new accounts in order to fully realize this new sales potential.

One of the first tasks that Head had undertaken as sales manager was a review of the field operations and performance of each sales representative. Head traveled with the sales representatives for a week in order to obtain as much information on each representative as possible. Head also spent two days with each person compiling a territorial analysis. This analysis broke each representative's district into trade areas that were then analyzed in terms of established accounts, competitive accounts, potential of the trade territory, market position of competitive manufacturers, and selection of target accounts. Head believed that a properly prepared territorial analysis could reveal whether the sales representatives really knew and worked their districts. Some pertinent statistics uncovered by the analysis are reported in Exhibits 17–3 and 17–4.

John Little's Performance.   Head concluded, after reviewing the results of the territorial analysis, that John Little's sales performance could be improved. Little had been with the company for over twenty years. A tall, handsome individual with a polished, articulate manner, he appeared to be a perfect salesperson, yet his performance never seemed to equal his potential.

While evaluating Little's accounts, call reports, and expense accounts, Head uncovered a pattern of infrequent travel throughout Little's district.

Exhibit 17–3 Sales Performance of the Individual Sales Representatives: 1982–83

Sales Representative	Sales Volume	
	1982	1983
Peters	$2,732,464	$2,636,832
Little	1,366,232	1,315,916
Homer	1,639,420	1,879,880
Cough	2,368,136	2,443,844
Stiles	1,001,903	1,127,928
Totals	$9,108,216	$9,399,402

Exhibit 17–4 Results of Territorial Analysis

Sales Representative	Number of Accounts	New Accounts in 1983	Average Daily Calls
Peters	63	3	4
Little	34	0	2
Homer	52	2	5
Cough	78	4	2
Stiles	47	2	3
Averages	54.8	2.2	3.2

Little sold only thirty-four active accounts, well below the company average of approximately fifty-five. With the low number of accounts and a daily call rate of two, it appeared that Little simply was not working very hard. When Little's sales performance was compared to his district's estimated potential, it appeared that Little was realizing only about 60 percent of the potential sales of his area. When compared with the other territories, Little's district ranked last in terms of sales volume per 1000 housing starts and sales volume per 100,000 population.

Head had questioned Little concerning coverage in his Georgia district. Head recalled part of their conversation:

Head: John, it appears that you simply are not calling on the potential customers in the outer areas of your district. For example, last month you spent twelve out of twenty days working in Atlanta. I know you live in Atlanta, and there is a tendency to work closer to home, but I believe that we are missing a lot of business in your area simply by not calling on people.

Little: Look, I have been selling roofing for a long time, even when the plant couldn't produce and ship it. Why get upset when we have a little extra product to sell?

Head: Look, John, we have increased production by 20 percent. You will have all the product you can sell. This means extra income to you, better services to your accounts, and more profit to the company. I will be happy to assist you in working out a plan for coverage of your district.

Little: Bob, don't you ever look at the volume of our customers? If you did, you would know that the Republic Roofing Supply in Atlanta is the second largest account of Dunn. Upchurch, the owner of Republic, is very demanding concerning my servicing Republic on ordering, delivery, and product promotion. It has taken a long time, but I have gained the trust and respect of Upchurch. That is why he looks to me to take care of the account. The reason that we have not lost the account to our competitors is that I give the type of service demanded by Upchurch.

Head: John, I agree that service to all of our accounts is extremely important. However, service does represent a cost, not only in terms of an outlay of money, but also in the potential loss of business from other accounts. I seriously question the profitability of spending approximately 40 percent of your time with one account.

Little: What do you mean, profitability? My district has always made money. Just because we have new management, why does everything have to change?

Head had continued the conversation by suggesting that he and Little meet at some future date for the purpose of laying out a travel schedule. It was Head's intention to structure the schedule so that Little could make a minimum of four calls per day. Little, however, refused to even consider setting up a schedule or to increase the number of calls per day. His refusal was based on the contention that he needed at least two days a week to service Republic properly. Little further stated that if Dunn would not allow him the two days a week to service Republic, other roofing manufacturers would.

Robert Head pondered his decision regarding John Little and the Georgia territory. He felt that he had three options. First, he could simply fire Little with the possibility of losing the Republic account. Because Republic was Dunn's second largest account, Head realized that this might be a dangerous course of action. Second, Head considered rearranging Little's district by transferring some of the outer counties to other sales representatives. Finally, Head realized that he could simply accept the situation and leave things as they were now. He remembered once being told by a close friend with years of management experience that sometimes a "don't rock the boat" strategy is the best way to handle difficult situations.

Question:

What should Robert Head do regarding John Little and his Georgia territory?

Notes

Chapter 1

1. John Hancock Mutual Life Insurance Corporation.
2. Dale C. Alsop and Gary Grikscheit, "Sales Personnel—The Outlook for Demand and Supply," *Journal of College Placement* 38 (Fall 1977), pp. 58–63; Gary M. Grikscheit, "Personal Selling: A Position Paper," in *Controversy and Dialogue in Marketing,* ed. Ross Lawrence Goble and Roy T. Shaw (Englewood Cliffs, N.J.: Prentice-Hall, 1975), pp. 269–82; U.S. Department of Labor, Bureau of Labor Statistics, *Occupational Projections and Training Data,* Bulletin 2053, September 1980 (Washington, D.C.: U.S. Government Printing Office, 1980), pp. 85–86.
3. Tex Schramm, "Texas Executives Comment on Philosophy of Management," *Texas Business Executive,* Fall 1978, p. 36.
4. Xerox Corporation sales literature.
5. Personal correspondence.
6. Robert L. Shook, *Ten Greatest Salespersons* (New York: Harper & Row, 1978), p. 34.
7. "How They Make It to the Top," *Sales and Marketing Management,* September 14, 1981, p. 57.
8. Personal correspondence.
9. Personal correspondence.
10. Personal correspondence.
11. Shook, *Ten Greatest Salespersons,* p. 65.
12. Personal correspondence.

Chapter 3

1. Patrick J. Robinson, Charles W. Faris, and Yoram Wind, *Industrial Buying and Creative Marketing* (Boston: Allyn & Bacon, 1967).
2. Philip Kotler, *Marketing Management: Analysis, Planning and Control* (Englewood Cliffs, N.J.: Prentice-Hall, 1980), p. 134.
3. John A. Howard and Jagdish N. Sheth, *The Theory of Buyer Behavior* (New York: John Wiley & Sons, 1969).
4. Abram Maslow, "A Theory of Human Motivation," *Psychology Review,* 1943, pp. 370–396; and *Motivation and Personality* (New York: Harper & Row, 1954).
5. G. H. Smith, *Motivation Research and Advertising in Marketing* (New York: McGraw-Hill, 1954), pp. 19–21.
6. John Douglas, George A. Field, and Lawrence X. Tarpey, *Human Behavior in Marketing* (Columbus, Ohio: Charles E. Merrill Publishing, 1967), p. 65.

Chapter 4

1. Albert Mehrabian, *Silent Messages* (Belmont, Calif.: Wadsworth), 1971.
2. Ellen McCardle, *Nonverbal Communication* (Dekker, 1974), p. 3.
3. Mehrabian, *Silent Messages.*
4. Ibid.
5. Sally Scanlon, "Every Person a Psychologist," *Sales and Marketing Management,* February 1978, pp. 34–35.
6. Henry L. Sisk, *Organization and Management* (Cincinnati, Ohio: South-Western Publishing, 1977), pp. 350–74.
7. Keith Davis, *Human Behavior at Work* (New York: McGraw-Hill, 1972), p. 394.

Chapter 5

1. "Gillette Spends $17.4 Million to Introduce Aapri," *Marketing News,* May 29, 1981, p. 6.
2. James F. Bender, "Training and Developing Sales Personnel," in *Handbook of Modern Marketing,* ed. Victor P. Buell (New York: McGraw-Hill, 1970), pp. 12–44.
3. Edgar Speer, "The Role of Training at United States Steel," *Training and Development Journal,* June 1976, pp. 18–21.
4. "Mail-Ins Bounce Back," *Incentive Marketing,* March 1981, p. 30.

Chapter 6

1. The Telemarketing section was written by John I. Coppett, Ph.D. Dr. Coppett is an internal consultant for AT&T Long Lines, Bedminster, New Jersey.
2. Bob Schiffman, "Confessions of a Cadillac Salesman," *Marketing Times,* May–June 1979, p. 24.
3. Thayer C. Taylor, "Information With Your Bacon and Eggs," *Sales and Marketing Management,* June 6, 1983, p. 61.

Chapter 7

1. Richard D. Nordstrom, *Introduction to Selling: An Experiential Approach to Skill Development* (New York: Macmillian, 1981) pp. 203–4.
2. Ibid.
3. *SPIN Sales Program,* Huthwaite Research Group, 1977.
4. Dennis DeMaria "Keep Quiet and Get the Order," *Personal Selling Power* 3, no. 2 (March/April 1983), p. 17. Copyright © 1983 by *Personal Selling Power.* Reprinted with permission of the publisher.

Chapter 8

1. "Dr. Pemberton's Pick-Me-Up" from *Paul Harvey's The Rest of the Story* by Paul Aurandt, copyright © 1977 by Paulynne, Inc. Rephrased by permission of Doubleday & Company, Inc.

Chapter 9

1. "You've Got to Do Better than That," *Personal Selling Power* 3, no. 2 (March/April 1983), p. 17. Copyright © 1983 by *Personal Selling Power.* Reprinted with permission of the publisher.

Chapter 10

1. Stewart A. Washburn, "You Have to Earn the Right to Close," in *Closing the Sale* (special

report), *Sales and Marketing Management* 118, no. 8 (June 13, 1977), pp. 10–12.
2. Mike Radick, "Training Salespeople to Get Success on Their Side," *Sales and Marketing Management,* August 15, 1983, pp. 63–65.

Chapter 11

1. Robert L. Shook, *Ten Greatest Salespersons* (New York: Harper & Row, 1978), p. 95.
2. Ibid., p. 155.
3. Ibid., p. 67.
4. Somerby Dowst, "This Year's Winners: All-Around Performers," *Purchasing,* August 22, 1979, p. 43.
5. Ibid., p. 45.

Chapter 12

1. Robert L. Shook, *Ten Greatest Salespersons* (New York: Harper & Row, 1978), pp. 7–24.
2. Ibid.
3. 1977 Census of Retail Trade.
4. U.S. Department of Labor, "Employment and Earnings," January 1980, p. 172.
5. Shook, *Ten Greatest Salespersons,* pp. 135–54.
6. Ibid., pp. 7–24.
7. Arch G. Woodside and Taylor J. Sims, "Retail Sales Transactions and Customer 'Purchase Pal' Effects on Buying Behavior," *Journal of Retailing* 52, pp. 57–64.
8. Edgar J. Bracco, "The Unsold Prospect," *Pet Age,* November 1980, p. 45.
9. Adapted from information in Richard D. Nordstrom's *Introduction to Selling: An Experimental Approach to Skill Development* (New York: Macmillan, 1981) pp. 202–3.

Chapter 13

1. Somerby Dowst, "This Year's Winners: All-Around Performers," *Purchasing,* August 22, 1979, pp. 38–46; "Buyers Give Top Honors to Quality Salesmen," *Purchasing,* August 22, 1981, p. 65.
2. *Standard Industrial Classification Manual*

(Washington, D.C.: U.S. Government Printing Office, 1972).

3. Adapted from Philip Kotler, *Marketing, Management: Analysis Planning and Control,* 4th ed. (Englewood Cliffs, N.J.: Prentice-Hall, 1980), p. 172.

4. Patrick J. Robinson, Charles W. Faris, and Yoram Wind, *Industrial Buying and Creative Marketing* (Boston: Allyn & Bacon, 1967).

5. Somerby Dowst, "This Year's Winners: All-Around Performers," *Purchasing,* August 22, 1979, pp. 38–46; "Buyers Give Top Honors to Quality Salesmen," *Purchasing,* August 22, 1981, p. 65.

Chapter 14

1. Robert L. Shook, *Ten Greatest Salespersons* (New York: Harper & Row, 1978), p. 79.

2. "Problem Areas for Salespeople," *Training: The Magazine of Human Resources Development,* April 1977, p. 7.

3. Franklin Evans, "Selling as A Dyadic Relationship—A New Approach," *American Behavioral Scientist,* May 1963, p. 76.

4. Paul J. Halvorson and William Rudelius, "Is There a Free Lunch?" *Journal of Marketing,* January 1977, pp. 44–49.

Chapter 15

1. Raymond Baumhart, "How Ethical Are Businessmen?" *Harvard Business Review,* July–August 1961, p. 6; *Ethics in Business* (New York: Holt, Rinehart & Winston, 1968); James S. Bowman, "Managerial Ethics in Business and Government," *Business Horizons,* October 1976, pp. 48–54; Archie Carroll, "Managerial Ethics: A Post-Watergate View," *Business Horizons,* April 1975, pp. 75–80; and W. Blumenthal, "Rx for Reducing the Occasion of 'Corporate Sin.'" *SAM Advanced Management Journal* 42 (1977), pp. 4–13.

2. "It's Time to Repeal the Right to Do Wrong," *Sales and Marketing Mangement,* October 11, 1976, pp. 39–42; "Marketing Observer," *Business Week,* July 13, 1974, p. 50.

3. Ibid.

Chapter 16

1. John D. Rockefeller as quoted in Garret L. Berger and William V. Haney, *Organizational Relations and Management* (New York: McGraw-Hill, 1966), p. 3.

2. Charles M. Futrell, *Sales Management: Behavior, Practice, and Cases* (New York: Dryden Press, 1981), pp. 200–202.

3. Edgar Speer, "The Role of Training at United States Steel," *Training and Development Journal,* June 1976, pp. 18–21.

4. *The Challenge of Sales Management at Procter & Gamble* (Cincinnati, Ohio: Procter & Gamble Corporation, 1980).

5. Ibid.

6. "Good Grief, Salesmen Training Each Other," *Training: The Magazine of Human Resources Development,* May 1976, p. 35.

7. William A. Fynes, "Self-Development for Salespeople: It's Easy with a Cassette Tape Library," *Training: The Magazine of Human Resources Development,* July 1978, p. 28.

Chapter 17

1. James L. Taylor and Charles M. Futrell, "Sales Force Management and the Motivation Mix: Role of the Nonfinancial Reward as a Sales Incentive" (Southern Marketing Association Proceedings, University of South Western Louisiana, 1978).

2. "A Conversation with Jim Dittman," *Incentive Marketing,* November 1978, pp. 34–36.

3. Sally Scanlon, "Who's Keeping Score on Incentive Results?" *Sales and Marketing Management,* September 1978, p. 63.

4. "The Beauty of It All: Jafra Incentives Spur Sales, Recruiting," *Incentive Marketing,* October 1978, pp. 59–62.

5. "Real Estate Developer Building Fast with Sales and Production Awards," *Incentive Marketing,* October, 1978, pp. 57–58.

6. "Sara Lee—Top Dough Sales Contest," *Incentive Marketing,* July 1978, pp. 42–44.

7. "Lots of Laughs and Sales," *Incentive Marketing,* July 1978, pp. 40–42;

8. Charles M. Futrell, *Factors Important in Managing the Sales Force* (working paper, Texas A&M University, 1980).

9. Robert Tannenbaum and Warren Schmidt, "How to Choose a Leadership Pattern," *Harvard Business Review*, 51, May 1973.

10. Charles M. Futrell, John E. Swan, and John T. Todd, "Job Performance Related to Management Control Systems for Pharmaceutical Salesmen," *Journal of Marketing Research*, February 1976, pp. 25–33.

Company Index

Name Index

Subject Index

*This book has been set Computer Assisted Photocomp in
10 and 9 point Zapf Light. Section titles are 28 point Zapf
Demi. Chapter numbers are 36 point Zapf Demi and chapter
titles are 24 point Zapf Demi. The size of the type page is
36 by 45 picas.*